UYGHUR

AN INTERMEDIATE TEXTBOOK

Gulnisa Nazarova
Kurban Niyaz

Library of Congress Cataloging-in-Publication Data

Names: Nazarova, Gulnisa, author. | Niyaz, Kurban, author.
Title: Uyghur : an intermediate textbook / Gulnisa Nazarova, Kurban Niyaz.
Description: Washington, DC : Georgetown University Press, 2016. | Includes bibliographical references and index.
Identifiers: LCCN 2016002414 | ISBN 9781626163645 (pb : alk. paper)
Subjects: LCSH: Uyghur language--Textbooks for foreign speakers--English.
Classification: LCC PL54.62 .N393 2016 | DDC 494/.32382421--dc23
LC record available at http://lccn.loc.gov/2016002414

© This book is printed on acid-free paper meeting the requirements of the American National Standard for Permanence in Paper for Printed Library Materials.

22 21 20 9 8 7 6 5 4 3

Printed in the United States of America

Administrative and pedagogical support by Öner Özçelik, Dave Baer and Amber K. Kent
Book design by Sukhrob Karimov and Kurban Niyaz
Cover design by Pam Pease
Cover image by emerson matabele

تەڭرىتاغدىن سادا

VOICES FROM THE TENGRITAGH

**This book is dedicated in honor of and reverence to our Uyghur ancestors.
It is they who, in holding steadfast to their language, have made
it possible for us to teach it to future generations
-- Uyghur and otherwise -- across the globe.**

CONTENTS

Scope and Sequence

Grammar	Functions	Chapter
- Review of the tenses - The conditional mood - Review of noun cases - Review of ability form - The verb بولماق	- Introducing yourself and others - Telling and writing dates - Describing past events - Describing future plans and abilities	ئۆتكەنگە نەزەر: ئۇيغۇرچە ئىسمىم يالقۇن
- The narrative past with the word ئىكەن - The narrative past with the suffix -پتۇ - The hearsay or reportative past with the suffix -پتۇ	- Expressing compliments and surprise - Narrating stories - Expressing apologies and regrets - Comparing Uyghur and English names - Describing personal interests and hobbies	1. ئۇيغۇر ئىسىملىرى
- The passive voice - The present/future narrative & hearsay - The reflexive pronoun ئۆز - The first person optative (imperative) mood	- Describing one's family - Describing the Uyghur مەھەللە and هويلا - Comparing traditional and modern families - Comparing Uyghur and American families - Describing Uyghur and American host etiquette - Writing a biographical sketch	2. ئۇيغۇرلاردا ئائىلە
- Past, present-continuous, Present/future participles - Postpositions of: • means or manner with بىلەن • place and instrument with ئارقىلىق • time with باشلاپ - The conditional بولماق + -سا - The construction -غۇدەيمەن	- Asking for and giving advice - Making suggestions - Giving instructions - Expressing politeness - Expressing wishes	3. ئاق يول بولسۇن!

Grammar	Functions	Chapter
- The postposition قارىغاندا - Sentence coordination with -پ \ -ىپ \ -ۇپ \ -ۈپ - The particles: -لا، -غۇ، -ە	- Describing Uyghur and Chinese food - Narrating a sequence of events - Recognizing Chinese borrowings - Ordering food using Chinese loan words - Comparing food - Expressing emphasis	4. ئۇيغۇر تائام ناملىرى
- The auxiliary verbs ئالماق and بەرمەك - The gerund of purpose: • with - غىلى • with the verbal noun + postposition ئۈچۈن • with the verbal noun + suffix -غا \ -قا \ -گە \ -كە - The construction -غۇم \ -غۇڭ بار - Super polite form with -سىلا \ -سىلە	- Expressing goals - Describing places - Giving sightseeing information - Expressing opinions about buildings and people - Expressing desire - Expressing politeness - Narrating past events	5. تەڭرىتاغ باغرىدا
- Noun formation suffixes - Word formation for onomatopoeia (imitative words) - The word ئەمەسمۇ - Subordinate clause of reason	- Describing Uyghur traditional occupations - Describing artisans in Uyghur bazaars - Bargaining at a bazaar - Recognizing onomatopoeias - Explaining reasons	6. ئۇيغۇرلاردا ھۈنەر - كەسىپ
- The auxiliary verb كەتمەك - Verb formation with the suffix -لى (-لا \ -لە) - Reciprocal constructions - Causative constructions in Uyghur (Part 1) - Adjective forming suffix -ىي	- Describing educational backgrounds - Comparing educational systems in Xinjiang and the US - Describing life in a dorm - Describing a typical day on campus - Describing the University - Reading advertisements - Reading Uyghur street signs	7. مەكتەپ ھاياتى

Grammar	Functions	Chapter
- The auxiliary verbs بولماق and ئەتمەك - Compound verbs with the verb بارماق - The remote past tense with ئىدى - The habitual past - Simultaneous actions	- Describing extra-curricular activities - Describing free time activities - Narrating past events - Describing ئولتۇرۇش and مەشرەپ	8. ئولتۇرۇش ۋە مەشرەپ
- "You may/can" in Uyghur - The auxiliary verb ئولتۇرماق - The causative constructions (Part 2)	- Expressing permission - Describing your health - Expressing obligations - Complaining at the hospital - Describing the history of Uyghur sports - Telling scores in Uyghur - Describing sand therapy	9. ساغلام تەندە - ساپ ئەقىل
- The suffix -مىكىن - Another use of the word گەپ - Another use of the conditional - The construction "if only" in Uyghur - Connecting clauses with -غان/-قان/-گەن/-كەن + -لىق/-لىك + possessive + -نى - The suffix -مىش	- Making assumptions - Describing important life events - Comparing Uyghur and American weddings: then and now - Discussing concepts of هالال and هارام - Describing some challenges of modern Uyghur society - Expressing condolences - Expressing "supposedly"	10. ئۇيغۇر جەمئىيىتىدە
- The repeated conjunction بىرتۇرۇپ...بىرتۇرۇپ - Another use of the suffix -مىش - The first person of the Interrogative present–future form - Relative clauses with the word بولۇپ - The construction -غۇم (-غۇڭ...) كېلىدۇ	- Describing places and people - Making reservations at a hotel - Making friends - Describing things: Uyghur silk and rugs - Expressing wishes - Buying gifts at the Khotan bazaar - Recognizing the Khotan dialect	11. ئاخىرقى سەپەر - خوتەن

Grammar	Functions	Chapter
- The suppositional future with -ار \ -ەر \ -ر - The particle جۇمۇ - The short form of the first person plural optative -يلى - The word دەپ	- Describing gift-related etiquette - Expressing probability - Describing social issues - Talking to the taxi agent - Expressing suggestions - Expressing appreciation and gratitude - Expressing future plans	12. خەير - خوش، ئۈرۈمچى!

FOREWORD

The 'Central Asian Language Series,' prepared by the Center for Languages of the Central Asian Region (CeLCAR), is the first set of Central Asian language textbooks published in the United States that is based on the Communicative Approach. *Uyghur: An Intermediate Textbook*, authored by Gulnisa Nazarova and Kurban Niyaz, is the fourth intermediate level textbook in this series.

The textbook provides learners with activities that are aimed at helping them perform tasks and functions that native speakers of Uyghur perform in their appropriate cultural context. The grammar and the vocabulary covered in the textbook are also chosen carefully to help learners perform these tasks and functions at the intermediate level and beyond.

The textbook aims to provide students with a foundation of listening, speaking, reading, and writing, all four basic skills of language, while offering them various authentic and culturally relevant materials, including videos taped in various regions of Xinjiang, China, the area where the Uyghur language is predominantly spoken. In addition to demonstrating different aspects of the Uyghur culture, the book also provides contemporary topics of universal interest and does so in meaningful and communicative ways.

Uyghur: An Intermediate Textbook incorporates the latest innovations in foreign language teaching, and has been prepared with the input of various second language acquisition and language pedagogy experts, as well as linguists. The way new information is presented and the tasks and activities used in the textbook to consolidate this information are all in line with the findings of the latest research in second language acquisition, linguistics, and language pedagogy.

A textbook such as this is possible with the vision and labor of many. We are, first of all, grateful for the support from the Department of Education through Title VI funds that helped establish and continue to sustain CeLCAR, our Language Resource Center. The contents of this textbook were developed under grant #P229A140007 and #P229A100015 from the U.S. Department of Education (Principal Investigator: Öner Özçelik). However, those contents do not necessarily represent the policy of the U.S. Department of Education, and you should not assume endorsement by the Federal Government. In addition to the excellent work done by the authors, I would like to acknowledge the members of our textbook development committee, Dave Baer, Sukhrob Karimov, and Amber Kennedy Kent, for their administrative, pedagogical, technological, and editing help throughout the process of preparing this textbook. The project would not have been possible without their contributions.

We are also grateful to Indiana University's School of Global and International Studies and the College of Arts and Sciences for providing us with logistical support as well as significant internal funds. We would also like to extend special thanks to the Department of Central Eurasian Studies (CEUS) at Indiana University for providing us with the linguistic and cultural expertise needed in creating various aspects of this textbook, and for sharing many resources.

Dr. Öner Özçelik
Director, CeLCAR
Assist. Prof., CEUS
Indiana University, Bloomington

PREFACE

The purpose of this intermediate Uyghur textbook is to provide learners with a wide selection of intermediate-level materials and task-oriented, communicative activities that facilitate the development of the four language skills—speaking, listening, reading, and writing—in a balanced way. It is designed for students who have completed an introductory level of Uyghur instruction based on the first volume of the book, *Uyghur: An Elementary Textbook*, developed at the Center for Languages of the Central Asian Region (CeLCAR), as well as for students who have learned Uyghur at home or abroad and want to continue studying the language at the intermediate level. This textbook is developed specifically for classroom use; however, it can be used for self-study as well.

The materials presented in this textbook require a minimum of 160 hours of intensive language instruction to be completed. In terms of proficiency, this textbook prepares learners to perform at levels 1+, 2, or even 2+ (for highly motivated learners) on the ILR scale, or from Intermediate High to Advanced Mid/High level proficiency as defined on the ACTFL scale.

The textbook is designed as a virtual tour of the Uyghur homeland and is based on the imaginary experiences of John, a fictitious American student who receives a scholarship to travel to Xinjiang and study at Xinjiang University. Accompanying each of John's adventures are short blog entries, in which John relates to learners some of his experiences with the Uyghur language and culture. Throughout the book students will have the chance to visit various cities in this remarkable region. In so doing, students will enrich their knowledge of the Uyghur language and they will learn a great deal about many important aspects of Uyghur culture.

Unique features of the intermediate Uyghur textbook include the following:

- Topics carefully selected for maximum relevance and utility, and organized to optimize seamless and self-reinforcing learning
- Reading passages which include both authentic original and modified texts to challenge students with natural language and style while ensuring appropriate levels of comprehension
- Easy-to-follow texts with concise vocabulary lists, which build on and reinforce prior knowledge
- Important language concepts communicated through culture in naturalistic

settings that prepare students for real-life interaction within the region
- Interactive exercises which engage students by helping them express their personal needs and share their own opinions
- Activities presented in a balanced way to help students improve the four basic language skills: speaking, listening, reading, and writing
- Grammar lessons tied to specific cultural topics and explained in simple language to avoid complicated grammar terms
- Recorded dialogues so that students can fine-tune their pronunciation with an emphasis on correct intonation
- Authentic video segments filmed in Beijing, Ürümchi, Turpan, Kashgar, and Khotan.

ACKNOWLEDGMENTS

This Intermediate Textbook is a result of four years of hard and tireless work, and the collaborative efforts of many people.

We want to express our deepest gratitude to Professors William Fierman and Christopher Atwood, the former directors of the Center for Languages of the Central Asian Region (CeLCAR) at Indiana University (IU) Bloomington for providing the critical financial assistance which enabled us to start working on this project, as well as to Prof. Edward Lazzerini, the current director of the Inner Asian and Uralic National Resource Center (IAUNRC) at IU, for providing additional financial support. We would also like to thank Gardner Bovingdon, Associate Professor of the Department of Central Eurasian Studies (CEUS) for his immense support for our work. Finally, we are especially indebted to Prof. Öner Özçelik, current CeLCAR Director, for providing all the necessary conditions for the successful completion of this project, in addition to ensuring continuation of funds for the project as the PI of the two grants supporting our work, #P229A140007 and #P229A100015 from the U.S. Department of Education.

We are also very much indebted to Dr. Beatrix Burghardt, a pedagogy specialist at IU, whose help, comments, and constructive criticism regarding content, pedagogical methods, organization of topics, and detailed chapter layouts were extremely helpful in improving the overall academic quality of the textbook. Thanks also to Dave Baer, Assistant Director of CeLCAR, who assisted us in overcoming all manner of job-related obstacles before, during, and after the completion of the project. Nicholas Kontovas, a PhD student at IU and instructor of Turkish at IU's Summer Language Workshop and Boğaziçi University in Istanbul, has shown his brilliance in linguistics and the Uyghur language through his editing of texts and comparisons of Uyghur and English vocabulary and example sentences, in addition to his contribution of grammar explanations. Amber Kennedy Kent, CeLCAR's Language Instructional Specialist, completed a final edit of the English text and provided helpful comments.

Much appreciation goes to Sukhrob Karimov, an energetic IT professional at CeLCAR, for his generous help in designing the textbook, as well as Tiffany Joy C. Ignalaga, a graduate student at the Henry Radford School of Fine Arts for her valuable input regarding the design work for the last six chapters.

We were very lucky to have two visiting scholars from Xinjiang University at CeLCAR this year. We would like to express our gratitude to Samat Mamitimin for his valuable feedback regarding the book, as well as his proofreading of the Uyghur text, editing of all the audio files, and help with the recording of audio and video materials. We also would like to thank Omerjan Kurban, who assisted in the recording of audio materials. In addition, we greatly appreciate Muyassar Ghalip's help with the recording of the female voice for the first six chapters.

We would like to express our appreciation to Nigora Azimova, an Uzbek language developer at CeLCAR with whom we shared many ideas during our work on the textbook. The same appreciation is extended to the rest of the CeLCAR staff as well for their immense support.

We would like to thank CEUS graduate student Michael Krautkraemer, who took Intermediate Uyghur during the 2014-2015 academic year, for his great help in providing excellent feedback and valuable suggestions for the textbook, in addition to all the other learners who took Intermediate Uyghur while this textbook was being developed for their generous support and suggestions.

Special thanks go to Colin Legerton, Elise Anderson, and Vincent Malic for providing passages about their experiences while they were studying in Xinjiang. Also, we greatly appreciate Nicholas Kontovas and Timothy Grose for their help with some of the cultural notes that are in English.

We wish to extend special thanks to the photographer of our cover image, emerson Matabele (http://www.silkroadcollection.com/ or http://www.silkroadcollection.com/), and his assistant, Adonis Mouna, for their wonderful work and support in allowing us to use this photograph, entitled "Elders."

We are very grateful to the individuals who have very generously provided all the photographs for this textbook project. Their personal photo collections are the result of various field studies, sightseeing tours, and language immersion programs from Ürümchi to Khotan, from Turpan to Altay. These materials greatly enhance the authenticity of each chapter of the textbook. We would like to express our appreciation to McKay Barrow, Aygul Mipo, Lewis Traveler, Brian Cwiek, Vincent Malic, Elise Anderson, Michael Patrick, Sandrine Catris, Timothy Grose, David Straub, James Nagler, Aybike Tezel, Ondřej Klimeš, Nicholas Kontovas, Valeri Hardin, Michael Krautkraemer, Kara Abramson, Li Xuan, Benjamin Burnett, Jia Jianfei, Li Xuan, Alissa Davis, Miriam Woods, Alex Daniel McRae, Andrew Morris, Josh Summers (Xinjiang 新疆: Far West China), Rahman Arman, Kurbanjan Rozi, Colin Legerton, Jewher Ilham, Ilyar Nazarov, Zulpiqar Barat, Adil Turahmetov, Ed Pulford, Marc van der Chijs, Omaq Sadvakasova, Rayhongul Kakhakharova, Anders Öfverström, and Stefan Geens.

We also would like to express our gratitude to those people who kindly agreed to let us use their images in our video clips. They are: Zulpiqar Barat, Mirshad Ghalip, Helimigul Abliz, Ondřej Klimeš, Benjamin Burnett, Vincent Malic, Gulchehra Keyum, Elise Anderson, Ablet Abdureshit Berqi, Samat Mamitimin, Turahmet Turahmetov, Nazugum Turahmetova, the Uyghur samsa makers at the Uyghur restaurant "Qeshqer" in Beijing, the Uyghur man who served as our guide at the Turpan Kareez Museum and provided us with interesting information about Turpan grapes and wine production, the Uyghur tevip Abdugheni from Turpan, and the Uyghur socks merchant at the Khotan market for his beautiful song. We also thank all the other unnamed people who appear in the video clips.

Particular acknowledgment is due to Wikimedia Foundation, as well as all those who have contributed to its collaborative wiki projects, such as Wikipedia and Wikimedia Commons, which have granted unrestricted use of numerous images in the public domain. We also would like to applaud the creators of the Uyghur online dictionary at yulghun.com for creating such an incredible resource which we used throughout the development of this textbook.

As in our previous project, excerpts of well-known songs from the repertoire of late Uyghur musician Nurmuhammad Tursun have been used as background music for some of the video files accompanying this textbook. The melodious sound of his tembur not only gives pleasure and comfort to users while they study, but also indirectly exposes them to the beauty of Uyghur traditional music. We would like to give our special thanks to him. God bless him, and may he rest in peace!

We also want to express our deep appreciation to the anonymous reviewers of this textbook. Their feedback and critiques were crucial.

Last, and perhaps most importantly, we would like to thank the Uyghur people for using and preserving one of the oldest Central Asian languages, which has made possible the initialization and completion of our textbook projects.

Despite all the help we have received from numerous people, we know that some mistakes may still remain. We take full responsibility for all potential errors in the textbook, and we would be grateful if readers could draw them to our attention for further correction. Meanwhile, we apologize for any confusion they may cause the reader.

NOTE TO THE INSTRUCTOR

We worked very hard to make this textbook available and we believe that our efforts will make a difference in the classroom. This textbook offers a thematically organized, integrative approach to the Uyghur language, combined with current innovations in foreign language teaching. The innovations include an emphasis on integrated skills development with a large number of the activities intended to develop strong speaking, listening, reading, and writing skills. The texts and activities in the book provide sufficient materials for students to learn the language within a cultural context.

Upon successful completion of the courses contained herein, learners should be able to:

- Hold different conversations on concrete topics such as family, work, school, places of interest, and occupations, as well as some topics related to current events, health problems, and social issues faced by Uyghur society today.
- Read fairly complex authentic materials with the goal of comprehending the main ideas of the text, as well as a level of detail commensurate with intermediate knowledge of the language.
- Express their opinions on different topics presented in the textbook, providing some supporting arguments.
- Give written and oral descriptions of people, places, and social events with some level of detail.
- Talk about and compare Uyghur and American culture.

The textbook is structured as follows:

1. Preliminary Chapter

This chapter is designed as a review of the knowledge and skills assumed to have been covered during elementary-level language instruction. Here students will reinforce their knowledge of the Uyghur language gained from previous study.

2. Twelve thematic chapters

This textbook contains twelve chapters in total. A short description of things to come is provided at the beginning of each chapter.

Each chapter contains authentic and modified passages from various sources for reading comprehension purposes; short notes describing some elements of Uyghur culture in English for students' cultural education and enrichment; audio and video activities for listening comprehension purposes; grammar points related to the content being presented; prompts for student projects and presentations; and authentic pictures illustrating contemporary life among the Uyghurs.

Most of the activities are designed as a set of activities and have their own title based on the content of the task. For example in Chapter 7, Exercise 9 is titled ئوقۇغۇچىلار ھاياتى *Students' Life* and has three tasks numbered 9.1, 9.2, and 9.3. However, there are also some separate single activities without any title; these are usually grammar activities.

Every odd chapter contains a section called *Do you know this person?*, in which learners are introduced to a famous Uyghur person. Every even chapter contains a section titled *Pulling it all together*, in which students reinforce their knowledge and check the progress they have made during each two chapters by completing a limited selection of focused exercises. In addition to this, every even chapter concludes with a *Self-check* section, in which students also can self-assess their knowledge of the topics they have covered in each set of two chapters.

The end of each chapter features a vocabulary list containing all of the new words and phrases introduced throughout the chapter.

At the end of Chapter Twelve there is a sort of end-of-course review. It concludes with a brief *Comprehensive Culture Quiz*, the purpose of which is to sum up some of the most interesting points from students' virtual tour of the Uyghur homeland. Like the *Self-check* sections of previous chapters, it is also intended to help learners self-assess their knowledge of the most memorable aspects of Uyghur culture touched upon during their studies.

3. Three appendices at the end of the book:

Appendix A: Transcriptions of audio activities
Appendix B: Transcriptions of videos
Appendix C: Uyghur - English and English - Uyghur glossaries

4. CD with Audio and Video exercises.

NOTE TO THE STUDENT

As you have already experienced, language learning requires time, motivation, and effort. At the intermediate level you may face some new challenges regarding structure and vocabulary, however, do not let them discourage you! We have tried to make learning Uyghur fun and enjoyable for you. This textbook will transport you to the homeland of the Uyghur people, allowing you to explore a number of aspects of Uyghur culture, as well as the language.

Some suggestions while using the textbook:

Even though there are a number of good printed Uyghur-English dictionaries, they can be difficult to find. We would suggest using the online dictionary *Yulghun* http://dict.yulghun.com/. In addition to translating between Uyghur, English, and Chinese, it also provides an internal (monolingual) dictionary for each of these languages, in which you can find a word's definition in that language. You can refer to this dictionary whenever you read passages or work on definition-related exercises.

We tried to avoid overloading explanations of structure or usage in the grammar points, so any time you have additional questions, you can ask your instructor/tutor for help. In order to help with digesting some of the heavy (complicated) grammar points, we have divided them into two or three parts. For example, you can find the grammar explanation for the causative voice split between chapters 7 and 9.

The videos used in this textbook are not studio quality. This is because most of them were shot by the authors on location in Xinjiang and Bloomington. Do not worry if you do not understand them fully. When you read the instructions for the video activities, you will see that the tasks that go along with the videos are appropriate to your assumed level. For better comprehension of the video clips, we suggest using the transcripts of the videos provided in Appendix B.

To the left of each of John's blog entries we have provided a Uyghur proverb. We tried to choose these based on the topic presented in each chapter. We encourage you to read these proverbs with the help of your instructor/tutor and discuss them in class. You might know that using proverbs in your target language makes your language closer to native speakers' and heightens your overall language proficiency.

Additional tips:

Work on your vocabulary!

As you may know after taking Elementary Uyghur, it is very important to learn vocabulary. At the intermediate level you will be provided with more complicated words and expressions. You may have your own way to work with new words. Some learners use flash cards, while others make a list, or divide up the words based on themes. Other strategies may include writing the words several times or developing catchy mnemonic devices using the new vocabulary. No matter what you do, make sure to go back to your vocabulary list or flash cards often, even once the chapter is over.

Read ahead!

The structural points in the textbook are explained in clear, accessible language. You do not need to wait for your instructor or tutor to explain each grammar point in the classroom. Instead, come to class prepared by studying the grammar points ahead of time. That way you will have more time to practice instead of trying to understand and process what was just explained to you.

Participate and speak up!

Remember that actively engaging in conversations with your instructor/tutor or classmates helps you to acquire Uyghur faster and better. Listen actively to your instructor/tutor's speech; concentrate on the structures and vocabulary (s)he is using. When working in small groups or in pairs, listen to your classmates and improve upon their efforts, if possible. Most importantly: speak up! Do not be afraid to make mistakes! That is how we learn languages.

Create an environment!

As you have experienced, learning a less commonly taught language such as Uyghur might feel isolating. You instructor/tutor and the textbook may seem to be the only source for learning about Uyghur and its speakers. However, you can find a number of sources on the web: listen to Uyghur online radio, watch Uyghur movies, and listen to Uyghur songs on YouTube! Always remember that in language acquisition ample input is key! These extra activities can be an excellent source of input. Even though you might not understand everything, you will still be exposed to Uyghur outside the classroom. Try to make Uyghur friends on Facebook or LinkedIn to find some opportunities to practice your language skills.

Stay motivated!

Remember that motivation is very important in language learning. Set realistic objectives for yourself and try to achieve them. Always stay positive!

We hope that this textbook will prove an invaluable tool as you journey along with John to enrich your knowledge of Uyghur language and culture.

Good luck! ئۇتۇق سىلەرگە يار بولغاي!

REFERENCES

A. Grammar references:

1. The Modern Uyghur Grammar (Morphology) by Hämit Tömür (translated by Anne Lee), Istanbul, Turkey: Dil ve Edebiyat, 2003.
2. A Grammar of Modern Uyghur by Frederick De Jong, Utrecht, the Netherlands: M. Th. Houtsma, 2007.

B. Authentic reading and listening samples were taken from the following sources:

1. Uyghur Örp-Adätliri [Uyghur Traditions and Customs], Ürümchi, Xinjiang Yashlar-Ösmürlär Näshriyati, 1996.
2. Uyghur Tili Oqushluqi 1 [Uyghur Reader], Ürümchi, Xinjiang Pän - Texnika Sähiya Näshriyati, 2001.
3. Uyghur Tili Oqushluqi 2 [Uyghur Reader], Ürümchi, Xinjiang Pän - Texnika Sähiya Näshriyati, 2001.
4. Novel "Qum Basqan Shähär" [The Sand- Buied City] by Memtimin Hoshur, Ürümchi, Xinjiang Yashlar-Ösmürlär Näshriyati, 2003.
5. Novel "Amät ve Apät" [Luck and Disaster] by Jalalidin Bähram, Ürümchi, Xinjiang Xälq Näshriyati, 2003.
6. "Qutadghu Bilik" Unchiliri, Ürümchi, Xinjiang Xälq Sähiya Näshriyati, 2012.
7. Some excerpts from poems by Dolqun Yasin were taken from the magazine "Güldästä" [A Bouquet of Flowers] Bishkek, Kyrgyzstan, 2003.
8. Uyghur proverbs were taken from Uyghur Xälq Maqal-Tämsilliri Izahlhiq Lughiti [Dictionary of Uyghur Proverbs], Ürümchi, Xinjiang Xälq Näshriyati, 2008.

C. Dictionaries:

1. Uyghur Online dictionary *Yulghun*: http://dict.yulghun.com/
2. Hazirqi Zaman Uyghur Tilining Izahliq Lughiti [A Uyghur Modern Annotated Dictionary], Ürümchi, Xinjiang Xälq Näshriyati, 2011.
3. Hazirqi Zaman Uyghur Ädäbiy Tilining Imla vä Talläpüz Lughiti [An Orthography and Pronunciation Dictionary of Standard Uyghur], Ürümchi, Xinjiang Xälq Näshriyati, 2000.

ئۆتكەنگە نەزەر
PRELIMINARY CHAPTER

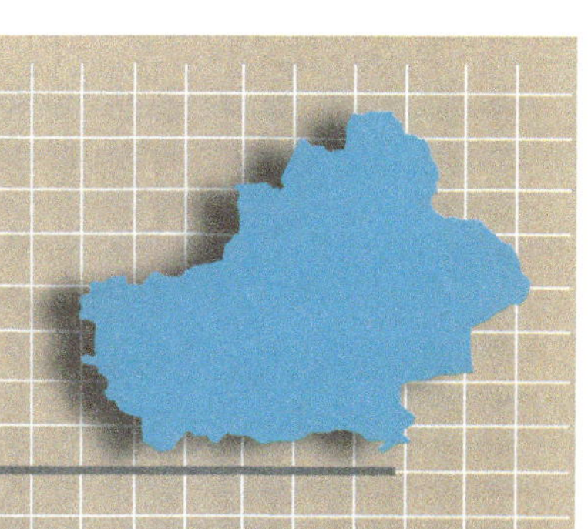

ئۇيغۇرچە ئىسمىم يالقۇن
MY UYGHUR NAME IS YALQUN

IN THIS CHAPTER

Functions
- Introducing yourself and others
- Telling and writing dates
- Describing past events
- Describing future plans and abilities

Grammar
- Review of the tenses
- The conditional mood
- Review of noun cases
- Review of ability form
- The verb بولماق

In this chapter you will get to know John, the main character of this textbook. John arrives at Indiana University and becomes acquainted with some students who are learning Uyghur. This chapter will give you an opportunity to refresh your knowledge of basic Uyghur verb tenses. By completing the activities herein, you will reinforce the common vocabulary and structures used to talk about yourself and others.

Exercise 1: سىز شىنجاڭغا بارغانمۇ؟

Look at the people in the pictures below. What do all these pictures have in common? Where were they taken? How do you know? What do you think the people in these pictures are doing in this region?

يالقۇن

ئىپارخان

باتۇر

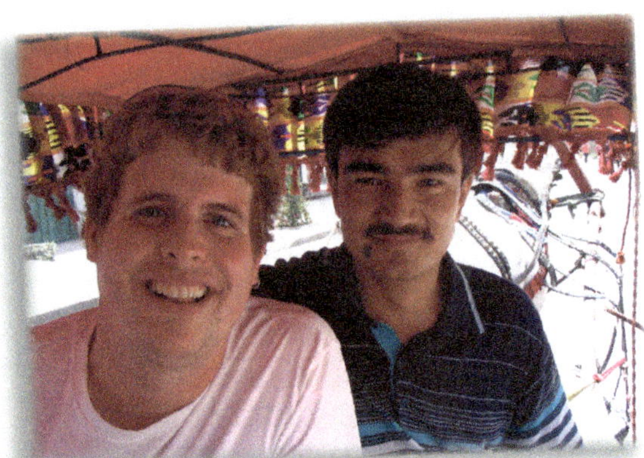

ئۆتكۈر

Note:
Ordinal numbers are formed by adding the suffix نچى- after vowels and ىنچى- after consonants to the end of the number. In writing, a hyphen is used to represent this suffix; it is still pronounced نچى-/ىنچى-.

3 - سىنىپ   234 - ئۆي

1949 - يىل   10 - قىسىم

Exercise 2: مېنىڭ ئىسمىم جون

Exercise 2.1: Listen to a passage about John and fill in the blanks with the appropriate dates.

مېنىڭ ئىسمىم جون. ئۇيغۇرچە ئىسمىم يالقۇن. مەن ئامېرىكىلىق. ______
- يىلى ______ - ئاينىڭ ______ - كۈنى نيۇ يوركتا تۇغۇلدۇم. ______ -
يىلى جورجتاۋن ئۇنىۋېرسىتېتىنى پۈتتۈردۈم. ______ - يىلى يازدا ئىندىيانا
ئۇنىۋېرسىتېتىغا كېلىپ ئىككى ئاي ئۇيغۇرچە ئۆگەندىم.
______ - يىلى تۇنجى قېتىم شىنجاڭغا باردىم. ئۇ يەردە ئۈچ ئاي تۇردۇم.
بۇ ماكاننى بەك ياخشى كۆردۈم. پۇرسەت بولسا، ئۇيغۇر دىيارىنى يەنە بىر قېتىم
زىيارەت قىلىمەن. مەن ئۇيغۇر تىلىغا قىزىقىمەن. ئىندىيانا ئۇنىۋېرسىتېتىغا
كېلىشىمنىڭ سەۋەبى ئۇيغۇر تىلىنى ۋە ئوتتۇرا ئاسىيا تارىخىنى تېخىمۇ ياخشى
ئۆگىنىش.

Exercise 2.2:  Read the following questions about John and answer the questions based on the passage above. In your response, write down the dates in words.

1. جون قاچان تۇغۇلدى؟

______

2. ئۇ قاچان ئۇنىۋېرسىتېتنى پۈتتۈردى؟

______

3. ئۇ (قاچان) نەچچىنچى يىلى ئىندىيانا ئۇنىۋېرسىتېتىغا كەلدى؟

______

4. ئۇ تۇنجى قېتىم شىنجاڭغا قاچان باردى؟

______

Exercise 2.3: Now ask your partner three questions about John.

.1

.2

.3

Exercise 3:  ساۋاقداشلىرىڭىز بىلەن تونۇشۇڭ!

Exercise 3.1: Skim the following questions and mark those which are commonly used when meeting people for the first time.

☐	نەچچە ياشقا كىردىڭىز؟	☐	ئىسمىڭىز نېمە؟
☐	سىز توي قىلغانمۇ؟	☐	سىز پولۇغا ئامراقمۇ؟
☐	ئائىلىڭىزدە نەچچە جان بار؟	☐	سىز قەيەرلىك؟
☐	سىز ئوقۇمسىز يا (ياكى) ئىشلەمسىز؟	☐	سىز ئالدىراشمۇ؟
☐	كۈتۈپخانىغا بارامدۇق؟	☐	تۇنۇگۈن نەگە باردىڭىز؟

Exercise 3.2:  Ask your classmates appropriate questions from the table above and fill in the blanks below with information according to their responses.

ئىسمى: ______________________ يۇرتى: ______________________

تۇغۇلغان كۈنى: ______________________

ئېيشى: ______________________ ئوقۇغان مەكتىپى: ______________________

ئائىلىسى: ______________________

The Verb بولماق

1. The verb بولماق is commonly used in introductions. Look at the following examples:

مەن ئەنۋەر بولىمەن.
I am Enwer.
بۇ يېڭى دوختۇرىمىز بولىدۇ.
This is our new physician.
بۇلار بىزنىڭ تۇغقانلىرىمىز بولىدۇ.
They are our relatives.

2. This verb is also used in the -ۇپ form as a part of a compound followed by the verb ئىشلىمەك to describe a person's profession.

ئانام شۇ مەكتەپتە ئوقۇتقۇچى بولۇپ ئىشلەيدۇ.
My mother is a teacher at this school.
سىز كىم بولۇپ ئىشلەيسىز؟
What is your occupation?

Exercise 3.3: Introduce your classmate to the class using the information gathered above. Pay attention to cases and possessive endings of nouns and pronouns. Use the verb بولماق in your introduction.

Exercise 4: قىسقا سۆھبەت

ماھىنۇر

دولقۇن

Exercise 4.1: Listen to the conversation between Mahinur and Dolqun, then complete the table below.

ماينۇر	دولقۇن	سوئاللار
		ئۇلار قەيەرلىك؟
		ئۇلار نەچچە ياش؟
		ئۇلار نېمە ئىش قىلىدۇ؟
		كىم ساياھەت شىركىتىدە ئىشلەيدۇ؟
		كىم تارىخقا قىزىقىدۇ؟
		كىمنىڭ دەرسى بار؟

Exercise 4.2: Now listen to the conversation again and rehearse it with your partner.

Exercise 4.3: Based on the dialogue you just heard, create your own dialogue and act it out with a partner.

Exercise 5: مېنىڭ ئىسمىم نازۇگۇم

Exercise 5.1:  Watch this video in which Nazugum introduces herself and circle the answer that best reflects the information provided in it:

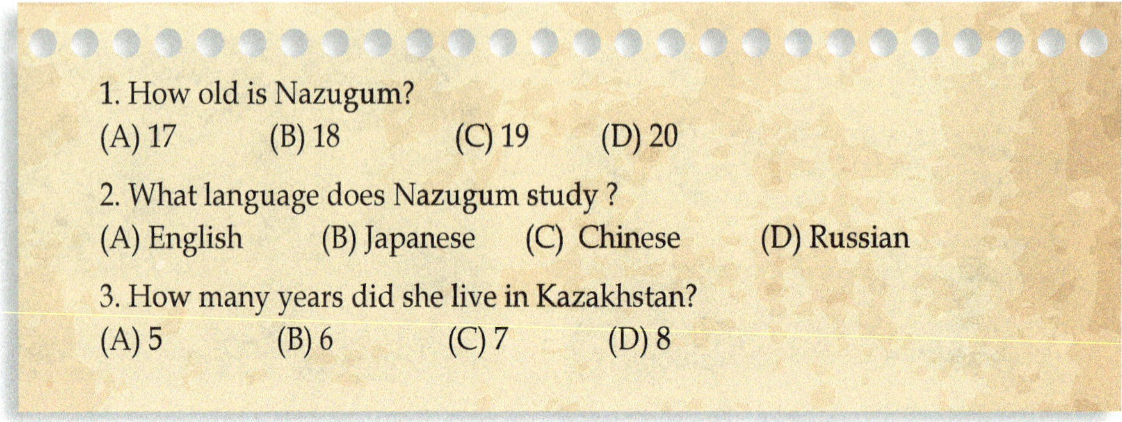

1. How old is Nazugum?
(A) 17 (B) 18 (C) 19 (D) 20

2. What language does Nazugum study ?
(A) English (B) Japanese (C) Chinese (D) Russian

3. How many years did she live in Kazakhstan?
(A) 5 (B) 6 (C) 7 (D) 8

Exercise 5.2: Watch the video one more time and answer the following two questions:

1. When was Nazugum born? Write out the full date including month, day, and year on the line provided.

____

2. In which city was she born?

____

Exercise 6:  You are getting ready for the first presentation in your Uyghur class. Using John's and Nazugum's introductions as an example, write a short paragraph about yourself.

Note:
You already know about basic Uyghur verb tenses, such as the present/future, simple past, indefinite past, present-continuous, and intentional future. Next you will have a chance to review them.

Exercise 7:  قەشقەرگە بارىمەن!

Read the following passage about Niko, one of John's classmates, and put all the verbs you find into the appropriate columns below.

مېنىڭ ئىسمىم نىكو. مەن ئامېرىكىلىق. يۇرتۇم كالىفورنىيە. مېنىڭ ئاتا-ئانام، ئاكام ۋە ئىككى سىڭلىم بار. ئاكام كانادادا تۇرىدۇ. ئۇ توي قىلغان. ئۇنىڭ بەك ئوماق بىر قىزى بار. چوڭ سىڭلىم چىكاگو ئۇنىۋېرسىتېتىدا ئوقۇيدۇ. كەلگۈسىدە ئۇ رەسسام بولماقچى. كىچىك سىڭلىم بۇ يىل تولۇق ئوتتۇرا مەكتەپنى پۈتتۈرىدۇ. ئۇ دوختۇرلۇقنى ئوقۇماقچى. مەن ئىندىيانا ئۇنىۋېرسىتېتىنىڭ ئاسپىرانتى. بۇ يەردە مەن ئۇيغۇرچە ئۆگىنىۋاتىمەن. مېنىڭ ئۇيغۇرچە ئىسمىم ئارسلان*. بۇ سۆزنىڭ كۆچمە مەنىسى "باتۇر، قورقماس" ئىكەن. مەن ئۇيغۇر تىلىغا بەك قىزىقىمەن.ئۇيغۇر تىلىنى ياخشىراق ئۆگەنسەم، شىنجاڭغا بارغاندا قىينالمايمەن. شىنجاڭ توغرۇلۇق كۆپ نەرسىلەرنى ئوقۇدۇم. ئۇ ناھايىتى گۈزەل ۋە باي تارىخقا ئىگە ئۆلكە ئىكەن. ئۇ يەرگە بارسام، چوقۇم تۇرپان، قەشقەر، خوتەن، غۇلجا قاتارلىق شەھەرلەرنى زىيارەت قىلىمەن.

*ئارسلان - lion cub

كەلگۈسى زامان	ھازىرقى زامان	ئۆتكەن زامان

Exercise 8: مەن شىنجاڭغا باردىم!

Exercise 8.1:  Read a second passage about Elise. Fill in the blanks with verbs expressing past events.

مېنىڭ ئىسمىم ئېلىس ئاندېرسون. ئۇيغۇرچە ئىسمىم نازاكەت. بۇ سۆزنىڭ مەنىسى "نازۇك، لاتاپەت". مەن ئۆزۈم ئامېرىكىلىق. ئوكلاخوما شتاتىدا تۇغۇلۇپ چوڭ ________. ھازىر ئىندىيانا ئۇنىۋېرسىتېتىنىڭ مۇزىكا فاكۇلتېتىدا ئوقۇيمەن. مەن ئۇيغۇرچە ئۆگەنگىلى تۆت يىل بولدى. ئۈچ قېتىم شىنجاڭنى زىيارەت ________. بىرىنچى قېتىم 2004 - يىلى يازدا ئۈرۈمچىگە ________. ئۇ يەردە شىنجاڭ ئۇنىۋېرسىتېتىدا بىر ئاي ئىنگلىزچە دەرس ________ لېكىن شۇ چاغدا ئۇيغۇرچە بىر سۆزمۇ بىلمەيتتىم. ئامېرىكىغا قايتقاندا ئۇيغۇر تىلى ۋە مەدەنىيىتىگە قىزىقىپ قالدىم. ئىككى يىلدىن كېيىن ئۇيغۇرچە ئۆگىنىشنى ________.

2007 - يىلى ئىككىنچى قېتىم شىنجاڭغا ________. بۇ قېتىم ئىككى يېرىم ئاي قەشقەردە تۇرۇپ ئۇيغۇرچە ________ ھەم مۇزىكا توغرۇلۇق تەتقىقات ________. شۇ چاغدىمۇ ئۇيغۇرچەم ئانچە ياخشى ئەمەس ئىدى، شۇڭا مەن خېلى قىينالدىم. ئەمما ئۇيغۇرچەم كۈندىن كۈنگە ياخشىلاندى. دائىم ئۇيغۇرلار بىلەن ________. 2010 -يىلى تەتقىقات قىلىش ئۈچۈن يەنە بىر قېتىم شىنجاڭغا باردىم. ئۈچ ئايچە ئۈرۈمچىدە ________. بۇ قېتىم بۇرۇنقىدەك قىينالمىدىم، چۈنكى ئۇيغۇرچەم خېلى ياخشى ئىدى. ئۇيغۇر دوستلىرىممۇ كۆپەيدى. بوش ۋاقتىمدا دوستلىرىم بىلەن شەھەر ئايلاندىم. ئۇلاردىن جانلىق تىلنى خېلى ياخشى ________ ئۇيغۇر تىلىنى ئۆگىنىش ئاسان ئەمەس. ھەر كۈنى مەشق قىلىشڭلار كېرەك. ئەمما تىرىشىپ ئۆگەنسەڭلار، شىنجاڭغا بارغاندا قىينالمايسىلەر.

Exercise 8.2:  Now listen to Elise's introduction to check your answers.

Exercise 8.3:  Ask your partner three questions about Elise.

.1

.2

.3

Exercise 9: ئۇلار قەيەردە؟ ئۇلار نېمە قىلىۋاتىدۇ؟

Exercise 9.1:  It is 4:00PM. John and his classmates have just finished their classes. Look at the pictures below and describe where the students are and what they are doing.

Exercise 9.2:  You want to invite your friend to a casual dinner. Call him and find out what he is doing now. Tell him you were passing by and are currently in front of his house.
The phone rings and your friend picks up.
You say ...

Exercise 10: مەن چىكاگوغا بارماقچى!

Exercise 10.1:  Watch a video in which Batur and Nazaket are talking about a trip they are planning to take to Chicago. Before watching it, practice the following words and expressions.

International Service	خەلقئارا بۆلۈم
even though I am an American	ئامېرىكىلىق بولغىنىم بىلەن
to register	تىزىملىتىپ قويماق
to take advantage of an opportunity	پۇرسەتتىن پايدىلانماق
to bring	ئاپارماق (ئېلىپ بارماق)
I was going to visit	كۆرۈپ كېلەي دېۋىدىم (دېگەن ئىدىم)
is it possible to...	بولامدىكەن (بولامدۇ ئىكەن)

Exercise 10.2: After watching the video, circle the best answer.

1. نازاكەت بىلەن باتۇر نەدە كۆرۈشۈپ قالدى؟
ئا: كۇتۇپخانىدا ب: كىتابخانىدا س: قىزىل چىراقنىڭ يېنىدا د: پەلەمپەيدە

2. باتۇر نەگە ماڭدى؟
ئا: خەلقئارا مەركەزگە ب: خەلقئارا بۆلۈمگە س: خەلقئارا سارايغا د: خەلقئارا يىغىنغا

3. باتۇر نېمە ئۈچۈن چىكاگوغا بارماقچى؟
ئا: ئۇ چىكاگوغا ئامراق ب: ئۇ چىكاگوغا بارمىغان
س: ئۇ تۇغقىنىنى يوقلىماقچى د: دوستى توي قىلماقچى

4. ئۇلار قاچان چىكاگودىن يولغا چىقىدۇ؟
ئا: كەچ سائەت يەتتىدە ب: كەچ سائەت سەككىزدە
س: كەچ سائەت توققۇزدا د: كەچ سائەت ئوندا

Exercise 10.3: Watch the video one more time and decide if the following statements are true or false:

خاتا	توغرا

1. باتۇر چەتئەللىك، شۇڭا ئۇ چىكاگوغا بارماقچى.
2. چىكاگوغا بېرىش ئۈچۈن ئاتمىش دوللار تاپشۇرۇش كېرەك.
3. ئۇلار چىكاگوغا شەنبە كۈنى سەھەر سائەت ئالتىدە ماڭىدۇ.
4. چىكاگوغا ئامېرىكىلىقلارمۇ بارسا بولىدۇ.

Exercise 11:  Look at these two sentences.

مەن ماشىنا ھەيدىيەلەيمەن. ئەمدى بىز چىكاگوغا بارالايمىز.

In these sentences you see two uses of the suffix -الا\ -ەلە. In the first sentence, it expresses "ability." In the second sentence, it expresses "possibility." Look at the following statements and decide which meaning of the suffix is intended.

Possibility	Ability	Statements
		1. مەن سۈ ئۈزەلەيمەن.
		2. ئۇ خەنزۇچە گېزىتلەرنى ئوقۇيالايدۇ.
		3. بۇ يازدا ئىشلىرىم كۆپ، ھېچنەگە بارالمايمەن.
		4. سىڭلىم ئات مىنەلمەيدۇ.
		5. كېلەر ھەپتە ھاۋا ئوچۇق بولىدۇ، ئەمدى تاغقا چىقالايمىز.
		6. ئۇلار ھازىر تورغا چىقالامدۇ؟
		7. ئۇيغۇرچە ناخشىلارنى چۈشىنەلەمسىز؟
		8. دادام ماشىنا ھەيدىيەلمەيدۇ.
		9. ئۇكام ئاچچىق تاماق يېيەلمەيدۇ.
		10. جۇڭگودا خىزمەتچىلەر باشلىقلا ھېچنەرسە دېيەلمەيدۇ.

Exercise 12:  Go back to Elise's introduction and find the one sentence which makes use of the conditional suffix -سا \ -سە (Exercise 8.1). Translate this sentence into English.

Exercise 13:  Get together with your classmates and discuss the following questions. Do they express ability or possibility?

1. بۇ يىل مەن شىنجاڭغا بارماقچى. سىلەر بارالامسىلەر؟
2. يازدا مەن جۇڭگودا بولىمەن، شۇڭا ئاتا- ئانامنى زىيارەت قىلالمايمەن. سىلەرچۇ ؟
3. مەن لەگمەنگە بەك ئامراق، لېكىن ئۆزەم ئېتەلمەيمەن. سىزچۇ، لەگمەن ئېتەلەمسىز؟
4. ئىنىم رۇسچە سۆزلىيەلەيدۇ. سىلەرچۇ؟ قايسى تىلدا سۆزلىيەلەيسىلەر؟
5. مەن ماشىنا ھەيدىيەلمەيمەن. سىلەرچۇ؟ ماشىنا ھەيدەش تەسمۇ؟
6. سىلەر ئاچچىق تاماققا ئامراقمۇ؟ ئاچچىق تاماق يېيەلەمسىلەر؟
7. مەن پۇتبول ئوينىيالمايمەن. سىلەرچۇ؟

Exercise 14:  Name the actions that these animals are able or not able to perform. Follow the example:

قۇش ئۇچالايدۇ، ئەمما سۇ ئۈزەلمەيدۇ.

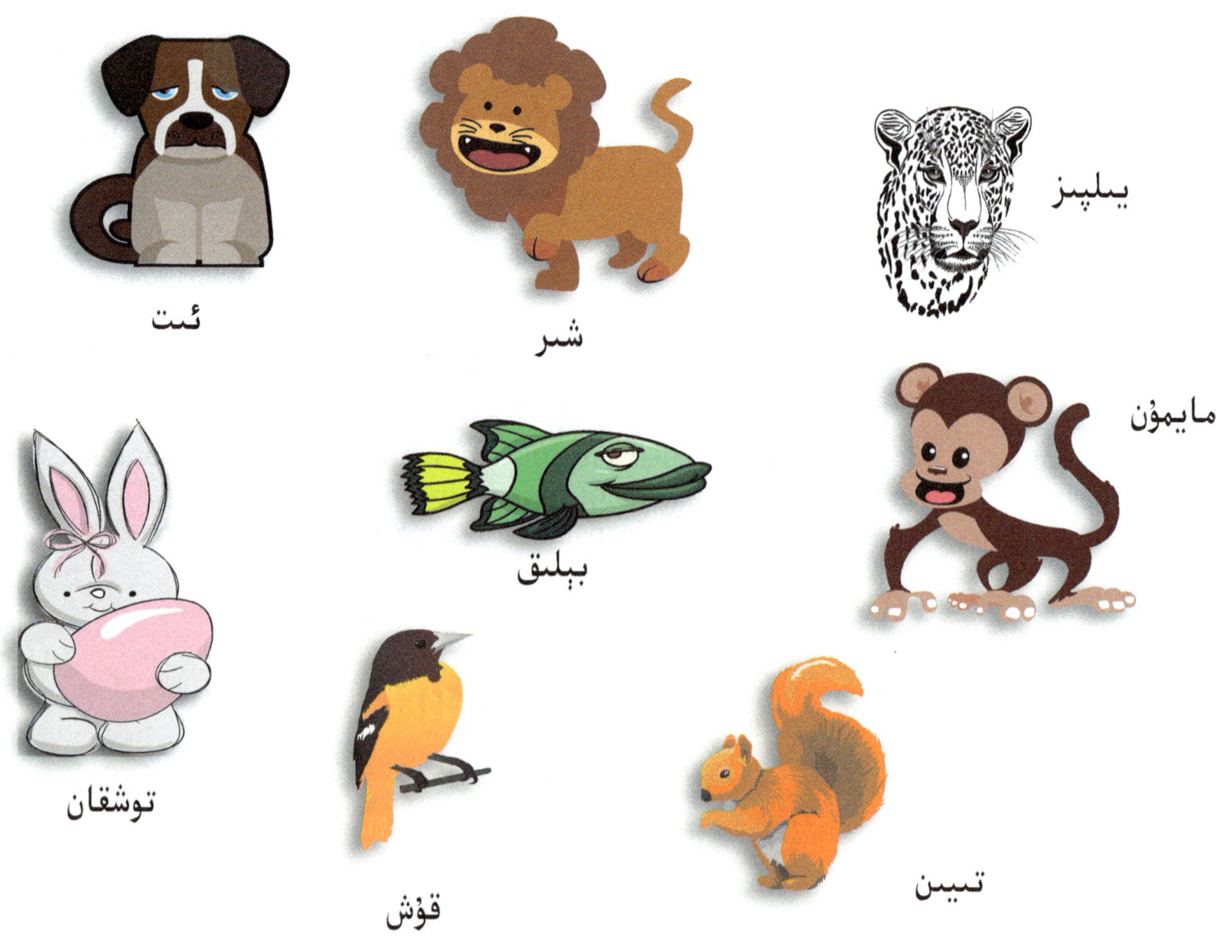

Exercise 15:  Pretend that you are an animal and describe yourself. Include what you can and cannot do. Your partner will guess which animal you are.

Exercise 16:  Your Uyghur friend Ilghar from Urumchi has been admitted to the University of Chicago for the fall semester. Write a brief email in which you tell him about the places he can stay, visit, and shop in Chicago. In your message, use verbs which express ability and possibility as much as you can. Follow this model:

چىكاگودا مىللىي ئاشخانىلار كۆپ، ئۇ يەردە سىز مۇسۇلمانچە تاماق يېيەلەيسىز...

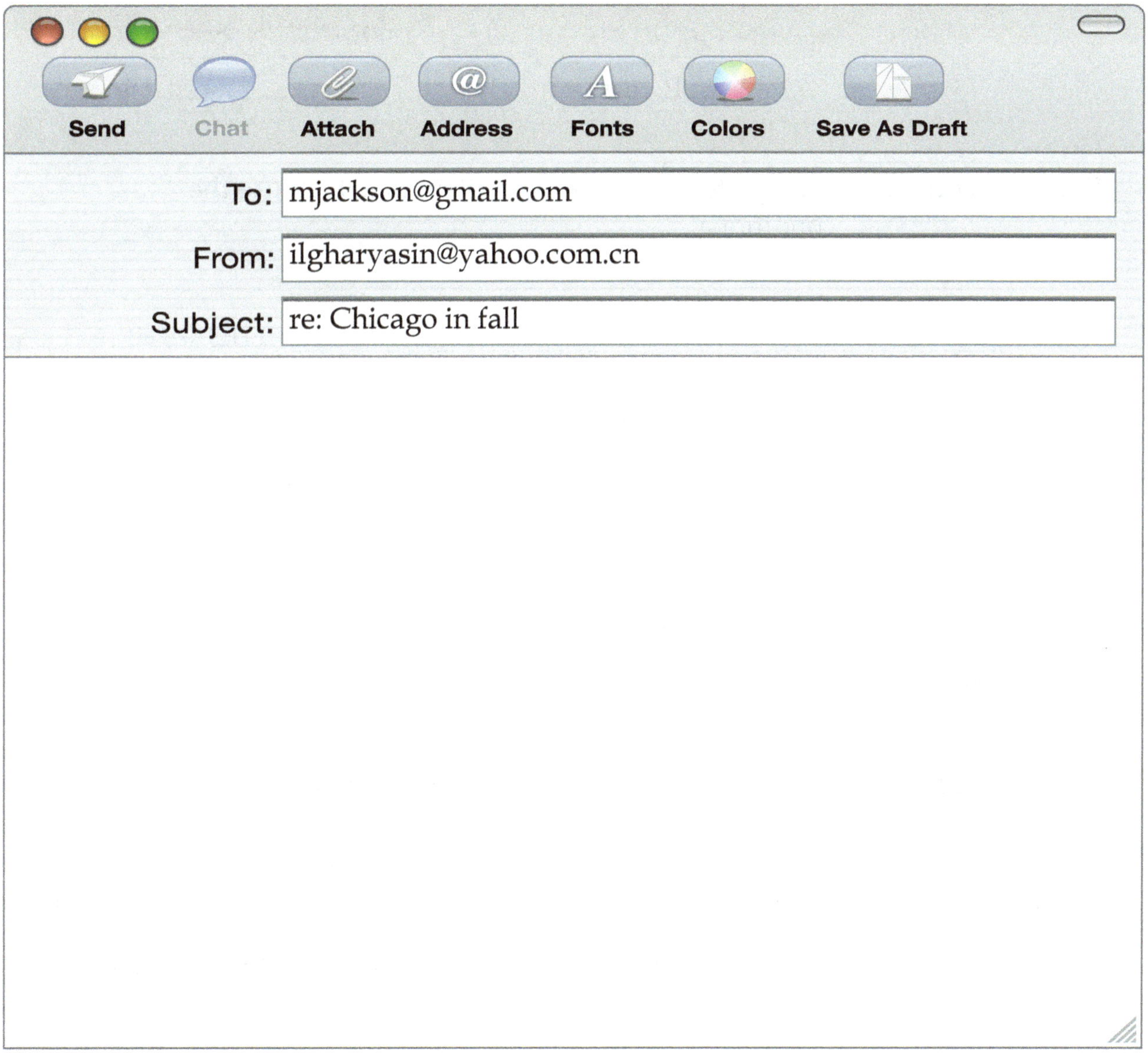

Send | Chat | Attach | Address | Fonts | Colors | Save As Draft

To: mjackson@gmail.com

From: ilgharyasin@yahoo.com.cn

Subject: re: Chicago in fall

Exercise 17: (ئەگەر) پۇلۇم بولمىسا، شىنجاڭغا بارالامدىم؟

Exercise 17.1:  Match the fragments in the righthand column with those in the lefthand colum in order to form complete sentences. The first one has been done for you.

شىنجاڭغا بارىمەن.	___	(ئەگەر) پۇلۇم بولسا،	1
كىنو كۆرىمەن.	___	ئاغىنەم كەلسە،	2
دۇكانغا بارىمىز.	___	پۇرسەت چىقىپ (بولۇپ) قالسا،	3
يولغا چىقمايمىز.	___	ۋاقتىم بولسا،	4
سۇ ئۈزگىلى بارىمىز.	___	دەرستىن بالدۇرراق چۈشسەك،	5
گىلەم ئالىمەن.	1	يامغۇر يېغىپ كەتسە،	6

Exercise 17.2:  Complete the following sentences, which use the conditional.

1. ئاغىنەم كەلسە، ______________________________
2. ئاپتوبۇسنى ساقلىساق، ______________________________
3. ماشىنىنى بۇ يەرگە قويساق، ______________________________
4. دوستۇمغا خەت يازسام، ______________________________
5. ئادىلنى كۆرسەم______________________________
6. ئۇلار دەرستىن چۈشسە، ______________________________
7. ئەگەر خالىسىڭىز، ______________________________

Exercise 18: شىنجاڭغا بارسام...

Exercise 18.1:  Write a short composition about a trip you would like to take in the future.

Exercise 18.2: A. Look at your composition. What verb forms and suffixes did you use?

B. Rewrite your composition using as many conditionals as you can.

Exercise 19: مېنىڭ ئىسمىم باھادىر

Exercise 19.1:  Watch the video where Bahadir (Benjamin) is introducing himself. Take some notes, then answer the following two questions:

1. What did you learn about Bahadir? Provide as many details as you can.
2. What did you learn about his family?

Exercise 19.2: Watch the video one more time and tell if the following statements are true or false:

	T	F
1. Bahadir came to Indiana nine years ago.		
2. He studied history.		
3. When he graduated from the University, he found a job.		
4. He is married.		
5. Now he is a graduate student at Indiana University.		
6. He studied Farsi as well.		

Project

Shooting a Video

You are interested in spending a couple months, or maybe a semester, somewhere in Xinjiang. You have been browsing several websites and found information on an internship program. You decide to apply for it.

As a part of your application, you must submit a two to three minute video presentation of yourself.

Shoot your own video using Bahadir's video as an example. Remember to:

- Introduce yourself (name, nationality, date of birth)
- Explain why you want to stay in Xinjiang
- Let the viewer know about your special skills
- Describe your language skills and other abilities
- Ask if it is possible for you to live with an Uyghur family to improve your Uyghur language skills

Vocabulary سۆزلۈك

Vocabulary is given according to the Uyghur alphabetical order. The right column precedes the left column on each page.

graduate student	ئاسپىرانت
as usual; like before	بۇرۇنقىدەك
opportunity	پۇرسەت
to take advantage of an opportunity	پۇرسەتتىن پايدىلانماق
to pay	پۇل تاپشۇرماق
to graduate	پۈتتۈرمەك
to research	تەتقىق قىلماق
high school	تولۇق ئوتتۇرا مەكتەپ
to get to know, to get acquainted	تونۇشماق
to marry	توي قىلماق
to be born	تۇغۇلماق
the first time	تۇنجى قېتىم
still; even more	تېخىمۇ
to study hard	تىرىشىپ ئۆگەنمەك
to register	تىزىملىتىپ قويماق

spoken language	جانلىق تىل
foreigner	چەتئەللىك
a corner	دوقمۇش
to visit	زىيارەت قىلماق
tour company	ساياھەت شىركىتى
reason	سەۋەب
to tour a city	شەھەر ئايلانماق
at that time	شۇ چاغدا
to return	قايتماق
to be interested in	قىزىقماق
stoplight	قىزىل چىراق
to suffer	قىينالماق
from day to day	كۈندىن كۈنگە
to drive a vehicle	ماشىنا ھەيدىمەك
place; area	ماكان
to practice	مەشق قىلماق
to visit	يوقلىماق

بىرىنچى دەرس

CHAPTER ONE 1

ئۇيغۇر ئىسىملىرى

UYGHUR PERSONAL NAMES

IN THIS CHAPTER

Functions

- Expressing compliments and surprise
- Narrating stories
- Expressing apologies and regrets
- Comparing Uyghur and English names
- Describing personal interests and hobbies

Grammar

- The narrative past with the word ئىكەن
- The narrative past with the suffix پتۇ -
- The hearsay or reportative Past with the suffix پتۇ -

In this chapter John and his friends meet Ekber, a native speaker of Uyghur from Urumchi. Through the blog entries, reading passages, and conversations in this chapter you will learn about the history of Uyghur naming customs, as well as the ancient city of Kashgar and the ways in which it has changed. In addition, you will also gain some experience with Uyghur stories and learn to tell stories in Uyghur yourself.

Exercise 1: سوئاللارغا جاۋاب بېرگىلار

1. كىشىلەر بىلوگىغا نېمە يازىدۇ؟
2. كىشىلەر نېمە ئۈچۈن بىلوگ يازىدۇ؟
3. دوستلىرىڭىز بىلوگ يازامدۇ؟
4. سىزچۇ؟ سىزنىڭ بىلوگىڭىز بارمۇ؟
5. بىلوگىڭىزغا كۈنىگە نەچچە قېتىم كىرىسىز؟

سىزنىڭچە، تۆۋەندىكى خاتىرىنى كىم يازغان؟

14 - ئاۋغۇست، يەكشەنبە

بۈگۈن بىزنىڭ ئائىلە ئۈچۈن قىزىق بىر ئىش بولدى: تاغام ئۆتكەن

ھەپتە بىر دانە لاتارىيە ئالغان ئىكەن (ئۈچ سوملۇق)، بۇ ھەپتە 50 مىڭ

سوملۇق مۇكاپات چىقىپتۇ. تاغام ماڭا بىر كومپيۇتېر ئېلىپ بېرىشكە

ماقۇل بولدى. كومپيۇتېر ئالغاندىن كېيىن كۈندىلىك خاتىرەمنى

كومپيۇتېردا يازىمەن. ئۇ چاغدا...

Exercise 2: ئۇيغۇرلارنىڭ ئىسمى

Exercise 2.1: Before reading John's first blog entry, practice the following words.

prophet	پەيغەمبەر
coin style	تەڭگىسىمان
messenger	ئەلچى
spot	داغ
planet	سەييارە
rights	ھوقۇق
property	مال- مۈلۈك
servant	چاكار
ferocious	ۋەھشى

lion cub	ئارسلان
tiger	يولۋاس
leopard	قاپلان
star	چولپان
gold	ئالتۇن
moon	ئاي
sun; day	كۈن
slave	قۇل
sword	قىلىچ

Exercise 2.2:  Read the following definitions and write down the appropriate words from the list above.

_______________	پۇل ۋە زىننەت بۇيۇملىرى ياسىلىدىغان قىممەت باھالىق مېتال
_______________	قۇياش
_______________	يۇلتۇز
_______________	ۋەھشى ھايۋان، "ھايۋاناتلارنىڭ پادىشاھى" دېگەن نامى بار
_______________	ھېچقانداق ھوقۇق ۋە مال - مۈلۈككە ئىگە بولمىغان چاكار
_______________	قارا يوللۇق بارس
_______________	ئاللاھنىڭ ئەلچىسى
_______________	يولۋاسقا ئوخشاپ كېتىدۇ، لېكىن ئۇنىڭدىن كىچىكرەك بولىدۇ، دەرەخكە چىقالايدۇ. تېنىدە تەڭگىسىمان داغلار بار.
_______________	ئۇرۇش قورالى
_______________	يەر شارىنى ئايلىنىدىغان سەييارە

Exercise 2.3:  Read the blog entry and answer the questions that follow.

Uyghur John's Blog

ئامېرىكىلىق يالقۇننىڭ تورتۇراسى

Search

كۈندە بىر ماقال:
ياشلىقتا بىلىم ئال، قېرىغاندا ئىشقا سال.

1 - سېنتەبىر

بۈگۈن ئۇيغۇر تىلى دەرسىنى باشلىدۇق. ساۋاقداشلىرىمنىڭ ئۇيغۇرچىسى خېلى ياخشىكەن. ئۇلار ئامېرىكىنىڭ ھەر قايسى شتاتلىرىدىن كەلگەن ئىكەن. بۈگۈن ئۇيغۇرچە ئىسمى يوق ئوقۇغۇچىلار ئۆزىگە ئۇيغۇرچە ئىسىم تاللىدى. دېمەك ساۋاقداشلىرىمنىڭ ئۇيغۇرچە ئىسىملىرى ئالىم، ئارسلان، نازاكەت، باتۇر ۋە ئادىل. ئوقۇتقۇچىمىز ئۇيغۇرچە ئىسىملار توغرۇلۇق قىسقىچە چۈشەنچە بېرىپ ئۆتتى. ئىسلام دىنىنى قوبۇل قىلىشتىن بۇرۇن ئۇيغۇرلار ئىسىملار ئۈچۈن تۈركىي سۆزلەرنى ئىشلەتكەن ئىكەن. مەسىلەن: ئارسلان، بارس، قاپلان، چولپان، ئاي، كۈن، ئالتۇن قاتارلىقلار. ئۇيغۇر خەلقى ئىسلام دىنىنى قوبۇل قىلغاندىن كېيىن، ئىسلام دىنى ئۇيغۇرلارنىڭ ئىسىملىرىغىمۇ تەسىر كۆرسىتىپتۇ. شۇنىڭدىن باشلاپ، ئۇيغۇرلارنىڭ ئىسىملىرىدا ئەرەبچە ۋە پارسچە سۆز بىلەن قويۇلغان ئىسىملار كۆپىيىشكە باشلىغان ئىكەن. مەسىلەن، ئابدۇللا (ئاللانىڭ قۇلى)، ھەبىبۇللا (ئاللانىڭ دوستى)، سەيپۇللا (ئاللانىڭ قىلىچى) دېگەن ئىسىملارغا ئوخشاش. ئىسلام دىنىغا بولغان ئېتىقاد كۈچەيگەندىن كېيىن ساپ ئۇيغۇرچە سۆز بىلەن قويۇلغان ئىسىملارنىڭ ئورنىنى ئەرەبچە ۋە پارسچە سۆز بىلەن قويۇلغان ئىسىملار ئىگىلەشكە باشلاپتۇ. ھەر بىر مۇسۇلمان ئۇيغۇر ئۆزىنىڭ ئاللاغا، پەيغەمبەرلەرگە بولغان سېغىنىشىنى ئىزھار قىلىش ئۈچۈن، ئۇلارنىڭ ئىسمىنى ئۆزلىرىگە ئىسىم قىلىپ قويۇشنى ئادەت قىپتۇ. لېكىن ئىسلامىيەتتىن كېيىن ئۇيغۇرچە سۆز بىلەن ئىسىم قويۇش ئادىتى پۈتۈنلەي يوقاپ كەتمەپتۇ. مەسىلەن: بۇلاق، ئالما، ئاي، چولپان، ئارسلان دېگەندەك ئىسىملارمۇ قويۇلۇپتۇ. ئىسلامىيەتتىن كېيىن ئەرەبچە سۆزلەر ئىچىدىن مەنىسى ياخشى، دىنىي تۈس ئالمىغان ئىسىملار قويۇلۇپتۇ، مەسىلەن: ئادىل، ئالىم، ئازاد، پەزىلەت، سائادەت، زۆھرە دېگەندەك. بۇنىڭدىن باشقا، ئۇيغۇر تىلىنىڭ ئۆزىگە خاس سۆز ياساش ئۇسۇلى ئارقىلىق ياسالغان ئىسىملارمۇ كۆپىيىپتۇ. مەسىلەن: ئەركىن، ئۆتكۈر، ئۆركەش، تۇرغۇن، يالقۇن دېگەندەك ئىسىملار.

بۇ مەلۇماتلار مەن ئۈچۈن بەك قىزىقارلىق بولدى. ئاڭلىسام، بۇ يەردە ئۇرۇمچىلىك بىر بالا بار ئىكەن. ئوقۇتقۇچىمىز ئۇنىڭ ئىسمىنى ئېيتقان ئىدى، ئەمما مەن ئۇنتۇپ قاپتىمەن.

1. ئىسلامىيەتتىن بۇرۇن ئۇيغۇرلار ئىسىملار ئۈچۈن قانداق سۆزلەرنى ئىشلەتكەن؟
2. ئىسلام دىنى قوبۇل قىلىنغاندىن كېيىن ئىسىم قويۇش ئادەتلىرىدە قانداق ئۆزگىرىشلەر يۈز بەرگەن؟
3. ئابدۇللا، ھەبىبۇللا، سەيپۇللا ئىسىملارنىڭ مەنىسى نېمە؟
4. نېمە ئۈچۈن ئۇيغۇرلار ئاللا ۋە پەيغەمبەرلەرنىڭ ئىسىملىرىنى ئۆزلىرىگە ئىسىم قىلىپ ئالغان؟
5. ئىسلامىيەتتىن كېيىن قانداق ئىسىملار ئىشلىتىلگەن؟

Exercise 2.4:  Read the proverb on the left side of the blog entry. What does it mean to you? Discuss its meaning with your instructor.

Exercise 2.5:  Which of the given options best matches the following words and expressions from the text?

تەرجىمىسى			سۆز - ئىبارىلەر
a. to describe	b. to choose	c. to drop	تاللىماق
a. concept	b. introduction	c. understanding	چۈشەنچە
a. belief	b. religion	c. worship	ئېتىقاد
a. fresh	b. clear	c. pure	ساپ
a. to express	b. to describe	c. to affect	ئىزھار قىلىش
a. whole	b. completely	c. plural	پۈتۈنلەي
a. aspect	b. nuance	c. flat	تۈس
a. dance	b. method	c. master	ئۇسۇل
a. custom	b. hobby	c. interest	ئادەت
a. to attract	b. to match	c. to reflect	ئەكس ئەتمەك

Exercise 2.6:  Working with a partner, discuss the following: What did you learn about the history of Uyghur names from John's blog? What do you know about names in your culture? What are some similarities and differences between Uyghur and English names?

1 The Narrative Past Tense

In the blog, the word ئىكەن appears in these forms:

ئىشلەتكەن ئىكەن، كەلگەن ئىكەن، باشلىغان ئىكەن

The word ئىكەن is used to form a narrative past tense. The narrative past is used to talk about things that happened in the distant past. It is also used to tell stories and fairy tales.

There are two forms of the narrative past in Uyghur. One is formed with the word (ئى+كەن) ئىكەن , which usually occurs after verbs in the indefinite past tense, at the very end of the sentence. Look at the following examples from the blog:

ئىسلام دىنىنى قوبۇل قىلىشتىن بۇرۇن ئۇيغۇرلار ئىسىملار ئۈچۈن تۈركىي سۆزلەرنى ئىشلەتكەن ئىكەن.
Before converting to Islam, Uyghurs used to use Turkic words for personal names.

ئۇيغۇرلارنىڭ ئىسىملىرىدا ئەرەبچە ۋە پارسچە سۆز بىلەن قويۇلغان ئىسىملار كۆپىيىشكە باشلىغان ئىكەن.
Among Uyghur names, the use of Persian and Arabic words gradually increased.

The second narrative past tense is formed by adding the suffix (پ+تۇ) -پتۇ (after vowels) and -ىپتۇ (after consonants) to the verb stem. Here are some examples from the blog:

ئۇيغۇرچە سۆز بىلەن قويۇلغان ئىسىملارنىڭ ئورنىنى ئەرەبچە ۋە
پارسچە سۆز بىلەن قويۇلغان ئىسىملار ئىگىلەشكە باشلاپتۇ.
Names based on Arabic and Persian words began to replace the names based on Uyghur words.

لېكىن ئىسلامىيەتتىن كېيىن ئۇيغۇرچە سۆز بىلەن ئىسىم قويۇش ئادىتى پۈتۈنلەي يوقاپ كەتمەپتۇ.
However, after Islam the custom of picking Uyghur names didn't |entirely vanish.

As you may have noticed, in narrations and stories, both forms of the narrative past can be used.

Exercise 3:  Now, using both forms of the narrative past and the words provided form grammatically correct sentences.

1. زاماندا \\ بىر دېھقان\\ بۇرۇنقى \\ياشىماق
2. ئاتا- بالا \\ يولغا چىقماق\\ سەھەردە
3. مېھمانلار\\ باغقا كىرمەك\\ ئاۋۋال\\ كېيىن\\ مىۋە يېمەك
4. دوست بولماق \\ چاشقان\\ ئىت\\ مۈشۈك \\ ئاخىرىدا \\ ۋە
5. كېسەل \\ دوختۇرغا\\ پۇل تاپشۇرماق\\ ئاندىن \\ داۋالانماق
6. كېيىن \\ مۇزېيغا بارماق\\ ئوقۇغۇچىلار\\ ئەتىگەندە\\ ئىمتىھان بەرمەك

Exercise 4: From John's blog, you learned that foreigners who learn Uyghur often take Uyghur names. Look at the following popular Uyghur names and their meanings. Try to remember at least five of them.

ئايالچە ئىسىملار	
مەنىسى	ئىسىم
خاتىرجەم	ئامىنە
ئانار گۈلى	گۈلنار
چىرايلىق	جەمىلە
ئازادلىق	ھۆررىيەت
مەڭگۈ	خالىدە
ئەقىللىق	رەشىدە
بەك گۈزەل	رەنا
چولپان يۇلتۇزى	زۆھرە
خۇش پۇراق	زەينەب
بەختلىك	سەئىدە
ساغلام، ساق	سالامەت
قۇياشتەك نۇرلۇق	شەمسىيە
ئېگىز	ئالىيە
سۆيۈملۈك	ئەزىزە
ياخشى مۇسۇلمان	فاتىمە
يالغۇز	پەرىدە
پادىشاھنىڭ قىزى	مەلىكە
نۇرلۇق	مۇنىرە

ئەرەنچە ئىسىملار	
مەنىسى	ئىسىم
بىر پەيغەمبەر	ئىلياس
ناھايىتى نۇرلۇق	ئەنۋەر
ئەخلاقلىق	ھەسەن
بىر پەيغەمبەر	داۋۇد
زېرەك	زاكىر
قىلىچ	زۇلپىقار
قەھرىمان	رۇستەم
پادىشاھ	سۇلتان
بىر پەيغەمبەر	سۇلايمان
تەشەككۈر ئېيتقۇچى	شاكىر
نەتىجە	سادىر
راستچىل	سادىق
پاكىز	تاھىر
ھەققانىي	ئادىل
غەلىبەقىلغۇچى	غالىب
تاللانغان	مۇختار
غەلىبە قىلغۇچى	مەنسۇر
بىر پەيغەمبەر	ئىبراھىم

Exercise 5: مومام ئېيتقان چۆچەكلەر

Exercise 5.1: Check the list of Uyghur men's names above and find the names Zakir and Shakir. What do they mean?

Exercise 5.2:  Read the passage below and circle any verb which displays one of the two forms of the narrative past. Then translate these sentences into English.

زاكىر بىلەن شاكىر

بۇرۇنقى زاماندا زاكىر بىلەن شاكىر ئىسىملىك ئىككى دوست بولغان ئىكەن. ئۇلار كىچىكىدىن بىللە ئويناپ چوڭ بولۇپ، مەكتەپكىمۇ تەڭلا كىرىپتۇ.

شاكىر ئىرادىلىك، تىرىشچان، زېرەك بالا بولغاچقا كۈندىن- كۈنگە ئەقىل- پاراسەتكە تولۇشقا باشلاپتۇ. زاكىر بولسا سىنىپقا كىرسە، بېشى ئاغرىيدىغان، سىرتقا چىقسا قۇشقاچ مارايدىغان بالا ئىكەن. شۇڭا ئۇ ياخشى ئوقۇيالماپتۇ.

ئارىدىن بىر نەچچە ۋاقىت ئۆتۈپتۇ. شاكىر مەكتەپتە "ئەقىللىق بالا" دېگەن نامنى ئاپتۇ. زاكىر كۈندىن- كۈنگە ئارقىدا قېلىپ، "ئويۇنخۇمار" دېگەن ئاتاققا قاپتۇ.

كۈنلەرنىڭ بىرىدە زاكىر شاكىردىن:

- ئاداش، ئىككىمىز مەكتەپكە تەڭ كىردۇق. بىر سىنىپتا ئوقۇۋاتىمىز، ھەيرانمەن، سېنىڭ ئۆگىنىش ئەھۋالىڭ مېنىڭكىدىن كۆپ ياخشى، بۇنىڭ سەۋەبى نېمە؟ - دەپ سوراپتۇ.

- تىرىشىپ ئۆگىنىشنى سەندىن ئۆگەندىم، بۇنىڭدىن باشقا سەۋەب يوق، - دەپ جاۋاب بېرىپتۇ شاكىر.

شاكىرنىڭ بۇ جاۋابى زاكىرنى رەنجىتىپتۇ. ئۇ: "شاكىر مېنىڭ ئەڭ يېقىن دوستۇم تۇرۇپ، مېنى زاڭلىق قىلىۋاتىدۇ" دەپ ئويلاپتۇ ۋە شۇنىڭدىن تارتىپ شاكىرغا گەپ قىلمايدىغان بوپتۇ.

بۇ ئىككى دوستنىڭ ئارىسىدا بولغان پاراڭدىن خەۋەر تاپقان ئۇستازى ئۇلارنى چاقىرىپتۇ ۋە شاكىردىن:

- زاكىرغا بەرگەن جاۋابىڭنىڭ مەنىسى نېمە؟ - دەپ سوراپتۇ.

- سىز بىزگە، - دەپتۇ شاكىر ئۇستازىغا قاراپ، - "ئەقىللىق بولاي دېسەڭ، ئەقىلسىزدىن ئۆگەن" دەپ تەلىم بەرگەن ئىدىڭىز. مەن سىزنىڭ شۇ تەلىمىڭىزنى ئېسىمدە چىڭ تۇتۇپ، زاكىرنىڭ ئويۇنغا بېرىلىپ كەتكەنلىكىنى كۆرۈپ، ئۆگىنىشكە كۆپرەك كۆڭۈل بۆلدۇم، - دەپتۇ. زاكىر شاكىرنىڭ سۆزىنىڭ مەنىسىنى چۈشىنىپ، تىرىشىپ ئۆگىنىشكە بەل باغلاپتۇ.

to make fun	زاڭلىق قىلماق
conversation	پاراڭ
to teach	تەلىم بەرمەك
to keep in mind	ئېسىدە چىڭ تۇتماق
to be diligent	كۆڭۈل بۆلمەك
clever	زېرەك
smart	ئەقىللىق

determined	ئىرادىلىك
to make a resolution	بەل باغلىماق
bird	قۇشقاچ
to peep; peer	مارىماق
a person who loves to play	ئويۇنخۇمار
to find out	خەۋەر تاپماق
to get upset	رەنجىمەك

Exercise 5.3: Now answer the following questions about Zakir and Shakir.

1. زاكىر بىلەن شاكىر كىم؟
2. ئۇلار بىر بىرىدىن قانداق پەرق قىلىدۇ؟
3. نېمىشقا زاكىر ياخشى ئوقۇيالماپتۇ؟
4. نېمە ئۈچۈن زاكىر شاكىردىن خاپا بوپتۇ؟
5. سىزنىڭچە شاكىرنىڭ جاۋابى توغرىمۇ؟ نېمىشقا؟
6. شاكىر ئۇستازىغا نېمە دەيدۇ؟

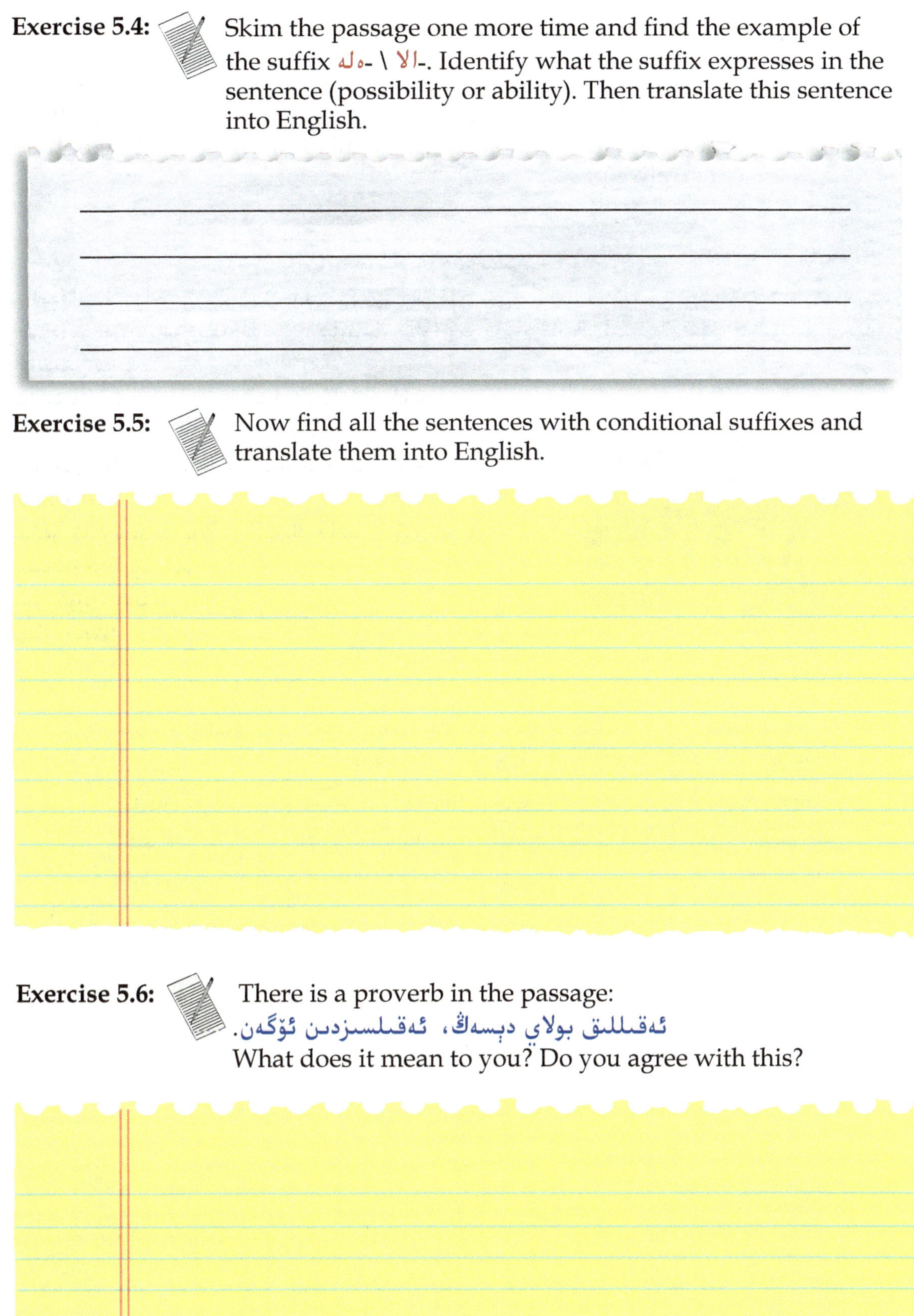

Exercise 5.4: Skim the passage one more time and find the example of the suffix -ەله \ -الا. Identify what the suffix expresses in the sentence (possibility or ability). Then translate this sentence into English.

Exercise 5.5: Now find all the sentences with conditional suffixes and translate them into English.

Exercise 5.6: There is a proverb in the passage:
ئەقىللىق بولاي دېسەڭ، ئەقىلسىزدىن ئۆگەن.
What does it mean to you? Do you agree with this?

Exercise 6: مومام ئېيتقان چۆچەكلەر

Exercise 6.1:  Look at the following passage. You are only given the first part of the text. Read it and, based on the meaning, finish the story in your own words. Remember to use both forms of the narrative past.

ئات ئوغرىسى

بىر دېھقاننىڭ ياخشى بىر ئېتى بار ئىكەن. بىر كېچىسى ئۇنىڭ ئېتىنى ئوغرىلاپ كېتىپتۇ. دېھقان ئېتىنى ئىزدەپ تەرەپ- تەرەپكە چېپىپتۇ. قارىسا، يولدا بىر ئادەم ئۇنىڭ ئېتىنى مىنىپ كېتىۋېتىپتۇ. دېھقان ئۇنىڭ ئالدىنى توسۇپ:

- بۇ مېنىڭ ئېتىم! - دەپ ۋارقىراپتۇ. ئاتلىق ئادەم:

- ياق، ياق. بۇ مېنىڭ ئېتىم، - دەپتۇ.

دېھقان دەرھال چاپىنىنى سېلىپ، ئاتنىڭ بېشىنى ئوراپتۇ-دە، ئاتلىق ئادەمدىن سوراپتۇ:

- ئەگەر ئات سېنىڭ بولسا، ئاتنىڭ قايسى كۆزى كور؟

ئاتلىق بىرئاز ئويلىنىۋېلىپ:

- سول كۆزى- دەپتۇ.

دېھقان دەپتۇ:

immediately	دەرھال	to steal	ئوغرىلاپ كەتمەك
blind	كور	to look for	ئىزدىمەك
coat	چاپان	to run	چاپماق
to take off	سالماق	to mount	مىنمەك
to cover	ئورىماق	to shout out	ۋارقىرىماق

Exercise 6.2:  Now read the original ending of the story. Was your ending close to it?

the public	خالايىق
to laugh together	كۈلۈشمەك
to be revealed	پاش بولماق
prison	تۈرمە

- سول كۆزى ئەمەس.

ئاتلىق دەپتۇ:

- توغرا، توغرا، مەن خاتالىشىپتىمەن، ئوڭ كۆزى كور.

دېھقان دەرھال ئاتنىڭ بېشىدىكى چاپاننى ئېلىپ، ئەتراپتا تاماشا كۆرۈپ تۇرغانلارغا قاراپ دەپتۇ:

- ھەي، خالايىق، كۆردۈڭلارمۇ، ئاتنىڭ ھېچقايسى كۆزى كور ئەمەس!

ئەتراپتىكىلەر ئۇنى كۆرۈپ كۈلۈشۈپتۇ ۋە دېھقاننىڭ سۆزىنى توغرا تېپىپتۇ. شۇنداق قىلىپ، ئوغرىنىڭ يالغان سۆزى پاش بولۇپتۇ. كىشىلەر ئاتنى ئىگىسىگە بېرىپ، ئوغرىنى تۈرمىگە ئېلىپ كېتىپتۇ.

Exercise 6.3:  Skim the whole story and tell if these statements are true or false.

توغرا	خاتا

1. دېھقاننىڭ ئېتىنى قوشنىسى ئوغرىلاپ كېتىپتۇ.
2. دېھقان ئېتىنى ئىزدەپ بازار تەرەپكە چېپىپتۇ .
3. يولدا ئۇ بىر ئاتلىقنى كۆرۈپ قاپتۇ.
4. ئاتلىق دېھقاننىڭ ئېتىنى دەرھال قايتۇرۇپ بېرىپتۇ.
5. دېھقان "ئاتنىڭ بىر كۆزى كور" دەپتۇ.
6. ئاتنىڭ ئىككى كۆزى كور ئىكەن.
7. دېھقان ئەقىل ئىشلىتىپ ئېتىنى قايتۇرۇپ ئاپتۇ.

Exercise 6.4:  What is the moral of this story? Share your ideas with your classmates.

Exercise 7: Tell a story or a fairy tale your parents or grandparents told you when you were young. Use both forms of the narrative past. Did you like the story? Why or why not? What is the moral of the story?

Useful expressions ئەسقاتىدىغان ئىبارىلەر

1. Compliments

In line one of the blog entry, you see the word ياخشىكەن, which is actually a combination of ياخشى and ئىكەن. The word ئىكەن is used in different contexts and has different functions. In this case, this word expresses approval, surprise, or a compiment on the part of the speaker. Note that ئىكەن in this case is usually used with adjectives. Look at the following examples:

Wow, your Uyghur is so good! ئۇيغۇرچىڭىز بەك ياخشىكەن!
Your daughter is beautiful! قىزىڭىز چىرايلىق ئىكەن!

In Uyghur, compliments can also be expressed by verbs using the suffix -پتۇ:

This juwawa is so tasty! بۇ جۇۋاۋا بەك ئوخشاپتۇ!
Your child has grown. بالىڭىز چوڭ بولۇپ قاپتۇ.
Your dress suits you so well! كۆڭلىكىڭىز ئەجەب يارىشىپتۇ!

Note that constructions with ئىكەن are also used to mark events that the speaker is able to infer from looking at hearing, touching, reading, or otherwise experiencing the results, traces or circumstances of the event. It is also used to mark discovery of information which the speaker has just learned.

This movie is so funny. بۇ كىنو ناھايىتى قىزىق ئىكەن.
Mac (Apple) computers are so handy! "ئالما" كومپيۇتېرلىرى بەك پەيزىكەن!
The food at this restaurant is not very good. بۇ ئاشخانىنىڭ تاماقلىرى ئانچە ياخشى ئەمەس ئىكەن.

The word ئىكەن may be written either together with or separately from the word which immediately precedes it.

2. Apologies and Regrets

At the end of the blog entry, you see the expression ئۇنتۇپ قاپتىمەن, which means "I forgot." In the word قاپتىمەن = قا+پتۇ+مەن, the suffix -پتۇ indicates the regret mood. This expresses a regret or an apology. Look at the following sentences:

Sorry, I forgot to bring my book. كەچۈرۈڭ، كىتابىمنى ئۆيدە ئۇنتۇپ قاپتىمەن.
Sorry, I did not know about that. مەن بۇنى بىلمەپتىمەن.
Sorry, I did not see that. مەن بۇنى كۆرمەپتىمەن.

The suffix -پتۇ may also denote the unexpected past. Compare the following sentence with the sentences above:

بالامنى ئېلىپ كەلمەكچى ئىدىم، لېكىن ئۇ كىنوغا كېتىپ قاپتۇ.
I was going to bring my son, but he (unexpectedly) went to the movie.

Exercise 8: How would you say the following compliments in Uyghur? Remember to use forms with both ئىكەن and -پتۇ.

1. Your *pilaf* is so tasty!	
2. His car is very expensive.	
3. This city is very beautiful!	
4. This *doppa* suits you very much.	
5. His bike is very old.	
6. This *Dapanji* is very spicy.	

Exercise 9:  What would you say in the following situations?

1. You were late for a class.	
2. You left your friend's book at home.	
3. You stepped on somebody's bag.	
4. You forgot your wallet at home.	
5. You fell asleep at a meeting.	
6. You missed a friend's phone call.	

Exercise 10: ئاڭلىسام قەشقەردە...

Exercise 10.1: 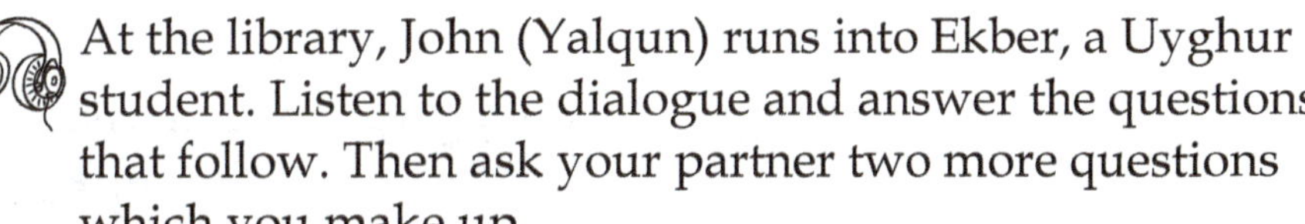
At the library, John (Yalqun) runs into Ekber, a Uyghur student. Listen to the dialogue and answer the questions that follow. Then ask your partner two more questions which you make up.

1. جون ئەكبەرنىڭ ئۇيغۇر ئىكەنلىكىنى نەدىن بىلدى؟
2. جون ئەكبەرنىڭ ئىسمىنى قانداق بىلىدۇ؟
3. نېمە ئۈچۈن جون ئۆزىگە يالقۇن دېگەن ئىسىمنى تاللىدى؟
4. جون قايسى فاكۇلتېتتا ئوقۇيدۇ؟ ئەكبەرچۇ؟
5. "ئاخبارات" دېگەن سۆزنىڭ مەنىسى نېمە؟
6. ئەكبەر شىنجاڭغا بارمىغىلى قانچىلىك بوپتۇ؟
7. جون شىنجاڭغا قاچان باردى؟
8. ئۇ قايسى شەھەردە تۇردى؟
9. جون شىنجاڭدا قانچىلىك تۇردى؟

Exercise 10.2:  Look at the following words and provide their English equivalents.

چاقماق	
كوزا	
خەۋەر	
تور	
تالاشماق	
تونۇشۇۋالماق ~ تونۇشۇپ ئالماق	

ئۆرۈشۈپ قالماق	
مۇسادىرە قىلماق	
ھەقىقەتەن	
قىزىق ئىش بولماق	
ئەسكە كەلمەك	
سۆھبەت سائىتى	

Exercise 10.3: Listen to the second part of the conversation and tell if the following statements are true or false.

توغرا	خاتا

1. قەشقەرنى ھازىر چېقىۋاتىدۇ.
2. بۇ خەۋەرنى يالغۇز رادىئودا ئاڭلىدى.
3. بىر كونا ئۆينى چاققاندا بىر كوزا ئالتۇن چىقىپتۇ.
4. ئالتۇن تاپقانلار ئۆرۈشۈپ قاپتۇ.
5. ئالتۇننى ھۆكۈمەت مۇسادىرە قىپتۇ.
6. سۆھبەت سائىتى ھەر جۈمە سائەت تۆتتە بولىدۇ.
7. سۆھبەت سائىتى خەلقئارا بۆلۈمدە بولىدۇ.

Exercise 10.4: Now read the dialogue aloud with your partner.

جون: ھازىر قەشقەرنى چېقىۋاتىدۇ. بىر كونا ئۆينى چاققاندا بىر كوزا ئالتۇن چىقىپتۇ.
ئەكبەر: نېمە چىقىپتۇ دېدىڭىز؟
جون: ئالتۇن.
ئەكبەر: ھە، كەچۈرۈڭ، مەن خاتا ئاڭلاپتىمەن.
جون: بۇ خەۋەرنى مەن توردىن كۆردۈم. كېيىن ئالتۇن تاپقانلار ئۆرۈشۈپ قاپتۇ.
ئەكبەر: نېمىشقا؟
جون: ئالتۇننى تالىشىپتۇ. كېيىن ئۇ ئالتۇننى ھۆكۈمەت مۇسادىرە قىپتۇ.
ئەكبەر: ھەقىقەتەن قىزىق ئىش بوپتۇ...
جون: ھە راست، سىز بىزنىڭ ئۇيغۇرچە سۆھبەت سائىتىمىزگە قاتنىشالامسىز؟
ئەكبەر: سۆھبەت سائىتى؟ ئۇ قاچان بولىدۇ؟
جون: ھەر جۈمە كۈنى سائەت ئۈچتە. ۋاقتىڭىز بارمۇ؟
ئەكبەر: ھەئە، بۇنداق ئىشقا ۋاقىت تاپىمىز ئەلۋەتتە. ئۇ قەيەردە بولىدۇ؟
جون: خەلقئارا بۆلۈمدە.
ئەكبەر: ئەمىسە جۈمە كۈنى شۇ يەردە كۆرۈشەيلى. خوش.
جون: خوش. سىزنى كۈتىمىز.

Exercise 11: قەدىمىي قەشقەر

Exercise 11.1:  Read the following passage about ancient Kashgar and answer the questions below.

قەشقەر - شىنجاڭنىڭ غەربىي جەنۇبىدىكى مەدەنىيەت ئەنئەنىلىرىگە باي قەدىمىي شەھەر. ئۇ تارىم ئويمانلىقىنىڭ غەربىي تەرىپىگە جايلاشقان. قەشقەر ھاۋاسى مۆتىدىل، يېرى مۇنبەت، سۈيى ئەلۋەك، مول ھوسۇللۇق، بوستانلىق ماكان. ئۇ خۇددى تەكلىماكان قۇملۇقىغا ئورنىتىلغان يېشىل ياقۇتقا ئوخشايدۇ. قەشقەر ئۇزاق تارىخقا ئىگە قەدىمىي شەھەر، شۇنداقلا تارىخنىڭ گۇۋاھچىسى. ئۇ قەدىمدىن تارتىپ يىپەك يولىنىڭ مۇھىم تۈگۈنى بولۇپ كەلگەن.

چاڭئەندىن باشلانغان يىپەك يولى تارىم ئويمانلىقىغا كىرگەندىن كېيىن جەنۇبىي ۋە شىمالىي يوللارغا بۆلۈنگەن. ئاندىن بۇ ئىككى يول قەشقەردە قوشۇلۇپ، پامىر ئېگىزلىكى ئارقىلىق غەربتىكى ئەللەر بىلەن تۇتاشقان. قەشقەر شەرق بىلەن غەرب ئوتتۇرىسىدىكى سودا تۈگۈنى ھەم شەرق مەدەنىيىتى بىلەن غەرب مەدەنىيىتىنىڭ ئۆز ئارا ئالمىشىش نۇقتىسى بولغان.

مىلادى 1- ئەسىردە بۇددا دىنى خوتەن رايونىغا، ئاندىن قەشقەرگە تارقالغان. شۇنىڭدىن كېيىن، خېلى ئۇزۇن مەزگىلگىچە قەشقەر بۇددا دىنى مەدەنىيىتىنىڭ مەركىزى بولۇپ قالغان. 10 - ئەسىرنىڭ باشلىرى ئىسلام دىنى قەشقەر رايونىغا كىرىشكە باشلىغان. شۇنىڭ بىلەن قەشقەر ئىسلام مەدەنىيىتىنىڭ مەركەزلىرىدىن بىرىگە ئايلانغان.

قەشقەر ئاھالىسىنىڭ قۇرۇلمىسى ئىنتايىن مۇرەككەپ بولغان. كېيىنكى دەۋرلەردە، ھەر خىل تارىخىي ئۆزگىرىشلەر سەۋەبىدىن باشقا قەبىلىلەر ۋە مىللەتلەر بۇ رايونغا كىرگەن. شۇنىڭ بىلەن قەشقەرنىڭ ئاھالە قۇرۇلمىسىدا زور ئۆزگىرىش يۈز بەرگەن. داڭلىق ئەسەرلەر ئارقا- ئارقىدىن يېزىلغان. شۇنىڭ بىلەن قەشقەر ئوتتۇرا ئاسىيادىكى مەشھۇر مەدەنىيەت مەركەزلىرىنىڭ بىرىگە ئايلانغان. مەدرىسلەر، كۇتۇبخانىلار كەينى- كەينىدىن قۇرۇلغان. ئوتتۇرا ئاسىيادىكى ھەر قايسى ئەل شائىر ۋە ئالىملىرى بۇ شەھەرگە توپلىشىپ بىلىم ئالماشتۇرغان. "تۈركىي تىللار دىۋانى" ۋە "قۇتادغۇ بىلىك" مانا موشۇنداق تارىخىي جەريانىنىڭ مەھسۇلى.

to connect	تۇتاشماق
to spread	تارقالماق
population structure	ئاھالە قۇرۇلمىسى
complicate	مۇرەككەپ
epoch; era	دەۋر
product	مەھسۇل
ruby	ياقۇت

mild	مۆتىدىل
fertile	مۇنبەت
abundant	ئەلۋەك
fruitful	ھوسۇللۇق
oasis	بوستانلىق
witness	گۇۋاھچى
hub; knot	تۈگۈن

1. قەشقەر قەيەرگە جايلاشقان؟
2. قەشقەرنى قانداق تەسۋىرلەش مۇمكىن؟
3. قەشقەرنىڭ "يىپەك يولى" دىكى رولى قانداق بولغان؟
4. نېمە ئۈچۈن قەشقەر ئىسلام مەدەنىيىتىنىڭ مەركەزلىرىنىڭ بىرىگە ئايلانغان؟

Exercise 11.2:  Match the sentence fragments in the right column with those in the left by drawing a line between them in order to form complete sentences describing Kashgar.

ئىنتايىن مۇرەككەپ بولغان
غەربىي تەرىپىگە جايلاشقان
مۇھىم تۈگنى بولغان
قەدىمىي شەھەر
مەركىزىگە ئايلانغان

قەشقەر ئۇزاق تارىخقا ئىگە
قەشقەر يىپەك يولىنىڭ
قەشقەر تارىم ئويمانلىقىنىڭ
قەشقەر ئىسلام مەدەنىيىتىنىڭ
قەشقەر ئاھالىسىنىڭ قۇرۇلمىسى

Exercise 11.3:  How would you title the following pictures?

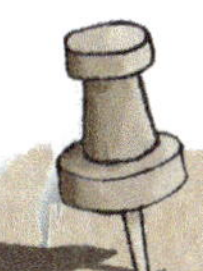

2 Hearsay or Reportative Past Tense with the Suffix -پتۇ

The suffix -پتۇ (-ىپتۇ / -ۇپتۇ / -ۈپتۇ) also indicates the hearsay or reportative past tense. This tense also expresses actions that happened in the past, but that you did not witness. Compare the following two sentences:

ئا. ئەكبەر ماشىنا ئالدى.　　　ب . ئەكبەر ماشىنا ئاپتۇ.

Both these sentences may be translated into English as:

Ekber bought a car.

In Uyghur, however, they have different meanings. In the first sentence, the information is witnessed firsthand. The speaker heard about the event straight from Ekber, or he saw the car himself. In the second sentence, the speaker heard about it from another source. In the conversation above, John shares some information about Kashgar. He did not witness the events firsthand, but he knows about them from the Internet.

بىر كونا ئۆينى چاققاندا بىر كوزا ئالتۇن چىقىپتۇ.

(I heard that) when they were tearing down an old house they found a jar full of gold.

ئالتۇننى ھۆكۈمەت مۇسادىرە قىلىپتۇ.

(I heard that) the government confiscated the gold.

To form the negative of the hearsay or reportative past tense add the suffix -ما/-مە to the stem of the verb.

I heard that Ekber did not go to this museum. ئەكبەر بۇ مۇزېيغا بارماپتۇ.

I heard that he did not hear about this. ئۇ بۇ خەۋەرنى ئاڭلىماپتۇ.

I heard that he did not buy a carpet. ئۇ گىلەم ئالماپتۇ.

If you add the suffix -پتۇ to a verb stem ending in the consonant ل, this ل will be dropped. Look at the following examples:

Yesterday Adil came to Kashgar. تۈنۈگۈن ئادىل قەشقەرگە كەپتۇ.

He stayed in his mother's house. ئۇ ئانىسىنىڭ ئۆيىدە قاپتۇ.

He bought a hat, but he did not buy a knife. ئۇ دوپپا ئاپتۇ، لېكىن پىچاق ئالماپتۇ.

This rule does not apply to the negative form.

Exercise 12:  Read the following sentences and fill in the blanks with the Uyghur versions of the accompanying verbs in the hearsay past tense.

to come	1. جون ئۈرۈمچىگە ______________________
to go	2. ئاگۈلسام ئۇ خوتەنگىمۇ ______________________
to stay	3. تۇرپاندا ئۇ ئۈچ كۈن دوستىنىڭ ئۆيىدە ______________
to visit	4. ئادىلنىڭ ئاتا- ئانىسى بېيجىڭنى ________________
to run away	5. ئاگۈلسام ئۇ تۇرمىدىن ______________________

Exercise 13: ئاگۈلسام\ ئاگۈلشىمچە...

Exercise 13.1:  Read the following short excerpt from John's blog entry. Rewrite it using the hearsay past form to tell what you heard.

بۈگۈن شەنبە. سائەت ئونغىچە ئۇخلىدىم. ئون يېرىملاردا ناشتا قىلدىم. ئاندىن تېلېۋىزور كۆردۈم. سائەت ئون ئىككىلەردە دوستۇم تېلېفون قىلدى. ئىككەيلەن كۆكتات بازىرىغا باردۇق. مەن بىر قوغۇن، ئىككى كىلو ئالما، ئىككى كىلو پەمىدور ئالدىم. دوستۇم تاۋۇز بىلەن ھەسەل ئالدى. چۈشلۈك تاماقنى بىزنىڭ ئۆيدە يېدۇق. سائەت تۆتلەردە كۇتۇبخانىغا باردۇق. سائەت يەتتىگىچە دەرس تەييارلىدۇق. ئاندىن تۈرك ئاشخانىسىغا بېرىپ كەچلىك تاماق يېدۇق.

Note that the suffix -لار/-لەر in this context expresses an approximate time (around ten, around twelve).

Exercise 13.2:  Get together with your partner and ask what (s)he did yesterday. Then present this information in class using the hearsay past.

> ***Note:***
> The narrative or hearsay past, formed with the word ئىكەن or the suffix -پتۇ is frequently used in Uyghur proverbs. This reflects the wisdom and past experiences of the Uyghur people, as if their ancestors were trying to send a message to younger generations.

Exercise 14: ئۇيغۇر ماقال - تەمسىللىرى

Exercise 14.1:  Read the proverbs below and match them with their definitions. The words and expressions that follow will help you understand the proverbs.

1. ئارپا- بۇغداي ئاش ئىكەن،
ئۈنچە- مارجان تاش ئىكەن.

2. ئاغزى يۇمشاق گۆش يەپتۇ،
ئاغزى قاتتىق مۇشت يەپتۇ .

3. يېنىدا بىر پۇلى يوق، تۆگىنىڭ
چىشىنى ساناپتۇ.

4. يېمەيمەن دەپ 70 قۇيماق
يەپتۇ.

___ كەمتەر، گېپى يۇمشاق كىشى توق ياشايدۇ، قوپال ئادەم ئاھانەت ئاڭلاپ ياشايدۇ.

___ ئاش بولمىسا جان ساقلىغىلى، كۈن كەچۈرگىلى بولمايدۇ؛ قىممەت باھالىق بۇيۇملارنى ئاشلىقنىڭ ئورنىدا يېگىلى بولمايدۇ، شۇڭا ئاشلىقنى قەدىرلەپ، زايە قىلماسلىق كېرەك.

___ كۆرۈنۈشتە تارتىنچاق، ئىنساپلىق بولۇۋېلىپ، پايدا- مەنپەئەتنى كۆرگەندە ئۆزىنى تۇتۇۋالالمايدىغان كىشىلەرنىڭ ئاچ كۆزلۈكىنى بىلدۈرىدۇ.

___ ئىقتىسادىي ئەھۋالى ناچار، ماددىي شارائىتى يامان بولسىمۇ چوڭ ئىشلارنى قىلمەن دەيدىغان ماختانچاقلارنىڭ چوڭلىقىنى بىلدۈرىدۇ.

benefit, advantage	پايدا- مەنپەئەت
braggart	ماختانچاق
fist	مۇشت
grain	ئاشلىق
humiliation	ئاھانەت
protecting oneself	جان ساقلىماق

greedy	ئاچ كۆز
material condition	ماددىي شارائىت
modest	كەمتەر
to live	كۈن كەچۈرمەك
shy	تارتىنچاق
conscientious	ئىنساپلىق

Exercise 14.2: Can you find English proverbs that explain the same ideas? How similiar or different are the meanings and forms of the equivalent proverbs in the two cultures?

Exercise 15:  John and his classmates run into Ekber as they are going to a Turkish restaurant. Read their conversation, and in the next page provide brief information about each student.

جون: ئەكبەر! كۆرۈشۈپ قالغىنىمىز ئەجەب ياخشى بولدى. ئەمدى باللارمۇ سىز بىلەن تونۇشۇۋالسۇن.
ئەكبەر: ياخشى، ياخشى. كېلىڭلار، بىللە تاماق يەيلى. ھەممىڭلار ئۇيغۇرچە ئۆگىنىدىغان ئوقۇغۇچىلارمۇ؟
جون: ھەئە. مەن سىلەرنى تونۇشتۇرۇپ قوياي. باللار، بۇ مەن سىلەرگە ئېيتقان ئەكبەر. ئۇ ژۇرنالىزىم
فاكۇلتېتىدا ئوقۇيدۇ. كەچۈرۈڭ ئەكبەر، ھېلىقى ئۇيغۇرچە سۆز نېمە ئىدى؟
ئەكبەر: قايسى سۆز؟
جون: سىز "ژۇرنالىزىم" دېگەننى يەنە بىر خىل دېگەن.
ئەكبەر: ھە، "ئاخبارات".
جون: رەھمەت! ماۋۇ باتۇر، ئۇمۇ ئاخبارات فاكۇلتېتىدا ئوقۇيدۇ. ئۇنى كومپيۇتېر ماھىرى دېسەكمۇ بولىدۇ.
كومپيۇتېرىڭىزدا بىر چاتاق چىقىپ قالسا، ئۇ ئوڭشاپ بېرىدۇ.
ئەكبەر: مۇنداق دەڭ. ياخشى! بىز سىز بىلەن بىر فاكۇلتېتتا ئىكەنمىز.
باتۇر: شۇنداق. تونۇشقانلىقىمىزدىن خۇشالمەن.
جون: ماۋۇ نازاكەت، ئۇ مۇزىكا فاكۇلتېتىدا ئوقۇيدۇ؛ نازاكەت ئۇيغۇر مۇقامىغا قىزىقىدۇ. بۇ بولسا ئالىم،
تارىخ فاكۇلتېتىدا ئوقۇيدۇ؛ ئۇ شىنجاڭ تارىخىنى ئۆگەنمەكچى. ئاۋۇ ئادىل، ئۇ سېلىشتۇرما ئەدەبىيات
فاكۇلتېتىدا ئوقۇيدۇ. ئۇ كەلگۈسىدە ئۇيغۇر يازغۇچىلارنىڭ ئەسەرلىرىنى ئىنگلىز تىلىغا تەرجىمە قىلماقچى.
بۇ ئۆتكۈر، ئۇ چېخىيەلىك. ئۇمۇ ئۇيغۇرلارنىڭ تارىخىغا بەك قىزىقىدۇ. ئۇ بىر نەچچە ماقالىمۇ ئېلان قىلغان.
ئەكبەر: ياخشى، ياخشى... سىزمۇ ئۇيغۇرچە ئۆگىنەمسىز؟
ئۆتكۈر: ھەئە. مەن ئۇيغۇرچە ئۆگىنىۋاتقىلى تۆت يىل بولدى.
ئەكبەر: ئەمىسە يېرىم ئۇيغۇر ئىكەنسىزدە.
ئۆتكۈر: ياق، مەن پۈتۈن ئۇيغۇر بولماقچى.
جون: ئەكبەر، سىزمۇ تۈرك تاماقلىرىغا ئامراقمۇ؟
ئەكبەر: مەن بۇ ئاشخانىنىڭ كاۋىپىغا ئامراق. بۇلارنىڭ كاۋىپى يۇرتۇمنى ئەسلىتىدۇ.
ئالىم: يۇرتىڭىزنى سېغىنىپسىزدە...
ئەكبەر: سېغىندىم. بولۇپمۇ ئوغلۇمنى.
باتۇر: نېمە؟ سىزنىڭ ئوغلۇڭىز بارمۇ؟
ئەكبەر: ھەئە، تۆت ياشلىق ئوغلۇم بار. ئۇ ئايالىم بىلەم ئۈرۈمچىدە قالدى.
نازاكەت: نېمىشقا ئۇلارنى بىللە ئەكەلمىدىڭىز؟
ئەكبەر: ئۇلار كېيىنرەك كېلىدۇ... مانا تاماقمۇ كەلدى. قېنى، تاماق يەيلى.

ئالىم
ئەكبەر
باتۇر
ئۆتكۈر
نازاكەت
ئادىل

Exercise 16: سىز نېمىگە قىزىقىسىز؟

Exercise 16.1: Listen to the short passages in which Zohre and Dawut describe their interests and decide if the following statements are true or false.

خاتا	توغرا	
		1. زۆھرە ئۇيغۇر مۇقاملىرىغا ئامراق.
		2. داۋۇت بالىلىقىدىن تارتىپ تارىخقا ئامراق.
		3. زۆھرە بەزىدە ئۇيغۇرچە خىپ-خوپ ئوينايدۇ.
		4. داۋۇت تارىخقا ئائىت ماتېرىياللارنى يىغىشنى ياخشى كۆرىدۇ.
		5. زۆھرە ياخشى ئۇسسۇلچى.
		6. داۋۇت تارىخ ئوقۇتقۇچىسى.
		7. زېرىككەندە زۆھرە ئۇيغۇر خەلق ناخشىلىرىنى ئېيتىدۇ.
		8. ھازىر تارىخقا قىزىقىدىغانلار ئاز.
		9. زۆھرە پات - پات ياتاقداشلىرى بىلەن دىسكوخانىغا بېرىپ تۇرىدۇ.
		10. داۋۇت تارىخىي رومانلارنى ئوقۇپ تۇرىدۇ.

Exercise 16.2:  Now read the paragraphs about Zohre and Dawut to check your answers.

مېنىڭ ئىسمىم زۆھرە. مەن ناخشا - مۇزىكا ئاڭلاشقا بەك ئامراق. مەن كۆپىنچە ھىندىستان، ئۆزبېكىستان ناخشىلىرىنى ئاڭلايمەن. بەزىدە ئۇيغۇرچە خىپ-خوپ ئوينايمەن. دوستلىرىم مەن ئوينىغان خىپ-خوپنى كۆرۈشنى ياخشى كۆرىدۇ. بىز بەزىدە ياتاقداش قىزلار بىلەن دىسكوخانىغا بېرىپ دىسكو ياكى تانسا ئوينايمىز. بەزىدە ھىندىچە ۋە ئەرەبچە ئۇسسۇلمۇ ئوينايمىز. زېرىكىپ قالساق كارا ئوكەي مۇزىكىسىغا ناخشا ئېيتىمىز.

مېنىڭ ئىسمىم داۋۇت. مەن شىنجاڭ ئۇنىۋېرسىتېتىنىڭ تارىخ فاكۇلتېتىدا ئوقۇيمەن. مەن كىچىكىمدىنلا تارىخقا بەك قىزىققان ئىدىم. شۇڭا ئالىي مەكتەپتە مۇشۇ كەسىپنى تاللىدىم. دەرستىن سىرتقى ۋاقىتلاردا تورغا چىقىپ ئۇيغۇر تارىخىغا دائىر ماتېرىياللارنى ئوقۇشنى ۋە توپلاشنى ياخشى كۆرىمەن. بەزىدە تارىخىي رومانلارنى ئوقۇيمەن. ھازىر تارىخ تېمىسىدىكى ئەسەرلەرنى ئوقۇيدىغانلار كۆپىيىۋاتىدۇ. زېرىككەندە ئۇيغۇر مۇقاملىرىنى ئاڭلايمەن. چۈنكى ئۇيغۇر مۇقاملىرىدا ئۇيغۇرلارنىڭ تارىخى ئەكس ئەتكەن.

Exercise 16.3: Using the paragraphs which you have just read as a guideline, invent some hobbies and interests for the people portrayed in the pictures below. Then briefly explain them to the class.

Exercise 17: Share your interests and hobbies with your classmates.

Have you ever heard about...? بۇ كىشىنى بىلەمسىز...؟

In this section you will read and learn about a famous Uyghur person.

Exercise 18: مەھمۇد قەشقەرى

Exercise 18.1:  Read the following passage about Mahmud al-Kashgari, an 11th century pioneer of Turkic linguistics. Then, answer the questions that follow. The words and expressions provided before the questions will help you to understand the passage better.

2014 - يىلى 18 - ئاۋغۇست
دۈشەنبە

1231 - سان پوچتا ۋاكالەت نومۇرى: 54 ـ 66

ئۇيغۇرخەلقىنىڭ ئاتاقلىق ئالىمى مەھمۇد قەشقەرى (كاشغەرى) مىلادى 1008 -يىلى قەشقەردىكى ئوپال يېزىسىدا تۇغۇلغان. ئۇ ئۆز يۇرتى قەشقەردە مەدرىسەنى تۈگەتكەندىن كېيىن، قوچۇ (تۇرپان)، ئىلى، بالاساغۇن(توقماق)، سەمەرقەند قاتارلىق شەھەرلەردە ساياھەتتە بولغان. تىلشۇناسلىق ۋە لۇغەتشۇناسلىققا دائىر مەخسۇس تەتقىقات بىلەن شۇغۇللانغاندىن باشقا، ئالىم يەنە ئىسلام تارىخى، ئىسلام پەلسەپىسى، قۇرئاننىمۇ پۇختا ئۆگەنگەن. ئۇ تۈركىي تىللارنى پىششىق بىلىشتىن تاشقىرى يەنە ئەرەب ۋە پارس تىللىرىنىمۇ تولۇق ئىگىلىگەن.

مەھمۇد قەشقەرى ئەينى زاماندا تۈركىي تىلدا سۆزلەشكۈچى خەلقلەرنىڭ تىللىرى بىلەن ئىنچىكىلەپ تونۇشۇش ئۈچۈن ئۇلار ئولتۇراقلاشقان جايلارنى تولۇق ئايلىنىپ چىققان. بۇ جەرياندا ئالىم تۈرلۈك تىل پاكىتلىرىنى، شېئىر-قوشاقلارنى، ماقال-تەمسىللەرنى، سۆز-ئىبارىلەرنى يىغقان. ئون نەچچە يىللىق ئەمەلىي تەكشۈرۈش، تەتقىق قىلىش نەتىجىسىدە توپلىغان بارلىق تىل ماتېرىياللىرىنى رەتلەپ چىقىپ، تۈركىي سۆزلەر ئەرەبچە ئىزاھلانغان سەككىز جىلدلىق ئىزاھلىق لۇغەتنى ئىشلەپ چىققان ۋە "دىۋان لۇغەتىت تۈرك" ("تۈركىي تىللار دىۋانى") دەپ نام بەرگەن. لۇغەتكە تۈركىي تىللاردا كۆپ ئىشلىتىدىغان سۆزلەر، گراماتىكىلىق قائىدىلەر، ھەربىي-مەمۇرىي ئاتالغۇلار، يېزا ئىگىلىك، يېمەك-ئىچمەك، سودا، قول ھۈنەرۋەنچىلىك، تىببىي-دورىگەرلىك، ھايۋانات، ئۆسۈملۈك ۋە ئاسمان جىسىملىرىغا دائىر سۆزلەر، قەبىلىلەرنامىلىرى، مۇھىم جۇغراپىيىلىك ناملار، قەدىمكى زاماندىكى خەلق داستانلىرى، رىۋايەتلىرى كىرگۈزۈلگەن.

ئۇلۇغ ئالىم مەھمۇد قەشقەرى مىلادى 1105 - يىلى 97 يېشىدا ۋاپات بولغان. ئالىمنىڭ "تۈركىي تىللار دىۋانى"ناملىق ئۆلمەس ئەسىرى دۇنيا مەدەنىيەت تارىخىدىكى ئۆچمەس نامايەندە ھېسابلىنىدۇ. شۇڭا بىرلەشكەن دۆلەتلەر تەشكىلاتى (ب د ت) پەن- مائارىپ باشقارمىسى 2008 - يىلنى "خەلقئارا مەھمۇد قەشقەرى يىلى" دەپ ئېلان قىلدى.

an epic poem	داستان
legend	رىۋايەت
an exponent	نامايەندە
valuable	ئېسىل
approximately	تەخمىنەن
to learn	ئۆگىنىمەك

military	ھەربىي
official	مەمۇرىي
a term	ئاتالغۇ
property	ئىگىلىك
celestial bodies	ئاسمان جىسىملىرى
a tribe	قەبىلە

famous	ئاتاقلىق
immortal	ئۆلمەس
specialist	مۇتەخەسسىس
to organize	رەتلەپ چىقماق
expression	ئىبارە
annotation	ئىزاھ

1. مەھمۇد قەشقەرى قايسى ئىلىملەرنى ئۆگەنگەن؟
2. ئۇ نېمە ئۈچۈن تۈركىي خەلقلەرنىڭ يۇرتلىرىنى ئايلىنىپ چىققان؟
3. مەھمۇد قەشقەرىنىڭ لۇغىتىگە قانداق سۆزلەر كىرگۈزۈلگەن؟
4. نېمە ئۈچۈن 2008 - يىلى "مەھمۇد قەشقەرى يىلى" دەپ ئېلان قىلىنغان؟

Exercise 18.2: Based on the passage, ask your partner three more questions about Mahmud al-Kashgari.

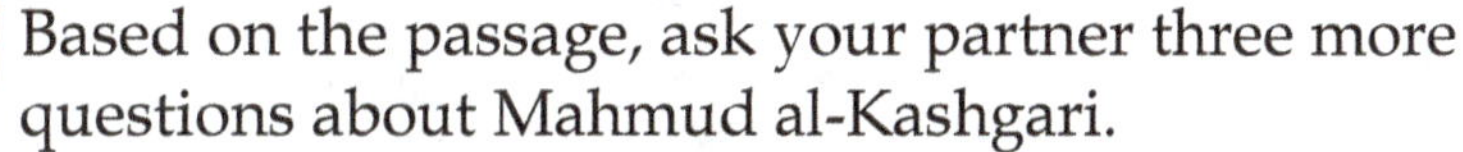

Vocabulary سۆزلۈك

Vocabulary is given according to the Uyghur alphabetical order. The right column precedes the left column on each page.

nickname	ئاتاق
mounted	ئاتلىق
covetous	ئاچكۆز
buddy	ئاداش
to make a habit	ئادەت قىلماق
fair	ئادىل
barley	ئارپا
free	ئازاد؛ ئەركىن
gold	ئالتۇن
to change	ئالماشماق
inhabitants	ئاھالە
to revolve; to become	ئايلانماق
around	ئەتراپ
smart	ئەقىللىق
literary work	ئەسەر
to recall	ئەسكە كەلمەك
century	ئەسىر
to reflect	ئەكس ئەتمەك
tradition	ئەنئەنە
to be determined (to do something)	بەل باغلىماق
wheat	بۇغداي
talk/chat	پاراڭ
to be revealed	پاش بولماق
benefit	پايدا - مەنپەئەت
moral character	پەزىلەت
Prophet	پەيغەمبەر
shy	تارتىنچاق
to be spread	تارقالماق
stone	تاش

to argue	تالاشماق
to choose	تاللىماق
to see the fun	تاماشا كۆرمەك
translation	تەرجىمە
to influence	تەسىر كۆرسەتمەك
to teach	تەلىم بەرمەك
to gather	توپلىماق
net	تور
to think it right	توغرا تاپماق
to introduce	تونۇشتۇرماق
to get acquainted	تونۇشۇۋالماق
to connect	تۇتاشماق
camel	تۆگە
jail	تۈرمە
knot	تۈگۈن
process	جەريان
coat	چاپان
to chop; to dig out; to run	چاپماق
time	چاغ
to crack; lightning	چاقماق
star	چولپان
concept	چۈشەنچە
memory; diary	خاتىرە
to find out	خەۋەر تاپماق
immediately	دەرھال
epoch; era	دەۋر
to get upset	رەنجىمەك
to mock	زاڭلىق قىلماق
clever	زېرەك
to be bored	زېرىكمەك

complicated	مۇرەككەپ
to confiscate	مۇسادىرە قىلماق
punch	مۇشت
A.D.	مىلادى
bad	ناچار
truly	ھەقىقەتەن
that	ھېلىقى
to steal	ئوغرىلاپ كەتمەك
basin	ئويمانلىق
to fight	ئۇرۇشۇپ قالماق
Uyghur dance	ئۇسسۇل
sharp	ئۆتكۈر
billow	ئۆركەش
mutual	ئۆزئارا
changes	ئۆزگىرىش
pearls and jewels	ئۈنچە - مارجان
to yell	ۋارقىرىماق
faith	ئېتىقاد
plateau	ئېگىزلىك
to search	ئىزدىمەك
to express	ئىزھار قىلماق
to use	ئىشلەتمەك
owner	ئىگە
to possess	ئىگىلىمەك
merciful; caring	ئىنساپلىق
to disappear	يوقاپ كەتمەك
homeland	يۇرت
the Silk Road	يىپەك يولى

happiness	سائادەت
handle; pure	ساپ
to put	سالماق
reason	سەۋەب
conversation hour	سۆھبەت سائىتى
to miss	سېغىنماق
comparative	سېلىشتۇرما
since then	شۇنىڭدىن تارتىپ
to accept	قوبۇل قىلماق
to agree	قوشۇلماق
to pour	قۇيماق
briefly	قىسقىچە
humble	كەمتەر
one after another	كەينى - كەينىدىن \\ ئارقا - ئارقىدىن
jar	كوزا
to increase	كۆپەيمەك
to care for	كۆڭۈل بۆلمەك
to live	كۈن كەچۈرمەك
witness	گۇۋاھچى
self-boasting; braggart	ماختانچاق
proverbs	ماقال - تەمسىل
article	ماقالە
to agree	ماقۇل بولماق
a home; place to stay	ماكان
religious school	مەدرىس
period	مەزگىل
information	مەلۇمات

ئىككىنچى دەرس

CHAPTER TWO

ئۇيغۇرلاردا ئائىلە

THE UYGHUR FAMILY

IN THIS CHAPTER

Functions

- Describing one's family
- Describing the Uyghur مەھەللە and هويلا
- Comparing traditional and modern families
- Comparing Uyghur and American families
- Describing Uyghur and American host etiquettes
- Writing a biographical sketch

Grammar

- The passive voice
- The present/future narrative & hearsay
- The reflexive pronoun ئۆز
- The first person optative (imperative) mood

In this chapter you will learn about the traditional multi-generational Uyghur family, along with some new kinship terms. Through the reading passages, John's blog entries and conversations, you will familiarize yourself with the Uyghur customs of hospitality and etiquette towards guests. You will also become acquainted with some important concepts in Uyghur culture such as هويلا and مەھەللە.

Exercise 1: تۆۋەندىكى سوئاللارنى مۇزاكىرە قىلىڭلار

1. ئائىلىڭىز چوڭمۇ؟
2. قېرىنداشلىرىڭىزدىن كىملەر بار؟
3. ئۆگەي دادىڭىزا\ ئاپىڭىز ياكى ئۆگەي قېرىنداشلىرىڭىز بارمۇ؟
4. سىز توي قىلغانمۇ؟ ئۆيۈڭلاردا نەچچە جان بار؟ باللىرىڭىز بارمۇ؟
5. ئائىلىڭىزدە قوشكېزەكلەر بارمۇ؟

Note:
While Uyghur does not have grammatical gender, there are some verbs and nouns in Uyghur which are only used when referring to either males or females. A similar phenomenon sometimes occurs in English, for example 'bachelor' (which is used to refer to men) and 'bachelorette' (which refers only to women).

Exercise 2: ئەرلەر ۋە ئاياللار

Exercise 2.1: Read the following sentences. Can you guess the speaker's gender?

1. مەن توي قىلغان \ توي قىلمىغان.	☐
2. مەن بويتاق.	☐
3. يولدىشىم بىلەن ئۇنىۋېرسىتېتتا ئوقۇپ يۈرگەندە تونۇشقان.	☐
4. مەن سودا قىلىمەن، ئايالىم ئىشلىمەيدۇ.	☐
5. مەن ئۆيلەنمىگەن.	☐
6. مەن غۇلجىدا ئەرگە تەگكەن.	☐
7. مەن توي قىلغان. ھازىر بىر قىزنىڭ ئاپىسى مەن.	☐

Exercise 2.2:  In the following passage Sultan aka talks about his family. Read the passage, then answer the following questions.

ئايالىم بىلەن توي قىلغىلى ئوتتۇز يىل بولدى. ئۇنىڭ بىلەن ئالىي مەكتەپتە ئوقۇپ يۈرگەندە تونۇشقان ئىدۇق. ئۇ ھازىر ئىشلىمەيدۇ، ئۆيدە. چوڭ قىزىمىز رازىيە يىگىرمە يەتتىگە كىردى. ئۇ يېقىندا يەنە بىر ئوغۇل كۆردى. ئۇلار مانا ئىككى ئوغۇللۇق بولدى. چوڭ ئوغلى مامۇت ھازىرچە بىز بىلەن تۇرىۋاتىدۇ. ئاتا- ئانىسىنىڭ ئۆيىگە كۆپ بارمايدۇ. رازىيە ئۆزى دوختۇرلۇقنى ئوقۇغان، ئەمما ھازىر بالىسىغا قاراپ ئۆيدە. ئۇنىڭ كىچىك ئوغلى بۇ يىل بىر ياشقا تولدۇ. رازىيەنىڭ يولدىشى چوڭ بازاردا بىر دۇكان ئېچىپ سودا- سېتىق ئىشلىرى بىلەن ئاۋارە. ئوغلىمىز شۆھرەتمۇ بۇلتۇر ئۆيلەندى. ئۇ تەرجىمان بولۇپ ئىشلەيدۇ. ئۇنىڭمۇ ئىشلىرى ياخشى، دائىم چەتئەلدە يۈرىدۇ. زامان ئۆزگىرىپ كەتتى، ھازىر نەگە بارىمەن دېسەڭ، شۇ يەرگە بارالايسەن. بىزنىڭ ياشلىقىمىزدا بۇنداق ئىشلار يوق ئىدى. كىچىك قىزىمىز ماھىرەمۇ چەت تىللار ئىنستىتۇتىغا ئوقۇشقا كىرگەن ئىدى. ئەمما بالىسى تۇغۇلۇپ، ئوقۇشنى ھازىرچە توختاتتى. ئۇنىڭ يولدىشى شۇ ئىنستىتۇتتا دەرس بېرىدۇ. ھازىر بىز بىلەن كەنجىمىز نۇرەخمەت تۇرىدۇ. ئۇ بۇ يىل مەكتەپنى پۈتتۈرۈپ شەھەرگە بېرىپ ئوقۇشقا كىرمەكچى. مەن بىر ئۆمۈر ئوقۇتقۇچىلىق قىلدىم. ھازىر مانا پېنسىيىگە چىقتىم.

1. سۇلتان ئاكىنىڭ نەچچە بالىسى بار؟
2. ئۇ ئايالى بىلەن قانداق تونۇشقان؟
3. ئۇلارنىڭ چوڭ كۈيئوغلى نېمە ئىش قىلىدۇ؟
4. كىچىك كۈيئوغلىچۇ؟
5. ئۇلارنىڭ چوڭ ئوغلى قاچان ئۆيلەنگەن؟
6. ئۇلار كىچىك قىزىنى ئەرگە بەرگەنمۇ؟
7. ئۇلارنىڭ نەچچە نەۋرىسى بار؟
8. ئۇلارنىڭ كەنجى ئوغلى توي قىلغانمۇ؟ ئۇ نېمە ئىش قىلىدۇ؟

Exercise 3: ئەنئەنىۋى ئۇيغۇر ئائىلىسى

Exercise 3.1:  Ekber gave a short presentation about the traditional Uyghur family. Below is the transcript of the presentation along with some questions from the audience. Read it and answer the underlined questions.

ئەكبەر: ئۇيغۇرلار ئادەتتە بىرنەچچە ئەۋلاد بىر قورۇدا (هويلا) ئولتۇرىدۇ، ئادەتتە كىچىكرەك مەهەللە 20 ~ 30 ئائىلىدىن تۈزۈلىدۇ.

باتۇر: مەهەللە دېگەن نېمە؟ ئۇ يېزىمۇ؟

ئەكبەر: ياق، ئاشۇنداق جىق ئائىلىدىن شەكىللەنگەن جاي "مەهەللە" دەپ ئاتىلىدۇ. چوڭراق مەهەللىلەر 50 ~ 60 تىن بىرەر يۈزگىچە ئائىلىدىن تۈزۈلىدۇ. شەهەرلەر بىلەن يېزىلاردىكى ئۇيغۇر ئائىلىلىرىنىڭ ئەھۋالى بىر- بىرىگە ئانچە ئوخشىمايدۇ. شەھەرلەردە هازىر چوڭ ئائىلىلەر ئاساسەن تېپىلمايدۇ. چوڭ ئائىلىلەر يېزىلاردا كۆپرەك ساقلانغان.

ئۆتكۈر: چوڭ ئائىلىدە قانچىلىك ئادەم بولىدۇ؟

ئەكبەر: چوڭ ئائىلىلەردە 20 ~ 30 جان بولىدۇ. بەزىلىرىدە 15~20 جان بولىدۇ.

نازاكەت: بۇنداق جىق ئادەمنى كىم باقىدۇ؟ هۆكۈمەت پۇل بېرەمدۇ؟

ئەكبەر: ياق، ئۇلار ئۆزىنى ئۆزى باقىدۇ. ئۇلار ئادەتتە ئائىلە بويىچە بىرلىكتە ئەمگەك قىلىدۇ. ئاشۇ چوڭ ئائىلىگە تەۋە نەرسىلەر ئادەتتە ئورتاق ئىشلىتىلىدۇ.هەتتا ئۇچ ۋاق تاماقمۇ بىللە يېيىلىدۇ.

باتۇر: ئۇلارنىڭ هەممىسى بىر ئۆيدە ئۇخلامدۇ؟

ئەكبەر: ياق. توي قىلمىغان ئوغۇللار بىر ئۆيدە، توي قىلمىغان قىزلار باشقا بىر ئۆيدە ئۇخلايدۇ. توي قىلغانلار بولسا ئاشۇ چوڭ قورونىڭ ئىچىدىكى ئايرىم ئۆيدە تۇرىدۇ، ئەمما هەممەيلەن بىللە ئەمگەك قىلىدۇ. شۇڭا مۇشۇنداق چوڭ قورولاردا ئادەتتە يىگىرمە نەچچە ئېغىز ئۆي سېلىنىدۇ. ئۇندىن باشقا يەنە چوڭ قورولاردا كۆمۈرخانا، تونۇر، ئوچاق، ئېغىل، كاتەك، هاجەتخانا قاتارلىقلارمۇ ياسىلىدۇ.

يالقۇن: كۆمۈرخانا، تونۇر، ئوچاق، ئېغىل، كاتەك... بۇلار نېمە؟

ئەكبەر: "كۆمۈر" سۆزىنى بىلەمسىلەر؟ كۆمۈر ساقلايدىغان جاينى ئۇيغۇرلار "كۆمۈرخانا" دەيدۇ. تونۇردا ئۇيغۇرلار نان ياقىدۇ. ئوچاقتا تاماق پىشۇرىدۇ. ئات، ئېشەك، كالا، قوي قاتارلىق ئۆي هايۋانلىرىنى باقىدىغان، سولايدىغان مەخسۇس ئۆينى "ئېغىل" دەيدۇ. ئۇيغۇرلاردا يەنە "قوتان" دېگەن سۆزمۇ بار. بۇ سۆزنىڭ مەنىسى "چوڭ ئېغىل"، "مالخانا" . "كاتەك" بولسا توخۇ، توشقان، كەپتەر قاتارلىقلار تۇرىدىغان كىچىك ئۆي.

ئالىم: جىق ئادەم بىر ئۆيدە تۇرسا، ئۆي ئىشىنى قانداق قىلىپ بۆلىدۇ؟

ئەكبەر: ئادەتتە ئەرلەر كۆپرەك ئېتىز ئىشىنى قىلسا، ئائىلىدىكى قىز باللار كىر يۇيۇش، تاماق ئېتىش دېگەندەك ئۆي ئىشلىرىنى قىلىدۇ. ئۆي ئىشلىرى دائىم شۇ ئۆيدىكى ئاياللارغا ۋە قىزلارغا مۇۋاپىق تەقسىملىنىدۇ. يەنە بىر قىزىق ئىش. ئۇيغۇر ئائىلىلىرىدە قازان، ياغاچ قوشۇق، يۇلغۇندىن ياسالغان چويلا، مىس چۆگۈن قاتارلىق ئەنئەنىۋى ئاشخانا سايمانلىرى هازىرمۇ ئىشلىتىلىدۇ.

يالقۇن: مېنىڭچە، ئاشۇنداق چوڭ ئائىلىلەردە چوقۇم بىردىن ئېشەك بار. شۇنداقمۇ؟

ئەكبەر: بەزىلىرىدە بىر ئەمەس، بىرنەچچە ئېشەك بېقىلىدۇ. چۈنكى ئېشەك دېهقانلارنىڭ ئەڭ كۈچلۈك ياردەمچىسى.

ئۆتكۈر: مېنىڭ ئاشۇنداق ئۇيغۇر ئائىلىلىرىنى كۆرگۈم بار.

ئەكبەر: شىنجاڭغا بارغاندا يېزىغا بېرىڭلار. بۇنداق ئائىلىلەر يېزىلاردا كۆپ.

Exercise 3.2:  Name each of the following pictures with the appropriate words in red from the passage.

Exercise 3.3:  Answer the following questions and support your answers based on the text.

1. Explain how the notion of sharing is understood in the Uyghur family.
2. What is the role of government, if any, in supporting families?
3. Boys and girls do not sleep in the same room. What do you think about this tradition?
4. How does a مەھەللە differ from an American neighborhood?

Exercise 3.4: Can you define each of the following words from the passage? The first one is done for you as an example.

كۆمۈرخانا	كۆمۈرخانىدا ئۇيغۇرلار كۆمۈر ساقلايدۇ.
تونۇر	
ئوچاق	
ئېغىل	
كاتەك	
قازان	

Exercise 4: Skim both the passage about Sultan aka's family (Exercise 2.2), and Ekber's presentation about the traditional Uyghur family (Exercise 3.1). How does the traditional Uyghur family differ from the modern Uyghur family? Fill in the table and compare the two family types.

Comparison A: Uyghur traditional families & modern families

زامانىۋى ئائىلە	ئەنئەنىۋى ئائىلە

Comparison B: The Uyghur & American families

Describe the strucuture, relationship, and traditions of the typical family in your culture. How does it compare to the modern Uyghur family?

ئۇيغۇرلاردا	سىزنىڭ مەدەنىيىتىڭىزدە

1 The Passive Voice

In his presentation (Exercise 3.1), Ekber talks about Uyghur traditional families in general terms. When we describe actions or instructions in general, there is often no subject in the sentence. Instead, the passive voice is used. In the presentation, you see verbs such as:

تۇزۇلىدۇ (تۇزۇلمەك)، ئاتىلىدۇ (ئاتالماق)، ئىشلىتىلىدۇ (ئىشلىتىلمەك)، يېيىلىدۇ (يېيىلمەك)

The suffix (ۇل- \ۈل- \ىل-) ل- in these words expresses the passive voice of the verbs تۈزمەك، ئاتىماق، ئىشلەتمەك، يېمەك.

The passive voice is used to express things that happen to someone or something without emphasizing who performed the action, as in the sentence "I was mugged!" Compare the following sentences:

Passive	*Active*
بۇ بازاردا گىلەم سېتىلىدۇ. The carpets are sold at this bazaar.	ئادىل بازاردا گىلەم ساتىدۇ. Adil sells carpets at the bazaar.
تاماقتىن كېيىن چاي ئىچىلىدۇ. Tea is served after food.	ئۇيغۇرلار تاماقتىن كېيىن چاي ئىچىدۇ. Uyghurs drink tea after eating.

If the final consonant of the verb stem is ل-, the suffix ن- (or after consonants, ىن-) should be added to make the passive voice. In Ekber's presentation you see the following examples:

سېلىنىدۇ (سالماق ~ سېلىنماق)؛ تەقسىملىنىدۇ (تەقسىملىمەك ~ تەقسىملەنمەك)
يېيىلىدۇ (يېمەك~ يېيىلمەك)؛ ياسىلىدۇ (ياسىماق ~ ياسالماق)؛
يېقىلىدۇ (ياقماق~يېقىلماق)؛ ئاتىلىدۇ (ئاتىماق ~ ئاتالماق)

Remember that vowels ئا and ئە become ي after the passive voice suffix is added.

Exercise 5:  Skim Ekber's presentation (Exercise 3.1) one more time and find all the sentences with the passive voice. Study each sentence.

Exercise 6:  Rewrite the following sentences using the passive voice in both the present and past tenses. The first is one is done for you.

تاماققا تۇز سېلىنىدۇ // سېلىندى.	تاماققا تۇز (سالماق)
	دۇكان سائەت سەككىزدە (تاقىماق)
	ناشتا ۋاقتىدا (قىلماق)
	ئادەملەر ۋاقتىدا (ئاگاھلاندۇرماق)
	كىتابلار ئۈستەلدىن (ئالماق)
	بايرامدىن بۇرۇن ئۆي (تازىلىماق)
	مېھمانلارغا تاماق (بەرمەك)

2 Present/Future Narrative & Hearsay

As is the case with many hearsay and narrative verb forms in Uyghur, to build the hearsay or narrative form of the present/future tense, we use the word ئىكەن. Look at the following examples:

He will (apparently) be living with his mother. ئۇ ئانىسى بىلەن تۇرىدىكەن.
He (apparently) works in the garden every day. ئۇ ھەر كۈنى باغدا ئىشلەيدىكەن.
ئۇلار سەھەردە يولغا چىقىدىكەن.
They are supposed to hit the road early in the morning.

As you can see, instead of being attached to the suffix -پتۇ as in the hearsay past, here the word ئىكەن is attached to the third person form of the verb in the present/future tense. Note that the last vowel ۇ is dropped and the word ئىكەن is written together with the main verb.

While the third person form of the hearsay/narrative is (for obvious reasons) most common, it is also possible to conjugate a verb in this way for the 1st and 2nd person. However, instead of being built upon the regular present/future forms for these persons, the 1st and 2nd person are simply composed of the hearsay/narrative present/future of the 3rd person above followed by the appropriate personal endings سەن ,مەن, etc... Look at the examples below:

(Apparently) I'm going with you. مەن سىز بىلەن بارىدىكەنمەن.
(Oh, so) you guys live in the bigger house. سىلەر چوڭراق ئۆيدە تۇرىدىكەنسىلەر.
(Apparently) we're all going to the forest together. ئورمانلىققا ھەممىمىز بارىدىكەنمىز.

2 Present/Future Narrative & Hearsay (cont'd.)

To form the negative of the present/future hearsay/narrative, simply add the suffix -ما\-مە as in the regular present/future. Here are some examples:

ئەزىز دادىسى بىلەن بارمايدىكەن.
Eziz will (apparently) not be going with his father.
ئۇنىڭ بالىسى زادى يىغلىمايدىكەن.
(He says) His kid never cries.
ئۇ بالىسىنى بېيجىڭغا ئەۋەتمەيدىكەن.
He (apparently) will not send his son to Beijing.

Exercise 7: Finish the sentences with the appropriate verbs and the corresponding endings for the present/future hearsay/narrative. When you see the symbol Ø, write a negative sentence.

بالىلار ئەتىگەندىن كەچكىچە سىرتتا (play) ________________
Ø بىز مېھمانخانىدا (stay) ________________
ئانىسى تاماقنى ئۆزى (cook) ________________
Ø بۇلارنىڭ ئائىلىسى قەشقەردە (live) ________________
سەن خەنزۇچە (know) ________________
ئەكبەرنىڭ ئانىسى ئۈرۈمچىگە ئاپتوبۇس بىلەن (come) ________________
Ø ئۇ ئاچچىق تاماق (eat) ________________

Exercise 8: مېھمان قانداق كۈتۈلىدۇ؟

Exercise 8.1: What is the proper etiquette for a host in your culture? Share your opinions with the class. Follow the model:

ئالدى بىلەن مېھمانغا ئىچىملىك بېرىلىدۇ.

Exercise 8.2:  Read John's blog entry and tell if the following statements are true or false.

Uyghur John's Blog

ئامېرىكىلىق ياڭۇننىڭ تورتۇراسى

Search

بۈگۈن سۆھبەت سائىتىمىزگە ئەكبەر كەلدى. بىز ئۇنىڭدىن ئۇيغۇر ئائىلىلىرى ۋە ئۇيغۇرلارنىڭ مېھماندوستلۇقى توغرۇلۇق كۆپ نەرسىلەرنى ئۆگىنىۋالدۇق. بىز ئۈچۈن بۇ بەك قىزىق بولدى. مەن شىنجاڭغا بارغاندا چوقۇم ئۇيغۇرلارنىڭ ئۆيىگە مېھمانغا بارىمەن. ئەكبەرنىڭ ئېيتىشىچە، ئۇيغۇر خەلقىدىكى مېھماندوستلۇق قەدىمدىن تارتىپ كېلىۋاتقان ئېسىل ئەنئەنىلەرنىڭ بىرى ئىكەن. ئۇيغۇر خەلقى مېھمان كەلسە بەكمۇ خوش بولىدىكەن. شۇڭا ھەرقانداق شارائىت ئاستىدا مېھمان كەلسە ئۇنى قىزغىن قارشى ئالىدىكەن. ئامېرىكىدا بۇنداق ئەمەس. بىزنىڭ ئادەملىرىمىز بەك ئالدىراش، ئۇلارنىڭ مېھمان كۈتۈشكە ئۇنداق كۆپ ۋاقتى يوق. ئۇلار ئۆزلىرىمۇ بەزىدە تاماقنى ئۆيدە ئەتمەي، رېستورانغا بېرىپ يەيدۇ.

ئۇيغۇرلاردا مەيلى چاقىرىلغان مېھمان بولسۇن، مەيلى تاسادىپىي كېلىپ قالغان مېھمان بولسۇن، ئوخشاش كۈتىدىكەن. مېھماننى ئەڭ ئېسىل، ئەڭ ياخشى تاماق بىلەن كۈتىدىكەن.

مېھمان كەلگەندە ھەرقانداق ئائىلە ئۇنىڭ قولىغا سۇ بېرىپ داستىخان سالىدىكەن. ئالدى بىلەن مېھماننىڭ ئالدىغا سىنچاي بىلەن نان قويىلىدىكەن. ئۆي ئىگىسى مېھماننىڭ چېپىغا قەنت ياكى ناۋات سېلىپ قويىدىكەن. بەزىدە سىنچايدىن كېيىن ئەتكەن چاي ئېتىپ كىرىدىكەن. چايدىن كېيىن، ياز بولسا ھۆل مېۋە كەلتۈرىدىكەن. ئۆي ئىگىسى مېھمان خالىغان تاماقنى ئېتىدىكەن. ئېمىدېگەن ياخشى ھە! ئادەتتە مېھمانلارغا پولۇ، گۆشنان، پېتىر مانتا، بولاق مانتا، چۆچۈرە، لەغمەن دېگەندەك تاماقلاردىن بىرىنى ئېتىدىكەن. كۆپ ھاللاردا مېھمان تامىقى جۈپ بولۇپ، پولۇ ئەتسە ئارقىدىن ئۇگرە، چۆچۈرە؛ مانتىدىن كېيىن شورپا دېگەندەك تاماقلار قوشۇپ ئېتىلىدىكەن... بىز بۇنداق ئادەتلەرنى ئاڭلاپ ھەيران قالدۇق. ئۇيغۇرلار ھەممە يەردە شۇنداق مېھمان كۈتەمدىكەن ياكى بۇنداق ئادەتلەر پەقەت يېزىلاردا ساقلىنىپ قالدىمۇ؟ ئۇ يەرگە بارغاندا مەن ئۆزۈم مۇشۇنداق ئۆرپ- ئادەتلەرگە دىققەت قىلىمەن. ئۇيغۇر تاماقلىرى توغرۇلۇق يېزىپ قورسىقىم ئېچىپ كەتتى... ئاشخانىغا بېرىپ تاماق يەپ كېلەي...

كۆزدە بىر ماقال: ئۆيۈڭ تار بولسىمۇ، كۆڭلۈڭ كەڭ بولسۇن.

ئىسىم

ئىم

خاتا	توغرا

1. چاقىرىلغان مېھمان ئالاھىدە كۈتۈلىدۇ.
2. چاقىرىلمىغان مېھمانغا تاماق ئېتىلمەيدۇ.
3. ئالدى بىلەن مېھمانغا ئەتكەن چاي بېرىلىدۇ.
4. ساھىبخان مېھماننىڭ چېپىغا ناۋات سېلىپ قويىدۇ.
5. مېھمانلارغا تاماق جۈپ ئېتىلىدۇ.

Exercise 8.3:  Skim John's blog entry again and list all the new information John has learned about Uyghur hospitality on the lines provided below. Since you are relating new information, it is appropriate to use the hearsay/narrative form of the present/future tense.

1.
2.
3.
4.

Exercise 8.4:  Now compare Uyghur host etiquette with that of your own culture by filling in the chart below.

ئۇيغۇر مەدەنىيىتىدە	سىزنىڭ مەدەنىيىتىڭىزدە	
		ئوخشاش تەرەپلىرى
		پەرقلىرى

Exercise 9:  Skim John's blog one more time and find all the sentences with the present/future narrative & hearsay and translate them into English.

Exercise 10: تۇغقاندارچىلىق ناملىرى

Exercise 10.1:  Do you remember kinship terms in Uyghur? Match the following Uyghur terms with their English equivalents.

grandchild	قېيناتا
daughter-in-law	ئۆگەي ئانا
nephew/niece	تاغا
father-in-law	هامما (هامماچا)
cousin	جىيەن
stepmother	كۈيئوغۇل
uncle	كېلىن
aunt	نەۋرە
son-in-law	نەۋرە ئاكا (ئاچا)
sister-in-law	چەۋرە
brother-in-law	ئەۋرە
great grandchild	يەڭگە
a great-great grandchild	قېيىن ئاچا(ئىگىچە) \\ قېيىن سىڭىل
elder brother's wife	قېيىن ئاكا \\ قېيىن ئىنى

Exercise 10.2:  Get together with your partner and ask him/her to solve the following puzzles.

1. دادامنىڭ ئىنىسى سىڭلىم ئۈچۈن كىم بولىدۇ؟
2. مېنىڭ بالام مومامنىڭ نېمىسى بولىدۇ؟
3. سىڭلىمنىڭ يولدىشىنىڭ ئانىسى ئۇنىڭغا كىم بولىدۇ؟
4. ئاكامنىڭ بالىسى ھەدەم ئۈچۈن كىم بولىدۇ؟
5. ئانامنىڭ ئاكىسىنىڭ قىزى مېنىڭ نېمەم بولىدۇ؟
6. دادامنىڭ ئەڭ چوڭ ھەدىسى مېنىڭ ھەدەمگە كىم بولىدۇ؟

Exercise 11: زۇلپىقارنىڭ ئائىلىسى

Exercise 11.1: Watch the first video segment and answer the following questions:

1. What are the names of the people in this video?
   Man: ______________________
   Woman: ______________________
   Boy: ______________________
2. What does the man say about his extended family?
   ____
   ____
3. Where is his wife from? ______________________
4. Who lives in Kashgar? ______________________
5. How many siblings does the man have and where are they now?
   ____
6. What does the word نەۋرە mean in his introduction?
   ____
7. Who in this video was introduced twice?
   ____

Exercise 11.2: Watch the second video segment and tell what this video is about. While watching, take some notes on the lines provided below.

____

____

____

Exercise 11.3: Watch the video again and put the following statements in order.

___	His father-in-law is a merchant.
___	Two of his brothers are traders.
___	He has a sister in Uch Turpan.
___	His mother-in-law is a business woman.
___	One of her sisters is a translator.
___	His mother-in-law is a house wife.
___	One of his brothers is a teacher.

Kinship Terms in Uyghur

Like every language, Uyghur can be divided up into regional dialects. In addition to differences in pronunciation, dialects often differ from one another in terms of certain elements of their vocabulary. For example, kinship terms display considerable variety from one dialect of Uyghur to the next.

In northern Xinjiang (Ghulja and Chöchek), and among Uyghurs in the Central Asian republics, the words موما and بوۋا are used for 'grandma' and 'grandpa', respectively. The terminology for aunts and uncles is slightly more complicated: If the person in question is older than the parent to whom they are related, they are referred to as چوڭ ئاپا 'aunt' (i.e., parent's older sister) and چوڭ دادا 'uncle' (i.e., parent's older brother), whereas if they are younger than the parent, they referred to as كىچىك ئاپا 'aunt' (i.e., parent's younger sister) or كىچىك دادا 'uncle' (i.e., parent's younger brother).

In southern Xinjiang, things are a bit simpler: Much as in English, چوڭ دادا means 'grandfather' and چوڭ ئاپا (or چوڭ ئانا) means 'grandmother'; كىچىك دادا and كىچىك ئاپا (or كىچىك ئانا) refer to any uncle or aunt, respectively, regardless of their age.

Exercise 12: 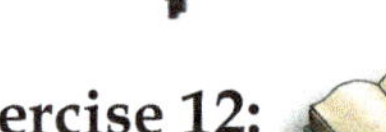 Read the following exerpt about the extended family of Dolqun, a native of Ghulja, and then replace the words in parantheses with their alternative forms given in the above note.

مەن چوڭ ئائىلىدە تۇغۇلدۇم. بىز ھەممىمىز بىر چوڭ قورۇدا تۇرىمىز. ئۆيىمىزدە بوۋام، مومام، دادام، ئاپام، ھامام ۋە بىز ئالتە بالا تۇرىمىز. قورۇدا يەنە (دادامنىڭ ئاكىسى) __________ ۋە (ئىنىسى) __________ ئائىلىلىرى بىللە تۇرىدۇ. (چوڭ تاغامنىڭ) __________ بەش بالىسى بار، ئۇلارنىڭ ئىككىسى ئوغۇل، ئۈچى قىز. كىچىك تاغام يېقىندا ئۆيلەنگەن. (دادامنىڭ سىڭلىسى) __________ ئىلى پېداگوگىكا مەكتىۋىدە ئوقۇيدۇ. (تاغامنىڭ) __________ چوڭ ئوغلى مەندىن ئۈچ ياش چوڭ. (تاغامنىڭ) __________ ئايالى تىككۈچى، ئۇ ناھىيىلىك تىكىمچىلىك كارخانىسىدا ئىشلەيدۇ. تاغامنىڭ چوڭ قىزىمۇ شۇ يەردە ئىشلەيدۇ. (كىچىك تاغامنىڭ) __________ ئايالى ئۆيدە، ئۇ ئىشلىمەيدۇ. (كىچىك تاغام) __________ شوپۇرلۇق قىلىدۇ. (ئاپامنىڭ چوڭ ھەدىسى) __________ ئۈرۈمچىدە. ئۇ ھازىر داڭلىق ناخشىچى. (ئاپامنىڭ ئىككىنچى ھەدىسى) __________ مۇخبىر، ئۇ "ئىلى گېزىتى" دە ئىشلەيدۇ. (ئاپامنىڭ ئىنىسى) __________ بار. ئۇ ئائىلىسى بىلەن چۆچەكتە تۇرىدۇ.

Exercise 13: نەۋرەمنىڭ ئىسمى تۈرەخمەت

Exercise 13.1: Watch the video and mark all the kinship terms you hear from the list below:

نەۋرە چوڭ ئاپا ئاپا تاغا ئاچا هامما چوڭ دادا

Exercise 13.2: Watch the video one more time and tell what you learned about Turehmet from his grandmother's narration. Provide at least four statements.

Exercise 13.3: Watch the video again and answer the following questions.

1. How many grandchildren does the woman have alive?

2. Why did she name her grandson Turehmet?

Exercise 14: مېنىڭ دادام

Exercise 14.1:  Read the following passage. Which of the following does the narrator mention about his father? Place a mark next to the traits which are mentioned in the list below.

bath house	مۇنچا
kind, sincere	ئاق كۆڭۈل
calm	ئېغىر - بېسىق
model worker	ئەمگەك نەمۇنىچىسى
to encourage	تۈرتكە بولماق
to scold	تىللىماق
to ignore	پەرۋا قىلماسلىق
warm treatment	ئىللىق مۇئامىلە
to be proud of	پەخىرلەنمەك
neat; tidy	رەتلىك
quarrel; fighting	جېدەل- ماجرا
a smile on someone's face	كۈلكە ئويناپ تۇرماق

مېنىڭ دادام مۇنچا خىزمەتچىسى. دادام ھەر كۈنى سەھەردە تۇرۇپ خىزمەتكە كەتسە، كەچ قايتىپ كېلىدۇ. ئۇ ئاق كۆڭۈل، ئېغىر - بېسىق ئادەم. ئۇ خىزمەتتىن ھېرىپ كەلسىمۇ، ھەرگىز ھاردىم دېمەيدۇ، دائىم ئۆگىنىشىمگە ياردەم بېرىدۇ. دادامنىڭ ئىشى ئاددىي بولسىمۇ*، ئۇ ئۆز ئىشىنى ياخشى كۆرىدۇ. دادامنىڭ تىرىشچانلىقى، ھەر يىلى ئەمگەك نەمۇنىچىسى بولۇپ باھالىنىشى مېنىڭ تىرىشىپ ئۆگىنىشىمگە تۈرتكە بولىدۇ. مەن دادامدىن پەخىرلىنىمەن. مەكتەپتە بەزى ساۋاقداشلىرىم مېنى "مۇنچىكەشنىڭ بالىسى" دەپ مازاق قىلىدۇ. لېكىن مەن بۇنداق گەپلەرگە ھېچ پەرۋا قىلمايمەن. دادامنىڭ خىزمەت ئورنى تۆۋەن بولسىمۇ، ناھىيىمىزدە دادامنى تونۇيدىغانلار كۆپ، ھەتتا چوڭ - كىشىلەرمۇ دادام بىلەن ئۇچرىشىپ قالسا، قىزغىن كۆرۈشىدۇ. دادام دائىم ساقال - بۇرۇتلىرىنى پاكىز ئېلىپ، رەتلىك كىيىنىدۇ. سىز ئۇنى كوچىلاردا ئۇچرىتىپ قالسىڭىز، مۇنچە خىزمەتچىسى ئەمەس، بەلكى بىرەر سەنئەت ئۆمىكىنىڭ ئارتىسىمىكىن دەپ قالىسىز. ئۇ كىشىلەرگە ھەمىشە ئىللىق مۇئامىلە قىلىدۇ. قوشنىلار ياكى باشقا كىشىلەر بىلەن جېدەل- ماجرا قىلمايدۇ. ئۆيدىمۇ شۇنداق، دادامنىڭ يۈزىدە دائىم كۈلكە ئويناپ تۇرىدۇ. دادام ئانامنىمۇ خاپا قىلمايدۇ. ئۇ ھېچ قاچان مېنىمۇ قوپال گەپلەر بىلەن تىللىمايدۇ. مەن دادامغا بەك ئامراق!

* بولسىمۇ - even though

☑	profession	☐	appearance
☐	personality	☐	father's achievements
☐	daily routine	☐	his feelings towards his father
☐	father's attitude towards job	☐	father's attitude towards life
☐	influence of father on the narrator	☐	narrator's friends' attitude

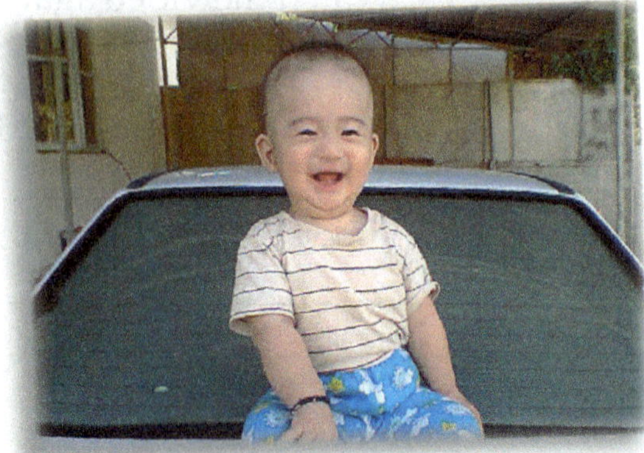

Exercise 14.2:  Read the passage again and add details to each category below in English.

Job ______________________________

Appearance ______________________________

Personality ______________________________

Father's attitude towards his family ______________________________

____

Father's influence on narrator ______________________________

Narrator's feelings towards his father ______________________________

____

Friends' attitude towards his father ______________________________

Exercise 14.3:  Based on the passage above, write a description of your own father/mother/uncle/aunt. Include as much details as you can.

Project

My Family

Prepare a presentation introducing your extended family. Include a detailed description of two of the most important people to you. Explain what they do and what they think about their lives, jobs, and families.

Exercise 15: مېھماننىڭ قولىغا سۇ بېرىلىدۇ

Exercise 15.1: Listen to the conversation between John and Ekber and answer the questions below.

1. ئۇيغۇر ئائىلىلىرىدە چاي ۋە تاماق قانداق سۇنۇلىدۇ؟
2. چاي ياكى تاماق ساھىبخانىنىڭ قولىدىن قانداق ئېلىنىدۇ؟
3. سىزنىڭچە، نېمە ئۈچۈن ئۇيغۇرلارنىڭ مەدەنىيىتىدە مېھماننىڭ قولىغا سۇ بېرىلىدۇ؟

Exercise 15.2: Listen to the conversation one more time while following along with the script. Circle the verb you hear from each pair of verbs provided in parentheses.

(تاك... تاك...)

ئەكبەر: جون! كېلىڭ، كېلىڭ.

جون: قانداق ئەھۋالىڭىز؟

ئەكبەر: ياخشى. كەلگىنىڭىز ياخشى بولدى. بىزدە "ياخشى مېھمان ئاش ئۈستىگە" دېگەن ماقال بار. مەن پولۇ ئېتىۋاتىمەن. كېلىڭ، بىللە يەيمىز.

جون: شۇنداقمۇ؟ مەن پولۇغا بەك ئامراق. قولۇمنى قەيەردە يۇيۇمەن؟

ئەكبەر: ئۇيغۇرلاردا ئۆيگە كەلگەن مېھماننىڭ قولىغا سۇ (بېرىدۇ\بېرىلىدۇ). بۇ يەر ئامېرىكا بولغاندىكىن سۇخانىدا يۇسىڭىز بولىدۇ.

جون: بۇ ياخشى ئادەت ئىكەن. ھەر بىر مېھماننىڭ قولىغا سۇ (بېرەمدۇ\ بېرىلەمدۇ؟)

ئەكبەر: شۇنداق. ئۇيغۇرلارنىڭ ئادىتىدە مېھمان بەك (ھۆرمەتلەيدۇ\ ھۆرمەتلىنىدۇ.)

جون : ئۇيغۇرلاردا يەنە قانداق ئادەتلەر بار ؟

ئەكبەر : چاي ۋە تاماق ئالدى بىلەن چوڭلارغا (بېرىدۇ\ بېرىلىدۇ.) چاي ياكى تاماق ئىككى قوللاپ (سۇنىدۇ\ سۇنۇلىدۇ) ۋە ئىككى قول بىلەن (ئالىدۇ\ ئېلىنىدۇ.)

Exercise 15.3: Now listen to the dialogue and repeat. While listening, you may take some notes.

Exercise 16: مومام ئېيتقان چۆچەكلەر

Exercise 16.1:  Read the following short story about a disaster (ئاپەت) in a forest and underline all the verbs in the passive voice.

بۇرۇنقى زاماندا تەكلىماكاندا بىر چوڭ ئورمان بولغان ئىكەن. ئورمانغا يېقىن جايدا بىر شەھەر بار ئىكەن. كېيىن شەھەردە ئادەم كۆپىيىپتۇ، شۇنىڭ بىلەن شەھەرگە نۇرغۇن يېڭى ئۆيلەر سېلىنىپتۇ. ئۆي سېلىشقا نېمە ئىشلىتىلىدۇ؟ ياغاچ. شۇنىڭ بىلەن كىشىلەر ئورمانلىقتىن دەرەخ كېسىشكە باشلاپتۇ. بىر-ئىككى ئايدىلا نۇرغۇن دەرەخلەر كېسىلىپتۇ. دەرەخلەر ئۈچۈن بۇ بىر ئاپەت بولۇپتۇ. شۇنىڭ بىلەن دەرەخلەر بۇنى ئورمان پادىشاھى قارىغايغا مەلۇم قىلىپتۇ.

- ئۇلار دەرەخنى قانداق كېسىدىكەن؟ - سوراپتۇ قارىغاي.
- ئۇلاردا "پالتا" دەيدىغان بىر قورال بار ئىكەن، ئالىيلىرى. شۇنىڭ بىلەن كېسىدىكەن،- دەپتۇ دەرەخلەر.
- ئۇنداق بولسا بېرىپ شۇ قورالنى ئوبدانراق كۆرۈپ كېلىڭلار،- دەپتۇ قارىغاي.

دەرەخلەر بېرىپ كۆرۈپ كەلگەندىن كېيىن ئورمان پادىشاھىغا مەلۇم قىلىپتۇ:

- ئالىيلىرى، بىز كۆردۇق. "پالتا" دېگەن بىر پارچە تۆمۈر ئىكەن. ئۇنىڭغا ياغاچتىن دەستە سېلىنىدىكەن.
- نېمە؟ پالتىنىڭ دەستىسى ياغاچمىكەن؟ - ئورمان پادىشاھى ھەيران بولۇپ سوراپتۇ.
- شۇنداق، ئالىيلىرى. ئەگەر پالتىغا تۆمۈردىن دەستە سېلىنسا قولنى ئاغرىتىدىكەن. ياغاچتىن دەستە سېلىنسا قولنى ئاغرىتمايدىكەن.
- كۆردۈڭلارمۇ؟ - دەپتۇ ئورمان پادىشاھى، - سىلەرنى كەسكەن پالتىنىڭ دەستىسى ياغاچ ئىكەن. پالتىغا ئۆزۈڭلار دەستە بولۇپ بەرگەندىن كېيىن بۇ ئۆزۈڭلارنىڭ خاتالىقى!

"پالتىنىڭ دەستىسى ياغاچ" دېگەن تەمسىل شۇنىڭدىن قالغان ئىكەن.

to cut	كەسمەك	forest	ئورمان
to report	مەلۇم قىلماق	to build a house	ئۆي سالماق
axe	پالتا	wood	ياغاچ
weapon	قورال	Your Highness	ئالىيلىرى
to be surprised	ھەيران بولماق	handle	دەستە
to hurt	ئاغرىتماق	iron	تۆمۈر
a pine tree	قارىغاي	a saying	تەمسىل

Exercise 16.2:  Give a title to the story. Explain in Uyghur why you think your title is appropriate to the story.

Exercise 16.3:  Now translate the sentences from the passage which use the passive voice into English.

Exercise 16.4: Using the following words and expressions in the boxes below, retell the story in your own words. Remember to use the passive voice suffixes whenever possible. Do not look at the original!

ھەيران بولماق	ئاپەت بولماق	ياشىماق
قولنى ئاغرىتماق	ئېيتماق	سالماق
كۆرمەك	مەلۇم قىلماق	ئىشلەتمەك
دەستە بولۇپ بەرمەك	كۆرۈپ كەلمەك	باشلىماق
قالماق	دەستە سالماق	كەسمەك

3 Reflexive Pronoun ئۆز

In the blog entry (Exercise 8.2) you see the word ئۆز 'self, own'. This word can have a number of functions within a sentence. In general, ئۆز refers to the person or a possessive pronoun and emphasizes the subject or the object of the sentence.

1. It is used as a simple noun to emphasize the doer of the action, as in English "him/her ... self."

ئەنۋەر ماشىنىنى ئۆزى تۈزەتتى. Anvar fixed the car himself.
خەتنى قىزىم ئۆزى يازدى. My daughter wrote the letter herself.

2. It may replace the personal pronouns for the purposes of emphasizing the subject of the sentence. In this case ئۆز takes the possessive ending.

ئۆينى مەن تازىلىدىم. I cleaned the house.
ئۆينى ئۆزۈم/ئۆزەم تازىلىدىم. I cleaned the house myself/by myself.
چىنىنى سەن چاقتىڭ. You broke the cup.
چىنىنى ئۆزەڭ/ئۆزۈڭ چاقتىڭ. It was you (yourself) who broke the cup.

3. As the object of a sentence, it takes the possessive ending and the accusative (-نى) or dative (-گە، -غا، -كە، -قا) endings.

ئۆزىنى كۆرمىدىم، ئۆكىسى بىلەن سۆزلەشتىم.
I did not see him (himself), but I talked to his brother.
نازاكەت ئۆزىگە ئالتۇن ھالقا سېتىۋالدى.
Nazaket bought a pair of golden earrings for herself.

4. When ئۆز is used without any ending of its own, it plays the role of adjective and it may be translated into English as 'own' (as in 'his own ', 'their own', 'her own'). In this case, it usually modifies the noun that follows it, which is marked with a possessive ending.

كىشىنىڭ ھۆرمىتى ئۆز قولىدا. Lit: Every person's dignity is in his own hands.

Exercise 17: مەن ئۆزۈم قىلىمەن!

Exercise 17.1:  Look at the sentences below. Choose the form of ئۆز that works best for each sentence.

1. ئۇ پەقەت ئۆزى/ ئۆزىنى/ ئۆزىنىڭ ئويلايدۇ، باشقىلار بىلەن ئىشى/ كارى يوق.
2. ئادىل ئۆزىگە/ ئۆزىدىن/ ئۆزىدە يېڭى ماشىنا ئاپتۇ.
3. ئۆزىگە/ ئۆزەمنىڭ/ ئۆزەم ئىسمىم نىكو، لېكىن ئۇيغۇرلار مېنى نىجات دەيدۇ.
4. باتۇر ئۆزى/ ئۆزىنىڭ/ ئۆزىگە ئۆيۈمىزنى تېپىپ كەپتۇ.
5. ئىشكنى ئۆزى / ئۆزىڭىزنىڭ / ئۆزىنى ئاچقۇچىڭىز بىلەن ئاچتىڭىزمۇ؟

Exercise 17.2: Draw lines between the sentence fragments in each colum below to form the Uyghur proverbs using the word ئۆز. Then, discuss their meaning.

دوستۇڭغا شۇنى قوي.	ئۆزەم تاپقان بالاغا*،
بولغاننى كۆرەلمەيدۇ.	ئۆزۈڭ نېمە يېسەڭ،
نەگە باراي داۋاغا؟	ئۆزۈڭگە ياخشىلىق تىلىسەڭ،
ياخشى تامىقىڭنى دوستۇڭغا بەر.	ياخشى تونۇڭنى ئۆزۈڭ كىي،
كۆزى تويماس.	ئۆزى بولالمايدۇ،
كىشىگە يامانلىق قىلما.	ئۆزى تويسىمۇ

*بالا - problem; trouble

Exercise 17.3:  Read the following short excerpt from John's blog and fill in the blanks with appropriate forms of the word ئۆز.

بۈگۈن شەنبە. دەم ئېلىش كۈنلىرى ئونغىچە ئۇخلايدىغان ئادەم، نېمىشقىدۇر بۈگۈن بالدۇر ئويغاندىم. قارىسام ئۆيۈم بەك قالايمىقان بولۇپ كېتىپتۇ. ناشتا قىلىپ، ئۆيۈمنى تازىلىدىم. ياتاقدىشىم بىلەن بازارغا بارماقچى ئىدۇق، ئەمما ئۇنىڭ مىجەزى يوق ئىكەن. بازارغا __________ باردىم. ئۇ يەردىن خېلى كۆپ نەرسە ئالدىم. چۈشلۈك تاماق يېگىلى ئاشخانىغا بارماي، ئۆيگە قايتىپ __________ تاماق ئەتتىم. ئاندىن دوستۇمنىڭ ئۆيىگە باردىم. ئۇ بۇزۇلۇپ قالغان كومپيۇتېرىنى __________ ئوڭشىتىپتۇ. بىز كومپيۇتېردا ئازراق ئويۇن ئوينىدۇق. كېيىن دوستۇم ئايلىنىپ كېلەيلى دېدى. بىز باغچىغا باردۇق. ئۇ يەردە باللار پۇتبول ئويناۋاتقان ئىكەن. بىزمۇ ئوينىدۇق. سائەت ئالتىلەردە ئۆيگە قايتتۇق. كەچلىك تاماقنى دوستۇمنىڭ ئۆيىدە يېدۇق. ئۇ __________ پولو ئەتتى. ئۇ پولوغا ئۇستىكەن!

4 The 1st Person Optative (Imperative) Mood

The optative mood is like the imperative, but you use it to command yourself. It is similar to the English 'Let's' as in 'Let's go!' in the plural, or 'Let' as in 'Let me do it' in the singular.

In the negative form, it is similar to 'shouldn't' as in 'I shouldn't say that.' The 1st person singular optative is formed by adding the suffix -اي / -ەي to the verb stem. The 1st person plural optative is formed by adding the suffix -يلى / -ەيلى.

As usual, the negative suffix -مە / -ما is added to the verb stem to form the negative. These are the forms of the optative:

Negative		Positive		Verbs
Plural	Singular	Plural	Singular	
كۆرمەيلى	كۆرمەي	كۆرەيلى	كۆرەي	كۆرمەك
كۈلمەيلى	كۈلمەي	كۈلەيلى	كۈلەي	كۈلمەك
يازمايلى	يازماي	يازايلى	يازاي	يازماق
ماڭمايلى	ماڭماي	ماڭايلى	ماڭاي	ماڭماق
سۆزلىمەيلى	سۆزلىمەي	سۆزلەيلى	سۆزلەي	سۆزلىمەك

Let's cook in our house. تاماقنى بىزنىڭ ئۆيدە ئېتەيلى.
Let me do it myself. بۇ ئىشنى مەن ئۆزەم قىلاي.
Let's not go to the movie today. بۈگۈن كىنوغا بارمايلى.
Let me not bother you. مەن سىزنى ئاۋارە قىلماي.
Let's go. قېنى، ماڭايلى.

In order to form the interrogative form of this mood, the question particle -مۇ is added.

Should we go to the market together? بازارغا بىللە بارايلىمۇ؟
Should we do this work tomorrow? بۇ ئىشنى ئەتە قىلايلىمۇ؟

Exercise 18: ئەتە بارايلى!

Exercise 18.1:  Using the 1st person optative, change the words given in brackets to the appropriate forms. If you see the Ø symbol after the verb in parentheses, write a negative sentence.

1. مەن ئۆزەم سىزگە تېلېفون ________________ (قىلماق)
2. ئەتە قەشقەرگە ________________ (بارماق).
3. ئەمدى ھەممەيلەن تاماق ________________ (يېمەك)!
4. ئاغىنىلەر، تاماقتىن كېيىن كىنو ________________ (كۆرمەك)!
5. ئۇ يەرگە ئىككىنچى ________________ (بارماق ø)!
6. قېنى مېھمانلار، ئۆيگە ________________ (كىرمەك)!
7. بۇ سوۋغات بەك ئاددىي ئىكەن، بۇنى سىزگە ________________ (بەرمەك ø) .
8. سائەت 12 بولۇپتۇ، مەن ________________ (ماڭماق).
9. قېنى، سىز سۆزلەڭ، مەن ________________ (ئاڭلىماق)!
10. بۇ يەردە ئورۇن بار ئىكەن، قېنى، ________________ (ئولتۇرماق)!

Note:

The 1st person optative (imperative) mood is also sometimes followed by the verb دېمەك, in which case it expresses a decision to perform the action of the verb (I am going to…) Literally, this means something like "I am saying I should go." Examples:

I'm going to the bazaar tomorrow. ئەتە بازارغا باراي دەيمەن.

I'd like to learn French. مەن فرانسۇزچە ئۆگىنەي دەيمەن.

Are you sure you will do that? سەن راستىنلا شۇنداق قىلاي دەمسەن؟

They would like to go to Kashgar. ئۇلار قەشقەرگە بارايلى دەيدۇ.

He is saying "Let's go to bed earlier." ئۇ بۈگۈن بالدۇرراق ئۇخلايلى دەۋاتىدۇ.

Exercise 18.2:  Ask your partner the following questions.

1. دەرستىن كېيىن نېمە قىلايلى دەيسىلەر؟
2. شەنبە-يەكشەنبە كۈنلىرى نېمە قىلاي دەيسىز؟
3. سەن يازدا شىنجاڭغا باراي دەمسەن؟
4. دوستۇڭ بۇ يەرگە كېلەي دەمدۇ؟
5. سىلەر رۇسچە ئۆگىنەيلى دەمسىلەر؟

Pulling it all together خۇرجۇندا

In this section, you will reinforce your knowledge and check the progress you have made during chapters 1 and 2 by completing a limited selection of focused exercises.

Exercise 19: ئۆتكۈرنى زىيارەت Here you will watch a video interview with Ondrej Klimes (Ötkür), a scholar of Uyghur studies.

Exercise 19.1: Before watching:
If you had a chance to interview Ötkür, which questions would you ask? Write at least six questions.

Exercise 19.2: Now watch the video and fill in the table below with the information provided.

	يېشى
	يۇرتى
	ئائىلىسى
	تۇغۇلغان ۋاقتى
	ئوقۇغان مەكتىپى

Exercise 19.3: Watch the video one more time and fill in the table below with the appropriate answers.

نېمە بولدى \ قىلدى؟	قاچان \ قەيەردە؟

Exercise 19.4: Answer the following questions about Ötkür.

1. ئۆتكۈر نېمە ئۈچۈن ئۇيغۇرچە ئۆگەندى؟
2. نېمە ئۈچۈن ئۇ ئامېرىكىغا كەلدى؟
3. ئۇنىڭ تەتقىقات ماقالىسىنىڭ ماۋزۇسى نېمە؟
4. ئۇنىڭ كەلگۈسى پىلانلىرى نېمە؟
5. قۇربان ھېيت ئۈچۈن ئۆتكۈر ئۇيغۇرلارغا نېمە دېدى؟

Exercise 20: ئابدۇمۇتەللىپنىڭ تەرجىمىھالى

Exercise 20.1: Here you will read about Abdumutellip, an Uyghur student from Kashgar. Before reading his biographical sketch, match the Uyghur words with their English equivalents.

to continue	___
to be enrolled	___
to exercise	___
Technical College	___
to participate in	___
major	___
anecdote	___
biography	___
internet, web	___
exhibition	___
to sit idle	___
to pay attention to	___

تەرجىمىھال	1
تېخنىكوم	2
كەسىپ	3
قوبۇل قىلىنماق	4
كۆرگەزمە	5
لەتىپە	6
تور	7
ئەھمىيەت بەرمەك	8
بەدەن چېنىقتۇرماق	9
بىكار تۇرماق	10
قاتناشماق	11
داۋاملاشتۇرماق	12

مەن ئابدۇمۇتەللىپ ئابلىمىت، 1992 - يىلى 2 - ئاينىڭ 2 - كۈنى قەشقەردە تۇغۇلدۇم. 1999 - يىلى 9 - ئايدا باشلانغۇچ مەكتەپكە كىردىم ۋە 2005 - يىلى 6 - ئايدا پۈتتۈردۈم. 2005 -يىلى 9 -ئايدا ئوتتۇرا مەكتەپكە ئوقۇشقا كىردىم. 2008 - يىلى 6 - ئايغىچە تولۇقسىز ئوتتۇرىنى شۇ مەكتەپتە ئوقۇدۇم. شۇ يىلى 6 - ئايدا يەنى تولۇقسىز ئوتتۇرىنى پۈتتۈرۈش ئالدىدا، ئوتتۇرا تېخنىكومغا سەنئەت (ئاككوردىيون) كەسپىدىن ئىمتىھان بېرىپ، قەشقەر سەنئەت مەكتىپىگە قوبۇل قىلىندىم. لېكىن بۇ مەكتەپتە ئوقۇماي، 2008 - يىلى 9 - ئايدىن 2011 - يىلى 6 - ئايغىچە تولۇق ئوتتۇرىنى ئوقۇدۇم. 2011 - يىلى 6 - ئاينىڭ 7 - كۈنى دۆلەتلىك ئالىي مەكتەپ ئىمتىھانىغا قاتناشتىم ۋە 278 نومۇر ئالدىم. ئەمما ئىمتىھان نەتىجەم نومۇر سىزىقىغا يەتمىدى. شۇ سەۋەبتىن ماڭا ھېچقانداق يەردىن چاقىرىق كەلمىدى. ئەسلىدە مەن شىنجاڭ پېداگوگىكا ئۇنىۋېرسىتېتىنىڭ ئىنگلىز تىلى كەسپىنى تاللىغان ئىدىم. ئەمما كېيىنرەك قەشقەر پېداگوگىكا ئىنستىتۇتىنىڭ ئاخبارات كەسپىدىن چاقىرىق كەلدى. لېكىن قەشقەردە ئوقۇشنى خالىمىدىم. بىر يىلدىن كېيىن 2012 - يىلى ئالىي مەكتەپ ئىمتىھانىدا يۇقىرى نومۇر بىلەن ئۆزۈم تاللىغان مەكتەپ ۋە كەسپكە قوبۇل قىلىندىم. بىرىنچى يىلى ئالىي مەكتەپتە خەنزۇ تىلى تەييارلىقىدا ئوقۇدۇم ۋە بىر يىلدىن كېيىن كەسپىمنى باشلىدىم. شۇنىڭدىن كېيىن يەنە بىر چەتئەل تىلىنى ئۆگىنىشنى توغرا تاپتىم. 2014 - يىلى 9 - ئايدا بېيجىڭغا كېلىپ فرانسۇز تىلىنى ئۆگىنىشنى باشلىدىم. كەلگۈسىدە فرانسىيەگە بېرىپ ئوقۇشمنى داۋاملاشتۇرماقچىمەن.

بوش ۋاقىتلىرىمدا مەن كىتابخانا، كۆرگەزمىلەرگە بېرىشنى ياخشى كۆرىمەن. ئەڭ ياخشى كۆرىدىغىنىم، ھەر خىل جايلارنى ئايلىنىش، مەسىلەن بازارلىرىمىز، دۇكان- سارايلىرىمىزنى. كۆپ كىتاب ئوقۇيمەن، بولۇپمۇ تارىخىي كىتاپلارغا قىزىقىمەن. يەنە لەتىپىلەر، يۇمۇرلارنى ئوقۇيمەن. بەزىدە تورغا چىقىمەن. توردا ئىنگلىزچە ھەم ئۇيغۇرچە نەرسىلەرنى كۆرىمەن. يېڭى ناخشا، سۈرەت، ئۇچۇرلارنى ئىزدەيمەن. ئادەتتە تەنتەربىيەگە ئانچە ئەھمىيەت بېرىپ كەتمەيمەن، ئەمما بەدەن چېنىقتۇرۇشقا ئامراق. بەزىدە ئەتىگەنلەردە يۈگۈرۈپ تۇرىمەن. ئۆيدە ئولتۇرۇشنى يامان كۆرىمەن. قەشقەردە بولسام، ھېيتگاھ ئەتراپىدا، ياكى كەچلىك بازارلاردا بولىمەن. ئۇرۇمچىدىمۇ ئاساسەن دۆڭكۆۋرۈككە بېرىپ كېلىمەن. ئەڭ ئۆچ كۆرۈدىغان ئىشىم - بىكار تۇرۇش.

Exercise 20.2:  Based on the information in the passage above, answer the following questions.

	ئابدۇمۇتەللىپ تولۇقسىز ئوتتۇرا مەكتەپنى قاچان پۈتتۈردى؟
	ئۇ تولۇق ئوتتۇرا مەكتەپنى نەدە ئوقۇدى؟
	نېمە ئۈچۈن ئۇ قەشقەر پېداگوگىكا ئىنستىتۇتىنىڭ ئاخبارات كەسپىدە ئوقۇمىدى؟
	2000 -يىلى ئۇ قايسى كەسپكە قوبۇل قىلىندى؟
	نېمە ئۈچۈن ئابدۇمۇتەللىپ بېيجىڭغا باردى؟
	بوش ۋاقىتلىرىدا ئۇ نېمە قىلىدۇ؟
	ئۇنىڭ نېمە بىلەن خوشى يوق؟

Exercise 20.3:  The verbs and expressions below are commonly used in biographical sketches. How many synonyms can you provide for each of these words?

	دۇنياغا كەلمەك
	چوڭ بولماق
	پۈتتۈرمەك
	ئوقۇماق
	ئۆيلەنمەك
	ئەرگە تەگمەك
	ئالەمدىن ئۆتمەك

Exercise 20.4:  Based on the passage about Abdumutellip, write your own biographical sketch. Use the words and expressions from below.

تۇغۇلماق چوڭ بولماق ئوقۇماق پۈتتۈرمەك
ئىمتىھان بەرمەك كەسىپ ئىمتىھان نەتىجىسى
قوبۇل قىلىنماق قاتناشماق قىزىقىش چېنىقماق
ساياھەت قىلماق ئامراق خوشام يوق

Self-check 

Use the following list to check your knowledge of the topics you have covered in chapters 1 and 2. Mark whether you know and can do the following in Uyghur. If you think you may need more work to fully understand something, you can go back to the relevant section in the chapters and review it.

1. I can talk and write about:

The history of Uyghur names	☐
The traditional multi-generational Uyghur family	☐
Old Kashgar	☐
Uyghur hospitality	☐
Kinship terms	☐
My life (biographical sketch)	☐
Mahmud Qeshqeri and his famous work "تۈركىي تىللار دىۋانى"	☐

2. I can also:

Recognize Uyghur male and female names	☐
Tell fairy tales	☐
Discuss my interests and hobbies	☐
Describe my family and family members	☐
Compare Uyghur and American families	☐
Conduct an interview with an Uyghur scholar	☐

3. I can explain the following words and concepts:

كاتەك	☐
چوڭ ئاپا	☐
چوڭ دادا	☐
كىچىك ئاپا	☐
كىچىك دادا	☐
ئاق كۆڭۈل	☐
ھاجەتخانا	☐

مەھەللە	☐
قورۇ	☐
مېھماندوست	☐
كۆمۈرخانا	☐
تونۇر	☐
ئوچاق	☐
ئېغىل	☐

4. I can use grammar to …

Give a compliment and express surprise with ئىكەن	☐
Express regret with the suffix پتۇ-	☐
Narrate stories by using both forms of the narrative past (with the word ئىكەن and the suffix پتۇ-)	☐
Tell some proverbs in Uyghur using the hearsay past	☐
Talk about myself using the reflexive pronoun ئۆز	☐
Give commands/suggestions to myself (and my companions) using the optative mood	☐
Relate what I have heard using the hearsay past	☐
Make general statements without a clear subject by using the passive voice	☐

Vocabulary سۆزلۈك

Vocabulary is given according to the Uyghur alphabetical order.
The right column precedes the left column on each page.

disaster	ئاپەت
finally	ئاخىرى
to cause pain	ئاغرىتماق
to warn	ئاگاھلاندۇرماق
to pass away	ئالەمدىن ئۆتمەك
your Majesty	ئالىيلىرى
solution	ئامال
family member	ئائىلە ئەزاسى
labor	ئەمگەك
to pay attention	ئەھمىيەت بەرمەك
generation	ئەۋلاد
to take care of	باقماق
to exercise	بەدەن چېنىقتۇرماق
single	بويتاق
to sit idle	بىكار تۇرماق
axe	پالتا
to clean/wash	تازىلىماق
accidental	تاسادىپىي
to close	تاقىماق
to choose	تاللىماق
approximately	تەخمىنەن
biography	تەرجىمىھال
to distribute	تەقسىملىمەك
belonging to	(-غا) تەۋە
rabbit	توشقان
tandoor	تونۇر
iron	تۆمۈر
pair	جۈپ
to grow up	چوڭ بولماق
strainer	چويلا

kettle	چۆگۈن
error	خاتالىق
to continue	داۋاملاشتۇرماق
bunch	دەستە
to be born	دۇنياغا كەلمەك
to visit	زىيارەت قىلماق
to get preserved	ساقلىنىپ قالماق
tool	سايمان
to trade	سودا قىلماق
to lock up	سولىماق
condition	شارائىت
to be formed	شەكىللەنمەك
to participate in	قاتناشماق
pine tree	قارىغاي
to receive; to accept	قوبۇل قىلماق
animal pen	قوتان
weapon; tool	قورال
courtyard	قورۇ
to escape (from)	قۇتۇلماق
enthusiastic, fervent	قىزغىن
chicken coop	كاتەك
dove	كەپتەر
to cut	كەسمەك
coal	كۆمۈر
diary	كۈندىلىك خاتىرە
to report; to inform	مەلۇم قىلماق
neighborhood	مەھەللە
appropriate	مۇۋاپىق
hospitality	مېھماندوستلۇق

custom	ئۆرپ - ئادەت
to build a house	ئۆي سالماق
to marry	ئۆيلەنمەك
field	ئېتىز
excellent	ئېسىل
corral	ئېغىل
to use	ئىشلەتمەك
wood	ياغاچ
countryside	يېزا

copper	مىس
condition	ھال
everyone	ھەممەيلەن
to be surprised	ھەيران بولماق
courtyard	ھويلا
government	ھۆكۈمەت
stove	ئوچاق
forest	ئورمان
thief	ئوغرى
to steal	ئوغرىلاپ كەتمەك

ئالىملار سۆھبىتى

نان ئېلىۋېلىڭ!

ئۈچىنچى دەرس

CHAPTER THREE

ئاق يول بولسۇن!

HAVE A SAFE TRIP!

IN THIS CHAPTER

Functions
- Asking for and giving advice
- Making suggestions
- Giving instructions
- Expressing politeness
- Expressing wishes

Grammar
- Past, present-continuous, present/future participles
- Postpositions of:
  - means or manner with بىلەن
  - place and instrument with ئارقىلىق
  - time with باشلاپ
- The conditional بولماق + -سا
- Construction -غۇ دەيمەن

In this chapter, John has received a scholarship and is getting ready for a trip to Xinjiang. After making some pre-departure preparation, his first stop is Beijing. Through the conversations, readings, and entries from John's blog which follow, you will become acquainted with مىللەتلەر ئۇنىۋېرسىتېتى (the University of Nationalities ~ Minzu University) in Beijing. You will also take a virtual trip to some of Beijing's important historical sites, such as خان سارىيى \ گۇگۇڭ (the Forbidden City) and سەددىچىن (the Great Wall).

Exercise 1: تۆۋەندىكى سوئاللارنى مۇزاكىرە قىلىڭلار

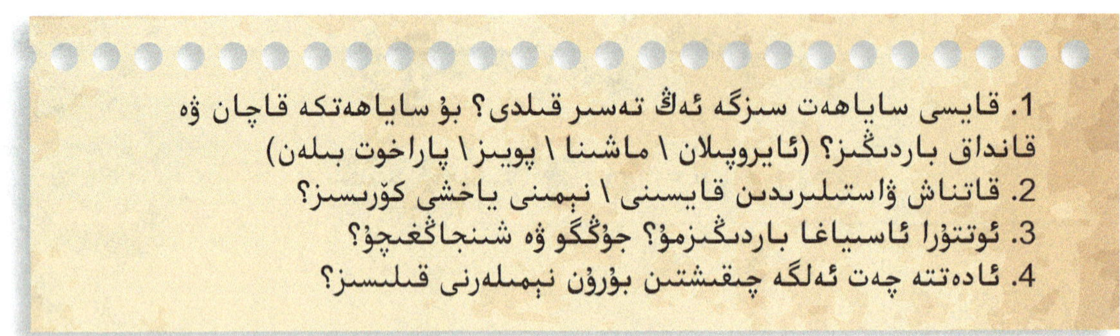
1. قايسى ساياھەت سىزگە ئەڭ تەسىر قىلدى؟ بۇ ساياھەتكە قاچان ۋە قانداق باردىڭىز؟ (ئايروپىلان \ ماشىنا \ پويىز \ پاراخوت بىلەن)
2. قاتناش ۋاستىلىرىدىن قايسىنى \ نېمىنى ياخشى كۆرىسىز؟
3. ئوتتۇرا ئاسىياغا باردىڭىزمۇ؟ جۇڭگو ۋە شىنجاڭغىچۇ؟
4. ئادەتتە چەت ئەلگە چىقىشتىن بۇرۇن نېمىلەرنى قىلىسىز؟

Exercise 2:  Match the following pictures with the appropriate words.

Group 1 قاتناش ۋاستىلىرى

پويىز	—
ئايروپىلان	—
ئاپتوبۇس	—
ۋېلسىپىت	—
پاراخوت	—

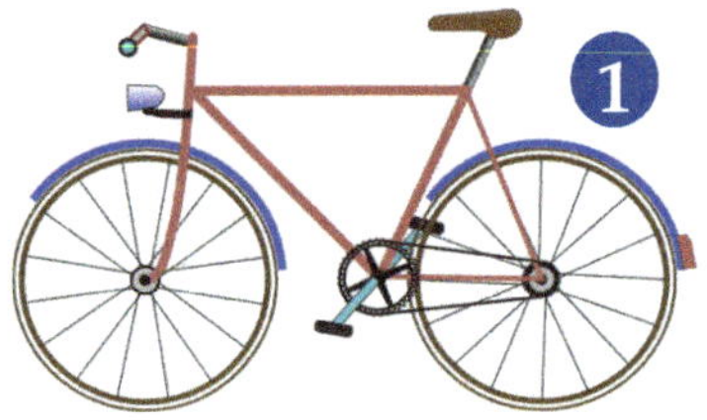

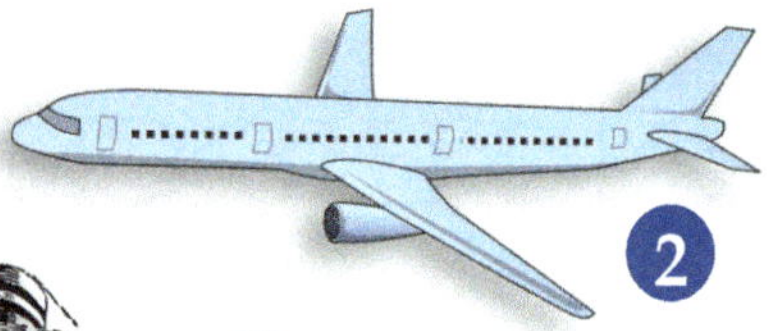

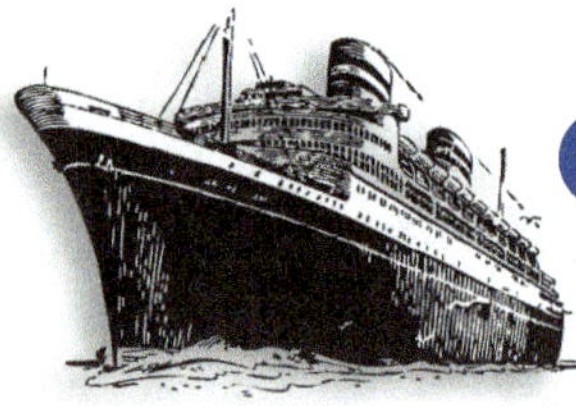

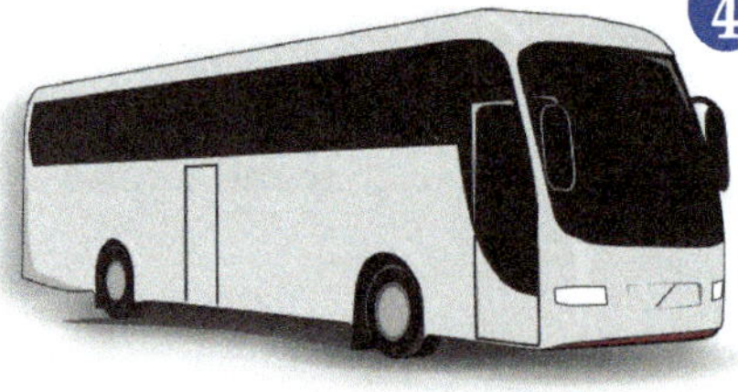

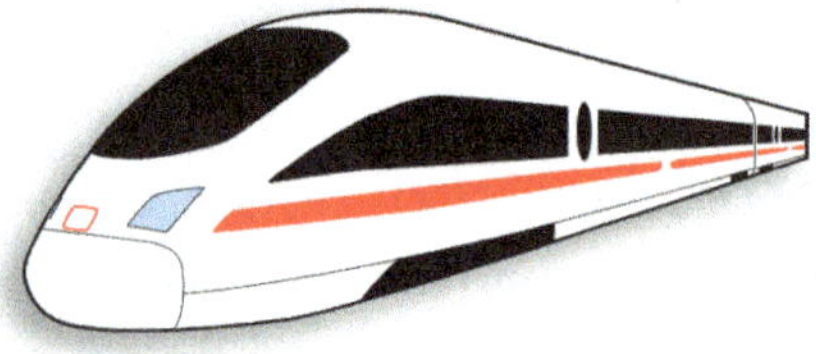

Group 2 ساياھەت بۇيۇملىرى

چامادان	—
بىلەت	—
ھۆججەت	—
يۇك/ يۇك - تاق	—
سىنئالغۇ / ۋىدېئو كامېرا	—
فوتو ئاپپارات	—
خەرىتە	—

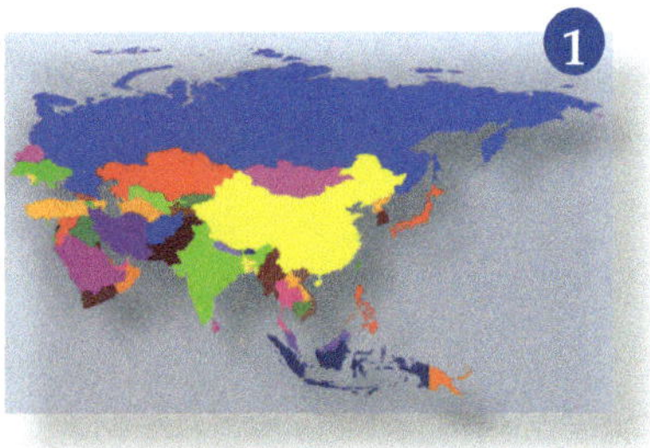

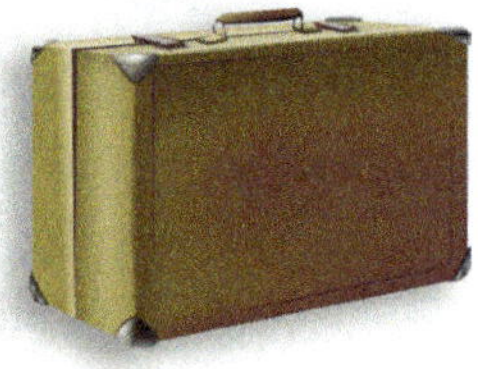

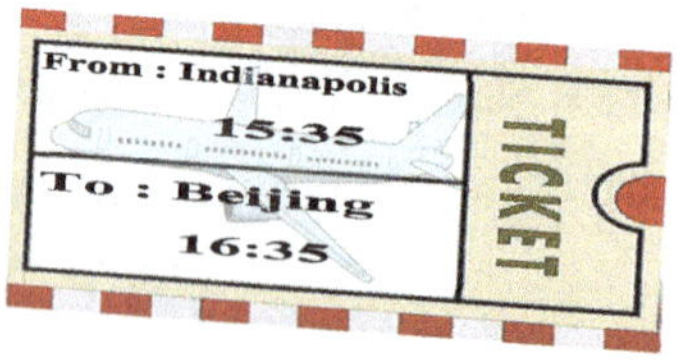

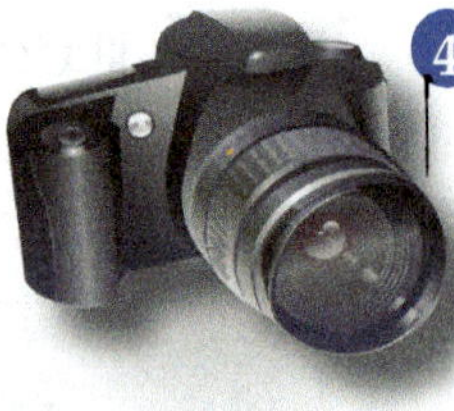

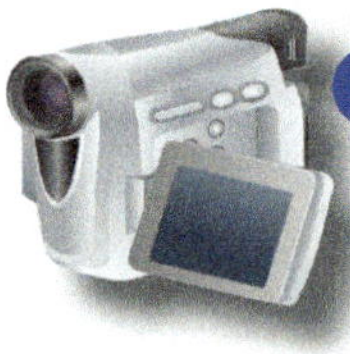

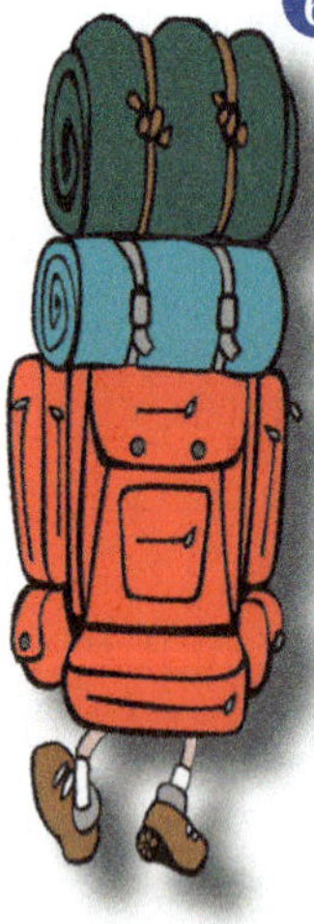

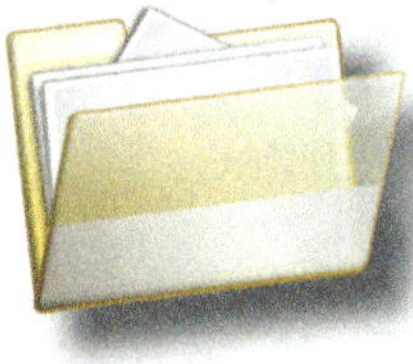

Exercise 3: نېمە قىلىندى/قىلىنمىدى؟

Exercise 3.1 :  Imagine that you are going on a long trip in a few days. You prepare a list of all the things you need to do before you head out. Check your to-do list below. In the boxes to the right of the statements, mark a few of the tasks done (√) and the rest as not-yet-done (!). Use your imagination!

چامادانلارنى تەييارلاش/ قاچىلاش	__	ئايروپىلان بېلىتىنى ئېلىش	__
كىتابلارنى كۇتۇپخانىغا قايتۇرۇش	__	ئۆي تازىلاش	__
بانكىدىن پۇل ئېلىش	__	كىيىم - كېچەكلىرىمنى يۇيۇش	__
دوستۇمدىن ئالغان قەرزنى قايتۇرۇش	__	شىنجاڭدىكى دوستلىرىمغا سوۋغات ئېلىش	__
ماشىنامنى سېتىش	__	كېرەكلىك دورىلارنى ئېلىش	__

Add at least two things you will need to do.

Exercise 3.2 :  Now rewrite each of the statements above using the passive voice. Use the negative for things which you have not done yet.

Exercise 4: مۆكاپات پۇلى تەستىقلاندى!

Exercise 4.1:  Read the blog entry below, then answer the questions that follow.

Uyghur John's Blog

ئامېرىكىلىق يالقۇننىڭ تورتۇراسى

كۈندە بىر ماقال:
كۆزۈڭنىڭ باردا شەھەر كۆر، چىشىڭنىڭ باردا گۆش يە.

Search

1 - ماي: بۈگۈن مەن ئۈچۈن قوش خوشاللىق بولدى: تىل ئۆگىنىش مۇكاپات پۇلى ھەققىدىكى ئىلتىماسىم تەستىقلاندى ھەم بۈگۈن مېنىڭ تۇغۇلغان كۈنۈم! بەك ھاياجانلىنىۋاتىمەن، چۈنكى بىر ئايدىن كېيىن مەن يەنە شىنجاڭغا بارىمەن! ئۇ يەردە ياشاۋاتقان ئۇيغۇرلار بىلەن ئۇيغۇرچە سۆزلىشىمەن! ئۈرۈمچى، قەشقەر، خوتەنگە يەنە بارىمەن! قەشقەردە تونۇشقان ئۇيغۇر بوۋاي "بىر كۈنلۈك سەپەرگە ئون كۈن تەييارلىق" دېگەن ئىدى. بۇنىڭ مەنىسىنى مانا ھازىر چۈشەندىم. قىلىدىغان ئىشلار بەك كۆپ. ئەندىشە قىلىدىغان ئىشلارمۇ بار. ئالدى بىلەن ئايروپىلان بېلىتىنى ئالىمەن. يازدا جۇڭگوغا بارىدىغان كىشىلەر بەك كۆپ، شۇڭا ئايروپىلان بېلىتىنى بالدۇرراق ئېلىشىم كېرەك. ھازىر قولۇمدا پاسپورت بار، لېكىن مۇكاپات پۇلىنىڭ ھۆججەتلىرى تېخى كەلمىدى. بۇنىڭدىن باشقا ھۆججەتلەر خەنزۇچىغا تەرجىمە قىلىنىشى لازىم ئىكەن. بۇنىڭغا كىم ياردەم بېرىدۇ؟ بۇنى يەنىلا ئۆزۈم قىلىشىم كېرەك. بۇ يەردىن ئۈرۈمچىگە بىۋاستە ئايروپىلان يوق، شۇڭا ئاۋۋال بېيجىڭغا بېرىپ، بېيجىڭ ئارقىلىق ئۈرۈمچىگە بارىمەن. بېيجىڭدا ياشاۋاتقان ئۇيغۇرلار ھازىر قانچىلىك؟ ئۇلارنى زىيارەت قىلىش مۇمكىنمۇ؟

بېيجىڭدىن ئۈرۈمچىگە ئايروپىلان بىلەن بارامدىم يا پويىز ياخشىمۇ؟ ھازىرچە ئۇنى ئۆزەممۇ بىلمەيمەن. بېيجىڭدىن ئۈرۈمچىگە يېڭى تۆمۈر يول سېلىنىدى دەپ ئاڭلىدىم. ئەمما پويىز بېلىتى ئېلىش خېلى تەس دەيدۇ. قېنى، شۇ يەرگە بارغاندا بىر گەپ بولار... ئەپسۇس، بېيجىڭدا مەن تونۇيدىغان باللار ھازىر يوق. ئۈرۈمچىدىن كەلگەن ئەكبەرنىڭ بېيجىڭدا ئوقۇۋاتقان ئۇيغۇر دوستلىرى بارمىكىن؟

ئاڭلىسام، شىنجاڭ ھازىر بۇرۇنقىغا ئوخشىمايدىكەن، مەن كۆرگەن قەشقەرمۇ يوق ئىكەن. فوتو ئاپارات ياكى ۋىدېئو كامېرا ئېلىپ كىرىشكە بولامدىكىن؟ بۇ تېخى نامەلۇم، بىلىدىغان كىشىلەردىن سورىشىم كېرەك. بەزىلەر "چەتئەللىكلەر تاموژنىدىن ئۆتكەندە ئۇلارنى ئالاھىدە تەكشۈرىدۇ"، "ئۇلارنىڭ سومكىسىنى ئاختۇرىدۇ" دەيدۇ. بۇ گەپلەر راستمىكىن؟ بۇلارنى ئەكبەردىن سورايمەن. ئىككى يىلنىڭ ئالدىدا ئۈرۈمچىدە تونۇشقان ئۇيغۇر دوستۇم ياسىندىنمۇ ياردەم سورايمەن. ئۈرۈمچى ۋە قەشقەردە ئوقۇۋاتقان باللار ھازىر مەكتەپنى پۈتتۈرگەن بولۇشى مۇمكىن. بارغىنىمدا ئۆزۈم ئۇلارنى تاپىمەن. بۇنىڭدىن تاشقىرى بېيجىڭدىن ئۈرۈمچىگە كەلگەندىن كېيىن شىمال ۋە جەنۇبتىكى بارىدىغان جايلارنىڭ ئاپتوبۇس بېلىتى ھەققىدە بىر خام چوت تەييارلىشىم لازىم. ئەتىدىن باشلاپ سەپەرنىڭ تەييارلىقىنى باشلايمەن.

قىلىدىغان ئىش نېمىدېگەن كۆپ! تېخى ئەڭ مۇھىم نەرسىنى ئۇنتۇپ قاپتىمەن: بانكىدىن پۇل ئېلىشىم كېرەك!

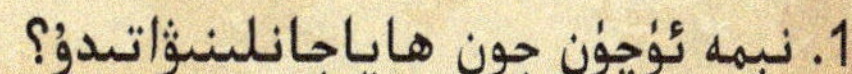

1. نېمە ئۈچۈن جون ھاياجانلىنىۋاتىدۇ؟
2. جون شىنجاڭدا نېمە قىلماقچى؟
3. بېيجىڭدا ئۇ كىملەرنى تونۇيدۇ؟
4. جون نېمىگە ئەندىشە قىلىدۇ؟
5. نېمە ئۈچۈن ئۇ خام چوت تەييارلىشى كېرەك؟
6. شىمال ۋە جەنۇبتىكى شەھەرلەرگە ئۇ نېمە بىلەن بارماقچى؟

Exercise 4.2:  Which of the given options best matches the meanings of the following words and expressions from the text?

تەرجىمىسى			سۆز - ئىبارىلەر	
a. to answer	b. to apply	c. to order	ئىلتىماس قىلماق	1
a. education	b. preparation	c. studying	تەييارلىق	2
a. take a look	b. take care	c. to check	ئاختۇرماق	3
a. major	b. important	c. necessarily	مۇھىم	4
a. to participate	b. to visit	c. to see	زىيارەت قىلماق	5
a. to order	b. to receive	c. to bring	بۇيرۇماق	6
a. to tie	b. to contact	c. to put together	ئالاقىلاشماق	7
a. to be excited	b. to be embarrassed	c. to be confused	ھاياجانلانماق	8
a. to feel	b. to worry	c. to weep	ئەندىشە قىلماق	9

1 Past Participle

A participle is an adjective derived from a verb. It functions like an adjective, insomuch as it usually modifies a noun. In Uyghur, participles generally correspond to English participles or relative clauses, ex. the boy (who is) reading the book.

Past participles are formed by adding the suffix -غان (-قان/ -گەن/ -كەن) to the verb stem. Look at the following sentences from a blog.

ئۈرۈمچىدىن كەلگەن ئەكبەرنىڭ بېيجىڭدا ئوقۇۋاتقان ئۇيغۇر دوستلىرى بارمىكىن؟
Does Ekber, who came from Urumqi, have Uyghur friends studying in Beijing?
ئۈرۈمچىدە تونۇشقان ئۇيغۇر دوستۇم ياسىندىنمۇ ياردەم سورايمەن.
I will ask my Uyghur friend Yasin, whom I met in Urumqi, for help.

The negative is formed by adding -ما / -مە before the participle ending. Remember that a vowel in the negative reduces in this position, yielding -مى.

سىنىپتا قەشقەرگە بارمىغان بالا بارمۇ؟
Is there anyone in class who has not been to Kashgar?
بۇ خەۋەرنى ئاڭلىمىغان كىشى يوق.
There is no one who hasn't heard this news.

Exercise 5: سۈپەتداشلار

Exercise 5.1:  How would you translate the past participles in the following sentences?

1. يېقىندا قەشقەردىن كەلگەن قىزغا نېمە بوپتۇ، ئاڭلىدىڭلارمۇ؟
2. ئادىل بۇزۇلغان كومپيۇتېرىنى رېمونتخانىغا ئېلىپ باردى.
3. ئولتۇرغان كىشىلەر دەرھال ئورنىدىن تۇردى.
4. ناخشا ئېيتقان قىز سەھنىدىن چۈشتى.
5. يېنىمدا ئولتۇرغان بالىنى تونۇمايمەن.

Exercise 5.2:  Use participles to combine each of the following pairs of sentences into one. Then check your sentences with your partner. The first one has been done for you.

خەت يازغان بالا ئورنىدىن تۇردى.	بالا خەت يازدى. ئۇ ئورنىدىن تۇردى.
	شوپۇر ماشىنا ھەيدىدى. ئۇ بىزنىڭ قوشنىمىز.
	ساجىدە ناخشا ئاڭلىدى. ئۇ دىسكو ئوينىدى.
	بوۋاي بازارغا باردى. ئۇ گۆش ئالدى.
	خېرىدار تاماق يېدى. ئۇ پۇل تۆلىدى.
	مۇئەللىم رەسىم سىزدى. ئۇ ئۆيگە قايتتى.
	قىزچاق تېلېفون بەردى. ئۇ ئۆيگە كىردى.

2 Present-Continuous Participle

The present continuous participle is formed by adding the suffix ۋاتقان- / ىۋاتقان- / ۋۇاتقان- / ۇۋاتقان- to the verb stem (ياشاۋاتقان). Note that this is actually the same suffix as the past participle, but attached to the progressive suffix / ۋات- / ىۋات- / ۋۇات- / ۇۋات-. Remember that the vowel ئا/ئە is reduced in monosyllabic verbs.

شۇ يەردە ياشاۋاتقان ئۇيغۇر ئائىلىسى بىلەن تونۇشتۇم.
I became acquainted with the Uyghur family (who is) living there.
The girl who's selling airline tickets is Uyghur. ئايروپىلان بېلىتى سېتىۋاتقان قىز ئۇيغۇركەن
Do you know the boy who's buying a knife? پىچاق ئېلىۋاتقان بالىنى تونۇمسىز؟

The negative is formed by adding -ما/-مە before the participle.

Who is the boy (who is) not eating? تاماق يېمەيۋاتقان بالا كىم؟

Certain verbs are not used in the present progressive form. For example: ياتماق, تۇرماق، ئولتۇرماق، يۈرمەك. They take the past tense ending غان- to show that somebody is sitting, walking, lying, or standing. This is because in Uyghur, the verb ئولتۇرماق (i.e., who sat and is now seated) expresses the act of sitting down, and not the state of being seated, whereas in English it can express either.

The girl sitting in chair looked at me. ئورۇندۇقتا ئولتۇرغان قىز ماڭا قارىدى.
ئەكبەر يەردە تۇرغان سومكىنى قولىغا ئالدى.
Ekber picked up the bag laying
(i.e., which was placed, and is now laying) on the ground.

Exercise 5.3:  Fill in the blanks with the appropriate forms of the present-continuous participle for each of the verbs given in parentheses.

1. تاپشۇرۇق (ئىشلىمەك) ____________ بالا سائەتكە قاردى.
2. تاماق (ئەتمەك) ____________ ئايال ئانامنى ئەسلەتتى.
3. دەرس (ئۆتمەك) ____________ ئوقۇتقۇچى ياپونچە بىلمەيدۇ.
4. كىتاب (ئوقۇماق) ____________ بالا بەك تىرىشچان.
5. ۋېلىسىپىت (مىنمەك) ____________ ئوقۇغۇچى كالىفورنىيەلىك.
6. چاي (ئىچمەك) ____________ كىشى مۇسابىقىگە تاللاندى.
7. سالام (بەرمەك) ____________ قىز ئۇلارنىڭ نەۋرىسى.

3 Present/Future Participle

The present/future participle is formed by adding -ىدىغان (after consonants) and -يدىغان (after vowels) to the verb stem (تونۇيدىغان / ئالىدىغان). This participle can refer to present or future actions. Remember that only vowel ئە is reduced in monosyllabic verbs. Examples:

بېيجىڭدا مەن تونۇيدىغان باللار ھازىر يوق.
There is nobody in Beijing now whom I know.
يازدا جۇڭگوغا بارىدىغان كىشلەر بەك كۆپ.
There are many people who go to China in the summer.
ۋىزا بېرىدىغانلار بۈگۈن ئىشلىمەيدۇ.
The visa officials don't work today.
شىنجاڭدا قىلىدىغان ئىشلار بەك كۆپ.
There are so many things to do in Xinjiang.

The negative is formed by adding -مە / -ما before the participle ending (قىلمايدىغان).

Is there anybody in class who does not know Uyghur?
سىنىپتا ئۇيغۇرچە بىلمەيدىغانلار بارمۇ؟

Exercise 5.4:  Using the present/future participle, form grammatically correct sentences from the provided words below. Follow the model:

يازماق / ماقالەم / بار / ئىككى. يازىدىغان ئىككى ماقالەم بار.

1. قىلماق \ كۆپ \ ئىشلىرىم \ ئەمەس. ______
2. كۆرۈشمەك \ ئوقۇتقۇچىم \ ئالدىراش \ بوگۈن. ______
3. ئوقۇماق \ ئۇيغۇرچە \ كىتاب \ يېزىلغان. ______
4. ئالماق \ تىزىملاندى \ كېلەر\ھەپتىگە \ بىلەتىم. ______
5. تونۇماق \دوستلىرىم\ ئوقۇيدۇ \ ئۇرۇمچىدە. ______
6. ياتماق \ ئەمەس \ ئەرزان \ مېھمانخانام. ______
7. ساتماق\ يوق \ دوللار! ______

Exercise 5.5:  The blog entry (Exercise 4.1) contains a number of underlined participles. Write them into the appropriate columns below.

Past Participle	Present- Continuous Participle	Present/Future Participle

Exercise 5.6:  Translate the following words into English based on their meaning in the blog entry.

	كەلگەن
	بىلىدىغان
	ياشاۋاتقان
	بارىدىغان
	تونۇشقان
	ئوقۇۋاتقان

4 The Postposition of Means or Manner: بىلەن

The postposition بىلەن describes the means by which the action of the verb is conducted. It can often be translated into English as 'by.' Examples:

بېيجىڭدىن ئۈرۈمچىگە ئايروپىلان بىلەن بارامدىم يا پويىز بىلەنمۇ؟
Shall I go from Beijing to Urumqi by plane, or by train?

The postposition بىلەن can also indicate the person which accompanies the subject in performing the action of the verb. In this case, it is best translated into English as 'with.' Examples:

I spoke with my mother for two hours. ئانام بىلەن ئىككى سائەت سۆزلەشتىم.
Yesterday I went to the movie with my friend. تۈنۈگۈن كىنوغا دوستۇم بىلەن باردىم.

The Postposition ئارقىلىق

The postposition ئارقىلىق can be translated into English as 'through,' 'via,' or 'by way of.' This postposition may be used in expressions of place. Examples:

ئاۋۋال بېيجىڭغا بېرىپ، بېيجىڭ ئارقىلىق ئۈرۈمچىگە بارىمەن.
First I'll go to Beijing, then via Beijing I'll go to Urumqi.

The postposition may also be used in an abstract sense to indicate an instrument or medium. Examples:

I talked to him via/through Skype. ئۇنىڭ بىلەن سكايپ ئارقىلىق سۆزلەشتىم.

The Postposition of Time from Which: باشلاپ

The postposition باشلاپ indicates the time from which the action of the verb begins. It is coupled with a noun in the ablative case. Look at the following example from the blog entry.

ئەتىدىن باشلاپ سەپەرنىڭ تەييارلىقنى باشلايمەن.
I will get ready for my trip starting tomorrow.

In this sentence the postposition باشلاپ can be translated into English as 'starting.'

Exercise 6:  Fill in the blanks with the appropriate postpositions
.بىلەن، ئارقىلىق، باشلاپ

1. نيو-يوركقا چىكاگو ________________ كەلدىم.
2. ئۇ كونسېرتقا سىز________________ بارماقچى.
3. پۇلنى پوچتا ________________ ئالدىم.
4. قەشقەرگە سىز________________ بارسام بولامدۇ؟
5. يەكشەنبىدىن ________________ ھەر كۈنى چېنىقىمەن.
6. قەشقەرگە خوتەن ________________ بارالامدىم؟
7. بۈگۈندىن ________________ تاپشۇرۇقلىرىمنى ۋاقتىدا ئىشلەيمەن.
8. ئۇ بىز________________ بارالمايدۇ، ئۇنىڭ ئىشلىرى بار ئىكەن.

Exercise 7: شىنجاڭغا سەپەر... شىنجاڭ؟

Exercise 7.1: How would you describe the following pictures? Try to use participles.

Exercise 7.2:  Study the following words, then read the passage below.

political	سىياسىي
ancient	قەدىمكى
to congregate	توپلاشماق
to establish; to build	قۇرماق
capital (city)	پايتەخت
to spread out	تارقالماق
cradle	بۆشۈك
to turn into; to wander around	ئايلانماق

land	زېمىن
times (as in two times more)	ھەسسە
basin	ئويمانلىق
culture	مەدەنىيەت
province	ئۆلكە
desert	چۆل
Silk Road	يىپەك يولى
important	مۇھىم

شىنجاڭ ئوتتۇرا ئاسىيانىڭ شەرقىگە جايلاشقان. ئۇ جۇڭگونىڭ ئەڭ چوڭ ئۆلكىسى. ئۇنىڭ زېمىنى فرانسىيەدىن ئۈچ ھەسسە چوڭ، كالىفورنىيەدىن تۆت ھەسسە چوڭ. شىنجاڭنىڭ شىمالىدا ئالتاي تېغى، ئوتتۇرىسىدا تەڭرى تېغى، جەنۇبىدا قاراقۇرۇم (كوئېنلۇن) تېغى، غەربىدە پامىر ئېگىزلىكى بار. تەڭرى تېغىنىڭ شىمالىدا جۇڭغار ئويمانلىقى، جەنۇبىدا تارىم ئويمانلىقى بار. تارىم ئويمانلىقىنىڭ ئوتتۇرىسىغا تەكلىماكان چۆلى جايلاشقان. بۇ چۆل -- دۇنيادىكى ئىككىنچى چوڭ چۆل ھېسابلىنىدۇ.

ئۈرۈمچى -- شىنجاڭ ئۇيغۇر ئاپتونوم رايونى (ش ئۇ ئا ر) نىڭ سىياسىي مەركىزى. ئۇيغۇرلار تەڭرى تېغىنىڭ شىمالىدىكى ئۈرۈمچى، قاراماي، بۆرتالا، غۇلجا، چۆچەك ۋە ئالتاي قاتارلىق شەھەرلەردە، شۇنداقلا تەڭرى تېغىنىڭ شەرقى ۋە جەنۇبىدىكى قۇمۇل، تۇرپان، كورلا، كۇچا، ئاقسۇ، قەشقەر، خوتەن قاتارلىق شەھەرلەردە توپلىشىپ ياشايدۇ.

قەشقەر، خوتەن ۋە ئىلى -- ئۇيغۇرلار ئەڭ كۆپ تارقالغان رايون. قەشقەر - ئۇيغۇرلارنىڭ مەدەنىيەت تارىخىدا ناھايىتى مۇھىم ئورۇن ئىگىلەيدۇ. قەشقەرنىڭ يازما تارىخى ئىككى مىڭ يىلدىن ئۇزۇن. قەشقەر قەدىمكى زاماندا "سۇلۇق" دەپ ئاتالغان ۋە "يىپەك يولى" دىكى بىر مۇھىم مەركەز بولغان. شۇ سەۋەبتىن شەرق مەدەنىيىتى بىلەن غەرب مەدەنىيىتى بۇ يەردە ئۇچراشقان. قاراخانىيلار دۆلىتى قۇرۇلغاندىن كېيىن قەشقەر بۇ دۆلەتنىڭ پايتەختى بولغان. پادىشاھ سۇلتان ساتۇق بۇغراخان 925 - يىلى قەشقەردە ئىسلام دىنىنى قوبۇل قىلغان. شۇنىڭدىن كېيىن قەشقەر ئۇيغۇرلارنىڭ يەنە بىر مۇھىم مەدەنىيەت مەركىزىگە ئايلانغان. قەشقەر -- ئۇيغۇر مەدەنىيىتىنىڭ بۆشۈكى، شۇنداقلا سىمۋولى.

Exercise 7.3: Based on the passage, answer the following questions.

1. شىنجاڭنىڭ شىمالىغا قايسى تاغ جايلاشقان؟
2. تەڭرى تېغى بىلەن قاراقۇرۇم تېغى قەيەردە؟
3. پامىر ئېگىزلىكى شىنجاڭنىڭ قايسى قىسمىغا جايلاشقان؟
4. شىنجاڭدا نەچچە ئويمانلىق بار؟ ئۇلار قەيەرگە جايلاشقان؟
5. تەكلىماكان چۆلى قەيەردە؟
6. ئۇيغۇرلار قايسى شەھەرلەردە توپلىشىپ ياشايدۇ؟
7. قەشقەر توغرىسىدا نېمىلەر ئۇققەندىڭىز؟

Exercise 7.4:  Here is a map of Xinjiang. Read the names, then sort them all into the columns which follow according to the type of geographical feature which they represent.

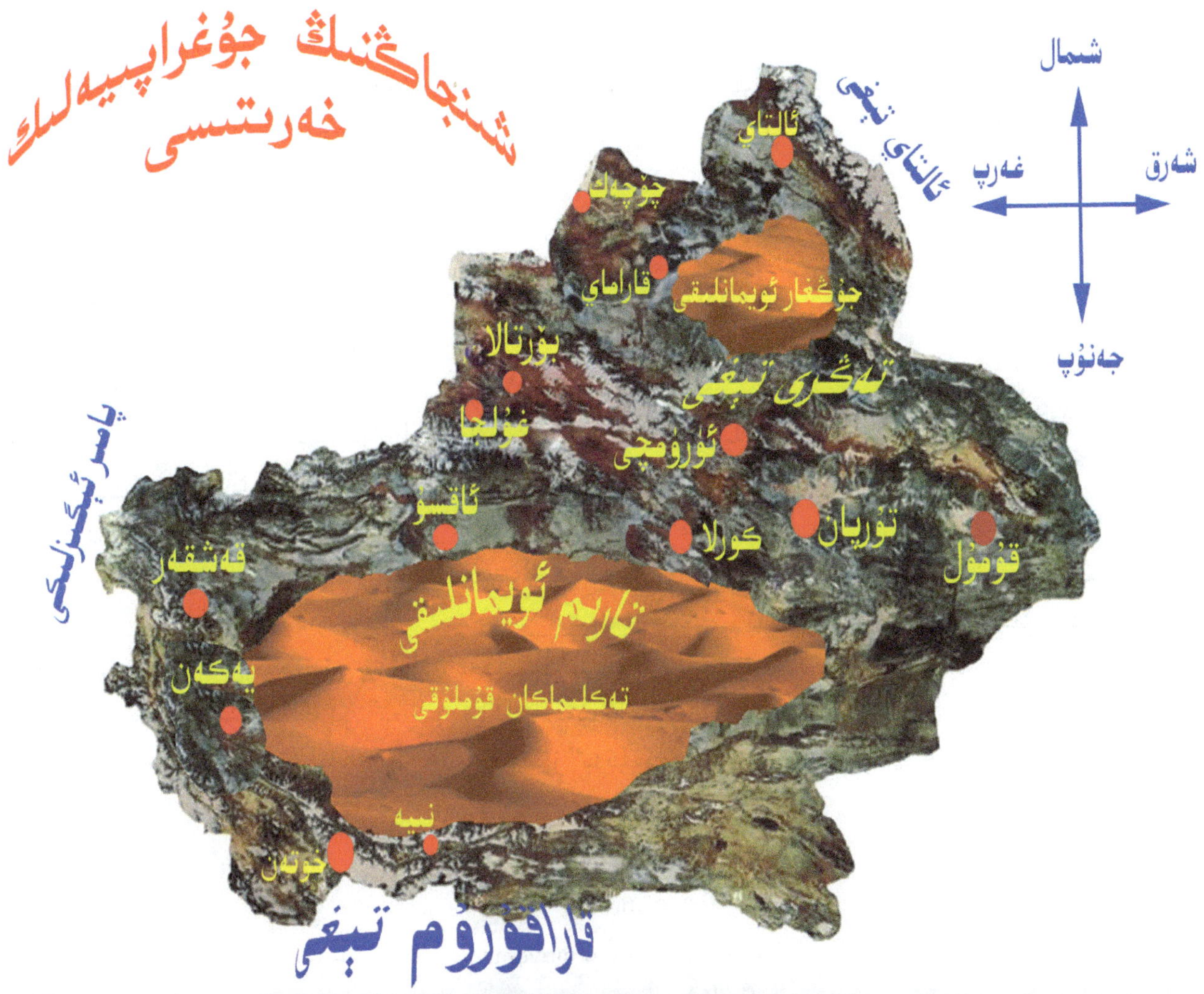

Cities شەھەرلەر	Mountains تاغلار	Deserts قۇملۇقلار	Basins ئويمانلىقلار

Exercise 8: "تەكلىماكان" سۆزى نەدىن كەلگەن؟

Exercise 8.1:  Read the following short passage about the Taklimakan desert and fill in the blanks with the provided words below.

كۆلىمى يەنى ماكان ئۇزۇنلىقى ئېگىزلىكى ئۆتۈشى

كەڭلىكى قۇم كۆچۈش ئەتراپىغا مەنزىرىسى جايلاشقان

تەكلىماكان قۇملۇقى-تارىم ئويمانلىقىنىڭ ئوتتۇرىسىغا __________ .
بۇ قۇملۇقنىڭ شەرقتىن غەربكىچە __________ مىڭ كىلومېتىردىن
ئاشىدۇ، جەنۇبتىن شىمالغا سوزۇلغان __________ تەخمىنەن 400
كىلومېتىر. تەكلىماكان قۇملۇقى شىنجاڭ بويىچە ئەڭ چوڭ قۇملۇق.
ئۇنىڭ __________ 324 مىڭ كۋادرات كىلومېتىر. قۇم بارخانلىرىنىڭ
__________ 60 ~80 مېتىر، ئەڭ ئېگىز جايى 250 مېتىرچە كېلىدۇ.
تەكلىماكان ئەسلى "تەركىي ماكان" __________ "تاشلانغان ماكان"
دېگەن سۆزدىن كېلىپ چىققان. كىشىلەرنىڭ ئېيتىشىچە، قەدىمكى زاماندا بۇ يەر گۈللەپ ياشنىغان، سۈيى
كۆپ، __________ گۈزەل، ئاۋات بىر __________ بولغان ئىكەن. ئەمما __________ سەۋەبىدىن بۇ
يەردىكى كىشىلەر ئەسلى ماكانىنى تاشلاپ، تەكلىماكانىنىڭ __________ جايلاشقان ئىكەن.
شۇنىڭدىن كېيىن كىشىلەر بۇ يەرنى "تەركىي ماكان" دەپ ئاتىشىپتۇ. يىللارنىڭ__________ بىلەن
تىلدىكى ئىستېمالنىڭ ئۆزگىرىشىگە ئەگىشىپ، بۇ سۆز "تەكلىماكان" غا ئۆزگىرىپتۇ.

to follow	ئەگەشمەك
consumption	ئىستېمال
to exceed	ئاشماق
to extend	سوزۇلماق

desert	قۇملۇق
sand movement	قۇم كۆچۈش
abandoned place	تەركىي ماكان
area; scale	كۆلەم

Exercise 8.2: Now listen to the passage and check your answers.

Exercise 9: What new information did you learn about Xinjiang from Exercise 7.2 and Exercise 8.1? Share your answers with your classmates.

Exercise 10:  Prepare a short presentation about your country. Describe its geography, major districts/states, people, and major ethnic groups. Compare your country with Xinjiang.

Exercise 11: يول تەييارلىقى

Exercise 11.1:  What do you need in order to travel to Xinjiang? Read and decide if the following statements are true or false.

خاتا	توغرا

1. ۋىزا ئېلىشىڭىز كېرەك.
2. يېڭى پاسپورت ئېلىشىڭىز لازىم.
3. پۇل ئالغىلى بانكىغا بېرىشىڭىز كېرەك.
4. سالامەتلىك سۇغۇرتىسى ئېلىشىڭىز كېرەك.
5. لازىملىق دورىلارنى سېتىۋېلىشىڭىز كېرەك.
6. ئۇيغۇرلارنىڭ ئۆرپ - ئادەتلىرىنى ئۆگىنىشىڭىز كېرەك.
7. ئاتا- ئانىڭىز بىلەن خوشلىشىشىڭىز لازىم.
8. ئايروپىلان بېلىتى ئېلىشىڭىز كېرەك.
9. شىنجاڭ خەرىتىسى سېتىۋېلىشىڭىز كېرەك.

Exercise 11.2:  John calls his friend in Urumchi to get some advice about his upcoming trip. Listen to their conversation and decide if the following statements are true or false.

خاتا	توغرا

1. جون شىنجاڭغا كۈزدە بارماقچى.
2. جون بېلەتنى بېيجىڭغىچە ئالماقچى.
3. بېيجىڭدا جوننىڭ دوستلىرى بار.
4. جون بېيجىڭدىن ئۈرۈمچىگە ئاپتوبۇستا بارىدۇ.
5. ئۈرۈمچىدە جوننىڭ ئاغىنىسى پويىز ئىستانسىسىغا چىقىدۇ.

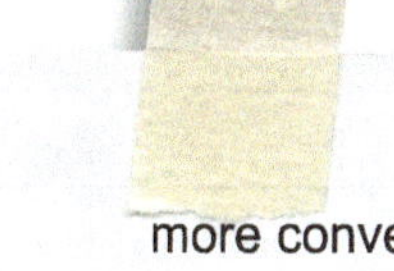

قولايراق: more convenient
كۆتۈۋالماق (كۈتۈپ ئالماق): to meet
ئايلانماق: to stroll
مەسلىھەت: advice
ئاغىنە: close friend
چۈشمەك: to stay over; to fall
نۇرغۇنلىغان: many

Exercise 11.3:  Here is an excerpt from the conversation between John and Yasin, in which John is asking for advice. Read it, then list the things John asks for.

جون: سىزنىڭ مەسلىھەتىڭىز كېرەك ئىدى.
ياسىن: خوش...
جون: نيۇ يوركتىن بېلەتنى قايسى شەھەرگە ئالسام قولايراق بولىدۇ؟
ياسىن: نيۇ يوركتىن بېلەتنى بېيجىڭغىچە ئالسىڭىز ياخشىراق بولىدىغۇ دەيمەن.
جون: شۇنداق قىلاي. بېيجىڭنىمۇ كۆرگۈم بار ئىدى. ئەمما بېيجىڭدا مېنىڭ تونۇشلىرىم يوق. ئۇ يەردە نەگە
چۈشسەم بولىدۇ؟
ياسىن: چاتاق يوق! ئۇ يەردە مەن تونۇيدىغان بىر نەچچە بالا بار. ئۇلارغا خەۋەر بېرىپ قويىمەن، ئۇلار
ئايرودرومغا چىقىپ سىزنى كۈتۈۋالىدۇ.
جون: رەھمەت سىزگە! بېيجىڭنىڭ داڭلىق ساياھەت ئورۇنلىرىنى زىيارەت قىلماقچى ئىدىم، ئۇنىڭغا
قانچىلىك ۋاقىت كېتىدۇ؟
ياسىن: بېيجىڭنى ئۈچ - تۆت كۈن ئايلانسىڭىز بولىدۇ. باللار سىزگە ياردەم بېرىدۇ.
جون: ئۈرۈمچىگە قانداق بارسام بولىدۇ؟
ياسىن: ئۈرۈمچىگە پويىز بىلەن كەلسىڭىز ياخشىراق بولىدۇ. چۈنكى پويىز ھەم ئەرزان ھەم قولاي. ئۈرۈمچىگە
كەلگۈچە نۇرغۇنلىغان جايلارنى كۆرەلەيسىز.

Exercise 11.4:  Now list the advice Yasin gives John in response.

5 Requesting and Providing Polite Suggestions

To ask for advice, you may use the verb in conditional mood (-سا) plus the verb بولماق. Example:

بېلەتنى قايسى شەھەرگە ئالسام قولاي بولىدۇ؟
To which city will it be more convenient to buy a ticket?

In order to make the above sentence more polite, use the comparative suffix -راق with the adjective. The construction can be translated into English as: it is better to.... Examples:

ئۈرۈمچىگە پويىز بىلەن كەلسىڭىز ياخشىراق بولىدۇ.
It would be better if you came by train.

6 The Construction -غۇ دەيمەن

In Yasin's response (line 4) you see a construction ياخشىراق بولىدىغۇ دەيمەن. This construction might be translated into English as "I think it would be better".

نيۇ يوركتىن بېلەتنى بېيجىڭغىچە ئالسىڭىز ياخشىراق بولىدىغۇ دەيمەن.
I am pretty sure it would be better if you bought a ticket from New York to Beijing.

As indicated by the translation of the sentence above, the construction -غۇ دەيمەن gives the meaning of 'I'm pretty sure that' or 'it looks to me as if'. It is used when a good deal of evidence suggests to the speaker that the action or state described by the thing that it modifies definitely did/does/will occur. This construction can attach to a wide range of clauses, so pay attention to how it is used in the reading and listening exercises which follow! Note that in this constructions the main verb is in the Present-Future tense.

There are some more examples:

I am pretty sure he will be coming later. .ئۇ كەچرەك كېلىدۇغۇ دەيمەن
I'm sure (s)he will be going, too. .ئۇمۇ بىز بىلەن بارىدۇغۇ دەيمەن

Exercise 12:  Now, practice asking for and giving advice with your partner. Decide with your partner what you should do in the following scenarios.

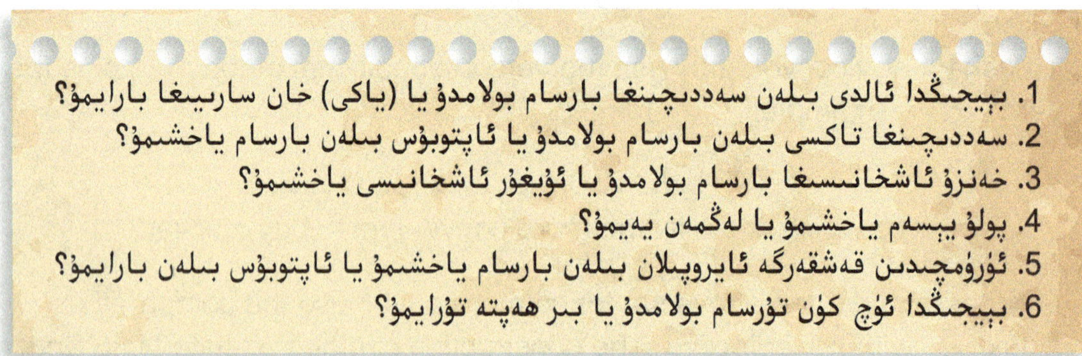

1. بېيجىڭدا ئالدى بىلەن سەددىچىنغا بارسام بولامدۇ يا (ياكى) خان سارىيىغا بارايمۇ؟
2. سەددىچىنغا تاكسى بىلەن بارسام بولامدۇ يا ئاپتوبۇس بىلەن بارسام ياخشىمۇ؟
3. خەنزۇ ئاشخانىسىغا بارسام بولامدۇ يا ئۇيغۇر ئاشخانىسى ياخشىمۇ؟
4. پولۇ يېسەم ياخشىمۇ يا لەڭمەن يەيمۇ؟
5. ئۈرۈمچىدىن قەشقەرگە ئايروپىلان بىلەن بارسام ياخشىمۇ يا ئاپتوبۇس بىلەن بارايمۇ؟
6. بېيجىڭدا ئۈچ كۈن تۇرسام بولامدۇ يا بىر ھەپتە تۇرايمۇ؟

Exercise 13: سىزگە ئېلخەت كەلدى!

Exercise 13.1:  Read Ekber's email and provide synonyms for the words and expressions in the table below.

To: yalquninbloomington@hotmail.com

From: akbar2012@gmail.com

Subject: Travelling again?

سالام يالقۇن:

ئىشلىرىڭىز ياخشىمۇ؟ خېلى بولدى سىز بىلەن كۆرۈشمىگىلى. مەن ئوقۇشلىرىم بىلەن بەكلا ئالدىراش بولۇپ كەتتىم. ئاخىرقى سۆھبەت سائىتىمىزگىمۇ بارالمىدىم. تۈنۈگۈن ئۆتكۈرنى كۆرۈپ قالدىم. ئۇ ماڭا بىر خوش خەۋەر ئېيتتى. ئاڭلىسام، شىنجاڭغا جابدۇنۇپسىز. ناھايىتى ياخشى بوپتۇ! مەن تولىمۇ خۇرسەن بولدۇم. ئەگەر مەندىن سورايدىغان سوئاللىرىڭىز بولسا، تارتىنماي سوراڭ. ھە راست، بېيجىڭدا مېنىڭ بىر ئاغىنەم بار. ئۇ مىللەتلەر ئۇنىۋېرسىتېتىدا ئوقۇيدۇ. ئۇ ئايرودرومغا چىقىپ سىزنى كۈتۈۋېلىشى مۇمكىن.

ماقۇل، خوش!
جاۋابىڭىزنى كۈتۈپ،
ئەكبەر

	خوش خەۋەر
	خۇرسەن بولماق
	جابدۇنماق
	تارتىنماق
	ئاغىنە

Exercise 13.2:  Now, respond to Ekber, asking him for suggestions about a place to stay, places to visit, and places to eat. Include three or more questions.

Send Chat Attach Address Fonts Colors Save As Draft

To: akbar2012@gmail.com

From: yalquninbloomington@hotmail.com

Subject: Re: Travelling again?

سالام ئەكبەر:

Exercise 14: قېنى، بىر گەپ بولارا!

Exercise 14.1: John has arrived in Beijing. At the airport one of Yasin's friends, Qavul, meets him. Listen to the conversation between them and circle the best answer.

1. John might get into trouble because he:
   - a. does not have a visa
   - b. said "Eastern Turkistan"
   - c. did not reserve a hotel room
   - d. likes pork

2. What does Qavul suggest taking?
   - a. the train
   - b. the airplane
   - c. the long distance bus
   - d. a bike tour

Exercise 14.2: Listen to the conversation one more time. Then fill in the blanks with missing words.

قاۋۇل: ياخشىمۇسىز !
جون: ياخشىمۇسىز !
- سىز ئامېرىكىلىق جونمۇ؟
- ھەئە. سىز قاۋۇلمۇ؟
- ھەئە، مەن قاۋۇل. بېيجىڭغا خوش كەپسىز !
- رەھمەت!
- جون، سىزنىڭ ئۇيغۇرچىڭىز بەك ________________ .
- رەھمەت. مەن ئامېرىكىدا ________________ ئۇيغۇرچە ئۆگەنگەن.
- سىز ________ شىنجاڭغا بارغانمۇ؟
- ھەئە. مەن شەرقىي تۈركىستاننى بۇرۇن زىيارەت قىلغان، ئەمما ئۇ چاغدا ئۇيغۇرچە بىلمەيتتىم.
- ھوي، دىققەت قىلىڭ. بۇ يەردە ________ "شەرقىي تۈركىستان " دېگىلى بولمايدۇ.
- كەچۈرۈڭ، ئۇنتۇپ قاپتىمەن.
- ئەمدى سىزنى مېھمانخانىغا ئاپىرىپ قوياي، ئاندىن تاماق يەيلى.
- قاۋۇل، مەن تېخى مېھمانخانا ئالمىغان. قانداق قىلىمەن؟
- چاتاق يوق. بۇ يەردە مېھمانخانىغا بېرىپلا ياتاق ئالسا بولىدۇ. قېنى، تاكسى توسايلى.
- بېيجىڭدا مېھمانخانا ________________؟
- قىممەتلىرىمۇ بار، ئەرزانلىرىمۇ بار. ھە راست، سىز بېيجىڭدىن ئۈرۈمچىگە قانداق بارىسىز؟
- ياسىن ________ بىلەن كەلسىڭىز ياخشى بولىدۇ دەپ ئېيتقان ئىدى.
- پويىز ياخشى، ئەمما بىر نەچچە كۈن ۋاقتىڭىز كېتىدۇ. سىزگە ________ ياخشىمىكىن.
- قېنى، بېيجىڭدا بەش - ئالتە كۈن تۇراي، ئاندىن بىر گەپ بولار.
- ئوھوي، سىز بۇنداق ئىبارىلەرنىمۇ بىلىدىكەنسىزغۇ! "بىر گەپ بولار" دېگەن گەپنى بەك ئورۇنلۇق ئىشلەتتىڭىز.
- شۇنداقمۇ؟ رەھمەت...
- مانا تاكسى، قېنى ماڭايلى!

Note:

Though many Uyghurs abroad tend to refer to their homeland as 'East(ern) Turkistan', the equivalent Uyghur term شەرقىي تۈركىستان is forbidden inside China. As a result, it is best to avoid using that name while you are in Xinjiang.

Exercise 14.3: Act out this conversation with your partner.

> **Note:**
>
> The word قېنى in the dialogue expresses an invitation to do something. Look at the following examples:
>
> Please, come in. !قېنى، ئۆيگە كىرىڭ
>
> Please, help yourself! .قېنى، تاماقتىن ئېلىڭ
>
> Let's pray. .قېنى، دۇئا قىلايلى
>
> Please, start! !قېنى، باشلاڭ

Exercise 15: مىللەتلەر ئۇنىۋېرسىتېتىدا

Exercise 15.1:  John is going to visit the University of Nationalities. Before visiting, he reads a short brochure about it.

مەركىزىي مىللەتلەر ئۇنىۋېرسىتېتى 1952- يىلى قۇرۇلغان.
جۇڭگودىكى ئاز سانلىق مىللەت ئوقۇغۇچىلىرى ئۈچۈن
قۇرۇلغان بۇ ئۇنىۋېرسىتېت ھازىر جۇڭگودىكى ئالدىنقى
100 ئۇنىۋېرسىتېتنىڭ بىرى ھېسابلىنىدۇ. ئۇنىۋېرسىتېتتا
60 تىن ئارتۇق ماگىستىرلىق كەسپى ۋە 25 دوكتورلۇق
كەسپى ئېچىلغان. بۇ ئۇنىۋېرسىتېتتا جۇڭگودىكى
ئۇيغۇر، موڭغۇل، تىبەت (زاڭزۇ)، جۇاڭزۇ ۋە باشقا مىللەتلەرنىڭ تولۇق كۇرس،
ماگىستىر ۋە دوكتور ئوقۇغۇچىلىرى ئوقۇيدۇ. ھەر يىلى بۇ
ئۇنىۋېرسىتېتقا 50 كە يېقىن ئۇيغۇر ئوقۇغۇچى ئوقۇشقا
كېلىدۇ. بۇ ئۇنىۋېرسىتېتتا ئۇيغۇر تىل- ئەدەبىياتى
فاكۇلتېتىمۇ بار. يېقىنقى مەلۇماتلارغا قارىغاندا،
مەكتەپ ئوقۇغۇچىلىرىنىڭ
70% ى خەنزۇلار، قالغىنى باشقا ئاز سانلىق مىللەت
ئوقۇغۇچىلىرى ئىكەن.

Exercise 15.2:  Use the following key words below and recreate the article in your own words.

25	قۇرۇلماق	ئاز سانلىق مىللەت	تىل- ئەدەبىيات فاكۇلتېتى	
ماگىستىرلىق كەسپى	60 تىن ئارتۇق	دوكتورلۇق كەسپى	قالغىنى	
1952	ھەر يىلى	70%	50 كە يېقىن	خەنزۇ

Exercise 15.3:  While walking on the campus of the University of Nationalities, John and Qavul run into one of Qavul's professors. Listen to the short dialogue between John and the Uyghur professor, then answer the questions that follow.

1. نېمە ئۈچۈن جون بېيجىڭغا كەلدى؟
2. ئۇ بېيجىڭدا قانچىلىك تۇرىدۇ؟
3. ئۇ شىنجاڭدا قانچىلىك تۇرىدۇ؟
4. ئۇ قايسى شەھەرلەرنى زىيارەت قىلماقچى؟

Exercise 15.4:  How would you reply to the Uyghur professor? Look at the questions below and write your own answers.

1. سىز ئامېرىكىدىن كەلدىڭىزمۇ؟ ____________________
2. قايسى شتاتتىن كەلدىڭىز؟ ____________________
3. ئۇيغۇرچىنى نەدە ئۆگەندىڭىز؟ ____________________
4. ئامېرىكىدا ئۇيغۇرچە ئۆگىنىدىغانلار كۆپمۇ؟ ____________________
5. بېيجىڭغا كېلىشتىكى مەقسىتىڭىز نېمە؟ ____________________
6. شىنجاڭغا قاچان ماڭىسىز؟ ____________________
7. ئۇ يەردە قانچىلىك تۇرىسىز؟ ____________________
8. قايسى شەھەرلەرنى زىيارەت قىلماقچىسىز؟ ____________________

Exercise 15.5:  Now listen to the professor's questions. Stop your audio after each question and speak your own answers aloud.

Useful phrases ئەسقاتىدىغان ئىبارىلەر

Wishing Well

1. To express wishes in Uyghur usually the 2nd person Imperative form of the verb is used. For example:

Be happy! بەختلىك بولۇڭ!
Have a long life! (lit."Live much") كۆپ ياشاڭ!

2. You can also express a wish to have or attain something by using the 3rd person Imperative form (-سۇن). Look at the following examples:

May your life be long! ئۆمرىڭىز ئۇزۇن بولسۇن!
May luck be with you! ئامەت سىزگە يار بولسۇن!
Bon voyage! (lit."May your road be white!") ئاق يول بولسۇن!

3. In literary language and on formal occasions people express wishes by using the suffix -غاي (-قاي، -كەي، -گەي). Look at the following examples:

May your life be long! ئۆمرىڭىز ئۇزۇن بولغاي!
May God give you strength! ئاللاھ سىلەرگە كۈچ - قۇۋۋەت بەرگەي!

Do you remember any special words and expressions used to congratulate people? Here are some common ones:

تەبرىكلەيمەن! مۇبارەك بولسۇن! قۇتلۇق بولسۇن!
Congratulations!

تۇغۇلغان كۈنىڭىزنى تەبرىكلەيمىز!
تۇغۇلغان كۈنىڭىزگە مۇبارەك بولسۇن!
Happy birthday!

يېڭى يىل بايرىمىڭىزغا مۇبارەك بولسۇن!
يېڭى يىل بايرىمىڭىز قۇتلۇق بولسۇن!
Happy New Year!

Exercise 16:  What might you say?

1. On your friend's birthday.	
2. Before your friend is going on a trip.	
3. At a wedding ceremony for a young couple.	
4. When your friend is going to take his exam.	
5. Upon the birth of your friend's baby.	
6. Whan your friend has bought a new car/house.	

Exercise 17: Look at the following excerpt from a toast at a traditional wedding ceremony. To whom do you think it was addressed? Discuss this with your instructor.

كۈيئوغۇل

ئەتىگەندە تۇرار بولغاي، كۆكۈلنى ئاچار بولغاي،
توققۇز ئوغۇل بىر قىزلىق مېھرىبان ئانا بولغاي!
قوتاندا قويلۇق بولغاي، يىلقىلىق، كالىلىق بولغاي،
تۇۋى يېيىلغاي، ئۇچى ئۇزارغاي، خۇدا يار بولغاي!

كېلىن

Useful phrases ئەسقاتىدىغان ئىبارىلەر

Expressions with the words خۇدا / ئاللاھ

Below are some useful expressions using the words خۇدا / ئاللاھ 'God' in Uyghur.

Thank God!	خۇداغا شۈكرى!
God willing.	خۇدا خالىسا/ بۇيرىسا!
God willing.	ئاللاھ بۇيرىسا/ ئىنشائاللاھ!
God save (you)!	خۇداغا/ خۇدايىمغا ئامانەت!
God save (you, him)! / God forbid!	خۇدا / خۇدايىم ساقلىسۇن/ ئاللاھ ئاسرىسۇن!
Oh my God!	يا ئاللاھ!
Oh my God!	تووۋا خۇدايىم/خۇدايىم تووۋا!
God forbid	خۇدا ئۆزى كەچۈرسۇن

Exercise 18: خۇدايىم بۇيرىسا...

Exercise 18.1:  Look at the following short dialogues and fill in the blanks with appropriate expressions containing the words خۇدا / ئاللاھ

1
ئەسسالامۇ ئەلەيكۇم، يۇسۇپكا. قانداق ئەھۋالىڭىز؟
__________________، بالام. مۇشۇنچىلىك تۇرىۋاتىمەن.

2
دادا، خوتەنگە قاچان ماڭىمىز؟
__________________ يەكشەنبە كۈنى.

3
__________________ كېلەر ھەپتە قارامايغا بېرىپ كېلىمەن.
ئەمىسە بىللە بارايلى.

4
__________________، بىر ئايدىن كېيىن يېڭى ئۆيگە كۆچىمىز.
ئۆي پۈتتىمۇ؟

5
__________________، قىزىم. بارغاندىن كېيىن تېلېفون قىلىشنى ئۇنتۇما!
خاتىرجەم بول، دادا. بېرىپلا تېلېفون قىلىۋېتىمەن.

6
خوش دادا، مەن ماڭدىم.
__________________، قىزىم.

7
ئەھمەدكا، تۇرپان قانداقراق ئىكەن؟
يازدا تۇرپانغا بېرىشتىن __________________، ئۇكا. ئوت دېگىنە، ئوت.

8
ئاڭلىدىڭمۇ، ياپونىيەدە توققۇز بال يەر تەۋرەپتۇ.
__________________ بۇنداق بالا- قازادىن.

9
__________________ئەجەب كېچىكتىڭلار!
ئاپتوبۇس يولدا بۇزۇلۇپ قالدى.

10
__________________، بۇ راست ئىشمىكەن؟
راستكەن. مەنمۇ باشتا ئىشەنمىگەن.

Exercise 18.2  Now listen to these dialogues to check your answers.

Exercise 19: سەددىچىنگە بارايلى!

Exercise 19.1: What do you know about the places in the pictures below? Share your knowledge with your classmates and take notes on the information which they provide.

Exercise 19.2:  John and Qavul are visiting some famous historical sites in Beijing. Read their conversation and answer the questions that follow.

جون: ياخشىمۇسىز قاۋۇل!

قاۋۇل: ياخشى. ئۆزىڭىزچۇ؟

جون: ياخشى. بۈگۈن نەگە بارىمىز؟

قاۋۇل: سەددىچىن بىلەن خان سارىيىغا بارايلى.

جون: خان سارىيى؟ بۇ قەيەر؟

قاۋۇل: خان سارىيى – بۇرۇن بېيجىڭدا ياشىغان مانجۇ پادىشاھلىرىنىڭ ئوردىسى. مىڭ سۇلالىسىدىن چىڭ سۇلالىسىغىچە نۇرغۇن پادىشاھلار بۇ جايدا تۇرغان.

جون: ھە، زىجىنچېڭ دېگەن شۇمۇ؟

قاۋۇل: ھەئە. ئۇ بۇ يەرنىڭ خەنزۇچە نامى. بەزى كىتابلاردا «شەھرىستان» دەپ تەرجىمە قىلىنغان.

جون: خان سارىيى بۇ يەرگە يېقىنمۇ؟

قاۋۇل: يىراق ئەمەس. بېيجىڭنىڭ ئوتتۇرىسىدا. ئاۋۇ ئاپتوبۇس شۇ يەرگە بارىدۇ. قېنى، مۇشۇنىڭغا چىقايلى.

جون: ئاڭلىسام، خان سارىيىدا بىر ئۇيغۇر مەلىكىسى ياشىغان ئىكەن. شۇنداقمۇ؟

قاۋۇل: شۇنداق. ئۇنىڭ ئەسلى ئىسمى ئىپارخان. مانجۇلار قەشقەرنى بېسىۋالغاندىن كېيىن ئۇ بېيجىڭغا ئېلىپ كېلىنگەن. كېيىن چيەنلوڭ پادىشاھقا خانىش بولۇشقا مەجبۇرلانغان. شۇنىڭ بىلەن ئىپارخان ئۆزىنى ئۆلتۈرىۋالغان.

جون: قەشقەردىمۇ بىر ئىپارخان مازىرى بار، شۇنداقمۇ؟

قاۋۇل: شۇنداق. ئاڭلىشىمچە، ئىپارخان ۋاپات بولغاندىن كېيىن جەستى قەشقەرگە ئېلىپ كېلىنگەن ۋە ئاپاق خوجا مازىرىغا دەپنە قىلىنغان ئىكەن.

جون: خان سارىيىدىن سەددىچىنگە بارىدىغان ئاپتوبۇس بارمۇ؟

قاۋۇل: بىۋاستە ئاپتوبۇس يوق. ئاپتوبۇس ئالمىشىپ بارغىلى بولىدۇ. سىز سەددىچىنگە بارغانمۇ؟

جون: ياق. بەك بارغۇم بار.

قاۋۇل: قېنى، ئاۋۋال خان سارىيىنى كۆرەيلى. ئەتە سىزنى سەددىچىنگە ئاپىراي.

جون: كۆپ رەھمەت سىزگە، قاۋۇل.

قاۋۇل: ئەرزىمەيدۇ.

1. "شەھرىستان" دېگەن سۆزنىڭ مەنىسى نېمە؟
2. خان سارىيى بېيجىڭنىڭ نەرىدە؟
3. خان سارىيىدا كىملەر ياشىغان؟
4. ئىپارخان كىم؟ ئۇ قاچان ۋە نېمە سەۋەبتىن بېيجىڭغا ئېلىپ كېلىنگەن؟
5. ئىپارخان كىم تەرىپىدىن ئۆلتۈرۈلگەن؟
6. ئىپارخانىنىڭ جەستى قەيەرگە دەپنە قىلىنغان؟

Exercise 19.3:  Now match the following words and expressions from the text with their English equivalents by drawing a line between one and the other.

to take	خان سارىيى
princess	دەپنە قىلىنماق
the king's palace	ئاپارماق
the great wall	جەسەت
to be forced	پادىشاھلارنىڭ ئوردىسى
the forbidden city	مەجبۇرلانماق
dynasty	سەددىچىن
corpse	مەلىكە
to be buried	سۇلالە

Exercise 20: سەددىچىن قەيەردە؟

Exercise 20.1:  The next day, John and Qavul are visiting the Great Wall. Listen to a conversation between them and decide if the following statements are true or false.

توغرا	خاتا

1. "سەددىچىن" سۆزىنىڭ مەنىسى "چىن دۆلىتىنىڭ پادىشاھلىقى".
2. چىن دۆلىتى بۇ سېپىلنى كۆچمەن مىللەتلەرنىڭ ھۇجۇمىنى توساش ئۈچۈن سالغان.
3. سەددىچىن جۇڭگونىڭ باشقا شەھەرلىرىدىمۇ بار.
4. بۇرۇن سەددىچىن سېپىلى چېگرا بولغان.

Exercise 20.2:  Now read the dialogue and give the English equivalent of the words and expressions that follow.

جون: سەددىچىن بۇ يەرگە يىراقمۇ؟
قاۋۇل: ھەئە. شەھەردىن يىراق. بۇ يەردىن 70 كىلومېتىر ماڭىمىز.
جون: "سەددىچىن" دېگەن سۆزنىڭ مەنىسى نېمە؟
قاۋۇل: بۇ پارسچە سۆز. مەنىسى "چىن دۆلىتىنىڭ توسمىسى" .
جون: نېمىشقا بۇنى "توسما" دەيدۇ؟
قاۋۇل: بۇرۇنقى ۋاقىتتا چىن دۆلىتى شىمالدىكى كۆچمەن مىللەتلەرنىڭ ھۇجۇمىنى توسۇش ئۈچۈن بۇ سېپىلنى سالغان. شۇنىڭ بىلەن كىشىلەر بۇنى "سەددىچىن" دەپ ئاتىغان.
جون: مۇنداق دەڭ. سەددىچىن سېپىلى بېيجىڭدىن باشقا يەنە قەيەردە بار؟
قاۋۇل: سەددىچىن بىر پۈتۈن سېپىل. ئۇ شەنخەيگۇەن شەھىرىدىن يۈمېنگۇەن شەھىرىگىچە سېلىنغان. شۇڭا جۇڭگونىڭ شىمالىدىكى ھەممىلا يەردە سەددىچىن بار.
جون: دېمەك، بۇ سېپىل بۇرۇنقى ۋاقىتتا چېگرا بولغان. شۇنداقمۇ؟
قاۋۇل: توپ-توغرا ئېيتتىڭىز. بۇرۇن شۇنداق بولغان. ھازىر ئۇنداق ئەمەس. مانا سەددىچىنگە كەلدۇق.
جون: پاھ، نېمە دېگەن كۆپ ئادەم!
قاۋۇل: قېنى، ئاۋۇ يەردە رەسىمگە چۈشەيلى.

	توسما
	كۆچمەن
	ھۇجۇم
	توسماق
	سىپىل
	چېگرا
	رەسىمگە چۈشمەك

Exercise 20.3: Act out the conversation with your partner.

Exercise 21: What did you learn about the Forbidden City and the Great Wall from the dialogues you have read?

Exercise 22: Look at Exercise 19.1 and compare what you knew before and what you know now. Share your notes with a group.

Have you ever heard about...? بۇ كىشىنى بىلەمسىز...؟

In this section you will read and learn about a famous Uyghur person.

Exercise 23: يۈسۈپ خاس ھاجىپ

Exercise 23.1:  Read the following passage about Yüsüp Khas Hajib, an 11th century philosopher of the Turkic world. Then, answer the questions that follow. The words and expressions provided before the questions will help you to understand the passage better.

قەشقەر كەچلىك گېزىتى

2014 - يىلى 18 - ئاۋغۇست
دۈشەنبە

1231 - سان پوچتا ۋاكالەت نومۇرى: 54 - 66

ئۇيغۇرلارنىڭ ئۇلۇغ مۇتەپەككۇرى، دۆلەت ئۇستازى ۋە شائىر يۈسۈپ خاس ھاجىپ تەخمىنەن 1018 – يىلى ئوتتۇرا ئاسىيادىكى بالاساغۇن شەھرىدە دۇنياغا كەلگەن. ئۇ مەملىكەتنى قانداق باشقۇرۇش ھەققىدىكى قوللانما خاراكتېرلىك پەلسەپۋى ئەسەر «قۇتادغۇ بىلىگ» ("بەخت ئېلىپ كېلىدىغان بىلىملەر") بىلەن مەشھۇر. ئۇنىڭ ھاياتى ھەققىدە تەپسىلىي مەلۇماتلار يوق. يۈسۈپ بالاساغۇنىنىڭ ئەسىرىدە بېرىلگەن مەلۇماتلارغا ئاساسلانغاندا، ئاپتور مەرىپەتلىك بىر ئۆلىما ئائىلىسىدە دۇنياغا كەلگەن، شۇنداقلا كىچىكىدىن ئەرەب ۋە پارس تىللىرىنى پىششىق ئۆگەنگەن. ئۇنىڭ ئەسىرى 1070 – يىلى قەشقەردە يېزىلغان ۋە قاراخانىلار دۆلىتىنىڭ پادىشاھى سۇلايمان تاۋغاچ بۇغراخانغا تەقدىم قىلىنغان. پادىشاھ بۇ ئەسەرنى ئوقۇغاندىن كېيىن ناھايىتى رازى بولغان ۋە ئۇنىڭغا ئالىي دەرىجىلىك مەسلىھەتچى- «خاس ھاجىپ» دېگەن ئۇنۋاننى بەرگەن. يۈسۈپ بالاساغۇنى شۇنىڭدىن كېيىن «يۈسۈپ خاس خاجىب» دەپ ئاتالغان. ئاپتور تەخمىنەن 1086 – يىلى قەشقەردە ۋاپات بولغان ۋە شۇ يەرگە دەپنە قىلىنغان.

ئوتتۇرا ئاسىيادىكى ئورتاق تىل بولغان قەدىمكى تۈرك تىلىدا يېزىلغان «قۇتادغۇ بىلىگ» جەمئىي 446 بەتلىك بولۇپ، 13 مىڭ مىسرالىق داستان 67 بابقا بۆلۈنگەن. ھازىر بۇ ئەسەرنىڭ ۋېنا نۇسخىسى، قاھىرە نۇسخىسى ۋە فەرغانە نۇسخىسى قاتارلىق ئۈچ خىل كۆچۈرۈلمە نۇسخىسى ساقلانماقتا. ئەسەرنىڭ يۈسۈپ خاس ھاجىپ ئۆز قولى بىلەن يازغان ئەسلى نۇسخىسى تېخى تېپىلمىدى.

"قۇتادغۇ بىلىگ" تىن پارچە:

ئىتلارغا گەر يولۋاس يولباشچى بولسا، ئىتلار ھەم يولۋاستەك باتۇر بولىدۇ،
يولۋاسقا ئىتلارنى يولباشچى قىلساڭ، يولۋاسلار ئىت كەبى لالما بولىدۇ.

stray (for animal)	لالما
advisor	مەسلىھەتچى
to bury	دەپنە قىلماق
verse (of poetry)	مىسرا
version; copy	نۇسخا
structure	قۇرۇلما
to be born	دۇنياغا كەلمەك
to be satisfied	رازى بولماق
senior; exalted	ئالىي

thinker	مۇتەپەككۇر
manual	قوللانما
leader	يولباشچى
philosophy	پەلسەپە
information	مەلۇمات
knowledge	مەرىپەت
scholar	ئۆلىما
to present	تەقدىم قىلماق
character	خاراكتېر

1. يۈسۈپ خاس ھاجىپ قايسى تىللارنى ئۆگەنگەن؟
2. "قۇتادغۇ بىلىگ" قانداق مەزمۇندىكى ئەسەر؟
3. "قۇتادغۇ بىلىگ" نىڭ قۇرۇلمىسى قانداق؟
4. "قۇتادغۇ بىلىگ" نىڭ ئەسلى نۇسخىسى ھازىر قەيەردە؟

Exercise 23.2: Based on the passage, ask your partner three more questions about Yüsüp Khas Hajip.

Vocabulary سۆزلۈك

Vocabulary is given according to the Uyghur alphabetical order. The right column precedes the left column on each page.

to search	ئاختۇرماق
extra	ئارتۇق
friend	ئاغىنە
to contact with	ئالاقىلاشماق
to replace	ئالماشتۇرماق
to revolve	ئايلانماق
a pity	ئەپسۇس
to follow	ئەگەشمەك
to be anxious	ئەندىشە قىلماق
calamity	بالا- قازا
to get broken	بۇزۇلۇپ قالماق
cradle	بۆشۈك
to occupy	بېسىۋالماق
directly	بىۋاستە
capital	پايتەخت
to hesitate	تارتىنماق
to be dispersed	تارقالماق
abandoned land	تاشلانغان ماكان
customs (airport)	تاموژنا
to translate	تەرجىمە قىلماق
to be approved	تەستىقلانماق
to affect	تەسىر قىلماق
to investigate	تەكشۈرمەك
preparation	تەييارلىق
to be gathered	توپلانماق
partition	توسما
undergraduate	تولۇق كۇرس
railway	تۆمۈريول
to get prepared	جابدۇنماق
corpse	جەسەت

suitcase	چامادان
a desert	چۆل
border	چېگرا
a rough calculation	خام چوت
queen	خانىش
map	خەرىتە
good news	خوش خەۋەر
to be happy	خۇرسەن بولماق
state	دۆلەت
true	راست
territory	زېمىن
to visit	زىيارەت قىلماق
tourist attractions	ساياھەت ئورۇنلىرى
the Great Wall	سەددىچىن
to stretch out	سوزۇلماق
dynasty	سۇلالە
city wall	سېپىل
political	سىياسىي
the Forbidden City	شەھرىستان\ خان سارىيى
transportation	قاتناش ۋاستىلىرى
ancient	قەدىمكى
debt	قەرز
to accept	قوبۇل قىلماق
double	قوش
to establish	قۇرماق
to be established	قۇرۇلماق
sand shift	قۇم كۆچۈش
desert area	قۇملۇق
major	كەسىپ
nomad	كۆچمەن

document	هۆججەت
to be considered	ھېسابلانماق
fire; grass	ئوت
palace	ئوردا
basin	ئويمانلىق
to encounter	ئۇچراشماق
province	ئۆلكە
consumption	ئىستېمال
to possess	ئىگىلىمەك
application; request	ئىلتىماس
written history	يازما تارىخ
earthquake	يەر تەۋرىمەك
luggage	يۈك - تاق
a horse	يىلقا

scale/scope	كۆلەم
to meet; to pick up	كۈتۈۋالماق
tomb	مازار
culture	مەدەنىيەت
princess	مەلىكە
meaning	مەنا
landscape	مەنزىرە
stipend	مۇكاپات پۇلى
unknown	نامەلۇم
numerous	نۇرغۇنلىغان
to get excited	ھاياجانلانماق
times	ھەسسە
attack	ھۇجۇم

تۆتىنچى دەرس

CHAPTER FOUR

ئۇيغۇر تائام نامىلىرى

THE LANGUAGE OF FOOD IN XINJIANG

IN THIS CHAPTER

Functions

- Describing Uyghur and Chinese food
- Narrating a sequence of events
- Recognizing Chinese borrowings
- Ordering food using Chinese loan words
- Comparing food
- Expressing emphasis

Grammar

- The postposition قارىغاندا
- Sentence coordination with -پ \ -ىپ \ -ۇپ \ -ۈپ
- The particles: -لا، -غۇ، -ە

In this chapter you will learn about Uyghur food and its vocabulary. With John you will visit some Uyghur restaurants in Beijing and learn more about Chinese borrowings among food-related vocabulary in Xinjiang. From the reading passages and video segments you will also obtain more information about authentic Uyghur food and will gain a familiarity with گۆش گىردە, باچكا شورپىسى, and ياپما.

Exercise 1: تۆۋەندىكى سوئاللارنى مۇزاكىرە قىلىڭلار

1. قايسى خەلقنىڭ مىللىي تائاملىرىنى ياخشى كۆرىسىز؟
2. جۇڭگو تاماقلىرى ھەققىدە نېمىلەرنى بىلىسىز؟
3. سىز ئۇيغۇر تائاملىرىنى يەپ باققانمۇ؟ قايسى ئۇيغۇر تاماقلىرى سىزگە ياقتى؟ قايسىسى ياقمىدى؟
4. تاماق ئېتىشنى ياخشى كۆرەمسىز؟ ئادەتتە قايسى تاماقلارنى ئېتىسىز؟ نېمىشقا\ نېمە ئۈچۈن؟

Exercise 2:  Look at the following food names, then write the number of the picture which corresponds to each name in the boxes to the right.

___	پىلتە قۇيماق
___	سامسا
___	پولۇ
___	توخۇ كاۋىپى

___	ساماۋەر شورپىسى
___	مانتا
___	لەڭمەن
___	كاۋاپ

3

2

1

7

6

5

4

8

Exercise 3: قېنى مېھمانلار، بۇ يەرگە ئولتۇرۇڭلار!

قاۋۇل: جون، ئاۋۇ خەتنى ئوقۇيالامسىز؟
جون: ئوقۇپ باقاي، ھە، قەشقەر رېستورانى. توغرىمۇ؟
قاۋۇل: توغرا. مۇشۇ ئاشخانىدا تاماق يەيلى!

Exercise 3.1:  While John and Qavul are ordering food, Qavul explains some special dishes to John. Read the first part of their conversation and match the words on the following page with their English definitions.

كۈتكۈچى: نېمە يەيسىلەر؟
قاۋۇل: جون، سىزنىڭ نېمە يېگۈڭىز بار؟
جون: مەن بىلمەيمەن. سىز بۇيرۇڭ.
قاۋۇل: مەيلى. ھوي تاڭجاڭ، بۈگۈن نېمە تاماقلار بار؟
كۈتكۈچى: پولو، مانتا، لەڭمەن، گاڭپەن، خۈيمەن، سومەن.
جون: "خۈيمەن" ۋە "سومەن" دېگەن نېمە؟
قاۋۇل: "خۈيمەن" دېگەن سۇيۇق ئاش، "سومەن" دېگەن قورۇما چۆپ.
جون: ھە، ھە، ئەمدى ئېسىمگە كەلدى. مەن بۇرۇن ئۈرۈمچىدە يېگەن. ئۇنتۇپ قاپتىمەن.
قاۋۇل: مەن بىر لەڭمەن يەي. سىز نېمە يەيسىز؟
جون: مەن سومەن يەيمەن.
قاۋۇل: ھەي تاڭجاڭ، بىزگە بىر گويرۇ لەڭمەن، بىر سومەن.
كۈتكۈچى: چاتاق يوق. دىڭ-دىڭ سومەنمۇ يا مەنپەر سومەنمۇ؟
جون: نېمە؟!
قاۋۇل: "دىڭ-دىڭ سومەن" دېگەندە جىزىنى قىسقا - قىسقا توغرايدۇ؛
"مەنپەر" دېگەندە جىزىنى سۇغا كىچىك-كىچىك ئۈزۈپ تاشلايدۇ.
جون: "جىزا" دېگەن نېمە؟
قاۋۇل: ھە، بۇ لەڭمەننىڭ پىلتىسى.
جون: مۇنداق دەڭ. ماقۇل، مەن دىڭ-دىڭ سومەن يەي.
كۈتكۈچى: مانا ھازىر. ھەي سوگوزا، ماۋۇ مېھمانلارغا بىر گۈيرو لەڭمەن، بىر دىڭ-دىڭ سومەن!!!

___	the person who communicates orders between the customer and the chef; a sort of combined server/expeditor (from Chinese tángjiāng 汤将)	سومەن	1
___	a sort of noodle soup, usually prepared by throwing pinched-off pieces of dough into a boiling broth containing previously prepared meat and vegetables (from Chinese huìmiàn 回面)	تاڭجاڭ	2
___	stir-fried noodles cut into larger pieces with meat and assorted vegetables (from Chinese chǎomiàn 炒面)	مەنپەر سومەن	3
___	stir-fried noodles cut into small pieces with meat and assorted vegetables (from Chinese dīngdīng chǎomiàn 丁丁炒面)	لەڭمەن پىلتىسى	4
___	stir-fried noodles pinched off into irregular pieces with meat and assorted vegetables (from Chinese miànpiān chǎomiàn 面片炒面)	دىڭ-دىڭ سومەن	5
___	long strands of dough made by pulling and stretching (probably from Chinese lāmiàn 拉面)	سوگوزا	6
___	the chef de cuisine/head cook (from Chinese chǎoguōzi 炒锅子)	خۇيمەن	7

Two Folk Etymologies of "Langman"

There are fewer dishes in the Uyghur culinary repertoire more iconic than لەڭمەن, the pulled noodle dish served with a meaty, peppery tomato sauce. Therefore, it may come as a surprise to learn that some people think that the origin of the word لەڭمەن / لەغمەن is ultimately derived from the Chinese lāmiàn 拉面 'pulled noodles', transmitted to the Uyghurs by way of Chinese-speaking Hui or Tungan Muslims. However, there is another school of thought which derives this word from an Old Turkic root *läg- 'to float', which may survive in Modern Uyghur as لەيلىمەك. Wherever the word comes from, there is one thing everyone can agree on: لەڭمەن is delicious!

Exercise 3.2:  Listen to the second part of the conversation between John and Qawul about food in Xinjiang. Then decide if these statements are true or false.

توغرا	خاتا

1. باشقا ئاشخانىلاردا خەنزۇچە سۆزلەر كۆپرەك ئىشلىتىلىدۇ.
2. ئۇيغۇرلار خەنزۇچە سۆزلەرنى ئىشلىتىشكە ئادەتلىنىپ قالغان.
3. "تاڭجاڭ" دېگەن سەي قورۇيدىغان ئۇستا.
4. "سوگوزا" دېگەن كۈتكۈچى.
5. گويرۇ لەڭمەنگە كۆپ لازا سالىدۇ.
6. "لازا" سۆزى لۇغەتتە "مۇچ" دەپ ئېلىنغان.
7. ئۇيغۇر تاماقلىرى جۇڭگو تاماقلىرىدەك ئاچچىق.
8. "سەي" سۆزى "قورۇما" مەنىسىدىمۇ ئىشلىتىلىدۇ.

Chinese Words in Uyghur

Some Uyghurs may have a preference for or against the use of Chinese loanwords in certain situations. You will also find it advantageous to be able to distinguish between Uyghur words of Chinese origin and those of non-Chinese origin. This can be difficult for a non-native speaker, but as you expand your Uyghur vocabulary you will be more readily capable of picking out Chinese loans.

To a native Uyghur speaker, Chinese words just "sound different". Nevertheless, there are some general rules to help you distinguish Uyghur words of Chinese origin. For example, Mandarin has a very simple syllable structure; syllables cannot begin with more than one consonant and can only end in a vowel, -n, -ng, or -r. In a word like ياڭيۇ, it's easy to see that the two syllables follow these rules. In pronunciation, each syllable of a Chinese loanword tends to be pronounced slightly long and with equal stress.

Exercise 3.3:  Now read the transcript of the conversation to check your answers.

جون: بۇ ئاشخانىدا خەنزۇچە سۆزلەرنى بەك كۆپ ئىشلىتىدىكەن.

قاۋۇل: بەزى ئاشخانىلارغا قارىغاندا بۇ يەردە ئانچە كۆپ ئەمەس. بەزى يەردە "لەڭمەن" دېيىشنىڭ ئورنىغا "بەنميەن" دەيدۇ.

جون: نېمىشقا بۇنچە كۆپ خەنزۇچە سۆزلەرنى ئىشلىتىسلەر؟ ئۇيغۇرچە سۆز يوقمۇ؟

قاۋۇل: ياق، ئۇيغۇرچە سۆز بار. لېكىن ئۇيغۇرلار ھازىر خەنزۇچە سۆزلەرنى ئىشلىتىشكە ئادەتلىنىپ قېلىۋاتىدۇ.

جون: مەن باياتىن ئاڭلىغانلىرىمنى يېزىۋالاي. سىز "تاڭجاڭ" دېدىڭىز. بۇ نېمە دېگەن گەپ؟

قاۋۇل: ھە، ئۇ "كۈتكۈچى" دېگەن مەنىدە.

جون: "تاڭجاڭ"، "خۇيمەن"، "سومەن"، "گاڭپەن"، "بەنميەن"، "گويرۇ"، ... ھە، يەنە "سوگوزا" دېگەنچۇ؟

قاۋۇل: ئۇ سەي قورۇيدىغان ئۇستا.

جون: ھە، يەنە "سەي". بۇ "قورۇما" دېگەن گەپ، شۇنداقمۇ؟

قاۋۇل: ھەئە.

جون: سىز بۇيرۇغان "گويرۇ لەڭمەن" ئاچچىق لەڭمەنمۇ؟

قاۋۇل: ئاچچىق، چۈنكى ئۇنىڭغا كۆپ لازا سالىدۇ. لېكىن جۇڭگو تاماقلىرىغا قارىغاندا ئۇيغۇر تاماقلىرى ئانچە ئاچچىق ئەمەس.

جون: مەن لۇغەتتىن "لازا" دېگەن سۆزنى تاپقان. لۇغەتتە ئۇ "مۇچ" دەپ ئېلىنغان.

قاۋۇل: راست دەيسىز. ھازىر تىلىمىز بەك بۇزۇلۇپ كېتىۋاتىدۇ. يەنە كېلىپ ئۆزىمىز بۇزۇۋاتىمىز.

1 Comparison with the Postposition قارىغاندا

The postposition قارىغاندا has a number of meanings such as 'based on' (مەلۇماتلارغا قارىغاندا) or 'from this' (بۇ يەردىن قارىغاندا). However, one of its most common meanings is 'in comparison'. Remember that قارىغاندا follows a noun in the dative case (-غا\\ -قا \\ -گە \\ -كە), much as in English we say 'in comparison to' something.

مەنپەرگە قارىغاندا، گويرۇ لەڭمەن ئاچچىق(راق).
In comparison to menper, goyru lengmen is spicy.
(i.e. Goyru lengmen is spicier than menper.)
بەزى ئاشخانىلارغا قارىغاندا خەنزۇچە سۆزلەر بۇ يەردە ئانچە كۆپ ئەمەس.
In comparison to some restaurants, there are few(er) Chinese words here.
جۇڭگو تاماقلىرىغا قارىغاندا ئۇيغۇر تاماقلىرى ئانچە ئاچچىق ئەمەس.
In comparison with Chinese dishes, Uyghur dishes are not very spicy.

Exercise 4:  Make comparisons by using the words/phrases below. Follow the model:

ئۆيلەرنىڭ چوڭلىقى: قەشقەر - ئۈرۈمچى
ئۈرۈمچىگە قارىغاندا قەشقەردە ئۆيلەر چوڭراق.

1. كوچىلارنىڭ كەڭلىكى: بېيجىڭ - ئۈرۈمچى ____________________
2. خېمىرنىڭ تومىلىقى: لەڭمەن - ئۈگرە ____________________
3. شىنجاڭنىڭ ھاۋاسى: ئالتاي - باشقا يەرلەر ____________________
4. ئادەملەرنىڭ ئېگىزلىكى: ئۇيغۇرلار - خەنزۇلار ____________________
5. تاماقنىڭ باھاسى: ئۈرۈمچى - خوتەن ____________________
6. تىل ئۆگىنىش: ئۇيغۇرچە - خەنزۇچە ____________________

Exercise 5: كۇتكۇچى ۋە خېرىدار

Exercise 5.1:  John went to an Uyghur restaurant. Read his conversation with a waiter, then match the words in the righthand column of the accompanying box with their synonyms in the lefthand column.

كۇتكۇچى: قېنى مېھمان، بۇ ياققا ئولتۇرۇڭ!
جون: رەھمەت!
كۇتكۇچى: سىز گېرمانىيەلىكمۇ؟
جون: ياق. مەن ئامېرىكىلىق.
كۇتكۇچى: مۇنداق دەڭ. ئۇيغۇرچىنى ياخشى بىلىدىكەنسىز.
جون: ئۇيغۇرچە؟ ياق، ئۇيغۇرچە دەڭ.
كۇتكۇچى: ئوخشاشقۇ؟ قېنى، نېمە يەيسىز؟
جون: نېمە تاماقلار بار؟
كۇتكۇچى: بۈگۈن شۇنداق ئوخشىغان باچكا تاڭ بار. بىرنى ئەكىلەيمۇ؟
جون: باچكا تاڭ؟ بۇ نېمە؟
كۇتكۇچى: باچكا شورپىسى.
جون: باچكا دېگەن نېمە؟
كۇتكۇچى: كەپتەرنىڭ بالىسى.
جون: رەھمەت، مەن شورپىنى ياخشى كۆرمەيمەن.
كۇتكۇچى: ئەمسە گەنزايۇدىن بىر تەخسە ئەكىلەيمۇ؟
جون: بۇ قانداق تاماق؟
كۇتكۇچى: ھە، بۇ ياغدا قورۇلغان بېلىق.
جون: ياق، ياق. مەن تۈنۈگۈن دوستۇم بىلەن كەلگەندە يەنە بىر تاماقنى ئاڭلىغان.
كۇتكۇچى: لەڭمەن؟ پولۇ؟ سومەن؟ خۇيمەن؟ ئۈگرە؟
جون: ياق. چۆچۈرە.
كۇتكۇچى: ئاشخانىمىزدا چۆچۈرە يوق. لەڭمەن يېمەمسىز؟
جون: مەيلى. بىر لەڭمەن يەي.
كۇتكۇچى: گويرۇمۇ ياكى سۇيرۇمۇ؟
جون: قانداق پەرقى بار؟
كۇتكۇچى: گويرۇ لەڭمەن دېگەن گۆش، پىياز، پەمىدور ۋە لازا سېلىنغان لەڭمەن. سۇيرۇ لەڭمەننىڭ
گۆشنى ئۇششاق چانىۋەتكەن.
جون: ئەمسە بىر سۇيرۇ لەڭمەن يەي.
كۇتكۇچى: پىجۇ ئىچەمسىز؟
جون: پىۋىمۇ؟
كۇتكۇچى: ھەئە.
جون: ماقۇل. بىر پىۋا بېرىڭ.
كۇتكۇچى: جەمئى 25 كوي.
جون: پۇلنى ھازىر تۆلەمدىم ؟
كۇتكۇچى: شۇنداق.
جون: مانا بۇ 30 يۈەن.

قورۇلغان بېلىق	تاڭ
پىۋا	باچكا
شورپا	گەنزايۇ
يۈەن	پىجۇ
كەپتەرنىڭ بالىسى	كوي

Exercise 5.2:  Read the dialogue one more time, then circle the best answer for each of the following questions.

1. What kind of food did John want to order in the restaurant?
   (A) pigeon soup (B) dumpling soup (C) tomato soup (D) noodle soup

2. The underlined word in the dialogue means:
   (A) square (B) small (C) round (D) wide

3. John paid:
   (A) before eating (B) while eating
   (C) after eating (D) nothing because he was an American

Urghuy or Uyghur - What's in a Name?

It might surprise you to know that the name 'Uyghur' hasn't always been the dominant name for the people we now call Uyghurs. In fact, the name originally came from the ruling ethnicity of the Uyghur Qaghanate, which ruled a large swath of land from modern day northern Xinjiang all the way north and east into Mongolia and Siberia. When this kingdom collapsed in the mid 9th century, a majority of the original Uyghurs fled and settled in parts of what are now Xinjiang and Gansu. However, with the expansion of Islam into the region starting around the 10th century, the name 'Uyghur' was gradually lost, and replaced by different terms in different places. When scholars attempted to reestablish the name for all the people whom we now refer to as Uyghurs, some regions with less-developed education and infrastructure either preserved older forms of the name, or couldn't pronounce the name quite right. As a result, in some areas you might find it pronounced 'Urghuy'. You should avoid doing so yourself, because it is generally considered a sign of poor education.

Exercise 5.3:  Match the following Uyghur phrases with their English equivalents.

English
Should I pay now?
Have a seat please!
What would you like to eat?
Ok, I will have lagman.
Shall I bring a pigeon soup?
Do you want lagman?

Uyghur
قېنى مېھمان، بۇ ياققا ئولتۇرۇڭ!
قېنى، نېمە يەيسىز؟
باچكا تاڭ ئەكېلەيمۇ؟
لەغمەن يېمەمسىز؟
پۇلنى ھازىر تۆلەمدىم ؟
ئەمسە بىر لەغمەن يەي.

Exercise 5.4: Here are two lists of dishes from the same restaurant. The list on the left is the menu given to customers; the list on the right tells the server which foods are (√) and are not (-) available at the moment. With a partner, act out a scenario in which a customer orders food using the menu on the left, while the server must respond whether the dishes being ordered are available or not available according to the list on the right.

Make sure that the person playing the role of the customer does not look at the waiter's list!

خېرىدار	
8 يۈەن	چۆچۈرە
15 يۈەن	لەغمەن
10 يۈەن	گۆشنان
4 يۈەن	كاۋاپ
12 يۈەن	سومەن
25 يۈەن	باچكا تاڭ
15 يۈەن	گەنزايۇ
10 يۈەن	ئۆپكە-ھېسىپ
2 يۈەن	سامسا

كۈتكۈچى	
–	چۆچۈرە
√	لەغمەن
–	گۆشنان
√	كاۋاپ
√	سومەن
√	باچكا تاڭ
√	گەنزايۇ
–	ئۆپكە-ھېسىپ
–	سامسا

Note:

Since Uyghur food is made fresh to order, it is common in Uyghur restaurants that some foods might run out in the middle of the day. Alternatively, some smaller restaurants may make some foods on some days, and other foods on other days.

2 Coordinating Clauses in Uyghur

Coordinating clauses are clauses linked in a series which mimics the chronological order in which they are performed. You already know how to coordinate clauses in Uyghur using the word ۋە 'and'.

Nazaket will go home and cook. نازاكەت ئۆيگە بارىدۇ ۋە تاماق ئېتىدۇ.
Adil will go to Xinjiang and learn Uyghur. ئادىل شىنجاڭغا بارىدۇ ۋە ئۇيغۇرچە ئۆگىنىدۇ.

Native speakers of Uyghur, however, are more likely to construct these types of sentences using the suffix ـىپ- (also پ- after vowels, or ۇپ- / ۈپ- according to vowel harmony). Compare the following sentences to the sentences above:

Nazaket will go home, then cook. نازاكەت ئۆيگە بېرىپ تاماق ئېتىدۇ.
Adil will go to Xinjiang, then learn Uyghur. ئادىل شىنجاڭغا بېرىپ ئۇيغۇرچە ئۆگىنىدۇ.

The sentences mean almost the same thing, except that the ـىپ- is more specifically sequential, whereas the ۋە is less clear in terms of the order in which the actions of the two verbs are conducted.

This suffix is often called a gerund or gerundial, which in this case means that it is a verb which acts in some ways like an adverb. Sentences with the ـىپ- gerund are actually easier to form in many ways, because a whole sequence of verbs can be strung together, but only the final verb is conjugated in the regular way. All the verbs preceding it just take the ـىپ- suffix, and the tense, aspect, mood, and person information is copied from the last verb in the sequence. For example:

قىزىم ئۆيگە كېلىپ، تاماق يەپ، ئازراق دەم ئېلىپ كۇتۇپخانىغا بارىدۇ.
My daughter is going to come home, eat a bit, rest a bit, then go to the library.

Keep in mind that the suffix ـىپ- causes the vowel in single-syllable roots containing ئا or ئە to raise to ئې (ex. بارماق- بېرىپ) while in two-syllable verb roots a ئا or ئە in the final syllable raises to ئى (ex. ئايلىنىپ < ئايلان).

جون ئاپتوبۇس بىلەن شەھەر ئايلىنىپ، دوستلىرىغا سوۋغا ئېلىپ قايتتى.
John strolled the city, then bought some gifts for his friends.

2 Coordinating Clauses in Uyghur (cont'd.)

You should also note that this is one verb form for which the negative looks very different from the affirmative. Its form is (مەستىن - \ ماستىن -)مەي / - ماي -.

ئادىلە دەرستىن كەچ چۈشۈپ، تاماقمۇ يېمەي يولغا چىقتى.
Adile left class late, and, without eating, set out on her trip.
ئۇ بىرسى بىلەن گەپلىشىپ، ماشىنامنى كۆرمەي ئۆتۈپ كەتتى.
She was talking to someone, and without seeing me she walked by.
ئۇ ئالدىراپ خوش دېمەستىن كېتىپ قالدى.
As rushed, he left without saying goodbye.
دادام يولدا دىققەت قىلماستىن پۇتىنى سۇندۇرىۋالدى.
On the road my dad broke his leg without paying attention.

As you saw in the example above, the negative does not copy from one verb in the string to the other; therefore, it must be placed on any verb which the speaker intends to be negative.

Exercise 6: چۆچۈرە

Exercise 6.1: Based on the pictures below, predict the process of making چۆچۈرە.

Exercise 6.2:  Read the following recipe for چۆچۈرە. Find all the sentences which contain the ending -پ (-ىپ / -ۇپ / -ۈپ). Translate them into English as accurately as possible.

ingredient(s)	خۇرۇج
bone	سۆڭەك
cilantro	ئاشكۆكى
tail	قۇيرۇق
cumin	زىرە
to chop	چانىماق
to grind	سوقماق
filling; ground meat	قىيما
to knead	يۇغۇرماق
to roll out	يايماق
dough wrapper	جىلت
to wrap	تۈگمەك

چۆچۈرە

خۇرۇجى: ئاق ئۇن، سۆڭەكلىك قوي گۆشى، پىياز، ئاشكۆكى، تۇز، زىرە، قارىمۇچ ، پەمىدۇر

ئېتىش ئۇسۇلى:

1. گۆشنىڭ سۆڭەكلىرىنى قايىنتىپ، ئۇششاق توغرالغان پىياز، پەمىدۇر، تۇز سېلىپ شورپا قايىنتىمىز.

2. گۆش، پىياز، ئاشكۆكىنى ئۇششاق توغراپ، سوققان قارىمۇچ ، زىرە، تۇز ئارىلاشتۇرۇپ قىيما تەييارلايمىز.

3. خېمىرنى يۇغۇرۇپ، نېپىز يېيىپ، تۆت- بەش سانتېمېتىر چوڭلۇقتا جىلت كېسىپ، ھەربىر جىلتنىڭ ئىچىگە ئاز- ئازدىن قىيما سېلىپ چۆچۈرە تۈگىمىز.

4. قايناۋاتقان شورپىغا چۆچۈرىنى سالىمىز. 3~ 5 مىنۇت پىشۇرۇپ، ئاشكۆكى سېلىپ ، چۆچۈرىنى شورپىسى بىلەن چىنىگە ئۇسىمىز.

Exercise 6.3:  Now watch a video of چۆچۈرە being prepared without sound, then explain what happened before the چۆچۈرە were put together.

Exercise 6.4:  Check the following elements of the چۆچۈرە making procedure and put them in order according to the video.

گۆش بىلەن پىياز توغرىلىدۇ	☐	خېمىر كېسىلىدۇ	☐
خېمىر يېيىلىدۇ	☐	خېمىر يۇغۇرۇلىدۇ	☐
چۆچۈرە تۈگۈلىدۇ	☐	قىيما تەييارلىنىدۇ	☐
شورپا قاينىتىلىدۇ	☐	چۆچۈرە پىشۇرۇلىدۇ	☐

Exercise 6.5: Now, watch the video (Exercise 6.3) with sound and describe how the people in the video made چۆچۈرە. Use the ـىپ- form with past tense.

Exercise 7: ئۇيغۇرلار ئۇچۇن تاماق ئېتىش بىر خىل سەنئەت!

Exercise 7.1:  Read the following passage about Uyghur cuisine and discuss the questions that follow.

ئۇيغۇر تائاملىرىنىڭ تۈرى كۆپ، تەمى لەززەتلىك ۋە سالامەتلىككە پايدىلىق. ئۇيغۇرلار ئۈچۈن تاماق ئېتىش بىر خىل سەنئەت ھېسابلىنىدۇ. ئۇيغۇر تاماقلىرىنىڭ ئەڭ ئاساسلىق خۇرۇچلىرى ئۇن، گۈرۈچ، گۆش ۋە ئوتياش (كۆكتات). بەزىدە كىيسەللەر ئۈچۈن گۆشسىز تاماقمۇ قىلىنىدۇ. ئادەتتە كۆپ ئېتىلىدىغان ئۇيغۇر تائاملىرىدىن لەڭمەن، پولو، شورپا، سۇيۇقئاش، چۆپ ئاش، چۆچۈرە، مانتا، شويلا، كاۋاپ، گۆشنان، دۇملىمە، گۆشگىردە قاتارلىقلار بار. ھازىرقى كۈندە ئۇيغۇرلارنىڭ لەڭمىنى پۈتۈن ئوتتۇرا ئاسىياغا تارقالغان. ئۇيغۇر لەڭمىنى ئەڭ داڭلىق. لەڭمەن دېسە كىشىلەر ھامان ئۇيغۇرلارنى ئەسلەيدۇ. مەھمۇد كاشغەرىنىڭ مىلادى 1074 – يىلى يېزىلغان «تۈركىي تىللار دىۋانى» ناملىق ئەسىرىدە بۇ تاماقلارنىڭ كۆپى مىسال قىلىپ ئېلىنغان. ئۇيغۇرلار ياشايدىغان ھەرقايسى رايونلارنىڭ ئۆزىگە خاس تائاملىرى بار. مەسىلەن، شىنجاڭنىڭ شەرقىدىكى قۇمۇل رايونىنىڭ «ياپما» ناملىق تامىقى خېلى داڭلىق. بۇنىڭدا گۆش، سەۋزە، بەرەڭگە (ياڭيۇ)، پىياز قاتارلىقلار مايدا قورۇلغاندىن كېيىن ئۈستىگە قاتمۇ قات قىلىپ نېپىز خېمىر يېپىلىدۇ. ئاندىن 20-15 مىنۇت ئەتراپىدا دۇملىنىدۇ. ئاندىن خېمىر ئايرىم تەخسىگە ئېلىنىدۇ ۋە قورۇما بىلەن يېيىلىدۇ. تۇرپاننىڭ ياپمىسى قۇمۇلنىڭ ياپمىسىدىن پەرق قىلىدۇ. تۇرپاندا ياپمىغا بولدۇرغان خېمىر باسىدۇ. خوتەن رايونىنىڭ ئالاھىدە تائاملىرىدىن بولغان گۆشگىردە قۇۋۋەتلىك تائاملارنىڭ بىرى ھېسابلىنىدۇ. ئۇ سامسىغا ئوخشايدۇ، ئەمما سامسىدىن يوغانراق بولىدۇ. ئۇنىمۇ تونۇردا ياقىدۇ. شىنجاڭنىڭ ھەممە جايلىرىدا دېگۈدەك ئۆپكە – ھېسىپ، سامسا، لەڭمەن، مانتا، پولۇ، شورپا، كاۋاپ قاتارلىق تائاملارغا ئېغىز تېگەلەيسىز.

almost	دېگۈدەك
meat stew	دۇملىمە
raised dough	بولدۇرغان خېمىر
a fried dish	قورۇما

to taste	ئېغىز تەگمەك
layer by layer	قاتمۇ - قات
to put on	باسماق
nutritious	قۇۋۋەتلىك

1. What does the author mean by "Cooking is an art for Uyghurs"?
2. Why is the dictionary "تۈركىي تىللار دىۋانى" mentioned in the text?
3. What is the difference between Qumul and Turfan ياپما?
4. What kind of food can you try in most places of Xinjiang?

Exercise 7.2:  Skim the passage one more time and provide a recipe for Turpan ياپما.

Exercise 7.3:  Now read the following three personifications. Which Uyghur foods are personified here? Circle the appropriate one from the given options below each personification. Explain your choice.

1

مەن ئۇيغۇرلارنىڭ ئەنئەنىۋى تائاملىرىنىڭ بىرى. مېنى تەييارلاش ئۈچۈن ئۇن، مايلىق قوي گۆشى، پىياز، مۇۋاپىق مىقداردا زىرە ۋە سوقغان قارىمۇچ لازىم. مېنى ھەم تونۇردا ھەم دۇخوپكىدا پىشۇرسا بولىدۇ. شەكلىم ھەر خىل: بەزىدە تۆت بۇرجەك ياكى ئۈچ بۇرجەك، بەزىدە دۇگىلەك بولىمەن. مېنى كىشىلەر ياخشى كۆرۈپ يېيىشىدۇ. تونۇردىن چىقىشىمنى ساقلاپ تۇرىدۇ. مەن نېمە؟

مانتا چۆچۈرە جۇۋاۋا سامسا

2

مەنمۇ ئۇيغۇرلارنىڭ تائاملىرىنىڭ بىرى. مېنى خوتەن رايونىدا كۆپرەك كۆرەلەيسىلەر. مېنىڭ ئىچىم گۆش بىلەن پىيازغا تولغان. ئىچىمدىكىنى كىشىلەر "قىيما" دەپ ئاتىشىدۇ. مېنىڭ قېرىندىشىم بار. ئۇنىڭغا كىشىلەر "سامسا" دەپ نام بەرگەن. بۇ قېرىندىشىم پۈتۈن ئوتتۇرا ئاسىيادا بار، مەن بولسام خوتەننىڭ ئۆزگىچە تائامى ھېسابلىنىمەن. مېنى سىلەر ئوتتۇرا ئاسىيادا تاپالمايسىلەر. ئۇ يەردىكىلەر ئىسمىمنىمۇ ئاڭلىمىغان. قېنى، تېپىڭلارچۇ، مەن نېمە؟

گۆشنان سامبۇسا پولو گۆشگىردە

3

ئۇيغۇر تائاملىرىنىڭ ئىچىدە مېنىڭ ئورنۇم ئالاھىدە. مېنىڭ ئىسمىمنى ئاڭلىغاندا، كىشىلەر ئۇيغۇرلارنى تىلغا ئالىدۇ، چۈنكى مەن ئۇيغۇرلار ئارقىلىق پۈتۈن ئوتتۇرا ئاسىياغا تارقالغان. مەن بەك چىرايلىق. ماڭا بىر قاراڭلار! قىپقىزىل قورۇلغان قوي گۆشى رەڭگارەڭ سەيلەر بىلەن ئىنچىكە خېمىرنىڭ ئۈستىدە... خېمىرىمنىڭ ئۇزۇنلىقى بىر نەچچە مېترغىچە يېتىدۇ. كىشىلەر مېنى يېگەندە: پاھ، نېمىدېگەن يېيىشلىك تاماق بۇ ھە، - دېيىشىدۇ. مېنى تونۇدىڭلارمۇ؟ مەن...

نېرىن لەغمەن سۇيۇقئاش چۆپ

Exercise 8: ئۇيغۇر سامسىلىرى

Exercise 8.1: Before watching another video, read the following excerpt from a poem by Muhämmädjan Rashidin about Uyghur cuisine. Guess the meaning of the word سامسىپەز from the context.

ماھارەتلىك سامسىپەزلەر سايراپ تۇرار،
سامسىپەزنىڭ ئىككى قولى ئويناپ تۇرار.
ئۇيغۇرلارنىڭ تائاملىرى بەرگەن لەززەت،
ئاغزىڭىزدىن كەتمەي ئايلاپ، يىللاپ تۇرار!

Exercise 8.2:  Now, watch the video without sound and put the following statements describing the steps of baking سامسا in order.

سامسىنى تونۇرغا ياقىمىز	
جىلىت ئاچىمىز	
گۆش بىلەن پىيازغا قارىمۇچ ، تۇز، زىرە قوشۇپ قىيما تەييارلايمىز	
سامسا تۈگىمىز	
تونۇرغا ئوت قالايمىز(سالىمىز)	1

Exercise 8.3: Watch the video again with sound. This time pay attention to the conversation, then answer the following questions:

1. What is the difference between سامسا and مانتا?
2. What do you think the word قاسقان means?
3. How long should the سامسا be baked in the تونۇر?
4. Before taking the سامسا out of the تونۇر, the سامسىپەز says: ئۇستام ياقسا ئالمايدىكەن، بىزلا ياقساق قالمايدىكەن. What does this phrase mean to you? Discuss your answer with the instructor.

Exercise 8.4: Watch the video with the sound turned off. This time, you will narrate the process of baking سامسا by using the -سپ form with the present/future tense.

Exercise 9: ئۇيغۇرلار گۆش يېمەمدۇ؟

Exercise 9.1:  Read the following passage which has been taken with minimal adaptation from the Uyghur novel ئامەت ۋە ئاپەت (Luck and Disaster) by Jalalidin Behram. This conversation is conducted by a Uyghur man, Khalmet, and a Burmese woman.

never	ھەرگىز
mouse	چاشقان
goat	ئۆچكە

- قورسىقىڭىز ئاچتىمۇ، نېمە يەيسىز؟
- ماڭا موما، گاڭپەن، چىلىغان سەي بولسىلا بولىدۇ.
- گۆشلۈك قورىمىچۇ؟
- يا... ياق، - خالمەت دەرھاللا قوللىرىنى شىلتىدى،
- مەن... مەن گۆش يېمەيمەن.
- جۇڭگولۇقلار ئىت، مۈشۈك، چاشقان گۆشلىرىنىمۇ يەيدىكەنغۇ.
- لېكىن مەن خەنزۇ ئەمەس، ئۇيغۇر!
- ئۇيغۇر دېگەن نېمە ئۇ؟
- مىللەت! جۇڭگودىكى 56 مىللەتنىڭ بىرى.
- ئۇلار نەدە ياشايدۇ؟
- شىنجاڭدا.
- شىنجاڭ دېگەن قەيەردە؟
- جۇڭگونىڭ غەربىدە.
- ئۇ يەرلەر چىرايلىقمۇ؟
- جەننەت دەڭە...
- نېمىشقا ئۇيغۇرلار گۆش يېمەيدۇ؟
- سىز خاتا چۈشىنىپ قالماڭ، - دېدى خالمەت، - بىز قوي، كالا، ئۆچكە، توخۇ، بېلىق، كەپتەر گۆشلىرىنى يەيمىز، لېكىن بايا سىز دېگەن ئىت، مۈشۈك، چاشقان، توڭگۇز گۆشلىرىنى ھەرگىز يېمەيمىز.
- توڭگۇز گۆشى ئوبدانغۇ، ئۇنى نېمىشقا يېمەيسىلەر؟
- دىنىمىز راۋا كۆرمەيدۇ، چۈنكى بىز ئىسلام دىنىغا ئېتىقاد قىلىمىز.

pig	توڭگۇز
dove	كەپتەر
to swing hands	قوللىرىنى شىلتىماق
to see as right	راۋا كۆرمەك
to believe	ئېتىقاد قىلماق
heaven	جەننەت
religion	دىن
a fried dish	قورۇما

Exercise 9.2:  What did you learn about Uyghurs and their eating habits from the passage?

3 Particles Expressing Emphasis: غۇ- , لا- , *and* ە-

In the passage, you saw three particles: غۇ- , لا- , and ە- . Particles are short words, usually one, rarely two syllables, which attach to the ends of other words. In Uyghur, these usually add some sort of emphasis.

The particle لا- is primarily restrictive; it generally gives the sense of 'only', 'just', 'just now', or occasionally 'right away'. One common use of لا- is after the conditional suffix سا- /سە- . Used in this way, it means something like 'just so long as'.

ماڭا موما، گاڭپەن، چىلىغان سەي بولسىلا بولىدۇ.
I just want steamed bread, rice, and pickles.
خالمەت دەرھاللا قوللىرىنى شىلتىدى.
Khalmet immediately gestured 'no' with his hands.

The particle غۇ- (قۇ-) also serves to emphasize a fact the speaker is stating. It expresses emphasis by adding the notion of 'as we all know...'. For example, in line 6:

جۇڭگولۇقلار ئىت، مۈشۈك، چاشقان گۆشلىرىنىمۇ يەيدىكەنغۇ.
As we all know Chinese people do eat all kinds of meat!
As we all know pork is indeed good! !توڭگۇز گۆشى ئوبدانغۇ

The particle ە- usually attaches to the 2nd person imperative mood and functions to deliver a meaning of polite request. Look at the following examples:

Please do not say that. .ئۇنداق دېمەڭە
Please come here. .يېنىمغا كەلگىنە
Please don't do that. .ئۇنداق قىلماڭە

Though the particle ە- , theoretically, can be added to all 2nd person imperative forms, you should remember that its use is mostly limited to friends of family. In more formal context, one should use another polite request form with the conditional suffix سە- \سا-. For example:

Could you please write a recommendation letter for me?
(appropriate) .ماڭا بىر تەۋسىيە خېتى يېزىپ بەرسىڭىز
(inappropriate) .ماڭا بىر تەۋسىيە خېتى يېزىپ بېرىڭە

Exercise 10: ئۆنداق دېمەڭ...

Exercise 10.1:  Attach the appropriate particle -لا، -غۇ، -ە to the correct words in the following sentences.

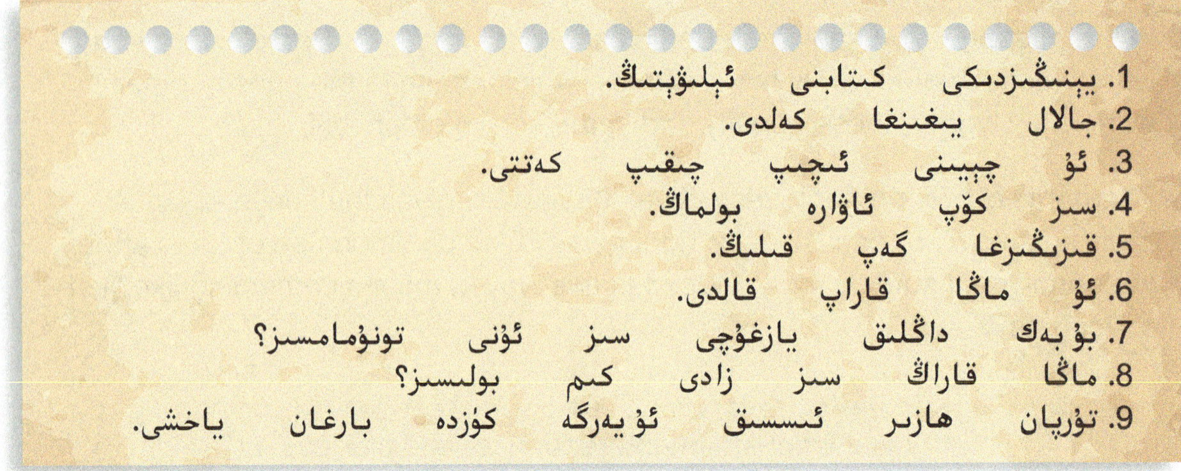

1. يېنىڭىزدىكى كىتابنى ئېلىۋېتىڭ.
2. جالال يېغىنغا كەلدى.
3. ئۇ چېيىنى ئىچىپ چىقىپ كەتتى.
4. سىز كۆپ ئاۋارە بولماڭ.
5. قىزىڭىزغا گەپ قىلىڭ.
6. ئۇ ماڭا قاراپ قالدى.
7. بۇ بەك داڭلىق يازغۇچى سىز ئۇنى تونۇمامسىز؟
8. ماڭا قاراڭ سىز زادى كىم بولىسىز؟
9. تۇرپان هازىر ئىسسىق ئۇ يەرگە كۈزدە بارغان ياخشى.

Exercise 10.2: Now listen to the audio recording to check your answers.

Exercise 11: Can you read the folowing menu? Try it!

Pulling it all together خۇرجۇندا

In this section, you will reinforce your knowledge and check the progress you have made during chapters 3 and 4 by completing a limited selection of focused exercises.

Exercise 12:  Read the following online posting from an internet forum about travelling in China. Write a response to the questions and make suggestions using the information you learned in these chapters.

خەۋەرلەر
مەسلىھەت
ناخشا - مۇزىكا
ئەڭ يېڭى فىلملەر
يېڭى ئەزالار
يۇمشاق دېتاللار
يېڭى يازمىلار

سالام ئۇيغۇر دوستلار! مەن بېيجىڭ ئارقىلىق شىنجاڭغا بارماقچى. ئەمما بېيجىڭدا ئارانلا ئۈچ كۈن تۇرالايمەن.

(1) ئۇيغۇرلارغا ئائىت بەزى ماتېرىياللارنى يىغاي دەيمەن. بەزىلەر مىللەتلەر ئۇنىۋېرسىتېتىغا بېرىشنى تەۋسىيە قىلدى. قانداق قىلاي؟ شۇ يەرگە بېرىش مۇۋاپىقمۇ؟ ئۇ يەردىكى ئوقۇتقۇچىلار بىلەن كۆرۈشۈش مۇمكىنمۇ؟ ئۇلارنىڭ تېلېفون نومۇرىنى بىلىدىغانلار بارمۇ؟

(2) بەزى ساياھەت ئورۇنلىرىغا باراي دەيمەن، ئەمما ۋاقتىم ۋە پۇلۇم كۆپ ئەمەس. بەزىلەر سەددىچىنگە بېرىشنى، يەنە بەزىلەر شەھىرىستان (خان سارىيى) غا بېرىشنى تەۋسىيە قىلىشۋاتىدۇ. سىلەرچە قەيەرگە باراي؟ ئۇ يەرلەرگە بېرىش ئۈچۈن قايسى ئاپتوبۇسقا چىقىشىم لازىم؟ تاكسىدا بارسام قىممەتمۇ؟

(3) باشقا مىللەتلەرنىڭ تاماقلىرىنىمۇ يەپ باقاي دەيمەن. بۇنىڭ ئۈچۈن قەيەرگە بارسام بولىدۇ؟ ئۇيغۇر تاماقلىرىدىن قايسىسىنى يەي؟ جۇڭگولۇقلار ھەرقانداق گۆشنى يەيدۇ دېگەن گەپ راستمۇ؟

 Contact: uyghurjan@bayanchur.com

Exercise 13: ئۇيغۇر تىلىدىكى "ياۋا" سۆزلەر

Exercise 13.1: Before watching: Listen to the words and decide if they are Chinese in origin.

Chinese	سۆزلەر	
	مال	1
	لەڭسەي	2
	مازار	3
	داڭلىق	4
	مەقبەرە	5
	جوڭياڭ مىندا	6
	گاۋكاۋ	7
	خېرىدار	8

Chinese	سۆزلەر	
	جوڭبا	9
	ئەردوچوزا	10
	سودىلىق	11
	شاڭچاڭ	12
	چاقىرىق	13
	داۋاملىق	14
	ساياھەت	15
	ناۋاي	16

Exercise 13.2:  Now watch the video clips. Listen to each excerpt carefully. Circle the Chinese loan words you hear from the following options below.

Excerpt #1: A Uyghur student's advice to an American student who is heading to Xinjiang

مىرشات	جاي	سودا	چاۋشى	ساياھەت
	يوۋخاۋ	جا	ئەڭ	سەنشىخاڭزا

Excerpt #2: A brief self-introduction of a Uyghur student who is currently studying in Beijing

ھەلىمە	ئارزۇ	ئوتتۇرا	شەھەرلىك	يەنجۇسىڭ
	ئاتۇش	يېڭي داشۆ	ئەسلى	بوشى

Excerpt #3: A restaurant manager talks about his restaurant in Beijing.

سۇلايمان	ئادەم	ئىككى	پىيسەي	كاۋاپچى
	فۇۋۇيۇەن	سامسىپەز	ئاشخانا	مەنجاڭ

Exercise 14: ئۇيغۇر تىلىم قەيەردە؟

Exercise 14.1:  At the end of his trip to Beijing, John writes a blog entry about recent changes in Uyghur vocabulary. Read it and answer the questions that follow based on the passage.

Uyghur John's Blog

ئامېرىكىلىق ياللقۇننىڭ تورتۇراسى

Search

كۈندە بىر ماقال: كىمنىڭ زۇلمى كۆپ بولسا، زاۋالى يېقىن بولار.

ئۇيغۇرلار ئارىسىدا خەنزۇچە سۆزلەرنى قوشۇپ سۆزلەش بەك ئومۇملاشقان ئىكەن. مېنىڭچە بۇنىڭ سەۋەبى شۇ: شىنجاڭدا خەنزۇلار بەك كۆپ، لېكىن ئۇيغۇرچە مەكتەپلەر ھازىر بەك ئاز. ئۇيغۇر بالىلارنىڭ كۆپى خەنزۇچە مەكتەپتە ئوقۇيدۇ. مەن بېيجىڭدا كۆرگەن ئۇيغۇرلارنىڭ ھەممىسى شۇنداق ئىكەن. تۈنۈگۈن مەركىزىي مىللەتلەر ئۇنىۋېرسىتېتىدىكى ئۇيغۇر تىلى پروفېسسورى بىلەن كۆرۈشتۈم. ئۇمۇ سۆزلىگەندە خەنزۇچە سۆزلەرنى ئارىلاشتۇرۇپ سۆزلىدى. مەن بەك ھەيران قالدىم. ئۇيغۇر تىلىدا بار سۆزلەرگىمۇ خەنزۇچە سۆزلەرنى ئىشلىتىدىكەن. تۈنۈگۈن بىللە تاماق يېدۇق، قارىسام كۈتكۈچىگە "ماڭا جامىيەن قىلىڭ" دەيدۇ. كېيىن ئۇقسام "يەنە ئازراق چۆپ (خېمىر) سېلىپ بېرىڭ" دېگەن گەپ ئىكەن.

ئۇيغۇر ئوقۇغۇچىلارمۇ سۆزلەشكەندە خەنزۇچە سۆزلەرنى كۆپ ئىشلىتىدىكەن. مەن ھېلىقى ئۇيغۇر پروفېسسوردىن بۇ ئىشنى سورىدىم. ئۇ كىشى "بۇنداق قىلىش خاتا" دەيدۇ. ئۇنىڭ ئېيتىشىچە، كۆپ قىسىم ئۇيغۇر زىيالىلىرى خەنزۇچە سۆزلەرنى ئارىلاشتۇرۇپ سۆزلەشكە قارشى ئىكەن، لېكىن سۆزلەشكەندە يەنىلا ئاشۇنداق ئارىلاش سۆزلەيدىكەن. ئاڭلىشىمچە خەنزۇ تىلىنى بىلمەيدىغان دېھقانلارمۇ تېلېفون نومۇرىنى خەنزۇچە ئوقۇيدىكەن. مەسىلەن، ساقچىدىن ياردەم سوراش نومۇرى 110 نى "ياۋ- ياۋ- لىڭ" دەيدىكەن. خەنزۇچە سۆزلەر يېمەك - ئىچمەك ۋە تۇرمۇش بۇيۇملىرى ئۈچۈن كۆپرەك ئىشلىتىلىدىكەن. مەن بىر ئۇيغۇر ئوقۇغۇچى بىلەن تونۇشتۇم. ئۇ بېيجىڭدا فىزىكا كەسپىدە ماگىستىرلىق ئۈچۈن ئوقۇيدىكەن. ئۇ ماڭا توردىكى بىر پارچە شېئىرنى بەردى. قارىسام بەك قىزىق ئىكەن. بۇ يەرگە كۆچۈرۈپ قويدۇم:

تۇڭلاتقۇنى "بىڭشياڭ" دەپ،
ياڭراتقۇنى "يىڭشياڭ" دەپ،
گۈرجەكنىمۇ "تىشياڭ" دەپ،
ئۇيغۇر تىلىم ئەلۋىدا.

شاۋقۇن- سۈرەن "زايىن"دەپ،
خەت باسقاننى "دايىن"دەپ ،
تەلەپپۇزنى "فايىن"دەپ،
ئۇيغۇر تىلىم ئەلۋىدا.

كۇتۇبخانا - "تۇشۇگۇەن"،
مۇلازىملار - "فۇۋۇيۇەن"،
"ساۋمېي"بولدى بۆلجۈرگەن،
ئۇيغۇر تىلىم ئەلۋىدا.

ئېرى ماڭدى "جيۇبا"غا،
خوتۇن چايغا "دىبا"غا،
بالا كۆندى "ۋاڭبا"غا،
ئۇيغۇر تىلىم ئەلۋىدا.

1. نېمە ئۈچۈن ئۇيغۇرلار خەنزۇچە سۆزلەرنى كۆپ ئىشلىتىدۇ؟
2. "تۇڭلاتقۇ"، "گۇرجەك"، "بۆلجۇرگەن" سۆزلەرنىڭ مەنىسى نېمە؟
3. "تەلەپپۇز" ۋە "كۇتۇپخانا" ئۈچۈن قايسى خەنزۇچە سۆزلەر ئىشلىتىلىدىكەن؟
4. سىزنىڭچە خەنزۇچە "جيۇبا"، "دىبا"، "ۋاڭبا" سۆزلەرنىڭ مەنىسى نېمە؟
5. "ئۇيغۇر تىلىم ئەلۋىدا" دېگەن گەپنى قانداق تەرجىمە قىلىسىز؟

Exercise 14.2: According to the passage, Uyghur intellectuals are against the use of Chinese borrowings in Uyghur. Do you agree with them? Explain your answer.
Does your language use borrowed vocabulary for food or any other subjects?

Project

On the Trial of Chinese Words in Uyghur

Prepare an interview with an Uyghur in your town or via Skype/Facebook. How many Chinese words can you find in this interview?

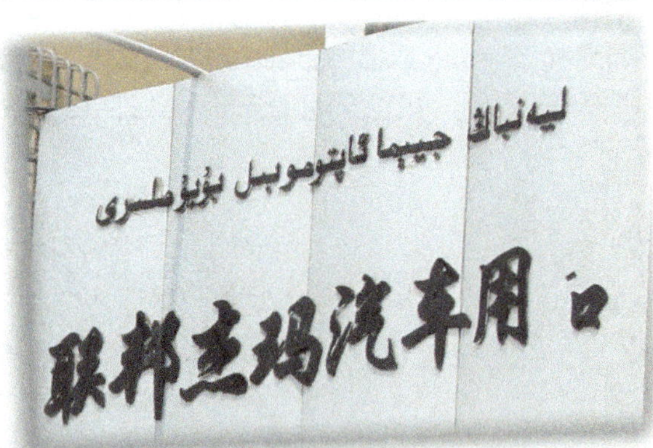

Self-check

Use the following list to check your knowledge of the topics you have covered in chapters 3 and 4. Mark whether you know and can do the following in Uyghur. If you think you may need more work to fully understand something, you can go back to the relevant section in the chapters and review it.

1. I can talk and write about:

The University of Nationalities in Beijing (مىللەتلەر ئۇنىۋېرسىتېتى)	☐
Some historical information about the Forbidden City and the Great Wall in Beijing	☐
Uyghur foods and how some of them are cooked	☐
Some recent changes in Uyghur vocabulary	☐
Yusup Xas Hajip and his famous work "قۇتادغۇ بىلىگ"	☐

2. I can also:

Describe Xinjiang's geographical location	☐
Describe places such as Kashgar and Taklimakan Desert	☐
Compare things and people	☐
Read Uyghur menus at restaurants with Chinese food names	☐
Order Uyghur food using some Chinese words	☐
Present my country for an Uyghur audience	☐
Compare the Xinjiang Uyghur Autonomous Region and my country	☐
Conduct a simple interview with native speakers	☐

3. I know how to:

Express good wishes at Uyghur weddings	☐
Understand and use some expressions containing the words خۇدا and ئاللاھ	☐
Recognize Chinese words in Uyghur	☐
Use some food-related Chinese borrowings	☐

4. I can explain the following words and concepts:

ياپما	☐
تاڭجاڭ	☐
سۇيۇقئاش	☐
بىر گەپ بولار	☐
سامسىپەز	☐
گۆشگىردە	☐
خېرىدار	☐
مەقبەرە	☐

قۇملۇق	☐
ئويمانلىق	☐
يىپەك يولى	☐
پامىر ئېگىزلىكى	☐
سەددىچىن سېپىلى	☐
خان سارىيى	☐
چۆچۈرە	☐
باچكا تاڭ	☐

5. I can use grammar to …

Describe things and people using past, present and future participles	☐
Use some expressions with the postpositions (بىلەن، ئارقىلىق and باشلاپ)	☐
Make some suggestions (ياخشىراق بولىدىغۇ دەيمەن/ ئۇ كېلىدىغۇ دەيمەن)	☐
Ask and give polite suggestions (conditional mood and the verb بولماق)	☐
Express polite commands (قېنى)	☐
Make comparisons (قارىغاندا)	☐
Emphasize a statement (-غۇ، -لا and -ە)	☐
Express good wishes (-سۇن and -غاي)	☐
Coordinate clauses -پ (-ىپ، -ۇپ)	☐

Vocabulary سۆزلۈك

Vocabulary is given according to the Uyghur alphabetical order. The right column precedes the left column on each page.

to mix	ئارىلاشتۇرماق
ethnic minority	ئاز سانلىق مىللەت
coriander, cilantro	ئاشكۆكى
farewell	ئەلۋىدا
pigeon soup	باچكا شورپىسى
we will see	بىر گەپ بولار
to be spread	تارقالماق
to drop, throw away, cast	تاشلىماق
to take a taxi	تاكسى توسماق
waiter	كۈتكۈچى
to cut	توغرىماق
to prepare for something	جابدۇنماق
to be located	جايلاشماق
water dumplings	چۆچۈرە
queen	خانىش
dough	خېمىر
to bury	دەپنە قىلماق
to infuse (tea), to brew	دەملىمەك
oven	دۇخوپكا
round, circular	دۈگىلەك
to braise	دۈملىمەك
samsa maker	سامسىپەز

a fried dish	سەي \ قورۇما
fried noodles	سومەن
insurance	سۇغۇرتا
noodle soup	سۇيۇقئاش
bone	سۆڭەك
mutton soup	شورپا
fried fish	قورۇلغان بېلىق
to fry	قورۇماق
tail fat	قۇيرۇق ياغ
filling; ground beef	قىيما
to copy	كۆچۈرمەك
to meet	كۈتۈۋالماق
place (to stay)	ماكان
advice	مەسلىھەت
to be reckoned, to be counted as	ھېسابلانماق
vegetables	ئوتياش \ كۆكتات
to understand, to know	ئۇقماق
province	ئۆلكە
to taste, to try	ئېغىز تەگمەك
expression	ئىبارە
potato	ياڭيۇ

بەشىنچى دەرس

CHAPTER FIVE

تەڭرىتاغ باغرىدا

ON THE HILLSIDE OF THE TENGRITAGH

IN THIS CHAPTER

Functions
- Expressing goals
- Describing places
- Giving sightseeing information
- Expressing opinions about buildings and people
- Expressing desire
- Expressing politeness
- Narrating past events

Grammar
- The auxiliary verbs ئالماق and بەرمەك
- The gerund of purpose:
  - with -غىلى
  - with the verbal noun + postposition ئۈچۈن
  - with the verbal noun + suffix -غا \ -قا \ -گە \ -كە
- The construction -غۇم \ -غۇڭ بار
- Super polite form with -سىلا \ -سىلە

In this chapter, John flies to Urumchi. He wants to visit some famous cities in Xinjiang before school starts. Through the conversations, reading passages, and excerpts from John's blog entries herein, you will take a virtual trip to cities located in the east and south of the Tengritagh, and learn more about grapes of Turpan, كارىز, the famous ھېيتگاھ mosque, as well as other well-known destinations.

Exercise 1: قەدىمي يۇرتلار

Exercise 1.1:  Look at the map of Xinjiang. Some cities have been marked with pictures of monuments, handcrafts, or products for which those cities are known, but the names of the cities are missing. Name each city and tell us what you know about them.

KAZAKHSTAN
MONGOLIA
ALTAY
CHÖCHEK
KARAMAY
BÖRTALA
KUYTUN
ÜRÜMCHI
GYZSTAN
GHULJA
SHIHENZI
QUMUL (HAMI)
KORLA
KUCHA
ATUSH
AQSU
YERKEN
CHARQLIQ
CHINA
TIBET

Exercise 1.2:  Can you add another thing (item, product) to each city?

Exercise 2: ئۈرۈمچىگە سەپەر

Exercise 2.1:  While waiting for his plane to take off for Urumchi, John wrote a brief blog entry about the Uyghurs. Read it and answer the questions that follow.

Uyghur John's Blog

ئامېرىكىلىق يالقۇننىڭ تورتۇراسى

Search

كۈندە بىر ماقال:

يۇرت قوغدىساڭ ئۆسەرسەن، قوغدىمىساڭ ئۆچەرسەن.

12-ئاۋغۇست: مانا، بۈگۈنمۇ كەلدى... بىرەر سائەتتىن كېيىن ئۈرۈمچىگە ئۇچىمەن. ئويلىسام ماڭا ئايروپىلان ياخشىكەن. تۆت سائەتتە ئۈرۈمچىگە يېتىپ بارىدىكەنمەن. ھازىر مەن ھاياجاندا. چۈنكى بۇ قېتىم ئۇيغۇرلارنىڭ ۋەتىنىدە بىر يىل تۇرىمەن! بۈگۈنگىچە ئۇيغۇرلار توغرۇلۇق خېلى كۆپ مەلۇماتلارغا ئىگە بولدۇم. بىر دوستۇم ئۇيغۇرلارنى تونۇشتۇرۇپ مۇنداق دېدى: "ئۇيغۇر" دېگەن سۆز 'ئىتتىپاقلىشىش'، 'ئۇيۇشۇش' دېگەن مەنىنى بىلدۈرىدۇ. ئۇيغۇر تىلى ئالتاي تىللىرى سىستېمىسىدىكى تۈركىي تىل تۈركۈمىگە كىرىدۇ. ئۇيغۇرلار ئەرەب ئېلىپبەسى ئاساسىدا تۈزۈلگەن ئۇيغۇر يېزىقىنى قوللىنىدۇ. ھازىرغىچە مەلۇم بولغان تارىخىي يادىكارلىقلارغا قارىغاندا، ئۇيغۇرلار 2000 يىللىق يېزىق تارىخىغا ئىگە ئىكەن. ئۇيغۇرلارنىڭ ئۆزىگە خاس مىللىي ئەنئەنىلىرى بەك كۆپ. ئۇلار ئەمگەكچان، باتۇر مىللەت... مەن ئۇيغۇرلار تارىخىغا تېخىمۇ قىزىقىپ قالدىم. ئەمدى، ئاللاھ بۇيرىسا، شىنجاڭدا ئۇيغۇرلارنىڭ ئارىسىدا يۈرۈپ ئۇلارنىڭ ئۆرپ-ئادەتلىرىنى ئۆز كۆزۈم بىلەن كۆرۈمەن ۋە تېخىمۇ كۆپ نەرسىلەرنى ئۆگىنىۋالىمەن. بۈگۈنگىچە تۇرغىنىمدا ئۇيغۇر ئاشخانىلارغا كۆپ باردىم. ئۇيغۇرلارنىڭ تائاملىرى خىلمۇخىل ھەم مەززىلىك ئىكەن. ئاڭلىسام نانىنىڭلا ئون نەچچە تۈرى بار ئىكەن. مەن گىردە نان، توقاچ، گۆشنانلارغا ئېغىز تەگدىم. كاۋاپنىڭ تۈرلىرىچۇ! تونۇر كاۋىپى، زىخ كاۋىپى، تاۋا كاۋاپ، قىيما كاۋاپ، قازان كاۋىپى... ئۇيغۇرلار كالا، قوي، ئۆچكە، تۆگە، ئات، بېلىق، توخۇ، ئۆردەك، غاز، توشقان ۋە بىر قىسىم ياۋايى قۇشلارنىڭ گۆشىنى يەيدىكەن...

پاھ، شىنجاڭنىڭ مېۋىلىرى نېمىدېگەن تاتلىق! مەن ئالما، ئۈزۈم، ئۆرۈك، نەشپۈت، ئانار، ياڭاق، ئەنجۈر، بادام قاتارلىق مېۋىلەرنى تويۇپ يەيمەن! ئامېرىكىدا بىر دوستۇمغا ئۇيغۇرلار توغرۇلۇق سۆزلەپ بەرسەم، ئۇ "ئۇيغۇرلار خەنزۇلارغا ئوخشامدۇ؟" دەپ سورىدى. ئەپسۇسكى كۆپ ئامېرىكىلىقلار ئۇيغۇرلارنى بىلمەيدۇ. مەن ئۇنىڭغا ئۇيغۇرلارنىڭ رەسىملىرىنى كۆرسەتتىم. دوستۇم دوپپا كىيگەن بوۋايلارنى، رومال ئورىغان مومايلارنى كۆرۈپ ھەيران قالدى، چۈنكى ئۇ ئۇيغۇرلارنى خەنزۇلارنىڭ بىر تۈرى دەپ ئويلىغان ئىكەن. مەن دوستۇمغا ئۇيغۇرلارنىڭ كلاسسىك مۇزىكىسى 12 مۇقام توغرۇلۇق سۆزلەپ بەردىم. ئۇ ئۇيغۇرلارغا قىزىقىپ قالدى. بەلكىم دوستۇممۇ بىر كۈنى ئۇيغۇرلار ماكانىنى زىيارەت قىلغىلى جۇڭگوغا كېلىدۇ... ۋوي، ماڭىدىغان ۋاقىت بوپ قاپتىغۇ... ئايروپىلانىمغا كېچىكىپ قالماي تېخى ...

ئىسىم

ئىم

1. جون خاتىرىسىدە نېمە توغرۇلۇق يازىدۇ؟
2. شىنجاڭدا ئۇ نېمە قىلماقچى؟
3. نېمە ئۈچۈن جون ئۈرۈمچىگە ئايروپىلان بىلەن بېرىشنى قارار قىلدى؟
4. "ئۇيغۇر" سۆزىنىڭ مەنىسى نېمە؟
5. ئۇيغۇر تىلى ۋە ئۇيغۇر يېزىقى توغرۇلۇق نېمە بىلىسىز؟
6. ناننىڭ قانداق تۈرلىرى بار؟ كاۋاپنىڭچۇ؟
7. جون قايسى مېۋىلەرنىڭ ناملىرىنى ئەسلىدى؟
8. ئۇيغۇرلار خەنزۇلاردىن قانداق پەرق قىلىدۇ؟

Exercise 2.2:  Read the proverb on the left side of the blog entry. What does it mean to you? Discuss its meaning with your instructor.

Exercise 2.3:  Based on the text, which of the given definitions best matches the following words and expressions?

تەرجىمىسى				سۆز - ئىبارىلەر	
a. excitement	b. enthusiasm	c. anticipation	d. expectation	ھاياجان	1
a. territory	b. homeland	c. county	d. province	ۋەتەن	2
a. knowledge	b. information	c. education	d. tutoring	مەلۇمات	3
a. to obtain	b. to contact	c. to catch	d. to tie	ئىگە بولماق	4
a. alliance	b. league	c. unity	d. society	ئىتتىپاقلىشىش	5
a. to be busy	b. to use	c. to work	d. to support	قوللانماق	6
a. remnant	b. relic	c. trace	d. reminder	يادىكارلىق	7
a. tradition	b. belief	c. habit	d. hobby	ئەنئەنە	8
a. custom	b. convention	c. norm	d. guidance	ئۆرپ - ئادەت	9
a. to taste	b. to experience	c. to touch	d. to speak	ئېغىز تەگمەك	10
a. manner	b. kind	c. brand	d. net	تۈر	11
a. to need	b. to hope	c. to call	d. to dream	ئۈمىد قىلماق	12

1 Auxilary Verb ئالماق

As you know from previous chapters, many Uyghur auxiliary verbs attach to a main verb to express a more nuanced aspect. These auxiliaries often take the place of English adverbs, though there is no single translation for any auxiliary which is appropriate for all contexts.

One such auxiliary verb is the verb ئالماق, literally 'to take.' When used as an auxiliary, it indicates that the action of the verb somehow benefits the person who performs it, either immediately or in the future.

Like many Uyghur auxiliaries, ئالماق follows a main verb ending in -ىپ \ -پ, at which point it takes all the necessary tense, aspect, and personal endings. However, there is also another way of forming compound verbs with the auxiliary ئالماق which is much more common. Look at this example from the blog entry you just read:

شىنجاڭدا ئۇيغۇرلارنىڭ ئارىسىدا يۈرۈپ ئۇلارنىڭ ئۆرپ-ئادەتلىرىنى
ئۆز كۆزۈم بىلەن كۆرۈمەن ۋە تېخىمۇ كۆپ نەرسىلەرنى ئۆگىنىۋالىمەن (ئۆگىنىپ ئالىمەن).
In Xinjiang I will be among Uyghurs and will see their traditions and customs with my own eyes. I will learn (I will have the opportunity to learn) many more things.

As you can see from the example above, instead of being written as two separate words, the main verb and the auxiliary in such constructions are contracted into one word, and the -پ from the full form changes to -ۋ.

In this case, the full form -ىپ ئالماق and the contracted form -ىۋالماق mean the same thing, but the latter is usually used to avoid confusion with the non-auxiliary use of the -ىپ \ -پ form. (This is not the case with other auxiliary verbs, as we shall see in Grammar Explanation 2.) Take a look at some more examples:

ئۇنىڭ تېلېفون نومۇرىنى ئېسىمدە تۇتۇۋالدىم (تۇتۇپ ئالدىم).
I memorized his telephone number.
ئۇنتۇپ قالماسلىق ئۈچۈن بۇ ماقالنى دەپتىرىمگە يېزىۋالدىم (يېزىپ ئالدىم).
I wrote this proverb down in my notebook so that I wouldn't forget it.
ۋاقتىم بولماي قالسا دەپ تاماقنى ئۆيدە يەۋالغان ئىدىم (يەپ ئالغان ئىدىم).
I ate at home in the event that I wouldn't have time.

1 Auxilary Verb ئالماق (cont'd.)

توختاپ تۇرۇڭ، پۇلۇمنى يانچۇقۇمغا سېلىۋالاي. (سېلىپ ئالاي)
Wait–let me quickly put my money in my pocket.
ھاجەتخانىغا كىرىۋالسام (كىرىپ ئالسام) بولامدۇ؟
Is it okay if I run to the restroom quickly?

As an auxiliary verb, ئالماق also has several other meanings. The examples below demonstrate its use to denote an action with an unexpected, negative result for the subject (usually a physical injury).

ئاپتوبۇستىن چۈشۈۋاتقاندا پۇتۇمنى قايرىۋالدىم (قايرىپ ئالدىم).
I sprained my foot getting off the bus.
سىڭلىم ئوچاقتا ئوت قالىغاندا قولىنى كۆيدۈرۈۋالدى (كۆيدۈرۈپ ئالدى).
My younger sister burned her hand while lighting the fire in the oven.
نازاكەت سەۋزە توغراپ قولىنى كېسىۋاپتۇ (كېسىپ ئاپتۇ).
I heard that Nazaket cut her hand chopping carrots.
يىقىلىپ بېشىمنى تامغا ئۇرۇۋالدىم (ئۇرۇپ ئالدىم).
I fell and hit my head on the wall.

Exercise 3: يېزىۋالدىڭلارمۇ؟

Exercise 3.1:  Look at the following contracted compound verbs which make use of the auxilary ئالماق. Identify the main verb and the auxiliary verb, write them separately in the second column from the right, then translate them into English. The first one is done for you as an example.

I saw it (or: I took the chance to see it)	كۆرۈپ ئالدىم	كۆرۈۋالدىم
		كېلىۋالدى
		تۇتۇۋالدۇق
		بىلىۋالدىڭ
		يەۋالدىم
		ئۇخلىۋالدۇق
		ئارام ئېلىۋالدۇق

Exercise 3.2:  Now, form sentences using the words provided and the auxilary verb ئالماق, which you just learned. Be aware that you may have to add additional words to form coherent sentence. Follow the models.

ئوقۇش   كەلمەك   تاماق   ئەتمەك   يېمەك

ئوقۇشتىن كەلسەم، ئانام تاماق ئېتىپ قويۇپتۇ، ئىسسىقىدا يەۋالدىم.

گۆش   توغرىماق   قول   كەسمەك

گۆش توغرىغاندا قولۇمنى كېسىۋالدىم (گۆش توغراپ قولۇمنى كېسىۋالدىم).

ئۇسساپ   كەتمەك   سۇ   ئىچمەك

قورساق ئاچماق   تاماق   يېمەك

ئۇيقۇ كەلمەك   ئازراق   ئۇخلىماق

تاماق ئەتمەك   قول كۆيدۈرمەك

پۇتبول ئوينىماق   پۇت سۇندۇرماق

ئىسسىق چاي   ئىچمەك   تىل كۆيدۈرمەك

خەرىتىگە قارىماق   تۇرپاننىڭ ئورنى   بىلمەك

خەرىتىگە قارىماق   تۇرپاننىڭ ئورنى   بىلمەك

مەشق قىلماق   خەت بېسىش   ئۆگەنمەك

ئاپتوبۇستىن چۈشمەك   پۇت   قايرىماق

2 Auxilary Verb بەرمەك

In the blog entry you read, you also saw a number of examples of the auxiliary verb بەرمەك attached to the form -پ \ -ىپ of the main verb:

ئامېرىكىدا بىر دوستۇمغا ئۇيغۇرلار توغرۇلۇق سۆزلەپ بەرسەم،
ئۇ "ئۇيغۇرلار خەنزۇلارغا ئوخشامدۇ؟" دەپ سورىدى.
When I told one of my friends in America about Uyghurs,
he asked, Are Uyghurs similar to Hans?
مەن دوستۇمغا ئۇيغۇرلارنىڭ كلاسسىك مۇزىكىسى 12 مۇقام توغرۇلۇق سۆزلەپ بەردىم.
I told my friend about the Twelve Muqams, the classic music of the Uyghurs.

As you can see from the translations of these examples, the auxiliary verb بەرمەك used in this way indicates that the action of the verb benefits someone other than the subject. This beneficiary is not always expressed, but when it is often done so with the dative case marker -غا (-قا، -كە، -گە) or the postposition ئۈچۈن. Look at the following examples:

I read a book to my little brother. ئۇكامغا (ئۇكام ئۈچۈن) كىتاب ئوقۇپ بەردىم.
Grandmother told us a story. مومام بىزگە چۆچەك ئېيتىپ بەردى.
Our neighbor cooked for us. قوشنىمىز بىزگە تاماق ئېتىپ بەردى.

The auxiliary بەرمەك also appears in a contracted form, in which the final -پ of the main verb and the initial -ب of the auxiliary both reduce to -ۋ , yielding -ىۋەرمەك . Look at the sentences below:

Please, keep eating! تامىقىڭىزنى يەۋېرىڭ! (يەپ بېرىڭ)
Keep sitting. (Sit back down.) ئولتۇرۇۋېرىڭلار! (ئولتۇرۇپ بېرىڭلار)
ئۇلار سۆزلەشتى، مەن خېتىمنى يېزىۋەردىم. (يېزىپ بەردىم)
They talked, and I continued writing my letter.
سوئاللىرىڭىز بولسا، تارتىنماي سوراۋېرىڭ! (سوراپ بېرىڭ)
If you have any questions, don't be shy–just ask!
ماشىنا بولمىسا، ئاپتوبۇستا كېتىۋېرەمدۇق؟ (كېتىپ بېرەمدۇق)
If there's no car, should we still go by bus?
مۇئەللىم كەلمىسە، كىنوغا ئۆزىمىز بېرىۋېرىمىز. (بېرىپ بېرىمىز)
If the teacher doesn't come, we can go ahead to the movie ourselves.

You will note from the translations of the examples above, however, that unlike with the auxiliary ئالماق , the contracted form of the auxiliary construction (-ىۋەرمەك) differs in meaning from the full form (-ىپ بەرمەك). In this case, the contracted form serves to indicate that the action of the verb occurs or continues despite some obstacle, impediment, or hesitation.

Exercise 4: ئىشىڭىزنى قىلىۋېرىڭ!

Exercise 4.1:  Look at the verb phrases below. Each of them employs a contracted compound verb with the auxilary بەرمەك. Identify the main verb and the auxiliary verb, write each one separately in the second column from the right, then translate them into English. Follow the example.

Why do you keep talking so much?	سۆزلەپ بېرىسىز	نېمانداق سۆزلەۋېرىسىز؟
		1. كىنو كۆرۈۋەرمەڭ!
		2. سوئال سوراۋەرمەڭ.
		3. سورىماستىن كېلىۋېرىڭلار.
		4. تارتىنماستىن ئېلىۋېرىڭ.
		5. ئۆزىمىز بېرىۋەردۇق.
		6. ئۇلار كېتىۋەردى.
		7. ماقالەمنى يېزىۋەردىم.
		8. باللار سىرتتا ئويناۋەردى.
		9. قارىسام، ھاراقنى ئىچىۋەردىڭ.
		10. بۇ ئىشنى ئۆزىڭىز قىلىۋېرىڭ.
		11. تۇرپانغا ئۆزۈڭلار بېرىۋېرىڭلار.
		12. باللار سىرتتا ئويناۋەرسۇن.
		13. مەن مۇشۇ يەردە قېلىۋېرەي.
		14. بىز تاماقىمىزنى يەۋېرەيلى.
		15. ئەخمەت كىتابىنى ئوقۇۋەردى.
		16. ئۇلار بىلگىنىنى قىلىۋېرىدۇ.

Exercise 4.2:  Join the sentences below using the auxilary verb بەرمەك to express a meaning of continuity. The verb in the second clause will take the auxilary, but you should add some other material in between the clauses (i.e., conjunctions) to make the sentence clearer. Follow the example.

ئانىسى بالىلارنى ئۆيگە چاقىردى. بالىلار سىرتتا ئوينىدى.

ئانىسى بالىلارنى ئۆيگە چاقىردى، ئەمما بالىلار سىرتتا ئويناۋەردى.

1. مۇئەللىم سىنىپقا كىردى. ئوقۇغۇچىلار سۆزلەشتى.

---

2. يالغۇن خەنزۇچە بىلىدۇ. ئۇ ئۇيغۇرچە سۆزلەيدۇ.

---

3. ئۆيدە گۆش يوق ئىدى. ئانام گۆشسىز پولۇ ئەتتى.

---

4. تىلەمچى ئۆيىمىزگە ھەر كۈنى كەلدى. مەن ئۇنىڭغا پۇل بەردىم.

---

5. ئۇ نۇرغۇن سوئال سورىدى. مەن توختىماي جاۋاب بەردىم.

---

6. يامغۇر ياغدى. جون يولغا چىقتى.

---

7. ئۇ چارچىدى. بىلوگنى يازدى.

---

8. ئەنۋەرنىڭ ئۇيقۇسى كەلدى. ئۇ ماشىنا ھەيدىدى.

---

9. ئۇنىڭ قورسىقى تويدى. ئۇ تاماق يېدى.

---

10. بالا يىغلىدى. ئاكىسى ئۇخلىدى.

Exercise 4.3:  Look at the lyrics of the Uyghur folk song transcribed below. Translate them into English, paying special attention to the use of the auxilary verb بەرمەك.

promise	ۋەدە
now, at the present time	ئەمدىلىكتە
to break one's promise	يانماق
to desire, to fancy	ئارزۇلىماق
to disown	تانماق
to run away	قاچماق
to be annoyed	رەنجىمەك

باشتا قىلغان ۋەدەڭدىن ئەمدىلىكتە ياندىڭمۇ؟
باشتا ئارزۇلاپ مېنى ئەمدىلىكتە تاندىڭمۇ؟
مەيلى، كەتسەڭ كېتىۋەر، مەيلى تانساڭ، تېنىۋەر،
مەيلى قاچساڭ، قېچىۋەر،
رەنجىمەيمەن سېنىڭدىن، مەيلى كەتسەڭ كېتىۋەر...
ئاھ دەيمەن، خۇدا دەيمەن، ئايرىلغانىغا ئۆلمەيمەن،
خۇدايىم شۇنداق بۇيرۇپتۇ، بۇنى سەندىن كۆرمەيمەن،
ئالا شەپكە كىيىۋاپلا، ئاپىچە بولاي دەملا،
يۇرەككە ئوتنى سېپ قويۇپ چوڭ يولچە كېتەي دەملا.
مەيلى، كەتسەڭ كېتىۋەر، مەيلى تانساڭ، تېگىۋەر
مەيلى قاچساڭ، قېچىۋەر،
رەنجىمەيمەن سېنىڭدىن، مەيلى كەتسەڭ كېتىۋەر...

Exercise 4.4:  Now summarize the lyrics of the song in one sentence. Use the words below.

يىگىت قىز تاشلاپ كەتمەك رەنجىمەك كېتىۋەرمەك

____

____

Useful phrases ئەسقاتىدىغان ئىبارىلەر

In Uyghur, there are a number of commonly used idiomatic expressions which employ the auxiliary بەرمەك. Two common ones feature the full form ـىپ بەرمەك- :

1. ئۆلۈپ بەرمەك 'to go crazy for,' 'to die for,' 'to go gaga over' (often used after the conditional)

بالىلار ئويۇن دېسە ئۆلۈپ بېرىدۇ.
Just say the word "game" and the kids will go gaga! (lit. die)
ۋۆي، قىزلار سەندەك كېلىشكەن يىگىتنى كۆرسە، ئۆلۈپ بېرىدۇ دەيمەن...
...I'm telling you, if the girls see a handsome young guy like you they'll go crazy

2. بولۇپ بەرمەك 'to be given over to' (passions, sins); 'to be obsessed with' or 'to be hung up on' (to the point of neglecting responsibilities) (takes the dative case)

ئاغىنىسى كېلىپ، ئۇنىڭغا بولۇپ (بوپ) بەردى. ھەر كۈنى قاۋاقخانىدا.
His friend came, and now he doesn't do anything else. They're at the bar every day.
ئۆتكەن ھەپتە بالامغا كومپيۇتېر ئالغان ئىدىم.
ئەمدى ئۇنىڭغا بولۇپ (بوپ) بەردى. ئۆيدىن چىقمايدۇ.
Last week I bought a computer for my child, and now he's obsessed with it.
He doesn't leave the house.
يېڭى ماشىنا ئېلىپ ئۇنىڭغا بولاپ (بولۇپ) بەردى-دە، ھە دەپ ئۇ شەھەردىن بۇ شەھەرگە يۈرىدۇ.
He bought a new car and now he just drives back and forth from one town to another.

3. بولىۋېرىدۇ! (بولاۋېرىدۇ!) 'It's okay'; 'okay'; 'no problem'; 'whatever'

- ھازىرچە مۇشۇ تېلېۋىزورنى ئىشلىتىپ تۇرسىڭىز، ئاندىن ياخشىراقى چىقىپ قالار...
- بولىۋېرىدۇ! (بولۇپ بېرىدۇ!) بۇ تېلېۋىزورمۇ بىر ئوبدان ئىكەن.
- It's okay. This TV is also good.
- If you use this TV for a while, maybe later you will get a better one.
- نېمە تاماق يەيسىز؟ What would you like to eat?
- نېمە بولسا، بولاۋېرىدۇ! Whatever is fine!

Exercise 4.5:  Translate the following sentences into English. Pay attention to the idiomatic expressions which make use of the auxilary verb بەرمەك.

	كرىس لەڭمەن دېسە ئۆلۈپ بېرىدۇ.
	دادىسى پۇل بېرىپ، ئۇنىڭغا بولاپ بەردى.
	- نېمە ئىچىسىز؟ - نېمە بولسا بولىۋېرىدۇ.
	ساۋاقدىشىڭ پۇتبول دېسە ئۆلۈپ بېرىدۇ.
	دادىسى ماشىنا ئېلىپ بەرگەندىن كېيىن ئۇنىڭغا بولۇپ بەردى.
	توي قىلىپ ئۇنىڭغا بولۇپ بەردى، ھېچنەگە چىقماي ئۆيدىلا ئولتۇرىدۇ.
	ئوقۇشقا كىرىپ ئۇنىڭغا بولۇپ بەردى، كۇتۇبخانىدىن چىقمايدۇ.
	خەنزۇچە ئۆگىنىپ ئۇنىڭغا بولۇپ بەردى، پەقەت خەنزۇچە كىتابلار ئوقۇيدۇ.
	ئۇسسۇل ئۆگىنىپ قىزىقمغا بولۇپ بەردى، ھەر كۈنى ئۇسسۇل ئوينايدۇ.

3 Expressing Purpose and Objectives

1. Suffixes: -غىلى (-قىلى، -گىلى، -كىلى)

پولۇ پىشۇرغىلى گۈرۈچ ئالدىم. I bought rice to cook pilaf.
قەشقەرگە مەن ئۇيغۇرچە ئۆگەنگىلى كەلدىم، ماڭا ئىگىز- پەس گەپ قىلماڭ.
I came to Kashgar to learn Uyghur – don't speak so inappropriately to me.
دوستۇمنى كۆرگىلى كورلىغا باردىم. I went to Korla to see my friend.

Remember that there is no negative form of the above suffix in this function.

2. Verbal noun + postposition ئۈچۈن

سودىلىق قىلىش ئۈچۈن بازارغا باردىم. I went to the bazaar to go shopping.
تاماق يېيىش ئۈچۈن ئاشخانىغا كىردۇق. We went into the restaurant to eat.
خەت سېلىش ئۈچۈن پوچتىخانىغا باردىم. I went to the post office to mail a letter.

3. Verbal noun + suffix (-قا، -كە)

بازارغا ئالما سېتىشقا چىقتىم. I went to the bazaar to sell apples.
خوتەنگە دادامنى يوقلاشقا باردىم. I went to Khotan to visit my father.
بۇ مەھەللىگە ئويناشقا كەلدىم. I came to this neighborhood to have fun.

The negative form of purpose and objectives is possible with a verbal noun + the postposition ئۈچۈن and verbal noun + suffix (-قا، -كە) .
Look at the following examples:

پۇل بەرمەسلىك ئۈچۈن (بەرمەسلىككە) ئۇ ئۆيدىن چىقىپ كەتتى.
He left the house to avoid giving money (to his family).
بۇ ئىشنى قىلماسلىق ئۈچۈن (قىلماسلىققا) ئۇ ئۇخلىۋالدى.
She fell asleep to avoid working.
ئۇ پۇل بەرمەسلىككە شۇنداق قىلدى.
He did it to save money.

Exercise 5:  Fill in the blanks with the appropriate words below, along with one of the constructions detailed in Grammar Point 3 to indicate purpose or objective. You may have to use the same verb twice.

بىلدۈرمەك　　ئۆگەنمەك　　قىلماق　　پىشۇرماق

ئالدىرىماق　　بولماق　　كۆرمەك　　ئالماق

1. يالقۇن ئۇيغۇرچىنى ياخشىراق ________ ئۇيغۇرچە ھېكايىلار ئوقۇيدۇ.
2. كىنو ________ ئۇلار شەھەرگە باردى.
3. گىلەم ________ خوتەنگە بېرىش لازىم.
4. ساغلام ________ چېنىقىش كېرەك.
5. ئائىلەمنى ________ جۇمە كۈنى يۇرتۇمغا بارىمەن.
6. تورت ________ دۇكانغا باردىم.
7. پولۇ ________ سەۋزە بولمىسا بولمايدۇ.

Exercise 6: نېمە ئۈچۈن؟! نېمىشقا؟

Exercise 6.1: What is your goal? Ask your partner the following questions about their goals/objectives.

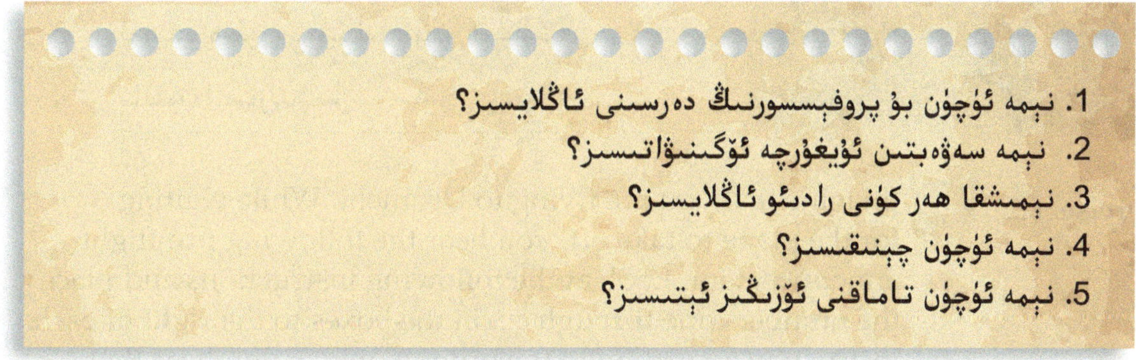

1. نېمە ئۈچۈن بۇ پروفېسسورنىڭ دەرسىنى ئاڭلايسىز؟
2. نېمە سەۋەبتىن ئۇيغۇرچە ئۆگىنىۋاتىسىز؟
3. نېمىشقا ھەر كۈنى رادىئو ئاڭلايسىز؟
4. نېمە ئۈچۈن چېنىقىسىز؟
5. نېمە ئۈچۈن تاماقنى ئۆزىڭىز ئېتىسىز؟

Exercise 6.2:  Write down five more questions to ask your partner regarding their goals or objectives.

Exercise 7:  Now write about your partner's goals and present your composition in class.

Exercise 8: ئايروپىلاندا

Exercise 8.1:  On the plane, John makes note of some safety instructions. Look at the following signs and match them with the statements below.

 ____  ____  ____  ____

ئۇچۇش جەريانىدا
تۆۋەندىكىلەر مەنئى قىلىنىدۇ:

رەسىم تارتىش	1
تاماكا چېكىش	2
ئېلېكترونلۇق ئۈسكۈنىلەرنى ئىشلىتىش	3
يانفوندا سۆزلىشىش	4

Exercise 8.2:  Imagine that you are flying to Urumchi. While waiting for the plane to take off, you hear the following pre-flight announcement. Look at the following instructions and place the numbers one through six in the boxes to the right of each instruction according to the order in which you hear them.

ھاجەتخانىدىكى «ئىس- تۈتەك كۆزەتكۈچ» كە چېقىلماڭ.	—
ئۇچۇش جەريانىدا تاماكا چېكىش مەنئى قىلىنىدۇ.	—
بىلىشكە تېگىشلىك ئىشلارنى دىققەت بىلەن ئاڭلاڭ!	—
يولۇچىلار بۆلمىسىدىكى خىزمەتچىلەرنىڭ قوماندانلىقىغا بوي سۇنۇڭ.	—
ئالدى بىلەن بىخەتەرلىك تاسمىسىنى باغلاڭ.	—
جىددىي ئەھۋال يۈز بەرگەندە ئوكسىگېن ماسكىسىنى ئىشلىتىڭ.	—

Exercise 8.3:  Because you are seated in an exit row, you recive a brochure which says that you may be asked to open the exit door and assist the crew in the event of an emergency. Read the brochure below, then look at the checklist that follows. For each item, tell whether the condition in question appears in the the brochure (Yes) or (No).

ئەگەر ئورنىڭىز جىددىي چىقىش ئېغىزى يېنىدا بولسا...

جىددىي ئەھۋال يۈز بەرگەندە، ئىشىكنى سىز ئاچىسىز ھەمدە ئايروپىلان خادىملىرىغا ھەمكارلىشىسىز. شۇڭا سىزدە تۆۋەندىكىدەك ئەھۋاللار بولسا، ئورۇن ئالماشتۇرۇشنى تەلەپ قىلىڭ:

1. بەدەن قۇۋۋىتىڭىز ۋە سالامەتلىكىڭىزنى ياخشى ئەمەس دەپ قارىسىڭىز؛
2. جىددىي ئەھۋالدا ئىشلارنى بىر تەرەپ قىلىش جۈرئىتىڭىز ۋە ئىقتىدارىڭىز كەم بولسا؛
3. ئاڭلاش، كۆرۈش، سۆزلەش ئىقتىدارىڭىز توسقۇنلۇققا ئۇچرىغان بولسا؛
4. مەزكۇر "بىلىشكە تېگىشلىك ئىشلار" نىڭ مەزمۇنىنى چۈشىنەلمىسىڭىز؛
5. كىچىك بالا ئېلىۋالغان بولسىڭىز؛
6. باشقىلارنى قۇتقۇزۇشنى خالىمىسىڭىز؛
7. يېشىڭىز 15 ياشتىن تۆۋەن بولسا.

You may ask to be reseated if:

	Yes	No
1. You believe that the physical exertion required to open the exit would injure you.		
2. You do not understand the instructions in this brochure.		
3. You do not wish to save others.		
4. You do not think you can reach the exit, open it, and get out quickly.		
5. You are less than 15 years of age.		
6. You are not able to give oral commands to others.		
7. You have a physical condition which may prevent you from helping.		
8. You have other responsibilities such as a small child to care for.		

Exercise 8.4:  Let's see how well you understand the following safety instructions. Match the Uyghur instructions with their English equivalents by drawing a line from one to the other.

بىخەتەرلىكىڭىز ئۈچۈن بىلىشكە تېگىشلىك ئىشلار:

Things you should know for your safety:

Follow all instructions given by crew members.	بىلىشكە تېگىشلىك ئىشلارنى تەپسىلىي ئوقۇپ چىقىڭ.
Do not tamper with the smoke detector in the lavatory.	جىددىي ئەھۋال يۈز بەرگەندە ئوكسىگېن ماسكىسىنى ئىشلىتىڭ.
During the flight smoking is prohibited.	بىخەتەرلىك تاسمىسىنى باغلاڭ.
Use the oxygen mask if there is an emergency.	يولۇچىلار بۆلمىسىدىكى خىزمەتچىلەرنىڭ قوماندانلىقىغا بوي سۇنۇڭ.
Read the safety instructions carefully.	ھاجەتخانىدىكى «ئىس- تۈتەك كۆزەتكۈچ» كە چېقىلماڭ.
Buckle your seatbelt.	ئۇچۇش جەريانىدا تاماكا چېكىش مەنئى قىلىنىدۇ.

Exercise 9: ئۆزۈمنى تونۇشتۇرىمەن!

Exercise 9.1:  Imagine that you have won a scholarship and are going to study in Urumchi for one year. Look at the list below and put the tasks in order to organize your first day in Urumchi. Note that there is no correct order, but be sure to make a logical sequence.

___	1. شىنجاڭ ئۇنىۋېرسىتېتىغا بېرىپ ئۆزۈمنى تىزىملىتىمەن.
___	2. ياتاققا بېرىپ، نەرسىلىرىمنى جايلاشتۇرىمەن.
___	3. تاماقتىن كېيىن باغچىغا بېرىپ دەم ئالىمەن.
___	4. ئۈرۈمچىگە كېلىپلا دوستۇمغا تېلېفون قىلىمەن.
___	5. ياتاق مەسىلىسىنى ھەل قىلىمەن.
___	6. دوستۇم بىلەن شەھەر ئايلىنىپ، ئۇيغۇر ئاشخانىسىدا تاماق يەيمەن.
___	7. بازارغا بېرىپ پۇل ئالماشتۇرىمەن.
___	8. ئوقۇغۇچىلىق كېنىشكىسى ئېلىپلا، بازاردىن تېلېفون سېتىۋالىمەن.
___	9. كىتابخانىغا بېرىپ دەرسلىك كىتاب ئالىمەن.
___	10. نىمكەشماللار بازىرىغا بېرىپ ئەرزانراق بىر ۋېلسىپىت ئالىمەن.
___	11. چوڭراق بىر ماگىزىننى تېپىپ ئازراق سودىلىق قىلىمەن.

Exercise 9.2: Get together with your partner and compare your answers.

Exercise 10: ئۈرۈمچىگە خوش كەپسىز!

Exercise 10.1: John arrives in Urumchi and gives a call to his friend Yasin. Listen to the dialogue between them and answer the following questions.

1. جون سائەت نەچچىدە ئۈرۈمچىگە كەلدى؟
2. نېمە ئۈچۈن ياسىن جوننى سائەت سەككىزدە كېلىدۇ دەپ ئويلىدى؟
3. ئۇلار قەيەردە //نەدە كۆرۈشىدۇ؟
4. 40 كوي قانچە دوللار بولىدۇ؟

Exercise 10.2: Now practice reading the dialogue between John and Yasin aloud with your partner.

ياسىن : ۋەي!
جون: ئەسسالامۇ ئەلەيكۇم!
ياسىن : ۋەئەلەيكۇم ئەسسالام! سىز كىم؟
جون : مەن جون.
ياسىن : جون؟ سىز ئۈرۈمچىگە كېلىپ بولدىڭىزمۇ؟
جون : شۇنداق.
ياسىن : قاۋۇل سىزنى سائەت سەككىزدە بارىدۇ دېگەن.
جون: مەن سائەت ئالتىدە كەلدىم.
ياسىن : ئاپلا! مەن خاتالىشىپتىمەن. قاۋۇل سىزنى بېيجىڭ ۋاقتى بىلەن سەككىزدە يېتىپ بارىدۇ
دېگەن ئىكەندە. مەن سىزنى ئۈرۈمچى ۋاقتى سائەت سەككىزدە كېلىدۇ دەپ ئويلاپتىمەن.
جون: ھېچقىسى يوق. شىنجاڭ ئۇنىۋېرسىتېتىغا قانداق بارىمەن؟
ياسىن : سىز قەيەردە؟
جون : مەن ھازىر ئايرودرومدا.
ياسىن : ھە، ئۇنداقتا تاكسىغا ئولتۇرۇڭ.
جون: تاكسى قىممەتمۇ؟
ياسىن : ئانچە قىممەت ئەمەس. قىرىق كويغا شىنجاڭ ئۇنىۋېرسىتېتىغا ئەكىلىدۇ.
جون : بەك ئەرزان ئىكەن. قىرىق كوي ئالتە-يەتتە دوللار دېگەن گەپ. ئەمىسە تاكسىغا ئولتۇراي.
سىز بىلەن نەدە كۆرۈشىمىز؟
ياسىن : مەن شىنجاڭ ئۇنىۋېرسىتېتىنىڭ ئالدىغا بېرىپ تۇرىمەن.
جون : ماقۇل ئەمىسە... مانا تاكسىمۇ كەلدى...

Exercise 10.3:  Imagine that you receive a phone call from your Uyghur friend. He says that he has just arrived in New York from Beijing, and he is asking for advice on how to get to Los Angeles. Get together with your partner and create your own dialogue. First, give your partner suggestions, then remind him about the time difference between New York and Los Angeles. Act out your dialogue.

Help:
(1) Your flight from New York to Los Angeles departs at 2:00 pm.
(2) Flight time is about four hours.
(3) Los Angeles time is three hours behind New York time.

Exercise 11: ساياھەتنىڭ باشلىنىشى

Exercise 11.1:  Before school starts, John's goals are to: (1) see the kariz; (2) try famous grapes in Turpan; (3) visit the Id Kah mosque; (4) visit the tombs of Mahmud Kashgari and Yüsüp Khas Hajib.
On the lines below, translate John's goals from the list above into Uyghur. The first is done for you as an example.

جون تۇرپانغا كارىزنى كۆرۈش ئۈچۈن (كۆرۈشكە، كۆرگىلى) بارىدۇ.

Exercise 11.2:  John makes a map of his journey. Based on his map below, summarize his upcoming trip. The first leg of his journey has been described for you.

جون ساياھەتنى ئۈرۈمچىدىن باشلايدۇ. ئۇ ئاۋۋال ئاپتوبۇستا
(ئاپتوبۇس بىلەن) تۇرپانغا بارىدۇ...

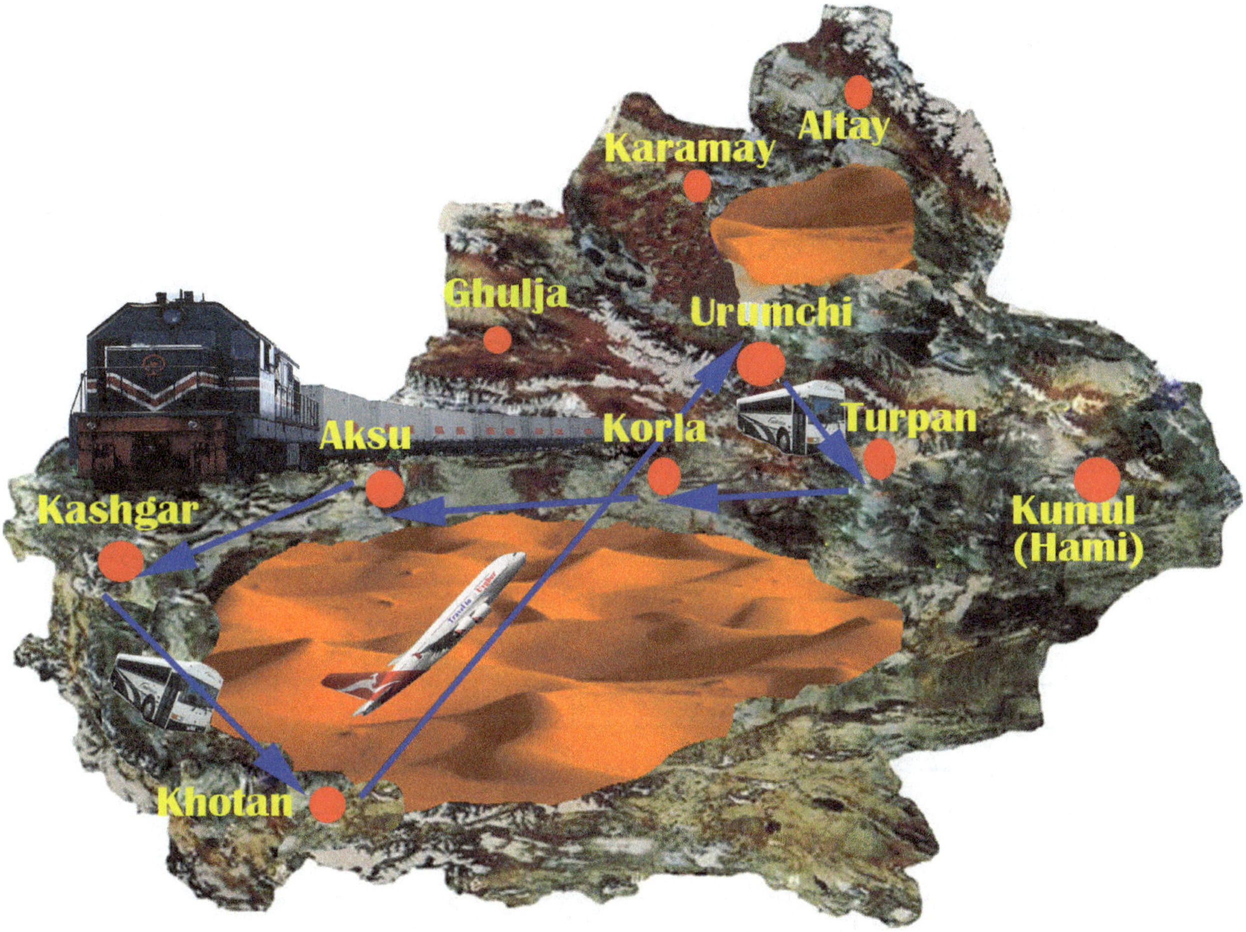

Exercise 12: ئۈزۈم ماكانى - تۇرپان

Exercise 12.1:  Read the following passage about Turpan and translate it into English.

تۇرپان شىنجاڭدىكى ئەڭ قەدىمىي شەھەرلەرنىڭ بىرى. تارىخىي مەنبەلەرگە قارىغاندا، تۇرپان مىلادىدىن ئىككى ئەسىر بۇرۇن قۇرۇلغان. بىر زامانلاردا تۇرپان ئىدىقۇت ئۇيغۇر خاندانلىقىنىڭ پايتەختى بولغان. ئۇ بۈيۈك يىپەك يولىنىڭ ئوتتۇرىسىغا جايلاشقان. تۇرپان دۇنياغا ئۆزىنىڭ قەدىمىيلىكى بىلەنلا ئەمەس، بەلكى ئاتاقلىق مىڭ ئۆي بىلەن، ئۈزۈمزارلىقى بىلەن، قەدىمىي كارىزلىرى بىلەن تونۇش. مىڭ ئۆي* يادىكارلىقى تۇرپاندىن 50 كىلومېتر يىراقلىقتا جايلاشقان. بۇددا دىنى دەۋرىدە شۇ يەردىكى تاغلارنىڭ ئىچىدە ئىبادەتخانىلار قۇرۇلۇپ، تاملىرى بۇددانىڭ ھاياتىغا بېغىشلانغان سۈرەتلەر بىلەن بېزەلگەن. بۇ سۈرەتلەر مىلادىدىن بۇرۇن ياسىلىپ، كۆپ قېتىم بۇزغۇنچىلىققا ئۇچرىغان بولسىمۇ، ئاتمىشتىن ئارتۇق ئۆڭكۈر ياخشى ساقلىنىپ قالغان. دۇنيانى ھەيران قالدۇرغان ھەيۋەتلىك تام سۈرەتلىرىنى باشقا ھېچ نەرسە بىلەن سېلىشتۇرۇشقا بولمايدۇ.

كارىز - يەرنىڭ ئاستىدا قېزىلغان قۇدۇق سىستېمىسى. ئۇزاق ئەسىرلەر داۋامىدا يەرلىك دېھقانلار ئېتىزلىرىنى سۇغۇرۇش ئۈچۈن چۆلدە كارىزلارنى كولاپ يەرنىڭ ئاستىدا سۇنى ساقلاپ قېلىش يولىنى تاپقان. بۇ كارىزلار ھازىرمۇ تەكلىماكان چۆلىدىكى ئاۋات يەرلەرنى سۇ بىلەن تەمىنلەيدۇ. تۇرپانىنىڭ "ئۈزۈم ماكانى" دېگەن نامى بار. سەۋەبى شەھەرنىڭ ئىچى ۋە تېشى ئۈزۈم بىلەن تولغان. شۇنداقلا 15 كىلومېتىرغا سوزۇلغان ئۈزۈم باراڭلىرى شەھەرنى سېپىلدەك ئوراپ تۇرىدۇ. تۇرپاندا ئۈزۈمدىن شاراب ۋە ھەر تۈرلۈك شىرنىلەرنى ياسايدۇ، ئۇرۇقسىز ئۈزۈمدىن كىشمىش قۇرۇتىدۇ. ھازىر تۇرپان شارابى دۇنياغا كەڭ تارقالدى ھەم ياۋروپانىڭ داڭلىق شارابلىرى بىلەن بىر قاتاردا تۇرىدۇ. تۇرپاندىكىدەك پۈتۈن شەھەرنى قاپلىغان ئۈزۈمزارلىقلار دۇنيانىڭ باشقا يېرىدە يوق دېسەك خاتالاشمايمىز. تۇرپانىنى قەدىمىي مۆجىزە شەھەر دېسەكمۇ بولىدۇ، سەۋەبى بۇ شەھەر تەكلىماكان چۆلىنىڭ شىمالىدىكى گۈلزارلىق شەھەر. يازدا تۇرپانىنىڭ ھاۋاسى ناھايىتى ئىسسىق ۋە قۇرغاق.

Thousand (Budda) Caves - مىڭ ئۆي

prosperous	ئاۋات
trellis	باراڭ
miracle	مۆجىزە
a flower bed	گۈلزارلىق
to devote (to)	بېغىشلىماق
magnificent	ھەيۋەتلىك
historical relics	يادىكارلىق
A.D.	مىلادى

source	مەنبە
temple	ئىبادەتخانا
to decorate	بېزىمەك
picture	سۈرەت
cave	ئۆڭكۈر
a well	قۇدۇق
to dig	قازماق / كولىماق
to preserve	ساقلاپ قالماق

Exercise 12.2:  In the rightmost column, there are a few main ideas from the passage. Look at each word or phrase, then draw a line to the sentence in the leftmost column that best fits it.

ئۇزاق ئەسىرلەر داۋامىدا يەرلىك دېھقانلار ئېتىزلىرىنى سۇغۇرۇش ئۈچۈن چۆلدە كارىزلارنى كولاپ يەرنىڭ ئاستىدا سۇنى ساقلاپ قېلىش يولىنى تاپقان.
سەۋەبى شەھەرنىڭ ئىچى ۋە تېشى ئۈزۈم بىلەن تولغان.
مەسىلەن، تۇرپاندا ئاتاقلىق مىڭ ئۆي، چۆلدە ئۆسكەن ئۈزۈمزارلىقلار، قەدىمي كارىزلار مەۋجۇت.
تارىخي مەنبەلەرگە قارىغاندا تۇرپان مىلادىدىن ئىككى ئەسىر بۇرۇن قۇرۇلغان.

قەدىمي شەھەر
داڭلىق يادىكارلىقلار
كارىز
ئۈزۈم ماكانى

Exercise 12.3:  Read the following sentences from the passage in Exercise 12.1 and fill in the blanks with the appropriate words below. Try to not look at the passage!

ئوتتۇرىسىغا	چېتىگە	باشقۇرىدۇ	تەمسىلەيدۇ	مۆجىزە	مەركىزى
چۆلنىڭ	ئۇرۇقسىز	پايتەختى	تەملىك	مىڭ ئۆي	ھەيۋەتلىك

1. قەدىمدە تۇرپان ئىدىقۇت ئۇيغۇر خانلىقىنىڭ ____________ بولغان.
2. تۇرپان دۇنياغا مەشھۇر ____________ بىلەن تونۇش.
3. كارىزلار ھازىرمۇ ئېتىزلارنى سۇ بىلەن ____________ .
4. ____________ قىزىل ئۈزۈمدىن شاراپ ياسايدۇ ۋە كىشمىش قۇرۇتىدۇ.
5. تۇرپاننى قەدىمي ____________ شەھەر دېسەكمۇ بولىدۇ.

Exercise 12.4: Now answer the following questions about Turpan.

1. مىڭ ئۆي يادىكارلىقى توغرۇلۇق نېمە بىلىسىز؟
2. كارىز توغرۇلۇقچۇ؟
3. نېمە ئۈچۈن تۇرپاندا كارىزلار پەيدا بولغان؟
4. نېمە ئۈچۈن تۇرپاننى "ئۈزۈم ماكانى" دەيدۇ؟
5. تۇرپان ئۈزۈملىرىدىن قانداق مەھسۇلاتلار ئىشلەپ چىقىرىلىدۇ؟

Exercise 13: تۇرپان ئۈزۈملىرى

Now you will watch an informational video about grape and wine production in the famous grape-growing region of Turpan.

Exercise 13.1:  Watch the first segment, in which a guide introduces different varieties of grapes in Turpan.

1. What sorts of grapes are grown in Turpan? The guide mentions six varieties. Mark at least five from the following:

كىشمىش   سېرىق ئۈزۈم   قاشقىر   قىزىل ئۈزۈم   بىجاقىي
قارا ئۈزۈم   قاپاق سايىۋى   غۇنچە ئۈزۈم

2. The guide said that farmers prefer to grow the grape variety know as كىشمىش. This type of the grape presents 90% of the whole grape growing industry in Turpan. What is the reason behind this?

Exercise 13.2:  Watch the second segment. After watching, answer the questions below.

1.What did you learn about the wine production in Turpan?
2. Do they export their wines to other countries?
3. Which type of wine do European people prefer?

Useful phrases ئەسقاتىدىغان ئىبارىلەر

Do you recall how to ask for advice/suggestions/directions? Use a main verb in the conditional mood with the verb بولماق. Look at the following examples:

How can I get to that restaurant? بۇ ئاشخانىغا قانداق بارسام بولىدۇ؟
Can I get to the library via 3rd street? كۈتۈپخانىغا ئۈچىنچى كوچا بىلەن بارسام بولامدۇ؟
Can I write the article at night (i.e. tonight)? ماقالىنى كەچتە يازسام بولامدۇ؟
Can I buy a ticket beforehand? بېلەتنى بالدۇرراق ئالسام بولامدۇ؟

Do you remember any words and phrases commonly used to give directions?

keep straight ئۇدۇل (توغرا) مېڭىڭ
take a right/left turn ئوڭغا// سولغا قايرىلىڭ (بۇرۇلۇڭ)
turn back ئارقىغا يېنىڭ (قايتىڭ)
walk until the crossroad تۆت كوچىغىچە مېڭىڭ
take right after the stop light قىزىل چىراقتىن ئوڭغا بۇرۇلۇڭ
follow the main road چوڭ يولنى بويلاپ مېڭىڭ
cross the street يولدىن ئۆتۈڭ

Exercise 14: Ask your partner for directions from your classroom to two of the following places: (the library, a nearby restaurant, the post office, an administration office).

Exercise 15: بۇ ئەتراپتا مېهمانخانا بارمۇ؟

Exercise 15.1: John is in Turpan. On the street, he meets an Uyghur man and asks him if there is a hotel nearby. Listen to the first part of their dialogue and write down John's question.

Exercise 15.2: From the dialogue you just have heard, you can tell that John did not understand the directions well. What about you? Listen to the passage one more time and explain how to get to the Turpan Hotel.

Exercise 15.3: *How can I get to…?* Ask your partner for the following directions.

1. بۇ ئەتراپتىكى ئەڭ ياخشى رېستوران قايسى؟ ئۇنىڭغا قانداق بارسام بولىدۇ؟
2. قولىڭىزدىكى كىتابنى قايسى دۇكاندىن ئالسام بولىدۇ؟ بۇ دۇكانغا قانداق بارىمەن؟
3. مەكتەپ دوختۇرخانىسىغا پىيادە بارسام بولامدۇ؟ قايسى ئاپتوبۇسقا چۈشسەم تېزرەك بارىمەن؟ بۇ ئاپتوبۇسنىڭ بېكىتى قەيەردە؟
4. بۈگۈن ئانامنىڭ تۇغۇلغان كۈنى ئىدى. ئانامغا قانداق سوۋغا ئالسام بولىدۇ؟ گۈل بازىرىغا قانداق بارىمەن؟

Exercise 15.4:  Now read the rest of the conversation between John and Arslan aka and translate all the underlined words and expressions.

جون: كەچۈرۈڭ، ئىسمىڭىزنى سورىماپتىمەن.

ئارسلان ئاكا: مېنىڭ ئىسمىم ئارسلان.

جون: ئارسلان ئاكا، ياردىمىڭىز ئۈچۈن رەھمەت. تۇرپاندا ھېچ كىمنى تونۇمايمەن دەپ ئەنسىرىگەن ئىدىم.

ئارسلان ئاكا: ئەنسىرەشنىڭ ھاجىتى يوق، بالام. ئۇيغۇرلار ناھايىتى مېھماندوست خەلق. ھېچ كىم سىزدىن ياردىمىنى ئايىمايدۇ. ئەگەر يەنە بىرەر نەرسە لازىم بولسا، تارتىنماي سوراۋېرىڭ.

جون: رەھمەت سىزگە. ئەتىلىككە شەھەر ئايلانغۇم بار*. نەلەرگە بارسام بولىدۇ؟

ئارسلان ئاكا: تۇرپاندا ساياھەت ئورۇنلىرى ناھايىتى كۆپ. مەسىلەن، ئىمىن ۋاڭ مۇنارى، ئىدىقۇت قەدىمىي شەھىرى، بۈيلۈق، بېزەكلىك مىڭ ئۆي، كارىز مۇزېيى، ئايدىڭ كۆل قاتارلىق جايلارغا بارسىڭىز بولىدۇ.

جون: پاھ، بارىدىغان يەرلەر ناھايىتى كۆپ ئىكەنغۇ.

ئارسلان ئاكا: شۇنداق. تۇرپاننى ساياھەتچىلەر بەكمۇ ياخشى كۆرىدۇ.

جون: بىلىمەن، شۇڭا مەنمۇ تۇرپاننى بىر كۆرۈپ كېتەي دەپ كەلگەن ئىدىم. ماقۇل ئەمسە، ئارسلان ئاكا، يەنە كۆرۈشۈپ قالارمىز.

ئارسلان ئاكا: ئەلۋەتتە. مەن ھەر كۈنى مۇشۇ يەردە. نېمە لازىم بولسا كېلىڭ، جۈمۇ.

جون: بولىدۇ، مەن ماڭاي. خوش!

ئارسلان ئاكا: خوش، بالام، خۇدايىمغا ئامانەت.

*-غۇم بار this expresses desire (see page 179)

Exercise 15.5:  The passage mentions **six** attractions in Turpan. Look at the following pictures and name them based on the descriptions in the previous passage.

____

____

____

____

____

____

Exercise 16: تۇرپان كارىزلىرى

Here you will watch another informational video about *kareez*, an underground water transportation and irrigation system commonly employed in the Turpan area.

Exercise 16.1: Before watching look up the following words:

brook	ئېرىق
to be connected	ئۇلانماق
deep	چوڭقۇر
shallow	تېيىز

a creation	كەشپىيات
underground	يەر ئاستى
well	قۇدۇق
stream	ئۆستەڭ

Exercise 16.2:  After watching the video, tell if the statements below are true or false.

توغرا	خاتا

1. تۇرپاننىڭ يازپەسلى ناھايىتى ئىسسىق، شۇڭا سۇنىڭ پارغا ئايلىنىش مىقدارى يۇقۇرى.
2. كارىز يەر ئاستى قۇدۇقلىرىدىن ئىبارەت.
3. يەر ئاستى قۇدۇقلىرى تۇرۇبا ئارقىلىق بىر- بىرىگە ئۇلىنىدۇ.
4. باش تەرەپتىكى قۇدۇقلار تېيىزرەك بولىدۇ.
5. ئەڭ ئۇزۇن كارىز ئون كىلومېتىرچە كېلىدۇ.
6. كارىزلارنىڭ ئومۇمىي ئۇزۇنلۇقى بەش مىڭ كىلومېتىردىن ئاشىدۇ.
7. كارىزنىڭ "سەددىچىن سېپىلى" دېگەن نامى بار.

Exercise 16.3: In the video you heard an Uyghur proverb:

ئەر ئۆلسە چىراغ ئۆچىدۇ، كارىز ئۆلسە ئەل كۆچىدۇ.

Translate it into English and then discuss its meaning with the instructor.

4 Expressing Desire

To express a wish (desire) the suffix -غۇم (-گۇم، -قۇم، -كۇم) is added to the verb stem + words بار//يوق.

In the dialogue, you see the sentence ئەتىلىككە شەھەر ئايلانغۇم بار.
It can be translated into English as "I would like to see the city tomorrow. // I want to see the city tomorrow." Look at the following chart:

	Singular	Plural
1st person	(مېنىڭ) -غۇم (-گۇم، -قۇم، -كۇم)	(بىزنىڭ) -غۇمىز (-گۇمىز، -قۇمىز، -كۇمىز)
2nd person	(سېنىڭ) - غۇڭ (-گۇڭ، -قۇڭ، -كۇڭ) (سىزنىڭ)-غۇڭىز(-گۇڭىز، -قۇڭىز، -كۇڭىز)	(سىلەرنىڭ) -غۇڭلار(-گۇڭلار، -قۇڭلار، -كۇڭلار)
3rd person	(ئۇنىڭ، ئۇلارنىڭ) -غۇسى (-گۇسى، -قۇسى، -كۇسى)	

Look at the following examples:

خوتەن قاش تېشىنى كۆرگۈم بار.
I would like to see the Khotan jade.
ماشىنا ئالغۇمىز بار، ئەمما پۇلىمىز يوق.
We want to buy a car, but we have no money.
Do you want to go to this wedding? بۇ تويغا بارغۇڭ بارمۇ؟
He does not want to do this. ئۇنىڭ بۇ ئىشنى قىلغۇسى يوق.
Don't you want to cook? تاماق ئەتكۇڭىز يوقمۇ؟
Would you like to eat pilaf today? بۈگۈن پولۇ يېگۈڭلار بارمۇ؟
They don't want to buy a knife. ئۇلارنىڭ پىچاق ئالغۇسى يوق.

Exercise 17: Using the construction explained above, ask your partner a few questions about his/her wishes or desires. Follow the example.

لەڭمەن يېگۈڭ بارمۇ؟ تۇرپانغا بارغۇڭلار بارمۇ؟

Exercise 18: What have you learned about Turpan from the materials presented thus far? Share your thoughts with your classmates.

Exercise 19: قەشقەرگە سەپەر

Exercise 19.1: Now you will take a trip to modern Kashgar. Before your journey begins, discuss the following questions.

1. سىز قەشقەرگە بارغانمۇ؟ بۇ شەھەرنى قانداق تەسەۋۋۇر قىلىسىز؟
2. يىپەك يولى ھەققىدە نېمىلەرنى بىلىسىز؟
3. مەھمۇد كاشغەرى ۋە يۈسۈپ خاس ھاجىپ كىم؟
4. ھېيتگاھ مەسچىتى توغرۇلۇق نېمە بىلىسىز؟

Exercise 19.2: Look at the words below. Place each word into the column beneath the appropriate category in the table that follows.

دۇتار ئۈزۈك مانتا سۇناي داپ نەي ئەتلەس ئۈزۈك گىلەم پىچاق
راۋاب ئۆپكە - ھېسىپ بىلەيزۈك غىجەك ياپما دوپپا ساپايى تەمبۇر

چالغۇ ئەسۋابلىرى	قول ھۈنەر بۇيۇملىرى	ئۇيغۇر تاماقلىرى	زىبۇ زىننەت بۇيۇملىرى

Exercise 19.3: Listen to the passage in which the narrator takes you on a tour of Kashgar. Then fill out the information section of the following table in English with details regarding each place.

مەلۇمات	ئورۇن
	ئاپئاق خوجا مەقبەرىسى
	مەھمۇت قەشقەرى مازىرى
	يۈسۈپ خاس ھاجىپ مازىرى
	ھېيتگاھ مەسچىتى

Exercise 19.4:  Now read the excerpt below from the passage you just listened to and answer the questions that follow in English.

قېنى، قەشقەرنىڭ چوڭ بازىرىغا ئۆتەيلى. نېمىلەر يوق بۇ بازاردا... ئەمگەكچان، مېھنەت سۆيەر خەلقىم... مانا تۈرلۈك قول ھۈنەر بۇيۇملىرى، مىللىي ئۇسلۇبتىكى زىبۇزىننەت بۇيۇملىرىدىن ھالقا، مارجان، ئۈزۈك، بىلەيزۈكلەر... مانا قولدا توقۇلغان گىلەملەر، ھەر خىل كىيىملەر، رەختلەر... نېمىدېگەن چىرايلىق ئەتلەسلەر... مانا مىللىي چالغۇ ئەسۋابلار: دۇتار، راۋاب، غېجەك، تەمبۇر، ساپايى، داپ، نەي، سۇناي... سەنئەتكار خەلقىمىنىڭ ئون ئىككى مۇقامى خىيالىمدىن ئۆتتى. بۇ مۇقاملاردا ئۇيغۇر خەلقىنىڭ ھاياتى، گۈزەل روھىي دۇنياسى، قايغۇ - ھەسرەتلىرى ناخشا، مۇزىكا، ئۇسسۇل ئارقىلىق ئىپادىلەنگەن.

1. How does the narrator describe the Kashgar bazaar?
2. What attracts most visitors to this bazaar?
3. Why does the narrator mention the "Uyghur Twelve Muqam" in the passage?
4. What do the Muqam tell us about the Uyghurs?

Uyghur Twelve Muqam

The Uyghur Twelve Muqam (i.e. musical modes or scales) were developed in Central Asia over 500 years ago after the appearance of the Arabic maqamat modal system, which had given birth to many musical genres among the various peoples of Eurasia and North Africa. The most well-known Uyghur muqam are the following twelve: Rak, Chäbiyat, Segah, Chahargah, Pänjigah, Özhal, Äjäm, Oshaq, Bayat, Nava, Mushavräk, and Iraq. The "Twelve Muqam" were revised and systematized by Queen Amannisakhan during the reign of Sultan Abdureshid Khan. Their history and the musical repertoire which employs them reflect the history, culture, wisdom, knowledge, lifestyle, and unique musical language of the Uyghur people. Uyghurs also have local muqam systems named after the places in which they originated, such as Dolan, Ili, Kumul, and Turfan.

Exercise 20: قەشقەردىكى ئۇيغۇر رېستورانىدا

Exercise 20.1:  John goes to an ئاشخانا in Kashgar and overhears a conversation between a foreigner and the waitress. Read their conversation and circle all the imperatives.

little, bit	سەل
delicious	ئوخشىغان
fluent	راۋان
noodle soup	سۈيۈقئاش
yoghurt	قېتىق
very	ئەجەب

كۈتكۈچى: كەلسىلە، ئولتارسىلا...
خېرىدار: ياخشىمۇسىز!
كۈتكۈچى: نېمە يەيلا ؟
خېرىدار: قانداق تاماق بار؟
كۈتكۈچى: ھەممە تاماق بار. پولۇ يەيمەن دېسىڭىز، سەل تۇرۇپ پىشىدۇ.
لەڭمەن، مانتا بۇيرىسىڭىز، ھازىرلا تەييار بولىدۇ. ئۆپكە-ھېسىپمۇ بار. يا
سۈيۈقئاش ئىچەملا؟ ھەراست، قېتىقمۇ بار...
خېرىدار: كاۋاپچۇ؟ كاۋاپ بارمۇ؟
كۈتكۈچى: ئۇيغۇر ئاشخانىسىدا ئەلۋەتتە كاۋاپ بولىدۇ! كاۋاپ يەملا؟
خېرىدار: ھەئە، مەن ئۇيغۇر كاۋىپىغا ئامراق. بەش زىق كاۋاپ، يەنە بەش
مانتا ئالاي.
كۈتكۈچى: ھازىر تەييار بولىدۇ. تاماق كەلگۈچە چاي ئىچىپ تۇرسىلا. كۆك چاي
ئىچەملا، پەمىل چايمۇ؟
خېرىدار: كۆك چاي ئىچەي.
كۈتكۈچى: قېتىقچۇ؟ شۇنداق ئوخشىغان قېتىق بار.
خېرىدار: ماقۇل، قېتىق ئىچەي.
كۈتكۈچى: مانا قېتىق. كەچۈرۈڭ، بىر ئىشنى سورىسام بولامدۇ؟
خېرىدار: سوراۋېرىڭ.
كۈتكۈچى: سىز بۇ يەرلىككە ئوخشىمايدىكەنسىز. سىز قەيەرلىك؟
خېرىدار: مەن ئاۋسترالىيەلىك.
كۈتكۈچى: شۇنداقمۇ؟ توۋا، ئۇيغۇرچىڭىز ئەجەب ياخشىكەنە. مەن تېخى سىزنى تاتار دەپ ئويلاپتىمەن.
خېرىدار: مەن شىنجاڭغا كەلگىلى تۆت يىل بولدى.
كۈتكۈچى: مۇنداق دەڭ، شۇڭا ئۇيغۇرچىنى راۋان سۆزلەيدىكەنسىز-دە.
خېرىدار: رەھمەت. لېكىن تېخى كۆپ نەرسىلەرنى ئۆگىنىشىم كېرەك.
كۈتكۈچى: ياخشى... مەن تاماقىڭىزنى ئەكىلەي.
خېرىدار: بۇ قېتىق نېمىدېگەن ياخشى! سىڭلىم، يەنە بىر چىنە ئەكەلسىڭىز*.
كۈتكۈچى: مانا ھازىر.
خېرىدار: رەھمەت، بۇ قېتىق ناھايىتى تەملىك ئىكەن.
كۈتكۈچى: شۇنداق، بۇ ئاشخانىدا تاماق يېگەنلەر قېتىق ئىچمەي كەتمەيدۇ.
مانا تاماقىڭىز تەييار بولدى، ئالسىلا. يەنە بىر نېمە لازىم بولسا، چاقىرسىلا.
خېرىدار: رەھمەت .

*ئەكەلسىڭىز (ئېلىپ كەلسىڭىز) - This type of compound verbs are introduced in chapter 8

5 Super Polite Form of Imperative With -سلا/-سله

1. There are two types of imperatives (commands and requests) in Uyghur: informal and formal. The informal imperative has two forms:

(1) Using the steam of the verb: بار، ئال، كەل
(2) Adding suffix -غىن (-قىن، -كىن، -گىن) to the stem of the verb:

يازغىن، دېگىن، كەتكىن

As you remember, the formal imperative is formed by adding the suffixes -ڭ،(-ىڭ، -ۇڭ، -ۈڭ) to the stem:

كەچۈرۈڭ، ئېلىڭ، ئولتۇرۇڭ، قاراڭ، ئاڭلاڭ...

However, there is another, "super polite" form of the formal imperative with the suffix -سلا/-سله in Uyghur: Look at the following examples:

ماڭا قارىسىلا، كەلسىلە، ئالسىلا، ئاڭلىسىلا...

The suffix -سلا/ -سله consists of the conditional suffix -سا/-سە plus plural ending -لار/ -لەر, in which the last consonsnt ر drops.

You will frequently hear this super polite form in southern Xinjiang. Usually it is used to express high respect to elder people and honored guests.

2. In line 3 of the dialogue, the waitress asks the question نېمە يەيلا؟ instead of نېمە يەيسىز؟ Here the suffix -لا is used in the interrogative form of the present-future tense in order to express the highest respect to elder people, guests, customers, and so forth. Compare the following examples:

سىلى بازارغا ئەتە بارامىلا؟
سىز بازارغا ئەتە بارامسىز؟
Will you go to the bazaar tomorrow?
سىلى چاي ئىچەمىلا ؟
سىز چاي ئىچەمسىز ؟
Would you like a cup of tea?
ئەرزانراق بەرسەم ئالامىلا؟
ئەرزانراق بەرسەم ئالامسىز؟
If I give it to you for a cheaper price, will you buy it?

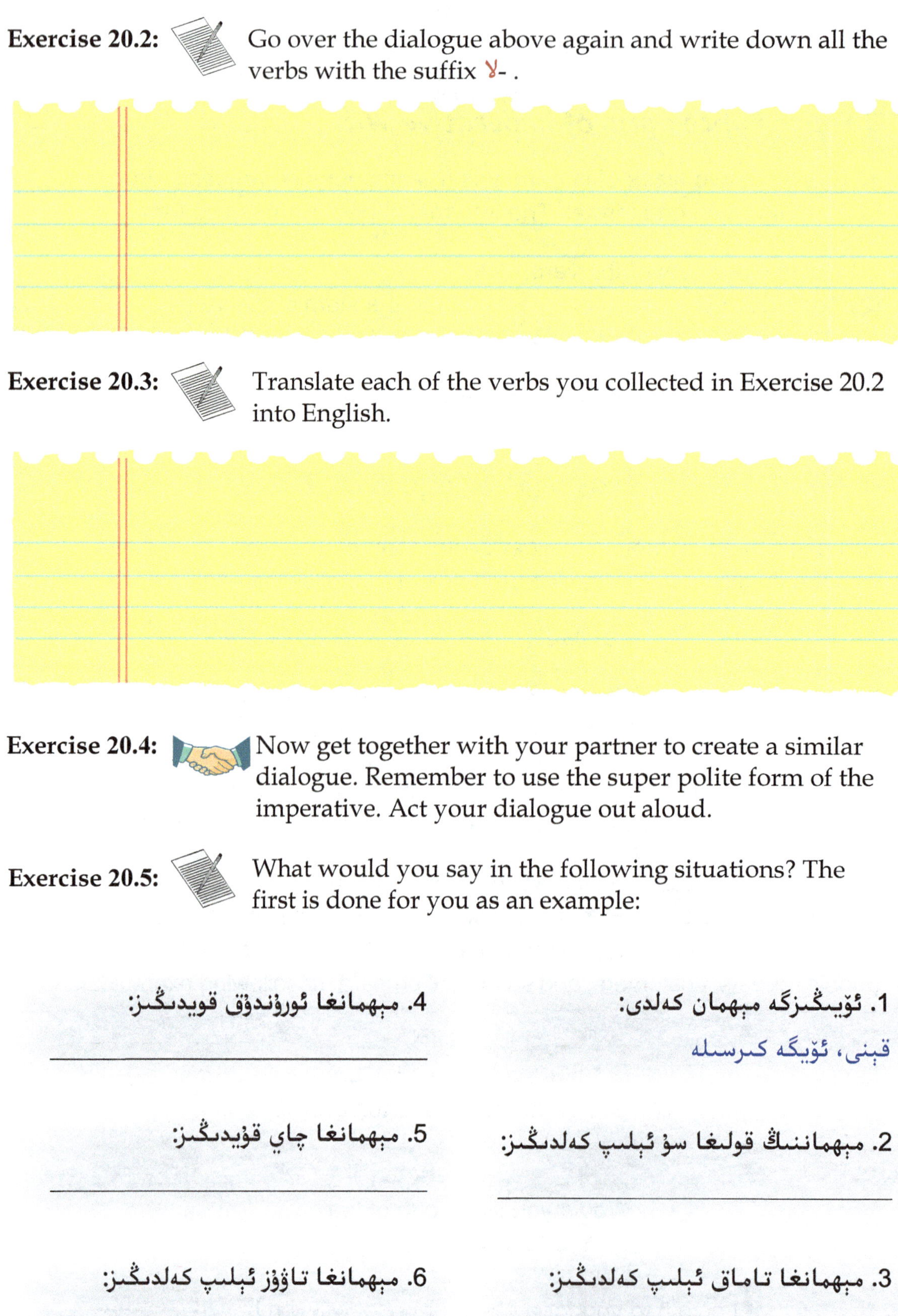

Exercise 20.2: Go over the dialogue above again and write down all the verbs with the suffix لا- .

Exercise 20.3: Translate each of the verbs you collected in Exercise 20.2 into English.

Exercise 20.4: Now get together with your partner to create a similar dialogue. Remember to use the super polite form of the imperative. Act your dialogue out aloud.

Exercise 20.5: What would you say in the following situations? The first is done for you as an example:

1. ئۆيىڭىزگە مېھمان كەلدى:

قېنى، ئۆيگە كىرسىلە

2. مېھماننىڭ قولىغا سۇ ئېلىپ كەلدىڭىز:

____

3. مېھمانغا تاماق ئېلىپ كەلدىڭىز:

____

4. مېھمانغا ئورۇندۇق قويدىڭىز:

____

5. مېھمانغا چاي قۇيدىڭىز:

____

6. مېھمانغا تاۋۇز ئېلىپ كەلدىڭىز:

____

Exercise 21: هېيتگاھ مەسجىتى

Exercise 21.1: In Kashgar, John visits the famous Héyt Gah mosque and takes some pictures. Look at those pictures. What you can say about the mosque?

Exercise 21.2:  Read the following excerpt from the website of an Uyghur travel agency about the Héyt Gah Mosque. Write a brief summary of the passage in Uyghur. You may use the vocabulary in the accompanying box.

One of the most frequently visited tourist attractions in Kashgar is Heyt-Gah Mosque. The name Heyt-Gah comes from the Persian "The place of religious festivals." The mosque was built in 1442, as a much smaller structure, however, now it is considered the biggest mosque in China. The whole area of the mosque is about 16,800 square meters. It consists of a main gate, a courtyard, a hall of prayer, a minaret, and a number of other, smaller structures. The main gate opens onto the courtyard which is surrounded on all sides by green trees.

The hall of prayer is located at the western side of the mosque. The roof of the hall is held up by light blue pillars. Around the ceiling and pillars are intricate carvings. The brick minaret looks out over Heyt-Gah Square. The inside of the minaret is decorated with green floral patterns.

Every Friday afternoon, thousands of Muslims gather in the mosque to worship. Five times a day during the festivals of Ramadan and Qurban, the mosque, the square, and the surrounding streets fill with Muslims.

hall of prayer	ئىبادەتخانا	minaret	مۇنار
main gate	چوڭ دەرۋازا	roof	ئۆگزە
courtyard	هويلا	pillars	تۈۋرۈك
ceiling	تورۇس	brick	خىش
carvings	ئويما نەقىش	floral patterns	گۈللۈك نەقىش

Have you ever heard about...? بۇ كىشىنى بىلەمسىز...؟

In this section you will read and learn about a famous Uyghur person.

Exercise 22: تاتا تۇڭا

Exercise 22.1:  Read the following passage about Tata Tonga, a 13th century Uyghur scholar from Turpan. Then, answer the questions that follow. The words and expressions provided before the questions will help you to understand the passage better.

قەشقەر كەچلىك گېزىتى

2014 - يىلى 18 - ئاۋغۇست
دۈشەنبە

1231 - سان پوچتا ۋاكالەت نومۇرى: 54 ـ 66

تاتا تۇڭا ئۇيغۇر مەدەنىيەت تارىخىدىكى مەشھۇر شەخسلەرنىڭ بىرى. ئۇنىڭ تۇغۇلغان ۋە ۋاپات بولغان ۋاقتى ھەققىدە ئېنىق مەلۇماتلار يوق. ئەمما "موڭغۇللارنىڭ مەخپىي تارىخى" ۋە "يۈەن سۇلالىسى تارىخى" ناملىق ئەسەرلەرگە ئاساسلانغاندا تاتا تۇڭا تۇرپاندا تۇغۇلغان. ئۇ كىچىك ۋاقتىدا ناھايىتى ئەقىللىق بولۇپ، كىچىكىدىن موڭغۇلچە ۋە خەنزۇچە تىللارنى پىششىق ئۆگەنگەن. مىلادىيە 1204 - يىلى چىڭگىزخان نايمان خانى تايان خان بىلەن ئۇرۇش قىلغان. شۇ ئۇرۇشتا تاتا تۇڭا ئىسىملىك ئۇيغۇر كاتىپ چىڭگىزخانغا ئەسىرگە چۈشكەن. شۇ ۋاقىتتا تاتا تۇڭا نايمانلار ئارىسىدىكى ئەڭ ھۆرمەتلىك كىشىلەرنىڭ بىرى ئىدى. چىڭگىزخان ئۇنىڭدىن ئۇيغۇر يېزىقى ھەققىدە ئاڭلىغاندىن كېيىن ھەيران بولغان ۋە ئۇنى ئۆزىگە ئۇستاز قىلغان. شۇنىڭدىن كېيىن تاتا تۇڭا موڭغۇللارنىڭ پوچتا، باج ، مەمۇرىيەت، دىپلوماتىيە، مالىيە، ئەدلىيە قاتارلىق كەسىپلىرىدە ئىشلىگەن. شۇنىڭ بىلەن بىر ۋاقىتتا چىڭگىزخاننىڭ بۇيرۇقى بويىچە موڭغۇللار ئۇيغۇر يېزىقىنى قوبۇل قىلغان. تاتا تۇڭا ئۇيغۇر يېزىقىنى موڭغۇل شاھزادىلىرى ۋە بەگلىرىگە ئۆگەتكەن. شۇنىڭدىن كېيىن موڭغۇللار ئۇيغۇر يېزىقى ئاساسىدىكى بۇ يېزىقنى ھازىرغىچە ئىشلىتىپ كەلمەكتە.

administration	مەمۇرىيەت
diplomacy	دىپلوماتىيە
finance	مالىيە
justice	ئەدلىيە

information	مەلۇمات
war	ئۇرۇش
to be captured	ئەسىرگە چۈشمەك
tax	باج

1. تاتا توڭا قايسى تىللارنى ئۆگەنگەن؟
2. تاتا توڭا چىڭگىزخان بىلەن قانداق ئۇچراشقان؟
3. ئۇ قايسى ساھەلەردە خىزمەت قىلغان؟
4. موڭغۇللار ئۇيغۇر يېزىقىنى قانچە ئۇزۇن ئىشلەتتى؟

Exercise 22.2: Based on the passag, ask your partner three more questions about Tata Tonga.

____

____

____

خەلق شائىرى لۇتپۇللا مۇتەللىپ
(1922-1945)

خەلق داھىسى ئەخمەتجان قاسىمى
(1914-1949)

Vocabulary سۆزلۈك

Vocabulary is given according to the Uyghur alphabetical order. The right column precedes the left column on each page.

to wish	ئارزۇلىماق
prosperous	ئاۋات
it's unfortunate that	ئەپسۇسكى
hard working	ئەمگەكچان
fig	ئەنجۈر
to worry	ئەنسىرىمەك
brave	باتۇر
almond	بادام
trestle	باراڭ
physical capability	بەدەن قۇۋۋىتى
to obey	بويسۇنماق
damage	بۇزغۇنچىلىق
section	بۆلمە
to decorate	(-نى) بېزىمەك
to be dedicated to	(-غا) بېغىشلانماق
safety belt	بىخەتەرلىك تاسمىسى
to dispose; to solve	بىر تەرەپ قىلماق
bracelet	بىلەيزۈك
architecture	بىناكارلىق
since then	(-دىن) تارتىپ
to shy	تارتىنماق
to demand	تەلەپ قىلماق
ceiling	تورۇس
hindrances	توسقۇنلۇق
rabbit	توشقان
type	تۈر
group	تۈركۈم
a knot; center	تۈگۈن
even more	تېخىمۇ كۆپ
process	جەريان

courage; a name for males	جۈرئەت
emergency	جىددىي
musical instruments	چالغۇ ئەسۋابلار
staff	خادىم
brick	خىش
gate	دەرۋازا
cloth	رەخت
to be upset	رەنجىمەك
spiritual world	روھىي دۇنيا
jewelry	زىبۇزىننەت بۇيۇملىرى
to preserve; to wait	ساقلىماق
to extract; to water	سۇغۇرماق
picture; speed	سۈرەت
city wall	سېپىل
cave	غار
to cover	قاپلىماق
to escape; to run away	قاچماق
to leave	قالدۇرماق
sorrow	قايغۇ - ھەسرەت
handicraft products	قول - ھۈنەر بۇيۇملىرى
hand fabricated	قولدا توقۇلغان
to use	قوللانماق
to rescue	قۇتقۇزماق
well	قۇدۇق
karez (underground irrigation channel)	كارىز

goat	ئۆچكە
duck	ئۆردەك
apricot	ئۆرۈك
roof	ئۆگزە
cave	ئۆڭكۈر\ غار
ring	ئۈزۈك
vineyard	ئۈزۈمزار
tools	ئۈسكۈنە
promise	ۋەدە
field	ئېتىز
fine	ئېسىل
to taste	ئېغىز تەگمەك
temple	ئىبادەتخانا
to express	ئىپادىلىمەك
to unite	ئىتتىپاقلاشماق
smoke	ئىس - تۈتەك
ability	ئىقتىدار
cultural relics	يادىكارلىق
cell phone	يانفون
to return; to light	يانماق
wild birds	ياۋايى قۇشلار
passenger	يولۇچى

to dig	كولىماق
spectator	كۆزەتكۈچ
raisin	كىشمىش
design	لايىھە
necklace	مارجان
delicious	مەززىلىك
source	مەنبە
to prohibit	مەنئى قىلماق
tower	مۇنار
miracle	مۆجىزە
A.D.	مىلادى
national tradition	مىللىي ئەنئەنە
pear	نەشپۈت
decoration	نەقىش
earring	هالقا
to cooperate	هەمكارلاشماق
magnificent	هەيۋەتلىك
to encounter	ئۇچرىماق
to fly	ئۇچماق
teacher	ئۇستاز
style	ئۇسلۇب
join together	ئۇيۇشۇش

ئالتىنچى دەرس

CHAPTER SIX

ئۇيغۇرلاردا ھۈنەر - كەسىپ

UYGHUR TRADITIONAL OCCUPATIONS

IN THIS CHAPTER

Functions

- Describing Uyghur traditional occupations
- Describing artisans in the Uyghur bazaars
- Bargaining at a bazaar
- Recognizing onomatopoeias
- Explaining reasons

Grammar

- Noun formation suffixes
- Word formation for Onomatopoeia (imitative words)
- The word ئەمەسمۇ
- Subordinate clause of reason

In this chapter you will learn about some common Uyghur jobs, including ancient Uyghur artisanal occupations such as پىچاقچى, ساپالچى, etc. You will travel with John and plunge headfirst into the Uyghur traditions at the cultural heart of Xinjiang – Kashgar. From the reading passages and blog entries contained herein, you will obtain some information about the culture of trading and bargaining among Uyghurs. You will also have a chance to experience this culture first-hand as you attempt to purchase a famous Yengisar knife and بەكە at the Kashgar bazaar. You will become acquainted with some concepts such as كاسىپ, قول ھۈنەرۋەنچىلىك, ھۈنەر, and مەدىكار.

Exercise 1: ھەرخىل كەسپلەر

Exercise 1.1: Look at the snapshots of professions commonly encountered in Uyghur bazaars. See if you can name each profession in Uyghur.

Exercise 1.2:  Match the following words with their English equivalents by drawing a line from one to the other.

clay pottery	ھۈنەر
tailor	ھۈنەرۋەن، كاسىپ
butcher	كۇلالچىلىق / ساپالچىلىق
baker	مىسكەرچى
metal-worker	تۈنىكىچى
carpet maker	گىلەمچى
craftsman	دوپپىچى
doppa maker	ياغاچچى
carpenter	قاسساپ/پوكانچى
coppersmith	ناۋاي
handicraft	تىككۈچى
day laborer	مەدىكار

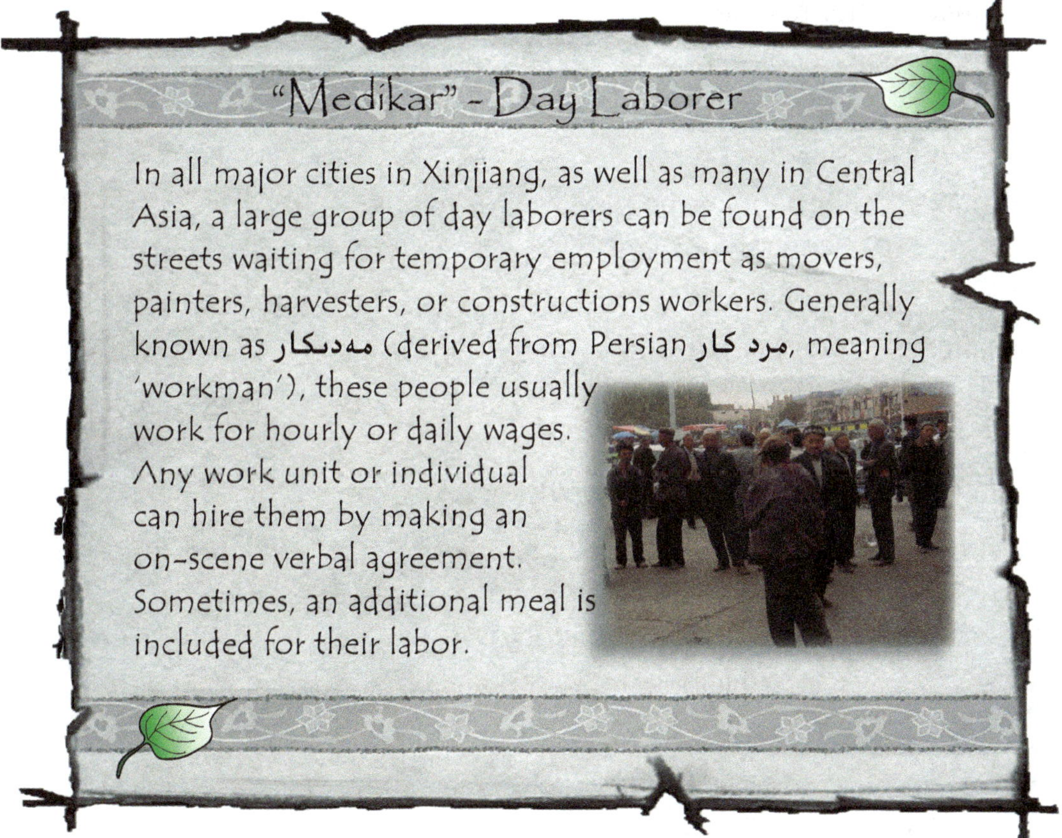

"Medikar" - Day Laborer

In all major cities in Xinjiang, as well as many in Central Asia, a large group of day laborers can be found on the streets waiting for temporary employment as movers, painters, harvesters, or constructions workers. Generally known as مەدىكار (derived from Persian مرد كار, meaning 'workman'), these people usually work for hourly or daily wages. Any work unit or individual can hire them by making an on-scene verbal agreement. Sometimes, an additional meal is included for their labor.

1 Noun Formation Suffixes in Uyghur: Occupations

As you know, the most common suffix used in Uyghur to indicate a profession is the all-purpose agentive -چى . This can be attached to a wide variety of different words. For example: ناخشىچى 'singer,' ئىشچى 'worker,' تۆمۈرچى 'blacksmith,' كىنوچى 'projectionist,' etc.

There are also a number of other suffixes (all derived from Persian verb stems) whose use is relatively restricted, but which are nevertheless found on some commonly used names for professions:

Suffix -كار\كەر\ گەر (general profession suffixes):
مەدىكار 'casual worker,' بىناكار 'architect'
خىزمەتكار 'servant,' پاختىكار 'cotton grower'
مىسكەر 'a coppersmith'
سودىگەر 'merchant,' زەرگەر 'jeweller'

Suffix -پەز (for people who cook):
ئاشپەز 'cook,' سامسىپەز 'samsa maker'

Suffix -كەش (for people who pull/consume):
ھارۋىكەش 'cart driver' ھاراقكەش 'drunkard'

Suffix -ۋاز (for people who play with or handle):
دارۋاز 'tightrope walker' كەپتەرۋاز 'pigeon raiser'
قىمارۋاز 'gambler' بۇيرۇقۋاز 'bossy person'

Suffix -ۋەن (for people who keep/manage):
باغۋەن 'gardener' سارايۋەن - 'inn keeper'
ھۈنەرۋەن 'craftsman'

Suffix -پۇرۇش (for people who sell):
دورىپۇرۇش 'medicine seller' كىتابپۇرۇش 'book seller'
چايپۇرۇش 'tea seller'

Suffix -شۇناس (for people who study):
تارىخشۇناس 'historian' تىلشۇناس 'linguist'

Exercise 1.3: Look at the pictures in Exercise 1.1 again, and provide a brief description for each person's occupation.

Exercise 2: Write a definition in Uyghur and in English for each of the following words below using the same pattern. The first one is done for you as an example.

پىچاقچى	پىچاق ياسايدىغان ۋە پىچاق ساتىدىغان كىشى Pichaqchi is a person who makes and sells knives
دوپپىچى	
گىلەمچى	
دارۋاز	
ياغاچچى	
باغۋەن	
ئاشپەز	
تارىخچى	
چايپۇرۇش	
سودىگەر	
هارۋىكەش	

Exercise 3: How do you imagine life in the bazaar? Think of ten adjectives to describe the colors, scents, and sounds you might encounter there.

____

____

____

Exercise 4: ئۇيغۇر بازارلىرى

Exercise 4.1:  The following passage was adaptated from the famous Uyghur novel "قۇم باسقان شەھەر" (*The Sand-Buried City*) by Memtimin Hoshur. Read it with your instructor and underline all the words related to occupations.

بازار ھەر تەرەپتىن كىرىۋاتقان كاسىپلار، دېھقانلار، مەدىكارلارنىڭ ۋاڭ- چۇڭى، ئېلىپ- ساتارلارنىڭ خېرىدار چاقىرىپ ۋارقىراشلىرى بىلەن جانلىنىپ كېتەتتى. بۇ يەردە يىراق شەرقنىڭ چىنە - قاچا، ئۈنچە - مەرۋايىت، يىپەكلىرى بار ئىدى، شۇنداقلا ھىندى، تىبەت سودىگەرلىرىنىڭ ھەر خىل بوياق، دورا- دەرمانلىرىنىڭ خۇش پۇراقلىرى كېلەتتى؛ بىر يەردە ئېلىپ - ساتارلار قەشقەر چەكمەنلىرى، كۇچا ئەلتېرىلىرى، خوتەننىڭ گىلەم، ئەتلەسلىرىنى ساتسا، يەنە بىر يەردە كۇلالچىلار چۆنەك بىلەن كوزىلىرىنى جاڭگىلدىتىپ ئۇرۇپ ماختايتتى. قايسىبىر ئۇستى يېپىق، سالقىن رەستىلەردە ئاجايىپ گۈللەر كەشتىلەنگەن دوپپىلارنى كۆتۈرۈشۈۋالغان ئايالار خېرىدارلىرى بىلەن قىزغىن سودىلاشسا، يەنە قايسىدۇر بىر كوچىلاردا مىسكەرلەر، تۆمۈرچىلەر جاڭگىلدىتىپ ئۇرغان بولقا ئاۋازلىرى قۇلاقنى زىڭگىلدىتاتتى...

Exercise 4.2:  Now read the list of words below and draw a line matching each word to its definition. Go back to the passage and find these words in context for clues.

رەختنىڭ يۈزىگە يىڭنە بىلەن تىكىپ چۈشۈرۈلگەن گۈل، تۈرلۈك رەسىم	ئەلتېرە
سۇ قاتارلىق سۇيۇق نەرسىلەرنى قاچىلاش ئۈچۈن ساپالدىن ياسالغان قاچا	چەكمەن
بىر ئايلىق قوزىنىڭ تېرىسى	كەشتە
پاختا ياكى يۇڭ يىپتىن پۇختا ، سىلىق قىلىپ توقۇلغان يەرلىك رەخت	رەستە
ئىككى ياقىسىغا ھەر خىل سودا دۇكانلىرى قاتار ئورۇنلاشقان ئاۋات كوچا	كوزا
دەرەخنىڭ يېغى ئۆسكەن ئىنچىكە شېخى	چۆنەك

Exercise 4.3: تۆۋەندىكى سوئاللارغا جاۋاب بېرىڭ

1. How would you describe the bazaar based on this passage?
   a) How does it smell?
   b) What colors do you see?
   c) What sounds can you hear?
2. What kind of goods can you find in this bazaar?
3. What jobs or occupations do the people in this bazaar have?

Exercise 5: ئۇيغۇرلاردا رەڭ چۈشەنچىسى

Exercise 5.1:  On the next page, you will read a cultural note about the symbolic meanings of colors in Uyghur culture. Before reading, provide definition in English for the following words. The first two are provided for you.

nobility	ئالىيجانابلىق
victory	غەلىبە
	مۇراسىم
	پەرىشانلىق
	جەڭگىۋارلىق
	ناغرا - سۇناي
	زىبۇزىننەت بۇيۇملىرى
	چۈشكۈنلۈك

Exercise 5.2:  Draw a line between the words in the righthand column and their antonyms in the lefthand column.

خوشاللىق	قايغۇ - ھەسرەت
تۇرلۇك	مۇسىبەت
بەخت - سائادەت	قارىلاش
ئاقلاش	بەشمەك
كىيمەك	ئوخشاش

Exercise 5.3:  Read the following passage with the help of your instructor.

رەڭلەر ئۇيغۇرلارنىڭ ئۆرپ - ئادەتلىرىدە مۇھىم بىر ئالاھىدىلىك بولۇپ شەكىللەنگەن. مەسىلەن: ئاق رەڭ ئۇيغۇرلارنىڭ ئەنئەنىۋى ئېڭىدە بەخت - ئامەت، ياخشىلىق، پاكلىق، ئالىيجانابلىق چۈشەنچىسىنى بەرگەن. سەپەرگە چىققانلارنى ئۇزىتىشتا ئاق يول تىلەش، سۈتنى ئۇلۇغلاش، قارنى بەخت - ئامەتنىڭ بەلگىسى دەپ بىلىش، قىزلار توي بولغان كۈنى ئاق رەڭلىك كۆڭلەك كىيىش، هازىدار ئەرلەر بېلىگە ئاق باغلاش، ئاياللار ئاق ياغلىق سېلىش، ئۆي - ئىمارەتلەرنى ئاقارتىش... قاتارلىق ئادەتلەرنىڭ ھەممىسىدە ئاق رەڭ ئۇلۇغلانغان. كۆك رەڭمۇ ئۇيغۇرلارنىڭ ئىپتىدائىي دىنىي ئېتىقادى بىلەن باغلانغان ھالدا ياخشىلىق ۋە ئامەتنىڭ سىمۋولى ھېسابلىنىدۇ. كۆك سۆزىنىڭ بىر نەچچە تۈرلۈك مەنىسى بار: مەسىلەن، تەڭرى، ئاسمان، ياشا، ياشارماق، ئوت- چۆپ قاتارلىقلار. بۇ رەڭ ئۇيغۇرلاردا مۇقەددەس رەڭ چۈشەنچىسىگە كۆتۈرۈلگەن. ئۇيغۇرلار قىزىل رەڭنى ياخشىلىقنىڭ، خوشاللىقنىڭ، بەخت - سائادەتنىڭ، گۈزەللىكنىڭ، جەڭگىۋارلىقنىڭ، غەلىبىنىڭ سىمۋوللۇق بېشارىتى دەپ بىلىدۇ. مەسىلەن، ئۇيغۇرلارنىڭ ئادىتىدە توي - تۆكۈن بولسا، قىز تەرەپكە ئېلىپ بارىدىغان قوينىڭ بېشىغا قىزىل رەخت باغلاپ قويۇلىدۇ. توي كۆچۈرۈش ھارۋىسىغا قوشۇلغان ئاتلارغا ياكى ھازىرقى زاماندىكى توي كۆچۈرۈش ماشىنىلىرىنىڭ ئالدىغا قىزىل رەخت باغلىنىدۇ. ھەتتا توينىڭ ناغرا- سۇنايلىرىغىمۇ قىزىل رەخت باغلاپ قويۇلىدۇ. سۈننەت توي مۇراسىمىدا سۈننەتنى قىلىنىدىغان بالىنىڭ بېلىگە قىزىل پوتا باغلىنىدۇ. قىزلار، ياش چوكانلار قىزىل رەڭلىك كۆڭلەك كىيىشنى ياخشى كۆرىدۇ. قىزىل رەڭنى ياشلىقنىڭ بەلگىسى دەپ بىلىدۇ.

سېرىق رەڭ ئۇيغۇرلارنىڭ ئېستېتىك ئادىتىدە قۇياشقا، مول ھوسۇلغا سىمۋول قىلىنىدۇ. ئۇيغۇرلار سېرىق رەڭنى ئالتۇن رەڭ دەپ ئاتايدۇ. ئەڭ ئەتىۋارلىق گۈزەل سەنئەت بۇيۇملىرى ۋە زىبۇزىننەت بۇيۇملىرىنىڭ رەڭگىمۇ ئالتۇن رەڭنى ئاساس قىلىدۇ. لېكىن بەزىدە سېرىق رەڭ چۈشكۈنلۈككە ، روھسىزلىققا، پەرىشانلىققا سىمۋول قىلىنغان ئەھۋاللارمۇ ئۇچرايدۇ. قارا رەڭ بولسا قايغۇ- ئەلەم ۋە مۇسىبەتنىڭ سىمۋولى قىلىنغان. ئەمما ھازىر بەزى ياشلار زامانىۋى مودىغا ئەگىشىپ، قارا رەڭلىك كىيىملەرنى كىيىدىغان بولغان.

Exercise 5.4:  Circle the correct answers to the questions below.

1.هازىدار ئەرلەر بېلىگە نېمە باغلايدۇ؟

ئا. پوتا ب. بەلۋاغ س. ياغلىق د. گالستۇك

2. قانداق رەڭ ئۇيغۇرلاردا ياخشىلىق، گۈزەللىك، غەلىبە سىمۋولى؟

ئا. كۆك ب. قىزىل س. ئاق د. سېرىق

3. قايسى رەڭ ئۇيغۇرلاردا قۇياشقا، مول ھوسۇلغا سىمۋول قىلىنغان؟

ئا. قىزىل ب. ئاق س. سېرىق د. قارا

4. قايسى رەڭ چۈشكۈنلۈككە ، روھسىزلىققا، پەرىشانلىققا سىمۋول قىلىنغان؟

ئا. قارا ب. ئاق س. سېرىق د. كۆك

5.قايسى رەڭ قايغۇ- ئەلەم ۋە مۇسىبەتنىڭ سىمۋولى ؟

ئا. قارا ب. سېرىق س. كۆك د. قىزىل

Exercise 5.5:  Does any color in your culture hold a special symbolic meaning? Compare the meanings of colors in your culture with those in Uyghur culture by filling in the chart below. Write your answers in Uyghur.

سىزنىڭ مەدەنىيىتىڭىزدە	ئۇيغۇر مەدەنىيىتىدە	رەڭلەر
		ئاق
		سېرىق
		قىزىل
		قارا
		كۆك
		يېشىل

Mämtimin Hoshur

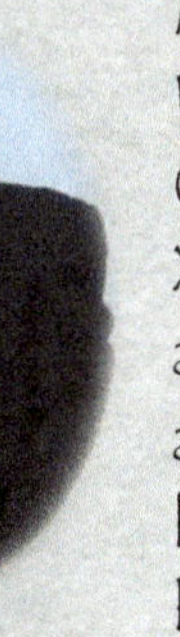

Mämtimin Hoshur, a leading novelist of modern Uyghur literature, was born in 1944 in Ghulja (Yining in Chinese). After graduating from Xinjiang University in 1967, Hoshur worked as a village cadre and interpreter until he found a job in 1980 with the "Ili River," a bimonthly literary magazine. Starting from the 1990s, his immensely well-received series of satiric novels - including "Qirliq Istakan" ("The Angular Glass"), "Sarang" ("Crazy"), "Char Horaz" ("A Speckled Rooster"), "Dap," "Altun Chishliq It" ("A Dog with Golden Teeth"), "Burut Majirasi" ("The Moustache Turmoil"), "Choshqilargha Bayram" ("Pigs' Holiday"), and "Qara Qorsaq Serke" ("The Black Belly Bellwether") has brought him a great public recognition. He is considered one of the most successful writers in modern Uyghur prose.

2 Onomatopoeia in Uyghur

The Uyghur language is very rich with words that imitate sounds - a phenomenon known as onomatopoeia. You may have heard some of them, but you probably did not know that these words were based on the sounds of things they described. For example:

شارقىراتما 'waterfall' (شار is the sound made by pouring liquid)
گۈلدۈرماما 'thunder' (from the sound گۈلدۈر rumbling)
ۋاراڭ - چۇرۇڭ 'noise'
غاجىماق 'to gnaw'
جاراڭلىماق 'to clang'
تاراقلىماق 'to make a racket'

It is very important to recognize imitative words because they are frequently used both in everyday speech describing events and, as you saw in the previous authentic passage, in Uyghur literature.

Single imitative words:

گۇر the sound of a large crowd (گۇرۇلدىمەك, گۇررىدە)
جىرىڭ the sound of a bell (جىرىڭلىماق)
گۈلدۈر 'clatter, crash' (گۈلدۈرماما)
پىژ 'hiss, sizzle' (پىژىلدىماق)
غىژ the sound of flies (غىژىلدىماق)

Paired imitative words (re-duplication): تىرىق-تىرىق 'scratch-scratch,' ۋىل-ۋىل 'gleaming', تاق-تۇق 'knocking and banging,' ۋال-ۋۇل 'flashing,' etc.

Here are some examples of adverbs formed on the basis of such words using the suffix -ىدە: پاققىدە 'with a flop,' شاررىدە 'with a splash,' غاچچىدە 'with a crack,' گۇپپىدە 'with a thump,' ۋىچچىدە 'with a hiss,' ۋاچچىدە 'with a soft squelchy sound,' etc.

Exercise 6: تەقلىدىي سۆزلەر

Exercise 6.1: Below you see some further examples of onomatopoeia taken from the same novel "قۇم باسقان شەھەر". These examples demonstrate that imitative words play a very important role in describing the nature of the actions which they imitate. Compare each sentence with a variant which doesn't make use of onomatopoeia.

The door opened. The door opened with a squeak.	ئىشىك ئېچىلدى. ئىشىك غىچىرلاپ ئېچىلدى.
The cold water coming up from underground. The cold water gurgling up from underground.	....يەرنىڭ ئاستىدىن چىقىۋاتقان مۇزدەك سۇ ...يەرنىڭ ئاستىدىن بۇلدۇقلاپ چىقىۋاتقان مۇزدەك سۇ
The doves moved from their place. The doves moved from their place with a flutter.	كەپتەرلەر ئورنىدىن قوزغىلىپ كەتتى. كەپتەرلەر ئورنىدىن گۇررىدە قوزغىلىپ كەتتى.
The water in the teapot was boiling. The water in the teapot was boiling with bubbling.	چەينەكلەر قايناۋاتاتتى. چەينەكلەر ۋاراقلاپ قايناۋاتتتى.

Exercise 6.2: Listen and repeat the following sentences. Identify the onomatopoeia in each sentence.

1. بۇ تاراق-تۇرۇق نەدىن كېلىۋاتىدۇ؟
2. شۇ ئارىدا تېلېفون جىرىڭلىدى.
3. ئۇلار قاقاقلاپ كۈلۈشتى.
4. يەرگە بىر نەرسە پوككىدە چۈشتى.
5.بۇ ۋاراڭ- چۇرۇڭدا نېمە ئىش قىلالايسىز؟

Exercise 6.3: Read the sentences below and underline the words that imitate sounds. Discuss their meanings with your partner.

1. دېرىزىدىن گۇر- گۇر شامال ئۇرىۋاتىدۇ.
2. ئۇنىڭ جاراڭلىق ئاۋازى شۇ يەرگىمۇ ئاڭلاندى.
3. ئۇ پۇلنى ئېلىپ موككىدە يانچۇقىغا سالدى.
4. مېھمان مەست بولۇپ ساپاغا گۇپپىدە يىقىلدى.
5. ئۇ ھۆركىرەپ يىغلىدى.
6. ئەنۋەر لىككىدە بازارغا بېرىپ كېلەي دەپ ئۆيدىن يۇگۇرۇپ چىقتى.
7. مۇختار، سەن كۆپ ۋالاقلىما، جۇمۇ.

Exercise 6.4:  Look at the following two words from the passage (Exercise 4.1) along with their definitions.

«چاك - چاك» قىلغان كۈچلۈك ئاۋاز چىقارماق	جاكىلدىماق
«زىك» قىلغان ئاۋاز چىقارماق	زىكىلدىماق

Below, you see a number of pictures of various animals. Match them with the verbs in the accompanying box that describe the sounds they make. Then, try to think of the English equivalents of these words, if they exist.

1	مۆرىمەك
2	مەرىمەك
3	ھاۋشىماق
4	گىژىلدىماق
5	ھۇۋلىماق
6	ھاڭرىماق
7	مىياۋلىماق

Exercise 7: كوزىچى يار بېشى

Exercise 7.1: 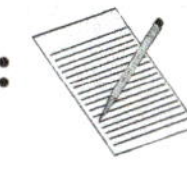 John pays a visit to the *High Terrace Folk Houses* during his stay in Kashgar. Look at the ticket quickly and make a note of everything you can understand based on the information presented on the ticket. You may use your knowledge of other languages as well.

Exercise 7.2:  Look at John's ticket again (Exercise 7.1). It is multilingual, but very little information is made available in Uyghur. Rewrite as much information from the ticket as you can using only Uyghur.

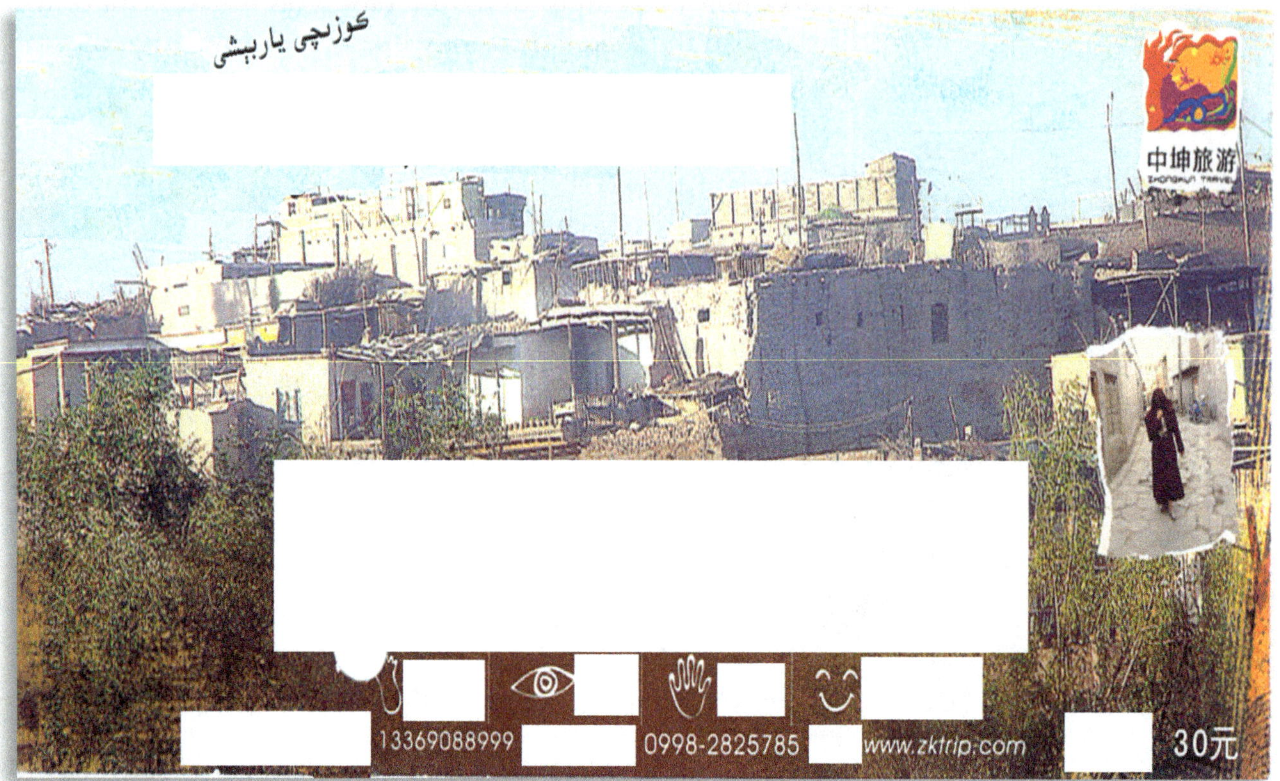

Exercise 8: ئۇيغۇرلاردا كۈلالچىلىق

Exercise 8.1:  Watch the video about Uyghur pottery. Try and guess what the profession of the man in the video might be in Uyghur. Refer to Exercise 1.2 if needed.

Exercise 8.2: This time watch the video and mark all the words below that you hear. What do these words mean? Look up the meanings of the vocabulary using the list at the end of this chapter.

ساپال بۇيۇملار　　ھۈنەر　　خۇمار　　ئۇستا　　دەرەخ　　سېغىز توپا

لاي　　ماي　　ئەسۋاب　　ئۆلچەملىك　　گۈزەللىك قىممىتى

قەدىمىي شەكىل　　ئۇسلۇب　　خۇمدان　　ماددا

Exercise 8.3: Watch the video again. Which of the statements below were made in this video? Put a check mark √ in the boxes to the right of the sentences which appear in the video.

	1. ئۇيغۇر ساپالچىلىقىدا ساپال بۇيۇملار قولدا ياسىلىدۇ.
	2. كۇلالچىلار ئاۋۋال سېغىز توپىدا لاي ئېتىدۇ.
	3. ساپال بۇيۇملار ئۇچار چاق ئارقىلىق ياسىلىدۇ.
	4. ساپال بۇيۇملارنىڭ شەكلى بىر بىرىگە ئوخشىمايدۇ.
	5. رەڭ بېرىلگەن ساپال بۇيۇملار خۇمداندا پىشۇرۇلىدۇ.
	6. ساپال بۇيۇملارغا گۈل - گىياھلار ۋە ئادەملەرنىڭ رەسىملىرى سىزىلىدۇ.
	7. ساپالچىلار بۇيۇملىرىنى ئۆزلىرى بويايدۇ.

Exercise 8.4: Watch the video one more time. Which colors are usually used in Uyghur pottery? The narrator mentions four colors. Write all of them on the line provided below.

Exercise 9: بەكە ئالالملا؟

Exercise 9.1:  Like many visitors to Kasghar, John goes to the bazaar to buy one of the famous Yengisar knives. Listen to the passage and answer the question below.

1. How does the seller know that John wants to buy a knife?
A. John looks like a foreigner B. John looks like a local
C. Foreigners usually buy knives D. both A and C

2. How does John know about Yengisar knives?
A. He read a newspaper article. B. A friend of his told him.
C. He saw an ad on TV. D. He Googled them.

Listen to the passage again. This time, pay attention to language use.
1. How does the seller invite John into his shop?
2. What verb form does the seller use?

Exercise 9.2:  Listen to the second part of the dialogue.

1. What is happening in this section?
A. John is bargaining for the knife
B. John is purchasing the knife

2. During the conversation, a misunderstanding occurs. What is it about?

Exercise 9.3:  Listen to the rest of the dialogue and answer the questions that follow.

1. What is the difference between پىچاق and بەكە?
2. How much does the knife in question cost? How about بەكە?
3. What is the exchange rate between the Chinese yuan and the American dollar, according to the text?
4. What does John buy in the end?
5. How much does he pay?

Exercise 9.4:  Read the whole dialogue and practice acting it out with your partner.

سېتىقچى : ھەي، ئۇكام، مەكەسىلە.
جون: مېنى چاقىرۋاتامسىز؟
سېتىقچى: ھەئە، سىلىنى. پىچاق ئالامىلا؟
جون: پىچاق ئالىدىغانلىقىمنى نەدىن بىلدىڭىز؟
سېتىقچى: قايلىسام چەتئەللىكلەرگە ئوخشايدىكەنلا، بۇ بازارغا كەلگەن ساياھەتچىلەر چوقۇم پىچاق ئالىدۇ ئەمەسمۇ.
جون: مەنمۇ پىچاق ئالاي دەپ كېلىۋېدىم...
سېتىقچى: ئۇنداقتا مېنىڭ پىچاقلىرىمنى كۆرۈپ باقسىلا.
جون: بۇ يېڭىسار پىچاقلىرىمۇ؟
سېتىقچى: نەق ئۆزى! پىچاق تونۇيدىكەنلا...
جون: ھە، بىر ئۇيغۇر دوستۇم يېڭىسار پىچاقلىرى ئەڭ ياخشى دېگەن...
سېتىقچى: قېنى، بىرەرنى تاللىدىلىما؟
جون: ھەممىسى ياخشىدەك تۇرىدۇ. بۇلار نەچچە پۇل؟
سېتىقچى: ئۆزلىرى بىر دېسىلە. قانچە پۇلغا ئالىلا؟
جون: سىز دەڭە، مەن بىلمەيدىكەنمەن. يەنە ئەرزان دېۋەتسەم خاپا بولىسىز...
سېتىقچى: بازاردا خاپا بولىدىغان ئىش يوق، ئۇكام، دەۋەسىلە...
جون: 50 كە بېرەمسىز؟
سېتىقچى: 50 دېگىنىڭىز دوللارمۇ يا ...؟
جون: دېگىنىم 50 كوي، دوللار ئەمەس...
سېتىقچى: ياق- ياق، بۇ پىچاقلارنى 50 كويغا بېرەلمەيمەن. 50 كويغا ئاۋۇ كىچىك بەكنى ئالسىلا...
جون: بەكە؟ بۇ نېمە؟
سېتىقچى: ھە، بەكە دېگەن قىسقا پىچاق، ئۇنىڭ تىغىنى دەستە ئىچىگە قايرىپ قويغىلى بولىدۇ. بۇمۇ ياخشى نەرسە، بولۇپمۇ ساياھەتچىلەر ئۈچۈن. ئالسىلا، بەردىم 50 كويغا...
جون: ھە، بۇمۇ بولىدىكەن. مەن بەكىنىمۇ ئالاي.
سېتىقچى: ئالسىلا... 50 دوللار بەرسىلە، بۇ پىچاقنىمۇ سىلىگە بېرەي، مېھمان ئىكەنلا. بىز بۇ پىچاقلارنى يۈز دوللاردىنمۇ ساتقان...
جون: مەن بىر ئوقۇغۇچى، مېنىڭ ئۇنچىلىك پۇلۇم يوق...
سېتىقچى: 200 كويغا ئالالامىلا؟
جون: بۇ قانچە دوللار بولىدۇ؟
سېتىقچى: 30 دوللارچە بولىدۇ. قانداق، ئالامىلا؟
جون: 100 دوللار قانچە يۈەن بولىدۇ؟
سېتىقچى: يۈز دوللار 680 يۈەن بولىدۇ، 50 دوللار 340... دېمەك 200 يۈەن دېگەن 30 دوللار، شۇنداقما؟
جون: شۇنداق ئوخشايدۇ... ماقۇل، مەن بۇ پىچىقىڭىزنى 30 دوللارغا ئالاي...

Exercise 10: Imagine that you are at the Kashgar bazaar looking for a gift for a friend. You see a nice doppa and a Yengisar knife. One of you will play the role of the seller (card A), the other one will play the role of the customer (card B).

CARD A: the seller

You are a doppa-maker but you also sell decorated knives. You notice a foreigner walking around.
Your task is to attract his attention. While praising your product try to agree on a price that is closest to what you want.

CARD B: the tourist

You are in the Kashgar bazaar shopping for a doppa and a decorated knife. One of the artisans attracts your attention. After you respond, choose the product you like most, and bargain for as low a price as you can. Make sure you know what currency the seller is talking about.

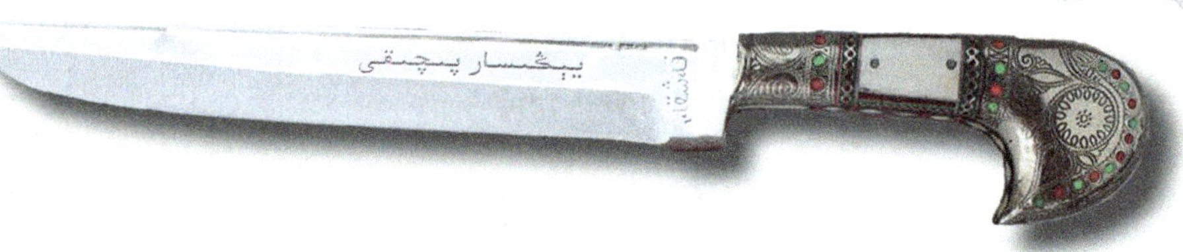

Note:

The word ئەمەسمۇ

In the dialogue (Exercise 9.4), you see the word ئەمەسمۇ, which is attached to the end of a statement. This word is frequently used by native speakers when they are confident that what they say is true, and that the listener will agree with what he hears. The following statement is from the dialogue:

قارىسام چەتئەللىكلەرگە ئوخشايدىكەنلا، بۇ بازارغا كەلگەن
ساياھەتچىلەر چوقۇم پىچاق ئالىدۇ ئەمەسمۇ.

It might be translated into English as:

You look like a foreigner. Every traveler who comes
to this bazaar definitely buys a knife.

Exercise 11:  Read the example and translate the following sentences using the word ئەمەسمۇ.

Example: As you may know, everybody loves *langman*.
ھەممە ئادەم لەڭمەنگە ئامراق ئەمەسمۇ.

1. (As you may know) This city is famous.

____

2. (As you may know) The grapes are sweet here.

____

3. (As you may know) This university is famous.

____

4. (As you may know) Khotan carpets are high quality.

____

Note:

The word ئەمەسمۇ is also used to explain that a proposition is not a surprise and implies that it is self-evident. Look at the following examples:

My son cries a lot... بالام بەك كۆپ يىغلايدۇ
It is ok; he is a little boy, isn't he? چاتاق يوق، ئۇ كىچىك بالا ئەمەسمۇ.
(Implying that little children usually cry a lot)
This girl is so pretty. بۇ قىز بەك چىرايلىق ئىكەن.
She is an actress, isn't she? ئۇ ئارتىس ئەمەسمۇ.
(Implying that being an actress also means being beautiful)

In these sentences, the usage of the word ئەمەسمۇ is close to the usage of the particle -غۇ.

3 Subordinate Clause of Reason

The examples below demonstrate how the word ئەمەسمۇ is also used with the conjunction شۇڭا to express reason.

هاۋا ئىسسىق ئەمەسمۇ، شۇڭا بالامغا سۇ ئېلىپ بەردىم.
The weather is hot, so I bought water for my son.
بالام بەك ئەتىگەن تۇرىدۇ ئەمەسمۇ، شۇڭا بالدۇرراق ياتسۇن.
My child wakes up early, so he should go to sleep earlier.

Another way to form subordinate clauses of reason is to add the suffix (كەچكە - ،قاچقا - ،گەچكە-) غاچقا - to the verb. Compare the following sentences with the examples above.

هاۋا ئىسسىق بولغاچقا، بالامغا سۇ ئېلىپ بەردىم.
Because the weather is hot, I bought water for my son.
بالام بەك ئەتىگەن تۇرغاچقا، بالدۇرراق ياتسۇن.
Because my son wakes up very early, he should go to sleep earlier.

In the negative form, simply add suffix مە- \ما- to the root of the verb. Remember, this reduces to مى- when followed by suffix گەچكە- \غاچقا-.
Look at the following example:

ۋاقتىم بولمىغاچقا، خوتەنگە بارالمىدىم.
Because I didn't have time, I couldn't go to Khotan.

Exercise 12: پۇلۇم بولمىغاچقا...

Exercise 12.1:  Look at the following examples of subordinate clause of reason. For each sentence, underline the verb root and circle the suffix expressing reason.

1. ئۇنىڭ ۋاقتى بولمىغاچقا، تويغا بارمىدى.
2. بالىسى كەچ كەلگەچكە، ئانىسى ئەنسىرىدى.
3. ئۇ بەكمۇ ئالدىراش بولغاچقا، مەن ئۇنىڭغا قاراشتىم.
4. پۇلۇم بولمىغاچقا، سەپەرگە چىقالمىدىم.
5. ئۇنى كۆرمىگەچكە، ئۇنىڭدىن بۇ ئىشنى سورىماپتىمەن.
6. ئۇنىڭ ئاۋازى ياخشى بولغاچقا، ئۇ داڭلىق ناخشىچى بولالىدى.
7. ماشىنا ئۇنىڭغا ياققاچقا، ئۇ ئۇنىڭ قىممەتلىكىگە قارىماي ئالدى.

8. ئۇ مېنى كۆرگەچكە، يېنىمغا كەلدى.
9. ئۇ بالدۇر كەتكەچكە، بىزنىڭمۇ ئولتۇرغىمىز كەلمىدى.

You will notice that the form of the suffix is different. List the different forms and explain why they are different:

____

____

____

There are three negative verb forms. Write them below and explain why the vowel changes in the negative suffix.

Exercise 12.2: Complete the sentences below to form subordinate clauses of reason. Change the verb as necessary. If you see the Ø symbol, write a negative sentence.

1. ۋاقتىم (بولماق) ______________________
2. ئۇ كىتابىمنى (ئەكەلمەك,ø) ______________________
3. دادام پۇل (بەرمەك, ø) ______________________
4. تاپشۇرۇقلىرىم كۆپ (بولماق) ______________________
5. ئۇنىڭ بېشى (ئاغرىماق) ______________________
6. بىز پىۋا (ئىچمەك, ø) ______________________
7. ئۇنىڭ دوستى (كەلمەك) ______________________
8. سىزنىڭ ماشىنىڭىز (بولماق) ______________________
9. هاۋا سوغۇق (بولماق) ______________________
10. ئۇلار بۇ كىنونى (كۆرمەك,ø) ______________________
11. ئانام تاماق (ئەتمەك) ______________________
12. ئۇ تاماكا (چەكمەك,ø) ______________________
13. سىلەر هاراق (ئىچمەك) ______________________

Exercise 13: يېڭىسار پىچىقى

Exercise 13.1: What have you learned about the Yengisar knife so far?

____

____

____

Exercise 13.2:  The following passage provides a brief description of the Yengisar knife, its history, and its importance in Uyghur culture. Read the text and complete the information on the museum display card that follows.

beautiful, fine	نەپىس
magnificent	كۆركەم
leather	خۇرۇم
copper	مىس
silver	كۈمۈش
jade	قاشتېشى
bravery	جاسارەت
dagger	خەنجەر
steel	پولات
the blade of a knife	پىچاقنىڭ بىسى
an exhibition	كۆرگەزمە
a horn	مۈڭگۈز
a bone	سۆڭەك
pearl	مەرۋايىت
raw materials	خام ئەشيا
handle	ساپ/دەستە

يېڭىسار پىچىقى - ئۇيغۇرلارنىڭ يەرلىك مىللىي قول- ھۈنەر بۇيۇملىرى ئىچىدە داڭلىق مەھسۇلاتلارنىڭ بىرى. ئۇ ئەسلىدە يېڭىسارنىڭ ئەنئەنىۋى ئىجادىيىتى بولغاچقا، "يېڭىسار پىچىقى" دەپ ئاتالغان. تارىم بوستانلىقىنىڭ غەربىي جەنۇبىي قىسمىغا جايلاشقان يېڭىسار ناھىيىسىدە پىچاق ياساش ھۈنەر كەسپى ناھايىتى تەرەققىي قىلغان. بۇ يەردە ئىشلەنگەن پىچاقلارنىڭ تۈرى يىگىرمە خىلدىن ئاشىدۇ. 1987- يىلى مەملىكەت بويىچە ھۈنەر- سەنئەت بۇيۇملىرىنى باھالاشتا، يېڭىسار پىچىقى بىرىنچىلىككە ئېرىشكەن. يېڭىسار پىچىقى ياسىلىش شەكلى جەھەتتىن نەپىس ۋە كۆركەم بولۇپ، ئىشلىتىشكە ناھايىتى قولاي. ئۇنىڭ تىغى، كېسىدىغان قىسمى ئۈچۈن سۇپەتلىك پولات تاللىنىدۇ. ئىشلىتىش ئورنىغا قاراپ، پىچاقنىڭ بىسى ۋە سېپى (تۇتىدىغان قىسمى) ھەر خىل شەكىللىك ياسىلىدۇ. ھەر بىر تۈرىنىڭ ئۆزىگە خاس نامى بولىدۇ. مەسىلەن، قاسساپ پىچىقى، ئائىلە پىچىقى، خەنجەر نۇسخىلىق پىچاق، يان پىچىقى، كۆرگەزمە پىچىقى قاتارلىقلار. يېڭىسار پىچىقىنىڭ سېپى ئۈچۈن ھەر خىل ھايۋانلارنىڭ مۈڭگۈزى ۋە سۆڭەكلىرى، مىس، كۈمۈش، قاشتېشى، مەرۋايىت قاتارلىق ئەتىۋارلىق ماتېرىياللار ئىشلىتىلىدۇ. بۇ خام ئەشيالار ئىنچىكە ھۈنەر ئارقىلىق بىر- بىرىگە كىرىشتۈرۈلۈپ گۈزەل - سەنئەت بۇيۇمىغا ئايلاندۇرۇلىدۇ. يېڭىسار پىچىقىنىڭ ھەممىسىگە ئۆزىگە ماس كېلىدىغان غىلاپ ياسىلىدۇ. غىلاپسىز يېڭىسار پىچىقى بولمايدۇ. غىلاپنىڭ كۆپچىلىكى ھەر خىل رەڭلىك كالا خۇرۇمىدىن ياسىلىدۇ. يەنە بەزى غىلاپلار مىس ياكى ئاليۇمىندىن ئىشلىنىپ، يۈزىگە ھەر خىل نەقىش ئويۇلىدۇ. پىچاق قەدىمدىن تارتىپ ئۇيغۇرلارنىڭ ئەنئەنىۋى ئادىتىدە ئەرلەر (يىگىتلەر) نىڭ كىچە - كۈندۈز يېنىدىن ئايرىلمايدىغان قورالى بولۇپ كەلگەن. ئۇيغۇرلارنىڭ ئەنئەنىسىدە پىچاق ئەرلىك جاسارىتىنىڭ سىمۋولى ھېسابلىنىدۇ.

شىنجاڭ مۇزېيى

Name of item on exhibit: ______________________________

Place of origin: ______________________________

Award: ____________ (country) ____________ (year)

Associated articles of traditional Uyghur clothing: ______________________________

____

Symbolic meaning: ______________________________

Part name: ____________

Materials: ____________

Part name: ____________

Materials: ____________

Decorated with: ____________

Part name: ____________

Materials: ____________

Materials: ____________

Exercise 13.3:  Below are some words from the passage. Match them with their definitions by drawing a line between the two.

كۆرستىش ئۈچۈن قويۇلغان نەرسىلەر ۋە شۇ نەرسىلەر قويۇلغان جاي	تەرەققىي قىلماق
مۇۋاپىق ، ئەپلىك	ناھىيە
مال سېتىۋالىدىغان ۋە گۆش ساتىدىغان ئادەم	ئېرىشمەك
راۋاجلىنىش ، ئىلگىرىلەش ، يۈكسىلىش	قولاي
نىشانغا يەتمەك ، قولغا كەلتۈرمەك	قاسساپ
ئويۇپ ئىشلەنگەن گۈل	كۆرگەزمە
يېزىدىن چوڭ بولغان مەمۇرىي رايون	نەقىش

Exercise 13.4:  Check your work on the display card by listening to the recorded passage.

Exercise 13.5:  Look at the statements below, and fill in the blanks with the appropriate words and expressions below.

خام ئەشيالار   سىپىي   بەلباغ   قورالى

تۆرى   مۆھىم   غىلاپسىز

1. بۇ يەردە ئىشلەنگەن پىچاقلارنىڭ ______________ يىگىرمە خىلدىن ئاشىدۇ.
2. يېڭىسار پىچىقىنىڭ تىغى ئۈچۈن سۆپەتلىك ______________ تاللىنىدۇ.
3. پىچاقنىڭ ______________ ھەر خىل شەكىللىك ياسىلىدۇ.
4. ______________ يېڭىسار پىچىقى بولمايدۇ.
5. پىچاق ئۇيغۇرلارنىڭ ئەنئەنىۋى ئادىتىدە ئەر (يىگىت) لەرنىڭ يېنىدىن ئايرىلمايدىغان ______________ بولۇپ كەلگەن.

Exercise 13.6: Using the information on the museum display card, provide an oral summary of the Yengisar knife.

Exercise 13.7:  Read the following proverbs. What do they mean to you? Are there any similar sayings in your language?

تىغ يارىسى ساقىيار،
دىل يارىسى ساقايماس.

Wounds of the flesh can heal, while wounds of the heart stay open.

ئاغزىدا كۈلكە - چاقچاق،
قوينىدا پالتا - پىچاق.

A smile on his mouth, but a dagger under his tongue.

پىچاقنى ئاۋۋال ئۆزۈڭگە سال،
ئاغرىمىسا باشقىلارغا سال.

Stab yourself with the knife; if it doesn't hurt use it on others.

سۆز قېلىپىدا ياخشى،
پىچاق غىلىپىدا.

A word is best in its place; a knife is in best in its sheath.

پىچاق ئۆز دەستىسىنى كېسەلمەس.

A blade can't cut its own handle.

Pulling it all together — خۇلاسە

In this section, you will reinforce your knowledge and check the progress you have made during chapters 5 and 6 by completing a limited selection of focused exercises.

Exercise 14.  Based on what you have learned, explain why you would like to go to different cities in Xinjiang.
Follow the model:

مەن تۇرپانغا كارىزنىڭ تارىخىنى ئۆگىنىش ئۈچۈن (ئۆگىنىشكە، ئۆگەنگىلى) بارىمەن.

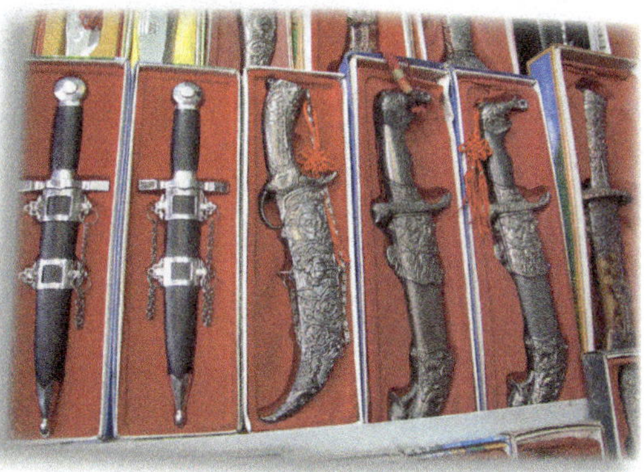

Exercise 15:  Imagine that you are planning a short business trip to Kashgar. Do some online research and find a hotel there. Read testimonies from previous guests. How did they like the hotels? Your task is to choose one of the hotels provided below and explain your choice.

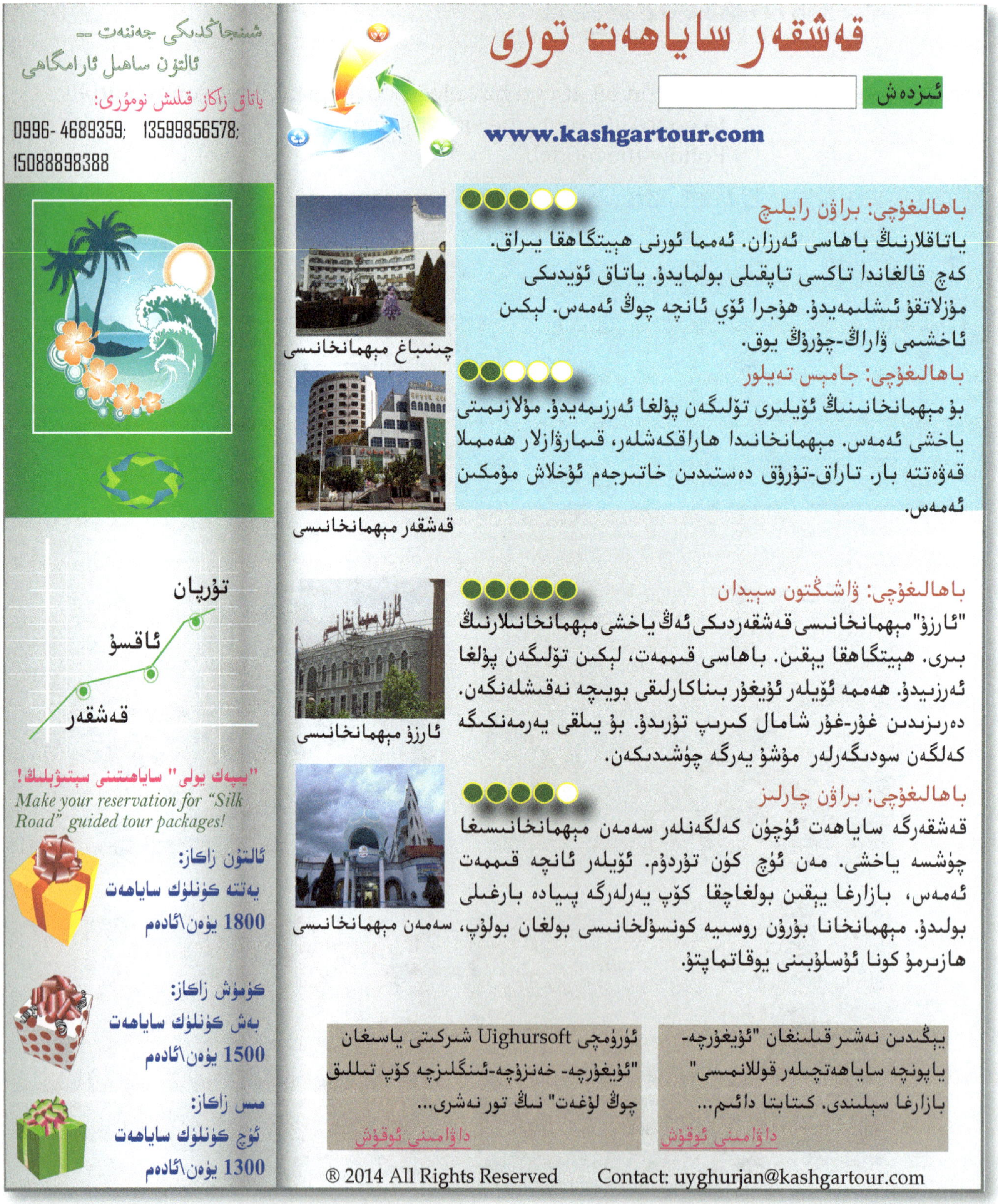

شىنجاڭدىكى جەننەت --
ئالتۇن ساھىل ئارامگاھى

ياتاق زاكاز قىلىش نومۇرى:
0996- 4689359; 13599856578; 15088898388

تۇرپان
ئاقسۇ
قەشقەر

"يىپەك يولى" ساياھىتىنى سېتىۋېلىڭ!
Make your reservation for "Silk Road" guided tour packages!

ئالتۇن زاكاز:
يەتتە كۈنلۈك ساياھەت
1800 يۈەن\ئادەم

كۈمۈش زاكاز:
بەش كۈنلۈك ساياھەت
1500 يۈەن\ئادەم

مىس زاكاز:
ئۈچ كۈنلۈك ساياھەت
1300 يۈەن\ئادەم

قەشقەر ساياھەت تورى

ئىزدەش

www.kashgartour.com

چىنباغ مېھمانخانىسى

باھالىغۇچى: براۋن رايلىچ
ياتاقلارنىڭ باھاسى ئەرزان. ئەمما ئورنى ھېيتگاھقا يىراق. كەچ قالغاندا تاكسى تاپقىلى بولمايدۇ. ياتاق ئۆيدىكى مۇزلاتقۇ ئىشلىمەيدۇ. ھۇجرا ئۆي ئانچە چوڭ ئەمەس. لېكىن ئاشخانىسى ۋاراڭ-چۇرۇڭ يوق.

قەشقەر مېھمانخانىسى

باھالىغۇچى: جامېس تەيلور
بۇ مېھمانخانىنىڭ ئۆيلىرى تۆلىگەن پۇلغا ئەرزىمەيدۇ. مۇلازىمىتى ياخشى ئەمەس. مېھمانخانىدا ھاراقكەشلەر، قىمارۋازلار ھەممىلا قەۋەتتە بار. تاراق-تۇرۇق دەستىدىن خاتىرجەم ئۇخلاش مۇمكىن ئەمەس.

ئارزۇ مېھمانخانىسى

باھالىغۇچى: ۋاشىڭتون سېيدان
"ئارزۇ" مېھمانخانىسى قەشقەردىكى ئەڭ ياخشى مېھمانخانىلارنىڭ بىرى. ھېيتگاھقا يېقىن. باھاسى قىممەت، لېكىن تۆلىگەن پۇلغا ئەرزىيدۇ. ھەممە ئۆيلەر ئۇيغۇر بىناكارلىقى بويىچە نەقىشلەنگەن. دەرىزىدىن غۇر-غۇر شامال كىرىپ تۇرىدۇ. بۇ يىلقى يەرمەنكىگە كەلگەن سودىگەرلەر مۇشۇ يەرگە چۈشىدىكەن.

سەمەن مېھمانخانىسى

باھالىغۇچى: براۋن چارلىز
قەشقەرگە ساياھەت ئۈچۈن كەلگەنلەر سەمەن مېھمانخانىسىغا چۈشسە ياخشى. مەن ئۈچ كۈن تۇردۇم. ئۆيلەر ئانچە قىممەت ئەمەس، بازارغا يېقىن بولغاچقا كۆپ يەرلەرگە پىيادە بارغىلى بولىدۇ. مېھمانخانا بۇرۇن روسىيە كونسۇلخانىسى بولغان بولۇپ، ھازىرمۇ كونا ئۇسلۇبىنى يوقاتماپتۇ.

بېيجىڭدىن نەشر قىلىنغان "ئۇيغۇرچە-ياپونچە ساياھەتچىلەر قوللانمىسى" بازارغا سېلىندى. كىتابتا دائىم...
داۋامىنى ئوقۇش

ئۈرۈمچى Uighursoft شىركىتى ياسىغان "ئۇيغۇرچە- خەنزۇچە-ئىنگلىزچە كۆپ تىللىق چوڭ لۇغەت" نىڭ تور نەشرى...
داۋامىنى ئوقۇش

 Contact: uyghurjan@kashgartour.com

Exercise 16: تۇرپاندا كۆرگەنلىرىم

Exercise 16.1: Tell a few things that you have learned about Turpan.

Exercise 16.2:  Now read John's blog entry about Turpan.

Uyghur John's Blog

ئامېرىكىلىق يالقۇننىڭ تورتۇراسى

Search

كۈندە بىر ماقال:
ئەلگە كىرسەڭ ئىلىگچە، سۇغا كىرسەڭ بېلىگچە.

17 - ئىيۇل، تۇرپان

بۈگۈن ئۇزاقتىن بېرى ئارزۇ قىلىپ كەلگەن قەدىمىي شەھەر تۇرپانغا كەلدىم. تۇرپاننىڭ "جۇڭگو بويىچە ئەڭ ئىسسىق جاي" دېگەن نامى بار ئىكەن. بۇ نام بىكارغا تارقالماپتۇ: بۈگۈن بۇ يەردە 45 سېلسىيە گرادۇسلۇق ئىسسىق بولدى. بۇ فەرېنخايت بويىچە 113 گرادۇس دېگەن گەپ. شۇنداقتىمۇ مەن "ئىدىقۇت قەدىمىي شەھىرى" ۋە "كارىز مۇزېيى" غا باردىم. مېنى ھەيران قالدۇرغان نەرسە شۇ بولدىكى، كارىز پۈتۈن شىنجاڭ بويىچە پەقەت تۇرپاندىلا بار ئىكەن. كارىز مۇزېيىغا كىرىپ، كارىز تارىخىغا ئائىت كۆپ نەرسىلەرنى ئۆگىنىۋالدىم. شۇ كارىزلار ئارقىلىق دېھقانلار ھازىرمۇ ئېتىزلىرىنى سۇغۇرىدىكەن.

تۇرپاننى "ئۈزۈم ماكانى" دەپ بىكار دېمەيدىكەن. شەھەرنىڭ ئىچى ۋە تېشى ئۈزۈمگە تولغان. بۇ يەرنىڭ ئۈزۈملىرى ھەقىقەتەنمۇ تاتلىق ئىكەن. مەن بىر ئۇيغۇر بوۋاينىڭ ئۆيىدە مېھمان بولدۇم. ئۇ ماڭا ئۈزۈم باراڭلىرىنى كۆرسەتتى. بۇلارنىڭ ئۈزۈمى ناھايىتى كۆپ ئىكەن. شۇنچە كۆپ ئۈزۈمنى نېمە قىلىسىلەر دەپ سورىدىم. بوۋاي مېنى ئالاھىدە بىر ئۆيگە باشلىدى. ئۇلار بۇ يەردە ئۈزۈملىرىنى قۇرۇتۇپ كىشمىش قىلىدىكەن. بۇ ئۆينىڭ تاملىرى تۆشۈك-تۆشۈك بولىدىكەن. تۆشۈكلەردىن ھاۋا كىرىپ ئۈزۈم سېسىپ قالمايدىكەن. بۇ ئۆيلەرنى چۈنچە دەيدىكەن. بۇ يەرنىڭ ئۈزۈم ھاراقلىرىمۇ بەك داڭلىق ئىكەن. تۇرپاندا مەن يەنە ئىنقىلابچى شائىر ئابدۇخالىق ئۇيغۇرنىڭ مازىرىنى زىيارەت قىلدىم. بۇ شائىر 1933 - يىلى شېڭ شىسەي تەرىپىدىن ئۆلۈم جازاسىغا ھۆكۈم قىلىنغان. بۇ شائىرنىڭ "ئويغان" شېئىرى ھازىرمۇ ئېسىمدە: "ھەي پېقىر ئۇيغۇر، ئويغان، ئۇيقۇڭ يېتەر!..."

What new information did you learn from John's blog entry?

Exercise 16.3:  Read the proverb on the left side of the blog entry. What does it mean to you? Discuss its meaning with your instructor.

Exercise 16.4: Answer the following questions about the blog entry.

1. تۇرپاندا جون نېمىگە ھەيران بولدى؟
2. چۈنچە دېگەن نېمە؟ نېمىشقا ئۇنىڭ تاملىرىدا كۆپلىگەن تۆشۈكلەر بار؟
3. تۇرپاندا جون قەيەرلەرنى زىيارەت قىلدۇ؟
4. ئابدۇخالىق ئۇيغۇر كىم؟ نېمە ئۈچۈن جون ئۇنىڭ قەبرىسىنى زىيارەت قىلدۇ؟

Exercise 16.5: At the end of the entry, John quotes a line from the famous poem by Abduxaliq Uyghur.

"ھەي پېقىر ئۇيغۇر، ئويغان، ئۇيقۇڭ بېتەرا!..."

What do you think this note means? How would you interpret it?

شائىرنىڭ قەبرى

ئابدۇخالىق ئۇيغۇر
(1933-1901)

Exercise 17: قەشقەردە كۆرگەنلىرىم

Exercise 17.1:  The second entry in John's blog is about Kashgar. What have you learned about old and modern Kasghar? Take notes here based on the headings provided. Go to Chapter 1 Exercise 11.1 if needed.

History: ______________________________
Role of the city on the Silk Road: ______________________________
Famous places: ______________________________
Famous people: ______________________________

Exercise 17.2:  Read John's blog entry about his trip to Kashgar and answer the questions that follow.

Uyghur John's Blog

ئامېرىكىلىق يالقۇننىڭ تورتۇراسى

Search

كۈندە بىر ماقال:

ئانا يۇرتۇڭ ئامان بولسا، رەڭگى - روھىڭ سامان بولماس.

21 - ئىيۇل، قەشقەر

قەشقەرنىڭ كۆپ جايلىرى چېقىلىپ، يېڭى بىنالار سېلىنىپتۇ. شۇنداق بولسىمۇ، بۇ شەھەرگە كەلگىنىمدىن بەك خوشال بولدۇم. مېھمانخانا تېپىشتا ئازراق قىينالدىم. بۇ يەردە چەتئەللىكلەر خالىغان مېھمانخانىدا تۇرالمايدىكەن. مەن ھېيتگاھ مەسچىتىنىڭ يېنىغا جايلاشقان "تىللا" مېھمانخانىسىدىن بىر ياتاق ئالماقچى ئىدىم، ئەمما ئۇ يەردە چەتئەللىكلەر تۇرسا بولمايدۇ دەيدۇ، شۇڭا "چىنىباغ" مېھمانخانىسىغا بېرىشقا مەجبۇر بولدۇم. بۇ مېھمانخانىمۇ يامان ئەمەس ئىكەن، ئەمما ھېيتگاھ مەسچىتىدىن ئازراق يىراق ئىكەن... بۇ مېھمانخانىنىڭ مۇلازىمەتچىلىرىنىڭ كۆپى خەنزۇ ئىكەن. خەنزۇ تىلىنى بىلسەممۇ، ئۇيغۇر مۇلازىمەتچىلەر بىلەن پاراڭلاشقۇم بار ئىدى. شۇڭا كۆڭلۈم ئازراق يېرىم بولدى. بۇ مېھمانخانىنىڭ ئاشخانىسىدىمۇ ئۇيغۇرلارنى كۆرمىدىم. چەتئەللىكلەر تۇرىدىغان مېھمانخانىغا ئۇيغۇرلارنى ئىشقا ئالمايدىغان ئوخشايدۇ...

قەشقەرنى ھۈنەرۋەنچىلىكنىڭ ماكانى دەيدىكەن. كوزىچى يار بېشى دېگەن مەھەللىگە بېرىپ ناھايىتى كۆپ ھۈنەرۋەنلەر بىلەن كۆرۈشتۈم. ساپالچى دەمسىز، گىلەمچى دەمسىز، زەرگەر دەمسىز... ھەممىسى بار. شۇ يەردە مەن بىر پەشمەتچى بىلەن تونۇشۇپ قالدىم. مېنىڭ ئامېرىكىدىن كەلگەنلىكىمنى ئاڭلاپ، يېگەن پەشمەتلىرىمگە پۇل ئالمىدى. ئۇيغۇرلار قىزىق خەلق ئىكەن...

بۈگۈن سەھەردە مال بازىرىغا باردىم. بۇ بەك قىزىق بازار ئىكەن. بۇ بازاردا قوي، كالا، ئات، تۆگە ۋە ئېشەك قاتارلىق ھايۋانلارنى ئېلىپ ساتىدىكەن. بۇ يەرگە چەتئەللىكلەرمۇ كۆپ كېلىدىكەن. چۈشتىن كېيىن ئاپئاق خوجا مەقبەرىسىنى كۆردۈم. ئاپئاق خوجا - ئۇيغۇر دۆلىتىنى جۇڭغارلارغا ساتقان كىشى ئىكەن. ئۇنداقتا ئۇيغۇرلار بۇ ئادەمنى نېمە ئۈچۈن بۇنداق ھۆرمەتلەيدۇ؟ مەن بۇنى چۈشەنمىدىم...

1. What new information have you learned from this entry about the workers in the hotel for foreigners?
2. In كوزىچى يار بېشى, John meets another artisan. What is this person's craft?
3. After this experience, John writes that ئۇيغۇرلار قىزىق خەلق ئىكەن. Why does he say this?
4. How does John react to Uyghur's feelings towards Afaq Khoja?
   A. He agrees with them B. He is surprised by them
   C. He disagrees with them D. none of the above
5. Why does he not understand that Uyghurs respect him?

Exercise 17.3:  Tell if these are true or false based on the text.

توغرا	خاتا

1. جون ھېيتگاھ مەسچىتىنىڭ يېنىدىن بىر ياتاق ئالدى.
2. ئۇ چۈشكەن مېھمانخانىدا مۇلازىمەتچىلەرنىڭ كۆپى خەنزۇ.
3. بۇ مېھمانخانىنىڭ ئاشخانىسىدا ئاشپەزلەرنىڭ كۆپى ئۇيغۇر.
4. بۇ خاتىرىدە جون زەرگەر سۆزىنى تىلغا ئالدۇ.
5. زەرگەر قىممەت باھالىق مېتاللاردىن زىننەت بۇيۇملىرى ياسايدىغان ئۇستا.
6. ئاپاق خوجا ئۇيغۇرلارنىڭ قەھرىمانى.

Exercise 18:  Based on the two cities you have learned about, plan a trip to one of them. Explain where you want to go and why; what you want to see and why. Also, describe what gifts you would chose (and why) to bring back for your parents and your best friend.

Exercise 19:  Following John's blog entry, think of a trip you took somewhere. Describe what you did and saw during this trip. Explain what unusual things you have experienced and explain what you have learned about the places and the people of that country during that trip.

Project

My City

Prepare a presentation introducing your hometown. Include a detailed descriptions such as places to stay, visit, and dining. Explain why do you like/dislike about your hometown.

Self-check

Use the following list to check your knowledge of the topics you have covered in chapters 5 and 6. Mark whether you know and can do the following in Uyghur. If you think you may need more work to fully understand something, you can go back to the relevant section in the chapters and review it.

1. I can talk and write about:

Turpan: the land of grapes	☐
Modern Kashgar	☐
The Id Kah Mosque in Kashgar	☐
The Uyghur Twelve Muqam	☐
Uyghur bazaars and Uyghur craftsmen	☐
Uyghur jobs and occupations	☐
The Yengisar knife	☐
Tata Tonga, a 13th century scholar from Turpan	☐

2. I can also:

Talk about my goals	☐
Read, listen, and understand flight safety instructions	☐
Place a phone call from the airport to an Uyghur friend	☐
Make a travel plan	☐
Ask for directions	☐
Ask for help regarding tourist attractions in Turpan	☐
Conduct conversations and bargain with knife sellers in Kashgar	☐
Recognize onomatoeias in Uyghur	☐
Use some Uyghur proverbs related to knife culture	☐
Tell about a memorable trip	☐

3. I can explain the following words and concepts:

☐	بىخەتەرلىك تاسمىسى	☐	ماكان
☐	جىددىي چىقىش ئېغىزى	☐	ئەنئەنە
☐	ھاجىتى يوق	☐	ئۆرپ - ئادەت
☐	بېزەكلىك مىڭ ئۆي	☐	ئېغىز تەگمەك
☐	ئىمىن ۋاڭ مۇنارى	☐	كارىز
☐	ئىدىقۇت قەدىمىي شەھىرى	☐	ھېيتگاھ مەسچىتى
☐	ھۈنەرۋەن	☐	مەھمۇد قەشقەرى مازىرى
☐	مەدىكار	☐	يۈسۈپ خاس ھاجىپ مەقبەرىسى
☐	كوزىچى يار بېشى	☐	بولىۋېرىدۇ!
☐	بەكە	☐	مەنئى قىلىنماق

4. I can use grammar to ...

Emphasize verbs with ئالماق and بەرمەك	☐
Express purpose and objectives (-غىلى\ -قىلى\ -گىلى\ -كىلى)	☐
Express purpose and objectives (-قا\ -كە)	☐
Express purpose and objectives (ئۈچۈن)	☐
Express a wish/desire (-غۇم\ -قۇم\ -كۈم\ -گۈم and the words بارايوق)	☐
Give polite commands (-سىلا\ -سىلە)	☐
Ask questions expressing a high level of respect (-لا)	☐
Name occupations using the noun formation suffixes	☐
Express reason (ئەمەسمۇ)	☐
Express reason (-غاچقا\-قاچقا\-گەچكە\ -كەچكە)	☐

Vocabulary سۆزلۈك

Vocabulary is given according to the Uyghur alphabetical order.
The right column precedes the left column on each page.

cook, chef	ئاشپەز
valuable, precious	ئەتىۋارلىق
gardener	باغۋەن
to value	باھالىماق
pocket knife	بەكە
oasis	بوستانلىق
dye	بوياق
to be proud (of)	پەخىرلەنمەك
knife-maker or seller	پىچاقچى
banging, crashing	تاراق - تۇرۇق
to choose	تاللىماق
to develop (something)	تەرەققىي قىلماق
sense, feeling	تۇيغۇ
tailor	تىككۈچى
bravery	جاسارەت
to ring, jingle, ding	جىرىڭلىماق
tea-seller	چايپۇرۇش
enduring	چىدامىلىق
fly (insect)	چىۋىن
raw materials	خام ئەشيا
dagger	خەنجەر
leather	خۇرۇم
tightrope walker	دارۋاز
time, epoch, period	دەۋر
to speak fluently	راۋان سۆزلىمەك
small, narrow street (with shops on either side)	رەستە
legend	رىۋايەت
pottery	ساپالچىلىق \ كۇلالچىلىق

to greet	ئەھۋال سوراشماق
sheath	غىلاپ
butcher	قاسساپ
to laugh heartily	قاقاقلاپ كۈلمەك
weapon	قورال
convenient	قولايلىق
earthenware jar	كوزا
exhibition	كۆرگەزمە
very quickly	لىككىدە
day laborer	مەدىكار
country	مەملىكەت
product	مەھسۇلات
coppersmith	مىسكەر
traditional; national	مىللىي
bread maker; baker	ناۋاي
carving	نەقىش
cart driver	ھارۋىكەش
to wail, to sob	ھۆركىرەپ يىغلىماق
craft; skill	ھۈنەر
craftsman	ھۈنەرۋەن
to be dug out	ئويۇلماق
method	ئۇسلۇب
triangle	ئۈچ بۇلۇڭ
noise	ۋاراڭ - چۇرۇڭ (ۋاڭ-چۇڭ)
to talk too much (slang)	ۋالاقلىماق
to express	ئىپادە قىلماق
need, requirement	ئېھتىياج
carpenter	ياغاچچى
wool	يۇڭ

ئاتۇش ئۈگرەخانىسى
阿图什面条馆
TAXNA

吐鲁番第一宾馆

بەتتىنچى دەرس

CHAPTER SEVEN

مەكتەپ ھاياتى

CAMPUS LIFE IN XINJIANG

IN THIS CHAPTER

Functions

- Describing the educational background
- Comparing educational systems in Xinjiang and the US
- Describing life in a dorm
- Describing a typical day on campus
- Describing the University
- Reading advertisements
- Reading Uyghur street signs

Grammar

- The auxiliary verb كەتمەك
- Verb formation with the suffix -لى (-لا \ -لە)
- Reciprocal constructions
- Causative constructions in Uyghur (Part 1)
- Adjective forming suffix -ىي

In this chapter, John comes back to Urumchi to get ready for his first semester at Xinjiang University. He meets with his Uyghur language instructor and learns more about the educational system in Xinjiang. Through the conversations, reading passages, and excerpts from John's blog contained in this chapter, you will learn about campus life in Xinjiang and Uyghur students' daily activities. You will also become acquainted with some important concepts such as ئۇنۋان, ساھە, and مۇتەخەسسىس.

Exercise 1: Have you ever studied abroad? Explain where and when. How would you describe your educational background? Respond to the following questions to provide some basic information about your school.

1. فاكۇلتېتىڭىزدا قايسى پەنلەر ئوقۇتىلىدۇ؟
2. سىزنىڭچە ئوقۇغۇچىلار تىلشۇناسلىق، سىياسەت، دىنشۇناسلىق، ئىنسانشۇناسلىق، گۈزەل سەنئەت ۋە سودا پەنلىرى قاتارلىق دەرسلەردىن قايسىسىغا بەكرەك قىزىقىدۇ؟
3. ئوقۇغۇچىلارنى دەرسكە تېخىمۇ قىزىقتۇرۇش ئۈچۈن ئوقۇتقۇچىلار نېمە قىلىشى كېرەك؟
4. مەكتىپىڭلاردا سىياسىي ئۆگىنىش قىلامدۇ؟
5. ئوقۇغۇچىلار خالىغان ۋاقىتتا ئوقۇتقۇچىلىرى بىلەن كۆرۈشەلەمدۇ؟
6. مەكتىپىڭلاردا ئۇيغۇر تىلىغا قىزىقىدىغانلار كۆپمۇ؟ سىلەرچە ئۇلار نېمە ئۈچۈن ئۇيغۇر تىلىغا قىزىقىدۇ؟
7. سىلەرنىڭ مەكتىپىڭلاردىمۇ ئوقۇغۇچىلارنى ئاشخانىدا ئىشلىتەمدۇ؟
8. ئامېرىكىدا ئوقۇغۇچىلار تاپشۇرۇقلىرىنى كۇتۇپخانىدا ئىشلەمدۇ يا ياتاقلىرىدىمۇ؟ نېمىشقا؟

Exercise 2: ئۈرۈمچى تەسىراتلىرىم

Exercise 2.1:  After his trip to southern Xinjiang, John comes back to Urumchi to start coursework at شىنجاڭ پېداگوگىكا ئۇنىۋېرسىتېتى. Read the brief blog entry, then answer the questions that follow.

Uyghur John's Blog

ئامېرىكىلىق يالقۇننىڭ تورتۇراسى

Search

كۈندە بىر ماقال:
بىلمەسلىك ئەيىب ئەمەس، سورىماسلىق ئەيىب.

28- ئاۋغۇست: مانا ئۈرۈمچىگە قايتىپ كەلدىم. بىر نەچچە كۈندىن كېيىن دەرسلىرىمىزنى باشلايمىز. مەن يەنە ھاياجانلىنىۋاتىمەن... سەپەردە ئۇيغۇرچەمنى خېلى ياخشى مەشق قىلىۋالدىم. شۇنداق بولسىمۇ، يەنىلا ئەنسىرەۋاتىمەن. ئۇيغۇر پروفېسسورلىرىم سۆزلىسە، ئۇلارنى تولۇق چۈشىنەلەمدىم يا قىينىلامدىم؟ قېنى، ئوقۇش باشلانسۇن، بىر گەپ بولار... ئوقۇش باشلانماي تۇرۇپ ئەنسىرىگەننىڭ پايدىسى يوق.

تۈنۈگۈن دۆڭكۆۋرۈك بازىرىغا بېرىپ ئايلاندىم. نېمىدېگەن چوڭ بازار بۇ! بۇ بازاردا ھەممە نەرسە بار ئىكەن. يېڭىسار پىچاقلىرى دەمسىز، خوتەن گىلەملىرى دەمسىز، قەشقەر دوپپىلىرى دەمسىز... لېكىن نەرخى ئازراق قىممەترەك ئىكەن. دۆڭكۆۋرۈك ئەتراپىدا ئۇيغۇرلار جىق ئىكەن، لېكىن ئاڭلىسام ئۈرۈمچىنىڭ باشقا جايلىرىدا ئۇيغۇرلار ئاساسەن يوق ئىكەن، ھەممە يەرنى خەنزۇلار بېسىپ كېتىپتۇ. كىشىلەرنىڭ دېيىشىچە، ئىچكىرىدىن* ئۈرۈمچىگە كۆنگە نۇرغۇن خەنزۇلار كېلىدىكەن. قىزىق... يېقىندا بىر گېزىتتا "جۇڭگو ھۆكۈمىتى ئۇيغۇر ياشلىرىنى ئىچكىرىگە يۆتكەپ ئىش بىلەن تەمىنلەيدۇ" دېگەن بىر خەۋەرنى ئوقۇدۇم. مەن بۇ ئىشنى چۈشەنمىدىم. ئۇيغۇر ياشلىرىنى ئىچكىرىگە يۆتكىمەي، شۇ يەرنىڭ ئۆزىدە، يەنى** ئۆزىنىڭ ماكانىدا ئىش بىلەن تەمىنلىسە بولمامدۇ؟ خەنزۇلارمۇ ئۆز ئۆلكىلىرىدە ئىشلىسە ياخشى بولاتتىغۇ... شۇ ھۆكۈمەتمۇ سىياسەتنى بەكمۇ مۇرەككەپلەشتۈرىۋېتىدۇ- دە...

دۆڭكۆۋرۈكتە يەنە بىر قىزىق نەرسىگە كۆزۈم چۈشتى. ھەممە ۋىۋېسكىلار تۆت تىلدا يېزىلغان، يەنى ئۇيغۇرچە، خەنزۇچە، ئىنگلىزچە ۋە رۇسچە. ئاڭلىسام، ئىنگلىز تىلىدىن باشقا بۇ يەردە رۇس تىلىغىمۇ قىزىقىش ئىنتايىن يۇقىرى ئىكەن. ھەممە يەردە رۇس تىلى كۇرسلىرى توغرۇلۇق ئېلانلار چاپلانغان. بۇ بازاردا روسىيە ۋە ئوتتۇرا ئاسىيادىن كەلگەن سودىگەرلەرمۇ بەك كۆپ ئىكەن. مېنىڭمۇ ئوتتۇرا ئاسىيانى زىيارەت قىلغۇم بار. غۇلجىغا بارغىنىمدا پۇرسەت چىقىپ قالسىلا، ئالمۇتىغا ئۆتىمەن. ئۇ يەردىن قىرغىزىستان، ئۆزبېكىستانلارغا بارىمەن... سائەت ئالتە بوپتىغۇ... ياسىنغا تېلېفون قىلاي، بىللە تاماق يەيمىز دەپ كېلىشكەنتۇق.

---

*ئىچكىرى - China proper (lit. inside land)
**يەنى - in other words

ئىسىم
ئىم

1. جوننىڭ ئۇيغۇرچىسى ياخشى بولسىمۇ ئۇ نېمىگە ئەندىشە قىلىدۇ؟
2. دۆڭكۆۋرۈك بازىرىدا نېمىلەر بار؟ بۇ بازارنى قانداق تەسەۋۋۇر قىلىسىز؟
3. نېمىشقا جون ھۆكۈمەتنىڭ ئىشىغا ھەيران قالىدۇ؟
4. دۆڭكۆۋرۈك بازىرىدا ئۇنىڭ نېمىگە كۆزى چۈشىدۇ؟ نېمىشقا؟
5. جون ئوتتۇرا ئاسىيانى قاچان زىيارەت قىلماقچى؟

Exercise 2.2:  Match the given Uyghur words with their English equivalents.

full/fully	تولۇق
basically/nearly	ئايلانماق
complicated	ئاساسەن
government	بېسىپ كەتمەك
politics	يۆتكىمەك
to post/hang (a poster)	تەمىنلىمەك
poster/placard	سىياسەت
to occupy	ھۆكۈمەت
to provide	مۇرەككەپ
to stroll	ۋىۋىسكا
to transfer	چاپلىماق

Migration to and from Xinjiang

If you visit Urumchi, you will see that most sections of the city are occupied by Han Chinese people. In recent years there has also been a surge in the migration of Han Chinese to other cities in Xinjiang, such as Kashgar, Turpan, and Khoten. At the same time, the Chinese government actively promotes the migration of Uyghur youth to Inner China (ئىچكىرى), generally to work at factories. The government claims that assisted migration of young Uyghurs to factories in Inner China is a way of alleviating the pressures of high unemployment in Xinjiang and providing Uyghur youth with a source of income. However, many Uyghurs view such actions as part of an unspoken policy of cultural and linguistic assimilation. Uyghurs who move to Inner China often adopt elements of Han Chinese language and culture, and are removed from the strong family and community ties traditionally instrumental in the transmission of Uyghur culture.

1 The Auxilary Verb كەتمەك

In the blog entry, you see another auxiliary verb كەتمەك. It appears in the sentence:

دۆڭكۆۋرۈك ئەتراپىدا ئۇيغۇرلار جىق ئىكەن، لېكىن ئاڭلىسام ئۈرۈمچىنىڭ باشقا
جايلىرىدا ئۇيغۇرلار ئاساسەن يوق ئىكەن، ھەممە يەرنى خەنزۇلار بېسىپ كېتىپتۇ.
There are apparently a lot of Uyghurs around the Döngköwrük bazaar,
but from what I hear there are not many Uyghurs in other parts of Urumchi.
The Chinese have gone and taken over everywhere (are all over).

You have already learned that Uyghur often uses auxiliary verbs where English would use an adverb. The auxiliary verb كەتمەك is used to indicate that the action of the main verb occurs quickly or unexpectedly, often with intense and dramatic results. As indicated by the translation of the example sentence above, this meaning is often reflected in some colloquial dialects of American English using phrases like 'done gone and' or 'up and.' Where such translations are not appropriate, a similar meaning can also be expressed with adverbs such as 'suddenly' or 'just.' Sometimes, the urgency is clear from context and cannot be translated into English with a single word or phrase. Look at the following examples to try and get a feel of the range of meanings for the auxiliary use of كەتمەك.

بېشىم يامان ئاغرىپ كەتتى.
My head started to ache really badly all of a sudden.
ئەجەب چارچاپ (ھېرىپ) كەتتىم.
I just got really tired (all of a sudden).
گەپلىرىمنى ئاڭلاپ كۈلۈپ كەتتىڭغۇ؟!
You just burst out laughing when you heard what I said!
ئاڭلىدىڭلارمۇ، ئابلەتنىڭ قىزى قېچىپ كېتىپتۇ.
Did you hear? Ablet's daughter up and ran away with her lover!
Uncle Sadir passed away unexpectedly. سادىركام تۈگەپ كېتىپتۇ.
It started snowing all of a sudden. قار يېغىپ كەتتى.
ھاۋا بىر دەمنىڭ ئىچىدە ئۆزگىرىپ كەتتى.
The weather up and changed all of a sudden!
قىزىم، چاي قايناپ كەتتى!
My daughter, the tea's gone and boiled over!

Exercise 3: بالا قاتتىق يىغلاپ كەتتى

Exercise 3.1:  Read the following sentences and circle the numbers of those in which كەتمەك is used as an auxiliary verb. Then translate those sentences into English.

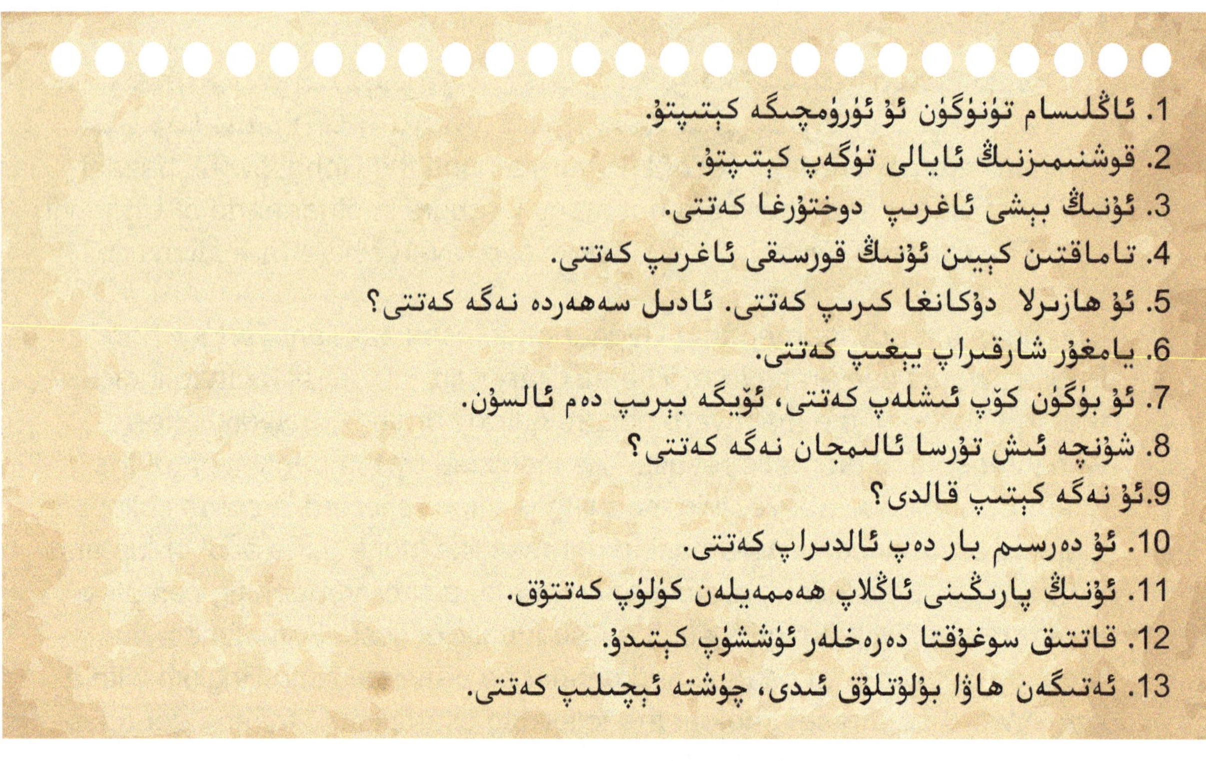

1. ئاڭلىسام تۈنۈگۈن ئۇ ئۈرۈمچىگە كېتىپتۇ.
2. قوشنىمىزنىڭ ئايالى تۈگەپ كېتىپتۇ.
3. ئۇنىڭ بېشى ئاغرىپ دوختۇرغا كەتتى.
4. تاماقتىن كېيىن ئۇنىڭ قورسىقى ئاغرىپ كەتتى.
5. ئۇ ھازىرلا دۇكانغا كىرىپ كەتتى. ئادىل سەھەردە نەگە كەتتى؟
6. يامغۇر شارقىراپ يېغىپ كەتتى.
7. ئۇ بۈگۈن كۆپ ئىشلەپ كەتتى، ئۆيگە بېرىپ دەم ئالسۇن.
8. شۇنچە ئىش تۇرسا ئالىمجان نەگە كەتتى؟
9.ئۇ نەگە كېتىپ قالدى؟
10. ئۇ دەرسىم بار دەپ ئالدىراپ كەتتى.
11. ئۇنىڭ پارىڭىنى ئاڭلاپ ھەممەيلەن كۈلۈپ كەتتۇق.
12. قاتتىق سوغۇقتا دەرەخلەر ئۈششۈپ كېتىدۇ.
13. ئەتىگەن ھاۋا بۇلۇتلۇق ئىدى، چۈشتە ئېچىلىپ كەتتى.

Exercise 3.2:  Now look at the remaining sentences, in which كەتمەك is not used as an auxiliary. Translate those sentences.

2 *Verb Formation with the Suffix* -لى (-لا \ -لە)

In the blog entry, you saw the verb سۆزلىمەك. You have seen before that many verbs have the suffix -لى between a root and the infinitive ending. For example: سۆز - سۆزلىمەك. This is the most commonly used verb forming suffix in Uyghur. It can be added to a noun, adjective, adverb, or pronoun to create verbs.

The suffix shows that the subject of the sentence 'created or did' the thing expressed by the root: work - ئىش, to work - ئىشلىمەك.

The suffix -لى is actually a reduced form of the suffix -لا، -لە, which changes to -لى as the result of vowel reduction. However, keep in mind that the vowel will not change in the present-future or present continuous tense forms: ئاق > ئاقلايدۇ \ ئاقلاۋاتىدۇ؛ سۆز > سۆزلەيدۇ \ سۆزلەۋاتىدۇ

In many cases, if you know the meaning of the original word, you can guess the meaning of the verb. However, occasionally the verb can have a distinct meaning (similar to English, c.f., rain and to rain; but arm and to arm). Look at more examples:

white - to whitewash; to justify ئاق - ئاقلا - ئاقلىماق

eye - to pursue, to have one's eye on كۆز - كۆزلە - كۆزلىمەك

you - to address a person using the polite form سىز - سىزلە - سىزلىمەك

good - to improve ياخشى - ياخشىلا - ياخشىلىماق

bad - to badmouth يامان - يامانلا - يامانلىماق

hand - to support قول - قوللا - قوللىماق

head - to start باش - باشلا - باشلىماق

Exercise 4:  Define the following words in Uyghur. Use an online dictionary if necessary. Follow the model.

ياخشىلىماق: بىرەر نەرسىنىڭ سۈپىتىنى بۇرۇنقىدىن ياخشىراق قىلماق، ئۆزگەرتمەك

يامانلىماق:

سۆزلىمەك:

قوللىماق:

باشلىماق:

تۈزلىماق:

تۈزلىمەك:

Exercise 5: مۇئەللىم بىلەن سۆھبەت

Exercise 5.1:  Listen to the dialogue between John and his Uyghur language instructor and decide if the following are true or false.

1. جون ئوقۇتقۇچىسى بىلەن بۇرۇن كۆرۈشكەن.
2. جون ئوقۇتقۇچىنىڭ ئىسمىنى تولۇق ئېيتىشى كېرەك.
3. جوننىڭ ساۋاقداشلىرىنىڭ ئارىسىدا جۇڭگولۇقلارمۇ بار.
4. ئۇنىڭ بىر ساۋاقدىشى ئامېرىكىلىق.
5. سىنىپتا ئىككى ياپونمۇ بار.
6. مۇئەللىم ئۇلۇشكۈن خەنزۇ ئوقۇغۇچىلىرى بىلەن كۆرۈشتى.
7. دەرس ئەتە باشلىنىدۇ.

توغرا	خاتا

Exercise 5.2: Listen to the dialogue again. Follow the script and fill in the blanks with the verbs that you hear.

جون: ئەسسالامۇ ئەلەيكۇم!

مۇئەللىم: ۋەئەلەيكۇم ئەسسالام! كېلىڭ، كېلىڭ، سىز جونمۇ؟

جون: ھەئە، مەن جون تومسون.

مۇئەللىم: مېنىڭ ئىسمىم پەرىدە داۋۇت، مەن سىزنىڭ ئۇيغۇر تىلى ئوقۇتقۇچىڭىز بولىمەن. ئېسىڭىزدە بولسا، سىز بىلەن بىر نەچچە قېتىم تېلېفوندا ______________

جون: ھەئە، ئېسىمدە بار ئەلۋەتتە. سىزنىڭ ئىسمىڭىزنى تولۇق ئېيتماي پەرىدە مۇئەللىم دېسەم بولامدۇ؟

مۇئەللىم: بولىدۇ، بولىدۇ... ئۈرۈمچىگە قاچان كەلدىڭىز؟

جون: مەن بۇ يەرگە كەلگىلى ئىككى ھەپتە بولدى. قارىسام ئوقۇشقا بىر نەچچە كۈن بار ئىكەن، شۇڭا تۇرپان بىلەن قەشقەرنى زىيارەت قىلىپ كەلدىم. ئۈرۈمچىگە تۈنۈگۈنلا قايتتىم.

مۇئەللىم: مۇنداق دەڭ... سەپىرىڭىز ياخشى بولدىمۇ؟

جون: ھەئە، بەك ياخشى بولدى. تۇرپان، قەشقەرلەرگە باردىم. ناھايىتى كۆپ ئۇيغۇرلار بىلەن____________ خېلى كۆپ نەرسىلەرنى ئۆگىنىۋالدىم. ئەمدى ۋاقتىم بولسا، غۇلجا تەرەپلەرنى كۆرگۈم بار...

مۇئەللىم: بۇنى ياخشى ئويلاپسىز. غۇلجىغا چوقۇم بېرىڭ. ھە راست، ساۋاقداشلىرىڭىز بىلەن؟
____

جون: ياق، تېخى، مەكتەپكە ھازىر كەلدىم. سىنىپتا قانچە ئوقۇغۇچى بار؟

مۇئەللىم: ھازىرچە ئالتە ئوقۇغۇچى ئۆزىنى تىزىملىتىپتۇ.

جون: ئۇلارنىڭ ھەممىسى چەتئەللىكلەرمۇ؟

مۇئەللىم: ياق، ئىككى خەنزۇمۇ بار.

جون: قىزىق، خەنزۇلارمۇ ئۇيغۇرچە ئۆگىنەمدۇ؟

مۇئەللىم: ئۆگىنىدىغانلارمۇ چىقىپ تۇرىدۇ.

جون: قالغان تۆتى قەيەرلىك ئىكەن؟

مۇئەللىم: بىرسى سىزنىڭ يۇرتدىشىڭىز ئىكەن، يەنە بىرسى گېرمانىيەلىك ئىكەن. مەن ئۇنىڭ بىلەن ئۈلۈشكۈن ____________. ئۇمۇ تونۇشاي دەپ كەلگەن ئىكەن. قالغان ئىككىسىنىڭ ئىسىملىرىغا قارىغاندا ياپونىيەلىك ئوخشايدۇ.

جون: مۇنداق دەڭ... مېنىڭ ئۇلار بىلەن تېزرەك تونۇشقۇم بار. دەرسلىرىمىزنى قاچان باشلايمىز؟

مۇئەللىم: ئۆگۈنلۈككە باشلايمىز.

جون: ياخشى! ئەمىسە ئۆگۈنلۈككە كۆرۈشەيلى!

مۇئەللىم: بولىدۇ. خوش!

Exercise 5.3: Practice the dialogue aloud with your partner.

3 Reciprocal (Mutual) Constructions: -ش (-ىش \ -ۇش \ -ۈش) + Verb

In the dialogue (Exercise 5.2), you saw some reciprocal constructions. They are used to describe an event in which two or more people perform the same action, either simultaneously or with each other. Compare the following verbs:

to talk	سۆزلىمەك
to chat, to talk with someone	سۆزلەشمەك
to be familiar with, to know	تونۇماق
to meet one another (for the first time), to get acquainted	تونۇشماق

Here are some examples:

He talked more than an hour. .ئۇ بىر سائەتتىن ئارتۇق سۆزلىدى

They taked more than an hour. .ئۇلار بىر سائەتتىن ئارتۇق سۆزلەشتى

He knows me. .ئۇ مېنى تونۇيدۇ

We got acquainted yesterday. .بىز تۈنۈگۈن تونۇشتۇق

In some cases, the primary meaning of the verb may take on a slightly different meaning when used in the reciprocal form. The following examples illustrate this point.

to pull	تارتماق
to argue	تارتىشماق
to come	كەلمەك
to agree	كېلىشمەك
to see	كۆرمەك
to meet	كۆرۈشمەك
to look	قارىماق
to help	قاراشماق

Exercise 6: ساۋاقداشلار بىلەن ئۇچراشتۇق

Exercise 6.1:  Decide when to use the reciprocal construction and complete these sentences.

كۆرمەك or كۆرۈشمەك

1. ئۇلۇشكۈن مەكتەپتە ئابدۇللانى ____________، لېكىن ئۇ مېنى ______________.
2. بىز ئۆي ئىگىسى بىلەن ______________ ئاندىن ئۇ بىزنى ئۆيگە باشلىدى.

قارىماق or قاراشماق

3. ئادىلە ئانىسىغا ______________. مېھمانلارنىڭ كېلىشىگە ھەممە تاماق تەييار ئىدى.
4. ئۇ ماڭا ھەيران بولۇپ -______________.

سۆزلىمەك or سۆزلەشمەك

5. ئۇ بالىسى ئويغىنىپ قالمىسۇن دەپ ئاستا ______________.
6. ئۇلار ئىككى سائەتتىن ئارتۇق ______________.

Exercise 6.2:  Read the following entry from John's blog about a day he spent hanging out with his friends. Circle the appropriate verb form based on the context in which it appears. In some sentences both forms could be correct, so circle both.

بۈگۈن ساۋاقداشلار بىلەن شەھەر ئايلىنىمىز دەپ (كەلگەن ئىدۇق، كېلىشكەن ئىدۇق). دەرستىن چۈشۈپلا دۆڭكۆۋرۈك بازىرىدا (ئۇچرىشىدىغان، ئۇچرايدىغان) بولدۇق. ياسىن ۋاقتىدا (كەلدى، كېلىشتى)، ئەمما غەيرەتنى يېرىم سائەت ساقلىدۇق. قورساقلىرىمىز بەكمۇ ئېچىپ (كەتتى، كېتىشتى)، شۇڭا ئالدى بىلەن تاماق يەۋالايلى دەپ بىر ئاشخانىغا (كىردۇق، كىرىشتۇق). مەن بىر تەخسە پولۇ، بىر چىنە قېتىق ۋە خامسەي بۇيرۇتتۇم. ياسىن 10 دانە پېتىر مانتا ۋە تۆت زىق كاۋاپ بۇيرۇتتى. غەيرەت بىر تەخسە لەڭمەن ۋە ئىككى دانە سامسا بۇيرۇتتى. ئاشپەز ئۇستاملار ناھايىتى چاققان ئىكەن. بۇيرۇتقان تاماقلىرىمىز بەك تېز تەييار (بولۇشتى، بولدى). ئاشخانا پاكىز ئىكەن. چىنە- قاچا، چوكىلارمۇ پاكىز يۇيۇلغان. بىز پاراڭلاشقاچ * تاماق (يېدۇق، يېيىشتۇق). كۆتكۈچى چاي دەملەپ (كەلدى، كېلىشتى). تاماقنى يەپ بولغاندىن كېيىن تاماقنىڭ پۇلىنى (تۆلىدۇق، تۆلەشتۇق). جەمئىي 52 كوي (بوپتۇ، بولۇشۇپتۇ). پۇلنى تۆلەپ، ئۇستاملارغا رەھمەت (ئېيتىپ، ئېيتىشىپ)، ئاشخانىدىن (چىقتۇق، چىقىشتۇق). بازارغا پاراڭلاشقاچ پىيادە (ماڭدۇق، مېڭىشتۇق).

---

*-  This expresses simultaneous actions. It is explained in chapter 8

Exercise 6.3:  Now listen to the passage and check your answers.

Exercise 6.4:  Based on the blog entry above, write about a time when you went out with your friends. Use the reciprocal construction as needed.

Have You Ever Seen Them?

Visitors to Xinjiang may notice typos, spelling mistakes, and other errors on billboards, signs, and advertisements in Uyghur. This is because in Xinjiang, the majority of sign-makers are usually not very well educated. Some of them have done their schooling in Chinese, and some of them have not completed formal education at all. As a result, machine translations and word-for-word translations from Chinese (which often sound awkward in Uyghur) are common. A government organization known as the XUAR Language and Script Committee has a Division of Terminology dedicated specifically to developing Uyghur words for modern concepts and technological developments; however, due to a lack of enforcement in schools or publications, these words are rarely used or understood by the wider public.

Exercise 7: John wants to meet his friend Yasin at the Döngköwrük bazaar. He decides to take a bus to get there. The bus moves slowly due to traffic, so John has plenty of time to look out the window. While reading some of the Uyghur signs he sees, he gets confused. What about you? Try to spot the mistakes in the signs that follow.

Exercise 8: ئۈرۈمچىدە قاتناش ۋاستىلىرى

Exercise 8.1: Here you will learn about transportation in Urumchi. Before reading the passage, check the following words.

to get on the bus, to take the bus	ئاپتوبۇسقا چىقماق
to get off the bus	ئاپتوبۇستىن چۈشمەك
bus stop	ئاپتوبۇس بېكىتى
full (bus)	لىق
passenger	يولۇچى
to run (as in a bus), to travel back and forth	قاتنىماق
to hail a taxi	تاكسى توسماق
to carry, to transport	توشۇماق (ئادەم، يۈك)
truck	قارا ماشىنا
a car, small vehicle	پىكاپ

Exercise 8.2:  Read the text below and fill in the blanks with the appropriate words and phrases provided in the table above.

ئىسمىم مارك. مەن ئەسلى ئامېرىكىلىق، لېكىن ھازىر ئۈرۈمچىدە تۇرىمەن. ئۈرۈمچىگە كەلگىلى
تۆت يىل بولدى. بۇ يەردە مەن ئىنگلىز تىلىدىن دەرس بېرىمەن ۋە قوشۇمچە بىر شىركەتتە تەرجىمان
بولۇپ ئىشلەيمەن. مەن مەكتەپ بەرگەن ياتاقتا تۇرىمەن، ئەمما ________ ھەر ھەپتە
دۆڭكۆۋرۈك بازىرىغا بېرىپ تۇرىمەن. ئۇ يەرگە بېرىش ئۈچۈن 7-يول ________. بۇ
ئاپتوبۇستىن باشقا دۆڭكۆۋرۈك بازىرىغا يەنە 101 - يول ئاپتوبۇسمۇ ________، ئەمما
ئۇ دائىم ________ كېلىدۇ، شۇڭا مەن ئۇنىڭغا چىقمايمەن. ئالدىراش بولسام، بەزىدە
________. بۇ يەردە تاكسى بەك ئەرزان. 10- 15 كويغا بازارنىڭ يېنىغا ئاپىرىپ
قويىدۇ. ئىشتىن چۈشكەندە قايسى ئاپتوبۇس بالدۇرراق كەلسە، شۇنىڭغا چۈشمەن، چۈنكى كەچتە
________ ئانچە كۆپ بولمايدۇ.

Exercise 8.3:  How do you get to work or school? Write an essay similar to the previous exercise.

Traffic Jams in Urumchi

Like many urban areas of China and Central Asia, Urumchi suffers from serious traffic problems. These include a failure to yield the right-of-way to pedestrians, even at designated crosswalks, as well as a general disregard for traffic laws. As you might imagine, this can and does lead to frequent and severe traffic jams.

Exercise 9: ئوقۇغۇچىلار ھاياتى

Exercise 9.1:  John and Yasin are talking about student life in Xinjiang. Listen to their conversation and take notes. Then compare your notes with those of a classmate and discuss what you learned from John and Yasin's conversation.

Exercise 9.2:  Now practice reading the dialogue aloud.

illegal	قانۇنغا خىلاپ
to spend the night	قونۇپ قالماق
to interrogate	سوراققا تارتماق
dislike, hate	ئۆچ

جون: ياخشىمۇسىز!

ياسىن: ياخشىمۇسىز! قانداق ئەھۋالىڭىز؟ قەشقەردىن قاچان قايتتىڭىز؟

جون: ئۈلۈشكۈن قايتتىم.

ياسىن: مۇنداق دەڭ. مەن سىزنى كېلىپلا تېلېفون قىلىدۇ دەپتىمەن.

جون: كەچۈرۈڭ، بەك كەچ كەلگەچكە تېلېفون قىلمىدىم.

ياسىن: كېرەك يوق. مەكتەپكە تىزىملاتتىڭىزمۇ؟

جون: ياق. تۈنۈگۈن ئۇيغۇر تىلى مۇئەللىمىم بىلەن كۆرۈشتۈم.

ياسىن: مۇئەللىم بىلەن كۆرۈشۈش ۋە تىزىملىتىش باشقا باشقا ئىككى ئىش.

جون: شۇنداقمۇ؟ چەتئەللىك ئوقۇغۇچىلار قانداق تىزىملىتىدۇ؟

ياسىن: مەكتىپىمىزدە "چەتئەللىك ئوقۇغۇچىلار ئىشخانىسى" دەپ بىر ئىشخانا بار. سىز شۇ يەرگە بارىسىز.

جون: دەرسلەرنىمۇ شۇ يەردە تىزىملامدۇ؟

ياسىن: ياق، دەرسلەرنى مەكتەپ سىزگە تاللاپ بېرىدۇ. سىز شۇ دەرسلەرنى ئوقۇيسىز.

جون: ئۆزۈم ياقتۇرغان دەرسلەرنى تاللاپ ئوقۇسام بولامدۇ؟

ياسىن: بولمايدۇ. سىز مەكتەپ سىزگە تاللاپ بەرگەننى ئوقۇشىڭىز شەرت!

جون: ياتاقچۇ؟ ياتاقنىمۇ مەكتەپ تاللاپ بېرەمدۇ؟

ياسىن: شۇنداق، چەتئەللىك ئوقۇغۇچىلار چوقۇم مەكتەپنىڭ چەتئەللىك ئوقۇغۇچىلار ياتاق بىناسىدا تۇرۇشى لازىم.

جون: شۇنداقمۇ؟ مېنىڭ ئۇيغۇرلارنىڭ ئۆيىدە تۇرغۇم بار ئىدى.

ياسىن: چەتئەللىكلەر ئۇيغۇرلارنىڭ ئۆيىدە تۇرۇشقا بولمايدۇ. بۇ قانۇنغا خىلاپ.

جون: مېنىڭ ئۈرۈمچىدە بىرقانچە ئۇيغۇر دوستلىرىم بار. مەن ئۇلار بىلەن ئىنتېرنېت ئارقىلىق تونۇشقان. ئۇلارنىڭ ئۆيىگە بارسام بولامدۇ؟

ياسىن: مېھمانغا بارسىڭىز بولىدۇ. بەلكىم ئۇيغۇرلارنىڭ مېھماندوست خەلق ئىكەنلىكىنى بىلىسىز. ئەمما قونۇپ قالسىڭىز، ئۆي ئىگىلىرىنى ساقچىلار سوراققا تارتىدۇ.

جون: نېمە؟ "سوراققا تارتىدۇ" دېگىنىڭىز "سوئال سورايدۇ" دېگەن گەپمۇ؟

ياسىن: بىرئاز ئوخشايدۇ. ساقچىلارنىڭ قوپال سوئال سورىشىنى بىز "سوراققا تارتماق" دەيمىز.

جون: مەن سوراققا تارتىشقا بەك ئۆچ!

ياسىن: مېنىڭمۇ سوراق بىلەن خوشام يوق.

Exercise 9.3:  Based on the previous conversation, mark the following sentences true or false. Try to mark your answers without looking back at the text.

	T	*F*
1. In order to be enrolled, you only need to meet with your teacher.		
2. International students need to go to the International Office to register.		
3. In Xinjiang, you may not choose the classes you wish to take.		
4. Foreign students live with local students in the same dorm.		
5. Foreign students may choose to stay with a family.		
6. Foreign students may visit local families.		
7. If you spend the night with a local family, the police will interrogate the host.		
8. The expression سوراقفا تارتماق is synonymous with the expression سوئال سورىماق.		

Exercise 9.4:  What do you think? Based on the dialogue in Exercise 9.2 discuss the following questions as a group.

1. سىزنىڭچە نېمىشقا شىنجاڭدا دەرسلەرنى مەكتەپ تاللاپ بېرىدۇ؟
2. نېمىشقا چەتئەللىك ئوقۇغۇچىلار ئۆزى خالىغان ياتاقتا/ئۆيدە تۇرالمايدۇ؟
3. سىزنىڭچە نېمە ئۈچۈن چەتئەللىكلەر ئۇيغۇرلانىڭ ئۆيىدە قوناپ قالالمايدۇ؟
4. ئەگەر ئامېرىكىدا ئوقۇغۇچىلارنىڭ دەرسلىرىنى مەكتەپ تاللاپ بەرسە، قانداق ئاقىۋەتلەر كېلىپ چىقىشى مۇمكىن؟
5. ئامېرىكىلىق ئوقۇغۇچىلار خالىغان جايدا تۇرالامدۇ يا چوقۇم ياتاقتا تۇرۇشى كېرەكمۇ؟ نېمىشقا؟

4 Causative Constructions in Uyghur

The Causative Constructions show that the action is caused by the subject of the sentence. These roughly correspond to English constructions with 'get', 'have' or 'make'.

She wrote an article. –> She made the students write an article.

In Uyghur, causatives are formed by adding the following suffixes:

(1) (-تۇر\-دۇر\-دۈر) تۇر and (-قۇز\ -گۈز\-كۈز) غۇز to verb stems ending with consonants, except those which end in اي، ەي or ەر. As you see from the examples below, causatives in دۇر- and غۇز- are interchangeable.

Causative verbs	*Active verbs*	
دوختۇر بىمارنى سائەت توققۇزدا ياتتۇردى(ياتقۇزدى). The doctor had the patient go to bed at nine.	دوختۇر سائەت توققۇزدا ياتتى. The doctor went to bed at nine.	A
ئەخمەت ئۇلارنى بۇ يولدا كۆپ ماڭدۇردى (ماڭغۇزدى). Ahmad had them walk a lot on this road.	ئەخمەت بۇ يولدا كۆپ ماڭدى. Ahmad walked a lot on this road.	B
خېمىرنى ئۇنىڭغا كەستۇردۇم (كەسكۇزدۇم) I made her cut the dough.	مەن خېمىرنى كەستىم. I cut the dough.	C
يۈكنى ئېشەككە ئارتتۇردۇم (ئارتقۇزدۇم) I made him load the donkey.	يۈكنى ئېشەككە ئارتتىم. I loaded the donkey.	D
دادام كىتابنى ماڭا ئالدۇردى (ئالغۇزدى). My father made me buy a book.	دادام كىتابنى ئۆزى ئالدى. My father bought the book himself.	E
مۇئەللىم ئوقۇغۇچىلارغا ماقالە يازدۇردى (يازغۇزدى). The teacher had the students write a paper.	مۇئەللىم ماقالە يازدى. The teacher wrote a paper.	F
ئادىلە بالىسىغا تاماق يېدۈردى (يېگۈزدى). Adile fed her son. (Adile made her son eat.)	ئادىلە تاماق يېدى. Adile ate the food.	G

4 Causative Constructions in Uyghur (cont'd.)

If a verb ends in a vowel, the causative is formed with the suffix ت-.

مۇئەللىم ئۇنىڭغا ماقالىنى قايتا ئوقۇتتى.

Note that there is an alternative form of the causative for verbs ending in a vowel which combines the suffix ت- with the aforementioned تۇر -تۇر\ -كۇز\ -قۇز suffixes, e.g. -تتۇر, -تقۇز . They mean the same, and are interchangeable. Look at the following examples:

Causative verbs	Active verbs	
ئۇ ئۆيىنى ياساتتى (ياساتقۇزدى، ياساتتۇردى). He had his home renovated.	ئۇ ئۆيىنى ياسىدى. He renovated his home.	H
ئەكبەر ئۇكىسىنى ئويناتتى (ئويناتقۇزدى، ئويناتتۇردى). Ekber let his younger brother play.	ئەكبەر ئۇكىسى بىلەن ئوينىدى. Ekber played with his younger brother.	I
ئۇ كىشىلەرنى كەچكىچە ئىشلەتتى (ئىشلەتكۈزدى، ئىشلەتتۈردى). He had the people work until sunset.	ئۇ كەچكىچە ئىشلىدى. He worked until sunset.	J
ئۇلار سادىرنىڭ قولىنى ئارقان بىلەن باغلاتتى (باغلاتقۇزدى، باغلاتتۇردى). They had Sadir's hands tied with rope.	ئۇلار سادىرنىڭ قولىنى ئارقان بىلەن باغلىدى. They tied Sadir's hands with rope.	K

If the original verb (i.e. without the causative) is intransitive (i.e. does not require an object) the new, causative form of that verb is transitive, and its object takes the accusative suffix نى- (examples a-b and h-k). However, if the original verb is already transitive (i.e., requires an object) (examples c-g) the original object keeps the accusative (if it is definite) and the new object takes the dative case ending غا-، قا-، گە-، كە-.

Note that there is a special class of derived or complex verb roots (usually, any root with two or more syllables ending in ي- ،ر-) which also take a causative ending ت-. You will learn more about these in Chapter 9.

All other verbal endings (passive, tense, negation, question) follow the causative ending:

Was the computer used? كومپيۇتېر ئىشلىتىلدىمۇ؟

Why wasn't this computer used? بۇ كومپيۇتېر نېمىشقا ئىشلىتىلمىدى؟

You didn't break your arm, did you? قولۇڭنى سۇندۇرىۋالمىدىڭمۇ؟

Exercise 10:  Fill in the blanks with the appropriate forms of the causative suffix.

1. ئادىل بوۋىسىنىڭ چەينىكىنى سۇن__________ۇپ قويدى.
2. پاتىگۈل بالىسىغا دورا ئىچ__________دى.
3. نازاكەت مېنىڭ كومپيۇتېرىمنى ئىشلە__________تى.
4. ئادىلە چېچىنى بويا__________ ماقچى.
5. خالمۇرات پىلانىنى ئۆزگەر_____تى.
6. ئاتا ئوغلىنىڭ چېچىنى ئال_____ دى.

Exercise 11:  Rewrite the following sentences using the causative suffix. Follow the example:

ئادىل چېچىنى ياسىدى. ئادىل چېچىنى ئۇستامغا ياساتتى (ياساتقۇزدى، ياساتتۇردى).

1. ئادىلە يېڭى كۆڭلەك ئالدى. ____
2. پاتىگۈل ئىلتىماسنامە يازدى. ____
3. ساۋاقداشلار كىنو كۆردى. ____
4. ئەنۋەر بۇزۇلغان ماشىنىسىنى ئۆزى رېمونت قىلدى. ______________________________
5. قاسىم كومپيۇتېرىنى ئۆزى ئوڭشىدى. ____________________________________

Exercise 12:  Go back to the questions provided in Exercise 1 and identify the causative suffixes in the sentences.

Exercise 13: ئوقۇغۇچىلارنىڭ كۈندىلىك مەشغۇلاتى

Exercise 13.1: Discuss the following questions in group.

1. Have you ever lived in a dorm?
2. Have you ever shared a room with someone?
3. Have you ever lived in a dorm abroad?

Note:

Many Uyghur students prefer not to stay in the same dormitories as Han Chinese, citing linguistic, cultural, and religious differences. In fact, the feeling is generally mutual. This two-way antipathy is due in large part to the stereotypes which each group ascribes to the other.

Exercise 13.2:  Read the first part of John's blog entry about students' daily routines and dorm life in Xinjiang. Then answer the questions below.

Uyghur John's Blog

ئامېرىكىلىق يالقۇننىڭ تورتۇراسى

Search

كۈندە بىر ماقال: كۈچلۈك بىرنى يېڭەر، بىلىملىك مىڭنى.

ئامېرىكىلىق ئوقۇغۇچىلارغا ئۇيغۇر ئالىي مەكتەپ ئوقۇغۇچىلىرىنىڭ تۇرمۇشى قىزىقارلىق تۇيۇلۇشى مۇمكىن. بۇ يەردە ئوقۇغۇچىلار بىزگە ئوخشاش مەكتەپكە ئوقۇش پۇلى ۋە ياتاق پۇلى تاپشۇرغان بىلەن ئوقۇيدىغان دەرسلەرنى ئۆزلىرى تاللىيالمايدىكەن، تۇرىدىغان ياتاقلارنىمۇ ئۆزلىرى تاللىيالمايدىكەن. ھەممىنى مەكتەپ ئورۇنلاشتۇرۇپ بېرىدىكەن. بۇ يەردىكى ئوقۇغۇچىلار ھەر كۈنى ئەتىگەن سائەت سەككىزدىن چۈشكىچە، ۋە بەزى كۈنلىرى چۈشتىن كېيىنمۇ بىر ئىككى سائەتتىن دەرس ئوقۇيدۇ. پۈتۈن مەكتەپتىكى ئوقۇغۇچىلار چۈش سائەت 12 دە تەڭلا دەرستىن چۈشكەچكە، بۇ ۋاقىتتا مەكتەپ قورۇسى بەكمۇ قىستاڭچىلىق بولۇپ كېتىدۇ. بۇ ۋاقىتتا پۈتۈن ئوقۇغۇچىلار مەكتەپ ئاشخانىسىغا تاماققا بارىدۇ. تۈنۈگۈن مەنمۇ ئۇيغۇر دوستلىرىم بارىدىغان ئوغۇللار 2 - ئاشخانىسىغا باردىم. تاماقلارنىڭ تۈرى كۆپ، شۇنداقلا باھاسى كوچىدىكى ئاشخانىلاردىن خېلىلا ئەرزان ئىكەن. ئەمما تاماقلارنىڭ سۈپىتى ئانچە ياخشى ئەمەس.

بارلىق ئوقۇغۇچىلار پۈتۈنلەي مەكتەپنىڭ ياتاق بىناسىدا تۇرۇشى لازىم ئىكەن. ئۇيغۇر دوستۇم ياسىننىڭ ياتىقىغا بېرىپ كۆرۈپ باقتىم. بىر ياتاقتا ئالتە ئوقۇغۇچى بىللە تۇرىدىكەن، شۇڭا ھەر بىر ئۆيدە قوش قەۋەتلىك كارىۋاتتىن ئۈچى بولىدىكەن. ئەمما ياتاقلاردا مۇنچا ياكى ھاجەتخانا بولمىغاچقا، ئوقۇغۇچىلار كوللېكتىپ ھاجەتخانىغا بارىدىكەن. ھەر بىر قەۋەتتە بۇنداق كوللېكتىپ ھاجەتخانىدىن ئىككىسى بولىدىكەن. ئۇلار بۇنى "سۇخانا" دەپ ئاتايدىكەن. ئادەتتە ئۇيغۇر ئوقۇغۇچىلار بىلەن خەنزۇ ئوقۇغۇچىلار بىر ياتاقتا تۇرۇشنى خالىمايدىكەن. ئۇيغۇرلار خەنزۇلارنى "مەينەت" دېسە، خەنزۇلار ئۇيغۇر ئوقۇغۇچىلارنى "ئوغرى" دەيدىكەن. بەزىدە ئۇيغۇر ئوقۇغۇچىلار بىلەن خەنزۇ ئوقۇغۇچىلار سۇخانىدا ئۇرۇشۇپ قالىدىكەن.

1. نېمىشقا چۈش سائەت 12 دە مەكتەپ قورۇسى قىستاڭچىلىق بولۇپ كېتىدۇ؟
2. مەكتەپ ئاشخانىسىنىڭ تاماقلىرى قانداق؟
3. مەكتەپ ياتىقىنى قانداق تەسۋىرلەيسىز؟
4. "كوللېكتىپ ھاجەتخانا" دېگەن نېمە؟
5. خەنزۇ ۋە ئۇيغۇر ئوقۇغۇچىلار بىر بىرىنى قانداق ئاتايدىكەن؟

Exercise 14: مەكتەپ ھاياتى

Exercise 14.1:  First, describe a typical day of your college life. Then describe a typical weekend when you were at college. Have you ever studied abroad? If so, what were your weekdays and weekends like?

Exercise 14.2:  Read the rest of John's blog entry and answer the questions below.

Uyghur John's Blog

ئامېرىكىلىق يالقۇننىڭ تورتۇراسى

Search

كۈندە بىر ماقال:
بىر بىكار كۈنتى بىكار قىلىپتۇ.

بۇ يەردىكى ئوقۇغۇچىلارنىڭ كۈندىلىك مەشغۇلاتى بەك ئاددىي: ئەتىگەن سائەت سەككىزدە دەرسكە بارىدۇ؛ تۆت سائەت دەرستىن كېيىن ئاشخانىغا بارىدۇ؛ تاماقتىن كېيىن ياتاققا ياكى كۇتۇپخانىغا بارىدۇ؛ ھەر چارشەنبە كۈنى چۈشتىن كېيىن ئوقۇغۇچىلارغا ئۆز سىنىپىدا "سىياسىي ئۆگىنىش" دەپ يىغىن ئاچىدۇ. بۇ يىغىندا ئوقۇغۇچىلار كوممۇنىستىك پارتىيەنىڭ ھەر خىل سىياسەتلىرىنى ئۆگىنىدىكەن، شۇڭا ھېچكىمنىڭ بۇ يىغىن بىلەن خوشى يوق ئىكەن. شەنبە ۋە يەكشەنبە كۈنلىرى ئوقۇغۇچىلار كىر يۇيۇش، مۇنچىغا بېرىش، بازار ئايلىنىش دېگەندەك ئىشلار بىلەن ئالدىراش بولىدىكەن. ئوقۇغۇچىلار بۇ يەردە تورغا چىقىشقا بەك ئامراق ئىكەن. مەكتەپنىڭ ئۆدۈلىدا بىرنەچچە تورخانا بار ئىكەن. ئوقۇغۇچىلارنىڭ ھەممىسى دېگۈدەك بوش ۋاقتى بولسىلا، تورخانىغا بېرىشنى ياخشى كۆرىدىكەن. توردا ناخشا ئاڭلاش ۋە دوستلىرى بىلەن پاراڭلىشىش ئاساسلىق ئورۇندا تۇرىدىكەن.

كەلگىنىمگە بىر ئاي بولمايلا ئامېرىكىنى ئەجەب سېغىندىم...

ئىسىم
ئىم

1."سىياسى ئۆگىنىش" دېگەن نېمە؟ نېمىشقا ئوقۇغۇچىلارنىڭ سىياسى ئۆگىنىش بىلەن خوشى يوق؟
2. شەنبە - يەكشەنبىلىرى ئوقۇغۇچىلار نېمە قىلىدۇ؟
3. تورخانىدا ئوقۇغۇچىلار ئادەتتە نېمە قىلىدۇ؟
4. سىزچۇ؟ سىزنىڭ ئوقۇش كۈنلىرىڭىز ئادەتتە قانداق ئۆتىدۇ؟
5. سىز كۈن بويى نېمە ئىشلار بىلەن ئالدىراش بولىسىز؟
6. سىزنىڭ ئەڭ ياخشى كۆرىدىغان ئىشىڭىز نېمە؟ نېمە بىلەن خوشىڭىز يوق؟

Mandatory Political Education in China

Throughout China, college students are obligated to take a political studies (سىياسىي ئۆگىنىش) course that serves to educate them in the Communist Party ideology and rhetoric. The course covers the history and tenets of "Marxism-Leninism-Mao Zedong Thought" as the foundation and guiding philosophy of the Peoples' Republic of China. It also covers the Party's official view of ethnic minorities and their role in Chinese history and society. Many Uyghurs find aspects of the "Party line" presented in this course objectionable – as do most other minorities, and many Han Chinese. However, in addition to being mandatory, the course imparts knowledge which is essential for any citizen who wishes to advance their career in politics within the PRC.

Exercise 14.3:  Based on the information given by John in his blog entry, what do you know about the average Uyghur student's daily routine? Fill in the blanks with appropriate words without looking at the passage.

ئوقۇغۇچىلارنىڭ كۈندىلىك ______________ بەك ئاددىي. ئۇلار ھەر
كۈنى ئەتىگەن سائەت سەككىزدىن ______________ دەرس ئوقۇيدۇ.
ھەر چارشەنبە كۈنى ______________ قىلىدۇ. سىياسى ئۆگىنىشتە
ئوقۇغۇچىلار ______________ ھەر خىل سىياسەتلىرىنى ئۆگىنىدۇ. شەنبە ۋە
يەكشەنبە كۈنلىرى ئوقۇغۇچىلار______________، ______________،
______________ دېگەندەك ئىشلار بىلەن ئالدىراش بولىدۇ. ئوقۇغۇچىلارنىڭ
ھەممىسى دېگۈدەك بوش ۋاقتىدا ______________ بىرىشنى ياخشى كۆرىدۇ.

Exercise 14.4:  Compare a Uyghur student's daily routines to your own. Fill in the table below.

پەرقى	ئوخشاشلىقى

Exercise 14.5: Now listen to the whole blog entry. Then, based on the text you hear, prepare an oral summary of your daily routine.

Exercise 15: تۇنجى ئوقۇش كۈنى

Exercise 15.1: Check the words below and listen to the conversation between John and a service assistant.

bank account	بانكا ھېساباتى
dining hall card	ئاشخانا كارتىسى
title, degree	ئۇنۋان
semester	مەۋسۇم

student ID	ئوقۇغۇچىلىق كىنىشكىسى
insurance	سۇغۇرتا
textbook	دەرسلىك كىتاب
History Department	تارىخ فاكۇلتېتى

Exercise 15.2: Listen to the conversation again and practice it aloud with your partner.

Exercise 15.3:  Now listen to a short question and answer session between two students and list the questions you hear in the lines provided below. The following vocabulary will help you understand the dialogue.

major, specialty	كەسىپ
expert, specialist	مۇتەخەسسىس

field, area of knowledge	ساھە
the chair (of a department)	مۇدىر

Exercise 15.4:  Now hold a similar conversation with a partner using the questions in Exercise 15.3 as a guide.

Exercise 15.5:  Add two more questions of your own for your partner to answer. Then, answer two of your partner's questions.

____

____

____

Exercise 15.6:  Match the following definitions with the appropriate words by drawing a line between the Uyghur word on the right and its appropriate definition on the left.

بىرەر ساھەدە مەخسۇس بىلىم ئىگىلەپ ھەم شۇ ساھەدە مول تەجرىبىگە ئىگە بولغان كىشى	دەرسلىك
ئىلمىي، كەسپىي ساھەدە ئىشلىگۈچىلەرنىڭ شۇغۇللىنىۋاتقان كەسپىدىكى ئىختىساسلىق دەرىجىسىنى بەلگىلەش ئۈچۈن مەخسۇس نام	مەۋسۇم
ئىلىم- پەن ، ئىدىيە ياكى ئىجتىمائىي پائالىيەت قاتارلىقلارنىڭ ھەر بىر تارمىقى	ئۇنۋان
بىر ئوقۇش يىلىنىڭ يېرىمى	مۇتەخەسسىس
ئوقۇغۇچىلارنىڭ دەرس ئۆگىنىشى ۋە دەرس تەكرارلىشى ئۈچۈن مەخسۇس تۈزۈلگەن كىتاب	ساھە

Exercise 16: شىنجاڭدا مائارىپ سىستېمىسى

Exercise 16.1: Look at the schematic of the education system in Xinjiang below and discuss it with your instructor. How does it differ from the American education system?

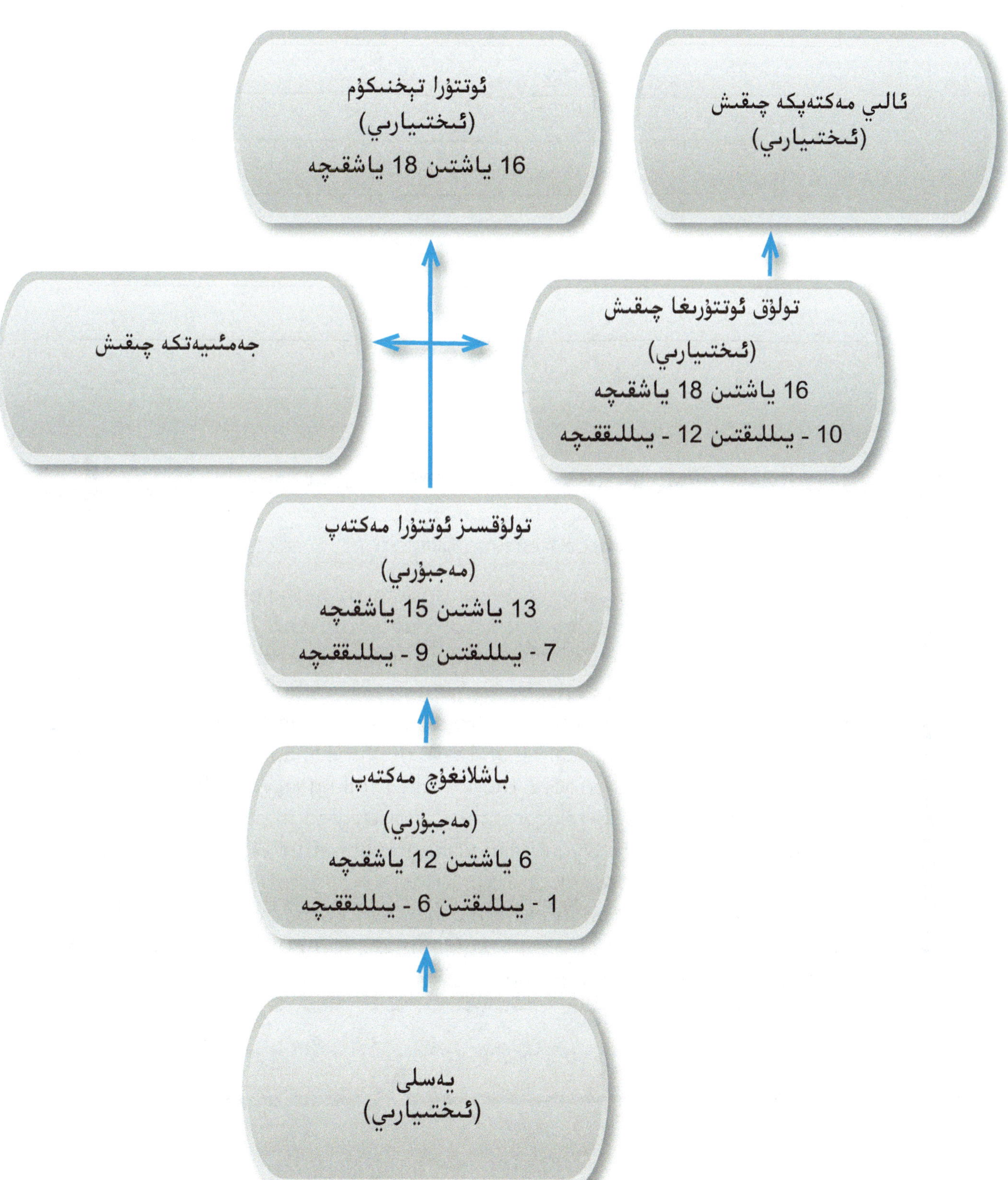

Exercise 16.2: Now write a summary of the information presented in Exercise 16.1 in Uyghur.

Education in Xinjiang

Since education in Xinjiang is only compulsory through the end of junior high school, many Uyghurs choose to drop out before completing their secondary education, often with the approval of their parents. This is because many Uyghurs feel that employment opportunities will be limited for them even if they graduate from college. In their eyes, it is better to enter the workforce earlier and save the time and money spent on higher education. Furthermore, the so-called "bilingual education" policy in Xinjiang effectively relegates the use of Uyghur in senior high school to classes specific to Uyghur language and literature (all university courses except Uyghur Literature are conducted in Chinese). This marginalizes students with an interest in other fields who have trouble with Chinese, and it is interpreted by many Uyghurs as a form of forced cultural assimilation or worse – brainwashing.

Exercise 17: شىنجاڭ ئۇنىۋېرسىتېتى

Exercise 17.1:  Read the following passage about Xinjiang University and complete the graph that follows in English according to the information contained therein.

شىنجاڭ ئۇنىۋېرسىتېتى – شىنجاڭدىكى تارىخى ئەڭ ئۇزۇن، كۆلىمى ئەڭ چوڭ، تەتقىقات سەۋىيىسى ئەڭ يۇقىرى ئالىي مەكتەپ. ئۇ شىنجاڭ ئۇيغۇر ئاپتونوم رايونىنىڭ مەركىزى ئۈرۈمچىگە جايلاشقان. شىنجاڭ ئۇنىۋېرسىتېتىنىڭ تارىخى 1924 - يىلى قۇرۇلغان "شىنجاڭ رۇسچە سىياسى- قانۇن مەكتىپى"دىن باشلىنىدۇ. بۇ مەكتەپ 1930 - يىلى "شىنجاڭ رۇسچە سىياسى - قانۇن ئىنستىتۇتى" بولۇپ قۇرۇلغان، 1935 - يىلىغا كەلگەندە نامى "شىنجاڭ ئىنستىتۇتى" غا ئۆزگەرتىلگەن. بۇ ۋاقىتتىكى مەكتەپ ئوقۇغۇچىلىرىنىڭ كۆپ قىسمى شىنجاڭنىڭ ھەرقايسى جايلىرىدىن كەلگەن ئۇيغۇر ئوقۇغۇچىلار بولۇپ، يەنە باشقا مىللەت ئوقۇغۇچىلىرىمۇ ئوقۇغان. 1950 - يىلى مەكتەپنىڭ نامى "شىنجاڭ مىللەتلەر ئىنستىتۇتى" غا ئۆزگەرتىلگەن. 1960- يىلى 10 - ئايدا رەسمىي "شىنجاڭ ئۇنىۋېرسىتېتى" دەپ ئاتالغان.

شىنجاڭ ئۇنىۋېرسىتېتى مەركىزىي مەكتەپ رايونى، شىمالىي مەكتەپ رايونى ۋە جەنۇبىي مەكتەپ رايونى دەپ ئۈچ قىسىمغا بۆلۈنىدۇ. رەسمىي مەلۇماتلارغا ئاساسلانغاندا مەكتەپنىڭ مۇقىم مۈلكى ئىككى مىليارد يۈەنگە يېتىدۇ. ھازىر شىنجاڭ ئۇنىۋېرسىتېتىدا ئىشلەۋاتقان مۇنتىزىم ئوقۇتقۇچىلار 1800 نەپەر (بۇنىڭ ئىچىدە دوكتورلۇق ئۇنۋانى بارلار 320 نەپەر، ماگىستىر ئۇنۋانى بارلار 800 نەپەر) بولۇپ، پۈتۈن مەكتەپ خىزمەتچىلەر سانىنىڭ % 49 نى تەشكىل قىلىدۇ.

شىنجاڭ ئۇنىۋېرسىتېتىدا ھازىر ئوتتۇز مىڭغا يېقىن ئوقۇغۇچى ئوقۇيدۇ. بۇنىڭ ئىچىدە تولۇق كۇرس ئوقۇغۇچىلىرى يىگىرمە ئالتە مىڭ، ماگىستىر ۋە دوكتۇر ئاسپىرانت ئوقۇغۇچىلار تەخمىنەن ئۈچ مىڭ. بۇ يەردە يەنە تۆت يۈزگە يېقىن چەتئەللىك ئوقۇغۇچىلار ھەر خىل كەسىپلەر بويىچە ئوقۇيدۇ. مەكتەپتە ماركسىزملىق پەلسەپە، ئەدەبىيات، قانۇن، ئىقتىساد، ئىلمىي باشقۇرۇش، تەبىئىي پەن (ئىجتىمائىي پەن) ۋە سانائەت پەنلىرى بويىچە 23 ئىنستىتۇت بار. شىنجاڭ ئۇنىۋېرسىتېتىنىڭ كۇتۇپخانىسى شىنجاڭدىكى ئەڭ چوڭ كۇتۇپخانا ھېسابلىنىدۇ. بۇ يەردە تەخمىنەن تۆت مىليون پارچىدىن ئارتۇق كىتاب بار. بۇ كىتابلارنىڭ يېرىمدىن كۆپرەكى باسما كىتاب شەكلىدە، قالغانلىرى ئېلېكترونلۇق كىتاب شەكلىدە بولۇپ، ئاساسەن مەكتەپ ئوقۇغۇچىلىرى ئۈچۈن خىزمەت قىلىدۇ. مەكتەپ رەھبەرلىكى شىنجاڭ ئۇنىۋېرسىتېتىنى 2020 - يىلىغا بارغاندا ئوتتۇرا ئاسىيادىكى ئەڭ داڭلىق ئالىي مەكتەپ قىلىپ قۇرۇپ چىقىش ئۈچۈن تىرىشماقتا. (تىرىشۋاتىدۇ.)

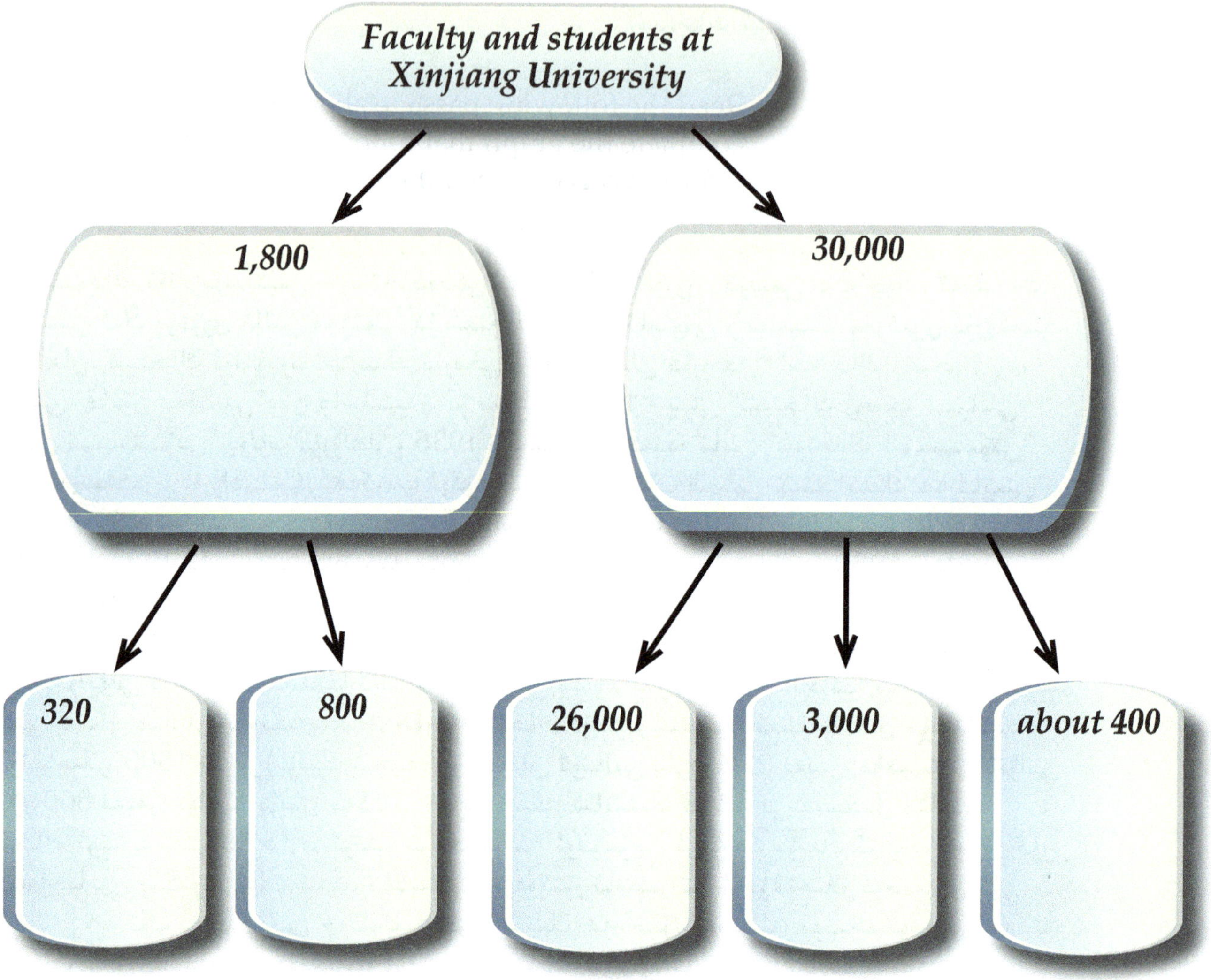

Faculty and students at Xinjiang University

- *1,800*
  - *320*
  - *800*
- *30,000*
  - *26,000*
  - *3,000*
  - *about 400*

Exercise 17.2:  Skim the text again and complete the timeline below with important events in the history of Xinjiang University.

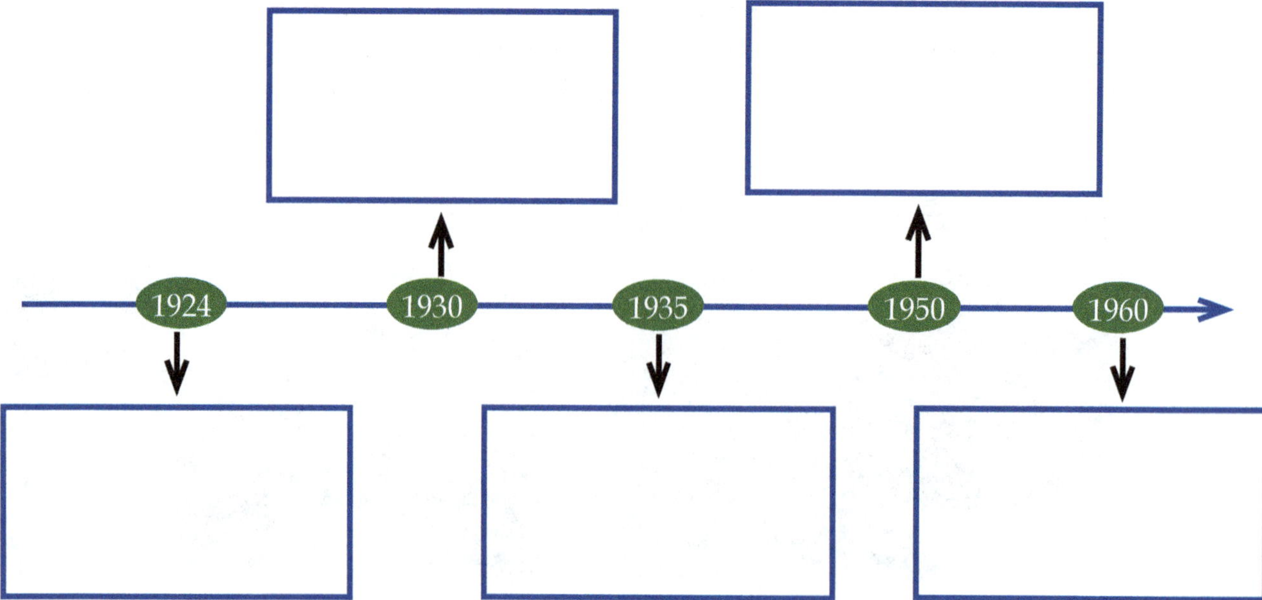

Exercise 17.3: Review the passage again and answer the following questions.

1. How many campuses does Xinjiang University have?
2. How many schools or divisions does the university comprise?
3. How many books does the library have?
4. In what forms are books available?

5 Adjective forming suffix ـىي-

The suffixes ـىي- and ـۋى- / ـۋىي- after a vowel (the two spellings are equivalent in meaning) are added to many nouns of Persian and Arabic origin to form adjectives. It is roughly equivalent to English suffixes such as -al, -ic, -ous, -ern, as in political, scientific, religious, eastern, etc.
Look at the following examples:

northern	شىمالىي	north	شىمال
southern	جەنۇبىي	south	جەنۇب
historical	تارىخىي	history	تارىخ
scientific	ئىلمىي	science	ئىلىم
religious	دىنىي	religion	دىن
the public	ئاممىۋى	the people	ئامما
modern	زامانىۋى	time	زامان
traditional	ئەنئەنىۋى	tradition	ئەنئەنە
personal	شەخسىي	person	شەخس
global	دۇنياۋى	world	دۇنيا
essential	ئاساسىي	basis, essence	ئاساس

Exercise 18: 

Match the adjectives given in column A to the nouns in column B to form expressions which make sense. Then make sentences with them.

A
دىنىي
شەخسىي
ئىلمىي
شىمالىي
تارىخىي

B
پائالىيەت
شىنجاڭ
ئۆي
ئۇنۋان
رومان

Exercise 19:  شىنجاڭ ئۇنىۋېرسىتېتىنىڭ ئوقۇتقۇچىسى

In this video, Zulpiqar Barat, an Uyghur professor from Xinjiang University, describes his educational institution. Watch the video and answer the following questions.

1. What institutions does Zulpiqar mention at Xinjiang University at the beginning of the video? Circle your answers from the followings:

ھاياتلىق ئىلمى ئىنستىتۇتى　　سودا مەكتىپى　　پەن - تېخنىكا ئىنستىتۇتى

ئاخبارات ئىنستىتۇتى　　ماتېماتىكا ئىنستىتۇتى　　فىلولوگىيە ئىنستىتۇتى

قانۇنشۇناسلىق ئىنستىتۇتى　　چەتئەل تىللىرى ئىنستىتۇتى

2. Which years did Zulpiqar study at Xinjiang University?

3. What does he say about the language of instruction at Xinjiang University?

4. Zulpiqar mentions some changes which have taken place at the فىلولوگىيە ئىنستىتۇتى over the last 20 years. What are they? Circle from the following:

1. فاكۇلتېتلار ئىسلاھ قىلىندى
2. يېڭى كەسپلەر ئېچىلدى
3. ئوقۇتقۇچىلارنىڭ مائاشى ئۆستى
4. جەمئىيەتشۇناسلىق فاكۇلتېتى قېتىلدى
5. مەكتەپنىڭ ئورنى يۆتكەلدى

5. Which of the following was not mentioned in Zulpiqar's narration about the degree programs offered at Xinjiang University?

باكالاۋۇرلىق　　ماگىستىرلىق　　دوكتورلۇق　　پوست دوكتورلۇق

6. Approximately how many students and teachers/staff are there at Xinjiang University?

Higher Education in Xinjiang

Although technically autonomous, the education system of the Xinjiang Uyghur Autonomous Region has conformed to most national standards of the People's Republic of China. As such, Uyghur students (like all students in China) must pass the national college entrance examination (ئالىي مەكتەپ ئىمتىھانى) before enrolling at a university. However, depending on their educational backgrounds, Uyghurs may take this examination in the Uyghur language (ئۇيغۇرچە ئوقۇغانلار) or in Chinese (خەنزۇچە ئوقۇغانلار). Furthermore, as minority students Uyghurs benefit from so-called 'preferential policies' (ئېتىبار سىياسىتى) which award 'bonus points' on this examination. There are over twenty institutions of higher education in Xinjiang to date. The most prestigious of these is Xinjiang University (شىنجاڭ ئۇنىۋېرسىتېتى), though a substantial number of young Uyghurs aspire to attend the Minzu University of China in Beijing (مەركىزىي مىللەتلەر ئۇنىۋېرسىتېتى). Unfortunately, in a reflection of broader efforts to strengthen Chinese as a national language, most university courses are conducted in Chinese.

Project

Prepare a video/audio interview with any professor from your university. Prepare a list of questions beforehand. Some examples are given below. When you are finished, translate the interview into Uyghur.
Present a summary of the interview in class.

Sample questions:

1. سىز ئىشلەيدىغان ئۇنىۋېرسىتېت/ بۆلۈم قاچان قۇرۇلغان؟
2. دەرسلىرىڭىزنى ئاڭلايدىغان ئوقۇغۇچىلار كىم؟
3. ئىمتىھان سوئاللىرىنى سىز چىقىرامسىز ياكى مەكتەپ چىقىرامدۇ؟
4. ئوقۇغۇچىلارغا ئادەتتە قانداق تاپشۇرۇقلار بېرىسىز؟

Have you ever heard about...? بۇ كىشىنى بىلەمسىز...؟

In this section you will read and learn about a famous Uyghur person.

Exercise 20: غوجەخمەت سەدۋاقاسوۋ

Exercise 20.1:  Read the following passage about Gojahmet Sadvaqasov, a famous Uyghur scholar and linguist, and answer the questions that follow. The words and expressions provided before the questions will help you to understand the passage better.

قەشقەر كەچلىك گېزىتى

2014 - يىلى 18 - ئاۋغۇست
دۈشەنبە

1231 - سان پوچتا ۋاكالەت نومۇرى: 54 ـ 66

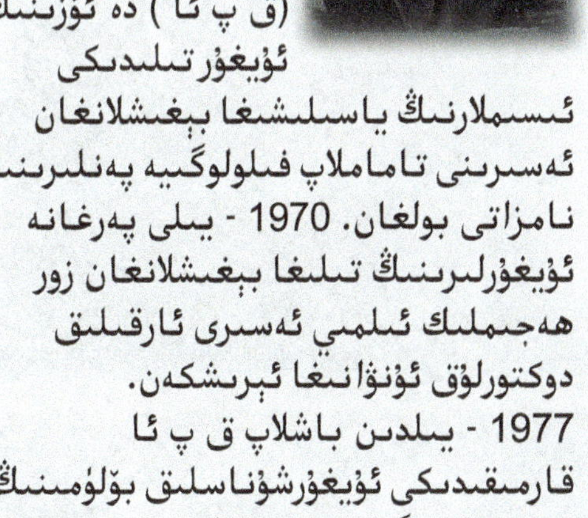

بۈيۈك تىلشۇناس غوجەخمەت سەدۋاقاسوۋ 1929 - يىلى ئالمۇتىدا دۇنياغا كەلگەن. 1957 - يىلى قازاقىستان پەنلەر ئاكادېمىيىسى (ق پ ئا) دە ئۆزىنىڭ ئۇيغۇر تىلىدىكى ئىسىملارنىڭ ياسىلىشىغا بېغىشلانغان ئەسىرىنى تاماملاپ فىلولوگىيە پەنلىرىنىڭ نامزاتى بولغان. 1970 - يىلى پەرغانە ئۇيغۇرلىرىنىڭ تىلىغا بېغىشلانغان زور ھەجىملىك ئىلمىي ئەسىرى ئارقىلىق دوكتورلۇق ئۇنۋانىغا ئېرىشكەن. 1977 - يىلدىن باشلاپ ق پ ئا قارمىقىدىكى ئۇيغۇرشۇناسلىق بۆلۈمىنىڭ خىزمەتلىرىگە يېتەكچىلىك قىلىپ 1986 - يىلى مەزكۇر بۆلۈمنى ئۇيغۇرشۇناسلىق ئىنستىتۇتىغا يۈكسەلدۈرگەن ۋە ئۇنىڭ تۇنجى قارارلىق باشلىقى بولغان. سەدۋاقاسوۋنىڭ ئۇيغۇر ئەدەبىياتى، سەنئىتى، تارىخى، ئېتنوگرافىيەسى، ئۇيغۇر تىلى گراماتىكىسى، جۈملىدىن ئۇيغۇر تىلىنىڭ ئىملا قائىدىسى بويىچە ئىشلىگەن ئەمگەكلىرى ئوتتۇرا ئاسىيا ئۇيغۇرلىرى، شۇنداقلا شىنجاڭ ئۇيغۇرلىرى تەرىپىدىن تولۇق ئېتراپ قىلىنىپ ھازىرغا قەدەر نوپۇزلۇق دەستۇر سۈپىتىدە قوللىنىلماقتا. ئۇنىڭ ئۇيغۇر تىلى گراماتىكىسىغا بېغىشلانغان ئەسەرلىرى 1980 - يىللىرى ئۈرۈمچىدە ئۇيغۇر ۋە خەنزۇ تىللىرىدا نەشر قىلىنغان. ئۇنىڭ ئىلمىي پېداگوگىكىغا بېغىشلانغان دەرسلىك ۋە ئۆگىنىش پروگراممىلىرىمۇ مۇھىم ئورۇندا تۇرىدۇ. سەدۋاقاسوۋنىڭ قەدىمكى ئۇيغۇر تىلى، خەلق ئېغىز ئەدەبىياتى مىراسلىرى ۋە ئەدەبىي تەرجىمە ساھەسىگە قوشقان تۆھپىسىمۇ ئالاھىدە گەۋدىلىك بولغانلىقى ئۈچۈن ئالىم كۆپ قېتىم شەرەپ مېداللىرىغا ئېرىشكەن. شۇنداقلا ئۇنىڭ ئىسمى "قازاقىستاننىڭ ھۆرمەت ئالتۇن قامۇسى"غا كىرگۈزۈلگەن. كۆپ قىرلىق ۋە مول ھوسۇللۇق بۈيۈك ئالىم 1991 - يىلى ئالەمدىن ئۆتتى.

the said, the designated	مەزكۇر
eminent	نوپۇزلۇق
as a guide	دەستۇر سۈپىتىدە
contribution	تۆھپە
branch	قارمىقى
first batch	تۇنجى قارارلىق
to cause to increase	يۈكسەلدۈرمەك
multi-talented	كۆپ قىرلىق
rule of orthography	ئىملا قائىدىسى
prolific	مول ھوسۇللۇق
honor	شەرەپ

Candidate of Philological Sciences	فىلولوگىيە پەنلىرىنىڭ نامزاتى
formation of nouns	ئىسىملارنىڭ ياسىلىشى
to be dedicated	بېغىشلانغان
academy of science	پەنلەر ئاكادېمىيىسى
to lead	يېتەكچىلىك قىلماق
large volume	زور ھەجىملىك
to receive a degree	ئۇنۋانغا ئېرىشمەك
significant	گەۋدىلىك
labor	ئەمگەك
to be recognized	ئېتىراپ قىلىنماق

1. ئالىم غوجەخمەت سەدۋاقاسوۋ توغرۇلۇق نېمە ئۆگەندىڭىز؟
2. ئالىمنىڭ ئىلمىي ئەسەرلىرى قايسى ساھەلەرگە بېغىشلانغان؟
3. ئۇيغۇرشۇناسلىقتا قوشقان تۆھپىسى ئۈچۈن غوجەخمەت سەدۋاقاسوۋ قانداق مۇكاپاتلارغا ئېرىشكەن؟

Exercise 20.2:  Based on the passage you have read and the pictures below, ask your partner three more questions about Gojahmet Sadvaqasov.

Vocabulary سۆزلۈك

Vocabulary is given according to the Uyghur alphabetical order. The right column precedes the left column on each page.

to be a priority	ئاساسلىق ئورۇندا تۇرماق
consequence	ئاقىۋەت
higher education	ئالىي مائارىپ
a literary work	ئەدەبىي ئەسەر
bank account	بانكا ھېساباتى
in association, together	بىر تۇتاش
piece; a measure word for book	پارچە
opportunity doesn't knock twice	پۇرسەت - غەنىيمەت
to lose the chance	پۇرسەتنى قولدىن بەرمەك
completely	پۈتۈنلەي
to argue	تارتىشماق
to choose	تاللاپ بەرمەك
natural science	تەبىئى پەن
to form, to organize	تەشكىل قىلماق
to provide, supply	تەمىنلىمەك
to carry, to transport	توشۇماق
to register	تىزىملاتماق
to be responsible	جاۋابكار بولماق
definitely	چوقۇم
field, area of knowledge	ساھە
art sciences	سەنئەت پەنلىرى
to interrogate	سوراققا تارتماق
insurance	سۇغۇرتا
to try	سىناپ باقماق
political	سىياسى
to run (as in a bus), to travel back and forth	قاتنىماق

to help	قاراشماق
to look	قارىماق
to accept	قوبۇل قىلماق
bunk bed	قوش قەۋەتلىك كارىۋات
to support	قوللىماق
to spend the night	قونۇپ قالماق
to interest someone in something	قىزىقتۇرماق
crowded	قىستاڭچىلىق
specialization; major	كەسىپ
to notice	كۆزى چۈشمەك
daily routine	كۈندىلىك مەشغۇلات
no problem	كېرەك يوق
to agree	كېلىشمەك
to do the laundry	كىر يۇماق
full (bus)	لىق
obligation, duty	مەجبۇرىيەت
responsibility	مەسئۇلىيەت
campus	مەكتەپ قورۇسى
to inform	مەلۇم قىلماق
based on the information	مەلۇماتلارغا ئاساسلانغاندا
dirty	مەينەت
expert, specialist	مۇتەخەسسىس
complicated, complex	مۇرەككەپ
fixed, stable	مۇقىم
service	مۇلازىمەت
regular, full time	مۇنتىزىم
bathroom	مۇنچا

street sign	ۋىۋېسكا
social science	ئىجتىمائىي پەن
to request; to apply	ئىلتىماس قىلماق
management	ئىلمىي باشقۇرۇش
passenger	يولۇچى
set of books	يۈرۈشلەشكەن دەرسلىك
to hold a meeting	يىغىن ئاچماق

property	مۈلۈك
to solve	ھەل قىلماق
to arrange, to organize	ئورۇنلاشتۇرۇپ بەرمەك
thief	ئوغرى
a title, name; degree	ئۇنۋان
the day after tomorrow	ئۆگۈن

سەككىزىنچى دەرس

CHAPTER EIGHT

ئولتۇرۇش ۋە مەشرەپ

UYGHUR PARTIES AND MESHREP

IN THIS CHAPTER

Functions

- Describing extra-curricular activities
- Describing free time activities
- Narrating past events
- Describing ئولتۇرۇش and مەشرەپ

Grammar

- The auxiliary verbs بولماق and ئەتمەك
- Compound verbs with the verb بارماق
- The remote past tense with ئىدى
- The habitual past
- Simultaneous actions

In this chapter, John makes some new Uyghur friends and gets involved in a number of different student activities, including a special sort of typical Uyghur gathering. Through the conversations, reading passages, and excerpts from John's blog entry contained in this chapter, you will learn about students' leisure activities at Xinjiang University. You will also learn the difference between تانسا and ئۇسسۇل, in addition to becoming acquainted with some important concepts pertaining to Uyghur culture, such as مەشرەپ, ئولتۇرۇش, and چاقچاق.

Exercise 1: Look at these pictures. In your free time, which of the following activities do you engage in? Talk a bit about your favorite leisure activity.

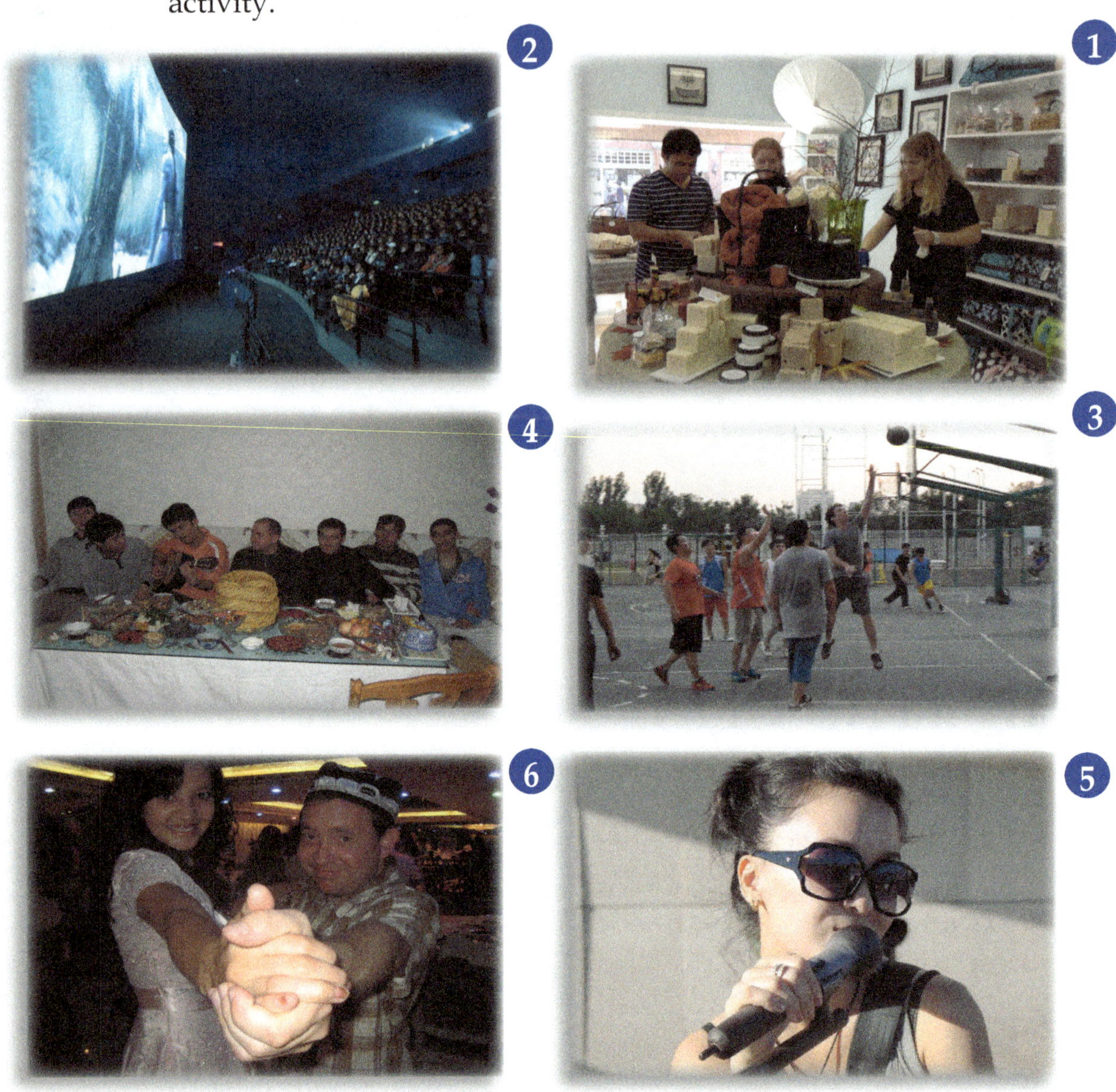

Exercise 2: تۆۋەندىكى سوئاللارنى مۇزاكىرە قىلىڭلار

1. بوش ۋاقتىڭىز چىقىپ قالسا نېمە قىلىسىز؟
2. تەتىلدە نېمە قىلىسىز؟
3. مەكتىپىڭلاردا ئولتۇرۇشلار بولامدۇ؟ ئۇلار ئادەتتە نەدە بولىدۇ ۋە قانداق ئۆتىدۇ؟
4. سىز ئولتۇرۇشلارغا ئامراقمۇ؟ نېمىشقا؟ سىز قانداق ئولتۇرۇشلارغا ئامراق؟
5. بۇ ئولتۇرۇشلار ئادەتتە قايسى كۈنى ۋە سائەت نەچچىدىن نەچچىگىچە بولىدۇ؟
6. بۇ ئولتۇرۇشلاردا نېمە قىلىسىلەر؟
7. ئولتۇرۇشتا ئادەتتە نېمە يەيسىلەر؟ قانداق ئىچىملىكلەر ئىچىسىلەر؟
8. ئەگەر ئولتۇرۇش بىلەن خۇشىڭىز بولمىسا، ئادەتتە نېمە قىلىسىز؟

Note:

Can you recall how to express likes and dislikes?

You can use various structures to talk about likes and dislikes:

ئۇ تاماق ئېتىشكە (ساياھەت قىلىشقا، پۇتبول ئويناشقا، كىتاب ئوقۇشقا) ئامراق.
He is fond of cooking (traveling, playing football, reading books).

ئۇ چېنىقىشنى (ناخشا ئاڭلاشنى، كىنو كۆرۈشنى، تورغا چىقىشنى) ياخشى كۆرىدۇ.
He likes to work out (listen to songs, watch movies, surf the web).

مەن پىۋاغا ئامراق، ئەمما ھاراق بىلەن خوشام يوق.
I'm fond of beer, but I'm not a fan of wine/hard liquor.

بىكار ئولتۇرۇشنى يامان كۆرىمەن.
I hate sitting around with nothing to do.

You can also use the auxiliary verb تۇرماق to show that the action of the verb is repetitive, frequent, or constant.

دەرستىن كېيىن پات-پات پۇتبول ئويناپ تۇرىمىز.
After classes, we often play soccer.

بەزىدە ساۋاقداشلار بىلەن پىۋىخانىغا بېرىپ تۇرىمىز.
Sometimes, we go to the bar with classmates.

Exercise 3: Practice the following short conversations (two follow on the next page) and construct similar ones using the structures reviewed in the note above.

1

- پۇتبول ئويناشنى ياخشى كۆرەمسىز؟
- ياق، پۇتبول بىلەن خوشام يوق، مەن ۋاسكېتبولغا ئامراق. سىزچۇ؟
- مەن پۇتبولغا بەك ئامراق، ئەمما ئۆزەم ئوينىمايمەن.

2

- سىز گىتار چېلىشنى بىلەمسىز؟
- ياق، مېنىڭ گىتار بىلەن خوشام يوق، مەن ئىسكرىپكىغا ئامراق. سىزچۇ؟
- مېنىڭ ئىسكرىپكا بىلەن خوشام يوق، مەن گىتارغا بەك ئامراق. مەكتەپتە گىتار كۇرژۇكىغا بارغان.
- شۇنداقمۇ؟ ناخشىمۇ ئېيتامسىز؟
- ھەئە، مەن ناخشا ئېيتىشنىمۇ ياخشى كۆرىمەن.

3

- سىز كومپيۇتېر ئويۇنلىرىغا ئامراقمۇ؟
- بالىلىقىمدا كومپيۇتېر ئويۇنلىرىنى بەكمۇ ياخشى كۆرەتتىم، ئەمما ھازىر ئۇنداق ئويۇنلارغا ۋاقتىم يوق. سىزچۇ، سىز كومپيۇتېر ئويۇنلىرىنى ياخشى كۆرەمسىز؟
- مېنىڭمۇ كومپيۇتېر ئويۇنلىرى بىلەن خوشام يوق. سىز دېگەندەك، بۇنداق ئويۇنلارغا كۆپ ۋاقىت كېتىدۇ. بۇنداق ئويۇنلارغا قارىغاندا چېنىققان ياخشى!

4

- سىز دىسكو ئويناشقا ئامراقمۇ؟
- دىسكو بىلەن پەقەتلا خوشام يوق. سىزچۇ؟
- مەن بەك ئامراق، بولۇپمۇ چاقماق ئۇسسۇلى (برېيك دانس) ئويناشنى ياخشى كۆرىمەن. بۇنىڭدىن باشقا يەنە سالسا، چاچا، تانگولارغىمۇ ئامراق.

Exercise 4: جوننىڭ ھەيرانلىقى

Exercise 4.1:  Read the first part of John's blog entry about his impression of Uyghurs.

What sort of stereotypes had John heard about Uyghurs before coming to Xinjiang? Did John find that these stereotypes accurately reflected reality?

Decide if the following statements are true or false. If a statement is false, give the correct answer.

توغرا	خاتا	
		1. ئۇيغۇر ئوقۇغۇچىلارنىڭ ئارىسىدا مىللىي سازلارنى چالىدىغانلار خېلى كۆپ.
		2. ئۇيغۇر ئوقۇغۇچىلار گىتارغا بەك ئامراق.
		3. ئوقۇغۇچىلار ئۇيغۇرچە سازلارنى ئۆگىنىش ئۈچۈن ھەر خىل كۇرژۇكلارغا قاتنىشىدۇ.
		4. مەكتەپتە مەخسۇس ئۇيغۇرچە سازلارنى ئۆگىتىدىغان ئۇستازلار بار.
		5. ئۇيغۇرچە سازلار سەنئەت ئىنىستىتۇتىدا ئۆگىتىلىدۇ.
		6. ئۇيغۇر خەلق ناخشىلىرىنى پەقەت قېرىلار ئاڭلايدۇ.

Exercise 4.2:  Read the rest of the blog entry and answer the questions that follow.

Uyghur John's Blog

ئامېرىكىلىق يالقۇننىڭ تورتۇراسى

Search

كۈندە بىر ماقال:
ھەسەلنى كۆپ يېسە ئۆرمەن تېتىيدۇ

بىر فولكلور پروفېسسورىنىڭ ئېيتىشىچە، ھازىر ئۇيغۇر بالىلارنىڭ كۆپى خەنزۇچە مەكتەپتە ئوقۇيدىغان بولغاچقا، كېيىنچە ئۇيغۇرچە ناخشىلارنى ئېيتىدىغان، ئۇيغۇرچە مۇزىكىلارنى چالىدىغان ئادەم قالماسلىقى مۇمكىن ئىكەن. ئۆتكەن ھەپتە يېڭىدىن تونۇشقان ئۇرۇمچىلىك دوستۇم مەردان مېنى بىر دوستىنىڭ تويىغا ئېلىپ باردى. تويدا ئاۋۋال مۇزىكانتلار ئۇيغۇر مۇقاملىرىدىن بىرنەچچە ئارىيە ئورۇنلىدى. مەن بەك خوشال بولدۇم، چۈنكى مەن ئۇيغۇر سازەندىلەرنىڭ ساز چېلىپ ناخشا ئېيتقانلىقىنى نەق مەيداندا كۆرۈپ باقمىغان ئىدىم. ئۇلار بەك ياخشى ناخشا ئېيتىدىكەن، مۇزىكىسىمۇ بەك ياخشىكەن. ئەمما زالدىكى بەزى ئۇيغۇرلار ھاراق ئىچىش بىلەن ئالدىراش ئىدى. ناخشا توختىغاندا، كىشىلەر ئاساسەن چاۋاك چالمايدىكەن، ئۇلارغا گۈل بەرمەيدىكەن. بىرنەچچە سائەتلىك توي ئاساسەن ئۇيغۇرچە ئۇسسۇل ۋە ياۋروپاچە تانسا بىلەن تۈگەيدىكەن. تويدا ھەممە ئۇيغۇرلار ئۇيغۇرچە ئۇسسۇل ئوينايدىكەن. ئۇلارنىڭ ئۇسسۇلى قارىماققا بەك ئاددىي، ئەمما ئويناش بىرئاز قىيىن ئىكەن. قەدەم ئالغاندا مۇزىكىغا ماسلىشىش بەك مۇھىم ئىكەن. مەن ئۇسسۇل ئوينىسام ھەممەيلەن كۈلۈپ كەتتى. ئۇيغۇرلارنىڭ ناخشا - ئۇسسۇلغا ئامراقلىقىنى قانداق چۈشىنىش لازىم؟

1. نېمىشقا فولكلور پروفېسسورى «كېيىنچە ئۇيغۇرچە ناخشىلارنى ئېيتىدىغان، ئۇيغۇرچە مۇزىكىلارنى چالىدىغان ئادەم قالماسلىقى مۇمكىن» دەيدۇ؟
2. تويدا جون بەكمۇ خوشال بولدى. بۇنىڭ سەۋەبى نېمە؟
3. تويغا بارغان مېھمانلار نېمە ئىشلار بىلەن ئالدىراش؟ ئۇلار چېلىنغان مۇزىكىدىن ھوزۇر ئالامدۇ؟
4. جون ئۇيغۇرچە ئۇسسۇلنى قانداق تەسۋىرلەيدۇ؟

Exercise 4.3:  Match the following words with their English equivalents by drawing a line from the Uyghur word on the right to its definition on the left.

to suit	ساز
to consider (as) superior	نەق مەيداندا
to clap	قەدەم
on the spot	ئەۋزەل كۆرمەك
a step, pace	چاۋاك چالماق
musical instrument	ماسلاشماق

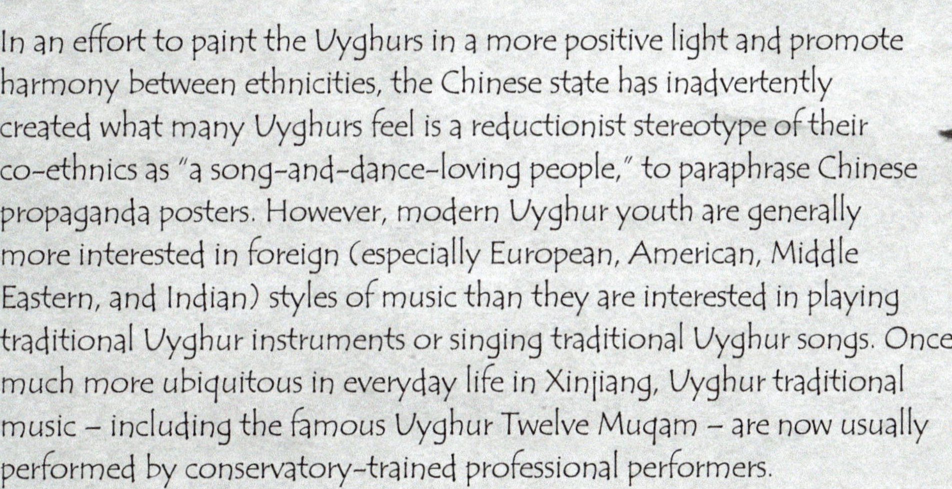

A Song-and-Dance-Loving People

In an effort to paint the Uyghurs in a more positive light and promote harmony between ethnicities, the Chinese state has inadvertently created what many Uyghurs feel is a reductionist stereotype of their co-ethnics as "a song-and-dance-loving people," to paraphrase Chinese propaganda posters. However, modern Uyghur youth are generally more interested in foreign (especially European, American, Middle Eastern, and Indian) styles of music than they are interested in playing traditional Uyghur instruments or singing traditional Uyghur songs. Once much more ubiquitous in everyday life in Xinjiang, Uyghur traditional music – including the famous Uyghur Twelve Muqam – are now usually performed by conservatory-trained professional performers.

Exercise 5: 

Exercise 5.1:  Listen to a short conversation between Mark and a Uyghur student who has just arrived in the US. Then answer the questions that follow.

1. What is the student asking Mark to do in this dialogue?
   A. help him move in.
   B. take him to the dorm.
   C. find him a dorm.
2. What are some differences between making housing arrangements in Xinjiang and in the US?

Exercise 5.2: Listen to the dialogue as many times as you need and provide the missing words in the transcript below.

سىز: ياتاقنى ئېلىپ بولدىڭىزمۇ؟
ئۇ: تېخى ئالمىدىم. مەن __________ مەكتەپ ئۆزى تاللاپ بېرىدۇ دەپ ئويلاپتىمەن.
سىز: ئامېرىكىدا بۇنداق __________ يوق. ئوقۇغۇچى ئۆزى خالىغان ياتاقنى __________.
ئۇ: مۇنداق دەڭ... سىزنىڭچە قانداق ياتاقنى ئالسام بولىدۇ؟
سىز: سىزگە قانداق ياتاق __________؟
ئۇ: ماڭا __________ ياتاق بولسا بولاتتى.
سىز: قېنى، يۈرۈڭ، مەن سىزنى ياتاق __________ ئاپىراي. شۇ يەردە مەسلىھەتلىشەيلى!

____

1 The Auxiliary Verb بولماق to Express Completion of an Action

In the dialogue (Exercise 5.2) you see the verb بولماق used as an auxiliary verb. It appears in the sentence:

Did you already get a room? ياتاقنى ئېلىپ بولدىڭىزمۇ؟

The use of the auxiliary verb بولماق indicates that the action of the main verb is performed to completion. Look at some more examples:

We finished eating. تاماقنى يەپ بولدۇق.
I finished my homework. تاپشۇرۇقۇمنى ئىشلەپ بولدۇم.
Have you finished washing up? يۇيۇنۇپ بولدۇڭلارمۇ؟
He finished writing the letter. ئۇ خېتىنى يېزىپ بولدى.

Most of the time, this can be translated into English using the construction "finish (doing something)"; however, sometimes the notion of completion has to be translated differently depending on context.

The guests have left. مېھمانلار كېتىپ بولۇشتى.
The child fell asleep. بالا ئۇخلاپ بولدى.
Did you already buy your ticket? بېلىتىڭىزنى ئېلىپ بولدىڭىزمۇ؟

Exercise 6: ماقالىنى يېزىپ بولدۇم!

Exercise 6.1:  Using the auxiliary verb بولماق, translate the following sentences into Uyghur.

1. I finished writing my article.
2. I finished reading this book.
3. After this semester, I am going to China. I already bought my ticket.
4. The driver already arrived in the city.
5. I came back from the gym and finished my shower already.
6. The new students already finished playing soccer.
7. The director finished drinking his coffee before reading the newspaper.
8. I assume that they already finished watching the movie.
9. Are you done with your exams?
10. She's already done with sending the letters.

Exercise 6.2:  You have volunteered to help some Uyghur students in the USA. Practice the following short exchanges. Then continue the dialogue. Use the following two phrases:

چەتئەللىك ئوقۇغۇچىلار بۆلۈمى
قاتناش ئىدارىسى

1. سىز: ئوقۇغۇچىلىق كىنىشكىسىنى ئېلىپ بولدىڭىزمۇ؟
ئۇ: ياق، تېخى ئالمىدىم.
...
2. سىز: شتات كىملىكىنى ئېلىپ بولدىڭىزمۇ؟
ئۇ: ياق، تېخى ئالمىدىم.
...
3. سىز: شوپۇرلۇق كىنىشكىسىنى ئېلىپ بولدىڭىزمۇ؟
ئۇ: پراۋىنى دەمسىز؟ ياق، تېخى ئالمىدىم.
...
4. سىز: سۇغۇرتا ئالدىڭىزمۇ؟
ئۇ: قايسى سۇغۇرتىنى؟
سىز: داۋالىنىش سۇغۇرتىسىنى.
ئۇ: ياق، ئالمىدىم.
...

2 Verbal Contractions with (-ئاپ\-ئەپ) -ئا\-ئە *Derived from the Verb* ئالماق

In the dialogue (Exercise 5.2) you also see a verb ئاپارماق. It appears in the sentence:

مەن سىزنى ياتاق باشقۇرۇش ئىشخانىسىغا ئاپىراي.
Let me bring you to the housing office.

This verb is a contraction of two verbs: ئېلىپ and بارماق. Its literal meaning is 'take and go'. There are a few verbs like this in Uyghur, all of which are composed of a contracted form of ئېلىپ, plus a verb of motion:

to take, to bring	ئېلىپ بارماق > ئېپ بارماق > ئاپارماق
to bring	ئېلىپ كەلمەك> ئېپ كەلمەك > ئەكەلمەك (ئەپكەلمەك)
to bring down	ئېلىپ چۈشمەك> ئېپ چۈشمەك> ئەچۈشمەك (ئەپچۈشمەك)
to bring up	ئېلىپ چىقماق > ئېپ چىقماق > ئەچىقماق (ئەپچىقماق)
to bring in	ئېلىپ كىرمەك > ئېپ كىرمەك > ئەكىرمەك (ئەپكىرمەك)

As you can see, in all of these contractions, all that remains of the verb ئالماق is the initial syllable ئا\ئە or -ئاپ\-ئەپ. The vowel of this syllable corresponds to the vowel in the first syllable of the following verb. The exception to this is ئەچىقماق.

As shown above, all of these verbs have an optional variant in which the پ of ئېپ is also retained, yielding -ئەپ\-ئاپ. However, in ئاپارماق, this پ takes the place of the initial ب of the original بارماق. Here are some more examples:

دادام مېنى موماملىنىڭ ئۆيىگە ئاپىرىپ قويدى.
My father took me to grandma's house.
He brought a carpet from Xoten. ئۇ خوتەندىن گىلەم ئەكەپتۇ.
ئەنۋەر كىتابلارنى بەشىنچى قەۋەتتىن ئۆزى ئەچۈشۈپتۇ.
Enwer brought the books down from the fifth floor himself.
مەن ئۆيگە كىرىپ سۇ ئەچىقتىم.
I went into the house and brought out some water.
Please, bring the things into the house. نەرسىلەرنى ئۆيگە ئەكىرسىڭىز.

Note that these verbs are very common in spoken Uyghur.

Exercise 7: كىتابلارنى ئەكەلدىم!

Exercise 7.1:  Using the sentences in the preceding grammar note as examples, write one sentence for each of the contracted verbs based on ئالماق which appear in the table.

Exercise 7.2:  Listen to the following sentences and write in the contracted verbs you hear.

1. سىزنى ئولتۇرۇشقا ئۆزۈم ________________.
2. ئايالىڭىزنى ئۆيۈمىزگە ________________، ئۇنىڭ بىلەن تونۇشايلى.
3. قىزىم، كىتابلارنى پەسكە ________________.
4. دادىڭىز ئۆكىڭىزنى مومىڭىزنىڭ ئۆيىگە ________________ قويسۇن.
5. بۇ ئۈستەلنى تۆپىگە ________________؟
6. دادا، ۋېلىسىپىتىمنى ئۆيگە ________________ قويسام بولامدۇ؟

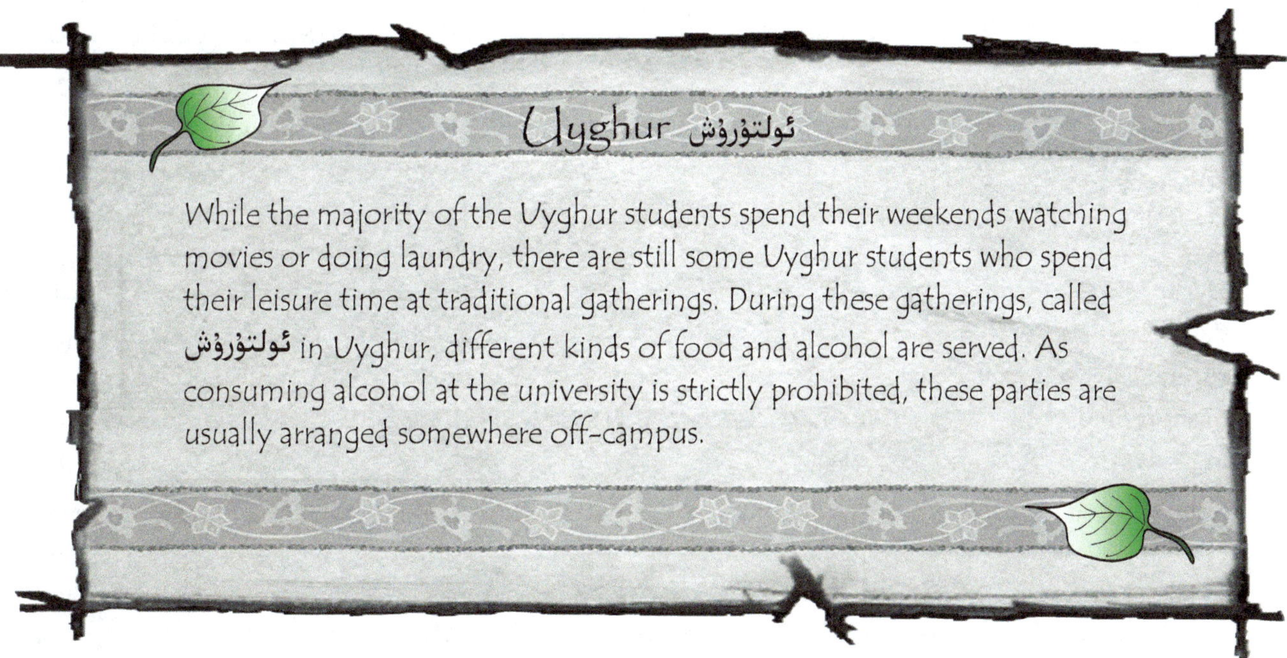

Exercise 8: ئۇيغۇر ئولتۇرۇشىدا

Exercise 8.1:  John has been invited to a party with some Uyghur students. Read the dialogue on the next page and discuss the questions that follow.

ياسىن: قېنى باللار، مەن سىلەرگە تونۇشتۇرۇپ ئۆتەي: بۇ بىزنىڭ ئامېرىكىلىق دوستىمىز جون. ئۇ شىنجاڭ ئۇنىۋېرسىتېتىغا ئۇيغۇرچە ئۆگەنگىلى كەپتۇ.

ئوقۇغۇچى ئا: قارشى ئالىمىز. ئۈرۈمچىگە خۇش كەپسىز!

جون: رەھمەت! مەن ئۇيغۇرلاردىن كۆپرەك دوستۇم بولسىكەن، دەيمەن.

ئوقۇغۇچى ئا: سىزنىڭ ئۇيغۇرچىڭىز ياخشىكەنغۇ! سىز ئۇيغۇرچىنى قەيەردە ئۆگەنگەن؟

جون: مەن ئامېرىكىدا ئىككى يىل ئۇيغۇرچە ئۆگەندىم. بۇ قېتىم بۇ يەرگە بىر يىللىق پراكتىكا ئۈچۈن كەلدىم.

ئوقۇغۇچى ب: ئامېرىكىدىمۇ ئۇيغۇرچە ئۆگىتىدىغانلار بارمۇ؟ بەك قىزىقكەن.

جون: ئامېرىكىدا ھەممە تىلنى ئۆگىتىدىغانلار بار.

ساقي*: ئەمىسە ئاغىنىلەر، سورۇننى باشلىۋەتتۇق. ياسىن بۇ ئامېرىكىلىق دوستىمىزنى ئەكەپتۇ. ھېلى ئۇ بىزگە مايكل جېكسوننىڭ ناخشىلىرىنى ئېيتىپ بېرىدۇ. قېنى، سورۇنىمىزنىڭ پەيزى بولۇشى ئۈچۈن، خوشە!

جون: مەن ناخشىچى ئەمەس. مەن ناخشا ئېيتالمايمەن.

ياسىن: ئۇ سىزگە چاقچاق قىلىۋاتىدۇ.... قېنى، خوشە!

ساقي: ئەمدى بۇ رومكا سىزنىڭ ھۆرمىتىڭىز ئۈچۈن. كەچۈرۈڭ، ئىسمىڭىز نېمىتى**؟

جون: جون. ئۇيغۇرچە ئىسمىم يالقۇن.

ساقي: ياخشى ئىسىمكەن. قېنى ئەمىسە سورۇنىمىزنىڭ يالقۇندەك قىزىپ كېتىشى ئۈچۈن، خوشە!

جون: مەن ھاراق ئىچمەيمەن.

ساقي: ياق، ياق. بۇ ھاراق ئەمەس، بۇ دېگەن كۆڭۈل!

جون: كۆڭۈل؟ بۇ نېمە دېگەن گەپ؟

ياسىن: سىزنىڭ ھۆرمىتىڭىز، دېگەن گەپ.

جون: رەھمەت. بۇنى چوقۇم ئىچىشىم لازىممۇ؟

ياسىن: ئىچسىڭىز بىز خۇشال بولىمىز.

جون: بوپتۇ، ئەمىسە بىر رومكا ئىچىپ باقاي.

ياسىن: ئامېرىكىلىقلار ھاراق ئىچمەمدۇ؟

جون: ئىچىدۇ، ئەمما مەن ئانچە ھاراق ئىچىپ كەتمەيمەن. بۇ ھاراقنى نېمە دەيسىلەر؟

ياسىن: بۇنى ئاق ھاراق دەيمىز. ئۈزۈم ھارىقىنى قىزىل ھاراق دەيمىز.

جون: ئەمىسە... خوشە!

ساقي: مانا قاراڭ، بىردەمدىلا "ئاق ھاراق، "قىزىل ھاراق" ۋە "خوشە" دېيىشنى ئۆگىنىۋالدىڭىز. مۇشۇنداق قىلسىڭىز، ئۇيغۇرچىنى تېخىمۇ ياخشى ئۆگىنىۋالىسىز. خوشە!

جون: ۋاي خۇدايىم، بۇ ھاراق بەك كۈچلۈك ئىكەن!

ياسىن: سەي يەڭ، سەي يېسىڭىز، ھاراقنى باسىدۇ.

جون: ياق، ھازىر ھاراق مېنى باستى.

Cheers!	خوشە!
occasion, gathering	سورۇن
wonderful, joyful	پەيز (پەيزى)
flame	يالقۇن
surely, definitely	چوقۇم
in short time	بىردەمدە
to press	باسماق

* ساقي: the one who pours the drinks (at a party, etc.)

** نېمىتى= نېمە ئىدى

1. What is the occasion for this party?
2. Who do you think is at this party? Are there any women?

Exercise 8.2:  Read the passage again. This time pay close attention to language use. Copy your answers to the following questions from the text.

1. The Uyghur students complimented John twice. What expressions do they use?

____

____

2. Who do you think is more direct in this conversation: John or his Uyghur friends? How do you know?

____

____

3. How does John react when they give him the drink? What does he say? How does he say it?

____

____

4. How do his Uyghur friends convince him to drink ھاراق? What do they say? How do they explain it to him?

____

____

5. There is a misunderstanding at the end of the dialogue. What is it about?

____

____

6. What do you say in the following situations?
- greeting a newcomer to a party: ______________
- offering a drink: ______________
- reassuring that someone was just kidding/joking: ______________

7. Explain the following concepts:

ئاق ھاراق: ______________________________

قىزىل ھاراق: ______________________________

سەي: ______________________________

Exercise 8.3:  Listen to and practice the dialogue with your classmates.

Exercise 9: ئولتۇرۇشتىن كېيىن

Exercise 9.1:  The following day, John and Yasin are discussing the previous night's ئولتۇرۇش. Listen and follow the script.

ياسىن: تۈنۈگۈن كۆپ ئىچىۋەتكەن ئوخشايمىز. سىزمۇ مەست بولۇپ قاپسىز.
جون: ئۇقمايمەن. ئەتىگەن ئويغانسام، سافادا يېتىپتىمەن. بېشىم بەك ئاغرىۋاتىدۇ.
ياسىن: هاراق چىشلىۋاپتۇ. بۇنىڭ ئۈچۈن پولۇ يەپ ئاندىن بىر ئۇخلىۋەتسىڭىز* ئوڭشىلىپ قالىسىز.
جون: مېنى هېچكىم چىشلىمىدى.
ياسىن: ياق، ئولتۇرۇشتىن كېيىن باش ئاغرىغانىنى "هاراق چىشلىۋاپتۇ" دەيمىز.
جون: شۇنداقمۇ؟ بۇ قىزىق گەپ ئىكەن. سىلەر ئادەتتە هەر شەنبە ئاشۇنداق ئولتۇرۇش قىلامسىلەر؟
ياسىن: دائىم ئەمەس. بۇرۇن شەنبە ياكى يەكشەنبە كۈنلىرى باشقا ئالىي مەكتەپلەرگە بېرىپ يۇرتلۇقلار ئولتۇرۇشى قىلاتتۇق. كېيىن مەكتەپلەر بۇنى چەكلىۋەتتى.
جون: هازىر ئۆز مەكتىپىڭلاردا ئولتۇرۇش قىلامسىلەر؟
ياسىن: ياق، ئوقۇغۇچىلار مەكتەپ ياتىقىدا هاراق ئىچسە بولمايدۇ. شۇڭا تۈنۈگۈنكىگە ئوخشاش سىرتتا ئۆيى بار باللارنىڭ ئۆيىدە ئولتۇرىمىز.
جون: ئۇيغۇر ئوقۇغۇچىلار ئادەتتە ئوقۇشتىن سىرتقى ۋاقىتلاردا ئىشلەمدۇ؟
ياسىن: بۇ يەردە ئىشلەيدىغان ئوقۇغۇچىلار ئاز. ئۇنىڭ ئۈستىگە ئىشمۇ جىق ئەمەس.
جون: ئەمىسە ئۇلار قانداق ياشايدۇ؟ مەكتەپ تۇرمۇش پۇلى بېرەمدۇ؟
ياسىن: بۇرۇن بېرەتتى. هازىر بىزدىن ئالىدۇ. ئوقۇش پۇلى، كىتاپ پۇلى، تاماق پۇلى، ياتاق پۇلى دېگەندەك پۇللارنىڭ هەممىسىنى بىز تۆلەيمىز. مەكتەپ بىزگە بىر تىيىن بەرمەيدۇ.
جون: ئۇنداقتا ئاتا- ئاناڭلار پۇل ئەۋەتىپ بېرەمدۇ؟
ياسىن: هەئە. هەممىمىزنىڭ بانكا كارتىسى بار. ئادەتتە ئانا- ئانىلار هەر ئايدا شۇ كارتىغا پۇل سېلىپ قويىدۇ.
جون: بىر ئايدا بىر ئوقۇغۇچىغا قانچىلىك پۇل كېتىدۇ؟
ياسىن: مەن يېڭى كەلگەندە بەش- ئالتە يۈز كوي بولسا يېتەتتى. هازىر ئايغا مىڭ كوي كېتىدۇ. مال باهاسى بەك ئۆسۈپ كېتىۋاتىدۇ. بىلەمسىز، بىر لەڭمەن بۇرۇن ئالتە كويتى**. هازىر 15 كوي.
جون: ئاخشامقى ئولتۇرۇشتا بەك كۆپ تاماق بار ئىدى. ئۇنىڭ پۇلىنى كىم چىقاردى؟
ياسىن: بىز ئادەتتە ئولتۇرۇش قىلساق پۇل يىغىش قىلىمىز. ئاخشاممۇ شۇنداق بولدى.
جون: مەن ئاخشام پۇل تۆلىمەپتىمەن. پۇلنى كىمگە بېرىمەن؟
ياسىن: ياق، ياق. سىز خاتا چۈشىنىپ قاپسىز. بىز ئادەتتە مېهمانلاردىن پۇل ئالمايمىز. بۇ ئۇيغۇرلارنىڭ ئادىتى.
جون: بۇنداق قىلساق مەن خىجىل بولۇپ قالىدىكەنمەن.
ياسىن: هېچقىسى يوق. ئامېرىكىغا ماڭىدىغاندا ئۇيغۇر ئاغىنىلىرىڭىزگە بىر خوشلىشىش ئولتۇرۇشى قىلىپ بەرسىڭىز بولىدۇ.
جون: ماقۇل، بۇ ياخشى مەسلىهەت بولدى.

---

* ئەتمەك: You will be introduced to this auxiliary verb later in this chapter

** كويتى= كوي ئىدى

Exercise 9.2:  Look at the following statements and decide if they are true or false. If you find a false statement, correct its content. Follow the example.

ئوقۇغۇچىلار ھەر شەنبە شۇنداق ئولتۇرۇشلار قىلىدۇ.

- ياق، ئۇنداق ئەمەس! بۇرۇن ئۇلار ھەپتە ئاخىرىدا شۇنداق ئولتۇرۇشلار قىلاتتى، ئەمما مەكتەپ بۇنى چەكلىدى.

1. ئولتۇرۇشنىڭ ئەتىسى جوننىڭ بېشى ئاغرىدى.
2. بۇرۇن ئالىي مەكتەپلەردە يۇرتلۇقلار ئولتۇرۇشى كۆپ بولاتتى.
3. ھازىر ئوقۇغۇچىلار ئۆز مەكتىپىدە ئولتۇرۇش قىلىدۇ.
4. ئوقۇغۇچىلارنىڭ كۆپى ئىشلەيدۇ.
5. مەكتەپ ئوقۇغۇچىلارغا ئوقۇش ۋە تۇرمۇش پۇلى بېرىدۇ.
6. ھازىر مال باھاسى قىممەتلەپ كېتىۋاتىدۇ.
7. بىر ئوقۇغۇچىغا بىر ئايدا بەش- ئالتە يۈز كوي يېتىدۇ.
8. جون ئولتۇرۇشقا پۇل بەردى.

توغرا	خاتا

Exercise 9.3:  You are having a conversation with a Uyghur friend about American parties. Ask and answer each other's questions based on the dialogue (Exercise 9.1). One of you will play the role of the American student, the other his/her Uyghur friend. Then switch roles and rehearse the dialogue again.

Exercise 10: جىرىم تىكىش پائالىيىتى

> ***Note:***
>
> University students in Xinjiang often engage in group activities aimed at conservation and environmental beautification. You might see such types of announcements (see the next page) on and around university campuses in Xinjiang.

Exercise 10.1:  While walking in the hallway of the University, John spots a poster on the wall. Can you tell what event this poster is announcing?

Exercise 10.2:  In order to familiarize yourself with the type of vocabulary which often appears in such announcements, study the words below.

(to plant) saplings	جىرىم/ كۆچەت (تىكمەك)
occasional	نۆۋەتلىك
wild	ياۋايى
zoo	ھايۋاناتلار باغچىسى
leading, guiding	يېتەكچىلىك
ten thousand	تۈمەن
an activity, an event	پائالىيەت
to hold, to have (an event, etc.)	ئۆتكۈزمەك
to participate	قاتناشماق
a leader	رەھبەر
propaganda	تەشۋىقات

3 The Remote Past Tense with -غان ئىدى\-غانتى

In Uyghur, the Remote Past Tense is used to describe two types of actions: (1) single, specific actions that occured in a very distant past, or (2) single, specific actions that occur in the past before another past action or frame of reference.

In very formal spoken and most written language, the Remote Past is formed in the following way:

Past Personal Endings	*Auxiliary Stem*
-دى (-دىم، دىڭ، ...)	-ئى

Past Participle Ending	*Verb Stem*
-غان (-قان، -گەن، -كەن)	-قىل

Examples:

ئۇلار مۇشۇ مەھەللىدە ياشىغان ئىدى (ياشىغانىدى).
They lived in this neighborhood a long time ago.
بۇرۇن مەن شۇ مەكتەپتە ئىشلىگەن ئىدىم (ئىشلىگەنىدىم).
Once I worked at this school.

However, in most written and spoken language the auxiliary stem is deleted. When this happens, the initial د of the past personal ending changes to ت, and the past personal ending is attached directly to the past participle ending on the main verb.

Past Personal Endings	*Auxiliary Stem*	*Verb Stem*
-تى (-تىم، -تىڭ، ...)	-غان (-قان، -گەن، -كەن)	-قىل

Look at the following examples:

They worked until early morning. ئۇلار تاڭ سەھەرگىچە ئىشلىگەنتى.
We had never seen them here. بىز ئۇلارنى بۇ يەردە ھېچ قاچان كۆرمىگەنتۇق.
My grandpa once lived with us. بوۋام بىز بىلەن ياشىغانتى.

The first use of the Remote Past, i.e. to indicate that the action of the verb occurred a very long time ago, is unlike any tense in English, but it is very easy to use and understand. Consider the following example:

كىچىك ۋاقتىمدا بىز بۇ شەھەردىن كۆچكەن ئىدۇق.
When I was young (i.e. a long time ago) we moved from this city.

3 The Remote Past Tense with -غان ئىدى\-غانتى *(cont'd.)*

Nevertheless, it is important to remember that this tense is not a hearsay tense, and is most often used for events which the speaker has witnessed him or herself.

The second use of the remote past, i.e. to indicate actions that occurred in the past before another past action, resembles that of the English past perfect or pluperfect (e.g. I had done). Compare the following example sentence to its English equivalent:

سەمەتلەر تۈنۈگۈن كىنوغا بېرىپتۇ. بىز ئۈلۈشكۈن بارغان ئىدۇق.
Semet and others went to the movies yesterday. We had gone the day before.

As with most Uyghur verb tenses, however, there is no exact English equivalent of the Uyghur remote past. In Uyghur, the remote past is often used in cases where English can use the simple past.

تۈنۈگۈن كىنوغا بارغانتۇق. قارىساق ھېچ كىم يوق. ئاڭلىساق كىنونىڭ ۋاقتىنى ئۆزگەرتىپتۇ.
We went to the movie yesterday. We looked and there was no one there.
We found out that they apparently changed the time of the film.

Another, related use of the remote past tense appears in sentences in which the speaker implies that something has occurred after the action of the verb in question, but does not know what. Consider the following conversations:

- ئادىلەنى ئامېرىكىغا كەتتى دەپ ئاڭلىدىم، راستمۇ؟
- ئۇقمايمەن، پاسپورت بېجىرىپ يۈرگەنتى.

- ئەكبەر دەرسكە كەلمىدىغۇ؟
- دادىسى كەلدىمىكىن. تۈنۈگۈن دادىسىنىڭ گېپىنى قىلغانتى.

In a telephone conversation:

- ياخشىمۇسىز!
- ياخشىمۇسىز! كىمنى ئىزدەيسىز؟
- مەن ئەكبەر، ئادىلجاننىڭ ساۋاقدىشى. ئادىلجان بارمۇ؟
- ئادىلجان يوق، ئۇ دۇكانغا چىقىپ كەتكەنتى...

Exercise 11: بۇرۇن رۇسچە ئۆگەنگەنتىم...

Exercise 11.1:  Complete each sentence with the appropriate remote past tense form for the verb in parentheses.

مەن بۇرۇن خەنزۇچە (ئۆگەنمەك) ________________ ، لېكىن ھازىر ئۇنتۇپ كەتتىم. تىلنى ئىشلەتمىسە، تېز ئۇنتۇلىدىكەن.

ئۇنىڭ ماشىنىسىنى شۇ يەردە (كۆرمەك) ________________

بۇرۇن ئۇ شۇ ئىداردە (ئىشلىمەك) ________________

- قىزىڭىز تەتىلدە ئۆيگە كېلەمدۇ؟
- ۋاي تاڭ، كېلىمەن دەپ تېلېفون (قىلماق) ________________

- تېلېۋىزورۇڭلار يوقمۇ؟
- تېلېۋىزورىمىز بۇزۇلۇپ (قالماق) ________________. ئۇنى رېمونتخانىغا ئاپىرىپ بەردۇق.

- كەلسىلە، ئاچا، نان ئالاملا؟
- ھەئە، ئۆيگە مېھمان (كەلمەك) ________________. سىڭىپ پىشقان ناندىن تۆتنى بېرىڭە.

Exercise 11.2:  Translate the following statements into English.

1. تاماق ئېتىشنى ماڭا دادام ئۆگەتكەنتى.

2. ئۇ ماشىنا ھەيدەشنى 15 يېشىدا ئۆگەنگەنتى.

3. پاسپورتىمنى 16 يېشىمدا ئالغانتىم.

4. ئۇنىڭ بىلەن ئىككى يىل بۇرۇن كۆرۈشكەنتىم.

5. ئېسىڭدە يوقمۇ، سەن ئۇنىڭ بىلەن تونۇگۈن بازاردا كۆرۈشكەنتىڭ.

6. ئانام بىلەن ئۆتكەن ھەپتە سۆزلەشكەنتىم.

7. ئۇنىڭ دوختۇر ئىكەنلىكىنى بىلمىگەنمىتىڭىز؟

4 The Habitual Past: (-ار ئىدى\-ەر ئىدى)-اتتى \ -ەتتى

In the dialogue between John and Yasin (Exercise 9.1), you saw a new form of the verb: the habitual past tense. Look at the following examples from the dialogue:

شەنبە ياكى يەكشەنبە كۈنلىرى باشقا ئالىي مەكتەپلەرگە بېرىپ يۈرتىلۇقلار ئولتۇرۇشى قىلاتتۇق.
On Saturdays or Sundays, we used to go to other universities and
have parties with the students in the dorms.
بۇرۇن مەكتەپ تۇرمۇش پۇلىنى بېرەتتى.
In the past, the school would pay for living expenses.
مەن يېڭى كەلگەندە بەش- ئالتە يۈز كوي بولسا يېتەتتى.
When I first came, five or six hundred kuai (RMB) used to suffice.

The Habitual past denotes an action that occurred frequently and regularly throughout some span of time in the past. It often corresponds to English constructions employing the phrase 'used to.'

In Uyghur, the habitual past takes the form -ات\-ەت attached to the stem of the main verb, plus the regular past tense personal endings beginning with ت, so as to match the final ت of the habitual past. When the verb stem ends in a vowel, the ئا or ئە of the habitual past ending reduces to ي , yielding -يت .

Past Tense Personal Ending	Habitual Past Ending	Verb Stem
-تى (-تىم، -تىڭ، ...)	-ات -يت	-قىل -ئاڭلا

ئۈرۈمچىدە تۇرغاندا ھەر كۈنى لەغمەن يەيتتىم.
When I lived in Urumchi I used to eat laghman every day.
بۇرۇن كۈنىگە ئون سائەتتىن ئىشلەيتتۇق.
We used to work more than ten hours a day.
ئۆپكە- ھېسىپنى "دىلبەر" ئاشخانىسىدىن ئالاتتىم.
We used to get lung sausage from the restaurant "Dilber."
بۇ ئاشخانىغا بىز ئەنجان پولۇسىنى يېگىلى باراتتۇق.
We used to go to this restaurant to have Andijan style pilaf.
بالىلىقىڭدا بەك كۆپ ئۇخلايتتىڭ.
During your childhood you used to sleep a lot.

4 The Habitual Past: -اتتى \ -ەتتى(-ار ئىدى\-ەر ئىدى) (cont'd.)

The negative of the habitual past is formed by adding the negative -ما/-مە directly to the verb stem, then employing the form of the habitual past tense ending introduced above for vowel-final stems (-يت) and conjugating accordingly.

Past Tense Personal Ending	*Habitual Past Ending*	*Negative*	*Verb Stem*
-تى (-تىم، -تىڭ، ...)	-يت	-ما -، -مە	قىل-، كەت-

بۇنداق ناخشىلارنى ئۆمرىمىزدە ئاڭلىمايتتۇق.

We would never ever (lit. 'in our lives') hear songs like this.

بالىلىقىدا ئۇ بىزنىڭ ئۆيگە كۆپ كەلمەيتتى.

When he was a child he wouldn't come to our home often.

You never used to do things like this before. بۇرۇن بۇنداق ئىشلارنى قىلمايتتىڭ.

This man never used to laugh. بۇ ئادەم ھېچ قاچان كۈلمەيتتى.

Although this is the most commonly used form of the habitual past in modern Uyghur, it is actually a contraction of an older form. Even today in some very formal speech or writing, the habitual past appears in its full, uncontracted form. This consists of the indefinite future tense -ار\-ەر (-ماس\-مە- in the negative) of the main verb, plus the past auxiliary copula ئىدى.

Past Tense Personal Ending	*Past Auxiliary Stem*
-دى (-دىم، -دىڭ،...)	ئى-

Indefinite Future	*Verb Stem*
-ار، -ماس	بار-

Exercise 12: ئۈرۈمچىدە ئۇيغۇرلار بىلەن كۆپ سۆزلەشتىم...

Exercise: 12.1:  Read Batur's (Vincent's) description of his time in Xinjiang. Circle all the verbs in both, the remote and the habitual past. Then translate these sentences into English on a separate sheet of paper.

2011- يىلى مەن شىنجاڭنىڭ كورلا شەھىرىدىكى بىر ئوتتۇرا مەكتەپتە ئىنگلىز تىلىدىن دەرس بەرگەنتىم. ئۇ يەردە مەن ناھايىتى ئالدىراش ئىدىم، شۇڭا ئۇيغۇر تىلىنى رەسمىي شەكىلدە ئوقۇيالمىدىم. خىزمەت توختامى تۈگىگەندىن كېيىن مەن ئامېرىكىغا قايتىپ كەتمەكچى بولدۇم، ئەمما ئۇيغۇر تىلىنى تېخىمۇ ياخشىراق ئۆگىنىش مەقسىتىدە ئۈرۈمچىگە بېرىپ ئۆزۈمنى شىنجاڭ يېزا- ئىگىلىك ئۇنىۋېرسىتېتىغا* تىزىملاتتىم.

ئۈرۈمچىدە ئۇيغۇر تىلىنى ئوقۇغانلىقىم مەن ئۈچۈن ناھايىتى ياخشى بىر تەجرىبە بولدى. كورلىدا مەن خەنزۇلار تۇرىدىغان جايدا ياشايتتىم، شۇڭا مېنىڭ خەنزۇچەم كۆپ ياخشىلاندى، لېكىن ئۇيغۇرچە ئاز سۆزلەيتتىم. بىراق ئۈرۈمچىدە مەن ئاساسەن ئۇيغۇرچە سۆزلىدىم، بۇ مېنىڭ تىل ئۆگىنىشىمگە بەكمۇ ياخشى بولدى.

ئۈرۈمچىدەك چوڭ شەھەردە سىز ھەر خىل ئادەملەر بىلەن تۈرلۈك تېمىلاردا سۆزلىشەلەيسىز. مەن ئەتىگەنلىرى بىرىنچى دەرسىمگە بېرىپ مۇئەللىمىم بىلەن پاراڭلىشاتتىم. بۇ دەرس مەخسۇس چەت ئەللىكلەر ئۈچۈن بولغاچقا، دەرسكە قاتناشقانلار ئاز ئىدى. شۇڭا بۇ دەرسنى "دەرس" دېمەي، بەلكىم "ئەركىن سۆھبەت" دېسەكمۇ بولاتتى. بىز خالىغان تېمىلارنى تاللاپ شۇ تېمىدا سۆزلىشەتتۇق. ئىككىنچى دەرسىم باشقىچە ئىدى. بۇ دەرستە مەن ئۇيغۇر تىلىنى كەسىپ قىلىپ تاللىغان خەنزۇ ئوقۇغۇچىلار بىلەن بىللە بولدۇم. سىنىپتا تەخمىنەن 30 ئوقۇغۇچى بار ئىدى. دەرستىن كېيىن مەن ساۋاقداشلىرىم بىلەن تاماققا چىقىپ ئۇلاردىن "نىمىشقا سىز ئۇيغۇر تىلىنى كەسىپ قىلىپ تاللىدىڭىز؟" دەپ سورايتتىم. ئۇلارنىڭ خىلمۇخىل ھېكايىلىرىنى ئاڭلاش مەن ئۈچۈن بەك قىزىق ئىدى.

ئۈرۈمچىدە ھەر خىل قىزىق پۇرسەتلەر بار. ئۇيغۇرچىنى تېخىمۇ ياخشىراق ئۆگىنەي دېسىڭىز، ئۇيغۇرلار ماكانىغا بېرىڭ!

*شىنجاڭ يېزا- ئىگىلىك ئۇنىۋېرسىتېتى: Xinjiang Agricultural University

Exercise 12.2:  Working with a partner, ask three questions each about Batur's life in Xinjiang. Use the habitual past tense.

Exercise 13:  Now read the following passage in which Professor Adilya Muhter describes her childhood. Fill in the blanks with the appropriate verbs in the habitual past.

بالىلىقىمدا ھەر تەتىلدە ئۇكام بىلەن موممىزنىڭ ئۆيىگە (go) ______________ .
مومام ئايكۆل كەنتىدە (live) ______________. دادىمىز بىزنى ئاپتوبۇستا (bring)
______________. ياز كۈنلىرى باللار بىلەن ئۆستەڭگە بېرىپ (swim) ______________، پۇتبول
(play)______________. بەزىدە تاماق يېيىشنىمۇ (forget) ______________. ئويۇن بىلەن
بولۇپ قورساقىمۇ ئاچمايتتى. بۇنداق چاغلاردا مومام (get angry) ______. ئىنىم مەندىن ئۈچ ياش
كىچىك ئىدى. ئۇ سۇ ئۈزۈشنى (know, neg.) ______________.
ئۆستەڭگە بارغاندا، مەن ئۇنىڭدىن بەكمۇ (worry) ______________.
بەزىدە ئېتىزلىقتا بېرىپ بوۋىمىزغا (help) ______________. بوۋىمىز بەكمۇ قىزىق ئادەم ئىدى.
ئۇ بىزگە ھەر خىل چۆچەكلەرنى (tell) ______________. ئۇكام چۆچەكلەرگە تولىمۇ ئامراق
ئىدى. ھويلىدا بىر تۈپ شاپتۇل دەرىخى بار ئىدى. ئەتىگەندە ئورنىمىزدىن تۇرۇپلا شاپتۇل يېگىلى
(to hurry) ______________. مومام بىزگە: " يۈزۈڭلارنى يۇيۇپ ئاندىن يەڭلار" (say) ______________ .
قىش كۈنلىرى سىرتقا چىقىپ قار (play) ______________. قوللىرىمىز مۇزلاپ كەتمىگىچە
ئۆيگە (enter neg.) ______________. ئۆيگە كىرگەندىن كېيىن ئوچاقنىڭ يېنىدا ئولتۇرۇپ
(to get warm) ______________. مومام بىزگە ئىسسىق چاي
(give) ______________.

Exercise14:  Look at the following pictures from Yasin's childhood. Based on these pictures make up five sentences using the habitual past.

Exercise 15: Describe your best childhood memory. How was it similar to or different from Yasin's?

5 The Auxiliary Verb ئەتمەك

In the dialogue (Exercise 9.1) you see an auxiliary verb ئەتمەك in the compound verbs چەكلىۋەتمەك and ئۇخلىۋەتمەك. It appears in the sentences:

كېيىن مەكتەپلەر بۇنى چەكلىۋەتتى (چەكلەپ ئەتتى).
Then the school suddenly prohibited this.
پولۇ يەپ ئاندىن بىر ئۇخلىۋەتسىڭىز (ئۇخلاپ ئەتسىڭىز) ئوڭشىلىپ قالىسىز.
If you eat pilaf and then sleep, you will recover.

The auxiliary verb ئەتمەك is often used to express that the action of the verb is surprising, or that it is performed quickly, suddenly, and unexpectedly from the perspective of those not performing the action.
Look at some more examples:

ئۇ يىغىلىپ قالغان ئەخلەتنى تاشلىۋەتتى.
He suddenly took up the fallen trash and tossed it aside.
ئادىل كىتابىنى ماڭا بېرىۋەتتى.
Adil (unexpectedly) gave me his book.
ئۇ ئۆيلەرنى ئۆزى تازىلىۋەتتى.
Surprisingly, he cleaned the rooms himself.
ئۇلار تاماقنى قالدۇرماي يەۋەتتى.
They ate up their food without even putting it down.

Occasionally, the auxiliary verb ئەتمەك appears on verbs whose only common feature is that something is being given, paid, or thrown in a direction away from the subject. Naturally, this usage is particular to a certain subset of verbs, and often there is no need to translate the auxiliary.

سىز خېتىڭىزنى سېلىۋەتتىڭىزمۇ؟
Did you send (out) your letter?
تاماقنىڭ پۇلىنى تۆلىۋەتتىڭلارمۇ؟
Did you (go ahead and) pay for the food?
دادام مەندىن "ئاناڭغا تېلېفون قىلىۋەتتىڭمۇ؟" دەپ سورىدى.
"Did you give your mother a call?" asked my father.
ئادىلدىن ئالغان قەرزنى بېرىۋەتتىم ؟
Did you give Adil the money you borrowed from him?

Exercise 16:  Follow the examples in Grammar Point 5 and write nine sentences on your own. Use each of the example compound verbs which employ ئەتمەك once.

Exercise 17:  Imagine that Ekber wrote a letter to his parents and asked you to give it to them when you are in Urumchi. Call Ekber's parents to arrange a meeting with them. Introduce yourself, explain the reason you want to meet them, tell them when you are available, then confirm the date and time of your meeting. Along with the other verbs, use the verb بېرىۋەتمەك to emphasize the urgency of this message.

Exercise 18: سالام خەت!

Exercise 18.1:  1. Before reading the letter, examine the words and expressions that are used in the letter.

excess	ئارتۇقچىلىق
pedestrians	پىيادىلەر
overcrowding	قىستاڭچىلىق
to swear	قەسەم قىلماق
concept	ئۇقۇم

to deliver free of charge	ھەقسىز توشۇماق
lawn, yard	چىملىق
to urge, admonish	تاپىلىماق
to sense	تۇيماق
polluted	بۇلغانغان

 2. Read the following phrases and statements taken from various parts of the letter.

1. كېلىپلا تىزىمغا ئالدۇرۇش، ئۆي تېپىش، تۇرمۇشقا لازىملىق نەرسىلەرنى تەييارلاش دېگەندەك ئىشلار بىلەن بىر ھەپتە ئۆتۈپ كەتتى.
2. پىيادە ماڭغاچ شەھەرنىڭ ساپ ھاۋاسىدىن ھوزۇرلاندىم، ھېچقاچان كۆرۈپ باقمىغان خىلمۇ - خىل دەرەخلەرنى تاماشا قىلدىم.
3. بۇ جاي بۈك- باراقسان ئورمانلىق بولغىنى ئۈچۈن 1820- يىلى ئىندىيانا ئۇنىۋېرسىتېتى قۇرۇلغاندا مەكتەپ ئورنى ئۈچۈن مۇشۇ شەھەر تاللانغان ئىكەن.
4. ئۈرۈمچىدە بىر سومغا ئالىدىغان نان بۇ يەردە بىر دوللار. بۇ - يەتتە سوم دېگەن گەپ.
5. مەنمۇ ھەر كۈنى تۆت سائەتتىن دەرس ئوقۇغاچ، كۇتۇپخانىدا تۆت - بەش سائەتتىن ۋاقىتلىق ئىشلەۋاتىمەن.
6. ئامېرىكىدا مەن ھەيران قالغان يەنە بىر ئىش - ماشىنا بولدى.

Exercise 18.2:  Based on the statements in the part B of Exercise 18.1, what do you think this letter is about? Identify at least three topics that Ekber writes about in his letter. Explain how you identified them.

Exercise 18.3:  Now read the letter and answer the questions that follow.

سالام قەدىرلىك دادا، ئاپا:

ياخشى تۇرىۋاتامسىلەر؟ بوۋام ۋە موماممۇ ئوبدان تۇرىۋاتامدۇ؟ ھەدەم ۋە سىڭلىمچۇ؟ ئۇرۇق- تۇغقان ۋە قولۇم- قوشنىلار تىنچلىقمۇ؟ مەن شۇنداق بولۇشىنى ئۈمىد قىلىمەن. خۇدا ھەممىمىزگە خاتىرجەملىك ۋە ئامانلىق ئاتا قىلسۇن.

ئامېرىكىغا كەلگەندىن بېرى سىلەرگە خەت يازالمىدىم. راستىنى دېسەم، بەك ئالدىراش بولۇپ كەتتىم. بۇ يەردە ۋاقىت بەك تېز ئۆتىدىكەن. بۇ يەردىمۇ بىر سوتكىدا يىگىرمە تۆت سائەت بولسىمۇ، ماڭا ئۇنداق ئەمەستەك بىلىنىدۇ. كېلىپلا تىزىمغا ئالدۇرۇش، ئۆي تېپىش، تۇرمۇشقا لازىملىق نەرسىلەرنى تەييارلاش دېگەندەك ئىشلار بىلەن بىر ھەپتە ئۆتۈپ كېتىپتۇ. ئاكام ئامېرىكىدا بولسىمۇ، ئۇنىڭ بىلەن تېخى تۈنۈگۈن تېلېفوندا سۆزلەشتىم. ئاكام مېنىڭ ئامېرىكىغا كەلگەنلىكىمنى* ئاڭلاپ بەك خوشال بولدى. قىشلىق تەتىلدە كالىفورنىيەگە كېلىپ ئويناپ كېتىشىمنى تاپىلىدى. ئۇنىڭ دېيىشىچە، كالىفورنىيەدە قىشتا سوغۇق بولمايدىكەن.

مەن تۇرۇۋاتقان بلۇمىڭتون شەھىرىنىڭ قانچىلىك چىرايلىق جاي ئىكەنلىكىنى بۇ يەرگە كېلىپ بىر ھەپتە بولغاندا ئاندىن بىلدىم. شۇ كۈنى يەكشەنبە ئىدى. بىرئاز دەم ئېلىش ئۈچۈن سىرتقا چىقتىم. قىزىق يېرى، شۇ كۈنى يەكشەنبە بولسىمۇ، شەھەرنىڭ كوچىلىرىدا ئادەم ئانچە كۆپ ئەمەس ئىدى. ئوقۇغۇچىلارنى ھەقسىز توشۇيدىغان شەھەر ئاپتوبۇسلىرىمۇ يەكشەنبە كۈنى ئىشلىمەيدىكەن. بۇنىڭ بىلەن شەھەر چۆلدەرەپ قالغاندەك كۆرۈنىدىكەن. مەن ئۈچۈن بۇمۇ ياخشى بولدى. پىيادە ماڭغاچ**، شەھەرنىڭ ساپ ھاۋاسىدىن ھوزۇرلاندىم، ھېچقاچان كۆرۈپ باقمىغان خىلمۇ - خىل دەرەخلەرنى تاماشا قىلدىم. بۇ يەردە زاۋۇتلار بولمىغاچقا، يەنە كېلىپ ھەممىلا يەر دەل- دەرەخلەر بىلەن قاپلانغاچقا، "بۇلغانغان ھاۋا" دېگەن ئۇقۇم بۇ يەردە مەۋجۇت ئەمەس. ئېيتىشلارغا قارىغاندا، بۇ جاي بۈك- باراقسان ئورمانلىق بولغىنى ئۈچۈن 1820- يىلى ئىندىيانا ئۇنىۋېرسىتېتى قۇرۇلغاندا مەكتەپ ئورنى ئۈچۈن مۇشۇ شەھەر تاللانغان ئىكەن. بۇ جاي ھازىرمۇ شۇنداق يېشىللىق بولۇپ، دەرەخ يوق جايلار پۈتۈنلەي چىملىق ئىكەن. "ئوتى بار يەرنىڭ سۈيى يوق" دېگەندەك، بۇ چىرايلىق شەھەردە ھەممىلا نەرسە شۇنداق قىممەت. ئۈرۈمچىدە بىر سومغا ئالىدىغان نان بۇ يەردە بىر دوللار. بۇ - يەتتە سوم دېگەن گەپ. شۇ كۈنى شەھەردە بىر ئىستاكان قەھۋەنى ئىككى دوللارغا ئالدىم ۋە شۇنىڭدىن كېيىن قەھۋە ئىچمەسلىككە قەسەم قىلدىم. بۇ يەردە ئەڭ قىممەت نەرسە - ئۆي. ھەر ئايدا ئۆي ئىجارىسىگە 500 دوللار تاپشۇرىمەن. شۇڭا كىشىلەرنىڭ "ئوقۇش مۇكاپات پۇلى بولمىسا، ئامېرىكىدا ئوقۇغىلى بولمايدۇ" دېگىنى بىكار ئەمەس ئىكەن. بۇنداق دېسەم يەنە ئەندىشە قىلىپ كەتمەڭلار، مېنىڭ مۇكاپات پۇلۇم تۇرمۇشۇمغا يېتىپ ئاشىدۇ.

بۇ يەردە ھەممە ئادەم بەكلا ئالدىراش كۆرۈنىدۇ. مەنمۇ ھەر كۈنى تۆت سائەتتىن دەرس ئۆقۇغاچ، كۈتۈپخانىدا تۆت - بەش سائەتتىن ۋاقىتلىق ئىشلەۋاتىمەن. ئۇنىڭ ئۈستىگە كۈنلۈك دەرسلەرنىڭ تاپشۇرۇقلىرىنى ئىشلەش ۋە قىسقا ماقالىلارنى يېزىش دېگەندەك ئىشلار بىلەن ئاۋارە بولىمەن. ئامېرىكىدا مەن ھەيران قالغان يەنە بىر ئىش - ماشىنا بولدى. بۇ يەردە مەندىن باشقا ھەممىلا ئادەمنىڭ ماشىنىسى باردەك قىلىدۇ. بۇ جايدا ماشىنا شۇنچە كۆپ بولسىمۇ، ئۈرۈمچىگە ئوخشاش ئۇنداق قىستاڭچىلىق ۋە قالايمىقانچىلىق يوق. ماشىنىلار ناھايىتى تېز ماڭىدۇ. قىزىل چىراقتىن باشقا توختاش بەلگىسى بار جايلاردا ساقچى بولمىسىمۇ، ھەممىلا ماشىنا ئۆزلىكىدىن توختاپ ئاندىن ماڭىدۇ. مېنىڭ تېخىمۇ ھەيران قالغىنىم بۇ يەردە ھەممە ماشىنا پىيادىلەرگە يول بېرىدۇ. ئەمما بىزنىڭ شەھەرلىرىمىزدە پىيادىلەرنىڭ ماشىنىغا يول بېرىشى ئومۇمىي قائىدە. مەن بۇنىڭدىن شۇنى چۈشەندىمكى، ئامېرىكىدا ئادەم ماشىنىدىن قىممەتلىك.

خەير، ھازىرچە مۇشۇنچىلىك يېزىپ تۇراي، قالغان گەپلەرنى كېيىنكى خەتلەردە دېيىشەرمىز. كۆرۈشكىچە ئامان بولۇڭلار. سىلەرنى سېغىنىپ:

ئوغلۇڭلار ئەكبەر

2014 - يىلى 20 - سېنتەبىر

---

*this construction is introduced in chapter 10

**this grammar is introduced later in this chapter

1. ئۇ يەكشەنبە كۈنى شەھەر ئايلانغاندا نېمىلەرگە دىققەت قىلىدۇ؟
2. نېمە ئۈچۈن ئەكبەر تۇرىدىغان شەھەردە "بۇلغانغان ھاۋا" ئۇقۇمى يوق؟
3. ئۇ خېتىدە ئىندىيانا ئۇنىۋېرسىتېتى توغرۇلۇق نېمىلەر يازىدۇ؟
4. "ئوقۇش مۇكاپات پۇلى بولمىسا، ئامېرىكىدا ئوقۇغىلى بولمايدۇ" دېگەن گەپكە قوشۇلامسىز؟ نېمىشقا؟
5. ئەكبەر ئامېرىكىدا يەنە نېمىلەرگە ھەيران قالىدۇ؟

Exercise 18.4: Summarize what you have learned about aspects that are particular to life in Urumchi from Ekber's letter.

Exercise 18.5:  Skim Ekber's letter again and answer the following questions.

1. To whom did Ekber write the letter? ______________________
2. What expression does he use in the greeting? ______________________
3. Look at the first paragraph. Who does Ekber ask about, and in what order? ______________________
4. What expression is used to close the introductory paragraph?

____

Now, look at the closing paragraph of the letter.

1. What wish does Ekber make before closing the letter?

____

2. How does he finish the letter?

____

3. Where and how is the date of the letter written?

____

Exercise 18.6:  Write your own letter to a Uyghur friend about your life in Xinjiang. Include the following information in your letter:

- Ask about your friend's family and your mutual acquaintances.
- Explain that you could not write earlier because you were busy registering and finding a place to stay.
- Briefly compare your life in Xinjiang with that in your hometown.
- Describe in detail one major difference you have noticed between life in the two places.
- Explain how you are covering your costs and fees and write about how your Uyghur has been improving.
- Promise that you will write more.
- Use appropriate greetings and conclude the letter following the format presented above, being sure to provide a date.

6 Expressing 'even if', 'although','even though':
verb + سا- \ سه- + مۇ-

In Uyghur, adding the particle مۇ- to the end of the conditional form of the verb changes the meaning of the condition slightly. Whereas the normal conditional generally corresponds to English 'if,' this form is used to mean 'even if' or 'even though.'

ماڭا مىلیون دوللار بەرسەڭمۇ بۇ يەردىن كەتمەيمەن.
Even if you give me a million dollars, I won't leave this place!
ئائىلىسى شۇنچىۋالا باياشات بولسىمۇ، بۇ بالا ئىنتايىن كەمتەر ئىدى.
Even though his family is very rich, he himself is an extremely humble child.
ئۇ بارسىمۇ، مەن بارمايمەن.
Even if he goes, I will not (go).
تاماق يېمىسەڭمۇ، چاي ئىچسەڭچۇ.
Even though you do not eat, have some tea.
ئۇ بېيجىڭدا ياشىسىمۇ، خەنزۇ تىلىنى بىلمەيتتى.
Even though he lived in Beijing, he did not know Chinese.

The full conjugation for the 'even if/though' form appears below.

مەن ... -سامۇ / -سەمۇ	بىز ... -ساقمۇ / -سەكمۇ
سەن ... -ساڭمۇ / -سەڭمۇ	
سىز ... -سىڭىزمۇ	سىلەر ... -ساڭلارمۇ / -سەڭلارمۇ
ئۇ ... -سىمۇ	ئۇلار ... -سىمۇ

Note that in the second (formal) and third person, the vowel of the conditional reduces to ى in this position.

بانكا ھېساباتىمدا پۇل بولسىمۇ بەزى سەۋەبلەر تۈپەيلىدىن ئۇنى ئالالمايمەن.
Even though there is money in my bank account, I can't take it out for some reason!

Exercise 19:  Look at Ekber's letter one more time and translate the underlined sentences.

Exercise 20:  Join the following pairs to make sentences using the structure found in Grammar Point 6. When you see the Ø symbol, write a negative sentence. Follow the example:

قەشقەرگە (بارماق) - يېڭى شەھەرگە (ئۆتمەك)
قەشقەرگە بارغان بولساممۇ، يېڭى شەھەرگە ئۆتمىدىم.

1. هاراق (ئىچمەك) Ø - بېشى (ئاغرىماق)

2. ئالدىراش (بولماق) - جىرىم تىكىش پائالىيىتىگە (قاتناشماق)

3. پۇل (بولماق) Ø - ماشىنا (ئالماق)

4. كەچ (بولماق) - كۇتۇپخانىغا (بارماق)

7 Simultaneous Actions

In Ekber's letter above you see constructions like: ماڭغاچ and ئوقۇغاچ. They appear in the following sentences:

پىيادە ماڭغاچ شەھەرنىڭ ساپ ھاۋاسىدىن ھوزۇرلاندىم.
I walked around, enjoying the city's fresh air.
مەنمۇ ھەر كۈنى تۆت سائەتتىن دەرس ئوقۇغاچ ، كۈتۈپخانىدا تۆت - بەش سائەتتىن ۋاقىتلىق ئىشلەۋاتىمەن.
I too was taking four hours of classes a day while working in the library for four to five hours.

The suffix -غاچ (-گەچ \ -قاچ \ -كەچ) is added to the verb stem to show that another action is performed at the same time. Look at the following examples:

They walked as they chatted. ئۇلار پاراڭلاشقاچ ماڭدى.
I read as I watched television. تېلېۋىزور كۆرگەچ ، كىتاب ئوقۇدۇم.
I drank my tea while reading the newspaper. گېزىت ئوقۇغاچ چاي ئىچتىم.

Note that when we translate these sentences into English, we put the second verb first, because this is a main verb. The second verb with the suffix in question is translated as 'while/as we, I' ...

This suffix can also be used to describe an action that should be performed while the action of the main verb is going on in the background. This usage of the suffix is usually followed by a command form.

دۇكانغا بارسىڭىز، نانمۇ ئالغاچ كېلىڭ.
If you go to the store, buy bread too (along with other stuff).
مەن بۈگۈن كەچ كېلىمەن، تاماق ئەتكەچ تۇرسىڭىز.
I'm coming late today, start cooking, please.
بازارغا بارسام، موماڭنى يوقلىغاچ كېلىمەن.
If I go to the market, I will visit my grandmother.
مەكتەپكە بارسىڭىز بۇ كىتابلارنى ئالغاچ كېتىڭ.
If you go to school, take these books, please.
Note that verbs with this ending are similar to those ending -ىپ
Compare the following sentences:
بىز چاي ئىچىپ پاراڭلاشتۇق.
بىز چاي ئىچكەچ پاراڭلاشتۇق.

Exercise 21:  Imagine that your Uyghur roommate left you a short note (باغاقچە). Read it, and then respond using the construction explained in Grammar Point 7. Follow the model after the note.

ياسىن:

ھازىر كىتاپلارنى قايتۇرۇشقا كۇتۇبخانىغا ماڭدىم. يېڭى كەلگەن ژۇرناللاردىن ئالغاچ كېلەمسىز؟ يېنىشىمدا سودىلىق ئۈچۈن تاللا بازىرىغا كىرمەكچىمەن. سوپۇن تۈگەپتۇ دېگەنتىڭ، تازىلىق بۇيۇملىرىدىن ئالغاچ كېلەمسىز؟ ئەگەر ئەتە ۋاقتىڭ بولسا، شەھەر كۆرگەچ ساڭا مەكتەپ رايونىنى كۆرسىتىپ كېلەمسىز؟

مۇختەر

كۇتۇبخانىغا بارساڭ، "شىنجاڭ ياشلىرى" ژۇرنىلىنىڭ يېڭى سانلىرىنى ئالغاچ كەلسەڭ.

Exercise 22: ئوقۇغۇچىلارنىڭ بوش ۋاقتى

Exercise 22.1:  After classes, John talks to Yasin about students' leisure activities at Xinjiang University. Read the conversation. Then answer the questions that follow.

جون: ياسىن، سىز ھازىر نەگە ماڭدىڭىز؟
ياسىن: ئاشخانىغا ماڭغان، بىللە بارامسىز؟
جون: باراي، سىز بىلەن ئازراق پاراڭلىشاي دېگەنتىم.
ياسىن: قېنى، ماڭغاچ پاراڭلىشايلى.
جون: سىزدىن بىر نەرسىنى سورىماقچى ئىدىم. ھېلىقى ئولتۇرۇشتا قىزلارنى كۆرمىدىم. قىزلار ئولتۇرۇشقا قاتناشمامدۇ؟
ياسىن: ئۇلارنىڭ ئۆزلىرىنىڭ ئولتۇرۇشى بولىدۇ. ئوغۇللار ئولتۇرۇشىدا كۆپ ھاراق ئىچىلگەچكە، ئۇلار قىزلارنى چاقىرمايدۇ.
جون: ئوغۇللار قىزلار ئولتۇرۇشىغا بارسا بولامدۇ؟
ياسىن: بارسا بولىدۇ، ئەمما كۆپىنچە قىزلار ئايرىم ئولتۇرۇش قىلىدۇ. تۇغۇلغان كۈن ئولتۇرۇشلىرىغا بەزىدە ئوغۇللارنىمۇ تەكلىپ قىلىدۇ.
جون: قىزلار ھاراق ئىچەمدۇ؟
ياسىن: ئىچىدىغانلارمۇ بار، ئەمما بىزدەك كۆپ ئىچمەيدۇ.
جون: قىزلار بوش ۋاقتى چىقىپ قالسا يەنە نېمىلەر قىلىدۇ؟
ياسىن: كۆپى مەكتەپ تانسىخانىسىغا بېرىپ كۆڭۈل ئاچىدۇ. ھەپتە ئاخىرلىرى ئۇ يەر بەك قىزىيدۇ.
جون: ئوغۇللارچۇ؟ ئۇلار تانسىخانىغا بارمامدۇ؟
ياسىن: بارمامدىغان*؟! تانسىخانىغا كىرىدىغان ئوغۇللار بەك كۆپ بولغاچقا، بەزىدە تانسىغا تارتىدىغانغا قىز قالمايدۇ. قوشنا مەكتەپتىنمۇ بىزنىڭ مەكتەپكە تانسا ئوينىغىلى كېلىدىغان ئوقۇغۇچىلار بار. ئۇلارنىڭ دېيىشىچە داشۆدە چىرايلىق قىزلار كۆپمىش**. يېڭى ئوقۇغۇچىلار تانسىنى ئانچە ياخشى ئوينىيالمايدۇ، ئەمما بىر ئايدىلا ئۇستا بولۇپ كېتىدۇ. بىز كۆپرەك سىبۇ ئوينايمىز، بەزىلەر يەنە ۋالىس ۋە رۇمبا ئوينايدۇ.

جون: سىبۇ دېدىڭىزمۇ؟ بۇ نېمە؟
ياسىن: ھە، بۇ تانسىنىڭ بىر تۈرى. بۇ خەنزۇچە سۆز. ئۇنىڭ مەنىسى "تۆت قەدەم". ھەر بىر يۈرۈش پۈت ھەركىتى تۆت قەدەملىك بولىدۇ. ئۆگىنىش بىرئاز ئاسان بولغاچقا كۆپ قىسىم ئۇيغۇر ئوقۇغۇچىلار مۇشۇنى ئوينايدۇ.
جون: مەكتەپ ئاشخانىسىغا كەپ قالدۇق-ھە؟
ياسىن: ھەئە، قېنى تاماق يەۋالايلى!

---

* Check page 283 for the explanation of this structure.

** The highlighted suffix indicates a slight sarcasm. This grammar is introduced in Chapter 10.

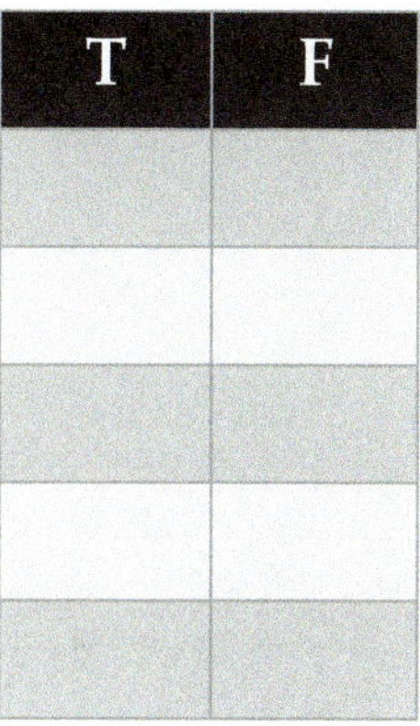

T	F

1. Girls are not invited to ئولتۇرۇش.
2. Men drink a lot of alcohol at ئولتۇرۇش.
3. Girls drink alcohol when they get together.
4. Girls and boys go to dance halls together.
5. Girls and boys like to dance سىبۇ.

Explain the concept of سىبۇ based on the passage.

What are the most common types of dances among Uyghur students?

Note:

The negative interrogative construction (بارمامدۇ+غان) بارمامدىغان expresses a certainty of the action and might be translated as: 'of course, definitely' (I/you/we/they... do). This construction is used with any verb. See more examples:

- بۇ ئاشخانىدا كاۋاپ بارمۇ؟
- بولمامدىغان؟!

- لەگمەن يەمسىز؟
- يېمەمدىغان؟!

- تەييار ماشىنىدا تۇرپانغا بىرىپ كەلمەمدۇق؟
- بارمامدىغان؟!

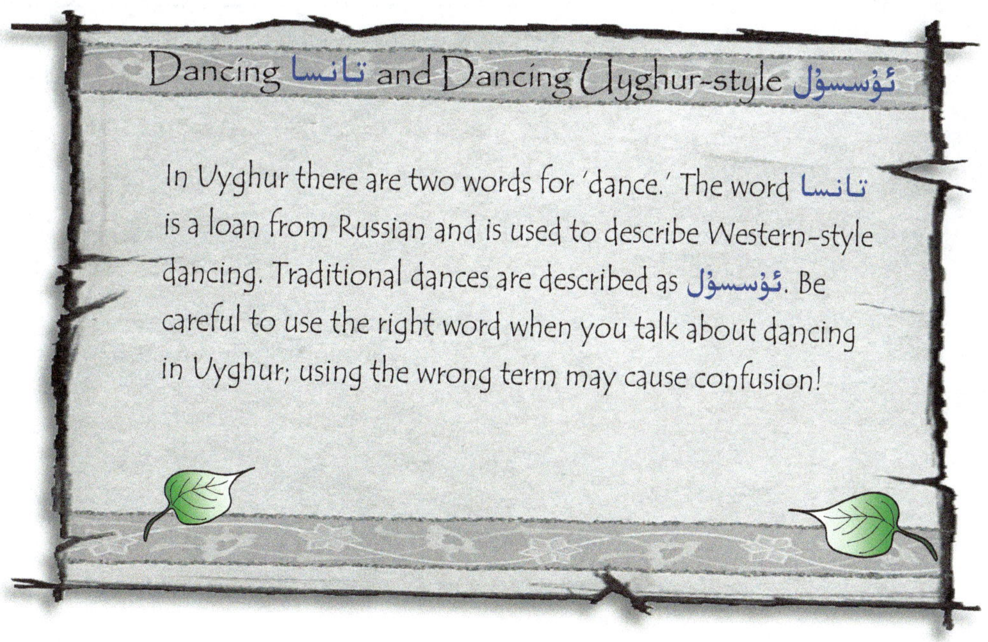

Exercise 22.2:  The next day Yasin ran into John at the library, where he introduced John to one of his female classmates. Read the first part of their conversation below and practice it with your partner.

ياسىن: ياخشىمۇسىز، جون!
جون: ياخشىمۇسىز! ياسىن، نېمانچە* جىق كىتاب ئالدىڭىز؟
ياسىن: ئالدىمىزدىكى ھەپتە مەۋسۇملۇق ئىمتىھان بار. بۇلارنى ئىمتىھانغا تەييارلىق قىلىش ئۈچۈن ئالدىم.
جون: ئوقۇغۇچىلار بىر قېتىمدا نەچچە كىتاپ ئالسا بولىدۇ؟
ياسىن: ئارىيەتكە دەمسىز؟
جون: ھەئە.
ياسىن: بىزدەك ئوقۇغۇچىلار ئون پارچە كىتاب ئالسا بولىدۇ. چەتئەللىك ئوقۇغۇچىلار يىگىرمە پارچە كىتاب ئالالايدۇ.
جون: بۇ بەك قىزىق ئىش ئىكەن. مېنىڭ يەنە باشقا ئىشلىرىم بار ئىدى. مەن ماڭاي ئەمسە.
ياسىن: توختاپ تۇرۇڭ. ئەنە، رەيھانگۈل كېلىۋاتىدۇ. مەن سىلەرنى تونۇشتۇرۇپ قوياي.
رەيھانگۈل: ياخشىمۇسىز ياسىن!
ياسىن: ياخشىمۇسىز! ئىمتىھانىڭىز باشلاندىمۇ؟
رەيھانگۈل: ھەئە. كېلەر ھەپتە بىر ئىمتىھانىم بار. شۇڭا كۈتۈپخانىدىن كىتاب ئالغاچ كۈتۈپخانىدا تەكرار قىلاي دېگەن.
ياسىن: ياخشى بوپتۇ. ھە راست، مەن سىلەرنى تونۇشتۇرۇپ قوياي: بۇ ئامېرىكىلىق جون. بىزنىڭ مەكتەپتە ئۇيغۇرچە ئۆگىنىۋاتىدۇ؛ جون، بۇ رەيھانگۈل. بىز بىر سىنىپتا ئوقۇيمىز.
جون: ياخشىمۇسىز!
رەيھانگۈل: ياخشىمۇسىز!

جون: رەيھانگۈل، مېنىڭ ئوقۇغۇچىلار ھەققىدە بەزى سوئاللىرىم بار ئىدى. سىزدىن سورىسام بولامدۇ؟
رەيھانگۈل: ئەلۋەتتە بولىدۇ. يۇرۇڭلار، بىرىنچى قەۋەتتىكى قەھۋەخانىدا پاراڭلىشايلى.
ياسىن: كەچۈرۈڭلار. مەن ھازىر ياتىقىمغا بېرىشىم لازىم. ھازىرچە سىلەر بېرىپ تۇرۇڭلار. مەن كىتابلارنى ئاپىرىۋېتىپ كېلەي.
جون: بولىدۇ ئەمسە، سىزنى ساقلايمىز.

---

* نېمانچە - why so much? (why on earth?)

Exercise 22.3:  Listen to the second part of the conversation between Räyhangül and John. Then tell if the following statements are true or false.

توغرا	خاتا

1. جون سۇتلۇك قەھۋەگە ئامراق.
2. ئوقۇغۇچى قىزلار شەنبە ۋە يەكشەنبىدىن باشقا ۋاقىتتا مەكتەپتىن چىقسا بولمايدۇ.
3. شەنبە كۈنلىرى قىزلار مونچىغا چۈشىدۇ.
4. شەنبە - يەكشەنبە كۈنلىرى قىزلار ئوغۇللار بىلەن بىللە ئولتۇرۇش قىلىدۇ.
5. دەم ئېلىش كۈنلىرى قىزلار بازارغا بېرىپ دۇكان ئارىلايدۇ.
6. تۇغۇلغان كۈن ئولتۇرۇشلىرىغا قىزلار ئوغۇللارنى تەكلىپ قىلىدۇ.
7. ئۇيغۇر قىزلار هاراق ئىچمەيدۇ.
8. بەزى ئولتۇرۇشلاردا ئوغۇل - قىزلار جۈپ بولۇپ تانسا ئوينايدۇ.
9. ئىمتىھان تۈگىگەندە ئوقۇغۇچىلار ئولتۇرۇش قىلىدۇ.

Exercise 22.4:  Compare the Uyghur ئولتۇرۇش with your college parties. What are the similarities and differences between the two? Write your observations in the space provided below.

پەرقى	ئوخشاشلىقى

Exercise 23: ئۇيغۇر مەشرىپى

Exercise 23.1: Discuss the following two questions as a group.

1. سىزنىڭ مەدەنىيىتىڭىزدە ياش ئوغۇل - قىزلارغا ئەدەپ - قائىدىلەر قانداق ئۆگىتىلىدۇ؟
2. مەشرەپ توغرۇلۇق ئاڭلىغانمۇسىز؟

Exercise 23.2:  Read the following passage about Meshrep with the help of your instructor.

مەشرەپ - ئۇيغۇرلاردىكى ئاممىۋى يىغىلىش پائالىيىتى. "مەشرەپ" سۆزى ئەرەبچە بولۇپ، ئۇنىڭ مەنىسى "جەم بولۇش ۋە ئىچىملىك (چاي ياكى شەربەت) ئىچىش". مەشرەپ - ئۇيغۇرلار ئارىسىدىكى ئۇزاق تارىخقا ئىگە جەم بولۇپ كۆڭۈل ئېچىش ئادىتى ئاساسىدا پەيدا بولغان. مەھمۇت كاشغەرى 11 - ئەسىردە يازغان "تۈركىي تىللار دىۋانى" دا بۇ خىلدىكى يىغىلىپ كۆڭۈل ئېچىش سورۇنلىرىدا كىشىلەرنىڭ ھاراق ئىچىپ ئۇسسۇل ئوينايدىغانلىقى ۋە ناخشا ئېيتىدىغانلىقىنى خاتىرىلىگەن.

ئۇيغۇرلار ئىسلام دىنىنى قوبۇل قىلغاندىن كېيىن بۇ خىل يىغىلىش پائالىيىتى داۋام قىلغان ۋە كېيىنچە "مەشرەپ" دەپ ئاتالغان. ئۇيغۇر مەشرىپىدە مەدەنىيەت بىلەن سەنئەت بىرلەشكەن بولىدۇ. مەشرەپتە ئۇيغۇرلار جەم بولۇپ ئولتۇرىدۇ ۋە ئۇسسۇل ئوينايدۇ، مەخسۇس سازەندىلەر مۇزىكا چېلىپ ناخشا ئېيتىدۇ. ئۇيغۇر خەلق ناخشىلىرىدا ئۇيغۇرلارنىڭ خوشاللىقى ۋە قايغۇسى سەنئەت شەكلىدە ئىپادىلەنگەن بولغاچقا، بۇ خىلدىكى ناخشىلار مەشرەپتىكى ئاساسلىق مەزمۇنلارنىڭ بىرى بولۇپ قالغان. شۇڭا بۇ خىل ناخشىلار ياشلاردا ئۇيغۇر سەنئىتىگە قارىتا قىزىقىش پەيدا قىلىش رولىغىمۇ ئىگە. مەشرەپتە يەنە تۈرلۈك تېمىدىكى چاقچاق ۋە خەلق ئويۇنلىرى بولىدۇ. مەشرەپتە ئۇيغۇرلاردىكى چوڭلارنى ھۆرمەتلەش، ئىناقلىق ۋە ئىتتىپاقلىق، سەمىمىيلىك، يامان ئىشلاردىن يىراق تۇرۇش قاتارلىق ئۆرپ - ئادەت ۋە ئەدەپ- ئەخلاققا دائىر مەزمۇنلار كومېدىيەلىك ئويۇنلار ئارقىلىق ياشلارغا جانلىق دەرس شەكلىدە ئۆگىتىلىدۇ . شۇڭا چوڭلار دائىم باللارنى مەشرەپكە ئېلىپ بارىدۇ. ئۇيغۇرلار ئارىسىدا ئەخلاقسىز كىشىلەرنى "مەشرەپ كۆرمىگەن كىشى" دەپ ئاتاش مۇشۇنىڭدىن كەلگەن.

مەشرەپ ئىختىيارلىق ئاساسىدىكى يىغىلىش بولغاچقا، ھەرقانداق كىشى قاتناشسا بولىدۇ، بۇنىڭ ئۈچۈن مەخسۇس تەكلىپنامە ئەۋەتىلمەيدۇ. ئوغۇللار مەشرىپى "ئوتتۇز ئوغۇل مەشرىپى" دەپ ئاتىلىدۇ، ئوغۇل-قىزلار مەشرىپى بولسا "ئوتتۇز ئوغۇل - توققۇز قىز مەشرىپى" دەپمۇ ئاتىلىدۇ، ئەمما مەشرەپكە كەلگەنلەرنىڭ سانى دائىم بۇنىڭدىن كۆپ بولىدۇ.

مەشرەپتە مۇقىم باشقۇرغۇچىلار بولىدۇ: ھۆرمەتلىك بىرەيلەن "يىگىت بېشى" بولۇپ سايلىنىدۇ ۋە مەشرەپنى باشقۇرىدۇ؛ مەشرەپتىكى ئويۇن، ناخشا - مۇزىكا ۋە يېمەك-ئىچمەك ئىشلىرىنى باشقۇرىدىغان كىشى " مىرشاپ " دېيىلىدۇ؛ تەرتىپ - ئىنتىزامغا مەسئۇل كىشى "پاششاپ" دەپ ئاتىلىدۇ؛ مەشرەپتىكى مۇكاپات ۋە جازانى ئېلان قىلىدىغان كىشى "قازىبەگ" دەپ ئاتىلىدۇ ۋە ئۇيغۇر ئۆرپ- ئادەتلىرىگە خىلاپ ئىشلارنى قىلغان كىشىلەرگە "جازا" بېرىدۇ. مەشرەپنىڭ باشقا خىلدىكى ئۇيغۇر سورۇنلىرىدىن ئەڭ چوڭ پەرقى - ئۇنىڭدا ھېچقاچان ھاراق ئىچىلمەيدۇ. 1990- يىللىرنىڭ ئاخىرىدىن باشلاپ ئۇيغۇرلارنىڭ بۇ خىلدىكى كوللېكتىپ مەشرەپ پائالىيىتى ھۆكۈمەت تەرىپىدىن چەكلەندى.

correct behavior	ئەدەپ- ئەخلاق
willingness	ئىختىيارلىق
fixed, stable	مۇقىم
discipline	تەرتىپ - ئىنتىزام
responsible	مەسئۇل
a punishment, penalty	جازا
towards, to, in regard to	قارىتا

public	ئاممىۋى
contrary to, against	خىلاپ
sincerity, honesty	سەمىمىيلىك
sadness	قايغۇ
content	مەزمۇن
to gather	جەم بولماق
friendly relations, harmony	ئىناقلىق

Exercise 23.3:  Match the words in the right-hand side of the column with their adjacent definitions in the left-hand column.

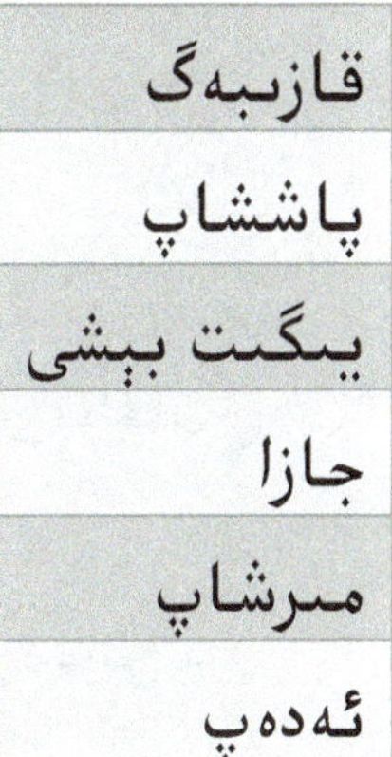

ئۆزئارا مۇئامىلىدە ئۆزىنى تۇتۇشنى بىلىش؛ ئەخلاق، تەربىيە ۋە ئۇنىڭ ئۆلچەملىرى	قازىبەگ
ناخشا- مۇزىكا ۋە يېمەك-ئىچمەك ئىشلىرىنى باشقۇرىدىغان كىشى	پاششاپ
ئەيىب ياكى جىنايىتى ئۈچۈن كۆرۈلىدىغان چارە	يىگىت بېشى
تەرتىپ - ئىنتىزامغا مەسئۇل كىشى	جازا
مەشرەپتىكى مۇكاپەت ۋە جازانى ئېلان قىلىدىغان كىشى	مىرشاپ
مەشرەپنى باشقۇرىدىغان كىشى	ئەدەپ

Exercise 23.4:  Read the passage one more time and answer the questions below.

1. مەشرەپ سۆزىنىڭ مەنىسى نېمە؟
2. مەشرەپ قانداق ئۆتكۈزىلىدۇ؟
3. نېمىشقا چوڭلار باللارنى مەشرەپكە ئېلىپ بارىدۇ؟
4. سىزنىڭچە، قانداق كىشىنى "مەشرەپ كۆرمىگەن كىشى" دەيدۇ؟
5. مەشرەپكە كىم قاتنىشالايدۇ؟
6. مەشرەپكە نەچچە ئادەم قاتناشسا بولىدۇ؟
7. كىم "يىگىت بېشى" بولۇپ سايلىنىدۇ؟ يىگىت بېشىنىڭ ۋەزىپىسى نېمە؟
8. مەشرەپتىكى ئويۇن، ناخشا- مۇزىكا ۋە يېمەك-ئىچمەك ئىشلىرىنى باشقۇرىدىغان كىشىنى نېمە دەپ ئاتايدۇ؟
9. تەرتىپ-ئىنتىزامغا مەسئۇل كىشىنچۇ؟

Exercise 23.5:  Now read the following example of the game often employed at مەشرەپ, then discuss it with your instructor.

مەشرەپتە جازا

مىرشاپ: خەپشۇك، ئوتتۇز ئوغۇل!
ئەخمەت: ئەسسالامۇ ئەلەيكۇم، مىرشاپ بېگىم! بىر ئارزۇيۇم بار ئىدى. ئېيتسام بولامدۇ؟
مىرشاپ: (يىگىت بېشى ۋە قازىبەگكە بۇرۇلۇپ) ئەسسالامۇ ئەلەيكۇم! ئوتتۇز ئوغۇلنىڭ بىرى بولغان ئەخمەتنىڭ بىر ئارزۇسى بار ئىكەن. ئېيتسا بولامدۇ؟
يىگىت بېشى ۋە قازىبەگ: بولىدۇ.
ئەخمەت: ئۆتكەن ھەپتە دوستىمىز مۇرادىل نەشە چېكىپتۇ. بىز بۇنىڭدىن بەك خاپا بولدۇق. بۇنى قانداق قىلىمىز؟
يىگىت بېشى: پاششاپ كىرسۇن!
پاششاپ: ئەسسالامۇ ئەلەيكۇم، ئوتتۇز ئوغۇل- توققۇز قىز!
يىگىت بېشى، قازىبەگ ۋە مىرشاپ: ۋەئەلەيكۇم ئەسسالام!
يىگىت بېشى: پاششاپ، دەرھال مۇرادىلنى بۇ يەرگە ئېلىپ كېلىڭلار!
پاششاپ: مانا، مۇرادىلنى ئېلىپ كەلدىم.
مىرشاپ: مۇرادىل، سول يەكتىز بولۇپ ئولتۇر!
يىگىت بېشى: مۇرادىل، ئۆتكەن ھەپتە نەشە چېكىپسەن. بۇ راستمۇ؟
مۇرادىل: راست.
يىگىت بېشى: نەشە چېكىش سالامەتلىككە زىيانلىق. بۇنى بىلەمسەن؟
مۇرادىل: بىلىمەن.
يىگىت بېشى: نەشىگە پۇل خەجلەش ئىسراپچىلىق بولىدۇ. بۇنى بىلەمسەن؟
مۇرادىل: بىلىمەن.
يىگىت بېشى: نەشە چېكىش - ئىسلام دىنىدا ھارام*. نەشە ئالغان پۇلغا بالىلىرىڭغا كىتاب ئېلىپ بەرسەڭ ياكى ئايالىڭغا كىيىم ئېلىپ بەرسەڭ تېخىمۇ ياخشى بولاتتى. بۇنى بىلەمسەن؟
مۇرادىل: مەن خاتا قىپتىمەن. مېنى كەچۈرۈڭلار!
يىگىت بېشى ۋە قازىبەگ: (پەس ئاۋازدا مەسلىھەتلەشكەندىن كېيىن) پاششاپ، مۇرادىل خاتالىقنى تونۇغانلىقى ئۈچۈن ئۇنىڭغا يېنىكرەك جازا بېرىمىز.
قازىبەگ: مۇرادىلغا تۆت پۇتلۇق بولۇپ مەيداننى ئۈچ قېتىم ئۆمىلەش جازاسى بېرىلسۇن!
پاششاپ: قېنى مۇرادىل، بۇ ياققا ماڭ!

* ھارام - This concept is explained in chapter 10

wasteful	ئىسراپچىلىق
light	يېنىكرەك
to crawl	ئۆمىلەش
voice	ئاۋاز

be quiet	خەپشۇك
marijuana	نەشە
on the knee	يەكتىز
harmful	زىيانلىق

Exercise 23.6:  Act out the above scenario in your classroom.

Pulling it all together

In this section, you will reinforce your knowledge and check the progress you have made during chapters 7 and 8 by completing a limited selection of focused exercises.

Exercise 24: Here you will watch two video segments reflecting a segment of the daily life of Uyghur students.

Exercise 24.1:  Watch the first segment and answer the following questions:

1. What is the name of the woman who came to introduce herself?

   (a) گۈلمىرە (b) گۈلچېھرە (c) گۈلبوستان (d) گۈلنۇر

2. What kind of help does she want from her interlocutor?

   (a) she is looking for a job (b) she wants to practice her English
   (c) she needs some money (d) she is going to borrow a book

3. When do they decide to meet?

   (a) Saturday morning (b) Saturday afternoon
   (c) Sunday afternoon (d) Sunday evening

4. How does the lady in glasses usually spend her weekends? Circle all the activities she does:

   (a) meets with her friends
   (b) spends time with her family
   (c) plays guitar
   (d) watches movies
   (e) does her homework
   (f) cooks

Exercise 24.2: Watch the segment one more time. This time pay attention to Gulchehra's question about the price of the English courses at the University. How does the lady in glasses respond?

____

____

____

Exercise 24.3:  In the second video, Gulchehra meets up with her new friend and they talk about their plan to spend time together. Watch the video and tell if the following statements are true or false.

توغرا	خاتا

1. ئۇلار كىنوغا بارماقچى.
2. ئۇلارنىڭ يەنە بىر دوستى كەلمەكچى.
3. ئۇلار بىللە تاماق ئېتىپ يېمەكچى.
4. ئۇلار تاماقنى سىرتتا يېمەكچى.

Exercise 24.4: Watch the video one more time. Note that here Gulchehra relates an Uyghur proverb regarding eating together. Try to catch the proverb. What do you think it means?

If you have a problem picking the proverb out by ear, refer to the transcript of the video located in Appendix B.

Exercise 25:  You have just met a new Uyghur student at your school. Listen to and read a transcript of his questions below. Then answer the questions providing specific details.

1. بۇ مەكتەپتە دەرسلەرنى ئۆزۈم تاللامدىم يا مەكتەپ ئورۇنلاشتۇرۇپ بېرەمدۇ؟
2. سىزنىڭچە قايسى ياتاقتا تۇرسام ياخشىراق بولىدۇ؟
3. ئوقۇغۇچىلىق كېنىشكىسىنى ئېلىش ئۈچۈن نېمە قىلىشىم كېرەك؟
4. كۇتۇبخانا كارتىسىنى بېجىرىشىم كېرەكمۇ؟ ئۇنىڭ ئۈچۈن نەگە بېرىشىم كېرەك؟
5. يېتەكچى ئوقۇتقۇچىم بىلەن كۆرۈشمەكچى بولسام، ئۇنىڭ بىلەن قانداق ئالاقىلىشىمەن؟
6. تەنتەربىيە زالىغا بارماقچى بولسام، ئۇنىڭغا ئايرىم پۇل تۆلەمدىم؟

Exercise 26:  Read the following story written by a student who spent some time at Xinjang University. Then translate it into Uyghur on a separate sheet of paper.

I first learned about Uyghur culture when I was studying Chinese for a year in Beijing. After graduating from university a couple years later, I decided to go to Xinjiang and study Uyghur for a year. Then in 2008, I moved back to Urumchi and lived there for about another year.

Urumchi is a lot like other big cities in China. However, the campus of Xinjiang University, where I studied, was a center of Uyghur culture and learning. All thc students in my classes there were foreigners. We lived together in the same dormitory, which was built specifically for foreign students, post-doctoral students, and younger teachers. The dormitory was nice, and it was relatively easy and inexpensive to get to and from the city center.

University life in Xinjiang is very different from university life in America. For example, in the dormitories there are usually six to eight people per room, curfew is at 11pm and the rules are very strict. Furthermore, students in Xinjiang choose their major before entering college. In America, students usually have the opportunity to choose most of their classes; however, in Xinjiang most students' classes are chosen for them.

For fun I enjoyed hanging out with some Uyghur friends, musicians, teachers, and artists, all of whom demonstrated a wonderful hospitality, kind nature, and great sense of humor. Sometimes we would play soccer, sing and dance, and go sightseeing. My favorite thing to do in my free time was to visit local restaurants and sample many different types of delicious Uyghur food!

Exercise 27:  You have been asked to prepare one of two sections of an online brochure for international students at Xinjiang University. On the next page, provide some basic information that helps students get oriented. Use the vocabulary presented earlier in this chapter.

Help:

1. Explain and describe campus life. Talk about enrollment, registration, living in a dorm, and using the library.
2. Explain and describe possible weekend activities such as going to the market, using the internet, and doing laundry.

ماﺋارىپ | تىل ئۆگىنىش | ئىنستىتۇتلار | ياتاق بۆلۈمى | خوجىلىق بۆلۈم | ئانا سەھىپە

新疆大学 شىنجاڭ ئۇنىۋېرستىتى

学院宗旨：
为社会主义建设培养优秀的接班人

مەكتەپنىڭ غايىسى:
سوتسىيالىزىم قۇرۇلۇشى ئۈچۈن مۇنەۋۋەر ئىزباسارلارنى يېتىلدۈرۈش

ئىزدەش

چەتئەللىك ئوقۇغۇچىلار | جۇڭگولۇق ئوقۇغۇچىلار | ئىشچى- خىزمەتچىلەر

مەكتەپ | كەسپلەر | خىراجەتلەر | ئىلتىماس

شىنجاڭ ئۇنىۋېرستېتىدا ________________________

____

____

____

____

____

____

____

____

____

____

____

____

____

____

____

____

ياردەم سوراش

ھەرخىل ياردەم ھەققىدىكى سوئاللارغا ئالاقىدار خادىملار 24 سائەت ئىچىدە جاۋاب بېرىدۇ. ياردەم سوراش ئۈچۈن ئوقۇغۇچىلىق نومۇرىڭىزنى مەلۇم قىلىڭ.

بۈگۈنكى خەۋەرلەر:

يېڭى ئوقۇغۇچىلارنى كۈتۈۋېلىش...

ئوقۇتقۇچىلار بايرىمى ...

"ئىككى يىغىن" روھىنى ...

باش بەت | بىز كىم | ئالاقىلىشىڭ | دوستانە ئۇلىنىشلار | قانۇنىي رەسمىيەتلەر

Exercise 28: چەتئەللىك ئوقۇغۇچىلارنىڭ نەزىرىدە

Exercise 28.1:  Read the passage where Kamal (Colin), a Uyghur learner, describes his experiences at Xinjiang University. Discuss the questions that follow.

2009- يىلى بېيجىڭدا بىر يىل خىتاي تىلىنى ئوقۇغاندا ئۇيغۇر مەدەنىيىتى بىلەن شىنجاڭ مەنزىرىسىگە قىزىقىپ قالدىم. ئاندىن 2010- يىلى ئالىي مەكتەپنى پۈتتۈرۈپلا، ئۈرۈمچىگە باردىم. ئۇ يەردە شىنجاڭ ئۇنىۋېرسىتېتىدا بىر يىل ئۇيغۇر تىلىنى ئوقۇدۇم. شۇنىڭدىن كېيىن، 2012- يىلى يەنە بىر يىلدەك ئۈرۈمچىدە تۇردۇم.

مېنىڭچە، ئۈرۈمچىنىڭ چوڭ قىسمى ئىچكىرى خىتاينىڭ ھەر قايسى شەھەرلىرىدىن ئانچە چوڭ پەرق قىلمايدۇ. لېكىن، شىنجاڭ ئۇنىۋېرسىتېتى جايلاشقان مەھەللە باشقىچە. ئۇ يەردە ئۇيغۇرلار جىق، شۇڭا تىل ئۆگىنىش شارائىتىمۇ ناھايىتى ياخشى. ئۇنىڭ ئۈستىگە ئېسىل ئاشخانىلار، دۆڭكۆۋرۈك بازىرى (دا بازار) قاتارلىق ئوتتۇرا ئاسىيا مەدەنىيىتىنىڭ پۇرىقى چىقىپ تۇرىدىغان جايلارمۇ ئاز ئەمەس.

شىنجاڭ ئۇنىۋېرسىتېتىدا ھەپتىدە يىگىرمە سائەت دەرس ئاڭلايتتۇق. ئون سائەت ئاساسىي دەرس بولۇپ، قالغان ئون سائەت ئاڭلاش، سۆزلەش، ئوقۇش قاتارلىقلار. بۇ دەرسلەردىن سىرت، ئۈچ - تۆتىمىز بىر مۇئەللىم بىلەن ھەپتىدە بىر قېتىملىق «شىنجاڭ يەرلىك تارىخى» دېگەن دەرسنىمۇ ئالدۇق. ئۇيغۇر تىلى سەۋىيىمىز تېخى بەك تۆۋەن بولغاچقا، مۇئەللىم بۇ دەرسنى خىتاي تىلىدا ئۆتەتتى.

ئۈرۈمچىدە ئوقۇغاندا مەكتەپتىكى ياتاق بىناسىدا تۇراتتىم. ئۇ ئادەتتىكى ئوقۇغۇچىلار تۇرغان ياتاق بىناسى ئەمەس، چەت ئەللىك ئوقۇغۇچىلار، ئاسپىرانتلار ۋە توي قىلمىغان ياش ئوقۇتقۇچىلار ئۈچۈن ئايرىم سېلىنغان بىر بىنا ئىدى. شارائىتى بەك ئاددىي بولسىمۇ، يامان ئەمەس ئىدى. بۇ بىنا مەكتەپنىڭ مەركىزىدە بولغاچقا، خېلى قولايلىق ئىدى، ھەم ئىجارە ھەققىمۇ ئانچە قىممەت ئەمەس ئىدى.

خىتايدىكى ئالىي مەكتەپلەرنى ئامېرىكىدىكى مەكتەپلەر بىلەن سېلىشتۇرساق، ھەر قايسى جەھەتلەردىن پەرقلەر خېلى چوڭ. مەسىلەن، ئامېرىكىدا بىر ياتاقتا پەقەت بىر- ئىككى بەلكى ئۈچ ئوقۇغۇچى تۇرىدۇ، لېكىن شىنجاڭدا ھەر ياتاقتا يا ئالتە يا سەككىز ئادەم تۇرىدۇ. ئوقۇغۇچىلار ھەر كۈنى كەچ سائەت ئون بىردىن بۇرۇن ياتاققا قايتمىسا بولمايدۇ. ئوقۇشقا كىرىشتىن بۇرۇن كەسپنى تاللاش كېرەك، ئاندىن كەسپنىڭ ھەممە دەرسىنى مەكتەپ ئۆزى ئورۇنلاشتۇرۇپ بېرىدۇ. كەسپىي دەرسلەردىن سىرت، ئوقۇغۇچىلار ھەر ھەپتە بىر سىياسىي دەرسنى ئاڭلىشى كېرەك (مەسىلەن ماركسىزم، ماۋ زېدوڭ ئىدىيىسى قاتارلىقلار). ناماز ئوقۇش، قۇرئان ئوقۇش، روزا تۇتۇش دېگەندەك ھەرخىل ئىسلام دىنىغا ئائىت ھەرىكەتلەر قەتئىي مەنئى قىلىنىدۇ. ئامېرىكىدا ئوقۇغۇچىلارنىڭ ھەر خىل ئەركىنلىكى بار، لېكىن خىتايدا ئوقۇغۇچىلارنىڭ ئەركىنلىكى چەكلەنگەن. كۆڭلۈمنى يېرىم قىلىدىغان ئىشلار كۆپ بولسىمۇ، ئۈرۈمچىدە تۇرغان ۋاقتىم ناھايىتى كۆڭۈللۈك ئۆتتى، بولۇپمۇ ئۇيغۇر ئاغىنىلىرىم بىلەن ئۆتكەن كۈنلىرىم. بىكار بولساق توپ ئوينايتتۇق، ناخشا ئاڭلاپ ئۇسسۇل ئوينايتتۇق، بەزىدە ساياھەتمۇ قىلاتتۇق. ھازىر شىنجاڭغا بارمىغىلى بەش يىل بولۇپ قالدى، مۇشۇ دوستلار بىلەن تور ئارقىلىق خەت يېزىشىپ، تېلېفون قىلىپ ئالاقە قىلىپ تۇرىمىز. خۇدايىم بۇيرىسا، بىر پۇرسەت تېپىپ ئۈرۈمچىگە بېرىپ كونا قەدىناس دوستلىرىمنى يوقلىغۇم بار.

1. How did Colin become interested in studying Uyghur?
2. What happened in the following years?

3. Why did he choose to study at Xinjiang University?
4. What was his daily schedule like at school?
5. What were the conditions like at the dorm?
6. At one point, Colin says the following:

ئامېرىكىدا ئوقۇغۇچىلارنىڭ ھەر خىل ئەركىنلىكى بار،
لېكىن خىتايدا بولسا ئوقۇغۇچىلارنىڭ ئەركىنلىكى چەكلەنگەن.
What does he mean? What examples does he give?

7. What was his best experience in Urumchi?
8. What are the differences he mentions between life in Xinjiang and life in America? Take notes below, then provide an oral summary.

Xinjiang	*America*

9. What methods do Colin use to study the Uyghur language?

Exercise 28.2:  Now read a passage in which Nazaket (Elise) describes her experiences at Xinjiang and American universities. Then, answer the questions that follow.

مەن ئۈرۈمچىگە بۇلتۇر كەلدىم. بۇ يەرگە كېلىشىمدىكى مەقسەت - تەتقىقات قىلىش. مەن ئۇيغۇرلارنىڭ سەنئىتىگە قىزىقىمەن. ھازىر مەن غەيرىي ماددىي مەدەنىيەت مىراسلىرىنى* قوغدايدىغان پائالىيەتلەر توغرۇلۇق تەتقىقات قىلىۋاتىمەن. ئىشلىرىم بەك كۆپ. ئىلمىي ماتېرىياللارنى ئوقۇپ توپلىشىم كېرەك. مۇزىكانتلارنى زىيارەت قىلمىسام يەنە بولمايدۇ. بۇنىڭدىن باشقا كۈندىلىك خاتىرەمنى يېزىشىم كېرەك. سەنئەت بىلەن مۇناسىۋەتلىك پائالىيەتلەرگە قاتناشمىسام تېخى بولمايدۇ. دۇتار چېلىشنى، ئۇسسۇل ئويناشنى ئۆگەنمەكچىمەن. خەنزۇچە دەرسكە قاتناشمىسام تېخى... ھەممە نەرسىگە ئۈلگۈرۈشۈم كېرەك.

شىنجاڭدا تەتقىقات قىلىش جەريانىدا مەن ئامېرىكا بىلەن جۇڭگونىڭ مائارىپ سىستېمىلىرىدىكى جىق پەرقلىرىنى ھېس قىلدىم. ئۇلارنى قىسقىچە ئېيتىپ ئۆتەي.

ھەپتىدە ئۈچ خىل دەرس ئاڭلايمەن: جۇڭگونىڭ ھازىرقى زامان سىياسىتى، ئومۇمىي تىلشۇناسلىق ۋە مەدەنىيەت ئالماشتۇرۇش. مەن دەرسكە قاتنىشىپلا، ئامېرىكا بىلەن جۇڭگونىڭ مائارىپ سىستېمىلىرىدىكى پەرقلەرنى بايقىدىم. بىرىنچىدىن، ئامېرىكىدا ئوقۇغۇچىلارنىڭ دەرستە ئاكتىپ پىكىر قىلىشى تەكىتلەنسە، جوڭگودا پەقەت ئاڭلاش تەكىتلىنىدىكەن. جۇڭگودا ئوقۇغۇچىلارنىڭ دەرس ۋاقتىدا سۆزلەيدىغان پۇرستى ئاز ئىكەن. ئىككىنچىدىن، ئامېرىكىدا بىز ئوقۇغۇچى بىلەن ئوقۇتقۇچى تەڭ دەپ قارايمىز، لېكىن جوڭگودا ئوقۇتقۇچىلار مۇنبەرگە چىقىپ ئوقۇغۇچىلاردىن ئېگىزرەك يەردە تۇرۇپ دەرس بېرىدىكەن. ئۈچىنچىدىن، دەرستە ئوقۇتقۇچى بىر خاتالىق ئۆتكۈزۈپ قويسا، ھېچ كىمنىڭ ئۇنى تۈزۈتۈپ قويۇشى مۇمكىن ئەمەس ئىكەن. بىر كۈنى خەنزۇچە ئوقۇتقۇچىمنىڭ بىر خاتاسىنى تۈزۈتۈپ قويغان ئىدىم، ئۇنىڭ چىرايى ئۆزگۈرۈپ كەتتى، ئۇ ھەم خاپا ھەم خىجىل بولۇپ قالدى.

ئويلىسام، تەتقىقات جەھەتتىمۇ چوڭ پەرقلەر بار ئىكەن. مەسىلەن، "تەتقىقات" سۆزىنىڭ مەنىسى ئىنگلىز تىلىدىكى مەنىگە ئانچە ئوخشىمايدىكەن. دېمەكچى بولغىنىم شۇكى، بۇ يەردىكى ماڭا ئوخشاش فولكلور بىلەن مۇزىكشۇناسلىق كەسپىدىكى تەتقىقاتچىلارنىڭ ئويلىشىچە، تەتقىقات پەقەت يازما ماتېرىياللارنى ئوقۇش ۋە دالا تەكشۈرۈشلەرنىلا ئۆز ئىچىگە ئالىدىكەن. بىراق، بىز ئامېرىكىدىكى تەتقىقاتچىلار كۆپ خىل ئوخشىمايدىغان ئۇسۇلدىن پايدىلىنىپ تەتقىقات قىلىمىز. مەسىلەن ئۈرۈمچىدە بەزىلەر مېنىڭ دۇتار چېلىش بىلەن ئۇسسۇل ئويناشنى ئۆگىنىشتىكى مەقسىتىمنى چۈشەنمەي، مەن قاتنىشىدىغان پائالىيەتلەرنى تەتقىقاتقا ھېچ قانداق مۇناسىۋىتى يوق دەپ قارايدۇ. لېكىن، مەن دۇتار چېلىش بىلەن ئۇسسۇل ئويناشنى ئۆگەنسەم، ئۇيغۇرلارنىڭ مەدەنىيىتىنى تېخىمۇ ياخشى چۈشىنەلەيمەن دەپ ئۆگىنىۋاتىمەن. ئۇنىڭ ئۈستىگە، مەن بىلەن ئۇيغۇر سەنئەتچىلەرنىڭ ئورتاق تىلىمىز بولسا، تەتقىقات قىلىشقا تېخىمۇ ئاسان بولىدۇ دەپ ئويلايمەن. مۇشۇنداق تەتقىقات قىلىش ئۇسۇلى ئىنسانشۇناسلىق ئىچىدىكى قاتنىشىش-تەكشۈرۈش ئۇسۇلى دېگەن گەپ. يەنە كېلىپ، تەتقىقات جەھەتتە باشقا چوڭ بىر پەرقىمىز بار ئىكەن. ئامېرىكىدا كىم بىر خەلقنى تەتقىق قىلاي دېسە، شۇ خەلقنىڭ ئانا تىلىنى ئۆگىنىشى كېرەك. لېكىن، جۇڭگودا مەيلى قايسى خەلقنىڭ (بولۇپمۇ ئاز سانلىق مىللەتلەرنىڭ) مەدەنىيىتىنى تەتقىق قىلسۇن، تەتقىقاتچىلارنىڭ كۆپىنچىسى ئۇ خەلقنىڭ تىلىنى ئۆگەنمەيدىكەن. بۇ راستىنلا ئەپسۇسلىنارلىق بىر ئەھۋال.

---

* غەيرىي ماددىي مەدەنىيەت مىراسلىرى - relics of intangible cultural heritage

stage	مۇنبەر	to defend, protect	قوغدىماق
a chance, opportunity	پۇرسەت	to emphasize	تەكىتلىمەك
field research	دالا تەكشۈرۈش	a method, way	ئۇسۇل
to be ashamed	خىجىل بولماق	related	مۇناسىۋەتلىك

1. What is Nazaket doing in Xijiang?

---

2. In what ways does she participate in cultural activities?

---

3. What does her daily schedule look like?

---

4. What differences does she mention between the Chinese and American educational systems?

---

5. She describes a strange classroom experience she had with a teacher. Explain what happened.

---

6. She uses the phrase قاتناشمسام تېخى to describe her participation in various cultural activities. Why do you think she uses this phrase? What does it imply?

---

7. What does she mean by the word تەتقىقات?

---

8. She noticed that the word research has different implications in the two cultures. Which are the definitions she mentions?

---

9. Do you agree with her definition? Why or why not?

---

10. What is the most important aspect of research in your opinion?

---

11. Nazaket has to visit and interview musicians as part of her research project. On a separate sheet of paper write 10 questions that you would ask in an interview with an Uyghur musician.

Exercise 28.3: Talk about your previous language learning experiences, such as where and how you studied other languages. What was the most beneficial method for you?

Exercise 29:  Would you like to study at Xinjiang University? Write a short composition using the information you learned in this chapter to explain in what activities you would like to participate and why if you were given the opportunity to study in Xinjiang.

Project

Prepare a presentation about your university. Be sure to include the following:

1. A short history of the university. In preparation for this task, complete a timeline and note the major events in your university's history.

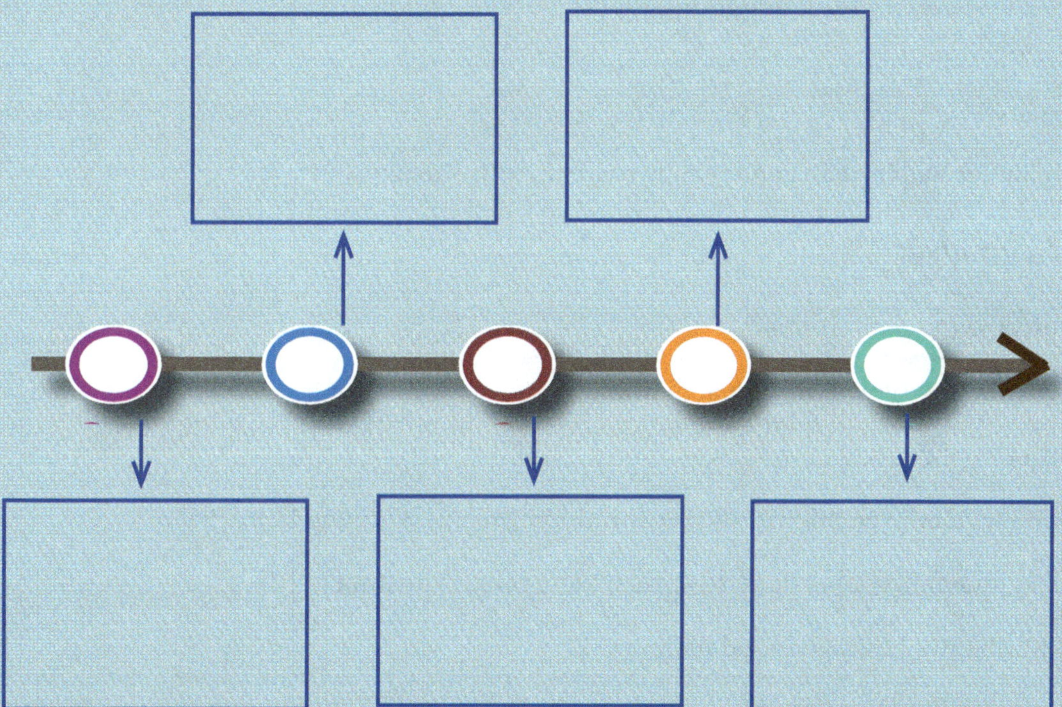

2. A description of the faculty and students at your university. Find specific numbers and statistics.
3. A description of the campus.
4. A description of a local place off-campus where students like to spend their time.

Self-check خامان

Use the following list to check your knowledge of the topics you have covered in chapters 7 and 8. Mark whether you know and can do the following in Uyghur. If you think you may need more work to fully understand something, you can go back to the relevant section in the chapters and review it.

1. I can talk and write about:

Life for a typical student in Urumchi	☐
The similarities and differences between the educational systems in Xinjiang Uyghur Autonomous Region and my country	☐
The history of Xinjiang University	☐
ئولتۇرۇش	☐
مەشرەپ	☐
Gojahmet Sadvakasov, an Uyghur scholar from Kazakhstan	☐

2. I can also:

Describe my daily routine	☐
Describe my typical leisure activities	☐
Describe the city where I live	☐
Conduct a conversation at the registration office in Xinjiang University	☐
Read and understand short advertisements related to student life	☐
Describe my best childhood memory	☐
Describe my educational institution	☐

3. I know how to:

Say that I like to do (or not do) certain things	☐
Give toasts at special occasions in Uyghur	☐

4. I can explain the following words and concepts:

☐	ھاراق چىشلىۋاپتۇ	☐	ئىچكىرى
☐	بۇ دېگەن كۆڭۈل	☐	ۋىۋېسكا
☐	بۇلغانغان ھاۋا	☐	سۇغۇرتا
☐	قەسەم قىلماق	☐	سىياسىي ئۆگىنىش
☐	جازا	☐	ساھە
☐	ئوقۇش مۇكاپات پۇلى	☐	مەۋسۇم
☐	تەتقىقات	☐	جەمئىيەتكە چىقىش
☐	مائارىپ سىستېمىسى	☐	ئولتۇرۇش and مەشرەپ
☐	تەبىئىي پەن	☐	خوشە!
☐	ئىجتىمائىي پەن	☐	ساقىي

5. I can use grammar to …

Emphasize verbs with auxiliaries ئەتمەك and كەتمەك	☐
Make verbs from nouns using (-لا\-لە) -لى	☐
Form mutual constructions using -ش \ -ىش	☐
Make adjectives using -ىي\-ۋى	☐
Express completion of action with the verb بولماق	☐
Form the causative with -غۇزا\-گۈز \-قۇزا\-كۈز؛ -دۇرا\-تۇرا\-دۇرا\-تۇر and -ت	☐
Form compound verbs like ئاپارماق and ئەكەلمەك	☐
Talk about the past using the remote past	☐
Talk about repeated actions using the habitual past	☐

Vocabulary سۆزلۈك

Vocabulary is given according to the Uyghur alphabetical order. The right column precedes the left column on each page.

superfluity	ئارتۇقچىلىق
wish, desire	ئارزۇ
public gathering	ئاممىۋى يىغىلىش
regrettable, unfortunate	ئەپسۇسلىنارلىق
badly behaved, immoral	ئەخلاقسىز
manners; etiquette	ئەدەب - ئەخلاق
impolite, rude	ئەدەبسىز
on the contrary	ئەكسىچە
reality, practice	ئەمەلىيەت
leader, manager	باشقۇرغۇچى
flourishing	بۈك- باراقسان
polluted	بۇلغانغان
splendid, wonderful	پەيزى
pedestrians	پىيادىلەر
to instruct, to urge	تاپىلىماق
to watch (an event, show)	تاماشا قىلماق
to invite someone to dance	تانسىغا تارتماق
experience	تەجرىبە
discipline	تەرتىپ - ئىنتىزام
luck	تەلەي
agreement, contract	توختام
to feel	تۇيماق
ten thousand	تۇمەن
punishment, penalty	جازا
stubborn; pigheaded	جاھىل
to gather	جەم بولماق
heaven	جەننەت
to plant saplings	جىرىم/كۆچەت تىكمەك
time, period	چاغ
to clap, to applaud	چاۋاك چالماق
to be limited, to be bounded by	چەكلەنمەك
to limit, to restrict	چەكلىمەك
fable, fairy tale	چۆچەك
to turn into a wilderness	چۆلدەرەپ قالماق
grassy area	چىملىق
to be ashamed, embarrassed	خىجىل بولماق
field research	دالا تەكشۈرۈشى
hell	دوزاق
officially	رەسمىي شەكىلدە
to fast	روزا تۇتماق
spirit, soul	روھ
necessity	زۆرۈرىيەت
harmful	زىيانلىق
play on musical instruments	ساز چالماق
occasion, gathering	سورۇن
swimming	سۇ ئۈزمەك
condition	شارائىت
peculiar	غەيرىي
to welcome	قارشى ئالماق
disturbance, chaos	قالايمىقانچىلىق
firm, absolute	قەتئىي
step	قەدەم
to take a step	قەدەم ئالماق
to swear	قەسەم قىلماق\ئىچمەك

haram (not permitted in Islam)	هارام
zoo	هايۋاناتلار باغچىسى
to carry for free	ھەقسىز توشۇماق
truth	ھەقىقەت
to perform	ئورۇنلىماق
to get better, to recover	ئوڭشالماق
concept	ئۇقۇم
of his own accord, voluntarily	ئۆزلىكىدىن
self-opinionated	ئۆزۈمچىل
a stream, small water channel	ئۆستەڭ
to increase	ئۆسۈپ كەتمەك
measure	ئۆلچەم
farmland	ئېتىزلىق
wastefulness	ئىسراپچىلىق
violin	ئىسكرىپكا
anthropology	ئىنسانشۇناسلىق
on one knee	يەكتىز
an agricultural	يېزا- ئىگىلىك

to defend, protect	قوغدىماق
overcrowding	قىستاڭچىلىق
village	كەنت
a group, club	كۇرژۇك
physical, material	ماددىي
to match	ماسلاشماق
to get drunk	مەست بولماق
responsible, in charge	مەسئۇل
goal	مەقسەت
view, scenery	مەنزىرە
result, outcome	مەھسۇل
to be cold, to get cold, to freeze	مۇزلاپ كەتمەك
fixed, stable	مۇقىم
stage, podium	مۇنبەر
heritage, legacy	مىراس
marijuana, hashish	نەشە
exact	نەق
on the scene	نەق مەيدان
occasional	نۆۋەتلىك

تانسا

ئۇسسۇل

族学与社会学学院一届一次教职工代表大会暨工会会员大会
五十六个民族大团结

新疆大学
XINJIANG UNIVERSITY

新疆教育学院
新东方

توققۇزىنچى دەرس

CHAPTER NINE

ساغلام تەندە - ساپ ئەقىل

HEALTH, SPORTS, AND MEDICINE

IN THIS CHAPTER

Functions

- Requesting & granting permission
- Talking to the doctor (complaints)
- Talking about your health
- Expressing obligation
- Describing problems at the hospital
- Talking about sports & leisure activities
- Describing practices in Uyghur folk medicine

Grammar

- Uyghur equivalents for 'can'/ 'may'
- The auxiliary verb ئولتۇرماق
- Causative constructions

In this chapter, John gets sick and is forced to pay a visit to the school hospital. Through the conversations, reading passages, video clips, and excerpts from John's diary contained in this chapter, you will learn about some common health issues in Xinjiang. You will also get some information about some types of Uyghur folk medicine, such as sand therapy. In addition to issues of medicine, you will enrich your knowledge of some popular sports activities in Xinjiang. Finally, you will become acquainted with some important health , exercise, and wellness related concepts such as كالتەك توپ, تىبابەتچىلىك, تېۋىپ, سۇغۇرتا, and پەرھىز.

Exercise 1:  John is sick. Read his blog and answer the questions that follow. The words and expressions provided before the questions will help you to understand the passage better.

Uyghur John's Blog

ئامېرىكىلىق ياڭقۇننىڭ تورتۇراسى

Search

كۈندە بىر ماقال: تەننىڭ ساقلىقى - جاننىڭ راھىتى.

28 - يانۋار: بۈگۈن پەقەتلا مىجەزىم يوق. كېچىچە ئۇخلىيالمىدىم. بۇرنۇمدىن سۇ ئېقىپ نەپەس ئالالماي بەك قىينالدىم. ئۈنىڭ ئۈستىگە يۆتەل بېسىپ بەكمۇ ئاۋارە قىلدى. ئەتىگەن ئورنىمدىن ئاران تۇردۇم. بېشىم زىڭىلداپ ئاغرىۋاتىدۇ. ئامېرىكىدىن ئەكەلگەن دورىلارنى ئىچىپ باقتىم، ئەمما پايدىسى بولمىدى. نېمە قىلىشىمنى بىلمەي، بىر ساۋاقدىشىمغا تېلېفون بەردىم. ئۇ "دوختۇرغا بارمىساڭ بولمايدۇ* " دېدى. "دوختۇرغا بېرىشتىن بۇرۇن دوختۇرخانىغا تېلېفون بېرىپ نومۇر ئېلىش لازىممۇ؟" دەپ سورىسام، "بۇ يەردە ئۇنداق ئىش يوق، تېلېفون قىلماستىن بېرىۋەرسەڭ بولىدۇ" دەيدۇ. ئۇ ماڭا مەكتەپ دوختۇرخانىسىغا بېرىشىمنى تەۋسىيە قىلدى. ئۇ يەر ئوقۇغۇچىلارغا ھەقسىز ئىكەن. بۇنى ئاڭلاپ خوش بولۇپ كەتتىم. چۈنكى ئامېرىكىدا دوختۇرغا بېرىش ئۈچۈن بىر نەچچە كۈن بۇرۇن تېلېفون قىلىشىڭىز كېرەك. ئۇلار دوختۇرنىڭ جەدۋىلىگە قاراپ، ئاندىن سىزگە بىر ۋاقىتنى بەلگىلەپ بېرىدۇ. كېسىلىڭىز بەك جىددىي بولسا، جىددىي قۇتقۇزۇش بۆلۈمىگە بېرىشىڭىز لازىم. ئۇ يەر بەك قىممەت. ئاڭلىسام ئۈرۈمچىدىمۇ دوختۇرخانىلارنىڭ ئايرىم كىشىلىك كېسەلخانىلىرى بار ئىكەن، ئەمما ئۇ يەرگە پەقەت ھۆكۈمەت ئەمەلدارلىرى ۋە بايلارلا بارىدىكەن ... تەلىيىمگە يارىشا، مەكتەپ دوختۇرخانىسى ياتىقىمىزدىن ئانچە يىراق ئەمەس. يۈزۈمنى يۇيۇپلا ناشتىمۇ قىلماي دوختۇرغا باردىم. گېلىم قاتتىق ئاغرىغاچقا، ھېچ نەرسە يېيەلمىدىم. دوختۇرخانا ھەقسىز بولغاچقا، ئادەم يامان كۆپ ئىكەن. بىر سائەت ئۆچىرەت ساقلىدىم، ئۆچىرەت دوختۇرنىڭ ئۈستىلىدىن كارىدورغىچە سوزۇلغاچقا، كېسەللەرنىڭ ئۆز ئەھۋالىنى دوختۇرغا ئايرىم چۈشەندۈرۈشى مۇمكىن ئەمەسكەن. "ياتاقتا يېتىپ داۋالىنىڭ" دېسە، قانداق قىلارمەن** دەپ قورقتۇم. دوختۇر ئايال مېنى چاقىرىپ "كىرسىڭىز بولىدۇ" دېگەندە، مەن قورقۇپ كەتتىم. ئۇ يامان تېز سۆزلەيدىكەن، ئۇنىڭ گېپىنى ئاران ئۇقتۇم. ئۇنىڭ دېيىشىچە، زۇكام بولۇپ قاپتىمەن. ھازىر زۇكام بولغانلار بەك كۆپ ئىكەن. بۇ كېسەل يۇقۇملۇق بولغاچقا، ئۆيدىن چىقماي داۋالىنىڭ دەيدۇ. ئۇ ماڭا بىر مۇنچە دورا يېزىپ بەردى. دورىلارنى ئېلىپ ياتاققا قايتتىم... راستىنى ئېيتسام، ھېچ ماغدۇرۇم يوق... قېنى، دورىلىرىمنى ئىچەي، بەلكىم ياخشىراق بولۇپ قالارمەن.*

This construction is explained later on page 306*

This grammar is introduced in Chapter 12 :قىل+ار+مەن**

to recommend	تەۋسىيە قىلماق
insurance	سۇغۇرتا
fortunately	تەلەيگە يارىشا
strength	ماغدۇر

feeling; temperament	مىجەز
to breathe	نەپەس ئالماق
barely, with difficulty	ئاران
to appoint, to arrange	بەلگىلىمەك

1. What differences did John notice between the clinic he visited in this passage and the medical facilities back home? Underline all the sentences in the passage that describe health practices in Xinjiang.
2. What were John's symptoms?
3. Why was he worried about visiting the doctor?
4. Which clinic did his friend suggest he visit? Why?
5. Why did he think it was fortunate that he chose this clinic?
6. What advice did the doctor give him? Why?
7. Based on the passage, what did John probably do after completing his blog entry?

The Region Without Health Care

Growing levels of air and water pollution, increasing desertification, decades of nuclear testing, and continued ecological damage have made Xinjiang one of the unhealthiest regions in China. Furthermore, health care resources are particularly difficult to access in rural areas, where many Uyghurs suffer from respiratory issues, cardiovascular diseases, and cancers which were previously rare or unheard of. While state employees in Xinjiang benefit from medical insurance covering about 70-80% of the cost of most medicines and procedures, the majority of rural Uyghurs live without any healthcare coverage.

1 Expressing may/can in Uyghur: بولماق + -سا/-سە + *verb*

In the passage (Exercise 1), you saw the following sentence:

You can/may go without calling beforehand. تېلېفون قىلماستىن بېرىۋەرسەڭ بولىدۇ.

In this sentence, the writer means that it is permissible to go to the clinic without calling first. To express the idea of may/can, we use the auxiliary verb بولماق in combination with the conditional form of the main verb. You will recall that بولىدۇ is often used with the meaning 'that's okay' in Uyghur; thus in this construction, what is really being said is 'It's okay if you' do something.

As illustrated by the translation accompanying the example above, the same idea can be expressed in English using the auxiliary verb 'may', as in "May I go to the bathroom." Note that in English we often replace this 'may' with 'can,' which can also be used to denote ability, whereas in Uyghur this construction is used for permission or suggestion. Look at the example from the preceding passage:

دوختۇر ئايال مېنى چاقىرىپ "كىرسىڭىز بولىدۇ" دېگەندە، مەن سەل جىددىيلەشتىم.
When the doctor called me and said "You may enter," I got a bit nervous.

Here are some additional examples:

For now you can/may use this dictionary. ھازىرچە بۇ لۇغەتنى ئىشلىتىپ تۇرسىڭىز بولىدۇ.
Can I take this chair? بۇ ئورۇندۇقنى ئالسام بولامدۇ؟

When the negative form is used with both verbs, it expresses a strong obligation and literally means 'it's not okay if I/you don't' do something. It is translated as 'must' or 'have to.' Look at the following sentences:

He said: You must go to the doctor! ئۇ "دوختۇرغا بارمىساڭ بولمايدۇ!" دېدى.
You must wake up earlier. بالدۇرراق تۇرمىساڭ بولمايدۇ.
You must eat your food faster. تاماقىڭنى ئىتتىكرەك يېمىسەڭ بولمايدۇ.
You must wash your hands. قولۇڭنى يۇمىساڭ بولمايدۇ.
You have to take your medicine on time. دورىنى ۋاقتىدا ئىچمىسەڭ بولمايدۇ.

Note: Remember that the same construction is used to ask and give advice politely. See Chapter 3 (page 93).

Exercise 3:  Read the following sentences and translate them by correctly identifying the meaning of each construction with -سا/-سە + بولماق.

1. دوختۇرغا ۋاقتىدا بارمىساڭ بولمايدۇ.
2. ھاۋا خېلى سوغۇق ئوخشايدۇ، پەلتو كىيمىسەم بولمايدۇ.
3. بازاردىن نان ئېلىۋالسىڭىز بولىدۇ.
4. بۇ ئالما تېخى پىشماپتۇ، ئۇنى يېسەڭ بولمايدۇ.
5. تاماق بەك ئوخشاپتۇ، ئۇنى يېمىسەك بولمايدۇ.
6. بۈگۈن بالدۇرراق ئۇخلىساڭ بولاتتى بالام، ئەتە سەھەردە يولغا چىقىسەن ئەمەسمۇ.
7. بۇ مەسىلىنى داداڭ بىلەن مۇزاكىرە قىلساڭ بولىدۇ.
8. ئاداش، بۇنداق قىلساق بولمايدۇ دەيمەن.
9. مالنىڭ پۇلىنى ھازىر تۆلىسەڭلار بولىدۇ.
10. يولغا چىقىشتىن بۇرۇن تاماق يەۋالمىساق بولمايدۇ.
11. ئاۋۇ ئادەم مۇشۇ مەھەللىنىڭ رەھبىرى، كۆرۈشۈپ قويمىساڭلار بولمايدۇ.
12. دورىنى يېنىمىزدىكى دورىخانىدىن ئالسىڭىز بولىدۇ.
13. مانا دوختۇر كېلىۋاتىدۇ، ئۇنىڭ بىلەن ئۆزىڭىز سۆزلەشسىڭىز بولىدۇ.

Exercise 4: تۆۋەندىكى سوئاللارغا جاۋاب بېرىڭلار

1. ساغلام بولۇش ئۈچۈن نېمە قىلىش كېرەك؟
2. سىز پەرھىز تۇتامسىز؟ قانداق تاماقلارنى يېمەسلىككە تىرىشىسىز؟ نېمىشقا؟
3. قايسى تەنتەربىيە تۈرىنى ياخشى كۆرىسىز؟ نېمىشقا؟
4. چەتئەلدە دوختۇرغا كۆرۈنۈپ باققانمۇ؟
5. دورا ئىچىش ياكى ئوكۇل سېلىشتىن قورقامسىز؟ نېمە ئۈچۈن؟
6. ئامېرىكىدا دوختۇرغا كۆرۈنۈش تەرتىپى قانداق؟

Exercise 5: دوختۇرخانىدا

Exercise 5.1:  At the clinic, John overhears a conversation between the doctor and another patient. Look up the definitions for the following words, then listen to the conversation and try to pick them out. Mark off each vocabulary item as you hear it in the box adjacent to that item in the chart below.

___	پايدا قىلماق	___	كۆڭۈل ئېلىشماق
___	رېتسېپ	___	قان بېسىمى
___	پەرھىز تۇتماق	___	ئۆلچىمەك
___	ماغدۇر	___	چىدىماق

Exercise 5.2: Listen to the dialogue again and circle the best answer to each question.

1. نېمە ئۈچۈن بىمار دوختۇرغا كېلىدۇ؟
(ئا) ئۇنىڭ ماغدۇرى يوق (ب) پۇتىنى سۇندۇرىۋالدى
(س) ئۇنىڭ قورسىقى ئاغرىدى (د) ئۇنىڭ مىجەزى يوق

2. بىمارنىڭ بېشى نەچچە كۈن ئاغرىدى؟
(ئا) بىر ھەپتە (ب) بەش- ئالتە كۈن
(س) ئۈچ - تۆت كۈن (د) بىر- ئىككى كۈن

3. دوختۇر بىمارغا قانداق دورا يېزىپ بەردى؟
(ئا) باش ئاغرىقىنى توختىتىدىغان (ب) قىزىتمىنى چۈشۈرىدىغان
(س) قان بېسىمىنى چۈشۈرىدىغان (د) كۈچ - قۇۋۋەت بېرىدىغان

4. بىمار قانداق تاماقلارنى يېمەسلىكى كېرەك؟
(ئا) تاتلىق (ب) مايلىق (س) ئاچچىق (د) تۇزلۇق

Exercise 5.3:  Now practice the dialogue with your partner. When finished, switch roles and practice the dialogue again.

كېسەل: ياخشىمۇسىز!
دوختۇر: ياخشىمۇسىز! سىزگە نېمە بولدى؟
كېسەل: نەچچە كۈندىن بېرى مىجەزىم يوق قاراڭ. بېشىم ئاغرىپ، كۆڭلۈم ئېلىشىپ، ھېچ ماغدۇرۇم يوق.
دوختۇر: گېپىڭىزگە قارىغاندا قان بېسىمىڭىز ئۆرلىگەن ئوخشايدۇ. قېنى، قان بېسىمىڭىزنى ئۆلچەپ باقايلى... قان بېسىمىڭىز خېلى يۇقىرى ئىكەن. بېشىڭىز ئاغرىغىنىغا نەچچە كۈن بولدى؟
كېسەل: بەش- ئالتە كۈن بولۇپ قالدىغۇ دەيمەن.
دوختۇر: دەرھال دوختۇرغا كۆرۈنمەي باش ئاغرىقىغا چىداپ ئولتۇردىڭىزمۇ؟
كېسەل: باش ئاغرىقىنى توختىتىدىغان دورىلارنى ئىچتىم.
دوختۇر: پايدا قىلدىمۇ؟
كېسەل: ئازراق ياردەم بەرگەندەك بولدى، لېكىن ئاغرىقى توختىمىدى، شۇڭا دوختۇرغا بېرىشنى قارار قىلدىم.
دوختۇر: ياخشى قىپسىز. سىزگە ھازىر باش ئاغرىقىنى توختىتىدىغان دورا ئەمەس، قان بېسىمىنى چۈشۈرىدىغان دورىلار كېرەك. مەن سىزگە رېتسېپ يېزىپ بېرەي. دورىلارنى بىرىنچى قەۋەتتىكى دورىخانىدىن ئالسىڭىز بولىدۇ.
كېسەل: رەھمەت، دوختۇر.
دوختۇر: دورىلارنى ۋاقتىدا ئىچىڭ. يەنە پەرھىز تۇتمىسىڭىز بولمايدۇ.
كېسەل: ئۇ نېمە دېگىنىڭىز؟
دوختۇر: مايلىق تاماقلارنى يېمەي تۇرۇڭ، كۆپرەك مېۋە- چېۋىلەردىن يەپ بېرىڭ. قېتىق ئىچىڭ. ئىلاجى بولسا ساپ ھاۋاغا كۆپرەك چىقىڭ.
كېسەل: يۈگۈرسەم بولامدۇ؟
دوختۇر: ھازىرچە يۈگۈرمەي تۇرۇڭ، لېكىن كۆپرەك مېڭىپ بەرسىڭىز بولىدۇ.
كېسەل: ماقۇل دوختۇر. رەھمەت سىزگە. خوش!
دوختۇر: خوش. ئامان بولۇڭ!

Translate the following sentences to Uyghur. Explain your choice of the particular grammatical forms for the highlighted expressions.

1. What are you doing here?
2. I'm just hearing about this from you now.

2 Auxiliary Verb ئولتۇرماق

In the dialogue (Exercise 5.3) you see the sentence:

باش ئاغرىقىغا چىداپ ئولتۇردىڭىزمۇ؟
Did you just endure your headache?

In this sentence, you see the verb ئولتۇرماق used as an auxiliary. When used in this way, it is meant to describe an action which is prolonged.

Note that the verb ئولتۇرماق is not very productive as an auxiliary verb. Its use is restricted to a handful of situations, and it is not commonly used, similar to previously auxiliary verbs which you have learned before. Therefore, at this level you are only expected to recognize it, and not to use it actively.

Compare the following pairs of sentences:

بۇ ئىش توغرۇلۇق كۆپ سۆزلىمەيلى.	بۇ ئىش توغرۇلۇق كۆپ سۆزلەپ ئولتۇرمايلى.
مەنمۇ بۇ ئىش توغرۇلۇق مانا سىلەردىن ئاڭلاۋاتىمەن.	مەنمۇ بۇ ئىش توغرۇلۇق مانا سىلەردىن ئاڭلاپ ئولتۇرۇۋېتىمەن.

Note that the auxiliary verb ئولتۇرماق can sometimes mimic the use of the auxiliary verb تۇرماق. The primary difference between the two is that the use of the auxiliary ئولتۇرماق implies that at least part of the action is completed while sitting down.

بۇ يەردە نېمە قىلىپ تۇرۇۋېسىلەر؟	بۇ يەردە نېمە قىلىپ ئولتۇرۇۋېسىلەر؟

Exercise 6: دوختۇرخانىدىكى شىكايەت

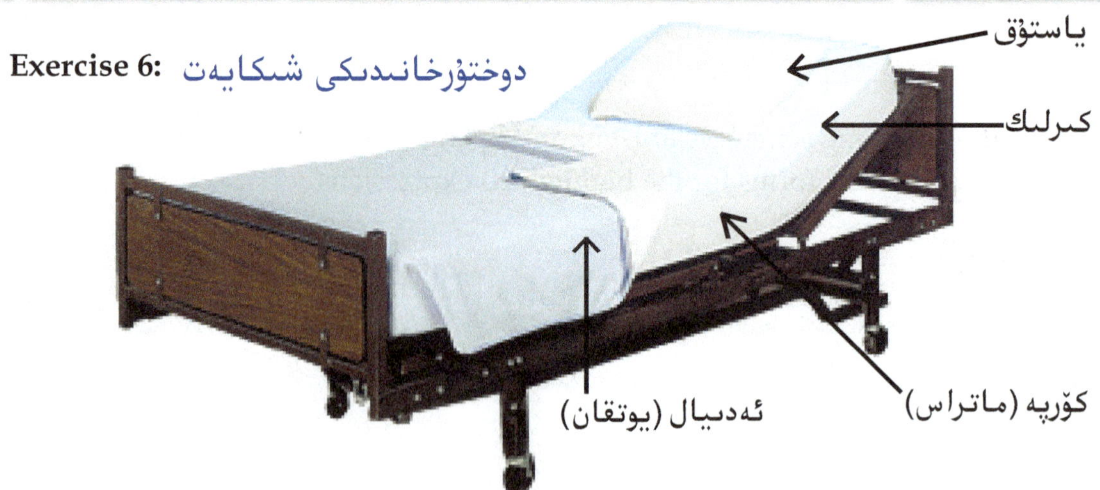

Exercise 6.1:  Listen to the dialogue between a patient and a nurse at the hospital and answer the questions that follow.

1. What is the problem?
2. What does the man want from the nurse? Why?
3. What is the nurse going to do about it?

Exercise 6.2: Listen and repeat. Follow the script below and act out the conversation with a partner.

بىمار: كەچۈرۈڭ دوختۇر، سىزدىن بىر ئىشنى سورىسام بولامدۇ؟
سېسترا: مەن سېسترا، دوختۇر لازىم بولسا چاقىرىپ بېرەي...
بىمار: ياق، ياق، بۇ ئىشنى سىزدىن سورىساممۇ بولىدۇ....مەن دوختۇرخانىدا ياتقىلى ئىككى كۈن بولدى، قاراڭ. شۇ كۈنلا كۆرپەمنى ئالماشتۇرۇپ بېرىڭلار دەپ ئىلتىماس قىلغانتىم، ئەمما ھازىرغىچە ئالماشتۇرۇلمىدى...
سېسترا: كۆرپىگە نېمە بوپتۇ؟
بىمار: سىڭلىم، بۇ كۆرپە بەكمۇ مەينەت ئىكەن... قاراڭ، ھەممە يەردە قاننىڭ داغلىرى* قېتىپ كېتىپتۇ. بۇنىڭدا يېتىشقا كۆڭلۈم تارتمايۋاتىدۇ. بىر ئامالىنى قىلىپ بەرسىڭىز.
سېسترا: ماقۇل، مەن مۇلازىمەتچىلەرگە دەپ قويىمەن.

* قاننىڭ داغلىرى: blood stains

Exercise 6.3:  Role-play. Use the above dialogue as a model to file complaints at a hospital. Choose from among the following problems.

ياستۇق - كىچىك ۋە قاتتىق
كۆرپە (ماتراس) - يىرتىق
ياستۇق قېپى - مەينەت
ئۆي (خانا) - سوغۇق
كىرلىك - قىسقا

Exercise 7: ئۇيغۇرلاردا تەنتەربىيە

Exercise 7.1: Discuss the following questions.

1. What is the most popular sport in your country?
2. Is there a specific type of sport, activity, or game that is only played in your country?
3. Is there a sport or game that people play in your country but which came from another country?

Exercise 7.2:  Look at the following pictures and match them with the appropriate words.

چېلىشىش	___	كالتەك توپ	___
بوكس	___	چويلا توپ	___
ئوغلاق تارتىشىش*	___	پەي توپ	___
نەيزە ئېتىش	___	دارۋازلىق	___
قىلىچۋازلىق	___	تېنىس - تاك توپ	___
قار تېيىلىش	___	بىليارد	___

* ئوغلاق تارتىشىش is a game played on horseback, in which two teams try to grab a goat carcass.

Exercise 8: ئوقۇغۇچىلار ۋە تەنتەربىيە

Exercise 8.1: Listen to Yasin's narration in which he describes their sport activities at Xinjiang University and fill in the blanks with the words below.

مۇسابىقە　　　خەنزۇ　　　ياتاق　　　توپ ئوينىشىمىز　　　ئامېرىكىچە

ۋاسكېتبول　　　تەنتەربىيە سارىيى　　　كىنولاردا

بىز ئادەتتە بوش ۋاقتىمىز بولسا پۇتبول ئوينايمىز. ھە راست، بۇ ئەنگلىيەچە پۇتبول، سىلەر
ئوينايدىغان ______________ پۇتبول ئەمەس. ئۇيغۇر ئوقۇغۇچىلار ئامېرىكىچە پۇتبولنى ئاساسەن
ئۇقمايدۇ، بىز ئۇنى پەقەت ______________ كۆرگەن. بەزىدە چۈشتىن كېيىنلىرى ئوغۇللار
______________ بىناسى ئارىلىقىدا فاكۇلتېتلار بويىچە كوماندىغا ئايرىلىپ توپ ئوينايمىز. بۇ
______________ رەسمىي پۇتبول مەيدانىدا بولمىغاندىكىن بىز پۇتبولنىڭ قائىدىلىرىگە ئانچە
رىئايە قىلىپ كەتمەيمىز. چۈنكى بىزنىڭ ______________ پەقەتلا كۆڭۈل خوشى ئۈچۈن. بىز ئادەتتە
خەنزۇ ئوقۇغۇچىلار بىلەن توپ ئوينىمايمىز. پۇتبولنى ______________ ئوقۇغۇچىلار بىرچىلىك
ئوينىيالمايدۇ، ئەمما داشۆنىڭ مەكتەپ پۇتبول كۇلۇبىدا ئاران ئىككى ئۇيغۇر ئوقۇغۇچى بار. بەزى
ئوغۇللار يەنە ______________ ۋە ۋالىبول ئوينايدۇ، ئەمما بۇ يەردە مەيدان تاپماق تەس. شۇڭا
توپ ئويناش ئانچە ئاسان ئەمەس. مەكتىۋىمىزنىڭ چوڭ ______________ بار، ئەمما ئۇنى پەقەت
مەكتەپ تەنتەربىيە كوماندىسىنىڭ مەشق قىلىشىغا ئىشلىتىدۇ، ئوقۇغۇچىلار كىرىشكە بولمايدۇ.

Exercise 8.2: Listen to the passage one more time. Then answer the following questions.

1. What type of football do Uyghur students play?
2. What happens in the تەنتەربىيە سارىيى ?
3. How often do Uyghur and Chinese students play football together?
4. What other ball games do students play?

Exercise 9: بۇگۈن پۇتبول ئوينايمىز!

Exercise 9.1:  Now read the conversation between John and Yasin and answer the questions that follow.

ياسىن: سائەت ئىككىدە باللار بىلەن پۇتبول ئوينىماقچىدۇق.
جون: پۇتبول؟ سىلەرمۇ پۇتبولنى بىلەمسىلەر؟
ياسىن: بۇ ئەنگلىيەچە پۇتبول، سىلەر ئوينايدىغان ئامېرىكىچە پۇتبول ئەمەس. ئۇيغۇر ئوقۇغۇچىلار ئامېرىكىچە پۇتبولنى ئاساسەن ئۇقمايدۇ، بىز ئۇنى پەقەت كىنولاردا كۆرگەن.
جون: مۇنداق دەڭ... پۇتبولنى شەنبە - يەكشەنبە كۈنلىرى ئوينامسىلەر؟
ياسىن: ياق، بەزىدە چۈشتىن كېيىنلىرىمۇ ئوينايمىز.
جون:پۇتبولنى نەدە ئوينايسىلەر؟
ياسىن: ياتاق بىناسى ئارىلىقىدا پۇتبول ئوينايدىغان جايلار بار. فاكۇلتېتلار بويىچە كوماندىغا ئايرىلىپ ئوينايمىز. بۇمۇسابىقە رەسمىي پۇتبول مەيدانىدا بولمىغاندىن كېيىن پۇتبولنىڭ قائىدىلىرىگە ئانچە رىئايە قىلىپ كەتمەيمىز. چۈنكى بىزنىڭ توپ ئوينىشىمىز پەقەتلا كۆڭۈل خوشى ئۈچۈن.
جون:ئۇ يەردە خەنزۇلارمۇ پۇتبول ئوينامدۇ؟
ياسىن: ھەئە، لېكىن بىز خەنزۇ ئوقۇغۇچىلار بىلەن ئوينىمايمىز. ئۇلار پۇتبولنى بىزچىلىك ئوينىيالمايدۇ. ئەمما داشۆنىڭ مەكتەپ پۇتبول كۇلۇبىدا ئاران ئىككى ئۇيغۇر ئوقۇغۇچى بار.
جون: ئامېرىكىدا ئوقۇغۇچىلار ۋاسكېتبولغا بەك ئامراق. ئۇيغۇرلارچۇ ؟
ياسىن: بەزى ئوغۇللار ۋاسكېتبول بىلەن ۋالىبول ئوينايدۇ، ئەمما بۇ يەردە مەيدان تاپماق تەس. شۇڭا توپ ئويناش ئانچە ئاسان ئەمەس. مەكتىپىمىزنىڭ چوڭ تەنتەربىيە سارىيى بار، ئەمما ئۇنى پەقەت مەكتەپ تەنتەربىيە كوماندىسىنىڭ مەشق قىلىشىغا ئىشلىتىدۇ، ئوقۇغۇچىلار كىرىشكە بولمايدۇ.
جون: قىزلارچۇ؟ ئۇلار تەنتەربىيەگە قىزىقامدۇ؟ ئۇلار بوش ۋاقىتلىرىدا نېمە قىلىدۇ؟
ياسىن: قىزلارنىڭ تەنتەربىيە بىلەن ئانچە خوشى يوق.

1. بوش ۋاقتى بولسا، ئۇيغۇر ئوقۇغۇچىلار نېمە قىلىدۇ؟
2. نېمە ئۈچۈن ئۇلار پۇتبول قائىدىلىرىگە ئانچە رىئايە قىلمايدۇ؟
3. ئوقۇغۇچىلار كىم بىلەن پۇتبول ئوينايدۇ؟
4. ئوقۇغۇچىلار پۇتبولدىن باشقا يەنە قانداق تەنتەربىيە ئوينايدۇ؟
5. قىزلارچۇ؟ ئۇلار بوش ۋاقىتلىرىدا نېمە قىلىدۇ؟

Exercise 9.2:  Practice the dialogue above with your partner.

Exercise 10: پۇتبول تارىخى

Exercise 10.1:  Read the following passage about the history of Uyghur football.

lamb's skin	قوزا تېرىسى
air	يەل
to fill	تولدۇرماق
a fur hat	تۇماق
jumping	سەكرەش
exercise	مەشغۇلات
to capture (take prisoner)	ئەسىر ئېلىش
to win	يەڭمەك
to lose	يېڭىلمەك

ئۇيغۇرلاردا ئۆزىگە خاس مىللىي ئالاھىدىلىككە ئىگە ھەرخىل تەنتەربىيە تۈرلىرى بار. بۇنىڭ ئىچىدە پۇتبول ئالاھىدە ئورۇندا تۇرىدۇ. تارىخىي پاكىتلارغا قارىغاندا، پۇتبول (توپ ئويۇنى) تۈركىي خەلقلەر تەرىپىدىن ئىجاد قىلىنغان. ئۇ چاغلاردىكى توپ ھازىرقى زاماندىكى توپقا ئوخشىمىغان. توپنىڭ ئورنىغا تولۇمچە سويۇلغان قوزا تېرىسىگە يەل (ھاۋا) بېرىلگەن ياكى تېرىنىڭ ئىچىگە سامان تىقىپ تىكىلگەن. بۇنىڭدىن تاشقىرى يۇمشاق نەرسىلەردىنمۇ (مەسىلەن كونا تۇماقلاردىن) توپ تىكىلىپ، ھاۋا ياكى سامان بىلەن تولدۇرۇلغان.

19- ئەسىرنىڭ 70- يىللىرى مەشھۇر سودىگەر مەرىپەتچى زات باۋۇدۇن مۇسابايوۋ شىنجاڭدىكى دىنىي مەكتەپلەردە پەننىي دەرس ئوقۇشنى يولغا قويۇپ، مەكتەپ ئەتراپىدا تەنتەربىيە مەيدانلىرىنىمۇ ياساتقۇزىدۇ*. ئوقۇغۇچىلار بۇ مەيداندا يۈگۈرۈش، سەكرەش، مېڭىش قاتارلىق ئاددىي تەنتەربىيە مەشغۇلاتلىرىدىن سىرت، پۇتبول، تارتىشما (ئارقان ۋە كالتەك)، "ئەسىر ئېلىش"، "تاش كەلدى - تاش كەتتى" قاتارلىق تەنتەربىيە پائالىيەتلىرى بىلەنمۇ مەشغۇل بولغان.

1902 - يىلى باۋۇدۇنباي ئۆز خىراجىتى بىلەن روسىيە، تۈركىيەگە ئوقۇغۇچىلارنى چىقىرىدۇ. ئۇلار ئوقۇشنى پۈتتۈرۈپ قايتقاندىن كېيىن، باشقا تەنتەربىيە تۈرلىرى قاتارىدا پۇتبولمۇ زامانىۋىلىشىدۇ ۋە نەتىجىدە ئۇيغۇر تۇنجى زامانىۋى پۇتبول كوماندىسى قۇرۇلىدۇ. 1927 - يىلى ئاتۇشتا قۇرۇلغان ئۇيغۇر پۇتبولچىلار كوماندىسى ئەنگلىيىنىڭ قەشقەردە تۇرۇشلۇق كونسۇلىنىڭ پۇتبول كوماندىسى بىلەن مۇسابىقىلىشىپ، ئۇلارنى بىرگە قارشى ئىككى** نەتىجە بىلەن، شۋېتسىيە كوماندىسىنى نۆلگە قارشى يەتتە نەتىجە بىلەن يېڭىدۇ.

يېڭى جۇڭگو قۇرۇلغاندىن كېيىن ئۇيغۇر پۇتبول كوماندىسىنىڭ ئەزالىرى يېڭى زامان پۇتبول مەيدانىدىن ئورۇن ئالىدۇ. 1951- يىلى بۇ كوماندا غەربىي شىمال رايونى بويىچە چېمپىيون بولىدۇ.

بۇ ئەھۋاللار بىزگە پۇتبول ئۇيغۇرلارنىڭ ئەنئەنىۋى مىللىي تەنتەربىيە تۈرلىرىدىن بىرى ئىكەنلىكىنى، ئۇنىڭ خەلقىمىز ئارىسىدا خېلى بۇرۇنلا كەڭ ئومۇملاشقانلىقىنى كۆرسىتىدۇ.

---

*Here the present/future tense is used to talk about the past

**This phrase is used to report scores in a game

Exercise 10.2:  Get together with your partner and read the following scores in Uyghur.

0:3 5:2 4:1 7:4 8:8 6:9

Exercise 10.3: Review the passage again and answer the following questions.

1. According to the passage, who invented the game of football? Do you think this theory is accurate?
2. How did Musabaev's work change religious schools?
3. What did the first balls used in football look like?

Exercise 10.4:  Skim the passage one more time and write down all the verb forms which make use of a causative construction. Which suffixes specifically express the causative voice in these examples?

Exercise 11: كالتەك توپ كوماندىسى

Exercise 11.1: تۆۋەندىكى سوئاللارنى مۇزاكىرە قىلىڭلار

1. Baseball seems to be a popular sport around the world. Why? What do you think about it?
2. Do you know of other countries where people play this sport?
3. Why do you think other cultures would choose to adopt baseball?
4. Do you think baseball is different from other team sports? Why or why not?

Exercise 11.2:  Read Colin's description of the Uyghur baseball team in Urumchi.

مەن 2005 - يىلى شىنجاڭ ئۇنىۋېرسىتېتىدا بىر يىگىتنى ئۇچرىتىپ قالدىم. ئۇنىڭ مۇرىسىدىكى سومكىدا بىر كالتەكنى كۆرۈپ بەك ھەيران بولدۇم. پەقەت ئۇرۇمچىدە ئەمەس، پۈتۈن مەملىكەتتە پۇتبول، ۋاسكېتبول قاتارلىق تەنتەربىيە تۈرلىرى بەك ئومۇملاشقان بولسىمۇ، كالتەك توپ يوق دەپ ئويلىغانتىم، لېكىن بار ئىكەن.

ئالدىنقى ئەسىرنىڭ 90 - يىللىرىدا ئۇرۇمچىدە ئوقۇۋاتقان ياپونىيىلىك ئوقۇغۇچىلار ياپونىيىگە قايتىشتىن بۇرۇن پەلەي، توپ، كالتەك قاتارلىق كالتەك توپ قوراللىرىنى قالدۇرغانىكەن. 2000- يىلدا بىر نەچچە ئوقۇغۇچى مۇشۇ قوراللارنى تېپىۋېلىپ بىر كوماندا قۇرغانىكەن. بىلىشىمچە، شۇ چاغلاردا شىنجاڭ ئۇنىۋېرسىتېتى كالتەك توپ كوماندىسى پۈتۈن شىنجاڭ بويىچە بىردىنبىر كوماندا بولغانىكەن. كوماندا ئەزالىرى ھەر ھەپتە ئاز دېگەندە ئۈچ قېتىم مەشىق قىلغانىكەن. قىشتا ھاۋا ناھايىتى سوغۇق بولغاندىمۇ، ئۇلار بىر ئوقۇتۇش بىناسىنىڭ يەر ئاستى ئۆيىگە كىرىپ مەشىق قىلىۋېرىدىكەن. بۇ كوماندا رايوندىكى بىردىنبىر كوماندا بولغاچقا، بەزىدە كوماندا ئەزالىرى ئىككىگە بۆلۈنۈپ كىچىك مۇسابىقە ئويناشتىن سىرت، ھېچقانداق رەسمىي مۇسابىقىگە قاتناشمايدىكەن. بەزىدە مەن ئۇلاردىن "مۇسابىقە ئوينىيالمىساڭلار نېمىشقا بۇنچە تىرىشىپ مەشىق قىلىسىلەر؟" دەپ سورايتتىم ۋە ئىككى خىل جاۋاب ئاڭلايتتىم. بەزىلەر "كالتەك توپقا قىزىقتىم" دېسە، يەنە بەزىلەر "قۇربان بېرىشنى ئۆگىنىش ئۈچۈن" دەيتتى. "نېمىنى قۇربان بېرىدۇ؟" دەپ ئويلايتتىم. ئۇلارنىڭ دېيىشىچە، كالتەك توپتىن باشقا ھېچقانداق تەنتەربىيەدە كوماندا ئۈچۈن ئۆزىنى قۇربان قىلىدىغان بىر ئىش يۈز بەرمەيدىكەن، بۇ پەقەتلا كالتەك توپتا بار ئىكەن. ئۇ چاغلاردا بۇ كوماندىنىڭ ترېنېرى بىر كورېيىلىك ئوقۇغۇچى بولغان ئىكەن. ئۇنىڭ ئايالى ۋە ئۈچ كىچىك بالىسى بار ئىكەن. ئۇ ئۆزىگە ھېچقانداق پايدا ياكى مائاش بولمىسىمۇ، ھەر ھەپتىدە ئۈچ قېتىم مەكتەپكە بېرىپ كوماندا ئەزالىرىغا كالتەك توپ ئۆگىتىش ئۈچۈن ئۆزىنىڭ ۋاقتىنى قۇربان بەرگەنىكەن. كوماندا ئەزالىرى بۇنىڭدىن چوڭقۇر تەسىرلىنىپتۇ. ئۇلارنىڭ دېيىشىچە، ئادەمنىڭ ھاياتىدا يا ئائىلىسى، يا خەلقى ئۈچۈن قۇربان بېرىش ناھايىتى مۇھىم بىر ئىش ئىكەن. ئۇلار كالتەك توپتىن مۇشۇ روھنى ئۆگەنگەنىكەن.

بۇ كوماندا ئەينى ۋاقىتتا پۈتۈن شىنجاڭ بويىچە بىردىنبىر كوماندا بولغان بولسىمۇ، ھازىر ئۇنداق ئەمەس. شۇنىڭدىن بېرى ئالىي مەكتەپ كوماندا ئەزالىرى تۆت - بەش باشلانغۇچ مەكتەپتە يېڭى كوماندا قۇرۇپ، ھازىرغىچە ھەر ھەپتىدە كىچىك بالىلارنى تەربىيەلەشكە ئۆزلىرىنىڭ ۋاقتىنى قۇربان بېرىدىكەن. 2005 - يىلدىن بۇيان ئالىي مەكتەپ كوماندىسى يازلىق تەتىلدە نەچچە ئون سائەتلىك پويىزغا ئولتۇرۇپ ئىچكىرى ئۆلكىلەرگە بېرىپ مەملىكەتلىك ئالىي مەكتەپ ئوقۇغۇچىلىرى كالتەك توپ مۇسابىقىسىگە قاتنىشىدىكەن. 2012- يىللىق مۇسابىقىدە ئۇلار پۈتۈن مەملىكەت بويىچە چېمپىيون بوپتۇ.

shoulder	مۇرە
tool	قورال
basement	يەر ئاستى ئۆيى

to sacrifice	قۇربان بەرمەك
salary	مائاش
spirit	روھ

Exercise 11.3:  Write the Uyghur words for the following items.

catcher	
pitcher	
bat	
ball	
glove	

helmet	
baseball cap	
chest protector	
mask	
kneepad	

Exercise 11.4: Skim the passage again and answer these questions in detail.

1. How did the team acquire baseball gear?
2. How was the first team organized?
3. What was their practice schedule like?

Exercise 11.5: تۆۋەندىكى سوئاللارنى مۇزاكىرە قىلىڭلار

1. According to the passage you just read, playing baseball teaches people about personal sacrifice. What does the author mean? Mention specific examples given in the text.
2. Do you think that baseball or any other team sport teaches the value of personal sacrifice?

3 Causative Constructions

As you remember, causative constructions show that the subject of the sentence does not perform the action of the verb directly but causes the action of the verb to be performed by someone/something else. Sentences with causative in Uyghur often correspond to English constructions using get, have, or make.

In Chapter 7 when we introduced causative constructions, we mentioned that the suffix ت- attaches to the verb to form the causative if the verb stem ends in a vowel.

Additionally, once the suffix ت- is used to form a causative, one can also make a double causative of the resultant verb by adding the regular causative suffixes تۇز- /تۇر- قۇز- /كۇز-. Look at the following example:

to fix	ياسىماق
to get something fixed	ياساتماق
to have someone get something fixed	ياساتقۇزماق

The suffix ت- is also used to form the causative of verbs whose stems end in اي، ىر، ار، ەر، ەي. The following verbs illustrate this form of the causative.

to make green	كۆكەرتمەك	to become green	كۆكەرمەك
to have (something) lifted	كۆتۈرتمەك	to lift	كۆتۈرمەك
to cause to increase	كۆپەيتمەك	to increase	كۆپەيمەك
to cause to decrease	ئازايتماق	to decrease in number	ئازايماق
to make yellow	سارغايتماق	to become yellow	سارغايماق
to widen	كېڭەيتمەك	to become wider	كېڭەيمەك
to whiten	ئاقارتماق	to turn white	ئاقارماق
to cause to water (as in a field)	سۇغارتماق	to water	سۇغارماق
to have someone called	چاقىرتماق	to call	چاقىرماق
to change (something else)	ئۆزگەرتمەك	to change (of one's own accord)	ئۆزگەرمەك

Exercise 12:  Fill in the blanks, where necessary, with the appropriate forms of the causative suffix.

1. ماۋۇ نان كۆكىر ______ىپ كېتىپتۇ.
2. باتۇر سادىرنى ئۇرۇپ يۈزلىرىنى كۆكەر______ىۋېتىپتۇ دەپ ئاڭلىدىم.
3. بازاردا بېدە* كۆپىي______ىپتۇ.
4. تۆتنى بەشكە كۆپەي______سە يىگىرمە بولىدۇ.
5. ئانامنىڭ چېچى ئاقىر______ىپ كەتتى.
6. ئۇ ئۆيلەرنى ئاقار______ىپ چىقتى.
7. ئۇنىڭ جىگىرى ئاغرىغاچقا، يۈزلىرى ساغىر______ىپ كېتىپتۇ.
8. ئادىل نانىنى سارغاي______ىپ پىشۇردى.
9. دوختۇر بىمارنى چاقىر______دى.
10. دوختۇر بىمارنى چاقىر______تى.
11. خالمۇراتنىڭ پىلانى ئۆزگەر______دى.
12. خالمۇرات پىلانىنى ئۆزگەر______تى.

---

* بېدە: alfalfa sprouts

3 Causative Constructions (cont'd.)

Some verbs with single syllable roots that end in ت-, ش-, or چ- take the causative endings ۇر- / ۈر- (sometimes ار-/ەر- in southern Xinjiang).

to make drink	ئىچۈرمەك	to drink	ئىچمەك
to send flying	ئۇچۇرماق (ئۇچارماق)	to fly	ئۇچماق
to drop/tip over	چۈشۈرمەك (چۈشەرمەك)	to go down	چۈشمەك
to move (something)	كۆچۈرمەك (كۆچەرمەك)	to move	كۆچمەك
to cause to increase	ئاشۇرماق	to increase	ئاشماق
to bring/send back	قايتۇرماق	to return	قايتماق
to make (something) fit	پاتۇرماق	to fit	پاتماق

Exercise 13:  Read the following sentences and fill in the blanks with the appropriate causative suffixes. Then translate the sentences into English.

1. ئۆي ئىگىسى ئىجارە پۇلنى ئاش ______ ماقچى.
2. باللار لەگلەك ئۇچ ______ دى.
3. ئانىسى بالىسىغا دورا ئىچ ______ مەكچى.
4. دوختۇر كېسەلگە ئوپېراتسىيە پۇلنى قايت ____ ىدۇ.
5. ھۆكۈمەت ئۇلارنى ئۆزى كۆچ ______ ىدۇ.
6. ئانامغا دېسىڭىز ئۇ ھەممە نەرسىلىرىڭىزنى بىر چامدانغا پات ______ ىدۇ.

3 Causative Constructions (cont'd.)

The following forms are irregular:

a. A few verbs that end in ق form causatives by taking the ending ۇت-/ىت-. Note that this ending also causes any ئە or ئا vowel in the root to raise to ئې.
The most common verbs in this category include:

to cause to flow	ئېقىتماق	to flow	ئاقماق
to get scared	قورقۇتماق	to fear	قورقماق

b. Some verbs take ار- to form causatives:

to send out	چىقارماق	to go out	چىقماق

c. The verb كۆرمەك 'to see' has its own special causative form which does not fit into any other category: كۆرسەتمەك 'to cause to see', i.e. 'to show'.

Exercise 14: شىپالىق تائاملار

Exercise 14.1: تۆۋەندىكى سوئاللارنى مۇزاكىرە قىلىڭلار

1. "سامساق، ئۇنى يېگەننىڭ تېنى ساق". بۇ گەپكە قوشۇلامسىز؟
2. سىزنىڭ مەدەنىيىتىڭىزدە قايسى تائاملار سالامەتلىككە پايدىلىق دەپ قارىلىدۇ؟
3. سالامەتلىككە پايدىلىق ئوزۇقلىنىش ئادەتلىرىدىن قايسىلارنى بىلىسىز؟

Exercise 14.2:   Read John's blog.

Uyghur John's Blog

ئامېرىكىلىق يالقۇننىڭ تورتۇراسى

Search

كۈندە بىر ماقال: سەھەر ھاۋاسى ئۆمرنىڭ داۋاسى.

قوشۇقتىكى كۆك نەرسىنى كۆردۈڭلارمۇ؟ ئەتىيازدا ئۈرۈمچىنىڭ كوچىلىرىدا بىردە باسقان ھارۋىلارنى ئىتتىرىپ* يۈرگەن كىشىلەر كۆپىيىپ قالدى. كۆپلىگەن ئاشخانىلارنىڭ ئىشىك بېشىغا "كۆك چۆچۈرە" دەپ يېزىلغان ۋىۋىسكىلارنى كۆردۈم. ھەيران بولۇپ ئۇيغۇر دوستۇمدىن " كۆك رەڭلىك چۆچۈرە دېگەن قانداق چۆچۈرە؟ " دەپ سورىدىم. سوئالىمنى ئاڭلاپ دوستۇم كۈلۈپ كەتتى. ئۇنىڭ ئېيتىشىچە، بۇنىڭ كۆك رەڭ بىلەن ھېچقانداق ئالاقىسى يوق ئىكەن. ئۇيغۇرلار ھەر يىلى ئەتىياز پەسلىدە، يەنى بىردە يېڭى كۆكلىگەندە، ئۇنىڭدىن چۆچۈرە تۈگۈپ يەيدىكەن. بىردە ئاشقازاننىڭ ھەزىم قىلىش** ئىقتىدارىنى ياخشىلايدىكەن. "كۆك چۆچۈرە" دېگەن گەپ ئەسلىدە يېڭى ئۆسكەن بىردىنىڭ رەڭگىگە قاراپ ئېيتىلغان ئىكەن. شۇنىڭدىن كېيىن مەنمۇ بىرنەچچە قېتىم كۆك چۆچۈرىنى يەپ باقتىم، ئۇنىڭ تەمى ماڭا ياقتى.....

مۇشۇ خىلدىكى ھەيران قالارلىق تائاملاردىن يەپ باققانلار بارمۇ؟ ئاشۇنداق غەلىتە، ئەمما تولىمۇ شىپالىق غىزالارنى كۆرگەنمۇسىز؟ ئەگەر سىزگە مۇشۇنداق ئىشلار ئۇچرىغان بولسا، ئىنكاس شەكلىدە ماڭا يوللاپ بەرسىڭىز.

---

* ئىتتەرمەك: to push

** ھەزىم قىلماق: to digest

ئىسىم

ئىم

Exercise 14.3: تۆۋەندىكى ئىككى سوئالغا جاۋاب بېرىڭلار

1. According to the blog entry which you have just read, what surprised John in Urumchi?
2. What did he learn from this experience?

Exercise 14.4:  Respond to John's blog post. Provide details about a food item of your choice. Include what it looked like, how it tasted, and what you thought about it.

Uyghur John's Blog

ئامېرىكىلىق يالقۇننىڭ تورتۇراسى

Search

كۈندە بىر ماقال:

توقلۇقتىن شوخلۇق چىقىدۇ.

ئىسىم

ئىم

Exercise 15: ئاممىۋى بىلدۈرگۈ

Exercise 15.1:  Read the following passage taken from a newspaper. Fill in the missing words from the table provided below. The table to the left of the reading contains words that will help you understand the passage better.

ياۋا پاكىز ئاسانلا تاغلىق مۇتەخەسسىسلەرنىڭ پايدىلىق
يۇقىرى تاللا

ياۋا كۆكتات ئىستېمال قىلغاندا ئېھتىيات قىلىڭ

to follow	ئەگەشمەك
peppermint	يالپۇز
alfalfa	بېدە
nutritional component	ئوزۇقلۇق تەركىبى
barren land	قاقاسلىق
rubbish	ئەخلەت
pile	دۆۋە
a stream	ئۆستەڭ
to poison	زەھەرلىمەك
to dip into	چىلىماق

ئۆز مۇخبىرىمىز: ھاۋانىڭ ئىللىشىغا ئەگىشىپ، شەھىرىمىزنىڭ ھەر قايسى چوڭ
يېزا - ئىگىلىك* مەھسۇلاتلىرى بازىرى ۋە __________ بازارلىرىغا يالپۇز، بېدە
قاتارلىق __________ كۆكتاتلار سېلىندى. شەھەرلىك
كېسەللىكلەرنىڭ ئالدىنى ئېلىش - كونترول قىلىش مەركىزىدىكى
ئالاقىدار __________ تونۇشتۇرۇشىچە،
ياۋا كۆكتات تەركىبىدە مىنېرال ماددا مول بولۇپ، ئوزۇقلۇق
تەركىبى __________ ئىكەن. __________
رايون، قاقاسلىقلاردا ئۆسكەن ياۋا كۆكتاتلار سالامەتلىككە
__________ بولسىمۇ، لېكىن خىمىيە سانائىتى
زاۋۇتىنىڭ ئەتراپى، يول بويى، ئاھالىلەر كۆپ ئولتۇراقلاشقان
رايون ھەمدە ئەخلەت دۆۋىلىرى ياكى بۇلغانغان ئۆستەڭ ئەتراپىدا
ئۆسكەن ياۋا كۆكتات ئادەمنى __________ زەھەرلەپ
قويىدىكەن. ئەتىياز - باكتېرىيىنىڭ كۆپىيىش مەزگىلى، شۇڭا ياۋا
كۆكتاتنى يېيىشتىن بۇرۇن __________ يۇيۇپ، سۇغا بىردەم
چىلاپ قويغاندىن كېيىن قورۇپ يېيىش، ھەرگىزمۇ خام يېمەسلىك
كېرەككەن.

*يېزا - ئىگىلىك: agriculture

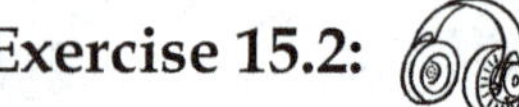 **Exercise 15.2:**  Now listen to the passage to check your answers.

Exercise 15.3: Below you will find some words and phrases from the text. Use them to give an oral summary of what you have learned from the preceding passage:

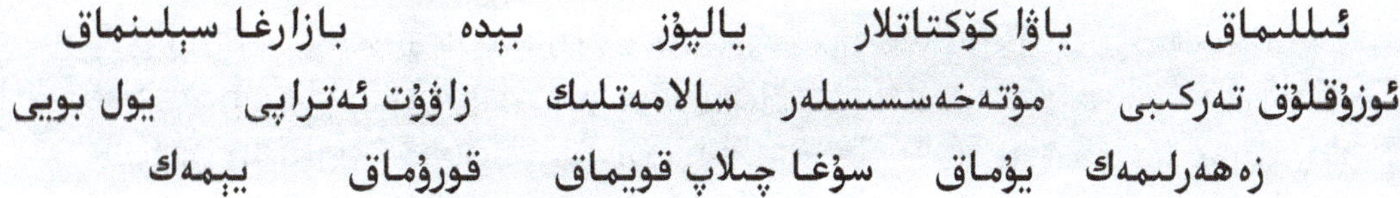

Exercise 16: ئۇيغۇرلاردا تېبابەتچىلىك

Exercise 16.1:  تۆۋەندىكى سوئاللارنى مۇزاكىرە قىلىڭلار

1. Do you always take medicine when you are sick? Why or why not?
2. What do you do when you are sick but do not want to see a doctor?
3. Have you ever tried any traditional medicine?

Exercise 16.2: For this exercise, watch the video and answer the questions below:

1. What does Ablet say about folk medicine in Khotan?
2. In his opinion, what is the reason for the development of folk medicine in this region?
3. What does he say about the eating habits of the Khotanese?

Exercise 16.3: Watch the video again and pay attention to what the narrator says about ئۇزۇن ئۆمۈر كۆرگۈچىلەر.

1. Who are the ئۇزۇن ئۆمۈر كۆرگۈچىلەر?
2. How does the narrator explain this phenomenon? What is the reason behind it?
3. Here the narrator mentions a statistic: 40%. What does it refer to?

Uyghur Traditional Medicine

Uyghurs are increasingly exposed to modern medical science, and most do not reject it outright. However, the majority of Uyghurs also continue to trust in an ancient and highly developed tradition of folk medicine. Uyghur traditional medicine relies on an impressive variety of herbs and plants to treat a wide range of physical and mental illness. The masters of this folk medicine are local doctors called 'tevip', and they usually make their diagnoses by checking the patients' veins. Most local people prefer to visit a *tevip* for common afflictions rather than going to a modern clinic. This is because traditional medicine is cheaper, and widely believed to have no adverse side effects.

Exercise 16.4:  Write the names of the following parts of the body in Uyghur.

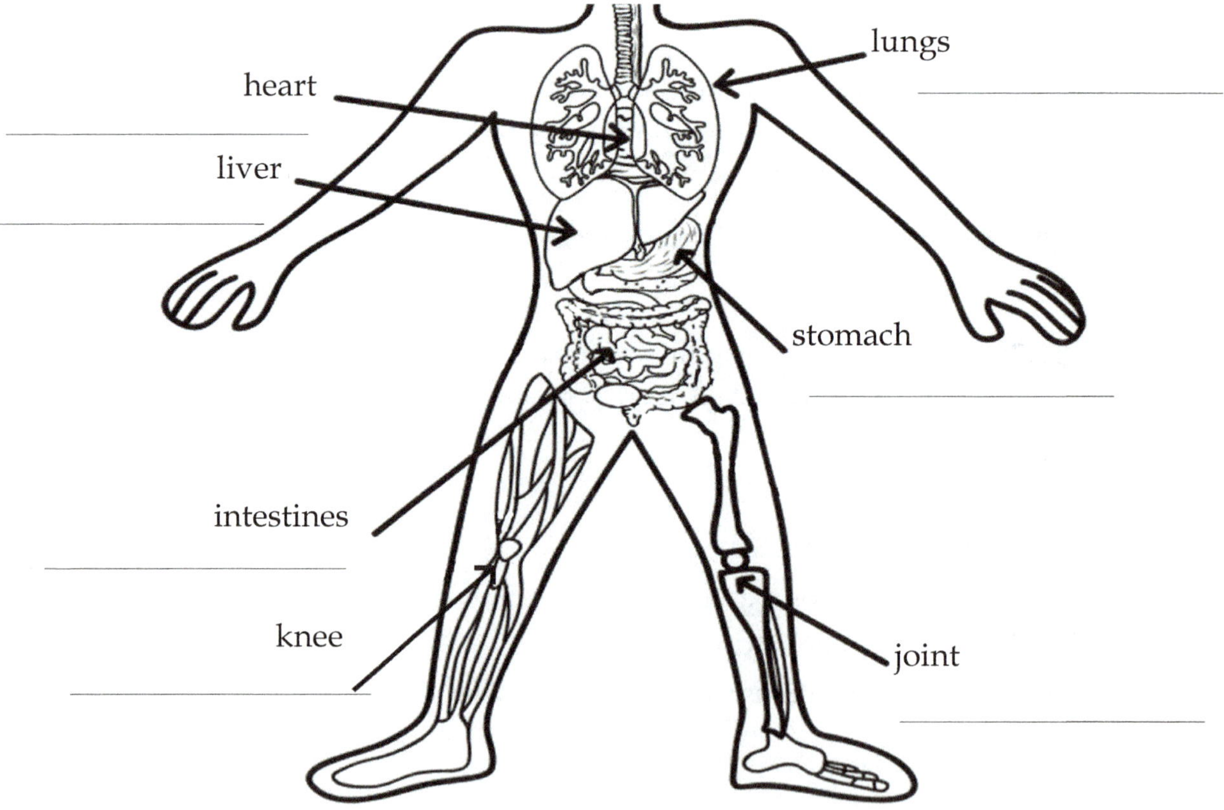

Exercise 16.5: تۆۋەندىكى رەسىمنى تەسۋىرلەپ بېرىڭ.

1. What do you think the people are doing in this picture?
2. Where do you think the picture was taken?

Exercise 17:  Here you will see parts of a video-interview with a تېۋىپ.

PART 1:
Watch the introduction to the interview and answer the questions that follow.

1. What is Abdugeni's educational background?
2. What were the major steps he took to develop his business?

PART 2:
Watch the next segment of the interview. In it, Abdugeni explains which health problems sand therapy can cure. While watching, take notes on what you see and hear.

PART 3:
In the third segment, the tevip explains when and how sand therapy should be done. Watch the video, then fill out the table that follows. List at least three important statements for each column.

Dos	*Don'ts*

PART 4:
Watch the next short segment and answer the questions below.

1. Where did this patient come from?
2. What is she being treated for?
3. When did she arrive for her treatment?
4. What does her treatment include?

PART 5:
Watch the final part and answer the questions below.

1. How are patients prepared for sand therapy?
2. What does the patient have to do right before digging themselves into the sand? Why?
3. What is the suggested length of time for a patient's first round of sand therapy?
   a. 11 days b. 13 days c. 21 days d. 23 days
4. How long should people stay in the sand for each session?
   a. 5-10 min. b. 15-20 min. c. 20-25 min. d. 50 min.
5. How long do returning patients typically stay? Circle all that apply.
   a. 11 days b. 13 days c. 15 days d. 17 days
6. True or false: Traditional medical practices such as sand therapy are not usually used in conjunction with modern medicine.
   True False

Exercise 18: تۆۋەندىكى سوئاللارنى مۇزاكىرە قىلىڭلار

1. What do you know about the weather and geography of Turpan that makes it an ideal place for sand therapy?
2. Why do you think sand therapy might help patients with the problems listed in this video?
3. Can you know of any similar treatments used in other places or by other cultures in the world?

Exercise 19:  Imagine you have gone to Turpan to experience sand therapy first-hand. Write a blog entry about what you have seen and experienced during your treatment. Use the information provided in the video.

Search

كۆزدە بىر ماقال:
قولى ئوچۇقنىڭ يولى ئوچۇق.

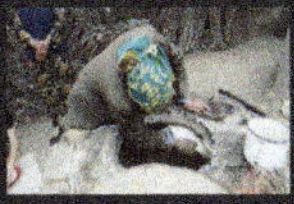

ئىسىم
ئىم

Have you ever heard about...? بۇ كىشىنى بىلەمسىز...؟

In this section you will read and learn about a famous Uyghur person.

Exercise 20: دولقۇن ياسىن

Exercise 20.1:  Read the following passage about Dolqun Yasin, a famous Uyghur poet. Then, answer the questions that follow. The words and expressions provided before the questions will help you to understand the passage better.

قەشقەر كەچلىك گېزىتى

2014 - يىلى 18 - ئاۋغۇست
دۈشەنبە

1231 - سان　　پوچتا ۋاكالەت نومۇرى: 54 - 66

شېئىرىمنى ياراتقان دەرد سەن، ۋەتىنىم.
قانچە دەرد تارتساڭمۇ مەرد سەن، ۋەتىنىم.

ئوت يۈرەك شائىر ۋە پېشقەدەم ژۇرنالىست دولقۇن ياسىن 1938 - يىلى ئىلى ۋىلايىتىگە قاراشلىق سۈيدۈڭ ناھىيىسىدە تۇغۇلغان. شائىرنىڭ دادىسى ش ئۇ ئا ر دا تونۇلغان سىياسىي ئەرباب ياسىن خۇدابەردى ئىدى. ئائىلە مۇھىتىنىڭ تەسىرىدە دولقۇن ياسىن كىچىكىدىنلا ئەدەبىياتقا ئىشتىياق باغلاپ ئۇيغۇر خەلقىنىڭ ھەقىقى شائىرى بولۇشقا بەل باغلايدۇ. 1956 - يىلى دولقۇن ئۈرۈمچىدە مىللەتلەر ئىنىستىتۇتىنى پۈتتۈرۈپ، شۇ يىلى تاشكەنت شەھرىدىكى ئوتتۇرا ئاسىيا دۆلەت ئۇنىۋېرسىتېتىغا فىلولوگىيە كەسپىگە ئوقۇشقا كىرىدۇ. 1961 - يىلى ئوقۇشنى ئەلا نەتىجە بىلەن پۈتتۈرۈپ ئۈرۈمچىگە قايتىدۇ ۋە 1963 - يىلغىچە "تارىم" ژۇرنىلىدا ئىشلەيدۇ. ئۆزىنىڭ ئۆتكۈر پىكىرلىك شېئىرلىرى بىلەن مۇستەبىت ھاكىمىيەتنىڭ كۆزىگە مىخ بولۇپ قادالغان ياش شائىر 1963 - يىلدىن 1968 - يىلغىچە قومۇلغا سۈرگۈن قىلىنىدۇ. داۋاملىق ئېغىرلىشىۋاتقان سىياسىي ۋەزىيەت ئاستىدا دولقۇن ياسىن 1968 - يىلى قازاقىستانغا قېچىپ كېتىشكە مەجبۇر بولىدۇ. ئۇيغۇر خەلقىنىڭ ئېغىر سىياسىي ۋە مىللىي دەردىنى تولۇق باشتىن كەچۈرگەن شائىر ئالمۇتىدا ۋەتەن دەردى، خەلق ئارمانى ۋە ئىنسانىي مۇھەببەتكە تويۇنغان، شۇنداقلا زور پەلسەپىۋى قىممەتكە ئىگە بىر قاتار ئۆلمەس شېئىرلارنى ۋە توپلاملارنى ئېلان قىلىدۇ. ئۆزىنىڭ بۇ بىر قاتار ئەمگەكلىرى بەدىلىگە شائىر قازاقىستاندا ۋە خەلقئارادا زور شەرەپلەرنى قولغا كەلتۈردى. ئۇيغۇر خەلقىنىڭ ئوت يۈرەك شائىرى ۋە جامائەت ئەربابى دولقۇن ياسىن 2005 - يىلى كېسەل سەۋەبىدىن ۋاپات بولدى.

ۋەتەننى باسقىنى زور توپان بولسا،
توپاننىڭ قەھرىگە تاشلاڭلار مېنى،
ۋەتەن يېنىۋاتقان بىر ۋولقان بولسا،
شۇ ۋولقاننىڭ ئىچىگە تاشلاڭلار مېنى،

مەن ئۇنىڭ قوينىدا كۆلگە ئايلىناي،
مەيلى يانغىن يېنىپ تۇرسا ئۇستۇمدە،
ئاشۇ يالقۇندىنمۇ كۈچلۈك بىر يالقۇن،
ۋەتىنىم سۆيگۈسى ياشار كۆكسۈمدە.

political situation	سىياسىي ۋەزىيەت
to escape	قېچىپ كەتمەك
to be forced to	مەجبۇر بولماق
pain	دەرد
to experience	باشتىن كەچۈرمەك
desire	ئارمان
to achieve	قولغا كەلتۈرمەك
social figure	جامائەت ئەربابى
enthusiastic	ئوت يۈرەك
generous; brave	مەرد

experienced, long in tooth	پېشقەدەم
the political figure	سىياسىي ئەرباب
to have zest	ئىشتىياق باغلىماق
to determine; to do something	بەل باغلىماق
sharp, fierce, keen	ئۆتكۈر
dictator, tyrant	مۇستەبىت
(political) power	ھاكىمىيەت
to be a thorn in (someone's) side	مىخ بولۇپ قادالماق
to be exiled	سۈرگۈن قىلىنماق
expense, cost	بەدەل

1. سىزنىڭچە دولقۇن ياسىننىڭ شائىر بولۇشىغا نېمىلەر تەسىر قىلدى؟
2. شائىر قايسى ئالىي مەكتەپنى پۈتتۈردى؟
3. ئوقۇشنى پۈتتۈرگەندىن كېيىن شائىر نېمە قىلدى؟
4. نېمە سەۋەپتىن دولقۇن ياسىن قازاقىستانغا چىقىپ كەتتى؟
5. "مىق بولۇپ قادالماق" دېگەن ئىبارىنىڭ مەنىسى نېمە؟

Exercise 20.2:  Based on the passage, ask your partner three more questions about Dolqun Yasin.

Exercise 20.3:  Read the following short excerpts from Dolqun Yasin's poems and translate them into English on a separate sheet of paper.

بۇ نۇرلۇق ۋەتەننى باستى جاھالەت،
ئۆزىمىز بولدۇقۇ ئۆز ۋەتەندە يات...

ئۆلدى دەپ بىلىڭلار ئىلىمدىن كەچسەم،
جاھالەت بوغدۇ بىلىمدىن كەچسەم.
ئۇيغۇرنىڭ تىزىمىدىن ئۆچۈرۈڭ دەرھال،
جان ئانام ئۆگەتكەن تىلىمدىن كەچسەم.

ۋەتەندىن ئايرىلىپ مەن گادا بولدۇم،
جاراڭلىق ناخشا ئىدىم، بىر سادا بولدۇم.
ئۆلۈمدىن بەتتەررەك ئىكەنغۇ ھىجران،
يەر دەسسەپ يۈرسەممۇ، مەن ئادا بولدۇم.

خورلىمىغىن، مېنىڭمۇ ئۆز ئېلىم بار.
خەلقىم ئوخشاش غەرەزسىز ساپ دىلىم بار.
گاچا دېمە، بۇلبۇل بىلەن بەسلىشىپ،
سۇلار بىلەن سۆزلەشكۇدەك تىلىم بار.

Vocabulary سۆزلۈك

Vocabulary is given according to the Uyghur alphabetical order. The right column precedes the left column on each page.

weakness	ئاجىزلىق
to decrease in number	ئازايماق
to preserve, take good care of	ئاسرىماق
to increase	ئاشماق
to turn white	ئاقارماق
to flow, to leak	ئاقماق
rubbish	ئەخلەت
member	ئەزا
to capture (take prisoner)	ئەسىر ئالماق
to follow	ئەگەشمەك
to put out for sale, to sell, to peddle	بازارغا سالماق
during this time	بۇ جەرياندا
kidney	بۆرەك
alfalfa	بېدە
to be disturbed, to be concerned	بىئارام بولماق
a lot	بىرمۇنچە
to fit	پاتماق
to have good effect	پايدا قىلماق
useful, beneficial	پايدىلىق
to be on a diet	پەرھىز تۇتماق
gloves	پەلەي
badminton	پەي توپ
opportunity	پۇرسەت
whole	پۈتۈن
tug of war (game)	تارتىشما

sequence	تەرتىپ
fortunately	تەلەيگە يارىشا
to recommend	تەۋسىيە قىلماق
to fill	تولدۇرماق
fur hat	تۇماق
folk medicine	تىبابەت
schedule, chart	جەدۋەل
emergency room	جىددىي قۇتقۇزۇش بۆلۈمى
to call	چاقىرماق
clean of dust	چاڭ - توزاڭدىن خالىي
tennis	چويلا توپ
wrestling	چېلىشىش
to endure, be able to stand	چىدىماق
to dip into	چىلىماق
to be insulted, to be humiliated	خارلانماق
humiliation	خورلۇق
tightrope walking	دارۋازلىق
stain, dirt, filth	داغ
to treat	داۋالىماق
to pay attention	دىققەت قىلماق
mental state	روھىي ھالەت
prescription	رېتسېپ
to pay attention to, to comply with, to observe	رىئايە قىلماق
to poison	زەھەرلىمەك
intellect, intelligence	زېھىن

related	مۇناسىۋەتلىك
shoulders	مۈرە
temperament	مىجەز
to breathe	نەپەس ئالماق
advice	نەسىھەت
to sign in (at a hospital)	نومۇر ئالماق
to produce; to obtain	ھاسىل قىلماق
to pass out	ھوشىدىن كەتمەك
the (government) authorities	ھۆكۈمەت ئەمەلدارلىرى
nutritional component	ئوزۇقلۇق تەركىبى
to give an injection	ئوكۇل سالماق
to be common, to become widespread	ئومۇملاشماق
stream	ئۆستەڭ
to measure	ئۆلچىمەك
fertility; productivity	ئۈنۈمدارلىق
careful, cautious	ئېھتىياتچان
to use	ئىستېمال قىلماق
if it is possible	ئىلاجى بولسا
pillow	ياستۇق
peppermint	يالپۇز
wild	ياۋا
basement	يەر ئاستى ئۆيى
to win	يەڭمەك
air	يەل
to develop a fungus infection	يەل تېشىش
blanket	يوتقان
infectious, contagious	يۇقۇملۇق
to wash	يۇماق
cough	يۆتەل
to happen	يۈز بەرمەك
to lose	يېڭىلمەك
to throb; to give a sharp, stabbing pain	زىڭىلدىماق
to become yellow	سارغايماق
industrial factory	سانائەت زاۋۇتى
jumping	سەكرىمەك
insurance	سۇغۇرتا
curing, healing	شىپالىق
ability, skill	قابىلىيەت
barren land	قاقاسلىق
blood pressure	قان بېسىمى
tools, weapons	قورال
lamb's skin	قوزا تېرىسى
to sacrifice	قۇربان بېرىش
sand therapy	قۇم بىلەن داۋالاش
an itch	قىچىشىش
a stick, bat	كالتەك
baseball	كالتەك توپ
to be discriminated	كەمستىلمەك
to increase	كۆپەيمەك
to lift	كۆتۈرمەك
to move	كۆچمەك
to become green, to go moldy	كۆكەرمەك
to want	كۆڭۈل تارتماق
to feel nauseous	كۆڭۈل ئېلىشماق\ ئاينىماق
to become wider	كېڭەيمەك
bed sheet	كىرلىك
salary	مائاش
mattress	ماتراس
strength, vigor	ماغدۇر
oil; gas	ماي
exercise; operation	مەشغۇلات
country	مەملىكەت
a measure word for land area	مو
competition	مۇسابىقە

ساغلاملىق دورا دۇكىنى
健康 药店
经营项目:中成药 化学药制剂 抗生素 各种保健品 监督电话: 6753809 联系电话: 133197938

李映芳口腔诊所
نەفس
چىش
سىلىش
داۋالاش
ئورنى

ئونىنچى دەرس

CHAPTER TEN

ئۇيغۇر جەمئىيىتىدە

IN UYGHUR SOCIETY

IN THIS CHAPTER

Functions

- Making assumptions
- Describing important life events
- Comparing Uyghur and American weddings: then and now
- Discussing concepts of هالال and هارام
- Describing some challenges of modern Uyghur society
- Expressing condolences
- Expressing 'supposedly'

Grammar

- The suffix -مىكىن
- Another use of the word گەپ
- Another use of the conditional
- The construction "if only" in Uyghur
- Connecting clauses with -غان/-قان/-گەن/-كەن + -لىق/-لىك + possessive + -نى
- The suffix -مىش

In this chapter, you will learn about social life in Xinjiang. Through the conversations, reading passages, video clips, and excerpts from John's diary contained in this chapter, you will learn about traditional Uyghur weddings (نىكاھ توي) and accompany John as he compares and contrasts this to a modern wedding which he attends in Urumchi. You will also learn about some social issues which plague Xinjiang, such as قىمار ئويناش, نەشە چېكىش , ئەيدىز, etc. Later on in the chapter, you will join John as he pays his respects at a Uyghur funeral ceremony and learns how to express condolences in Uyghur.

Exercise 1: The most important event in my life...

1. ھاياتىمىزدا بىزگە ئەڭ چوڭ تەسىر كۆرسەتكەن ئىشلار قايسى؟
2. ھاياتىڭىزدىكى ئەڭ مۇھىم ئىشنى تەپسىلىيرەك سۆزلەپ بېقىڭ.
بۇ ئىش سىزنىڭ ھاياتىڭىزغا قانداق تەسىر كۆرسەتتى؟

Exercise 2: جوننىڭ يەنە بىر ھەيرانلىقى

Exercise 2.1:  Read John's letter to Ekber, and answer the questions that follow. The provided words and expressions before the questions will help you to understand the passage better.

سالام ئەكبەر:

ياخشى تۇرىۋاتامسىز؟ قارىغاندا مەن يەنىلا خەت يېزىشتەك كونا ئەنئەنىنى تاشلىيالمايدىغان ئوخشايمەن. دوستلىرىمنىڭ مېنى "قەدىمي جون" دەپ مازاق قىلىشى بىكار ئەمەسكەن.

شىنجاڭغا كەلگىنىمگىمۇ بىر نەچچە ئاي بوپتۇ. ئۇيغۇر جەمئىيىتىنىڭ بەزى ئىشلىرىنى بىز ئامېرىكىلىقلار ھەرقانچە قىلساقمۇ چۈشىنەلمەيدىكەنمىز. ئۇيغۇرلار راستىنلا ئاجايىپ خەلق ئىكەن!

بۈرناكۈن بۇ يەردىكى ئۇيغۇر دوستلىرىم مېنى بىر تويغا ئېلىپ بارماقچى بولدى. مەن ئۆمرۈمدە ئۇيغۇرلارنىڭ توينى كۆرۈپ باقمىغاچقا، بەك قىزىقتىم. شۇنىڭ بىلەن ماڭىمۇ بىر توي باغىقى بەردى. باغاقىقا قارىسام، توي شەنبە كۈنى چۈشتىن كېيىن سائەت تۆتتە باشلىنىدىكەن. سائەت تۆتتە باغاقتا ئېيتىلغان "شاھ سەنەم" رېستورانىغا بارسام، رېستوراندا ھېچكىم يوق. "خاتا كېلىپ قالغان ئوخشايمەن" دەپ كۈتكۈچى قىزلاردىن سورىسام، توي بولىدىغان رېستوران مۇشۇ ئىكەن. باغاقنى كۆرسەتسەم ئۇلار كۈلۈپ كېتىپ تويىنىڭ سائەت يەتتىدە باشلىنىدىغانلىقىنى* ئېيتتى. شۇنىڭ بىلەن مەن ئۈچ سائەت كۈتتۈم. كېيىن ئۇقسام، توي باغاقلىرىغا "سائەت تۆتتە" ياكى "سائەت بەشتە" دەپ يېزىلغان بىلەن ھەممە ئۇيغۇرلار سائەت يەتتىدە ياكى سەككىزدە كېلىدىكەن.

ئۇيغۇرلارنىڭ تويى بەك قىزىق بولىدىكەن، ناخشا، ئۇسسۇل، دىسكو ۋە ياۋروپاچە تانسا توي تۈگىگىچە داۋام قىلىدىكەن. ئەرلەر ۋە ئاياللار ئىككى تەرەپتە ئايرىم ئولتۇرىدىكەن، ئامېرىكىدەك ئەر ئاياللار ئارىلاش ئولتۇرمايدىكەن. تويدا مەن ھەيران قالغان ئىشلارنىڭ بىرى ئۇيغۇرلارنىڭ ھاراق ئىچىشى بولدى. ئۇلار ئىچكەن ھاراق بېنزىندىنمۇ ئاچچىق، ئەمما ئەرلەرنىڭ كۆپى ھاراق ئىچتى. ئۆزلىرىنى مۇسۇلمان ھېسابلايدىغان ئۇيغۇرلارنىڭ ھاراق ئىچىدىغانلىقىنى زادىلا چۈشىنەلمىدىم. لېكىن ئۇلاردىن "ئۇيغۇرلار چوشقا يەمدۇ؟" دەپ سورىسا، ئۇلار بەك خاپا بولىدۇ. يەنە بىر ئىش، توي ئۈستىلىدىكى تاماقلار بەك كۆپ. ھەر بىر ئۈستەلدە ئوندىن ئادەم ئولتۇرىدىكەن، لېكىن ئۈستەلدىكى تاماقلارنى يىگىرمە ئادەممۇ يەپ بولالمايدۇ. تاماقلار ئارىسىدا "باچكا كاۋاپ" دەپ بىر تاماق بار ئىكەن. ئۇيغۇرلار كەپتەر باللىرىنى بوغۇزلاپ كاۋاپ قىلىدىكەن. ئۇلار "تىنچلىق سىمۋۇلى" دەپ قارىلىدىغان كەپتەرنى كاۋاپ قىلىپ يېيىشنى ياخشى كۆرىدىكەن. مەن بەك خاپا بولدۇم. مەن خاپا بولغان يەنە بىر ئىش - ئۇيغۇرلارنىڭ ئىسراپچىلىقى بولدى. دوستلىرىمنىڭ دەپ بېرىشىچە، توي ئۈستىلىدىن ئېشىپ قالغان تاماقلارنى ئەخلەت ساندۇقىغا تۆكىدىكەن. "ئېشىپ قالغان تاماقلارنى نېمىشقا ئۆيگە ئەپكەتمەيسىلەر؟" دەپ سورىسام، ئۇلار "باشقىلار زاڭلىق قىلىدۇ" دەيدۇ. ئۇيغۇرلارنىڭ نامرات تۇرۇپ بۇنداق ئىسراپخورلۇق قىلىشىنى زادىلا چۈشىنەلمىدىم.

* This grammar is explained later in this chapter

invitation	باغاق
gas	بېنزىن
to slaughter	بوغۇزلىماق
peace	تىنچلىق
wastefulness	ئىسراپچىلىق

a garbage can	ئەخلەت ساندۇقى
to throw out, pour out	تۆكمەك
to make fun of	زاڭلىق قىلماق/ مازاق قىلماق
to pay attention	ئېتىبار بەرمەك

1. نېمىشقا جوننىڭ دوستلىرى ئۇنى "قەدىمي جون " دەپ مازاق قىلدۇ؟
2. نېمىشقا جون رېستوراندا ئۈچ سائەت ساقلايدۇ؟
3. نېمىشقا مېھمانلار تاماقنى يەپ تۈگىتەلمەيدۇ؟
4. تويدا ئېشىپ قالغان تاماقلار نېمە قىلىنىدۇ؟
5. نېمىشقا جون ئۇيغۇرلارنىڭ باچكا كاۋىپىنى يېگىنىنى كۆرۈپ خاپا بولدۇ؟

Exercise 2.2:  Skim the letter on the preceding page one more time. What are some things John noticed at the wedding? Complete the list, following the example. Add at least four more observations and mark √ according to whether you think John's attitude towards a particular observation was positive or negative.

John's observations	*Positive*	*Negative*
ئۇيغۇرلار تويغا كېچىكىپ كېلىدۇ.		√

Exercise 2.3:  The following words have been taken from the letter on the preceding page. For each word, circle its synonym on the left.

تەكلىپنامە خەت	باغاق
تاشلاندۇق ئىسراپچىلىق	ئەخلەت
ماي نېفىت	بېنزىن
قۇش كەپتەر	باچكا

Exercise 3: مەدەنىيەت پەرقلىرى

Exercise 3.1: تۆۋەندىكى سوئاللارنى مۇزاكىرە قىلىڭلار.

1. چەت ئەلگە بارغاندا تويلارغا قاتنىشىپ باقتىڭىزمۇ؟ بارغان بولسىڭىز، شۇ تويىنى تەسۋىرلەپ بېرەمسىز؟
2. بۇ تويدا سىزنى نېمىلەر ھەيران قالدۇردى؟
3. سىلەرنىڭ مەدەنىيىتىڭلاردا تويلار قانداق ئۆتىدۇ؟

Exercise 3.2: Discuss the following question as a group.

ئۇيغۇرلارنىڭ توي ئادەتلىرى بىلەن سىزنىڭ مەدەنىيىتىڭىزدىكى توي ئادەتلىرىنى سېلىشتۇرۇڭ: سىزنىڭچە نېمىلەرنى قوبۇل قىلسا بولىدۇ، نېمىلەرنى قوبۇل قىلماسلىق كېرەك؟

Exercise 4: ئۇيغۇرلاردىكى مەيخورلۇق

Exercise 4.1: After the wedding, John talks to Yasin. Listen to the first part of their conversation and answer the questions that follow.

1. تويدا جون ئۇيغۇرلارنىڭ قايسى ئادىتىگە ھەيران قالدۇ؟
2. ئۇيغۇرلار ئادەتتە تويدا قانداق ئىچىملىكلەر ئىچىلىدۇ؟ ئامېرىكىلىقلارچۇ؟
3. نېمە توغرۇلۇق سۆزلەشكەندە جون قازاق دوستىنى ئەسلەيدۇ ؟
4. نېمىشقا ئۇلار رۇسلار بىلەن خەنزۇلارنى تىلغا ئالىدۇ* ؟

---

* تىلغا ئالماق: to mention

Exercise 4.2: Listen to the passage one more time and tell what the following expressions and phrases mean.

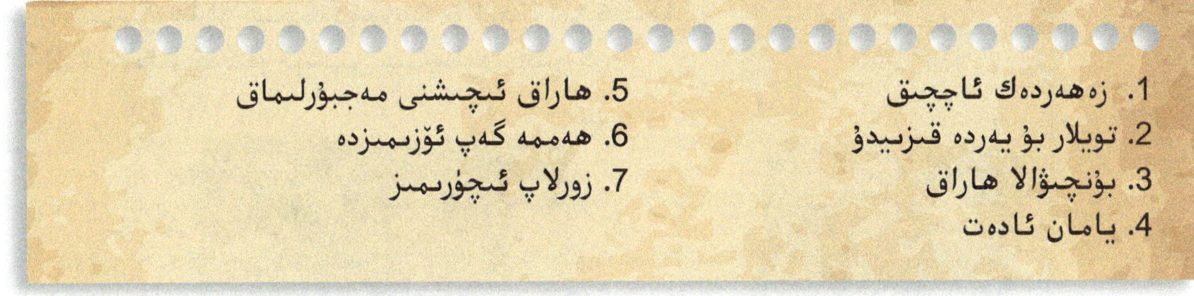

Exercise 4.3:  Do you agree with the following statement? List some arguments to support your view.

Agree and Disagree

قوشۇلىمەن	قوشۇلمايمەن
توغرا! مەنمۇ شۇنداق ئويلايمەن.	ياق، بۇ گەپكە قوشۇلالمايمەن.
بۇ (گەپ) گېپىڭىز توغرا، مەن قوشۇلىمەن.	ئۇنداق دېسەك بولماس.
شۇنداق، بۇ گەپنىڭ جېنى بار.	بۇ گەپكە قوشۇلساق بولمايدۇ.
ھەئە، توپ توغرا ئېيتتىڭىز!	ياق، ئۇنداق ئەمەس.
پىكرىڭىز ئورۇنلۇق.	بۇ گەپ ئاقمايدۇ.
مېنىڭچە چوقۇم شۇنداق.	يوق گەپنى قىلماڭلار.

Exercise 4.4: Using the phases on the preceding page, say if you agree or disagree with the following two statements. Explain why.

1. بىرسى ھاراق ئىچسە، سىزنىڭمۇ ئىچكۈڭىز كېلىدۇ.
2. ئادەملەر كەپتەر گۆشىنى يېمەسلىكى كېرەك.

Exercise 4.5:  Now practice the conversation with your partner. Read your line first, then try to look at your partner when you say it - not the text!

جون: ياسىن، تۈنۈگۈنكى تويغا تەكلىپ قىلغىنىڭلار ئۈچۈن كۆپ رەھمەت سىلەرگە، بەك كۆڭۈللۈك بولدى...

ياسىن: ھە، سىزگە ياققان بولسا، ياخشى بوپتۇ... تويلار بۇ يەردە قىزىيدۇ...

جون: تويدا مەن بىر نەرسىگە ھەيران قالدىم...

ياسىن: سىزنى تويدا نېمە ھەيران قالدۇردى؟

جون: ئۇيغۇرلارنىڭ ھاراق ئىچىشى....

ياسىن: سىلەردە تويدا ھاراق ئىچمەمدۇ؟

جون: ئىچىدۇ، ئەمما بۇنداق كۆپ ئەمەس... بىزدە ئادەتتە پىۋا بىلەن قىزىل ھاراق كۆپ ئىچىلىدۇ. بىراق تۈنۈگۈنكى تويدا قارىسام ھېلىقى زەھەردەك ئاچچىق ھاراقنى تازا ئىچىدىكەن. مەن تېخى مۇسۇلمانلار بۇنچىلىك ھاراق ئىچمەيدۇ دەپ ئويلاپتىمەن...

ياسىن: توغرا، ئەسلىدە بۇنچىۋالا* ھاراق ئىچىلمىسە ياخشى بولاتتى، ئەمما ھازىر بۇ يامان ئادەت بولۇپ قالدى. بىزگە بۇ ئادەت خىتايلاردىن ئۆتتىمىكىن...

جون: ئامېرىكىدا مېنىڭ بىر قازاق دوستۇم بار ئىدى، ئۇمۇ "ھاراق ئىچىش ئادىتى بىزگە رۇسلاردىن كەلدى" دېگەن. شۇ چاغدا مەن "رۇسلار سىلەرنى ھاراق ئىچىشكە مەجبۇر قىلغانمۇ؟" دەپ سورىسام، ئۇ كۈلۈپ كېتىپ: "ياق، بىز ئۇلارنىڭ ئىچكىنىنى كۆرۈپ ئىچىشنى باشلىدۇق" دېگەنتى.

ياسىن: توغرا دەيسىز، ھېچ كىم بىزنى مەجبۇرلىمىدى. ھەممە گەپ ئۆزىمىزدە... بۇ ئادەتتىن قۇتۇلساق ياخشى بولاتتى...

جون: ئۆتكەن ئاي مەن بىر ئولتۇرۇشقا بارغانتىم. ئۇ يەردىمۇ ساۋاقداشلار بىر نەچچە بوتۇلكا ھاراق كۆتۈرۈپ كەپتۇ. مەن "بۈگۈن ھاراق ئىچمىسەك بولامدىكىن" دېسەم، بىر دوستۇم: "ھاراق بولمىسا كۆڭۈل ئاچقىلى بولامدۇ؟" دەپ كۈلۈپ كەتتى. شۇ كۈنى ئىچمەي دېسەممۇ، ئىچىشكە مەجبۇر بولدۇم...

ياسىن: شۇنداق، ئىچمىگەنلەرنى ئۆزىمىز زورلاپ ئىچۈرىمىز...

---

* بۇنچىۋالا: so many

1 Making Assumptions Using the Suffix مىكىن- 'I suppose, I gather'

In the dialogue you see a verb ئۆتتىمىكىن (ئۆت+تى+مىكىن)

The suffix مىكىن- is originally a contraction of the question particle مۇ- and the evidential ئىكەن, which you have already encountered.

This suffix is used when the speaker makes an assumption based on a considerable amount of evidence. In other words, when this suffix is used, there is a high likelihood that the action in the sentence actually occured. While there is no single way to translate this suffix into English, it is roughly equivalent to adding a phrase like 'most likely' or 'I gather', or the word 'probably'. Here are some examples:

ئاڭلىسام تۈنۈگۈن ئۇنىڭ مىجەزى بولماي قاپتۇ، ئۇ تويغا بارمىدىمىكىن.
I heard that he wasn't feeling well yesterday, so I gather
he didn't go to the wedding.

OR: I heard that he wasn't feeling well yesterday, so he probably did not go to the wedding.

I gather he ate the food. .ئۇ تاماقنى يەپ بولدىمىكىن
Yasin most likely went to the doctor. .ياسىن دوختۇرغا باردىمىكىن

Note that since this suffix originally contained the question particle, the question particle reverts to its normal position when this suffix is used in conjunction with the third person of the present/future tense. This is to differentiate it from the past tense, with which it would otherwise be identical. In other words, in the present/future the question particle مۇ'- comes right after the verb root, followed by د- (a shortened form of the third person suffix دۇ-); then lastly the word ىكەن- (ئىكەن) is added.

هاۋا يامان سوغۇق، ئەتە قار ياغامدىكىن.
The weather's freezing! It'll probably snow tomorrow.
ئەنۋەر دادىسى بىلەن كېلەمدىكىن.
I assume that Enver will come with his father.
پىيادە بارساق بولامدىكىن.
I suppose we can just go by foot.

Exercise 5: ئەتە بارساق بولامدىكىن...

Exercise 5.1:  How would you translate the following sentences into Uyghur using Grammar Point 1?

1. It is very cold outside. I suppose we will go by bus.

____

2. Maybe he will come with his friend.

____

3. Look at these clouds; I suppose it will rain.

____

4. I am not sure if he will attend the meeting.

____

5. They will arrive late, so I suppose they will stay at the hotel.

____

Exercise 5.2:  What would you say next? Use the suffix مىكىن- to create a second sentence that follows logically from the first one. If you see the symbol Ø after the sentence provided, write a negative sentence.

يامغۇر يېغىۋاتىدىغۇ.______________________________؟

سائەت ئون بوپتۇ. (ø)______________________________؟

ئۇنىڭ ئانىسى كەپتۇ. (ø) ______________________________؟

بۈگۈن ياسىنىنىڭ تۇغۇلغان كۈنى. ______________________________؟

ئۇنىڭ ئايالى ئاغرىپ قاپتۇ. ______________________________؟

ئۇ هاراق ئىچىۋالدىم دېگەنتى. (ø) ______________________________؟

2 Using the Word گەپ

As you know, the word گەپ means 'a talk', 'words'. However, it also has other meanings such as 'a thing', 'matter', or 'question'. In the dialogue (Exercise 4.5) it appears in the following context:

توغرا دەيسىز، ھېچ كىم بىزنى مەجبۇرلىمىدى. ھەممە گەپ ئۆزىمىزدە...
Yes, you're right. No one forced us (to drink); it's our fault.

Look at more examples:

ھەي بالام، ھەممە گەپ سەندە (ئۆزۈڭدە)، تاماكا چەكمەيمەن دېسەڭ،
ھېچ كىم سېنى زورلىمايدىغۇ!
My boy, it's entirely up to you. If you say you don't smoke,
no one's going to force you!

گەپ ئۆزەمدە... كىم مېنى شۇ تويغا بار دەپتۇ. بارمىسام بۇ ئىشمۇ چىقمايتتى...
It's my fault... Whoever said I should go to that wedding! If I hadn't gone, none
of this would have happened...

گەپ سەندە ئەمەس، گەپ مەندە... پۇلۇم بولسا شۇ ئەھۋالغا قالمايتتۇق.
It's not your fault, it's mine... if I had the money, I wouldn't be stuck
in this situation.

گەپ ياشتا ئەمەس، گەپ باشتا.
It's a question of maturity, not age. (lit. "The matter is not one of age,
but of the head.") –Uyghur proverb

گەپ پۇلدا ئەمەس، دوستۇم، گەپ كۆڭۈلدە.
It's not a matter of money, my friend; it's a matter of desire.

3 Expressing Wishes Using Conditionals

In the dialogue (Exercise 4.5) you see the following constructions which employ the conditional mood.

ھاراق ئىچىلمىسە ياخشى بولاتتى.
It would be nice if there were no drinking.
(lit. "If alcohol were not drunk it would have been nice.")
بۇ ئادەتتىن قۇتۇلساق ياخشى بولاتتى...
It would be great if we got rid of this bad habit.

Depending on context, this construction is the equivalent of either the English 'would be' or 'would have been', however the habitual past is used in both sentences. This emphasizes that the idea expressed in the first clause is, in reality, not the case. Look at more examples:

ھاراق ئىچىلمىسە بۇ ئىش چىقمايتتى.
If no one had been drinking, (lit. "if alcohol were not drunk")
this wouldn't have happened.
ئانام بارسا، مەنمۇ باراتتىم.
If my mother had gone I would have gone, too.
ئۇلار بالدۇرراق كەلسە قاراڭغۇ چۈشمەستىن بۇرۇن قايتاتتۇق.
I wish they would come earlier so that we could leave before it gets dark.

Note that the verb بولماق is frequently used in these constructions to express approval, as you have seen on numerous previous occasions. Look at some more examples:

بالام تاماكا چېكىشنى (ھاراق ئىچىشنى) تاشلىسا بولاتتى.
It would be nice if my kid would quit smoking (drinking).
يامغۇر ياغمىسا بولاتتى.
It would be great if it stopped raining.
بۇ بىنا چېقىلمىسا بولاتتى.
It would be great if this building weren't torn down.

4 Using the "if only" Construction

If the verb بولماق (see the Grammar Point 3) is used in the simple past tense (not the habitual), these constructions emphasize urgency or desire, much like the English phrase 'if only'.

ئۇ ئۈلگۈرۈپ بارسا بولدى. If only he could make it on time.

دوختۇر ۋاقتىدا كەلسە بولدى. If only the doctor could come on time.

There is also another word كاشكى in Uyghur, used when a past event did not go as planned. In these situations, the speaker emphasizes his or her regret by putting كاشكى at the beginning of the statement. This is like saying 'if only' in English, and following it with a verb in the past perfect. Look at the following examples:

كاشكى ئادىل بۇ گەپنى بالدۇرراق دېگەن بولسا (ئىدى).
If only Adil had told us about this earlier.

كاشكى پۇلۇم بولسا, نېمە قىلىشنى ئۆزۈم بىلەتتىم.
If only I had money, I would know what to do.

Exercise 6: پۇلۇم بولسا، ماشىنا ئالاتتىم

Exercise 6.1:  Translate the following sentences into English on a separate sheet of paper.

1. بىر يامغۇر يېغىۋەتسە بولاتتى.
2. كاشكى ئوغلۇم بولسا، بۇ كۆنلەرگە قالماس ئىدىم.
3. بالىمىز ئامان - ئېسەن كېلىۋالسىلا بولدى.
4. بېلەتنى ۋاقتىدا ئېلىۋالساقلا بولدى.
5. بالىمىزنى ساقچى ئېلىپ كەتتى، بۇرۇنراق كەلسىڭىز كاشكى.
6. قېنى، شۇ چاغدا هازىرقى كۆچۈم بولسا ئىدى.

Exercise 6.2:  Based on the examples above, write three statements about your wishes for the future on a seperate sheet of paper.

Exercise 6.3:  Based on the examples above, write three statements about some regrets you have.

Halal and Haram for Uyghurs

In every religion, there are some things which are considered clean and some which are considered unclean. In Islam, things which are considered ritually clean are referred to as halal, whereas things which are ritually unclean are called haram. Among devout Muslims, much attention is paid to avoiding things or actions which are considered haram. The Qur'an and hadith (collected sayings of Prophet Muhammad and his followers) note some things which are universally haram across all Islamic sects and cultures. The most well-known of these is pork, which is almost never consumed even by the least strict of Uyghur Muslims. There are also some things which are considered haram by some Muslims and not by others, largely because of debate among scholars of Islamic law as to the scriptural foundations of various prohibitions. Often, these are said to fall under the category of makru – things which are not strictly forbidden, but are advised against.

Exercise 7:  Now read the second part of the dialogue between John and Yasin and tell if the statements which follow are true or false.

جون: مەن يەنە بىر نەرسىنى چۈشەنمىدىم. نېمىشقا ئۇيغۇرلار كەپتەر بالىسىنىڭ گۆشىنى يەيدۇ؟
كەپتەرنى تىنچلىق سىمۋولى دەيدىغۇ؟
ياسىن: ئۇ دېگەن خەلقئارالىق چۈشەنچە. ئۇيغۇرلار كەپتەرنى ئۇنداق چۈشەنمەيدۇ.
جون: دېمەك ئۇيغۇرلار تىنچلىقنى ياخشى كۆرمەمدۇ؟
ياسىن: ياق، ئۇيغۇرلار تىنچلىقنى سۆيىدۇ. ئەمما ئۇيغۇرلار كەپتەرنى دورىلىق گۆش ئورنىدا يەيدۇ.
جون: ئۇنداقتا سىلەر كەپتەرنى تىنچلىقنىڭ سىمۋولى دەپ قارىمامسىلەر؟
ياسىن: ياق. بىز كەپتەرنى پەقەت بىر تۈرلۈك قۇش دەپلا چۈشىنىمىز. خۇدا ئۇنى بىزگە ھالال گۆش قىلىپ بېكىتكەن. كېيىنكى قېتىم مەن سىزنى كەپتەر شورپىسى بىلەن مېھمان قىلاي.
جون: ياق، ياق. مەن كەپتەر گۆشى يېمەيمەن. مېنىڭ ئات گۆشى يەپ باققۇم بار.
ياسىن: چاتاق يوق. ئەمىسە ئەتە كەچتە ئات گۆشىدە ئەتكەن نارىن يەيلى!
جون: بولىدۇ. رەھمەت سىزگە.

1. Uyghurs do not consider the pigeon to be a symbol of peace. _______
2. In Uyghur culture pigeon meat is considered to be the healthiest meat. _______
3. John regrets that he did not try pigeon meat at the wedding. _______
4. John wants to try horse meat. _______

5 Joining Clauses with:

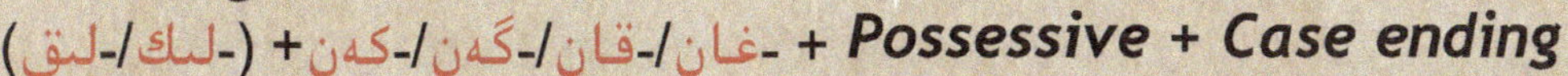

(لىق-/لىك-) +كەن-/گەن-/قان-/غان- + ***Possessive + Case ending***

You should remember from earlier lessons that Uyghur has three verb forms (often called 'participles') which act as adjectives, and are used to form what we might translate into English as relative clauses. You may also remember that each of these forms ends with كەن-/قان-/گەن-/غان-.

Continuous Participle	Present-Future Participle	Past Participle
ىۋاتقان/ -ۋاتقان-	ىدىغان/ -يدىغان-	غان/ -گەن/ -قان/ -كەن-

These forms can be used as nouns (called 'gerunds') in order to join two clauses together. When used in this way, they perform the function of the English word "that" in sentences like "I know that he came."

The phrase 'that he came' appears in the two following forms: كەلگەنلىكى or كەلگىنى.
These two forms are totally interchangeable in this context.
Look at the following example:

ئۇنىڭ كەلگىنىنى (كەلگەنلىكىنى) بىلىمەن.

I knew that he came.

As you can see in the chart below, all the gerund forms are built with this same basic formula:

Case Ending	Possessive Ending (corresponds to the subject)	(optional)	Gerund Ending	Verb Stem
نى، -گە/ -غا، ...-	ى، -ىم، ...-	لىك/-لىق-	غان/ -گەن/ -قان/-كەن- ىدىغان/ -يدىغان- ىۋاتقان/ -ۋاتقان-	كەل-، بار-، ...

You may have already noticed that one major difference between Uyghur and English is that Uyghur tends to treat a lot of its verb as nouns; they can take personal possessive endings and case endings just like nouns, and they often take the place of a noun in a sentence. This can seem daunting at first, but the nouns fit into Uyghur sentences in much the same way as their English counterparts do. Let's compare the example sentence above in English and Uyghur with a simpler sentence:

I know his secret. ئۇنىڭ سىرىنى بىلىمەن.

I know that he came. ئۇنىڭ كەلگىنىنى (كەلگەنلىكىنى) بىلىمەن.

5 Joining Clauses with:
-غان/-قان/-گەن/-كەن + (-لىك/-لىق) + Possessive + Case ending (cont'd.)

Just as the subordinate clause in English, introduced by the word 'that', comes after the verb like a normal object (for example 'his secret'), so too does the Gerund كەلگىنىنى\ كەلگەنلىكىنى in the corresponding Uyghur phrase. To get a better feeling for how this type of subordinate clause is formed in Uyghur, look at the following examples and their translations.

The past gerund: -غان/-گەن/-قان/-كەن

ئۇنىڭ كەتكىنىنى (كەتكەنلىكىنى) ئۆزۈم كۆردۈم. I saw that he left.
مېنىڭ بۇ تويغا بارغىنىمنى (بارغانلىقىمنى) ھېچ كىم بىلمەيدۇ.
No one knows that I went to this wedding.

The present/future gerund: -دىغان/ -دىغانلىق

Be careful, as in translating this into English we may use the simple present, the present progressive, or the future. What is most important it that the action expressed is constant, ongoing, or has yet happened by the time of the verb in the main clause:

ئۇنىڭ ھاراق ئىچىدىغىنىنى (ئىچىدىغانلىقىنى) بىلمەيدىكەنمەن.
I didn't know that he drinks alcohol.
ئۇنىڭ ئەتە بېيجىڭغا بارىدىغىنىنى (بارىدىغانلىقىنى) ئاڭلىماپتىمەن.
I didn't hear that he is going to Beijing tomorrow.

Note that when we have a verb ending in a vowel, we add ي- before the ending just as in the Present/Future Participle.

ئۇنىڭ سوئال سورايدىغىنىنى (سورايدىغانلىقىنى) بىلگەنتىم.
I knew he will ask a question.
بۇ بالىنىڭ كۆپ سۆزلەيدىغىنىنى (سۆزلەيدىغانلىقىنى) ئاڭلىغانتىم.
I had heard that this child talks a lot.

The present continuous gerund: -ۋاتقان\-ىۋاتقان\ -ۋاتقانلىق\ -ىۋاتقانلىق

ئۇنىڭ بۇ يەرگە كېلىۋاتقىنىنى (كېلىۋاتقانلىقىنى) نەدىن ئاڭلىدىڭىز؟

From where did you hear that he's coming here?
مېنىڭ ھاراق ئىچىۋاتقىنىمنى (ئىچىۋاتقانلىقىمنى) نەدە كۆردىڭىز؟
Where did you see me drinking alcohol?
ئەخمەتنىڭ بۇ زاۋۇتتا ئىشلەۋاتقىنىنى (ئىشلەۋاتقانلىقىنى) ئاكامدىن ئاڭلىدىم.
I heard that Exmet is working in this factory from my older brother.

5 Joining Clauses with:
(-لىق/-لىك) + -غان/-قان/-گەن/-كەن + Possessive + Case ending (cont'd.)

Note that as in the continuous gerund, if the verb stem ends with a consonant the vowel ى- is added, whereas if the verb ends in a vowel we maintain that vowel without reducing it (i.e. ئىشلەۋاتقان، ئاڭلاۋاتقان).

As with their corresponding participle endings, to make the negative forms of the gerunds, simply add the suffix -مە /-ما- between the verb stem and the gerund suffix.

ئانامنىڭ كەلمىگىنىنى (كەلمىگەنلىكىنى) ئاڭلاپ كۆڭلۈم يېرىم بولدى.
I heard that he didn't come and my heart was broken.
ئۇنىڭ گۆش يېمەيدىغىنىنى (يېمەيدىغانلىقىنى) بىلمەپتىمەن.
I didn't know that he didn't eat meat.

Finally, though all the examples above have featured gerunds in subordinate clauses with the accusative suffix نى-, this is not the case in every subordinate clause. For example, the verb ئىشەنمەك 'to believe' normally takes an object in the dative case -گە/-كە/-غا/-قا. Therefore, any subordinate clause that is the object of this verb will also have to take the dative ending. For example:

ئۇنىڭ هاراق ئىچمەيدىغىنىغا (ئىچمەيدىغانلىقىغا) ئىشەنمەيمەن!
I don't believe he doesn't drink alcohol!

The extensive use of these gerunds in Uyghur may seem overwhelming at first, but they appear very frequently in Uyghur and they distinguish a beginner student from an intermediate or advanced speaker. Take care to practice using and understanding these forms, and refer to the examples in this section whenever you need to.

Exercise 8:  For each of the following sentences, form a subordinate clause using the verb in parentheses with the tense indicated. Use the Grammar Points on gerunds on the preceding pages. If you see the symbol Ø after the tense, make the subordinate clause negative.

1. ئۈنىڭ ماشىنا (ئالماق) (Past) ______________ ئاڭلىدىم.
2. مېنىڭ توي (قىلماق) (Past Ø) ______________ نەدىن بىلىسىز؟
3. هاراق (ئىچمەك) (Past) ______________ ئۆز كۆزۈم بىلەن كۆردۈم.
4. بۇ تويغا ئۈچ قوي (سويۇلماق) (Past) ______________ بىلمەن.
5. ئۈنىڭ هازىر بۇ كارخانىدا (ئىشلىمەك) (Present Continuous Ø) ______________ بىلمەيتمەن.
6. ياسىنىڭ (كەتمەك) (Present Continuous) ______________ ئۆزۈم كۆردۈم.
7. ئۈنىڭ بېيجىڭغا (بارماق) (Present-Future) ______________ كىمدىن ئاڭلىدىڭىز؟
8. ئادىلنىڭ توي (قىلماق) (Present-Future Ø) ______________ ئېنىق بىلەمسىز؟
9. ئۈنىڭ ناخشا (ئېيتماق) (Present-Future) ______________ مەن ئاللىبۇرۇن ئاڭلىغان.

Exercise 9: ئۇيغۇرلارنىڭ ئەنئەنىۋى نىكاھ تويلىرى

Exercise 9.1: تۆۋەندىكى سوئاللارنى مۇزاكىرە قىلىڭلار

1. سىز قانداق تويلارغا قاتناشقان؟ بۇ تويلارنىڭ قانداق ئوخشاش ۋە پەرقلىق تەرەپلىرى بار؟
2. سىزنىڭ مەدەنىيىتىڭىزدە نىكاھ تويلىرىغا ئائىت ئالاھىدە ئادەتلەر/مۇراسىملار بارمۇ؟
3. سىزنىڭ مەدەنىيىتىڭىزدە ئەنئەنىۋى تويلار قانداق باسقۇچلار بويىچە ئېلىپ بېرىلىدۇ؟
4. ئۇيغۇرلارنىڭ ئەنئەنىۋى نىكاھ تويلىرىنى قانداق تەسەۋۋۇر قىلىسىز؟

Exercise 9.2:  John wrote a blog entry about traditional Uyghur wedding ceremonies. Before reading it, translate the following words into English.

	يىرتماق		قاراشماق		سورۇن
	قولداش		كۆچۈرمەك		ئەلچى
	رازىلىق		دەسسىمەك		لايىق تاپماق

Exercise 9.3:  Look at the table below. Which concept or part of the wedding do these terms refer to? Match the phrases in the two columns.

to transfer the wedding (from bride's to groom's house)	چاي ئاپارماق
to greet the bride's family	نىكاھ ئوقۇتماق
to send the matchmaker	ئەلچى ئەۋەتمەك
a meal given for in-laws after the wedding	توي كۆچۈرمەك
to take a dowry to the bride's family	چىللاق
to recite the marriage vows	سالامغا بارماق

Exercise 9.4:  Number the following events 1-6 to indicate the order in which you think they take place during and leading up to a traditional Uyghur wedding. The first has been done for you.

1	ئەلچى ئەۋەتىش		نىكاھ ئوقۇتۇش
	توي كۆچۈرۈش		چىللاق
	سالامغا بېرىش		چاي ئاپىرىش

Exercise 9.5:  Read the following six excerpts from John's blog entry and answer each question that follows in English on a separate sheet of paper.

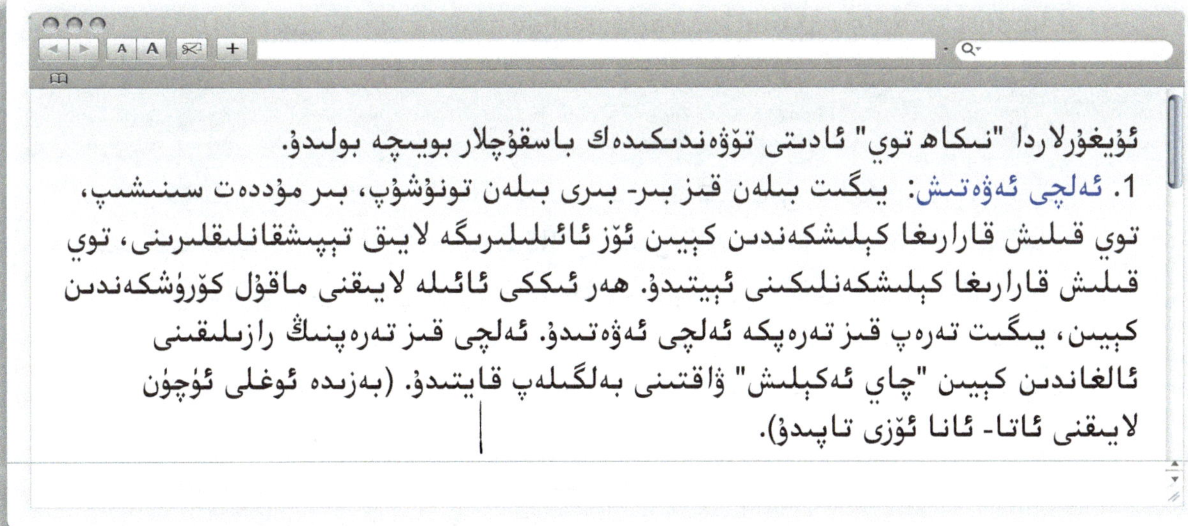
ئۇيغۇرلاردا "نىكاھ توي" ئادىتى تۆۋەندىكىدەك باسقۇچلار بويىچە بولىدۇ.
1. ئەلچى ئەۋەتىش: يىگىت بىلەن قىز بىر- بىرى بىلەن تونۇشۇپ، بىر مۇددەت سىنىشىپ، توي قىلىش قارارىغا كېلىشكەندىن كېيىن ئۆز ئائىلىلىرىگە لايىق تېپىشقانلىقلىرىنى، توي قىلىش قارارىغا كېلىشكەنلىكىنى ئېيتىدۇ. ھەر ئىككى ئائىلە لايىقنى ماقۇل كۆرۈشكەندىن كېيىن، يىگىت تەرەپ قىز تەرەپكە ئەلچى ئەۋەتىدۇ. ئەلچى قىز تەرەپنىڭ رازىلىقىنى ئالغاندىن كېيىن "چاي ئەكېلىش" ۋاقتىنى بەلگىلەپ قايتىدۇ. (بەزىدە ئوغلى ئۈچۈن لايىقنى ئاتا- ئانا ئۆزى تاپىدۇ).

1. Explain the ئەلچى ئەۋەتىش process. When do parents send the ئەلچى?

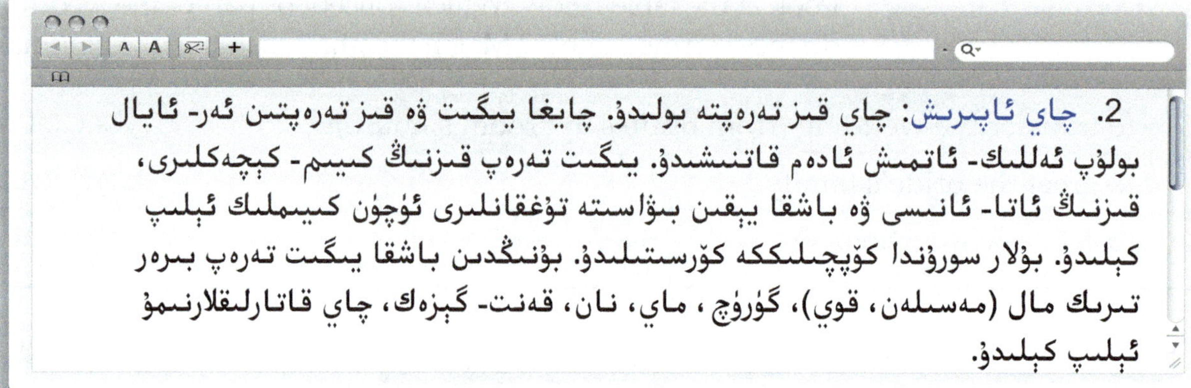

2. چاي ئاپىرىش: چاي قىز تەرەپتە بولىدۇ. چايغا يىگىت ۋە قىز تەرەپتىن ئەر- ئايال بولۇپ ئەللىك- ئاتمىش ئادەم قاتنىشىدۇ. يىگىت تەرەپ قىزنىڭ كىيىم- كېچەكلىرى، قىزنىڭ ئاتا- ئانىسى ۋە باشقا يېقىن بىۋاستە تۇغقانلىرى ئۈچۈن كىيىملىك ئېلىپ كېلىدۇ. بۇلار سورۇندا كۆپچىلىككە كۆرسىتىلىدۇ. بۇنىڭدىن باشقا يىگىت تەرەپ بىرەر تىرىك مال (مەسىلەن، قوي)، گۈرۈچ ، ماي، نان، قەنت- گېزەك، چاي قاتارلىقلارنىمۇ ئېلىپ كېلىدۇ.

2. Explain the چاي ئاپىرىش process. List all the items mentioned in the excerpt above which are crucial to it.

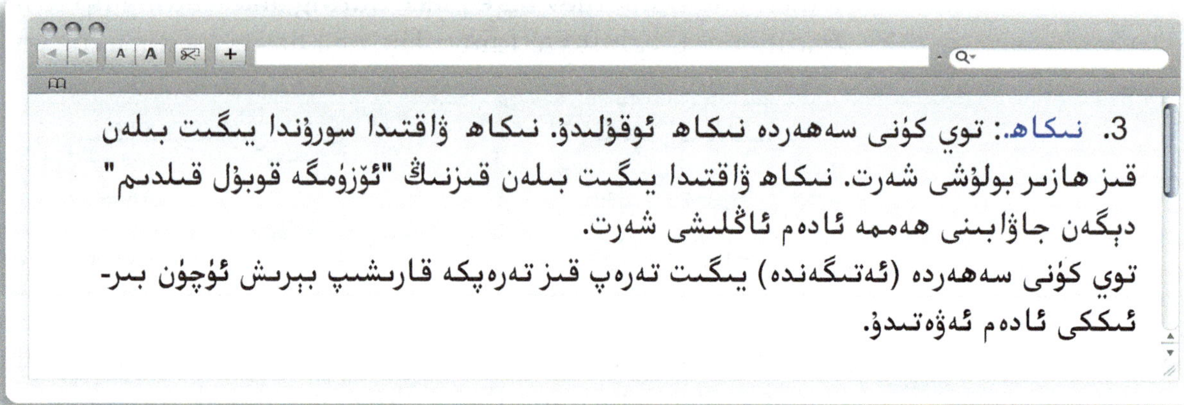

3. نىكاھ.: توي كۈنى سەھەردە نىكاھ ئوقۇلىدۇ. نىكاھ ۋاقتىدا سورۇندا يىگىت بىلەن قىز هازىر بولۇشى شەرت. نىكاھ ۋاقتىدا يىگىت بىلەن قىزنىڭ "ئۆزۈمگە قوبۇل قىلدىم" دېگەن جاۋابىنى ھەممە ئادەم ئاڭلىشى شەرت.
توي كۈنى سەھەردە (ئەتىگەندە) يىگىت تەرەپ قىز تەرەپكە قارىشىپ بېرىش ئۈچۈن بىر- ئىككى ئادەم ئەۋەتىدۇ.

3. What is the نىكاھ ceremony? What is the most important part of نىكاھ? Why is it important for everyone to hear the bride and groom's answers?

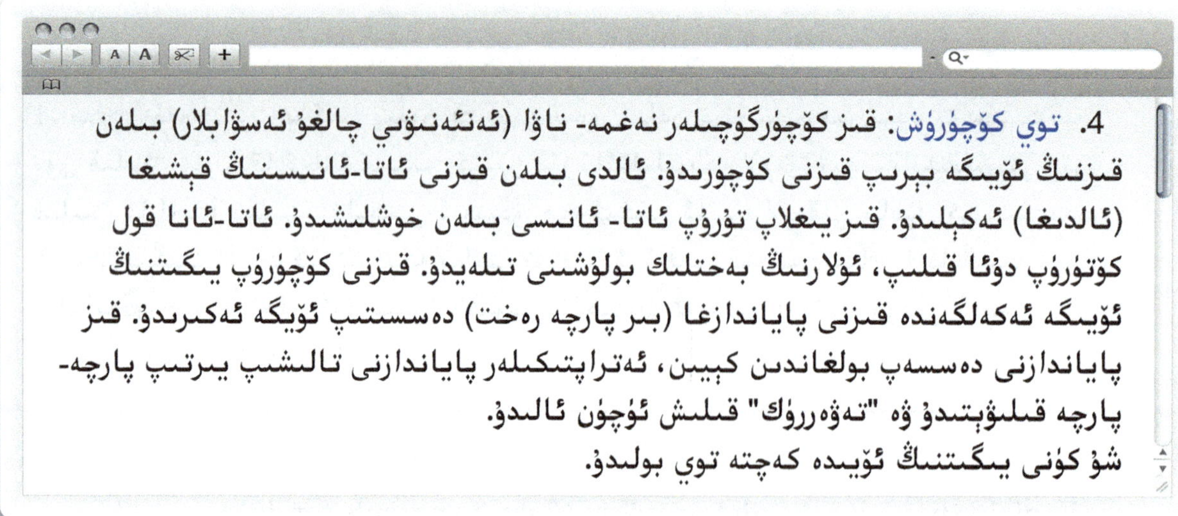

4. توي كۆچۈرۈش: قىز كۆچۈرگۈچىلەر نەغمە- ناۋا (ئەنئەنىۋىي چالغۇ ئەسۋابلار) بىلەن قىزنىڭ ئۆيىگە بېرىپ قىزنى كۆچۈرىدۇ. ئالدى بىلەن قىزنى ئاتا-ئانىسىنىڭ قېشىغا (ئالدىغا) ئەكېلىدۇ. قىز يىغلاپ تۇرۇپ ئاتا- ئانىسى بىلەن خوشلىشىدۇ. ئاتا-ئانا قول كۆتۈرۈپ دۇئا قىلىپ، ئۇلارنىڭ بەختلىك بولۇشىنى تىلەيدۇ. قىزنى كۆچۈرۈپ يىگىتنىڭ ئۆيىگە ئەكەلگەندە قىزنى پاياندازغا (بىر پارچە رەخت) دەسسىتىپ ئۆيگە ئەكىرىدۇ. قىز پاياندازنى دەسسەپ بولغاندىن كېيىن، ئەتراپتىكىلەر پاياندازنى تالىشىپ يىرتىپ پارچە- پارچە قىلىۋېتىدۇ ۋە "تەۋەررۈك" قىلىش ئۈچۈن ئالىدۇ.
شۇ كۈنى يىگىتنىڭ ئۆيىدە كەچتە توي بولىدۇ.

4. Explain the توي كۆچۈرۈش in detail.

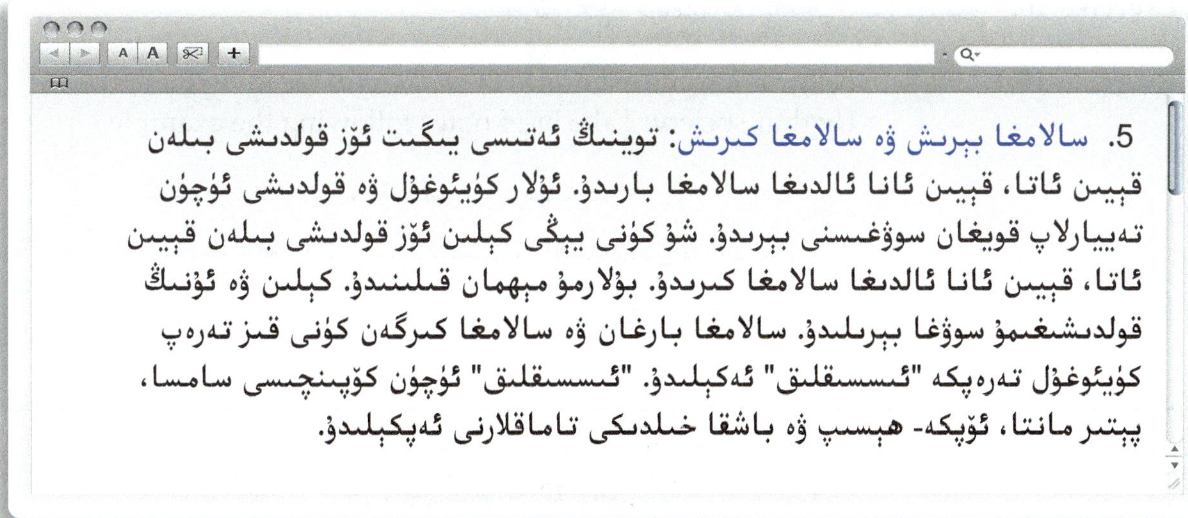

5. سالامغا بېرىش ۋە سالامغا كىرىش: توينىڭ ئەتىسى يىگىت ئۆز قولدىشى بىلەن قېيىن ئاتا، قېيىن ئانا ئالدىغا سالامغا بارىدۇ. ئۇلار كۈيئوغۇل ۋە قولدىشى ئۈچۈن تەييارلاپ قويغان سوۋغىسىنى بېرىدۇ. شۇ كۈنى يېڭى كېلىن ئۆز قولدىشى بىلەن قېيىن ئاتا، قېيىن ئانا ئالدىغا سالامغا كىرىدۇ. بۇلارمۇ مېھمان قىلىنىدۇ. كېلىن ۋە ئۇنىڭ قولدىشىغىمۇ سوۋغا بېرىلىدۇ. سالامغا بارغان ۋە سالامغا كىرگەن كۈنى قىز تەرەپ كۈيئوغۇل تەرەپكە "ئىسسىقلىق" ئەكېلىدۇ. "ئىسسىقلىق" ئۈچۈن كۆپىنچىسى سامسا، پېتىر مانتا، ئۆپكە- ھېسىپ ۋە باشقا خىلدىكى تاماقلارنى ئەپكېلىدۇ.

5. Explain the process of سالامغا بېرىش ۋە سالامغا كىرىش .

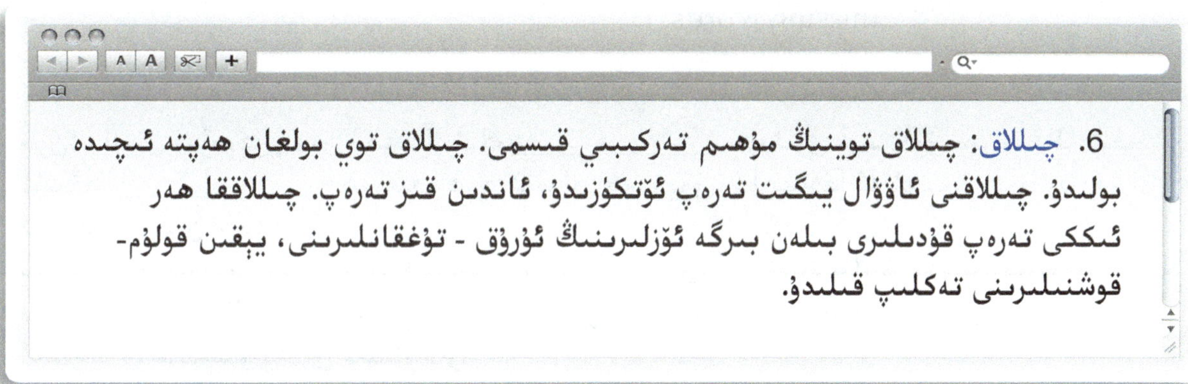

6. چىللاق: توينىڭ مۇھىم تەركىبىي قىسمى. چىللاق توي بولغان ھەپتە ئىچىدە بولىدۇ. چىللاقنى ئاۋۋال يىگىت تەرەپ ئۆتكۈزىدۇ، ئاندىن قىز تەرەپ. چىللاقتا ھەر ئىككى تەرەپ قۇدىلىرى بىلەن بىرگە ئۆزلىرىنىڭ ئۇرۇق - تۇغقانلىرىنى، يېقىن قولۇم-قوشنىلىرىنى تەكلىپ قىلىدۇ.

6. Explain the idea of the چىللاق .

Exercise 10: ئۇيغۇر جەمئىيىتىدىكى ئىللەتلەر

Exercise 10.1:  Below are some examples of challenges faced by modern Uyghur society. Take brief notes following the example.

قىمار ئويناش: پۇلدىن، ئۆيدىن ئايرىلىش.

خروئىن چېكىش: ئۆمرىنى بەربات قىلىش، ئائىلىسىدىن ئايرىلىش.

نەشە چېكىش:____

ئەيدىز:____

Exercise 10.2:  Now write some sentences about each problem on a separate sheet of paper. Follow the example:

قىمار ئويناپ كىشىلەر ئائىلىسىدىن، پۇلدىن، ئۆيدىن ئايرىلىدۇ.

Exercise 10.3:  Listen to John and Yasin's conversation and fill in the missing words.

جون: ياسىن، تۈنۈگۈن مەن ئۇيغۇرلارنىڭ ____________ تويلىرى توغرۇلۇق بىر ماقالە ئوقۇدۇم. ئۇنىڭدا ____________ ھەققىدە ھېچ قانداق گەپ يوق. قارىماققا ئەنئەنىۋى تويلاردا ھاراق ئىچىلمەيدىكەن - ھە؟
ياسىن: ھە، شۇنداق، ئەنئەنىۋى تويلاردا ھاراق ____________. ھاراق دېگەن كاساپەت مۇشۇ يېقىنقى يىللاردا پەيدا بولدى. ئەمما ئۇيغۇرلار جەمئىيىتىدە بۇ ئەڭ ئېغىر ____________ ئەمەس. بۇنىڭدىنمۇ يامان ئىشلار بار.
جون: قانداق ئىشلارنى دەيسىز؟
ياسىن: مەسىلەن قىمار ئويناش، نەشە، خروئىن چېكىش. ھازىر كۆپ ياشلار، بولۇپمۇ ئىشسىز قالغانلار، خروئىننىڭ ____________ كىرىپ، ئۆمرىنى بەربات قىلدى. بۇ كاساپەتنى ياشلىرىمىزغا يەنە ئۆزىمىز ساتىمىز.
جون: سىزمۇ خروئىن ساتامسىز؟
ياسىن: ياق، ياق، ئۆزىمىز دېگىنىم، ____________.
جون: مەسىلىلەر كۆپ دېدىڭىز. ئۇيغۇرلار ____________ يەنە قانداق مەسىلىلەر بار؟
ياسىن: ھە، "بالا كەلسە قوشلاپ كېلىدۇ، بىر- بىرىنى باشلاپ كېلىدۇ" دېگەندەك، خروئىن پەيدا بولغاندىن كېيىن ئەيدىز ____________ كۆپەيدى...
جون: ۋاي، كەچۈرۈڭ ياسىن، مەن ئۇنتۇپ قاپتىمەن. بۈگۈن ئابدۇكېرىم ئابلىزنىڭ* كېچىلىكى بار ئىكەن، سادىق ماڭىمۇ بىلەت ئەپ قويدۇم دېۋىدى، بارمىسام بولمايدۇ. بىز بۇ توغرۇلۇق كېيىنرەك پاراڭلاشساق بولامدۇ؟
ياسىن: بولىدۇ، بولىدۇ. مەن ئەتە تېلېفون قىلاي، ئاندىن بىللە تاماق يەيلى.
جون: خوش!

* ئابدۇكېرىم ئابلىز: a famous Uyghur comedian

Exercise 10.4:  Look at the following statements and decide if they are true or false based on the dialogue you have just heard. If you mark a statement false, correct its contents.

Example: ئۇيغۇرلارنىڭ ئەنئەنىۋى تويلىرىدا كوپ هاراق ئىچىلمەيدۇ. ***False***

- ياق، ئۇنداق ئەمەس! ئۇيغۇرلارنىڭ ئەنئەنىۋى تويلىرىدا هاراق ئومۇمەن ئىچىلمەيدۇ!

توغرا	خاتا

1. هاراق ئۇيغۇرلارنىڭ مەدەنىيىتىدە يېقىنقى يىللاردا پەيدا بولدى.
2. ئۇيغۇرلار جەمئىيىتىدە هاراق ئىچىش ئەڭ ئېغىر مەسىلە.
3. خروئىن سەۋەبىدىن ئەيدىز كېسىلى پەيدا بولدى.
4. خروئىننى پەقەت ئىشسىز قالغانلار چېكىدۇ.
5. جون ئابدۇكېرىم ئابلىزنىڭ كېچىلىكىگە بارماقچى.

Exercise 11: "بالا" سۆزى

Exercise 11.1: There is a proverb in the dialogue between John and Yasin.

بالا كەلسە قوش كەپتۇ، بىر- بىرىنى باشلاپ كەپتۇ.

Explain what it means. Is there a similar proverb in your language/culture?

***Note: The word* بالا**

You know that the word بالا in Uyghur means a child, guy, or a young person. However, based on the proverb above you may have guessed that this word has another meaning as well: trouble, disaster. These are actually two separate words, which are pronounced slightly differently. When بالا means 'child' etc., both of its vowels are of normal length; when بالا means 'trouble' the vowel in the final syllable is longer. This is even more noticeable when suffixes are attached to the word, because the last vowel of the بالا meaning 'trouble' does not reduce to ى when you might expect it to. Sometimes when بالا means 'trouble,' it appears in conjunction with another word قازا, which means roughly the same thing, i.e. بالا- قازا . The word بالا, either by itself or in the phrase بالا- قازا, is actively used in many Uyghur proverbs.

Exercise 11.2:  Read the following proverbs and place a mark under the meaning of the word بالا in the table to the left as intended according to the context. If this word is used twice in one example - once with one meaning, and once again with the other - note which use has which meaning.

child	trouble

1. بالا، قىلغان ئىشى چالا.
2. بالا كەلسە قوش كەپتۇ ، ئامەت كەلسە تاق كەپتۇ.
3. بالا بولسا شوخ بولسا، بولمىسا يوق بولسا.
4. بالىنىڭ چېچى ئاقارسىمۇ، ئاتىنىڭ ئالدىدا يەنىلا بالا.
5. بالاڭنى مەكتەپكە بەر، بولمىسا مەشرەپكە بەر.
6. بالا بالىلىقىدا بالا ئىكەن، چوڭ بولغاندا بالا ئىكەن.
7. بالا بالا بولغۇچە، ئانىسى موما بولار.

Exercise 12: خروئىن ئىلىپ كەلگەن ئاپەتلەر

Exercise 12.1: Describe the information presented on the graph below.

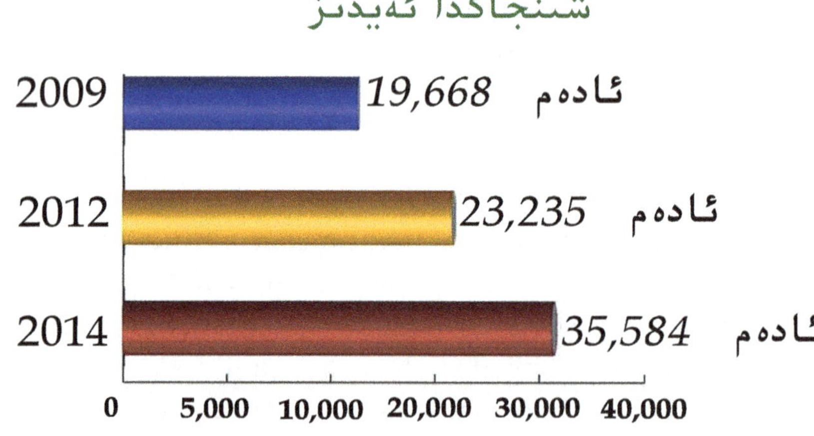

1. What does it say about the current health issues among people in Xinjiang?
2. What do you think the reason is for the current situation?
3. How do you think this impacts people's everyday lives?

Exercise 12.2:  The following quote is taken from the dialogue you are about to read. Translate it and explain what you think it means.

تۇڭگانلار ساتىدۇ، ئۇيغۇرلار چېكىدۇ، خىتايلار تۇتىدۇ.

Exercise 12.3:  Now read a conversation between John and Yasin about some social issues in Xinjiang and answer the questions that follow. The following words will help you to understand the passage better.

mortality rate	ئۆلۈش نىسبىتى	to be addicted	خۇمار بولماق
health/hygienic services	سەھىيە خىزمىتى	robbery	بۇلاڭچىلىق
funds	مەبلەغ	hepatitis	جىگەر ياللۇغى
existing	مەۋجۇت	cancer	راك
to confiscate	مۇسادىرە قىلماق	crime	جىنايەت
poison; drugs	زەھەر	transmission rate (of infectious disease)	تارقىلىش سۈرئىتى

AIDS in Xinjiang, 2014

Uyghurs (83.2%)
Han Chinese (6.2%)
Hui/Tun'gans (3.5%)
Kazakhs (1%)
Others

جون: ياسىن، سىز خروئىن چېكىش شىنجاڭدا بەك ئېغىر دېدىڭىز، شۇنداقمۇ؟

ياسىن: ئەپسۇسكى شۇنداق....

جون: مەن ئۇيغۇرلار ئىسلام دىنىغا ئىشىنىدۇ، شۇڭا ئۇلار خروئىن چەكمەيدۇ دەپ ئويلاپتىمەن.

ياسىن:ھەممىلا ئۇيغۇر چەكمەيدۇ. لېكىن ياشلار ئارىسىدا بىرئاز ئېغىر، بولۇپمۇ ئىشسىز ياشلاردا.

جون: ئۇلار ئىشسىز بولسا, خروئىننى قانداق ئالىدۇ؟ شىنجاڭدا خروئىن ئەرزانمۇ؟

ياسىن: ياق. شىنجاڭدا خروئىن جۇڭگو بويىچە ئەڭ قىممەت دەپ ئاڭلىدىم. زەھەرگە خۇمار بولغان باللار پۇل تېپىش ئۈچۈن جىنايەت يولىغا ماڭىدۇ.

جون: ئوغرىلىق ۋە بۇلاڭچىلىق قىلامدۇ؟

ياسىن: شۇنداق. ھازىر خەلق ئارىسىدا "تۇڭگانلار ساتىدۇ، ئۇيغۇرلار چېكىدۇ، خىتايلار تۇتىدۇ" دېگەن گەپ بار. ئاق ساتىدىغانلارنىڭ كۆپى تۇڭگانلار ئىكەن.

جون:"ئاق" دېگەن نېمە؟

ياسىن: بۇ خروئىننىڭ يەنە بىر نامى. بەزىلەر بۇنى "ئاق تاماكا" دەپمۇ ئاتايدۇ.

جون: مۇنداق دەڭ. شىنجاڭدىكى ئاق تاماكا نەدىن كېلىدۇ؟

ياسىن: ئىچكىرىدىن ۋە پاكىستاندىن كىرىدۇ. ھەر يىلى ساقچىلار ئاز دېگەندە يەتمىش- سەكسەن كىلوگرام خروئىننى مۇسادىرە قىلىدۇ.

جون: ۋاي خۇدايىم. ئاق تاماكا دېگەن شىنجاڭدىكەنغۇ!

ياسىن: تېخىمۇ يامىنى، ئاق تاماكىغا ئەگىشىپ ئەيدىزمۇ كۆپىيىۋاتىدۇ.

جون: شىنجاڭدا ئەيدىز بارمۇ؟

ياسىن: بار. ھۆكۈمەتنىڭ دېيىشىچە شىنجاڭدا ئەيدىز بولغانلار يەتمىش- سەكسەن مىڭ ئىكەن. شىنجاڭدىكى ئەيدىز كېسىلىنىڭ تارقىلىش سۈرئىتى جۇڭگو بويىچە 1- ئورۇندا ئىكەن. ھازىر شىنجاڭدا ئاق تاماكا بارمىغان يەر يوق. تېخىمۇ يامىنى، ھازىر ئەيدىزگە ئەگىشىپ باشقا كېسەللەرمۇ كۆپىيىۋاتىدۇ.

جون: قانداق كېسەللەر؟

ياسىن: جىگەر ياللۇغى، راك كېسىلى دېگەنلەر شىنجاڭدا بۇرۇن ئاساسەن يوق ئىدى. ھازىر بەك كۆپ. ئۇيغۇرلارنىڭ راك كېسىلى سەۋەبىدىن ئۆلۈش نىسبىتى دۇنيا بويىچە بىرىنچى ئورۇندا تۇرىدۇ.

جون: بۇ كېسەللەرنى ھۆكۈمەت داۋالامدۇ؟

ياسىن: سەھىيە خىزمىتى ئاساسەن ھۆكۈمەتنىڭ قولىدا، ئەمما مەبلەغ كەم بولغاچقا، ھەقسىز داۋالاش مەۋجۇت ئەمەس. ئۆز پۇلىغا داۋالىنىش كۆپ قىسىم ئۇيغۇرلارغا ئېغىر كېلىدۇ .

جون: مەن بۇلارنى ئاڭلىمىغان ئىكەنمەن. سىزدە مۇشۇ ھەقتە بىرەر ماتېرىيال بارمۇ؟

ياسىن: بار. مەن سىزگە ئېلخەت ئارقىلىق ئەۋەتىپ بېرەي.

جون: كۆپ رەھمەت!

1. Circle all that apply.

1. According to the passage, people who do not have enough money will most likely
   A. borrow B. steal C. commit murder D. find work
2. Which group is most likely to commit a crime to buy heroin in Xinjiang?
   A. Uyghurs B. young people
   C. young unemployed people D. women
3. Most of the heroin in Xinjiang comes from
   A. Pakistan. B. Afghanistan.
   C. Inner China. D. the US.A
4. How much heroin is confiscated by the police annually?
   A. 70-80 pounds B. 70-80 kilos
   C. 60-70 pounds D. 60-70 kilos
5. According to Yasin, which is the worst consequence of the heavy use of heroin?
   A. cancer B. AIDS C. hepatitis D. poverty
6. How many people are reported to be affected by AIDS in Xinjiang?
   A. 70,000 - 80,000 B. 17,000 - 18,000
   C. 7,000 - 8,000 D. 170,000 - 180,000

2. What do the following words literally mean in Uyghur? In what sense are they used in the text?

ئاق، زەھەر ، ئاق تاماكا

3. Check the definitions you provided to the words in the previous question with your instructor and your classmates. Did you guess the meaning of each word correctly?

Exercise 12.4: تۆۋەندىكى سوئاللارنى مۇزاكىرە قىلىڭلار

1. According to the text, HIV spreads faster in Xinjiang than in any other province or region of China. What reasons can you think of to explain this?
2. According to the text, health care is under government control and there is not enough funding for it. How do you think this influences people's lives?

Exercise 12.5:  Look at the following expressions taken from Exercise 12.3 and write a sentence with each of them in the lines provided below.

...دەپ ئويلاپتىمەن	... نىڭ دېيىشىچە
پۇل تېپىش ئۈچۈن...	.... كەم بولغاچقا
تېخىمۇ يامىنى...	...گە ئەگىشىپ
... دەپ ئاڭلىدىم	... ئارقىلىق ئەۋەتىپ بېرەي

1. ____________________
2. ____________________
3. ____________________
4. ____________________
5. ____________________
6. ____________________
7. ____________________
8. ____________________

Exercise 13: لوبنۇردىكى يادرو سىناقلىرى

Exercise 13.1: Look at the following pictures below. What do the pictures have in common? What do you think the relationship is between them?

Exercise 13.2:  One day on the street, John runs into Yasin. Listen to the first part of their conversation and decide if the following statements are true or false.

خاتا	توغرا

1.بالنىست سۆزىنىڭ مەنىسى دوختۇرخانا.

2. بۇ سۆز ئۇيغۇر تىلىغا رۇس تىلىدىن كىرگەن.

3. ياسىنىڭ مىجەزى يوق، ئۇ دوختۇرغا كۆرۈنمەكچى.

Exercise 13.3:  Now, read the rest of the conversation and answer the questions that follow. Before reading the passage, however, look at and give translations for the following words.

	تەسىر		ئوپېراتسىيە
	يادرو سىنىقى		مېيىپ
	قەرز ئالماق		سەزمەس

ياسىن: تاغامنىڭ ئوغلىنى بۈگۈن ئوپېراتسىيە قىلماقچى ئىكەن، شۇڭا كېلىپ دوختۇرلارغا تەرجىمانلىق قىلىشىپ بەرگىن دەيدۇ.
جون: نېمە كېسەل بوپتۇ؟
ياسىن: كېسەل ئەمەس، ئۇ تۇغۇلۇشىدىنلا مېيىپ ئىدى. ئەمدى يەنە بىر پۇتى سەزمەس بولۇپ قاپتۇ.
جون: ۋاي خۇدايىم. سەۋەبى نېمىدۇ دەمدۇ؟
ياسىن: ئۇقمايمەن. بۇنداق مېيىپ تۇغۇلغان باللار ھازىر بەك كۆپ.
جون: نېمىشقا؟
ياسىن: كىشىلەر شىنجاڭدىكى ئاتوم بومبىسىنىڭ تەسىرىدىن بولغان دەيدۇ.
جون: لوبنۇردىكى ئاتوم سىنىقىمۇ؟
ياسىن: ھەئە. بۇنداق يادرو سىنىقى ئەللىك يىلدىن بېرى توختىماي بولۇۋاتىدۇ.
جون: ئەمىسە ئوپېراتسىيە قىلىسا ھۆكۈمەت ھەقسىز داۋالامدۇ؟
ياسىن: ياق. تاغام يېزىدا دېھقان. دېھقانلارنىڭ سۇغۇرتىسى يوق. شۇڭا شەخسىي پۇلغا داۋالىنىدۇ.
جون: نەچچىلىك پۇل كېتىدۇ؟
ياسىن: بەك كۆپ. ئەمدى ئۇلارنىڭ بەش- ئون يىللىق تاپقىنى تۈگەيدۇ دېگەن گەپ.
جون: بەك كۆپ ئىكەن. ئەمدى ئۇلار قانداق قىلىدۇ؟
ياسىن: تۇغقانلاردىن ۋە تونۇشلاردىن قەرز ئالىدۇ، يەتمىسە قوي- كالىلىرىنى ساتىدۇ. باشقا ئامال يوق.
جون: ۋاي خۇدايىم. مەنمۇ بىللە بارسام بولامدۇ؟
ياسىن: ئەلۋەتتە. ئەمىسە يۈرۈڭ. ئەنە، ئاپتوبۇس كېلىۋاتىدۇ.

1. Why does Yasin go to the hospital?
2. How can Yasin help his uncle?
3. What happened to his uncle's son?
4. Why do many children have a disability at birth?
5. How do farmers pay for the expenses?

Project

Find out more detailed information about nuclear testing at Lobnur, then report your findings.

لوبنۇر

- قەيەردە؟ ____________________
- قاچان؟ ____________________
- نېمىشقا؟ ____________________
- قانچە؟ ____________________

Exercise 14: ياسىننىڭ ئائىلىسىدە ماتەم

Exercise 14.1:  John gets an email from Yasin. Read it and answer the questions that follow.

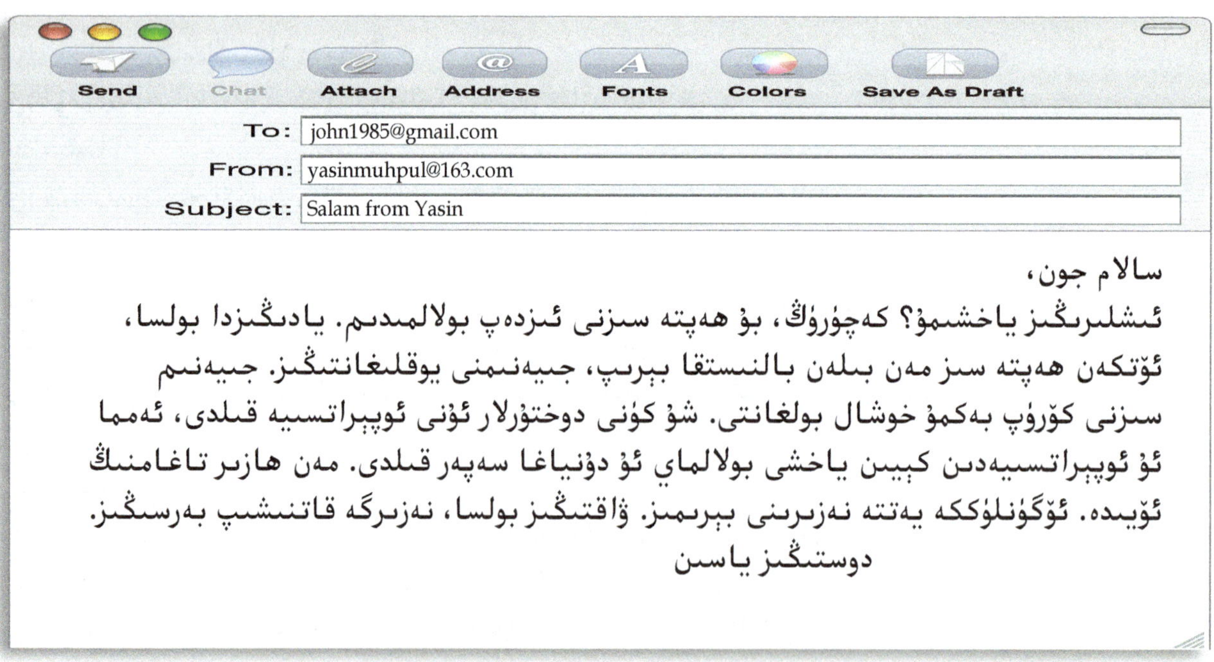

To: john1985@gmail.com

From: yasinmuhpul@163.com

Subject: Salam from Yasin

سالام جون،

ئىشلىرىڭىز ياخشىمۇ؟ كەچۈرۈڭ، بۇ ھەپتە سىزنى ئىزدەپ بولالمىدىم. يادىڭىزدا بولسا، ئۆتكەن ھەپتە سىز مەن بىلەن بالنىستقا بېرىپ، جىيەنىمنى يوقلىغانتىڭىز. جىيەنىم سىزنى كۆرۈپ بەكمۇ خوشال بولغانتى. شۇ كۈنى دوختۇرلار ئۇنى ئوپېراتسىيە قىلدى، ئەمما ئۇ ئوپېراتسىيەدىن كېيىن ياخشى بولالماي ئۇ دۇنياغا سەپەر قىلدى. مەن ھازىر تاغامنىڭ ئۆيىدە. ئۆگۈنلۈككە يەتتە نەزىرىنى بېرىمىز. ۋاقتىڭىز بولسا، نەزىرگە قاتنىشىپ بەرسىڭىز.

دوستىڭىز ياسىن

1. Why did Yasin write to John?
2. What does the expression ئۇ دۇنياغا سەپەر قىلماق mean?
3. Why is Yasin at his uncle's house?

Exercise 14.2:  Imagine that you are John. Write a reply to Yasin's message in Uyghur.

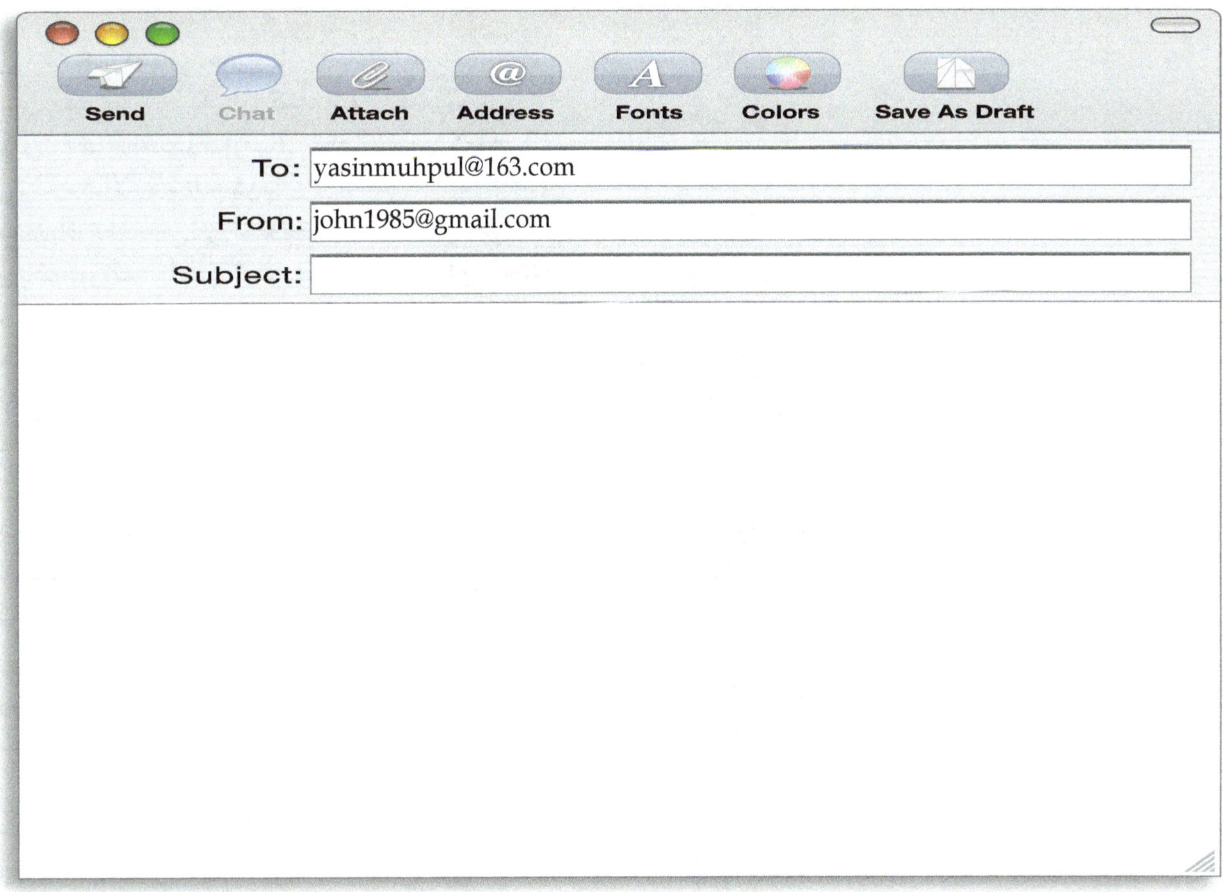

Exercise 14.3:  John visits Yasin's family. Listen to the conversation and circle the phrases you hear.

مانا، ئوغلىمىز بىزنى تاشلاپ كەتتى.	مانا، ئوغلىمىز كېتىپ قالدى.
رەھمەتلىك ئوغلۇم	ھۆرمەتلىك ئوغلۇم
راھەت كۆرمەيلا كۆز يۇمدى	ئۇنىڭ كۆزلىرى يۇمۇلدى
ئىچىم سىېرىلىپ كەتتى	ئىچىم سۇرۇپ كەتتى
تەسەللى بېرىشنى بىلمەيمەن	مەسلىھەت بېرىشنى بىلمەيمەن
خۇدا رەھمەت قىلسۇن	خۇدا ھۆرمەت قىلسۇن
جايى جەننەتتە بولسۇن	جەننەتتە بولسا بولدى

Exercise 14.4:  Now read the passage and define what the underlined words and phrases mean.

جون: ياخشىمۇسىز، ياسىن!

ياسىن: ھە جون، كېلىڭ، كېلىڭ، ياخشىمۇسىز!

ياسىن: (تاغىسىغا قاراپ): تاغا، جون كەلدى!

جون: ئەسسالامۇ ئەلەيكۇم!

ياسىننىڭ تاغىسى: ۋەئەلەيكۇم ئەسسالام جون، كېلىڭ!

جون: كەچۈرۈڭ، يامان ئىش بوپتۇ... بۇنداق ئەھۋالدا نېمە دېيىشنىمۇ بىلمەيمەن...

ياسىن: ھېچقىسى يوق، توغرا دېدىڭىز...

ياسىننىڭ تاغىسى جونغا: كەلگىنىڭىز ئۈچۈن رەھمەت، جون. مانا، ئوغلىمىز بىزنى تاشلاپ كەتتى. تەقدىرنىڭ ئىشىغا تەن بەرمىسەك بولمايدۇ، بالام... ئامال يوق. بىزدە "ئاللاھ بەردى، ئاللاھ ئالدى" دېگەن گەپ بار ...

جون: بالىڭىز نەچچە ياش ئىدى؟

ياسىننىڭ تاغىسى: ئەمدى ئون ئىككىگە كىرگەنتى...ھەەەي، ئۆلۈم ياشقا قارىمايدىكەن ئەمەسمۇ... رەھمەتلىك ئوغلۇم ھېچ بىر راھەت كۆرمەيلا كۆز يۇمدى، جېنىم بالام (يىغلايدۇ) .... تۇغۇلغاندىن بېرى بالىنىستتىن بالنىستقا كۆتۈرۈپ يۈردۈق سېنى، پايدىسى بولمىدىغۇ (يىغلايدۇ)....

جون: كەچۈرۈڭ...

جون(ياسىنغا قاراپ): ياسىن، سىزدىن سورايدىغان بىر نەرسە بار ئىدى...

ياسىن: ئا يەرگە ئۆتۈپ سۆزلىشەيلى.

جون: ياسىن، تاغىڭىزنىڭ ئالدىدا خىجالەت بولدۇم ...

ياسىن: نېمىشقا؟

جون: قاراڭ، مەن ھېچ قاچان بۇنداق مۇراسىملارغا قاتنىشىپ باقماپتىكەنمەن. نېمە دېيىشنىمۇ بىلمەيمەن... بۇ يەردىكى كىشىلەرنىڭ يىغىسىنى كۆرۈپ ئىچىم سىرىلىپ كەتتى، ئەمما نېمە دەپ تەسەللى بېرىشنى بىلمەيمەن...

ياسىن: بىزدە ئادەتتە تەسەللى بېرىش ئۈچۈن "خۇدا رەھمەت قىلسۇن"، "جايى جەننەتتە بولسۇن" دېگەندەك گەپلەرنى قىلىدۇ.

جون: توختاپ تۇرۇڭ، مەن بۇ گەپلەرنى يېزىۋالاي....

ياسىن: سىز يېزىپ تۇرۇڭ، مەن مېھمانلار بىلەن كۆرۈشۈپ قوياي. يېزىپ بولغىنىڭىزدىن كېيىن، ئاۋۇ ئۆيگە كىرىڭ، ھازىر ئاش تارتىلىدۇ...*

---

* ئاش تارتماق: to serve food

Exercise 14.5: Skim the passage again and answer the questions below.

1. جون نېمىشقا خىجالەت بولىدۇ؟
2. ياسىننىڭ تاغىسى نېمە دەپ يىغلايدۇ؟
3. دىئالوگدىكى ئاللاھ بەردى، ئاللاھ ئالدى دېگەن گەپنى قانداق چۈشىنىسىز؟
4. ئۆلۈم بولغان ئۆيگە بارغاندا نېمە دېيىش كېرەك؟

The Uyghur Funeral Ceremony

Uyghur funerals are considered community matters. They are usually organized and conducted on the very same day as the death, mostly before sunset. If a death occurs in the late afternoon or afterwards, the deceased is buried on the following day, generally right after the noon-time prayer. The family of the deceased informs all relatives and acquaintances, and people gather at the house of the deceased to pay their respects, express their condolences, and sometimes take part in the upcoming funeral ceremony. Until the body of the deceased is delivered to the cemetery, no food can be cooked in the house in which the deceased resided. Instead, neighbors, friends of the family, and relatives voluntarily bring cooked meals to the home of the deceased's family.

Exercise 15: ئاخىرەتلىك ئىشلار

Exercise 15.1:  There are fifteen expressions below. Eight of them are euphemisms for the verb 'to die.' Mark all eight expressions.

هالاك بولماق		بارلىققا كەلمەك		ئالەمدىن ئۆتمەك	
بۇ دۇنياغا كەلمەك		تۇگەپ كەتمەك		ئۇخلاپ قالماق	
ئۆلۈپ كەتمەك		ئارام ئالماق		ئۇ دۇنياغا سەپەر قىلماق	
پىيادە كەتمەك		كۆز يۇمماق		پەيدا بولماق	
قازا قىلماق		غايىب بولماق		ۋاپات بولماق	

Exercise 15.2:  Listen to the recording and check your responses.

Exercise 15.3:  What phrases do you use in your own language to express condolences when someone close to a person has died? Here are the phrases commonly used to express condolences in Uyghur. Listen to them and repeat.

- خۇدا/ئاللاھ رەھمەت قىلسۇن (قىلغاي)
- ياتقان يېرى جەننەتتە بولسۇن (بولغاي)
- سەۋر قىلىڭ
- ئۆلۈم دېگەن ياش - قېرى دېمەيدىكەن
- كەتكەننىڭ كەينىدىن كەتكىلى بولمايدۇ
- ئاللاھ ئۆزىنىڭ ياخشى بەندىلىرىنى ئاشۇنداق بالدۇر ئېلىپ كېتىدىكەن

Exercise 15.4:  Read the following باغاق. To what kind of event is the man invited? How do you know?

ئەسسالامۇ ئەلەيكۇم

ھۆرمەتلىك: بەيتۇل مەمۇر مەسجىد جامائەتلىرى

سىزلەرنى 8- ئاينىڭ 19- كۈنى (پەيشەنبە) ئۆتكۈزۈلىدىغان مەرھۇم ئوغلىمىز خالىقجاننىڭ قىرقى نەزىرىگە قاتنىشىپ بېرىشلىرىنى سورايمىز.

ھۆرمەت بىلەن: ئەخمەت توختى، سانىيە يۇسۇپ

ئۆتكۈزۈلۈش ۋاقتى: سائەت 11 دە

ئورنى: بارغۇت رېستورانى (رابىيە قادىر سودا سارىيىنىڭ ئارقىسىدا)

ئادرېسى: خەلقئارا چوڭ بازار ئۇدۇلىدىكى «شادلىق» باغاق بېسىش كوچىسىدا بېسىلدى. ئالاقىلاشقۇچى: نۇربىيە ئالاقىلىشىش تېلېفونى: 0991-2880972, 2876458

Exercise 16: تەزىيە بىلدۈرۈش/ كۆڭۈل ئېيتىش

Exercise 16.1: تۆۋەندىكى سوئاللارنى مۇزاكىرە قىلىڭلار

1. How do people in your culture show their respect for the deceased? What is the role of the family in communal mourning rituals, such as wakes?

2. What sort of people are invited to show their respect for the deceased? How do friends and neighbors participate in this event? Where do people gather to pay their respects?

3. When someone passes away, some cultural focus is on celebrating the life and achievements of the person through festivities in which people sing and dance joyously. Is this part of a normal funeral celebration in your culture?

Exercise 16.2: Describe the events presented in the following pictures. Go into as much detail as you can.

Exercise 17: ئۇيغۇرلارنىڭ ئۆلۈم- يىتىم ئادەتلىرى

Exercise 17.1:  Read the passage on the next page about some customs related to the funeral ceremony in Uyghur culture and answer the questions that follow. Before reading, check the words below:

to be in mourning	قارىلىق تۇتماق	top-quality; noble	ئېسىل
to see off	ئۇزاتماق	funeral prayers	جىنازا نامىزى
a visit to a bereaved family	ئۆلۈم پەتىسى	spirit, ghost	ئەرۋاھ
the ritual cooking of food during the mourning period in honor of the deceased	ياغ پۇرىتىش	feast in honor of the deceased	نەزىر

ئۇيغۇرلاردا ۋاپات بولغۇچى ئىنتايىن ھۆرمەتكە ئىگە. شۇڭا ۋاپات بولغۇچى ئۈچۈن ئەر بولسا "مەرھۇم"، ئايال بولسا "مەرھۇمە" دېگەندەك سۆزلەر ئىشلىتىلىدۇ. ۋاپات بولغۇچىنىڭ ھۆرمىتى ئۈچۈن جىنازا نامىزى ئوقۇلغاندىن كېيىن ئۇنىڭ تاۋۇتى قەبرىستانلىقچە كۆتۈرۈپ بېرىلىدۇ. قەبرىستانغا پەقەت ئەرلەر بارىدۇ، ئاياللار دۇئا قىلىپ ئۆيدە قالىدۇ. ئايالنىڭ تاۋۇتىغا گۈللۈك ئېسىل رەختلەردىن يوپۇق يېپىلىدۇ. ئەر بولسا، ئاق ياكى قارا سىدام رەختتىن قىلىنغان يوپۇق يېپىلىدۇ. ۋاپات بولغۇچىنىڭ بىۋاستە تۇغقانلىرى قارىلىق تۇتۇپ ئەرلەر بېلىگە ئاق باغلايدۇ، ئاياللار بېشىغا ئاق ياغلىق سالىدۇ. تاۋۇت ئىگىلىرى ئۆلۈم پەتىسىگە كەلگەن ئاياللارنىڭ بېشىغىمۇ ئاق ياغلىق سېلىپ قويىدۇ. ۋاپات بولغۇچىنىڭ "يەتتە نەزىرىسى" بېرىلمىگۈچە بىۋاستە ئەر تۇغقانلار بېلىدىكى ئاقنى يەشمەيدۇ، ساقال- بۇرۇتىنى ئالمايدۇ. بىۋاستە ئايال تۇغقانلار ۋاپات بولغۇچىنىڭ قىرىقى بولمىغۇچە(بەزىدە يىلغىچە) بېشىدىكى ئاقنى ئالمايدۇ."قىرقى نەزىر" ياكى "يىل نەزىر"دە ياشانغان بىرەر ئايال تەسەللى سۆزلەرنى قىلىپ ئاق سالغۇچىلارنىڭ بېشىدىكى ئاقنى ئېلىۋېتىپ، باشقا ياغلىق سېلىپ قويىدۇ. ھازىدار ئائىلىدە ئويۇن-كۈلكە ۋە باشقا تاماشا ئىشلىرى زادى بولمايدۇ. ھەتتا قولۇم- قوشنىلارمۇ ئۆز ئۆيىدە كۆڭۈل ئېچىش پائالىيەتلىرى قىلمايدۇ.
ۋاپات بولغۇچى ئۈچۈن "ئۈچ نەزىر"، "يەتتە نەزىر"،"قىرقى نەزىر" ۋە "يىل نەزىرى"* ئۆتكۈزىلىدۇ. نەزىر تۈگىگەندىن كېيىن ئائىلە ئەزالىرى قەبرىستانغا بېرىپ، قەبرىنى يوقلايدۇ. شۇنداقلا ھەر بىر روزا ھېيت ۋە قۇربان ھېيتلاردا نامازدىن كېيىن قەبرىستانغا بېرىپ قەبرىنى يوقلاش ئادىتى ھازىرمۇ داۋام قىلماقتا.

---

*نەزىر Feast that is held on specified days after a person's death in honor of the deceased.

1. From the passage, you learned that some activities related to funerary rituals among the Uyghurs are engaged in by specific genders. Look at each of the activities below and mark M for 'men' or W for 'women' according to the gender which generally engages in that activity.

Wears ئاق ياغلىق ________

Wears بەلۋاغ ________

Wears a mourning garment until the feast 7 days after the funeral ________

Wears a mourning garment until the feast 40 days after the funeral________

May wear a mourning garment until the feast 1 year after the funeral ______

2. Feasts which are held at certain intervals after a funeral are named after those intervals. What are the names of the special feasts prepared in honor of the deceased in Uyghur culture according to the passage you have just read? Circle all that apply (see the next page).

(a) 3-day feast
(b) 7-day feast
(c) 14-day feast
(d) 40-day feast
(e) 1-year feast
(f) 2-year feast

3. What do you think the color white symbolizes in this event? What does the color white symbolize in Uyghur culture in general? Refer to Chapter 6 Exercise 5.3 if needed.

Exercise 17.2:  Read the short excerpt below explaining some beliefs related to funerals which are commonly held among Uyghurs. Then, translate the passage into English in the provided lines below.

ئۇيغۇرلاردا ھەر پەيشەنبە كۈنى ئەرۋاھلارغا ئاتاپ ياغ پۇرىتىدىغان ئەھۋال داۋاملاشماقتا. ئۇلارنىڭ قارىشىچە، ھەممە ئەرۋاھلار جۈمە كۈنى مەككىگە توپلىنىپ جۈمە نامىزى ئوقۇرمىش. مەككىگە بېرىش ئۈچۈن ئەرۋاھ تېتىك بولۇشى لازىممىش. ھەر پەيشەنبە كۈنى ياغ پۇرىتىلسا*، ئەرۋاھلار تېتىكلىشىپ مەككىگە بالدۇر بارارمىش. گەرچە ئۇيغۇر زىيالىلىرى بۇنىڭ ئىسلام دىنىغا خىلاپ بىدئەت ئىشلار ئىكەنلىكىنى تەكىتلىسىمۇ، بۇ ئادەت يەنىلا ئۇيغۇرلار ئارىسىدا بەلگىلىك دەرىجىدە مەۋجۇت بولۇپ تۇرماقتا.

---

*ياغ پۇراتماق: frying food (usually dough) to release fragrance

6 Expressing 'supposedly' Using the Suffix مىش-

1. The suffix مىش- adds a sense of uncertainty or doubt to your statement. Its meaning is similar to the use of expressions like 'people say that' or 'supposedly' in English. Look at the following examples excerpted from the passage you have read:

ئەرۋاھلار جۈمە كۈنى مەككىگە توپلىنىپ جۈمە نامىزى ئوقۇرمىش.
(Supposedly) on Fridays ghosts gather in Mecca and perform the Juma prayer.
مەككىگە بېرىش ئۈچۈن ئەرۋاھ تېتىك بولۇشى لازىممىش.
In order to get to Mecca, ghosts (supposedly) need to be energetic.

2. This suffix is also sometimes used to express a slight sarcasm. Look at the following examples:

قولىدىن ئىش كەلمەيدۇ، تېخى دوختۇرمىش.
He can't do a thing, but he's a so-called "doctor".
ئۇ چەت ئەلگە چىقىپ كەپتۇمىش.
Well, he supposedly went abroad.
ئۇنىڭ ئوغلى مېنىڭ قىزىمغا ئاشىقمىش.
His son is apparently in love with my daughter.

3. Sometimes this suffix is used to describe things that have happened in dreams.

چۈشۈمدە بىر شاھزادە بىلەن توي قىپتىمەنمىش....

In my dream I (supposedly) got married to a prince.

4. The suffix also appears in the phrase (گەپ) مىش-مىش, meaning 'whispers', 'rumors', 'gossip', and 'word around town'.

يېڭى ئايفون ھەققىدە تارقالغان مىش-مىش خەۋەرلەر بەكلا كۆپىيىپ كەتتى.
All of a sudden there's been all this talk about the new iPhone.
بۇ مىش-مىش گەپ ئەمەس، بۇ گەپنى تۈنۈگۈنكى يىغىندا ئاڭلىدىم.
This isn't just some rumor; I heard during yesterday's meeting.

Exercise 17.3:  Read the following passage describing a dream and fill in the missing verbs from the box below.

تۇرارمىش　　يۈرەرمىش　　بېرىپتىمەنمىش
كېتىپتىمىش　　بوپتىمىش　　قايتىپ كەلمەيدۇ
دەرمىش　　سوراپتۇمىش　　ئىكەنمىشمەن

بۈگۈن بىر غەلىتە چۈش كۆرۈپتىمەن. چۈشۈمدە مەن بىر خانىش ____________
ئەتراپىمدا نۇرغۇن خىزمەتكارلار خىزمىتىمنى قىلىپ ____________. بىر كۈنى
شاھىم ئۇۋغا چىقىپ ____________. شۇ كۈنى يېنىمغا بىر قېرى موماي كېلىپ
بۇنداق ____________:
- ھەي خانىش، مەن سەندىن ئىككى سوئال سورايمەن، ئەگەر ئىككى كۈن ئىچىدە
سوئاللىرىمغا توغرا جاۋاب تاپالمىساڭ، شاھىڭ ئۇۋدىن____________!
قورقۇپ كەتكىنىمدىن ئاغزىمنى ئاچالماي قېتىپلا قاپتىمەن. ئەتراپىمدىكى
خىزمەتكارلىرىم غايىب ____________. موماي ماڭا قاراپ جاۋابىمنى ساقلاپ
____________.
- ماقۇل، سوئاللىرىڭنى سورا، مەن ئويلاپ باقاي دەپ جاۋاب____________.
موماي ماڭا قاراپ "دۇنيادا نېمە قاتتىق، نېمە تاتلىق؟ "دەپ ____________. شۇنىڭ
بىلەن ئويغىنىپ كېتىپتىمەن... خۇدايىم توۋا، بۇ چۈش زادى قانداق چۈش؟

Exercise 17.4: Now listen to the passage to check your answers.

Exercise 17.5: Below are two Uyghur tongue twisters that makes use of the مىش- ending. Practice saying them as fast as you can. Once you've succeeded, try saying them three times fast.

1. قىشتا كىشمىش پىشماسمىش، پىشسىمۇ يېگىلى بولماسمىش.
2. كالا گۆشىگە چوغ چاپلاشماسمىش.

Exercise 18: Now practice saying some other Uyghur toungue twisters. Try to say them fast three times in a row.

1. شال ئاقلاش ماشىنىسى شال ئاقلاۋاتىدۇ.
2. ئىشىكنىڭ ئالدىدا بىر كۈپ تۇرۇپتۇ، كۈپ تۈپىنى تۇتۇپ تۇرۇپتىمۇ، تۈپ كۈپىنى تۇتۇپ تۇرۇپتىمۇ؟
3. بىزنىڭ ئۆيدە تۆت تەكچە، چەتتىكى تەكچە چاك تەكچە.

Pulling it all together خۇرجۇندا

In this section, you will reinforce your knowledge and check the progress you have made during chapters 9 and 10 by completing a limited selection of focused exercises.

Exercise 19:  When you register for classes, what fees do you have to pay in addition to tuition? Circle those that apply from among the following:

تىزىملىتىش ھەققى　　قاتناش ھەققى　　تېخنولوگىيە ھەققى

رېمونت ۋە تازىلىق ھەققى　　داۋالىنىش ھەققى

1. What is covered in these fees?
2. What service do you receive in exchange for the fees?

Exercise 20: سىزگە ئېلخەت كەلدى

Exercise 20.1:  Adil is coming to study in the US but he is unfamiliar with the healthcare system there. Read his email below asking for advice and write a response in the email template provided on the next page.

To: mailinglist@uyghurlanguagestudents.com

From: adiljan1989@usa.com

Subject: Studying in the USA without insurance

سالام!

مېنىڭ ئىسمىم ئادىل. مەن شىنجاڭ ئۇنىۋېرسىتېتى ئوقۇغۇچىسى. بۇ يىل سىلەرنىڭ ئۇنىۋېرسىتېتىڭلارغا بېرىپ ماگىستېرلىق ئوقۇشۇمنى ئوقۇماقچىمەن. دوستۇم ياسىن سىزنىڭ ئېلخەت ئادرېسىڭىزنى بەرگەن ئىدى. سىزدىن بىر نەچچە سوئال سورىسام بولامدۇ؟ ئاڭلىشىمچە، ئامېرىكىغا بارغان ئوقۇغۇچىلار چوقۇم سۇغۇرتا سېتىۋېلىشى كېرەك ئىكەن. سىزنىڭچە سۇغۇرتا بولمىسا دوختۇرغا بارسام بولامدۇ ياكى دوختۇر مېنى قوبۇل قىلمامدۇ؟ سۇغۇرتىنى نەدىن ئالسام ياخشىراق بولىدۇ؟ ماڭا مۇشۇ ھەقتە بىر مەسلىھەت بەرگەن بولسىڭىز.

جاۋابىڭىزنى كۈتۈپ،

ئادىل

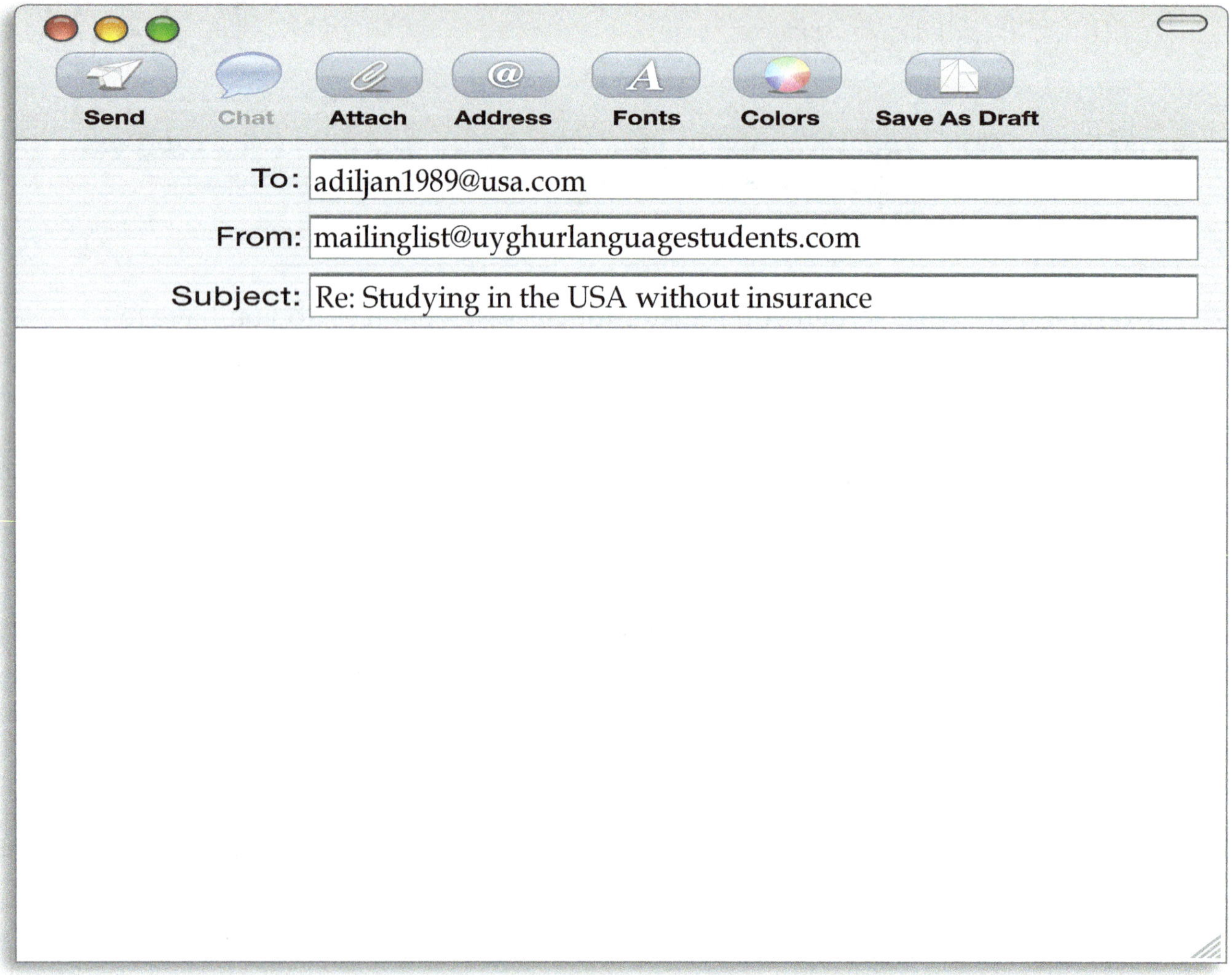

Send Chat Attach Address Fonts Colors Save As Draft

To: adiljan1989@usa.com

From: mailinglist@uyghurlanguagestudents.com

Subject: Re: Studying in the USA without insurance

Exercise 20.2:  Read the e-mail again. Identify the following forms and their functions:

1. There are three conditional forms. Circle each.
2. What is their function in this passage? Choose from below:
   (a) polite request (b) wish (c) advice (d) inquiry
3. Look at the highlighted suffix in the following excerpt. What does it express?

   بۇ يىل سىلەرنىڭ ئۇنىۋېرسىتېتىڭلارغا بېرىپ ماگىستېرلىق ئوقۇشۇمنى ئوقۇماقچىمەن.

4. Look at the highlighted word in the sentence below. What meaning does it add to the sentence?

   ئاڭلىشىمچە، ئامېرىكىغا بارغان ئوقۇغۇچىلار چوقۇم سۇغۇرتا سېتىۋېلىشى كېرەك ئىكەن.

Exercise 21: ئۇيغۇرلاردا بوكسچىلىق

Exercise 21.1: Here you will read a passage about Uyghur boxing. Look at the following numbers. What type of information do they probably refer to (e.g. date, age, weight, etc.)

1994 **91** **18:5** **15 - 19** **68**

Exercise 21.2:  Scan the following passage to check your answers. The words and expressions provided on the next page will help you to understand the passage better.

شىنجاڭ بوكس كوماندىسى شىنجاڭدىكى تەنتەربىيە كوماندىلىرى ئىچىدە تېز ئىلگىرىلەۋاتقان، شۇنداقلا كۆپچىلىكنىڭ ئېتىراپ قىلىشىغا ئېرىشكەن كوماندىلارنىڭ بىرى. مەزكۇر كوماندا 1994 - يىلى قۇرۇلغاندىن تارتىپ ئۆزىنىڭ ئەمەلىي كۈچى ئارقىلىق مەملىكەت ئىچى ۋە سىرتىدا چوڭ تەسىر قوزغاپ كېلىۋاتىدۇ. بولۇپمۇ 1997 - يىلى ئابدۇشۈكۈر مىجىتنىڭ مەملىكەتلىك بوكس مۇسابىقىسىنىڭ 91 كىلوگراملىقلار گۇرۇپپىسى بويىچە 5: 18 نەتىجە بىلەن چېمپىيون بولۇپ "جۇڭگو بوكس شاھى" دېگەن نامنى ئالدى. شىنجاڭ بوكس كوماندىسى باش تىرېنېرى ئابلىكىم ئابدۇرىشىتنىڭ يېتەكچىلىكىدە ھازىرغا قەدەر دۆلەت ئۈچۈن يىگىرمە نەچچە نەپەر مۇنەۋۋەر تەنھەرىكەتچى يېتىشتۈرۈپ بەردى. ئۇلاردىن ئالتە نەپەر تەنھەرىكەتچى جۇڭگوغا ۋاكالىتەن ئۇدا تۆت قېتىملىق ئولىمپىك مۇسابىقىسىگە قاتنىشىش سالاھىيىتىگە ئېرىشتى. مەملىكەتلىك ۋە خەلقئارا مۇسابىقىلەردە شىنجاڭ بوكس كوماندىسى جەمئىي 68 ئالتۇن مېدالنى قولغا كەلتۈردى. بۇ بىر قاتار نەتىجىلەرگە ئاساسەن جۇڭگونىڭ دۆلەتلىك بوكس كوماندىسى ھەر قېتىملىق خەلقئارالىق مۇسابىقىلەرگە شىنجاڭ بوكس كوماندىسىنىڭ مۇنەۋۋەر تەنھەرىكەتچىلىرىدىن ۋەكىل تاللاپ قاتناشتۇرىدىغان بولدى. بۇنىڭ بىلەن شىنجاڭ بوكس كوماندىسى ئۈچۈن ھەقىقىي مۇسابىقىلەرگە قاتنىشىش ۋە تەجرىبە توپلاش ئىمكانىيىتى تۇغۇلدى.

شىنجاڭ بوكس كوماندىسى مۇسابىقىلەردە ياخشى نەتىجىلەرنى قولغا كەلتۈرۈشكە ئەھمىيەت بېرىشتىن سىرت يەنە كوماندىنىڭ كەلگۈسى ئىستىقبالى ئۈچۈن ياشلارنى تەربىيەلەشنى چىڭ تۇتتى. ھازىرغا قەدەر كوماندا تەركىبىدە 15 ياشتىن 19 ياشقىچە بولغان ئەللىك نەچچە ئۆسمۈر مەشىق قىلماقتا. ئۆتكەن يىلى يەنە شىنجاڭنىڭ ھەرقايسى جايلىرىدىن 13 ياشتىن 14 ياشقىچە بولغان 30 ئۆسمۈر مەزكۇر كوماندىغا مەشىق ئۈچۈن تاللاندى. شۇنىڭ بىلەن بىر ۋاقىتتا كوماندا دەسلەپ قۇرۇلغان مەزگىللەردە قوبۇل قىلىنغان ماھىرلاردىن ئابدۇشۈكۈر، ئابدۇراخمان، ئەكرەم قاتارلىقلار بۈگۈنكى كۈندە شىنجاڭ كوماندىسىنىڭ ئاساسلىق تىرېنېرلىرىدىن بولۇپ قالدى. بۇنىڭ بىلەن شىنجاڭ بوكس كوماندىسى ھەم ئىزباسار بوكسچىلىرى بار، ھەم ئىزباسار تىرېنېرلىرى بار بولغان مۇكەممەل بىر كوماندىغا ئايلاندى.

representative	ۋەكىل	to recognize	ئېتىراپ قىلماق
possibility	ئىمكانىيەت	to achieve	ئېرىشمەك
future prospects	ئىستىقبال	outstanding	مۇنەۋۋەر
teenager	ئۆسمۈر	continuously	ئۇدا
period of time	مەزگىل	to train	يېتىشتۈرمەك
a successor	ئىزباسار	qualification	سالاھىيەت

Exercise 21.3: Read the passage again. Answer the following questions in detail.

1. What did you learn about "جۇڭگو بوكس شاھى"?
2. Who are the boxing coaches?
3. What is done to keep boxing alive?
4. There is one passive verb and two passive participles in the passage. Circle each and translate them into English.
5. What is the function of the highlighted suffix in the word بۇگۈنكى?

Exercise 22: ئۇيغۇرلار جەمئىيىتى

Exercise 22.1: Here you will read an excerpt from an article by Elise Anderson, who spent about two years in Urumchi. Before reading the passage, look at the sentence below:

ئۇيغۇرلار تۇرمۇشىنى قويۇق جەمئىيەت تورى ئىچىدە ئۆتكۈزىدىكەن.

What does the author imply about Uyghur society, in your opinion?

Exercise 22.2: تۆۋەندىكى ماقالىنى ئوقۇڭلار

يېقىنقى يىللاردىن بۇيان ئامېرىكىدا ھېچ كىمنىڭ ھېچ كىم بىلەن كارى بولمىسا ئەڭ ياخشى، باشقىلارنىڭ ئىشىغا بەك كۆڭۈل بۆلۈش ياخشى ئەمەس دەپ ھەر بىر ئادەمنىڭ شەخسىيەت - مەخپىيەتنى ھەممىدىن مۇھىم دەپ قارايدىغان كۆز قاراش شەكىللىنىپ قالغان. لېكىن، مېنىڭ ھېس قىلىشىمچە، ئۇيغۇرلاردا بۇنداق بىر كۆز قاراش يوق ئىكەن. ئەكسىچە، ئۇيغۇرلاردا "كىشىلەر ئۆز ئارا كۆڭۈل بۆلۈشسە ئەڭ ياخشى، ھېچ كىمنىڭ ھېچكىم بىلەن كارى بولمىسا يامان بولىدۇ" دەيدىغان بىر كۆز قاراش بار دېسەك توغرا كېلىدىكەن. مەن ئۆزۈم ھېچ كىمنىڭ ھېچكىم بىلەن كارى بولمايدىغان ئۆرپ - ئادەت ئىچىدە چوڭ بولغان بولساممۇ، ئەمما مەن ئۇيغۇرلار ئارىسىدىكى ئۆز-ئارا كۆڭۈل بۆلۈشنى ياخشى دەپ قارايمەن. ئۇيغۇرلار ۋە ئۇيغۇرلارغا ئوخشاش مىللەت خەلقى بىر - بىرى بىلەن كارى بولىدىغانلىقىنى ئاشكارا قىلىپ، پالانى ئىشنى قىلسام خەق نېمە دەيدۇ، پالانى ئىشنى قىلسام باشقىلارغا قانداق تەسىر بېرىپ قويارمەن دېگەن سوئاللارنى ھەرگىزمۇ نەزەردىن ساقىت قىلمايدۇ. بۇ ھەقىقەتەن ياخشى ئىش ئىكەن. ئۇيغۇرلارنىڭ باشقىلارغا كۆڭۈل بۆلىدىغانلىقى تۇرمۇشتىكى جىق ئىشلارغا تەسىر كۆرسىتىدىكەن. مەسىلەن، ئۇيغۇرلارنىڭ قويۇق جەمئىيەت تورى ئىچىدە ياشاۋاتقانلىقى ئۇلارنىڭ مېھماندوست خەلق ئىكەنلىكىنىڭ بىر سەۋەبىدۇر. بىر مېھمان كەلسە، ئۇيغۇرلار ئۆز ئىشنى تاشلاپ، پۇل ۋە ۋاقىتقا قارىماي، مېھمان ئالدىغا چىقىپ، ئۇنى قىزغىن كۈتىۋالىدىكەن. يولدا كېتىپ بارغاندا تونۇش ئادەم بىلەن ئۇچرىشىپ قالسا، چىرايلىق گەپ قىلىپ پاراڭ قىلىشىدىكەن. بەزىدە ئويلىسام، پۈتۈن شىنجاڭدىكى ئۇيغۇرلارنىڭ ھەممىسى بىر - بىرىگە تونۇشتەك بىلىنىدىكەن. بۇ خىل ئۆرپ - ئادەت بۈگۈنكى كۈنلەردە راستىنلا ئاز ئۇچرايدىغان بىر ئادەت ھېسابلىنىدۇ. ئۇيغۇرلارنىڭ باشقىلار بىلەن كارى بولىدىغانلىقى كىيىم - كېچەك، گىرىم قىلىش، گەپ - سۆز قىلىش قاتارلىق ئىشلارغىمۇ تەسىر كۆرسىتىدىكەن. ئامېرىكىدىكى ۋاقتىمدا مەن ئادەتتە "بولدىلا، نېمە كارىم" دەپ گىرىم قىلماي ئاددىي كىيىنىپ يۈرەتتىم، لېكىن شىنجاڭغا كېلىپ چىرايلىق كىيىنمەي، گىرىم قىلماي سىرتقا چىقمايدىغان بولدۇم.

to not care	كارى بولماسلىق	to reveal	ئاشكارا قىلماق
dignity	شەخسىيەت	a certain	پالانى
a secret	مەخپىيەت	to eliminate	ساقىت قىلماق
on the contrary	ئەكسىچە	make-up	گىرىم

Exercise 22.3: Answer the questions based on the passage.

1. As an American, what aspect of Uyghur society does Elise value?
2. What examples does she mention to support her view?
3. How has living among the Uyghurs changed her?
4. What words (nouns, adjectives, verbs) does she use to describe the Uyghurs?

Exercise 22.4: Now you will hear another excerpt written by Elise. In this later excerpt, Elise critiques some of the observations she made in her previous essay, which you read earlier. Listen carefully.

Exercise 22.5: Listen to the passage again and answer the following questions.

1. What are some negative aspects of attending a Uyghur wedding?
2. What are some negative aspects of always being friendly?
3. Elise says that "بۇ ھاياتتىكى ھەر قانداق ئىشنىڭ شەكلى بار". What does she mean?

Exercise 22.6: Listen to the passage again. Write down the missing adjectives in the transcript below based on what you hear.

يەنە بىر تەرەپتىن ئېيتقاندا، مۇشۇنداق ____________ جەمئىيەت تورى ئىچىدە
ياشاشنىڭ ياخشى بولمىغان يەرلىرىمۇ بار ئىكەن ۋە بەزى ئىشلار ئۇيغۇرلارغا بەك
____________ تەسىر كۆرسىتىدىكەن. مەن يېقىندا ئۇيغۇرلارنىڭ جەمئىيەتتىكى
مەسئۇلىيەتلىرىنىڭ ئېغىرلىقىنى ____________ھېس قىلدىم. تويلارنى مىسالغا ئالساق،
ئۇيغۇرلار توي ۋە نىكاھنى دۇنيادىكى ئەڭ ____________ ئىش دەپ قارايدىكەن. لېكىن،
باشقىلارنىڭ تويىغا بارىدىغان ۋاقىتلاردا، مەن تونۇيدىغان ئۇيغۇرلارنىڭ كۆپىنچىسى "توي دېگەن
ۋاقىتنى سۇدەك ئىسراپ قىلىدىغان بىر پائالىيەت" دەپ تويغا بېرىشنى يامان كۆرىدىكەن.
ئۇلارنىڭ تويغا بارغۇسى بولمىسىمۇ، بارمىسام____________ بولىدۇ دەپ بارىدىكەن.
قويۇق جەمئىيەت تورى ئىچىدە ياشاشنىڭ باشقا بىر ____________ يېرىمۇ بار. ئۇيغۇرلار
شەكىل دېگەن ئۇقۇمغا بەك ئېتىبار بېرىدىكەن. بۇ ھاياتتىكى ھەر قانداق ئىشنىڭ شەكلى
بار، لېكىن ئۇيغۇرلارنىڭ شەكىلگە شۇنچە كۆپ ئېتىبار بېرىدىغانلىقىنىڭ يامان تەرىپىمۇ بار
دەپ قارايمەن. مەسىلەن، كۆپ قىسىم ئادەملەر باشقىلارغا گەپ قىلغاندا "____________
گەپنى دېسەم ياخشى بولمايدۇ" دەپ، راستىنى ئېيتماي، ياخشىچاق بولۇپ ____________
گەپ قىلىپ يۈرىدىكەن. بىز ئامېرىكىلارنىڭ ____________ بىر يېرىمىز شۇكى، بىز گەپنى
ئۇدۇل قىلىدىكەنمىز. توغرىسىنى ئېيتمايدىغان بۇنداق ئىشنى بىر خىل ئالا كۆڭۈللۈك دېسەك
بولارمىكىن دەيمەن.

Note:

The suffix كى- in the word شۇكى acts much like a colon, or like the conjunction *that* in English, eg. "One good thing about us Americans is *that* we don't mince words."

Exercise 22.7:  In the excerpts in the previous exercises, Elise expresses her feelings and opinions regarding some aspects of Uyghur life. Look at the list below. Find each word/expression in Exercise 22.2 and Exercise 22.6.

ھېس قىلىشىمچە ئەكسىچە يەنە بىر تەرەپتىن ئېيتقاندا
دېسەك بولارمىكىن دەيمەن ئەكسىچە ياخشى دەپ قارايمەن

Exercise 22.8:  Do you agree or disagree with the following statements from Elise's excerpts? Explain your opinion using the phrases in Exercise 22.7. Give examples as part of your argument.

1. يېقىنقى يىللاردىن بۇيان ئامېرىكىدا ھېچ كىمنىڭ ھېچ كىم بىلەن كارى بولمىسا ئەڭ ياخشى، باشقىلارنىڭ ئىشىغا بەك كۆڭۈل بۆلۈش ياخشى ئەمەس دەپ ھەر بىر ئادەمنىڭ شەخسىيەت - مەخپىيىتىنى ھەممىدىن مۇھىم دەپ قارايدىغان كۆز قاراش شەكىللىنىپ قالغان.

2. ئۇيغۇرلارنىڭ قويۇق جەمئىيەت تورى ئىچىدە ياشاۋاتقانلىقى ئۇلارنىڭ مېھماندوست خەلق ئىكەنلىكىنىڭ بىر سەۋەبىدۇر.

3. بىز ئامېرىكانلارنىڭ ياخشى بىر يېرىمىز شۇكى، بىز گەپنى ئۇدۇل قىلىدىكەنمىز.

Exercise 23: نەشىنى قانۇنلاشتۇرايلى!

Exercise 23.1:  Read the internet discussion forum posts (on the next page) about the legalization of marijuana.

دېھقان: مەن بىر دېھقاننىڭ ئوغلى. نەشە ياساش ۋە نەشە چېكىش ئۇيغۇرلار ئارىسىدىكى ئۇزۇن تارىختىكى ئىگە ئادەتلەرنىڭ بىرى. تارىختىن بۇيان شىنجاڭدىكى ھېچقايسى ھۆكۈمەت نەشە چېكىشنى مەنئى قىلىپ باقمىغان ئىدى. ئەمما 1949 - يىلى جۇڭخۇا خەلق جۇمھۇرىيىتى قۇرۇلغاندىن كېيىن شىنجاڭدا قۇرۇلغان كوممۇنىستىك ھۆكۈمەت نەشە ياساش، نەشە سېتىش ۋە نەشە چېكىشنى جىنايەت دەپ بېكىتتى. شۇنىڭدىن بۇيان نۇرغۇنلىغان كىشىلەر مۇشۇ جىنايەتكە باغلىنىپ تۈرمىگە چۈشتى. ئەمىلىيەتتە نەشە ئۇيغۇرلار جەمئىيىتىدە نۇرغۇنلىغان پايدىلىق روللارنى ئوينىغان. ئۇنىڭ بىرى، نەشە كۆپلىگەن دېھقانلار ئۈچۈن مۇھىم ئىقتىسادىي كىرىم بولالايدۇ. نەشە ئادەتتە كەندىردىن ياسىلىدىغان بولۇپ، دېھقانلار كەندىرنى* كۆپىنچە ئېتىزنىڭ ئەتراپىغا تېرىيدۇ. كەندىر ئۆسۈپ چىققاندىن كېيىن ئۇنى پەرۋىش قىلىش، سۇغۇرۇش دېگەنلەر پۈتۈنلەي ھاجەتسىز. كەندىر ئۆسكەندىن كېيىن قۇرۇپ قالمايدۇ، تاكى كۈز بولغىچە كۆكلەيدۇ. دېھقانلار كەندىرنىڭ ئۇرۇقىدىن نەشە ياسايدۇ ۋە ئۇنى سېتىپ كىرىم قىلالايدۇ. ئېتىز ئەتراپىغا كەندىر تىكىشنىڭ يەنە بىر پەننىي ئاساسى بار: كەندىر ئۆسۈملۈكى ئۆزىدىن بىر خىل غەلىتە پۇراق چىقىرىدىغان بولغاچقا زىيانلىق ھاشارەتلەر بۇ پۇراقتىن قېچىپ كەندىر تېرىلغان تەۋەدىكى ئېتىزلىققا كىرمەيدۇ. مېنىڭچە نەشە قانۇنلاشتۇرۇلۇشى لازىم!

خوتەنلىك تېۋىپ: مەن سىزنىڭ پىكرىڭىزگە قوشۇلمەن! نېمىشقا دېسىڭىز، سىز كەلتۈرگەن سەۋەبلەردىن باشقا، تىبابەت ئىلمىدىن قارىغاندا نەشىنىڭ ناھايىتى يۇقۇرى دورىلىق قىممىتى بار. بولۇپمۇ نېرۋا كېسەللىكى ئۈچۈن ئىشلىتىلىدىغان دورىلارنىڭ كۆپىنچىسى كەندىر ئۇرۇقىدىن ياسىلىدۇ. نەشە چېكىش ئادەتتە مېڭىنى تىنچلاندۇرۇش رولىغا ئىگە. ھازىر تۇرمۇشنىڭ رېتىمى بەك تېز، شەھەر پۇقرالىرىنىڭ روھىي ۋە جىسمانىي جەھەتتىكى بېسىمى ئېغىر. روھىي جەھەتتە تىنچلىنىش ئۈچۈن ئۇنىڭغا تىنچ مۇھىت بولۇشى كېرەك. ئەمما ھازىرقى شەھەرلەردە تېز سۈرئەتتە كۆپىيىپ مېڭىۋاتقان نوپۇس سانى، ئۇنىڭغا ماس ھالدا چوڭىيىپ ماڭغان شەھەر كۆلىمى كىشىلەرگە تىنچ مۇھىت ئاتا قىلالمايدۇ. ئادەملەر سىغماي قېلىۋاتقان دىسكوخانىلار ۋە رېستورانلارمۇ چارچىغان كىشىلەرگە بۇنداق تىنچلىقنى بېرەلمەيدۇ. ئۇيغۇرلار ئىقتىسادىي جەھەتتە نامرات بولغاچقا، ساياھەت قىلىش ئارقىلىق روھىي جەھەتتىكى تىنچلىققا ئىگە بولۇش تېخىمۇ تەس. شۇڭا نەشە چېكىش كىشىلەرنىڭ چارچىغان مېڭىسىگە ئارام بېرىپ ئۇلارنىڭ روھىي جەھەتتىن ساغلام بولۇشىغا ياردەم بېرەلەيدۇ دەپ ئويلايمەن.

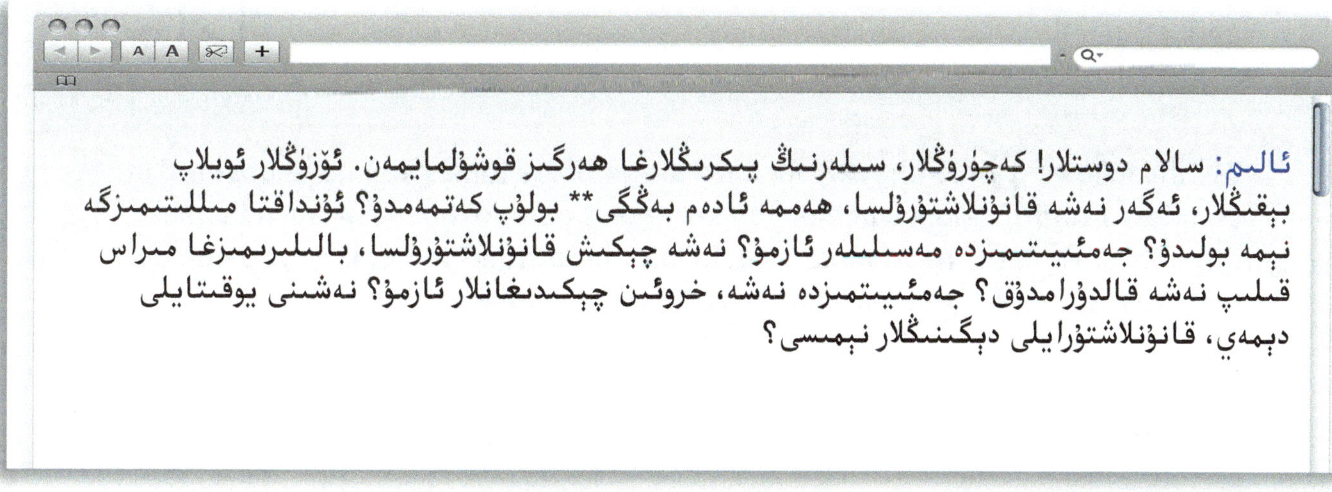

ئالىم: سالام دوستلار! كەچۈرۈڭلار، سىلەرنىڭ پىكرىڭلارغا ھەرگىز قوشۇلمايمەن. ئۆزۈڭلار ئويلاپ بېقىڭلار، ئەگەر نەشە قانۇنلاشتۇرۇلسا، ھەممە ئادەم بەڭگى** بولۇپ كەتمەمدۇ؟ ئۇنداقتا مىللىتىمىزگە نېمە بولىدۇ؟ جەمئىيىتىمىزدە مەسىلىلەر ئازمۇ؟ نەشە چېكىش قانۇنلاشتۇرۇلسا، بالىلىرىمىزغا مىراس قىلىپ نەشە قالدۇرامدۇق؟ جەمئىيىتىمىزدە نەشە، خروئىن چېكىدىغانلار ئازمۇ؟ نەشىنى يوقىتايلى دېمەي، قانۇنلاشتۇرايلى دېگىنىڭلار نېمىسى؟

*كەندىر: hemp

** بەڭگى: an opium addict

Exercise 23.2:  Outline the basic arguments of each of the comments on the preceding pages in the chart below. Fill the chart out in English.

	1st Entry	*2nd Entry*	*3rd Entry*
author			
opinion (for/against)			
argument			
other information			

Exercise 23.3: Prepare an oral summary answering the following questions.

قايسى پىكىرنى قوللايسىز؟ نېمىشقا؟

Self-check خامان

Use the following list to check your knowledge of the topics you have covered in chapters 9 and 10. Mark whether you know and can do the following in Uyghur. If you think you may need more work to fully understand something, you can go back to the relevant section in the chapters and review it.

1. I can talk and write about:

Typical Uyghur students' sports-related activities	
The history of Uyghur soccer	
The Urumchi baseball team	
The Urumchi boxing team	
Foods that heal, e.g. كۆك چۆچۈرە	
The importance of Uyghur folk medicine	
The tradition of sand therapy in Turpan	
The main parts of an Uyghur traditional wedding	
Health related social issues in the Uyghur homeland	
The details of Uyghur funeral ceremonies	
Modern Uyghur weddings and the weddings in my culture	
The nuclear testing at Lobnur	
The story of the ghosts who go to Mecca	
The Uyghur poet Dolqun Yasin	

2. I can also:

Explain my health problems/symptoms	
Describe important events in my life	
Make complaints at the hospital	
Describe my dream using the suffix مىش-	

3. I know how to:

Express condolences	
Talk about sport scores	
Express fault or responsibility with گەپ	
Use Uyghur proverbs related to health	
Recite a Uyghur tongue-twisters	

4. I can express my opinion on:

Drinking as a social habit	
The legalization of marijuana	

5. I know the following words and concepts:

	كۆڭۈل ئېلىشماق		قۇم بىلەن داۋالاش
	قان بېسىمى		ئىسراپچىلىق
	تەلەيگە يارىشا		ئىجابىي
	شىكايەت		سەلبىي
	مۇسابىقە		ھالال
	نەتىجە		ھارام
	يەڭمەك\ ئۇتماق		قىمار ئويناش
	يېڭىلمەك\ ئۇتتۇرماق		نەشە چېكىش
	كوماندا ئەزاسى		ئەيدىز
	بىرگە قارشى ئىككى		بالا- قازا
	مەشغۇلات		مېيىپ
	كالتەك توپ		يادرو سىنىقى
	نەزىر		تەزىيە بىلدۈرۈش/ كۆڭۈل ئېيتىش

6. I can use grammar to …

Express may/can (Verb بولماق + suffix: -سا \ -سە)	
Express obligation using double negative constructions with the auxiliary verb: بولماق	
Express the idea of 'sitting and doing' (auxiliary verb ئولتۇرماق)	
Make causative constructions (-ۋرا \ -ۋر \ -ارا \ -ەر)	
Express probability (-مىكىن)	
Express wishes (conditional and habitual past)	
Express if only (conditional and the verb بولماق)	
Connect clauses with نى + Possessive +(-گەن/-كەن+-لىك)	
Express doubt (-مىش)	

Vocabulary سۆزلۈك

Vocabulary is given according to the Uyghur alphabetical order.
The right column precedes the left column on each page.

habit	ئادەت
to tie on white (to show mourning)	ئاق باغلىماق
special	ئالاھىدە
way, method	ئامال
related to	ئائىت
trash bin	ئەخلەت ساندۇقى
spirit, ghost	ئەرۋاھ
messenger, matchmaker	ئەلچى
AIDS	ئەيدىز
to come into existence	بارلىققا كەلمەك
a stage, step	باسقۇچ
invitation	باغاق
to tie; to connect (together)	باغلىماق
disaster, calamity	بالا- قازا
hospital	بالنىست\ كېسەلخانا\ دوختۇرخانا
to ruin, to destroy	بەربات قىلماق
to slaughter	بوغۇزلىماق
according to	بويىچە
robbery	بۇلاڭچىلىق
petrol, benzene	بېنزىن
evil ways (in Islam)	بىدئەت
direct relative	بىۋاستە تۇغقان
to put out the welcoming carpet	پايانداز سالماق
speed of spreading	تارقىلىش سۈرئىتى
single, odd	تاق

coffin	تاۋۇت
to express condolences	تەزىيە بىلدۈرمەك\ كۆڭۈل ئېيتماق
to comfort, placate	تەسەللى بەرمەك
to imagine	تەسەۋۋۇر قىلماق
influence	تەسىر
to influence	تەسىر كۆرسەتمەك
destiny, fate	تەقدىر
to emphasize, stress	تەكىتلىمەك
to consent to; to give in to	تەن بەرمەك
an heirloom, cherished	تەۋەررۇك
to throw out, pour out	تۆكمەك
to pass away	تۈگەپ كەتمەك\ ئالەمدىن ئۆتمەك\ ۋاپات بولماق
to mention	تىلغا ئالماق
to wish	تىلىمەك
peace	تىنچلىق
heaven	جەننەت
hepatitis	جىگەر ياللۇغى
a crime, offense	جىنايەت
queen	خانىش
to be addicted	خۇمار بولماق
to be embarrassed, to be ashamed	خىجالەت بولماق
contrary to, against	خىلاپ
to step	دەسسىمەك

to get away from, to avoid	قۇتۇلماق
the Korban festival	قۇربان ھېيت
to be frozen (from fear, surprise or shock)	قېتىپ قالماق
to liven up, to reach a height	قىزىماق
to gamble	قىمار ئوينىماق
trouble, bad luck, misfortune	كاساپەت
to move	كۆچۈرمەك
to have fun	كۆڭۈل ئاچماق
entertainment	كۆڭۈل ئېچىش پائالىيىتى
happy, festive	كۆڭۈللۈك
cloth for a garment	كىيىملىك
to find a partner	لايىق تاپماق
funds	مەبلەغ
to be forced/ obliged	مەجبۇر بولماق
to force	مەجبۇرلىماق
deceased	مەرھۇم(ە)
existing	مەۋجۇت
ceremony	مۇراسىم
to confiscate	مۇسادىرە قىلماق
disabled	مېيىپ
rumors, word around town, gossip	مىش- مىش گەپ
feast in honor of deceased	نەزىر
to smoke marijuana	نەشە چەكمەك
songs and music	نەغمە- ناۋا
wedding	نىكاھ توي
a mourner	ھازىدار
to perish, to die	ھالاك بولماق
surgery	ئوپېراتسىيە
to hunt	ئوۋغا چىقماق

willingness; blessing	رازىلىق
cancer	راك
to live in ease	راھەت كۆرمەك
late (refers to a deceased person)	رەھمەتلىك
the Ramadan festival	روزا ھېيت
actually, really	زادى
to make fun of	زاڭلىق قىلماق/ مازاق قىلماق
poison; drugs	زەھەر
to force	زورلىماق
weighty words	سالمىقى بار گەپ
numb	سەزمەس
health department	سەھىيە خىزمىتى
to be patient, to forbear, to endure	سەۋر قىلماق
place (for meetings), an occasion, gathering	سورۇن
to test, try out	سىناشماق
to vanish, to disappear	غايىب بولماق
strange	غەلىتە
to help	قاراشماق
to be in mourning	قارىلىق تۇتماق
grave	قەبرە
cemetery	قەبرىستان
to borrow	قەرز ئالماق
sweets (such as cube sugar or candies that will be put out on the table for guests)	قەنت- گېزەك
bi-, double	قوش
bridesmaid, the best man (at a wedding)	قولداش

hot food	ئىسسىقلىق
nuclear test	يادرو سىنىقى
if you remember	يادىڭىزدا بولسا
scarf	ياغلىق
to untie, to take off (clothes)	يەشمەك
a cover, cover sheet	يوپۇق
to visit	يوقلىماق
to tear, to rip, to rend	يىرتماق
to see off	ئۇزاتماق
to pass	ئۆتمەك
death toll	ئۆلۈش نىسبىتى
a visit to a bereaved family	ئۆلۈم پەتىسى
to pay attention	ئېتىبار بەرمەك
high quality; noble	ئېسىل
e-mail	ئېلخەت
to be full of regrets, remorse	ئىچى سىرىلىپ كەتمەك
wastefulness	ئىسراپچىلىق

玉
入口处
精品和田玉
交易中心

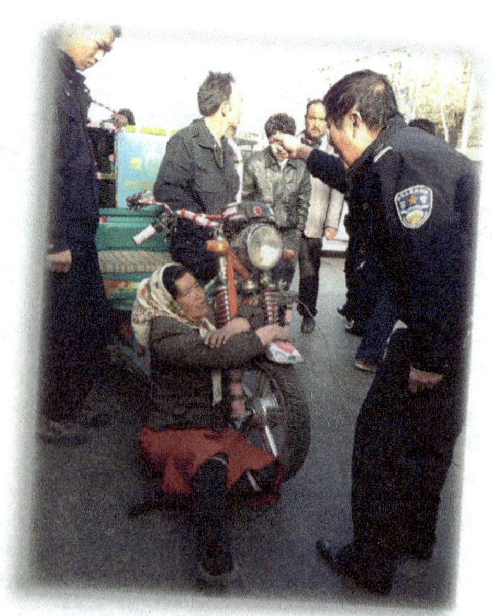

ئون بىرىنچى دەرس

CHAPTER ELEVEN

ئاخىرقى سەپەر- خوتەن

LAST TRIP - KHOTAN

IN THIS CHAPTER

Functions

- Describing places and people
- Making reservations at a hotel
- Making friends
- Describing things: Uyghur silk and rugs
- Expressing wishes
- Buying gifts at the Khoten bazaar
- Recognizing the Khoten dialect

Grammar

- The repeated conjunction بىر تۈرۈپ...بىر تۈرۈپ
- Another use of the suffix -مىش
- The 1st person of the interrogative present/future form
- Relative clauses with the word بولۇپ
- The construction -غۇم (-غۇڭ...) كېلىدۇ

In this chapter, you will accompany John on his trip to Khotan. You will catch a glimpse of the fascinating world of Uyghur traditional textiles like گەلەم and ئەتلەس in the silk and carpet making capital of the region. From the reading passages, video excerpts, and blog entries contained herein, you will obtain some information about the city and its peculiar dialect, and learn about a special naming tradition common among the Khotanese. You will become acquainted with some important cultural concepts and artifacts, such as قاشتېشى, شىۋە, and لەقەم.

Exercise 1: تۆۋەندىكى سوئاللارغا جاۋاب بېرىڭلار.

1. خوتەن توغرۇلۇق نېمىلەرنى بىلىسىز؟
2. خوتەن قاشتېشى ھەققىدە ئاڭلىغانمۇسىز؟
3. خوتەن گىلەمنى كۆرۈپ باقتىڭىزمۇ؟
4. گۆشگىردە يەپ باققانمۇسىز؟
5. خوتەن شېۋىسىنى ئاڭلاپ باقتىڭىزمۇ؟

Exercise 2: Look at the snapshots below. What can you tell about each picture?

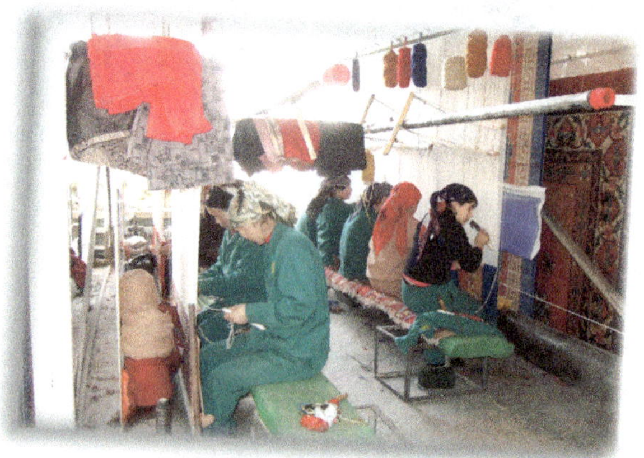

Exercise 3:  While on break from school, John wants to visit Khotan. Read his blog and answer the following questions:

Uyghur John's Blog

ئامېرىكىلىق ياللۇنىڭ تورتۇراسى

Search

26 - ماي:

ئۆتكەن قېتىم خوتەنگە بارالماي قالغانتىم، مانا ئەمدى ھازىر بارمىسام، باشقا بۇنداق پۇرسەت چىقمايدۇ. خۇدايىم بۇيرىسا، ئۈچ ئايدىن كېيىن ۋەتىنىمگە قايتىمەن. مېنى خوتەنگە ياسىن ئۆزى ئېلىپ بارماقچى بولغان، ئەمما ئۇنى ئاۋارە قىلغۇم كەلمىدى. ئۆزۈم ئۇيغۇرچە بىلگەندىن كېيىن ھېچ نەرسە بولماس دەپ ئويلايمەن. ئاڭلىسام، خوتەنلىكلەرنىڭ شېۋىسى ئەدەبىي تىلدىن خېلى پەرق قىلىدىكەن. ئۇلارنىڭ گېپىنى چۈشىنەلمىسەم قانداقمۇ قىلارمەن؟ بىرتۇرۇپ يالغۇز بارمايمىكىن دەيمەن، يەنە بىرتۇرۇپ ئۆزۈم بېرىۋېرەي دەيمەن.... بۈگۈن كەچنىڭ بېلىتىنى ئېلىپ قويدۇم. باللا (باللار) ئايرودرومغا ئەچىقىپ قويىمىز دېدى... مېنىڭ خوتەن بازارلىرىنى كۆرگۈم بار. كىشىلەرنىڭ دېيىشىچە، خوتەن بازارلىرى قەشقەر بازارلىرىدىنمۇ بەكرەك قىزىيدىكەن. خوتەن ئەزەلدىن يىپەك يولى توقۇمىچىلىقى بىلەن مەشھۇر بولۇپ كەلگەن ئىكەن. خوتەننىڭ گىلەم ۋە ئەتلەسلىرى پۈتۈن جۇڭگو بويىچە ئەڭ داڭلىق ھېسابلىنىدىكەن. خوتەنلىكلەرنىڭ ھەممىسى دېگۈدەك گىلەم توقۇيالايدىكەن. مېنىڭ شۇ گىلەم، ئەتلەس كارخانىلىرىغا بارغۇم بار. ئاڭلىسام خوتەنلىكلەر تېبابەتچىلىككىمۇ ئالاھىدە ئېتىبار بىلەن قارايدىكەن، ئۇ يەردە تېۋىپلەرمۇ خېلى كۆپ دەيدۇ. خوتەندىن كۆپ ئالىملار ۋە يازغۇچىلار چىققانىمىش. خوتەن خېلى ئاتىقى چىققان شەھەر بولسىمۇ، خوتەنلىكلەرنى ئاددىي - ساددا ياشايدۇ دەپ ئاڭلىدىم. ئۇلار بىلەن پاراڭلاشقۇم بار. قېنى، ئۇلار مېنىڭ ئۇيغۇرچەمنى چۈشىنەلەمدىكىن؟ مەنچۇ، مەن ئۇلارنىڭ شېۋىسىنى ئۇقالامدىمەن؟ ئەمدى بارغاندا بىر گەپ بولىدۇ-دە... ۋۇي، سائەتمۇ بەش بوپ قاپتۇ، ھازىر باللا كېلىدۇ، نەرسىلىرىمنى تەييارلاپ قوياي. ئايروپىلان مېنى تاشلاپ قويۇپ ئۇچۇپ كەتمىسۇن يەنە!

كۈندە بىر ماقال: ئوغۇل بالىغا قىرىق ھۈنەر ئاز

ئىسىم

ئىم

1. نېمىشقا جون خوتەنگە ياسىن بىلەن بارمايدۇ؟
2. جون خوتەن توغرۇلۇق نېمىلەر دەيدۇ؟
3. نېمە ئۈچۈن جون بىلوگىدا يىپەك يولىنى تىلغا ئالىدۇ؟
4. جون نېمىدىن ئەنسىرەيدۇ؟

Exercise 4:  Read the following sentence from the passage and translate it into English.

خوتەنلىكلەرنى ئاددىي - ساددا ياشايدۇ دەپ ئاڭلىدىم.

Use the same structure to create four statements similar to the one above. Follow the examples:

1. غوجەخمەت سەدۋاقاسوۋنى ھەقىقىي ئالىم دەپ بىلىمەن.
2. كالىفورنىيەدە قىش بولمايدۇ دەپ ئاڭلىدىم.

1 "One moment... and the next..." بىرتۇرۇپ... بىرتۇرۇپ

As you know, there are some conjunctions in Uyghur which require using the same word twice before two adjacent clauses. You have already encountered such conjunctions as: ھەم...ھەم، يا...يا

In John's blog you saw another repeated conjunction بىر تۇرۇپ ... (يەنە) بىر تۇرۇپ , which consists of two separate words بىر+ تۇرۇپ (one + the -پ form of the verb تۇرماق) .

In this context, however, بىر تۇرۇپ is roughly equivalent in meaning to the word گاھىدا 'for a time' or بىردەم 'for a moment.' When used twice, the resulting conjunction means that the subject of the verb does one thing at one moment and something else the next. It has the same meaning as another conjunction بىردەم ... بىردەم. Compare the following sentences:

بىرتۇرۇپ يالغۇز بارمايمىكىن دەيمەن، (يەنە) بىرتۇرۇپ ئۆزۈم بېرىۋېرەي دەيمەن...
One moment I was thinking "oh , I can't just go alone,"
the next I thought I should go myself...

كىچىك بالا دېگەن شۇ: بىرتۇرۇپ ئويناىمەن دەيدۇ، بىرتۇرۇپ ئۇخلايمەن دەيدۇ.
All kids are the same: one moment they want to play,
but next they want to sleep.

بۇ شەھەرنىڭ ھاۋاسى بىرتۇرۇپ ئېچىلىدىكەن، بىرتۇرۇپ تۇتۇلۇپ قالىدىكەن.
The weather in this town is clear one second and overcast the next.

ئەخمەت بىردەم كۆزلىرىنى ئاچاتتى، بىردەم يۇماتتى.
Exmet kept opening his eyes one second and shutting them the next.

ئۇ بىردەم كۈلەتتى، بىردەم يىغلايتتى.
He was laughing one moment and crying the next.

Exercise 5:  Compose your own sentences using the repeated conjunctions بىرتۇرۇپ ... (يەنە) بىرتۇرۇپ and بىردەم ... بىردەم. Follow the examples above.

___

___

___

2 Another Usage of the Suffix مىش-

In the previous chapter, you learned about the suffix مىش- and its functions. This suffix also appears in John's blog in the following sentence:

خوتەندىن كۆپ ئالىملار ۋە يازغۇچىلار چىققانمىش.
(It is said that) Many great thinkers and authors have come from Khotan.

As you see from the example above, the suffix مىش- here is used in much the same way as the normal hearsay past with پتۇ-, or the compound hearsay past with غان+ ئىكەن-. Compare the following sentences:

خوتەندىن كۆپ ئالىملار ۋە يازغۇچىلار چىققانمىش.
خوتەندىن كۆپ ئالىملار ۋە يازغۇچىلار چىقىپتۇ (چىققان ئىكەن).

Sometimes the suffix مىش- is even used in conjunction with the other hearsay tenses. Look at the following examples:

ئاڭلىسام ئۇ تۈنۈگۈن كەپتىمىش (كەپتۇمىش).
From what I hear he arrived yesterday.
ئۇ ئىشقا ئورۇنلىشىپتىمىش (ئورۇنلىشىپتۇمىش).
He apparently got hired.

It is important to note that as a hearsay past neither the پتۇمىش- construction, nor the ending مىش- by itself is very common. Usually only the suffix پتۇ- and the constraction غان+ ئىكەن- are used.

Exercise 6:  Translate the following sentences into English. Pay attention to the grammatical form of the last verb.

قېنى، ئۇلار مېنىڭ ئۇيغۇرچەمنى چۈشىنەلەمدىكىن؟ مەنچۇ، مەن ئۇلارنىڭ شېۋىسىنى ئۇقالامدىمەن؟

3 The 1st Person of the Interrogative Present/Future Form

You know that in the present/future tense to form the first person interrogative (yes/no question) the suffix -ام\ -ەم\ -م+ -دى+م is used.

بارامدىم؟ ئالامدىم؟ ئاڭلامدىم؟

However, in spoken Uyghur there is another form for the 1st person. As you can see from the underlined sentence (Exercise 3), in the 1st person of the interrogative present-future form the personal ending مەن is added. Compare the following verbs:

بارامدىم - بارامدىمەن (بارامدىم + مەن)
قىلامدىم - قىلامدىمەن (قىلامدىم + مەن)

As you can see from the examples above, the double م which results from the placement of the pronoun مەن after the verb ending in دى+م is reduced to a single م. The first person plural also displays an alternate interrogative ending, which is constructed in a similar way:

قىلامدۇق- قىلامدىمىز؟ بارامدۇق- بارامدىمىز؟

Exercise 7: مەنمۇ بارامدىمەن؟

Exercise 7.1:  Translate the following questions into Uyghur using the Grammar Point above.

1. Will I go home now?
2. Will we do this work?
3. Will I write this letter?
4. Will we read this book?

Exercise 7.2:  Now ask your partner some questions using the grammatical construction you just learned.

Exercise 8: مېھمانخانىدا

Exercise 8.1:  John arrives in Khotan. He tries to find a hotel. Listen to the first part of his conversation with the receptionist at a hotel front desk, and decide whether the following two statements are true or false.

1. John should have made a reservation. __________
2. The receptionist knew that John is a foreigner after greeting him. _________

Exercise 8.2:  Read the rest of the conversation and answer the questions below.

خىزمەتچى: سىز چەتئەللىك ئوخشىمامسىز؟!
جون: شۇنداق، مەن ئامېرىكىلىق.
خىزمەتچى: ئۇنداقتا سىز باشقا مېھمانخانىغا بېرىشىڭىز لازىم.
بۇ مېھمانخانىدا چەتئەللىكلەر تۇرسا بولمايدۇ.
جون: نېمىشقا؟
خىزمەتچى: خوتەندە چەتئەللىكلەر ئۈچۈن ئالاھىدە
مېھمانخانا بار، "ئەلچى" مېھمانخانىسى...
جون: مۇنداق دەڭ... سىز دېگەن مېھمانخانا بۇ يەردىن
يىراقمۇ؟
خىزمەتچى: يىراق ئەمەس، چوققۇ بازارنىڭ ئارقىسىدا.
ھازىر چىقىپلا تاكسى توسسىڭىز بولىدۇ، تاكسى سىزنى
بەش كويغا شۇ مېھمانخانىغا ئاپىرىپ قويىدۇ.
جون: رەھمەت.

1. John needs to go to another hotel because
   - A. it is expensive for him
   - B. there are no available rooms
   - C. he is a foreigner
   - D. he lost his passport
2. Which hotel does the receptionist tell him to go to?
3. How much does it cost to get to the hotel?

Exercise 8.3:  Listen to the whole conversation and repeat it aloud. Then act it out with a partner.

Exercise 8.4:  John arrives at another hotel. Listen to his conversation with a receptionist and tell if the following statements are true or false.

	توغرا	خاتا
1. جون بىر كىشىلىك ياتاق ئالدۇ.		
2. ئۇ تىزىملىتىش جەدۋىلىنى تولدۇردۇ.		
3. بۇ ياتاقنىڭ نەرخى 20 دوللار.		
4. جون خوتەندە تۆت كۈن تۇرماقچى.		
5. جوننىڭ ياتىقى 2- قەۋەتتە.		
6. ياتاقنىڭ نومۇرى 51.		
7. جوننىڭ بىرلا چامىدانى بار.		
8. جون يۈكىنى ياتىقىغا ئۆزى ئېلىپ چىقدۇ.		
9. بۇ مېھمانخانىنىڭ ئاشخانىسى يوق.		

Exercise 8.5:  Listen to and practice the dialogue. Then act out it with your partner.

Exercise 9: خوتەنگە خوش كەپسىز !

Here you will watch a video in which Ablet Abdureshit Berqi, a Khotanese writer, talks about Khotan.

Exercise 9.1:  Watch the video and answer the following questions.

1. What does the narrator say about the territory of Khotan?
2. What do چۆل كۆلىمى and بوستانلىق كۆلىمى mean to you? What does the narrator say about it?
3. What does he say about the population of خوتەن ۋىلايىتى ?
4. In your opinion, what does the expression تېرىلغۇ يەر كۆلىمى mean? Why does the narrator mention it?
5. At the end of the video Ablet says: خوتەندە توپا ياغىدىغان ئەھۋال بار. What does this mean?

Exercise 9.2: Watch the video again and tell what the following numbers refer to?

2 million ______________________________

96-97% ______________________________

365 ______________________________

150-200 ______________________________

Exercise 9.3: In this video the narrator uses several adjectives to describe Khotan. Watch the video one more time and circle adjectives you hear.

چىرايلىق   يەر كۆلىمى چوڭ   ھاۋاسى مۆتىدىل   سۈيى قىس   قالايمىقان
سۈيى ئەلۋەك   ئىسسىق   قۇرغاق   تىنچ   ھاۋاسى نەم

Exercise 10: خوتەن گىلىمى

Exercise 10.1: Have you heard of the Khotanese carpet? If so, what do you know about it? If you had a chance to ask a Khotanese person some questions about the carpet, what would you ask?

Exercise 10.2: Look at the picture of the famous Khotanese carpet and describe it. Talk about the colors, shapes, and design elements you see.

Exercise 10.3:  John wants to visit a گىلەم factory, where rugs are made. Before visiting, he reads a passage about this famous product of Khotan.

خوتەن گىلىمى

گىلەم - ئۇيغۇر قول ھۈنەر بۇيۇملىرى ئىچىدە ھەممىدىن ئەتىۋارلىق ۋە ئەڭ كەڭ ئومۇملاشقان مىللىي مەھسۇلاتلارنىڭ بىرى. خوتەننىڭ "گىلەم يۇرتى" دېگەن نامى بار.

گىلەم- خوتەن خەلقىنىڭ ئەنئەنىۋىي قول ھۈنەر مەھسۇلاتى بولۇپ، ئۇنىڭ تارىخى ناھايىتى ئۇزۇن. ئىككى مىڭ يىل بۇرۇن خوتەندە گىلەمچىلىكنىڭ بارلىقى ھەققىدە تارىخىي خاتىرىلەر بار. خەلق ئارىسىدا گىلەم ئەسلىدە گۈلەمجان ئىسىملىك بىر قىزنىڭ ئىجادىيىتى ئىكەنلىكى ۋە شۇ مۇناسىۋەت بىلەن شۇ قىزنىڭ نامىغا گۈلەم (ئاستا- ئاستا "گىلەم" گە ئۆزگەرگەن) دەپ ئاتالغانلىق ھەققىدە ھەر خىل رىۋايەتلەر بار. خوتەندە يەتتە ياشتىن يەتمىش ياشقىچە كىشىلەرنىڭ ھەممىسى گىلەم توقۇشقا ئادەتلەنگەن. خوتەن گىلىمى خوتەن قويىنىڭ يۇڭىدىن توقۇلىدۇ. خوتەندە يۇڭ يىپ بوياشقا ئىشلىتىدىغان تەبىئىي بوياق ماتېرىياللىرى (مەسلەن، ياڭاق پوستى، ئانار پوستى) ناھايىتى كۆپ چىقىدۇ.

خوتەن گىلەملىرى كىشىلەرنىڭ تۇرمۇش ئېھتىياجىغا ئاساسەن يەر گىلىمى (يەرگە سالىدىغان گىلەم)، تام گىلىمى (ئاسما گىلەم)، كارىۋات گىلىمى قاتارلىقلارغا بۆلۈنىدۇ. بۇ خىل گىلەملەرنىڭ چوڭ كىچىكلىكى ۋە رەڭ تۈرلىرى بىر - بىرىدىن پەرقلىنىدۇ.

گىلەم توقۇش يۈكسەك ئەقىل - پاراسەت ۋە گۈزەللىك تۇيغۇسى تەلەپ قىلىدىغان ئەمگەك بولغاچقا، ئۇيغۇرلار ئۇنى ناھايىتى قەدىرلەيدۇ ۋە پەخىرلىنىدۇ. گىلەم ناھايىتى چىدامlıق بولغاچقا، خەلق ئارىسىدا "كەمبەغەل بولساڭ گىلەم ئال" دەيدىغان گەپ بار. خوتەن گىلىمى بۈگۈنكى كۈندە تېخىمۇ تەرەققىي قىلىپ خەلقئارا

بازاردا رىقابەت كۈچىگە ئىگە بولغان بىر مىللىي قول ھۈنەر مەھسۇلاتى بولۇپ قالماقتا.

List three new pieces of information you have learned from this passage:

1. ______________________________
2. ______________________________
3. ______________________________

Answer the questions about the text.

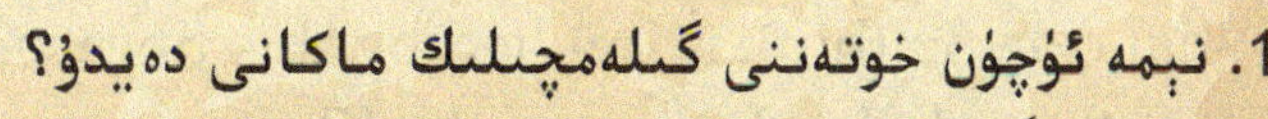

1. نېمە ئۈچۈن خوتەننى گىلەمچىلىك ماكانى دەيدۇ؟
2. خوتەن گىلىمى توغرۇلۇق قانداق رىۋايەتلەر بار؟
3. خوتەن گىلىمى قانداق يۇڭدىن توقۇلىدۇ؟
4. خوتەندە يۇڭ بوياشقا قانداق بوياقلار ئىشلىتىلىدۇ؟
5. نېمە ئۈچۈن كىشىلەر خوتەن گىلىمىنى ئەتىۋارلايدۇ؟

Explain the folk etymology of the word گىلەم based on this passage.

There is a saying in the text. Explain what is meant here:

كەمبەغەل بولساڭ، گىلەم ئال.

Exercise 10.4:  The following passage describes the various designs found in the Khotanese carpet. Read the passage and write the name of each design under the pictures of the objects which they represent.

خوتەن گىلىمى روشەن يەرلىك ئالاھىدىلىككە ۋە قويۇق مىللىي تۈسكە ئىگە. ئۇ نۇسخا جەھەتتىن "شەرق ئۇسلۇبى" غا تەۋە بولۇپ، ئۇنىڭ شەكلى خىلمۇ خىل ۋە رەڭدار، ئىشلىتىشكە قولايلىق. ئۇنىڭدا ئۇيغۇرلارنىڭ مىللىي ئېستېتىك تەلىپى ئەكس ئەتكەن. خوتەن گىلىمى نۇسخا جەھەتتىن ئانار نۇسخا (ئانار گۈل نۇسخا دەپمۇ ئاتىلىدۇ) ، چېچەك نۇسخا، لوڭقا نۇسخا، شام نۇسخا، يۇلتۇز نۇسخا قاتارلىق ئون نەچچە تۈرگە بۆلىنىدۇ. بۇ گىلەملەرنىڭ ھەممىسىدە بىر ئورتاق ئالاھىدىلىك بار، يەنى بۇ گىلەملەرنىڭ چۆرىسىگە ھەرە چىشلىق ئۇچ بۇلۇڭ شەكىل نەقشلەنگەن.

____

____

____

____

____

According to the text, the Khotanese carpet is ئىشلىتىشكە قولايلىق.
What do you think is implied by this phrase?
Even though the designs of the Khotanese carpet are different, they all have one thing in common. What is it?

Exercise 10.5:  Summarize what you know about the Khotanese carpet. Use the expressions given below and add details you have learned from the passages you read on the preceding pages.

گۈلەمجان، ئانا ماكان، تەبىئىي بوياق،
يەرلىك ئالاھىدىلىك، ئەقىل - پاراسەت، قويۇق مىللىي تۈس،
تۇرمۇش ئېھتىياجى، نۇسخا، شەرق ئۇسلۇبى، نەقىشلەنمەك،
خەلقئارا بازار، چىداملىق

4 Relative Clauses with the Word بولۇپ

The grammar point discussed in this section is mainly used in Uyghur literature and in news broadcasts. In spoken Uyghur, however, this structure is not active. It is important to recognize this structure when you see it, but you are not expected to produce it.

In the passage about the Khotan carpet, you saw two compound sentences using the verb form بولۇپ, where the word بولۇپ is used to connect two clauses as a conjunction.

1. گىلەم خوتەن خەلقىنىڭ ئەنئەنىۋىي قول ھۈنەر مەھسۇلاتى بولۇپ، ئۇنىڭ تارىخى ناھايىتى ئۇزۇن.

2. ئۇ نۇسخا جەھەتتىن "شەرق ئۇسلۇبى" غا تەۋە بولۇپ، ئۇنىڭ شەكلى خىلمۇ خىل ۋە رەڭدار، ئىشلىتىشكە قولايلىق.

These sentences might be translated into English as:

1. The carpet, as the people of Khotan's traditional handmade product, has a long history.
2. Belonging to the Eastern style, it (the carpet) has different forms and colors, and it is very convenient to use.

This construction might also be used as a stylistic device to avoid duplication of the verb forms. See the following example:

Instead of saying:

چۈشتىن بۇرۇن ھاۋا بۇلۇتلۇق بولىدۇ، پۈتۈن كۈن يامغۇر ياغىدۇ.

You can say:

چۈشتىن بۇرۇن ھاۋا بۇلۇتلۇق بولۇپ، پۈتۈن كۈن يامغۇر ياغىدۇ.

Besides that, this structure is often used in news reports to show that there are some other actions taking place. See the examples in Exercise 12.

Exercise 11:  Change the verb forms to avoid the duplicating tense endings.

1. چۈشتىن كېيىن ھاۋا ئوچۇق بولىدۇ، تېمپېراتۇرا 15 گرادۇس سېلسىيە بولىدۇ.

---

2. يېزا كوچىسىنىڭ ئىككى تەرىپىدە ئېرىقلار بولاتتى، بۇلاردا سۈپ - سۈزۈك سۇ ئېقىپ تۇراتتى.

---

3. خوتەن قاشتېشىنىڭ رەڭگى ئاق، سېرىق، كۆك، قاراۋە يېشىل بولىدۇ، ئاق قاشتېشى بىلەن سېرىق قاشتېشى ئەڭ ئەتىۋارلىق ھېسابلىنىدۇ.

Translate the sentences you wrote, and discuss how their meaning is different from the original sentences.

Exercise 12:  Look at the following sentences from Radio Free Asia news. Underline the coordinating words and explain their usage and meaning in the sentence.

ئۇيغۇر ئېلىنىڭ جەنۇبىي قىسمىدىكى تارىم ئويمانلىقىنىڭ ئەتراپىمۇ يەر تەۋرەش كۆپ يۈز بېرىدىغان جايلار بولۇپ، 2002- يىلى 2 - ئايدا قەشقەر ۋىلايىتىنىڭ مارالبېشى، پەيزىۋات ناھىيىلىرىدە 6.7 بال قاتتىق يەر تەۋرەپ 267 ئادەم ئۆلگەن، كۆپلىگەن ئادەم يارىلانغان ئىدى.

خەۋەرلەرگە ئاساسلانغاندا، تارىم ئويمانلىقىدا 8.4 تىرىلىيون كۇپمېتىر تەبىئىي گاز مىقدارى بار بولۇپ، بۇ پۈتۈن جۇڭگو چوڭ قۇرۇقلۇقىدىكى گاز زاپىسىنىڭ ئومۇمىي مىقدارىنىڭ تۆتتىن بىر قىسمىنى تەشكىل قىلىدىكەن.

ئۇيغۇر ئېلىنىڭ جەنۇبىي قىسمىدىكى تارىم ئويمانلىقىنىڭ ئەتراپىمۇ يەر تەۋرەش كۆپ يۈز بېرىدىغان جايلار بولۇپ، 2002 - يىلى 2 - ئايدا قەشقەر ۋىلايىتىنىڭ مارالبېشى، پايزىۋات ناھىيىلىرىدە 7.6 بال قاتتىق يارتەۋرەپ، 762 ئادەم ئۆلگەن، كۆپلىگەن ئادەم يارىلانغان ئىدى.

Exercise 13: يارده‌م كېره‌كمۇ؟

Exercise 13.1:  In Khotan, John meets a Uyghur man who offers to show him some well-known places in the city. Read a conversation between them and fill in the blanks with words or phrases which seem appropriate.

جون: كه‌چۈرۈك، بۇ ئه‌تراپتا بازار بارمۇ؟

مه‌تتۇرسۇن: ۋۇي، سىز ________________؟

جون: هه‌ئه، مه‌ن ________________.

مه‌تتۇرسۇن: يىراقتىن كه‌لگه‌ن ________________ ئىكه‌نسىز، بازارغا سىزنى ئۆزۈم ئاپىراي.

جون: ره‌همه‌ت ________________. تۈنۈگۈن گىلەم كارخانىسىغا بارغان ئىدىم، بۈگۈن بازارنى ئايلانغۇم كه‌لدى.

مه‌تتۇرسۇن: ياخشى بوپتۇ. بازارلىرىمىزنى كۆرمىسىڭىز هه‌رگىز بولمايدۇ. يۈرۈڭ، سىزنى چوققۇ ________________ ئاپىراي، پىيادىلا ________________. بازاردىن نىمه ئالماقچىسىز؟

جون: تۈنۈگۈن ئه‌تله‌س كىيگه‌ن ئاياللارنى كۆرۈپ، مېنىڭمۇ ئانامغا بىر پارچه ئه‌تله‌س ئالغۇم كه‌لدى.

مه‌تتۇرسۇن: بۇنى ياخشى ئويلاپسىز. خوته‌ن ئه‌تله‌س ماكانى ئه‌مه‌سمۇ... مه‌ن سىزگه ئه‌ڭ ئېسىل ئه‌تله‌سله‌رنى كۆرستەي.

جون: ره‌همه‌ت سىزگه. خوته‌نده ________________ بەك كۆپ ئىكه‌ن...

مه‌تتۇرسۇن: شۇنداق، بۇ ئۇيغۇرلار ماكانى ئه‌مه‌سمۇ، شۇڭا مه‌كته‌پنى پۈتتۈرۈپ بۇ يه‌ردىن كه‌تكۈم كه‌لمىدى. ساۋاقداشلىرىمنىڭ كۆپى هازىر ________________.

جون: هه راست، مېنىڭ ئىسمىم جون، ________________ ئىسمىم يالغۇن. سىزنىڭچۇ؟

مه‌تتۇرسۇن: مېنىڭ ئىسمىم مه‌تتۇرسۇن.

جون: مه‌تتۇرسۇن؟ مه‌ن تۇرسۇن دېگه‌ن ئىسىمنى ئاڭلىغان، ئه‌مما مه‌تتۇرسۇننى بىرىنچى ئاڭلىشىم.

مه‌تتۇرسۇن: هه، خوته‌نلىكله‌رنى ئۆلارنىڭ ئىسىملىرىدىن بىلىۋالغىلى بولىدۇ.

جون: ئۇلارنىڭ ________________ باشقىچىمۇ؟

مه‌تتۇرسۇن: باشقىچه ئه‌مه‌س، لېكىن خوته‌نلىكله‌رنىڭ ئىسىملىرىنىڭ كۆپىنچىسى "مه‌ت" بىله‌ن باشلىنىدۇ.

جون: قىزىق، مه‌ن بۇنى بىلمه‌يدىكه‌نمه‌ن...

مه‌تتۇرسۇن: بۇ يه‌رده كۆپره‌ك تۇرسىڭىز، خېلى نه‌رسىله‌رنى ئۆگىنىۋالىسىز... مانا بازارغىمۇ كېلىپ قالدۇق. قېنى، ئالدى بىله‌ن ئه‌تله‌س ________________ ئۆته‌يلى...

جون: شۇنداق قىلايلى!

Exercise 13.2:  Now listen to the dialogue and see if your answers are similar to the words you hear.

Exercise 13.3:  Look at the dialogue again. At the end of the dialogue John learns something new about male names used specifically in Khotan. Circle the Khotanese names from the collection of names below.

مەتنىياز ئۆمەرجان تۇنىياز تۇردىمەمەت مەتقۇربان

مەمتىمىن ئىمىنجان مەتروزى قاسىم ئابلىمىت

Exercise 13.4: Act out the dialogue with your partner.

5 Expressing Desire with the Verb كەلمەك

In the dialogue (Exercise 13.1) you have seen the following sentences:

بۈگۈن بازارنى ئايلانغۇم كەلدى.
Today I wanted to stroll around the city.
مېنىڭمۇ ئانامغا بىر پارچە ئەتلەس ئالغۇم كەلدى.
I also wanted to buy a piece of silk for my mother.
مەكتەپنى پۈتتۈرۈپ بۇ يەردىن كەتكۈم كەلمىدى.
After I graduated, I did not want to move from this place.

This construction shows a speaker's desire to do something and corresponds to the English 'would like', and 'want'.

The construction (Verb + -كۇ\-گۇ\-قۇ\-غۇ+-م\-ڭ... + the verb كەلمەك) is synonymous in meaning to the construction verb + غۇ+-م\-ڭ ... بار (Chapter 5).

Note that كەلمەك is conjugated for tense, person and negation, whereas the first verb functions as a noun ('my desire is to see,' 'his desire is to eat,' 'your desire is to live,' etc.). Look at the following examples:

مۇزدەك نەرسە ئىچكۈم كېلىۋاتىدۇ.
I want to drink something very cold.
دوستۇم بىلەن ئازراق مۇڭداشقۇم كېلىۋاتىدۇ.
I want to talk to my friend.
ئۇنىڭ كىنو كۆرگۈسى كەلدى.
He wanted to see a movie.
دائىم يۇرتۇمغا بارغۇم كېلىدۇ.
I always want to go to my home city.
سىزنى دائىم كۆرگۈم كېلىدۇ.
I always want to see you.
ئۇلارنىڭ بۇ ئىشنى قىلغۇسى كەلمىدى.
He did not want to do this work.
ئۇ يەرگە بارغۇڭ كەلمىدىمۇ؟
Did not you want to go there?

Exercise 14:  Using the grammatical structure from Grammar Point 5 and the verbs provided in parentheses, complete the following sentences. If you see the Ø symbol, write a negative sentence. Follow the examples.

كىتاب ئوقۇسام، (ئۇخلىماق) ئۇخلىغۇم كېلىدۇ.

بىز ماروژنى يېدۇق، تاماق (يېمەك) ø يېگۈمىز كەلمىدى.

1. خوتەنگە بارغاندا، ئۈنىڭ گىلەم (ئالماق) ________________.
2. گۆشنى كۆرۈپ كاۋاپ (يېمەك) ________________.
3. قورسىقىم توق بولغاچقا، ھېچ نەرسە (يېمەك) Ø ________________.
4. تويغا نېمىشقا بارمىدىڭىز؟ (بارماق) Ø ________________.
5. پەرىدەنىڭ مىللەتلەر ئۇنىۋېرسىتېتىدا (ئوقۇماق) ________ ، ئەمما دادىسى بېيجىڭغا ئەۋەتمىدى.
6. بۇ ماقالىنى ئوقۇدىڭىزمۇ؟ (ئوقۇماق) Ø ________________.

Exercise 15: How would you respond without hurting other people's feelings? Answer the questions using the construction above. Follow the examples:

دوستىڭىز: تۈنۈگۈن نېمىشقا ئولتۇرۇشقا كەلمىدىڭ؟

سىز: شۇنداق بارغۇم كەلدى، ئەمما قورسىقىم ئاغرىپ بارالمىدىم.

ساۋاقدىشىڭىز: كەچتە كىنوغا بارمامدۇق؟

كىنوغا بارغۇم كېلىۋاتىدۇ، ئەمما ۋاقتىم چىقمامدىكىن.

ئانىڭىز: نېمىشقا تاماقنى يېمىدىڭ؟

سىز: ________________________________

دادىڭىز: ئىشخانامغا كېلىمەن دەپ كەلمىدىڭغۇ؟

سىز: ________________________________

دوستىڭىز: بۈگۈن پۇتبول ئويناشقا بارامسەن؟

سىز: ________________________________

دادىڭىز: شەنبە- يەكشەنبە كۈنلىرى ماڭا قارىشالامسەن؟

سىز: ________________________________

ساۋاقدىشىڭىز: بۇ كىتابنى ئوقۇمىدىڭىزمۇ؟

سىز: ________________________________

Exercise 16: ئەتلەس ئالاملا؟

Exercise 16.1:  John is walking around the bazaar with Mettursun looking for a gift for his mother. Listen to the first part of the dialogue and answer the questions below.

1. What does John want to buy for his mother?
2. What are the basic colors for an Etles?

Statement	T	F
1. Young girls do not wear ئەتلەس.		
2. Middle-age women wear blue ئەتلەس.		
3. Older women usually wear black ئەتلەس.		
4. Women of any age can wear red ئەتلەس.		

Exercise 16.2:  Listen to the first part of the dialogue between Mettursun and the vendor and follow the transcript provided below. Circle the words that you hear pronounced differently from what you expect.

مەتتۇرسۇن: ئۇستام، ماۋۇ ئەتلەس شارپىلىرىنى نەچچە پۇلغا بېرىلا؟
دۇكاندار: سەھەردە كەلگەن خېرىدارنى قاچۇرما دەيدۇ. چاغلاپ بەرسىلە.
مەتتۇرسۇن: ئەتلەس ئارىلاش ئەمەستۇ؟
دۇكاندار: ھەممىسى تاللانغان ئەتلەسلەر.
مەتتۇرسۇن: ئەمسە ماۋۇنى نەچچىگە بېرىلا؟
دۇكاندار: قارىسام مەرد ئادەمكەنلا، سىلىگە ئوتتۇز كويدىن بېرەي.
مەتتۇرسۇن: مۇشۇ چىرايلىق گەپلىرى ئۈچۈن ئىككىنى ئالاي.
دۇكاندار: ئوبدان. ئانىلىرىغا ئالاملا يا ئاچىلىرىغا ئالاملا؟
مەتتۇرسۇن: دوستۇمنىڭ ئانىسىغا.

Exercise 16.3:  Read the rest of the dialogue in Khotan dialect. The provided words and expressions will help you to understand the passage.

ئەڭىل	كىيىم - كېچەك، بوي- تۇرق
سۇد بەرمەسلىك	پايدا يەتكۈزمەسلىك
سەركەشتە	ئاربلاش، ساختا
دىلخا	خللانغان، تاللانغان، ئەلا
ئانىكا	ئانا
ئاپا	ئاچا
خىلڭ	مەرد، نوچى
دەڭگىرەكلىمەك	پو ئاتماق، ماختاناماق
رەڭگىۋا	رەڭ، رەڭلىك

شاپ	تېز، چاپسان، ئىتتىك
مانتىلاش	ئاختۇرۇش، ئىزدەش
كات	ياغاچ كارىۋات
كاداڭ	تەجرىبىلىك
گىچاڭلاتماق	كۆز-كۆز قىلماق
مۇت	ھەقسىز، بىكار
ئۇز	چىرايلىق
سوم	كۆپ، جىق
گاداي	ئادەم

دۇكاندار (جونغا بىر قاراپ قويۇپ): ما گادايمۇ ئەتلەسنى بىلەمتا؟
مەتتۇرسۇن: بىلتۇ. كاداڭ گاداي ئۇ. ئانىكىسغا ئىككىنى ئالىتمەن دىيتۇ.
دۇكاندار: ئەڭلىگە قالىسا بىزگە ئوخشايتكىنيا. ھە بوپتۇ، مانى 60 كويغا بەدىم.
مەتتۇرسۇن: بىزگىمۇ سۇد بەسلە، ماقىما؟ 15 كويدىن بىرىييا.
دۇكاندار: ماندا رەڭگىۋا مالنى شاپ ئاممىسلا قامايتۇ. بازانى مانتىلىسا مۇندا مال چىقمايتۇ، مېلىنى گىچاڭلاتتى دېمىسلە، 25 كويدىن بىري.
مەتتۇرسۇن: ماندا دەڭگىرەكلىمىسلە. بازادا ئەتلەس دېگەن سوم تۇيۇپتۇ. 20 كويدىن بىري. قاندىغا؟
دۇكاندار: بوپتۇ، مۇت بەگىلى بۇمايتكەن. لەۋزىلىرىنى ئالاي. ما كاتتا جىندەك ئوتتۇراپ تۇسلا.
مەتتۇرسۇن: ھە، شاپ بوسلا.

Exercise 16.4: Compare the dialogue in Khotan dialect (Exercise 16.3) with the dialogue below in Standard Uyghur. What kind of differences did you notice? Discuss them with your instructor.

دۇكاندار (جونغا بىر قاراپ قويۇپ): ماۋۇ ئادەممۇ ئەتلەسنى بىلەمدۇ؟
مەتتۇرسۇن: بىلىدۇ. ئەقىللىق ئادەم ئۇ. ئانىسىغا ئىككىنى ئالىمەن دەيدۇ.
دۇكاندار: تۇرقىغا قارىسا بىزگە ئوخشايدىكەن. ھە بوپتۇ، مانى 60 كويغا بەردىم.
مەتتۇرسۇن: بىزگىمۇ پايدا بەرسىلە، ماقۇلما؟ 15 كويدىن بېرەي.
دۇكاندار: مۇنداق رەڭلىك مالنى تېز ئالمىسىلا قالمايدۇ. بازانى ئاختۇرسىڭىز مۇنداق مال چىقمايدۇ. مېلنى ماختىدى دېمىسىلە، 25 كويدىن بېرەي.
مەتتۇرسۇن: مۇنداق پو ئاتمىسىلا. بازاردا ئەتلەس دېگەن جىق تۇرۇپتۇ. 20 كويدىن بېرەي. قانداق؟
دۇكاندار: بوپتۇ، بىكارغا بەرگىلى بولمايدىكەن. سۆزىڭىزنى ئالاي. ماۋۇ كارىۋاتتا بىردەم ئولتۇراپ تۇرسىلا.
مەتتۇرسۇن: ھە، تېز بولسىلا.

The Khotan Dialect

As one of the major dialects of modern Uyghur, the Khotan dialect is mainly spoken within the areas between Guma and Charqiliq, the regions located in the southern rim of the Taklimakan Desert which were once bustling, cosmopolitan centers that flourished from the exchange of goods, languages, religions, and ideas. Particular features of this dialect include the addition of "t" after the verb stem, either the retroflexion of intervocalic "r" or its transformation into "y," the regular deletion of some intervocalic sounds, and the presence of voiced stops "b" and "d" in word-final positions.

Exercise 16.5:  Read the whole dialogue (Exercise 16.2 and Exercise 16.4). Then decide if the following statements are true or false.

توغرا	خاتا

1. بۇ دۇكاندارنىڭ ئەتلىسى سەركەشتە.
2. ئۇنىڭ ھەممە ئەتلىسى دىلخا مال.
3. دۇكاندار بىر شارپىنى 30 كويغا ساتماقچى.
4. مەتتۇرسۇن ئانىكىسىغا ئىككى شارپا ئالماقچى.
5. مەتتۇرسۇن دۇكاندار بىلەن سودىلاشتى.
6. دۇكاندار ئىككى شارپىنى 40 كويغا بەردى.

Exercise 16.6:  Listen and repeat the following words which contain particular phonological features of the Khotan dialect.

1. Addition of [ت] after the verb stem
Standard: بېرىلا Khotan dialect بىرتىلا

2. The sound [ر] becomes the sound [ي]
Standard: بىر Khotan dialect بىي

3. The sound [ر] becomes a retroflex sound*
Standard: بېرەي Khotan dialect بىرىي

4. The sound [ر] becomes sound [ل]
Standard: قارىسىلا Khotan dialect قالىسىلا

Note that some phonological reduction also occurs, for example:
- the verb بېرىدۇ becomes بىتۇ, ئالىدۇ becomes ئاتۇ , دەيدۇ becomes دىتۇ.

Exercise 16.7:  There is a saying in that dialogue سەدە كەگەن خىدانى قاچۇما. Rewrite it in standard Uyghur and tell what it means.

____

____

____

*If you study or familiar with Chinese, this sound is represented in Hanyu Pinyin by the letter 'r.'

Exercise 17: ئەتلەس توغرۇلۇق نېمە بىلىسىز؟

Exercise 17.1: Look at the following pictures of various types of ئەتلەس. What colors stand out in each? What do you think the colors represent?

Exercise 17.2: Here you will read a passage about Etles. Before reading, look at the following words and phrases.

aesthetic sensibility	ئېستېتىك تەپەككۇر
to express	ئىپادە قىلماق
to make threads from silkworms	پىلىدىن يىپ ئېگىرىش
weaving, knitting	ئەتلەس توقۇمىچىلىقى
ethnic (national) mark, emblem	مىللىي بەلگىسى
imitative	تەقلىدىي
to devote to	بېغىشلىماق
especially	بولۇپمۇ

Exercise 17.3:  Now read the passage and answer the following questions.

ئەتلەس - ئۇيغۇر يىپەكچىلىكىدىكى داڭدار مەھسۇلاتلارنىڭ بىرى ۋە ئۇيغۇر ئاياللىرىنىڭ ئەڭ ياخشى كۆرىدىغان يىپەك رەختلىرىدىن بىرى. شۇڭا ئۇيغۇر ئاياللىرىنىڭ كۆپچىلىكىدە بىر يۈرۈشتىن ئەتلەس كۆڭلىكى بولىدۇ. ئەتلەس كۆڭلەكنى ئۇيغۇر ئاياللىرىنىڭ مىللىي بەلگىسى دېيىشكە بولىدۇ. ئەتلەس ئۇيغۇر خەلقىنىڭ ئېستېتىك تەپەككۇرىدا ئۆز ماكانىنىڭ تۈزۈلۈشىنى، گۈزەل باغ - بوستانلىرىنى، يېشىل لېنتىدەك سوزۇلۇپ ئاققان دەريالىرىنى نەپىس ۋە رەڭدار يىپەك بىلەن تەقلىدىي ئىپادە قىلغان سەنئەت خەرىتىسىدۇر. ئەتلەس يىپەكتىن توقۇلغاچقا، سۈپىتى يۇقىرى، يۇمشاق ھەم نەپىس بولغاچقا، بەدەنگە ھوزۇر بېغىشلايدۇ.

شىنجاڭ قەدىمدىن باشلاپ يىپەكچىلىك بىلەن دۇنياغا مەشھۇر بولغان رايونلارنىڭ بىرى. بولۇپمۇ جەنۇبىي شىنجاڭنىڭ خوتەن ۋە قەشقەر رايونلىرىدا يىپەكچىلىك بىر قەدەر بۇرۇن تەرەققىي قىلغان. ئەتلەس - ئۇيغۇرلارنىڭ يەرلىك قول ھۈنەر مەھسۇلاتى. خوتەن شەھىرى، يەركەنت، يېڭىسار ۋە قەشقەر ئەتراپىدا ئەتلەس توقۇشنى ھۈنەر- كەسىپ قىلغان نۇرغۇن كاسىپلار بۇ ئەنئەنىۋى مىللىي ئادىتىنى يوقاتقىنى يوق. ئەتلەس توقۇمچىلىقى بىر قانچە باسقۇچلارنى بېسىپ ئۆتىدۇ: پىلىدىن يىپ ئېگىرىش، يىپنى بوياش، توقۇش.

ئادەتتە قولدا توقۇلغان يەرلىك ئەتلەسنىڭ ئۇزۇنلىقى ئالتە مېتىر قىرىق سانتىمېتىر، كەڭلىكى قىرىق بەش سانتىمېتىر بولىدۇ.

1. Why do Uyghur women like to wear ئەتلەس?
2. Where is ئەتلەس making most developed in Xinjang?
3. How many steps are included in producing ئەتلەس?
4. What are the measurements of handmade ئەتلەس?

Exercise 17.4:  Based on the passage, decide if the following statements are true or false.

خاتا	توغرا

1.خوتەن ۋە قەشقەر رايونلىرىدا يىپەكچىلىك بىر قەدەر بۇرۇن تەرەققىي قىلغان.

2. ئەتلەس كۆڭلەك ئۇيغۇر ئاياللىرىنىڭ مىللىي بەلگىسى.

3. ئەتلەس ئەڭ سۈپەتلىك پاختىدىن توقۇلىدۇ.

4. ئۇيغۇر ئەرلىرىنىڭمۇ بەلباغلىرى ئەتلەستىن تىكىلىدۇ.

Exercise 18: Read John's blog entry and answer the questions that follow.

Uyghur John's Blog

ئامېرىكىلىق يالقۇننىڭ تورتۇراسى

Search

كۈندە بىر ماقال:
گۆھەر ياتىدۇ سايدا، تونۇمىساڭ نېمە پايدا.

25 - ئىيۇل ، خوتەن

خوتەنگە كېلىپ ئۆزەمنى ئۇيغۇر دۆلىتىگە كېلىپ قالغاندەك ھېس قىلدىم، ئەمما يول بويىلىرىدىكى ئۇيغۇرچە ۋە خەنزۇچە يېزىلغان ۋىۋىسكىلار ماڭا بۇ يەرنىڭ يەنىلا جۇڭگو ئىكەنلىكىنى ئەسلەتتى.

خوتەننىڭ "گىلەم يۇرتى" ۋە "قاشتېشى ماكانى" دېگەن نامى بار ئىكەن. ئەمما خوتەندىكى ئۇيغۇرلارنىڭ گېپىنى چۈشەنمەك سەل تەسكەن. ئۇلار خوتەن دىئالېكتىدا سۆزلەيدىكەن. خوتەنلىكلەر بەك دوستانە ۋە سەمىمىي خەلق ئىكەن.

بىر كۈنى بازاردا ئۇيغۇرچە سۆزلەشسەم، كىشىلەر يېنىمغا ئولاشقىلى تۇردى. بىر بالا ماڭا قاراپ: ما سېرىق ئۇرغۇيچە بىلدىكەن، دېدى. قارىسام، ئۇ سېرىق دەپ مېنى دەپتۇ! مېنىڭ كۈلگۈم كەلدى، چۈنكى مەن ئۇيغۇرلار لەقەم قويۇشقا بەك ئۇستا دەپ ئاڭلىغان. بۇ بالا ماڭا دەررۇ لەقەم قويۇپتۇ!

مەتتۇرسۇن ئىسىملىك بالا بىلەن تونۇشۇۋالغان ئىدىم. ئۇ ماڭا بەكمۇ كۆپ ياردەم بەردى. ئۇ خوتەنلىك ئەرلەرنىڭ ئىسمى كۆپىنچىسى "مەت" سۆزى بىلەن باشلىنىدىغانلىقىنى ئېيتتى. ئىسىملار توغرۇلۇق يەنە قىزىق نەرسىلەرنى ئۆگىنىۋالدىم. ئەرلەر ئىسىملىرى "ئوبۇل" سۆزى بىلەن باشلانغان بولسا (ئوبۇلقاسىم، ئوبۇلنىياز)، بۇ كىشىلەر قەشقەرلىق ئىكەن، ئەگەر ئىسىملار "تۇ" ياكى "ئاق" سۆزى بىلەن باشلانسا (تۇنىياز، ئاقنىياز)، بۇ كىشىلەر كۆپىنچە ئاقسۇلۇق بولىدىكەن. ئىسىملارنىڭ ئاخىرىغا "قارى" سۆزى قوشۇلسا (قۇربان قارى، ئادىل قارى)، بۇلارنىڭ كۇچالىق ئىكەنلىكىنى بىلىۋالغىلى بولىدىكەن. غۇلجىلىق ئەرلەرنىڭ ئىسىملىرىنىڭ ئاخىرىغا "جان" سۆزى قوشۇلىدىكەن (ئابلاجان، تۇرسۇنجان)... نېمىدېگەن قىزىق- ھە....

خوتەندە قاشتېشى سېتىۋالغۇم كەلدى. بۇ يەرنى قاشتېشى ماكانى دەپ بىكار دېمەيدىكەن. شەھەرنىڭ ھەممە جايىدا قاشتېشى سېتىلىدىكەن. ئەمما ئۇنى بىلىدىغان ئادەم بىلەن ئالمىسا، تەس ئىكەن.

خوتەننىڭ نانلىرىنى ياخشى كۆردۈم. نېمىدېگەن مەززىلىك! گۆش گىردىلىرىمۇ ياخشىكەن، ئەمما ئىچىگە كۆپ ماي سالىدىكەن.

ئىسىم
ئىم

1. Why did John feel like he was in China?
2. What nickname was he given?
3. What regional names did he learn? List them all and underline the element which identifies them as coming from a particular region.
Follow the model:

غۇلجىلىق ئۇيغۇرلارنىڭ ئىسمى: ئابلا<u>جان</u>، تۇرسۇن<u>جان</u>

قەشقەرلىق ئۇيغۇرلارنىڭ ئىسمى: ______________________________

ئاقسۇلۇق ئۇيغۇرلارنىڭ ئىسمى: ______________________________

كۇچالىق ئۇيغۇرلارنىڭ ئىسمى: ______________________________

4. Which terms does John use for Khotan in this entry?
   A. land of ئەتلەس B. land of carpet
   C. land of jade D. land of oil

5. What advice does John give for foreigners who want to shop in the jade bazaar?

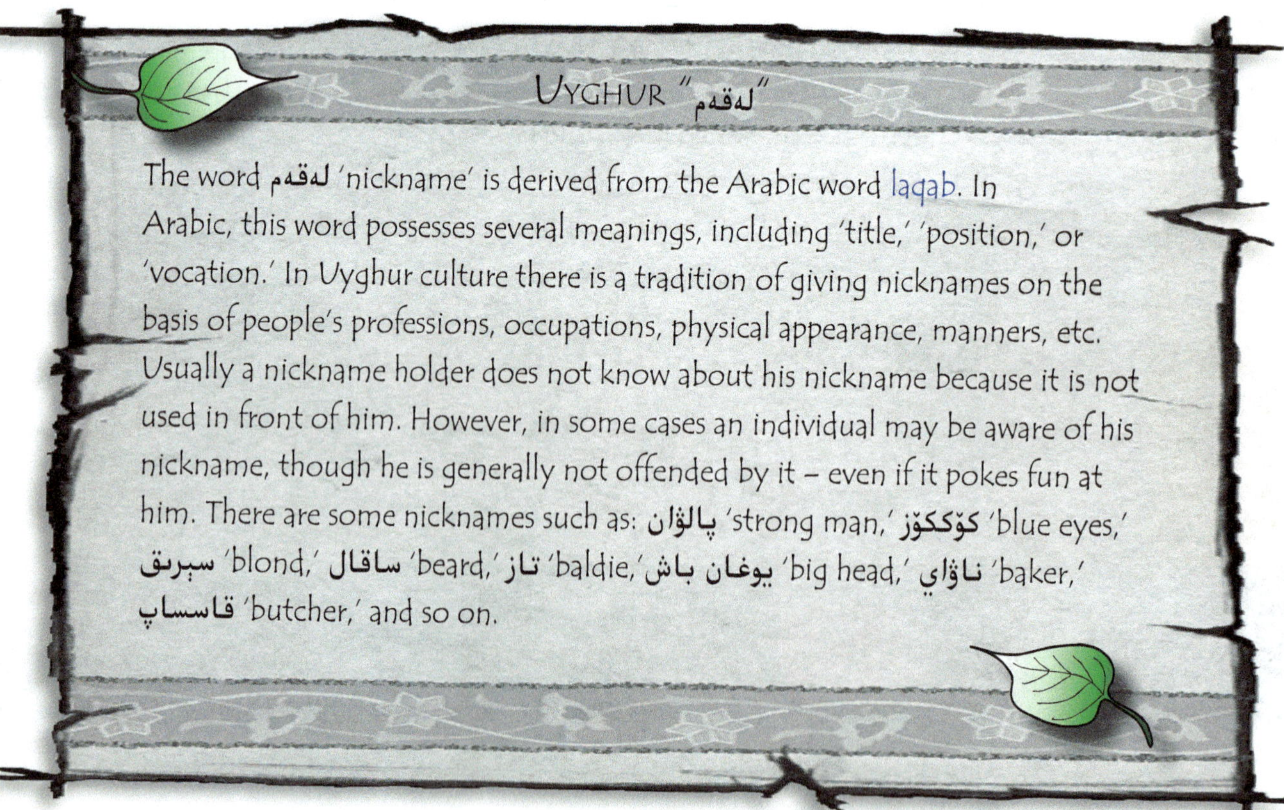

Uyghur "لەقەم"

The word لەقەم 'nickname' is derived from the Arabic word laqab. In Arabic, this word possesses several meanings, including 'title,' 'position,' or 'vocation.' In Uyghur culture there is a tradition of giving nicknames on the basis of people's professions, occupations, physical appearance, manners, etc. Usually a nickname holder does not know about his nickname because it is not used in front of him. However, in some cases an individual may be aware of his nickname, though he is generally not offended by it – even if it pokes fun at him. There are some nicknames such as: پالۋان 'strong man,' كۆككۆز 'blue eyes,' سېرىق 'blond,' ساقال 'beard,' تاز 'baldie,' يوغان باش 'big head,' ناۋاي 'baker,' قاسساپ 'butcher,' and so on.

Have you ever heard about...? بۇ كىشىنى بىلەمسىز...؟

In this section you will read and learn about a famous Uyghur person.

Exercise 19: ئابدۇكېرىم ئابلىز

Exercise 19.1: Read the following passage about Abdukerim Abliz, a famous Uyghur comedian. Then, answer the questions that follow. The words and expressions provided before the questions will help you to understand the passage better.

2014 - يىلى 18 - ئاۋغۇست
دۈشەنبە

قەشقەر كەچلىك گېزىتى

1231 - سان پوچتا ۋاكالەت نومۇرى: 54 ـ 66

ئۇيغۇر كىنو- تېلېۋىزىيە، ئېتوتچىلىق ساھەسىدە بەلگىلىك مۇۋەپپەقىيەتلەرنى قولغا كەلتۈرۈپ تاماشىبىنلارغا تونۇلغان داڭلىق كومېدىيە چولپىنى ئابدۇكېرىم ئابلىز 1970 - يىلى 3 - ئاينىڭ 27 - كۈنى قەشقەر شەھرىدە تۇغۇلغان. ئۇ ئۆزىنىڭ قىزىقىشى ۋە ئارزۇسى بويىچە 1987 - يىلى 9 - ئايدا شىنجاڭ سەنئەت ئىنستىتۇتىنىڭ ئاكتيورلۇق كەسپىگە قوبۇل قىلىندى. 1991 - يىلى 7 - ئايدا مەكتەپ پۈتتۈرۈپ تەڭرىتاغ كىنو ستۇدىيەسىگە ئاۋاز ئارتىسى بولۇپ ئورۇنلاشتى. ئابدۇكېرىم ئابلىز 1989- يىلى تېلېۋىزىيەدە «تۈيۈق يول» ناملىق ئېتوتنى ئويناپ تۇنجى قېتىم تاماشىبىنلار بىلەن يۈز كۆرۈشكەن. ئۇ 30 دىن ئارتۇق ئېتوت، كۆپلىگەن تېلېۋىزىيە تىياتىرلىرىدا ئوخشىمىغان خاراكتېر ۋە كەچۈرمىشكە ئىگە خىلمۇخىل پېرسوناژلارنىڭ ئوبرازىنى كۈچلۈك يۇمۇرىستىك ئالاھىدىلىككە ئىگە قىلىپ ياراتتى. بۇنىڭدىن باشقا ئابدۇكېرىم ئابلىز رېژىسسورلۇق كەسپىگە ئىشتىياق باغلاپ، «قۇربان تۇلۇمنىڭ بېيجىڭغا سەپىرى» ناملىق كىنو فىلمى، «داپ»، «ساراڭ»، «ئاخىرقى كۆل»، «قەبرىگە تۆكۈلگەن ياش» ناملىق تېلېۋىزىيە تىياتىرلىرىنىڭ مۇئاۋىن رېژىسسورلۇقىنى ئۆتىدى ۋە بىر نەچچە كۇلدۇرگە ۋە تېلېۋىزىيە تىياتىرلىرىغا مۇستەقىل رېژىسسورلۇق قىلىپ بەلگىلىك تەسىر قوزغىدى. ئابدۇكېرىم ئابلىز يەنە 500 دىن ئارتۇق كىنوغا ئاۋاز بېرىپ ئۆزىنىڭ ھەقىقىي بەدىئىي تالانتىنى نامايان قىلدى.

«سەنئەت بېغىدىكى بىر جۈپلەر» ژۇرنىلى 2004 - يىل، 3 - ساندىن ئېلىندى.

dead end	تۆيۇق يول
adventure	كەچۈرمىش
interest, pleasure	ئىشتىياق
to tie	باغلىماق
vice-, deputy	مۇئاۋىن
to fulfill, to do	ئۆتىمەك
to excite	تەسىر قوزغىماق
artistic	بەدىئىي

a studio theatre	ئېتوت
distinctive	بەلگىلىك
success	مۇۋەپپەقىيەت
to achieve	قولغا كەلتۈرمەك
an audience, spectators	تاماشىبىن
wish, desire	ئارزۇ
according to	بويىچە
celebrity	چولپان

1. ئابدۇكېرىم ئابلىز كىم؟
2. ئۇ قايسى ئالىي مەكتەپنى پۈتتۈردى؟
3. ئۇ ئوقۇش پۈتتۈرۈپ نېمە قىلدى؟
4. ئابدۇكېرىم ئابلىز «قۇربان تۇلۇمنىڭ بېيجىڭغا سەپىرى» ناملىق كىنو فىلىمنىڭ مۇئاۋىن رېژىسسورلۇقىنى ئۆتىگەن. قۇربان تۇلۇم ھەققىدە ئاڭلىغانمۇسىز؟ ئۇ نېمە مەقسەتتە بېيجىڭغا سەپەر قىلدۇ؟
5. ئابدۇكېرىم ئابلىزنىڭ بىرەر ئېتوتىنى كۆرگەنمۇ؟

Exercise 19.2:  Based on the passage above, ask your partner three more questions about Abdukerim Abliz.

Vocabulary سۆزلۈك

Vocabulary is given according to the Uyghur alphabetical order.
The right column precedes the left column on each page.

to take, to carry	ئاپارماق
to name; to be dedicated to	ئاتىماق
key	ئاچقۇچ
to look for, to search for	ئاختۇرماق
to get used to	ئادەتلەنمەك
in accordance with	ئاساسلانماق
gradually	ئاستا- ئاستا
hanging carpet	ئاسما گىلەم
pomegranate	ئانار
to bother	ئاۋارە قىلماق
to revolve, to rotate	ئايلانماق
nearby	ئەتراپ
valuable, precious	ئەتىۋارلىق
to provide a ride	ئەپچىقىپ قويماق
since long ago	ئەزەلدىن
to remind	ئەسلەتمەك
intelligence	ئەقىل - پاراسەت
to reflect	ئەكس ئەتمەك
stage	باسقۇچ
striped heavy silk	بەقەسەم
mark, emblem	بەلگە
dyestuff, tincture	بوياق
to dye	بويىماق
at one moment	بىرتۇرۇپ
to be proud of, to take pride in	پەخىرلەنمەك
to have an opportunity	پۇرسەت چىقماق
to make threads from a silk-worm	پىلىدىن يىپ ئېگىرمەك

on foot	پىيادە
very; clean	تازا
wall carpet	تام گىلىمى
natural	تەبىئىي
to develop	تەرەققىي قىلماق
to organize	تەشكىل قىلماق
demand	تەلەپ
to demand	تەلەپ قىلماق
weaving, knitting	توقۇمىچىلىق
life necessity	تۇرمۇش ئېھتىياجى
feeling	تۇيغۇ
folk doctor	تېۋىپ
folk medicine	تىبابەتچىلىك
an aspect, view	جەھەت
to be tired	چارچىماق
foreigner	چەتئەللىك
side, perimeter	چۆرە
enduring	چىدامىلىق
memory; diary	خاتىرە
various	خىلمۇ - خىل
immediately	دەررۇ
friendly	دوستانە
shop owner	دۇكاندار
cloth	رەخت
color	رەڭ
challenge	رىقابەت
olive	زەيتۇن
honest, sincere	سەمىمىي
art	سەنئەت
very clear	سۈپ- سۈزۈك
scarf	شارپا

to be decorated	نەقشلەنمەك
style, form	نۇسخا
saw design	ھەرە چىشلىق
to be reckoned	ھېسابلانماق
to cluster around	ئولاشماق
then	ئۇنداقتا
triangle	ئۈچ بۇلۇڭ
prefecture	ۋىلايەت
doorplate	ۋىۋىسكا
care, consideration	ئېتىبار
brook	ئېرىق
aesthetic thought	ئېستېتىك تەپەككۇر
excellent	ئېسىل
to flow	ئېقىپ تۇرماق
to express	ئىپادە قىلماق
invention	ئىجادىيەت
to be injured	يارىلانماق
age	ياش قۇرامى
walnut skin	ياڭاق پوستى
earthquake	يەر تەۋرەش
wool	يۇڭ
to occur, to happen	يۈز بەرمەك
luggage	يۈك- تاق
lofty, noble	يۈكسەك
thread, string	يىپ
silk-growing	يىپەكچىلىك
a type of thin silk	شايى
shape	شەكىل
dialect	شىۋە
jade	قاشتېشى
to launch, to develop	قانات يايماق
to value, esteem	قەدىرلىمەك
story, floor	قەۋەت
convenience	قولايلىق
dense, thick	قويۇق
mainland	قۇرۇقلۇق
small production unit	كارخانا
bed carpet	كارىۋات گىلىمى
craftsman	كاسىپ
major	كەسىپ
gas reserves	گاز زاپىسى
nickname	لەقەم
to praise	ماختىماق
to match up with	ماس كەلمەك
place	ماكان
products	مەھسۇلات
measure	مىقدار
national aspect	مىللىي تۈس
county	ناھىيە
delicate	نەپىس

ئون ئىككىنچى دەرس

CHAPTER **TWELVE**

خەير-خوش، ئۈرۈمچى!

GOOD BYE, URUMCHI!

IN THIS CHAPTER

Functions

- Describing gift-related etiquette
- Expressing probability
- Describing social issues
- Talking to the taxi agent
- Expressing suggestions
- Expressing appreciation and gratitude
- Expressing future plans

Grammar

- The suppositional future with -ار/ -ەر/ -ر
- The particle جۇمۇ
- The short form of the 1st person plural optative -يلى
- The word دەپ

In this chapter, John gets ready to go home. He invites his Uyghur friends for dinner to express his gratitude. He also goes shopping with Yasin to buy some gifts for his friends and relatives in the US. Along with John, you will learn about gift-related etiquette among Uyghurs. Through the conversations, reading passages, and excerpts from John's blog entries contained herein, you will also learn how to talk to taxi drivers and dispatchers, as well as what you might experience at the Urumchi airport.

Exercise 1:  مەركىزىي شەھەر - ئۈرۈمچى

Exercise 1.1: What do you know about Urumchi? Write some of your ideas in the lines provided below.

Exercise 1.2: Listen to the passage based on an inflight magazine article and write down any information about Urumchi which is new to you.

Exercise 1.3: Now you will read the passage. Before reading, look at the following words.

state-owned	دۆلەت ئىگىلىكىدىكى
county, district	ناھىيە
administrative	مەمۇرىي
prefecture	ۋىلايەت
advantage	ئەۋزەللىك
to develop (i.e. be developed)	روناق تاپماق

the lower slopes/ foot of a mountain	ئېتەك
science and technology	پەن - تېخنىكا
area	كۆلەم
auto manufacturing	ماشىنىسازلىق
use, consumption	ئىستېمال
to attract	جەلپ قىلماق

Exercise 1.4:  Read the passage and answer the questions that follow.

ئۈرۈمچى- شىنجاڭ ئۇيغۇر ئاپتونوم رايونىدىكى ئەڭ چوڭ شەھەر. ئۇ تەڭرىتاغنىڭ شىمالىي ئېتىكىگە، جۇڭغارىيە ئويمانلىقىنىڭ جەنۇبىي چېتىگە جايلاشقان. ئۈرۈمچى شىنجاڭ ئۇيغۇر ئاپتونوم رايونىنىڭ سىياسىي، ئىقتىسادىي، مەدەنىيەت، پەن- تېخنىكا مەركىزى. ئۈرۈمچىنىڭ كۆلىمى 11 مىڭ 440 كۋادرات كىلومېتىر، بۇنىڭ ئىچىدە شەھەر رايونىنىڭ كۆلىمى 51 كۋادرات كىلومېتىر.

ئۈرۈمچى شەھەر ئەتراپى رايونى بىلەن شەھەر رايونىنى ئۆز ئىچىگە ئالىدۇ. شەھەر ئەتراپى رايونى ئۈرۈمچى ناھىيىسى ۋە دۆلەت ئىگىلىكىدىكى ئالتە دېھقانچىلىق، چارۋىچىلىق مەيدانىنى ئۆز ئىچىگە ئالىدۇ. شەھەر رايونى يەتتە مەمۇرىي رايونغا بۆلۈنگەن.

ئۈرۈمچىنىڭ يىللىق ئوتتۇرىچە تېمپېراتۇرىسى 7.3 سېلسىيە گرادۇس، يازدا ئەڭ ئىسسىق بولغاندا، 37 سېلسىيە گرادۇس، قىشتا ئەڭ سوغۇق بولغاندا، نۆلدىن تۆۋەن 32 سېلسىيە گرادۇس بولىدۇ. بۇ يەرنىڭ ۋاقتى بېيجىڭ ۋاقىت رايونىدىن ئىككى سائەت كېيىن بولىدۇ.

ئۈرۈمچىدە ھازىر مېتاللچىلىق، كۆمۈر، ئېلېكتر، ئېلېكترون، ماشىنىسازلىق، نېفىت - خىمىيە سانائىتى، كۈندىلىك ئىستېمال بۇيۇملىرى، قۇرۇلۇش ماتېرىياللىرى، توقۇمىچىلىق، تېرە-خۇرۇم، قەغەزچىلىك قاتارلىق سانائەت سىستېمىلىرى بار.

ئۈرۈمچى شىنجاڭنىڭ قاتناش تۈگىنى. ئۈرۈمچىنى ھەرقايسى ۋىلايەت، شەھەر، ناھىيە ۋە دېھقانچىلىق-چارۋىچىلىق مەيدانلىرى بىلەن تۇتاشتۇرىدىغان تاشيوللار بار. شۇنداقلا ئۈرۈمچىنى بېيجىڭ، شاڭخەي، چۇڭچىڭ قاتارلىق چوڭ شەھەرلەر بىلەن تۇتاشتۇرىدىغان لەنجۇ – شىنجاڭ تۆمۈر يولى بار. ئۇنىڭدىن باشقا ئۈرۈمچىنى ئىچكى ئۆلكىلەر ۋە چەت ئەللەر بىلەن تۇتاشتۇرىدىغان ھاۋا قاتناش يوللىرىمۇ بار.

ئۈرۈمچى شەھرى ئۆز ۋاقتىدا يىپەك يولىنىڭ مۇھىم تۈگۈنى بولغان. ئۇ تارىخىي ۋە جۇغراپىيىلىك ئورنىنىڭ ئەۋزەللىكى، كۆپ مىللەتلىك قۇرۇلمىسى بىلەن مەملىكەت سىرتى ۋە ئىچىدىكى نۇرغۇنلىغان ساياھەتچىلەرنى ئۆزىگە جەلپ قىلىپ كېلىۋاتىدۇ. ھازىر ئۈرۈمچى ئەڭ روناق تاپقان ساياھەت رايونلىرىنىڭ بىرى.

1. ئۈرۈمچى نەگە جايلاشقان؟
2. ئۈرۈمچىنىڭ كۆلىمى قانچىلىك؟
3. ئۈرۈمچى قايسى رايونلارنى ئۆز ئىچىگە ئالىدۇ؟
4. ئۈرۈمچىدە قانداق سانائەت سىستېمىلىرى بار؟
5. ئۈرۈمچىنىڭ ھاۋاسى قانداق؟
6. نېمىشقا ئۈرۈمچى ساياھەتچىلەرنى ئۆزىگە جەلپ قىلىدۇ؟

Exercise 1.5:  Find the following numbers in the passage, then write down what the numbers are used to describe in English.

11, 440: ______________________________

51: ______________________________

7.3: ______________________________

37: ______________________________

32: ______________________________

Note:

As in English, decimals in Uyghur are written using a period. The number 7.3 is read as a decimal in Uyghur. When reading this number aloud, we say يەتتە پۈتۈن ئوندىن ئۈچ. This literally translates as 'seven wholes (and) three from ten;' it resembles the English 'seven and three tenths.' Note that when the number is written out in numerals, the three occupies the tens place - hence, "three from ten."

If the decimal extends to the hundreds place in Uyghur, the two digit number after the decimal point is read as a number "out of/from a hundred." The number 7.65 is pronounced: يەتتە پۈتۈن يۈزدىن ئاتمىش بەش

This is true even if the first of the two digits is a zero. The number 8.05 is pronounced: سەككىز پۈتۈن يۈزدىن بەش

Exercise 2:  Listen to the following numbers and repeat them aloud.

3	3.2	3.56
8	8.8	8.07
6	6.5	24.6
24	24.3	24.67
102	102.4	102.39

Exercise 3: دوستلارغا رەھمەت!

Exercise 3.1:  Before leaving Xinjing, John sent a message to his friends. You can see short parts of the message below. Read the sentences and put them in the correct order.

ئەزىز دوستلىرىم،

______ شۇڭا كېتىشتىن بۇرۇن ھەممىڭلارنى مېھمان قىلاي دەيمەن.

______ خۇدايىم بۇيرىسا، بىر نەچچە كۈندىن كېيىن ئامېرىكىغا قايتىمەن.

______ بۇ قېتىم سىلەر مېنىڭ مېھمىنىم بولۇڭلار.

______ مۇشۇ شەنبە سائەت يەتتىلەردە كۆرۈشسەك قانداق؟

______ سىلەر مېنى كۆپ مېھمان قىلدىڭلار.

______ مەن سىلەردىن بەك مىننەتدارمەن.

جاۋابىڭلارنى كۈتۈپ،

جون

Exercise 3.2: Now listen to the complete message. How does it compare with your answers above?

Exercise 3.3: Listen to the message again and take notes on any additional details that you understand.

Exercise 3.4:  Read the message and find the phrases that express the ideas below in different words:

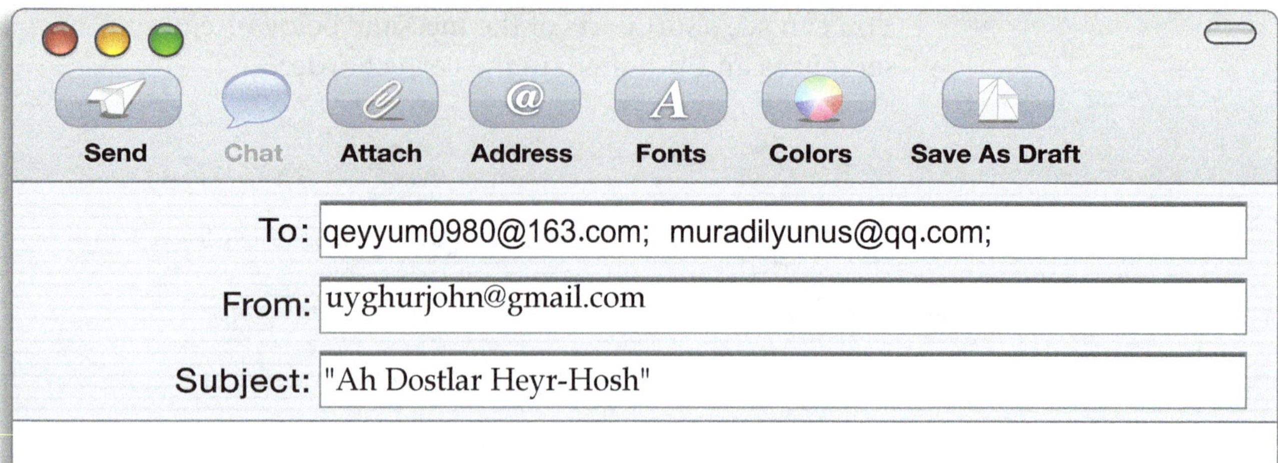

ئەزىز دوستلىرىم،

ۋاقىت نېمىدېگەن تېز ئۆتۈپ كەتتى. خۇدايىم بۇيرىسا، بىر نەچچە كۈندىن كېيىن ئامېرىكىغا قايتىمەن. راستىنى ئېيتسام، ئۈرۈمچىگە بەك كۆنۈپ قاپتىمەن. سىلەر بولغىنىڭلار ئۈچۈن بۇ يەردىكى ۋاقتىم بەك كۆڭۈللۈك ئۆتتى. مەن سىلەردىن بەك مىننەتدارمەن. سىلەر مېنى كۆپ مېھمان قىلدىڭلار. شۇڭا كېتىشتىن بۇرۇن ھەممىڭلارنى مەن ئامراق بولغان "قەشقەر رېستورانى"غا چاقىرىپ مېھمان قىلاي دەيمەن. سىلەر مېنى مېھمان دەپ ھېچ قاچان پۇل تۆلەتكۈزمىدىڭلار، ئەمما بۇ قېتىم سىلەر مېنىڭ مېھمىنىم بولۇڭلار. تاماقنىڭ پۇلىنى مەن تۆلەيمەن، بولامدۇ؟ قالغان گەپلەرنى كېيىن دېيىشەرمىز. مۇشۇ شەنبە سائەت يەتتىلەردە كۆرۈشسەك قانداق؟

جاۋابىڭلارنى كۈتۈپ،

جون

1. ۋاقتىم خۇشال - خۇرام ئۆتتى ____________________

2. سىلەرگە كۆپ رەھمەت ____________________

3. تەكلىپ قىلىمەن ____________________

4. مەن ياخشى كۆرگەن ____________________

Exercise 3.5:  Look at Johns's email and answer the following questions.

1. How does John address his friends?
2. How does he express his gratitude in this e-mail?
3. Why does he want to pay for his friends at the restaurant?
4. What phrase does he use to close the email?

Exercise 3.6:  Imagine, that after spending a year in Xinjiang, you are getting ready to go back to the US. Before leaving, you want to invite your Uyghur friends, who helped you a lot in Xinjiang, to a restaurant for a dinner. Write an email to your friends.

Send Chat Attach Address Fonts Colors Save As Draft

To:

From:

Subject:

Exercise 4: ئاخىرقى ئولتۇرۇش

Exercise 4.1:  John is at the restaurant with his friends. Listen to the first part of the conversation between John and his friends and answer the questions that follow.

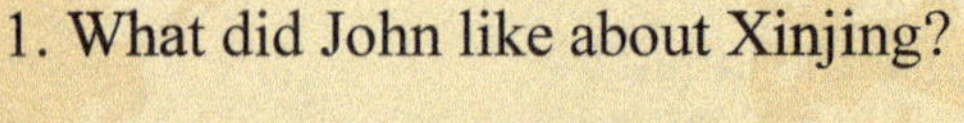

1. What did John like about Xinjing?
2. True or false: John thinks that Uyghurs are nicer than Americans. ________
3. What is the best translation of the phrase ۋاقىت نېمىدېگەن تېز ئۆتىدۇ - ھە!
   A. We are running out of time
   B. Time is money
   C. Time flies
   D: You may delay, but time will not.
4. What does the expression ئاق كۆڭۈل mean? ______________________

Exercise 4.2:  Listen to the second part of their conversation and answer the questions that follow.

1. What was most surprising for John in Xinjiang?
2. Why did his friend tell him to be quiet?
3. What unusual experience did John mention in relation to his trip to Kashgar?
4. Explain the saying:
   يولنىڭ يۈزىنى ئاچسا، خۇدايىم شۇ كىشىنىڭ بەختىنى ئاچىدۇ
5. What does the phrase ماڭا زادىلا ياقمىدى mean?
6. What is the function of the particle لا- in the word زادىلا?
   A. negation
   B. emphasis

Exercise 4.3:  Listen to the third part of their conversation and answer the questions that follow.

1. What is John's attitude towards the Uyghurs' drinking?
2. True or false?

   John refuses to drink هاراق. _______

   John will drink only beer. _______
3. Why do John's friends insist that he drink with them?
4. One of John's friends says: هاراقنى زورلىما What does this phrase mean? Why does he say that?

Exercise 4.4: Listen to the last part of their conversation and answer the questions that follow.

1. What are John's plans after returning home?
2. Where will John's friend take him next time?
3. What are John's plans for his future visit to Xinjiang?
4. How would you translate the phrase هە راست in the following context:

   هە راست، ئەتە مەن ئامېرىكىدىكى تۇغقانلىرىمغا بىرئاز سوۋغات ئالماقچىتىم.
   سىزنىڭ ۋاقتىڭىز بارمۇ؟
5. Read what Mejit told Qawul once again and translate it into English.

   هەي، قاۋۇل، هاراقنى زورلىما، جۇمۇ. بۇنداق قىلساڭ جون ئۇرۇمچىگە هەرگىز كەلمەيدۇ!

Use the same structure to form expressions of at least two sentences each similar to the one above.

1 The Suggestion Particle جۇمۇ

The particle جۇمۇ is often used after verbs in the imperative in order to make the command a sort of suggestion. In is roughly equivalent to the English use of the word 'okay?' with rising intonation which appears in the same location after the question. Look at the following examples:

- ھەي باللار، ئاستىراق گەپ قىلىڭلار. يەنە تۈرمىگە چۈشمەيلى، جۇمۇ.
Hey folks, be careful of your language. Let's not end up in jail.
بۇ يەرلەرگە يەنە كەلسىڭىز، مېنى ئىزدەڭ، جۇمۇ، مەن سىزنى غۇلجىغا ئاپىراي.
Look me up if you come here again, okay? Let me show you Ghulja.

Like its English counterpart, the suggestion implied by جۇمۇ may sometimes be more sarcastic than polite.

2 The Short Form of the 1st Person Plural Optative -ىلى

Look at the following excerpts taken from some dialogues you have read and heard.

- ئەمدى بۇ ئۇزىتىش ئولتۇرۇشى بولغاچقا، ئازراق ئىچىلى.
As this is a farewell party let's drink less.
- ئەمىسە ياتاققا بىللە بارىلى.
Let's go to the dorm together then.
Ok, let's do it. .- بولىدۇ، شۇنداق قىلىلى
Allright, guys let's go! !قېنى، ئاغىنىلەر، ماڭىلى

In Chapter Two, you learned about the 1st person plural Optative /-ەيلى -ايلى , which is used like English 'let's,' as in 'Let's go!.' In some parts of Xinjiang, a shortened form of the 1st person plural Optative -ىلى is used instead. It does not differ in meaning from the other form.

Note that this special form does not exist for verb roots which end in a vowel!

Exercise 5: سىز ساياھەت قىلىشقا ئامراقمۇ؟

Exercise 5.1:  Listen to the questions and answer them. The questions will be played automatically one after the other. Do not stop the CD! Practice until you can answer each question in the time allotted.

Exercise 5.2:  Imagine that one of your Uyghur friends is leaving the US after staying there for six months. What questions would you ask him? Write down at least seven questions.

Help:
Ask your friend about what he liked and did not like about the country, as well as any surprising situations he might have seen or experienced.

Exercise 5.3: Now get together with your partner. One of you will play the role of the Uyghur student. Ask and answer each other's questions.

Exercise 6: خوتەن بازىرىدا

Here you will watch two segments about a Uyghur bazaar filmed in Khotan.

Exercise 6.1:  Watch the first video and tell how you would describe a Uyghur bazaar? Note that this video does not have any words to focus on.

Exercise 6.2: Watch the video again and put the following sections of the bazaar in order based on how they appear in the video.

ئاياق بازىرى	
كۆڭلەك بازىرى	
ياغلىق بازىرى	
رەخت بازىرى	
چىنە بازىرى	
دوپپا بازىرى	

Exercise 6.3: Watch the video one more time and tell what would you buy as gifts for your friends or relatives from this bazaar?

Exercise 6.4:  Watch the second segment. Who is the man in this video? What is the purpose of his singing?

Exercise 6.5: Watch the video again. This time pay attention to the song. What is this song about? Circle the lines from the song you hear from the following options below.

1	ئا بالا ئېپ بولدى پايپاق.
2	مىشەدە بىر كويكەن پايپاق، ئا يەردە قىممەتكەن پايپاق.
3	مىشەدە ئەرزانكەن پايپاق.
4	ئانغا پايپاق بىر كويما؟
5	ئاچغا پايپاق بىر كويما؟
6	پايپاق نوچكەن باللا!
7	پايپاق ئىسلكەن باللا!
8	ئى يەردە ئۈچ كويكەن پايپاق.
9	پايپاق ھەر خىلكەن باللا.
10	ھەر ياڭزا پايپاق بىر كويما؟
11	ئاكغا پايپاق بىر كويما؟

Exercise 7: سوۋغات قائىدىلىرى

Exercise 7.1:  Discuss the following questions in group.

1. سىزنىڭ مەدەنىيىتىڭىزدە كىملەرگە ۋە قاچان سوۋغات بېرىلىدۇ؟
2. سوۋغات بەرگەندە/ ئالغاندا ئېيتىدىغان ئالاھىدە سۆزلەر بارمۇ؟
3. تۇغۇلغان كۈندە سوۋغات بەرگەندە ئادەتتە نېمە دەيسىز؟ ئالغاندىچۇ؟
4. بايراملاردا سوۋغات بەرگەندە ئادەتتە نېمە دەيسىز؟ ئالغاندىچۇ؟

Exercise 7.2:  While traveling around Xinjiang with John, you have been to a lot of places and learned about the famous products of various regions. Imagine you are returning to your home from Xinjiang. Which cultural artifacts would you bring back as gifts for the following people?

	يولدىشىڭىزغا/ ئايالىڭىزغا
	بالىلىرىڭىزغا/ جىيەنلىرىڭىزگە
	ئاتا- ئانىڭىزغا
	دوستلىرىڭىزغا
	خىزمەتداشلىرىڭىزغا
	باشلىقىڭىزغا

Exercise 7.3: John meets his friend, Yasin, to do some shopping. Before you read their conversation, study the following words and expressions.

تەرجىمىسى	سۆز - ئىبارىلەر
custom, habit	ئادەت
memory	خاتىرە
to be ashamed	ئىزا تارتماق
to feel shame	خىجىل بولماق
to express one's gratitude	مىننەتدارلىق بىلدۈرمەك
related to (takes the Dative)	(-غا) ئائىت
intention	نىيەت
real, true	چىن
to bother	ئاۋارە قىلماق

Exercise 7.4:  Read the conversation and answer the questions that follow.

ياسىن: جون، قانداق ئەھۋالىڭىز؟

جون: ياخشى، ئۆزىڭىزچۇ؟

ياسىن: مەنمۇ ياخشى، رەھمەت. تۈنۈگۈن سىزگە بىر سوۋغات ئالاي دەپ بازارغا بارغانتىم.

جون: مېنىڭ تۇغۇلغان كۈنۈم بولمىسا، نېمىشقا ماڭا سوۋغات ئالىسىز؟

ياسىن: بىزدە شۇنداق بىر ئادەت بار. سىز بىلەن قەدىناس دوست بولۇپ قالدۇق. سىز ئەمدى بۇ يەردىن كېتىۋاتىسىز، شۇڭا بۇ پىچاق مەندىن سىزگە بىر خاتىرە بولۇپ قالسۇن.

جون: پاھ، بۇ يېڭىسار پىچىقىغۇ! مەن قەشقەرگە بارغاندا ئالغانتىم، بۇ پىچاق ئۆزىڭىزدە قالسۇن!

ياسىن: ياق، ياق، بۇنداق قىلساق بولمايدۇ! ئېلىڭ! ئېلىڭ! ئۆزىڭىز سېتىۋالغان پىچاقنى بىرەر دوستىڭىزغا ياكى تۇغقىنىڭىزغا سوۋغات قىلارسىز، بۇ پىچاقنى ئۆزىڭىز ئىشلىتەرسىز.

جون: سەت بولدى، ئاۋارە قىلدىم سىزنى... كۆپ رەھمەت سىزگە! ئىزا تارتتىم...

ياسىن: ئىزا تارتىدىغان بىر ئىش يوق...

جون: مەن خاتا سۆزلىدىممۇ؟

ياسىن: ياق، خاتا ئەمەس. ئەمما ئۇيغۇرلار ئادەتتە مىننەتدارلىقنى بىلدۈرۈش ئۈچۈن "كۆپ رەھمەت، ئاۋارە بوپسىز" دەيدۇ.

جون: ھەەە، مەنمۇ شۇنداق دەي بولمىسا... كۆپ رەھمەت، دوستۇم ياسىن، ئاۋارە بوپسىز.

ياسىن: كېرەك يوق! بۇ مېنىڭ كۆڭلۈم.

جون: كۆڭلۈم؟ سىلەر بۇ گەپنى بەك كۆپ ئىشلىتىدىكەنسىلەر. ئۇنىڭ مەنىسىنى ئانچە ياخشى چۈشىنەلمىدىم.

ياسىن: ھە، بۇ سۆزنىڭ ئەسلى مەنىسى "يۈرەك ، قەلب".

جون: مەن بۇ سۆزنىڭ ئەسلى مەنىسىنى بىلىمەن، ئەمما ئېيتقان گېپىڭىزنىڭ مەنىسىنى ئانچە ياخشى چۈشىنەلمىدىم.

ياسىن: ئۇيغۇرلار چىن قەلبىدىن (كۆڭلىدىن) بىر نەرسە بەرسە "بۇ مېنىڭ كۆڭلۈم" دەيدۇ.

جون: ھە، مۇنداق دەڭ... مانا سىزدىن ئۇيغۇرلارنىڭ ئۆرپ-ئادەتلىرىگە ئائىت يەنە بىرمۇنچە نەرسىلەرنى ئۆگىنىۋالدىم!

ياسىن: سىز شىنجاڭغا يەنە كېلىڭ، تېخىمۇ كۆپ نەرسىلەرنى ئۆگىنىسىز.

جون: شۇنداق نىيىتىم بار! خۇدايىم بۇيرىسا، چوقۇم كېلىمەن!

ياسىن: بىز بۈگۈن بازارغا بارماقچىتۇق، شۇنداق ئەمەسمۇ؟

جون: شۇنداق!

ياسىن: قېنى ئەمىسە ، ماڭىلى!

1. نېمىشقا ياسىن جونغا سوۋغات ئېلىپ كېلىدۇ؟
2. ياسىن سوۋغاتنى بەرگەندە نېمىشقا جون ھەيران قالىدۇ؟
3. سوۋغاتنى ئالغاندىن كېيىن ئۇيغۇرلار ئادەتتە مىننەتدارلىقنى قانداق بىلدۈرىدۇ؟
4. "بۇ مېنىڭ كۆڭلۈم" دېگەن گەپنىڭ مەنىسى نېمە؟

Exercise 8:  From the passage on the preceding page, you learned an expression with the word كۆڭۈل. There are many Uyghur proverbs containing this word. Translate the proverbs provided below into English. Try to find a close equivalent in your own language and write them on the lines provided.

Uyghur Proverbs ئۇيغۇر خەلق ماقاللىرى

ئۆيۈڭ تار بولسىمۇ ، كۆڭلۈڭ كەڭ بولسۇن.

ئانىنىڭ كۆڭلى بالىدا، بالىنىڭ كۆڭلى دالىدا.

ئوق ئاتما، كۆڭۈل ساتما.

كۆڭۈل ئاغرىتقان دوست ئەمەس، مەيدە ئاغرىتقان ئاش ئەمەس.

ياخشىلىقنى ئۇنتۇما، يامانلىقنى كۆڭۈلدە تۇتما.

كالاڭغا كۆڭۈل بۆلگىچە، بالاڭغا كۆڭۈل بۆل.

3 Expressing Probability: The Suppositional Future -ار، -ەر، -ر

You already know that the present/future tense is usually used to express future actions in Uyghur. However, there is also another tense which is specifically used for things in the future which one supposes (but isn't sure) will happen. This tense is often called the suppositional future.

ماقۇل، ئەمىسە ئەتە كۆرۈشەرمىز!

Okay, then (I guess) I will see you tomorrow!

The suppositional future is formed by adding the ending ەر- / ار- or ر - (if the verb stem ends in a vowel) followed by the personal ending. The singular forms are:

مەن	بارارمەن	ئىشلەرمەن	ئوقۇرمەن
سەن	بارارسەن	ئىشلەرسەن	ئوقۇرسەن
سىز	بارارسىز	ئىشلەرسىز	ئوقۇرسىز
ئۇ	بارار	ئىشلەر	ئوقۇر

The plural forms are:

بىز	بارارمىز	ئىشلەرمىز	ئوقۇرمىز
سىلەر	بارارسىلەر	ئىشلەرسىلەر	ئوقۇرسىلەر
ئۇلار	بارار	ئىشلەر	ئوقۇر

The negative form of the suppositional future is formed by using the suffix -ماس\-مەس (according to vowel harmony) + personal endings.
Look at the following examples:

I don't think you will do that. سىز بۇنداق قىلماسسىز.
I don't think I will give my house to them. مەن ئۆيۈمنى ئۇلارغا بەرمەسمەن.
I don't think they will listen to this song. ئۇلار بۇ ناخشىنى ئاڭلىماس.

To make the interrogative form, simply add the question particle مۇ- after the suffix.

Would they listen to us? ئۇلار گېپىمىزنى ئاڭلارمۇ؟
Would you go with us? سىز بىز بىلەن بارارسىزمۇ؟
Would I do this? مەن بۇ ئىشنى قىلارمەنمۇ؟

Exercise 9: Look at the sentences below. What is similar in these sentences? What is different?

John will buy his father a knife.	جون دادىسىغا پىچاق ئالىدۇ.
John may buy his father a knife.	جون دادىسىغا پىچاق ئېلىشى مۇمكىن.
Maybe, John will buy his father a knife.	بەلكىم جون دادىسىغا پىچاق ئالار؟
Will John buy a knife for his father?	جون دادىسىغا پىچاق ئالامسىكىن؟

Exercise 10:  Using the exercise above as a model answer the following two questions.

1. جون ئولتۇرۇشقا بارامدۇ؟

____

____

____

2. جون پولۇ ئېتەمدۇ؟

____

____

____

Exercise 11: تەييارلىقىڭىز پۈتتىمۇ؟

Exercise 11.1: John and Yasin finished shopping at the market. They are on their way home. Listen to their conversation and do the following:

1. Tell if the following statements are true or false.

توغرا	خاتا

1. جون ئۈرۈمچىدىن بېيجىڭغا ئۇچىدۇ.
2. ئۇنىڭ يۈكى 20 كىلودىن ئاشسا بولمايدۇ.
3. جوننىڭ ئەكېتىدىغان تۆت پىچىقى بار.
4. جون پىچاقلارنى يېنىغا سېلىۋالىدۇ.

2. Answer the following questions:
   Why can't John's luggage weigh any more?
   Why can't John put the knives in his carry-on?

Exercise 11.2:  Now read a trascript of the conversation. Some words and expressions have been underlined. Can you guess their meaning based on the context?

ياسىن: ئالدىغان نەرسىلەرنىڭ ھەممىسىنى ئالدىڭىزمۇ؟

جون: ھەئە، مېنىڭچە بولدى... كۆپ نەرسە ئالمايمەن دېگەنتىم، ئەمما بۇ بازارغا كىرگەندە ئادەم ئۆزىنى <u>تۇتۇۋالالماي قالىدىكەن</u>...

ياسىن: بۇ يەردىن ئامېرىكىغا <u>قۇرۇق قول</u> <u>بىلەن</u> بارغىلى بولماس...

جون: ئۇغۇ شۇ، ئەمما بۇلارنى ئەكەتمەكمۇ <u>چوڭ گەپتە</u>... مەن بۇ يەردىن بېيجىڭغا ئۇچىمەن <u>ئەمەسمۇ</u>، شۇڭا يۈكۈم يىگىرمە كىلودىن <u>ئاشسا بولمايدۇ</u>.

ياسىن: ھە، توغرا، توغرا... ئەمما بېيجىڭدىن يەنە بەزى نەرسىلەرنى ئېلىۋالسىڭىز بولىدۇ...

جون: <u>ياقەي</u>، بولدى. مۇشۇ نەرسىلەرنى ئەكەتسەممۇ چوڭ گەپ...

ياسىن: چامادانلىرىڭىزنى قاچان تەييارلايسىز؟

جون: بۈگۈن كەچتە تەييارلايمىكىن...

ياسىن: ياردەم لازىم بولسا دەڭ، مەن قارىشىپ بېرەي.

جون: سىزنى <u>ئاۋارە قىلغۇم يوق</u>...ھېلىمۇ شۇنچە ۋاقتىڭىزنى ئالدىم.

ياسىن: ياق، ياق، ئاۋارە بولىدىغان ئىش يوق...

جون: ماقۇل، ئەمسە ياتاققا بىللە بارىلى.

ياسىن: <u>ئەكېتىدىغان</u> پىچاقلىرىڭىز كۆپمۇ؟

جون: ئۈچ پىچىقىم بار.

ياسىن: ئۇلارنى چامادانغا سېلىۋالسىڭىز ياخشىراق بولارمىكىن؟

جون: ھە، ئۆتكەن قېتىم بىر پىچىقىمنى <u>يېنىمغا</u> سېلىۋالغانتىم، ئايرودرومدا ئېلىۋالدى...

ياسىن: پىچاقنى كۆرسە ئۆتكۈزمەيدۇ...

جون: شۇنداقكەن...

ياسىن: ھە راست، ئايرودرومغا قانداق چىقىسىز؟

جون: شۇ ئىشنى سىز بىلەن <u>مەسلىھەت</u> قىلماقچىتىم. بۈگۈن كەچتە تاكسى <u>زاكاز</u> قىلىپ قويساق بولامدۇ؟

ياسىن: بولىدۇ، شۇنداق قىلىلى. مەن ئۆزەم تېلېفون قىلىپ بىر تاكسى بۇيرىتاي...

Exercise 12: تاكسى مۇلازىمىتى

Exercise 12.1:  Yasin calls the taxi company and asks for a cab for John to get him to the airport. Listen to the first part of the conversation and fill out the taxi-driver's note.

Time of pick-up: ____________________

Destination: ________________

Address: _______________________

Exercise 12.2: Listen to the conversation again, and repeat each line aloud.

Exercise 12.3:  With a friend, assume the roles of the taxi dispatcher and Yasin, acting out the conversation in pairs. Then, switch roles.

Exercise 12.4:  Read the second part of the conversation and answer the question that follows.

ئەر: نەگە بارىسىز؟

ياسىن: بىر دوستۇم ئايرودرومغا بارماقچى ئىدى. ئۇ سائەت توققۇزدا بېيجىڭغا ئۇچماقچى.

ئەر: ھمم... توققۇزدا ئۇچىدىغان ئايروپىلان بولسا، يەتتىدە ماڭسىڭىز ئۈلگۈرەلمەيسىز.

ياسىن: نېمىشقا؟

ئەر: سائەت يەتتىدە ھەممە ئادەم ئىشتىن چۈشىدۇ ئەمەسمۇ، بۇنداق ۋاقىتتا يولدا ماشىنا بەك كۆپ بولىدۇ. ئۇنىڭ ئۈستىگە ھازىر ئايرودروم يولىنى رېمونت قىلىۋاتىدۇ، شۇڭا 2- ئايلانما يولدا مېڭىش مۇمكىن ئەمەس.

ياسىن: مۇنداق دەڭ. ئۇنداق بولسا، سائەت نەچچىدە ماڭساق بولار؟

ئەر: سائەت ئالتىدە مېڭىڭ. چۈنكى ئايروپىلانغا چىقىشتىن بۇرۇن يەنە بىرمۇنچە رەسمىيەت ئۆتەيدىغان گەپ.

ياسىن: ماقۇل، شۇنداق بولسۇن. قانچە پۇل بولىدۇ؟

ئەر: ھە، يۈز كوي بولىدۇ.

ياسىن: سىزگە كۆپ رەھمەت! ئەمىسە بىز سائەت ئالتىدە كۈتىمىز.

ئەر: بولىدۇ. بىز ئەۋەتكەن ماشىنا دەل ۋاقتىدا ياتاق بىناسىنىڭ ئالدىغا بارىدۇ. ئىسمىڭىز؟

ياسىن: ياسىن خۇدابەردى.

ئەر: تېلېفون نومۇرىڭىز؟

ياسىن: بىر يۈز ئوتتۇز سەككىز - توقسان توققۇز - سەكسەن ئالتە - ئەللىك تۆت - قىرىق يەتتە.

1. Why does John need to take a taxi at 6:00 PM? The dispatcher mentions three reasons.Write them all down in the lines below.

____

____

____

2. What is Yasin’s phone number? Write it out in numerals.

3. How much will the trip cost? Write the price out, this time in words.

Exercise 12.5:  Now practice the whole dialogue with your partner.

(تېلېفون جىرىڭلايدۇ)
ئەر: ۋەي!
ياسىن: ئەسسالامۇ ئەلەيكۇم. بۇ دۆڭكوۋرۈك ساياھەت تاكسى شىركىتىمۇ؟
ئەر: شۇنداق. تاكسى كېرەكمۇ؟
ياسىن: ھەئە. بۈگۈن لازىم ئىدى.
ئەر: ھازىر دەمسىز؟
ياسىن: ياق. بۈگۈن كەچتە لازىم.
ئەر: سائەت نەچچىگە بولسۇن؟
ياسىن: كەچ سائەت يەتتىگە.
ئەر: ئادرېسىڭىزنى دەۋېتەمسىز؟
ياسىن: شىنجاڭ ئۇنىۋېرسىتېتى 8 – ياتاق بىناسى.
ئەر: نەگە بارىسىز؟
ياسىن: بىر دوستۇم ئايرودرومغا بارماقچى ئىدى. ئۇ سائەت توققۇزدا بېيجىڭغا ئۇچماقچى.
ئەر: ھىم... توققۇزدا ئۇچىدىغان ئايروپىلان بولسا، يەتتىدە ماڭسىڭىز ئۈلگۈرەلمەيسىز.
ياسىن: نېمىشقا؟
ئەر: سائەت يەتتىدە ھەممە ئادەم ئىشتىن چۈشىدۇ ئەمەسمۇ، بۇنداق ۋاقىتتا يولدا ماشىنا بەك كۆپ بولىدۇ.
ئۇنىڭ ئۈستىگە ھازىر ئايرودروم يولىنى رېمونت قىلىۋاتىدۇ، شۇڭا 2-ئايلانما يولدا مېڭىش مۇمكىن ئەمەس.
ياسىن: مۇنداق دەڭ. ئۇنداق بولسا سائەت نەچچىدە ماڭساق بولار؟
ئەر: سائەت ئالتىدە مېڭىڭ. چۈنكى ئايروپىلانغا چىقىشتىن بۇرۇن يەنە بىرمۇنچە رەسمىيەت ئۆتەيدىغان گەپ.
ياسىن: ماقۇل، شۇنداق بولسۇن. قانچە پۇل بولىدۇ؟
ئەر: ھە، 110 كوي.
ياسىن: سىزگە كۆپ رەھمەت! ئەمىسە بىز سائەت ئالتىدە كۈتىمىز.
ئەر: بولىدۇ. بىز ئەۋەتكەن ماشىنا دەل ۋاقتىدا ياتاق بىناسىنىڭ ئالدىغا بارىدۇ. ئىسمىڭىز نېمە؟
ياسىن: ياسىن ئوسمان.
ئەر: تېلېفون نومۇرىڭىزنى دەۋېتەمسىز؟
ياسىن: 138-9986-5437

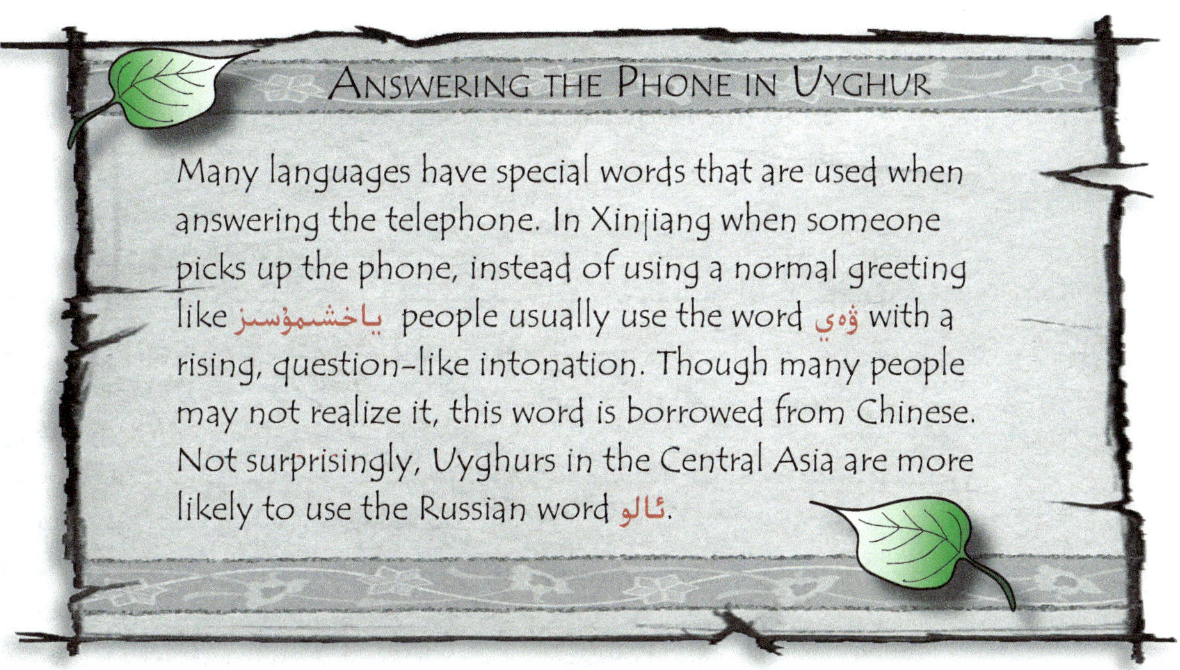

Answering the Phone in Uyghur

Many languages have special words that are used when answering the telephone. In Xinjiang when someone picks up the phone, instead of using a normal greeting like ياخشىمۇسىز people usually use the word ۋەي with a rising, question-like intonation. Though many people may not realize it, this word is borrowed from Chinese. Not surprisingly, Uyghurs in the Central Asia are more likely to use the Russian word ئالو.

Exercise 12.6: Use the conversation cards below to order a taxi.

CARD A: Wait for the agent to start. You need a taxi from Xinjiang University to the airport. Call the taxi agency and have them pick you up. Your partner will play the role of the dispatcher.

CARD B: You are the dispatcher at the taxi company. You will start the conversation.

CARD A: YOU

(Wait for dispatcher to start)

From: Xinjiang University

To: Airport

Time requested: 4.45am

Phone number: 158-9364-8475

CARD B: DISPATCHER

(Start by greeting the customer)

Ask for: address, pick-up/drop-off location, pick-up time

Suggest an earlier time because of traffic

Ask for a name and phone number

Exercise 13: تاكسىچى بىلەن سۆھبەت

Exercise 13.1:  Read the following conversation between John and the taxi driver.

جون: كەچۇرۇڭ، مەن سىزنى ئۈرۈمچى ۋاقتى سائەت ئالتىدە كېلىدۇ دەپ ئويلاپتىمەن.
تاكسىچى: ياق، بىز بېيجىڭ ۋاقتى ئىشلىتىمىز. سىز چەتئەللىك ئوخشىمامسىز؟
جون: ھەئە. ئۈرۈمچىدە بىر يىل تۇردۇم.
تاكسىچى: پاھ، ئۇرغۇيچىغا ئۇستا بوپ كېتىپسىز!
جون: ئۇرغۇيچە؟ مەن ئۇيغۇرچە ئۆگەندىم.
تاكسىچى: قارىسام، بۇبىنادا چەتئەللىكلەر كۆپكەن. ھەممىڭلار ئۇرغۇيچە ئۆگىنەمسىلەر؟
جون: ياق، ئۇلارنىڭ بەزىسى خەنزۇچە ئۆگىنىدۇ.
تاكسىچى: ھازىر ھەممە ئادەم خەنزۇچە ئۆگىنىۋاتسا، سىز نېمىشقا ئۇرغۇيچە ئۆگىنىسىز؟
جون: ئاكا، ئۇرغۇيچە ئەمەس، ئۇيغۇرچە دەڭ.
تاكسىچى: ھە بوپتۇ. بىزنىڭ تىلىمىزنى ئۆگىنىپ نېمە قىلىسىز؟
جون: مەن كەلگۈسىدە ئۇيغۇرلارنى تەتقىق قىلماقچى. شۇڭا ئۇيغۇرچە بىلىشىم شەرت.
تاكسىچى: مۇنداق دەڭ. سىز قەيەرلىك؟
جون: مەن ئامېرىكىلىق.
تاكسىچى: ئامېرىكىدا تاكسى نەچچە پۇل؟
جون: ئوخشاش ئەمەس. مەسىلەن، چىكاگودا شەھەر مەركىزىدىن ئايرودرومغا بارسا، ئەللىك دوللار ئەتراپىدا.
تاكسىچى: ئەللىك دوللار؟ بۇ ئۈچ يۈز نەچچە كوي دېگەن گەپ. ھەجەپ قىممەتكىنا.*
جون:شۇنداق، ئامېرىكىدا ماشىنا جىق بولغان بىلەن** تاكسى قىممەت.
تاكسىچى: سىز ئادەتتە تاكسىغا كۆپ چىقامسىز؟
جون: ياق، مېنىڭ ماشىنام بار.
تاكسىچى: ماشىنىڭىز قايسى ماركىلىق؟
جون: تويوتا.
تاكسىچى: تويوتا! مەنمۇ تويوتاغا ئامراق. مېنىڭ ماشىناممۇ تويوتا كامري.
جون: تويوتا ياخشى ماشىنا.
تاكسىچى:ئامېرىكىدا مايغا بىر ئايدا قانچىلىك پۇل كېتىدۇ؟
جون: مايغا؟ نېمە مايغا؟
تاكسىچى: بېنزىنغا نەچچە پۇل كېتىدۇ دەيمەن.
جون: ھە، كەچۈرۈڭ. ئادەتتە بىرەر يۈز دوللار كېتىدۇ.
تاكسىچى: 600 كوي دەڭ. توۋا، ئامېرىكىدا ماي بىزدىن ئەرزانكەن.
جون: شۇنداق. شىنجاڭدىن نېفىت چىققان بىلەن ئۈرۈمچىدە بېنزىن ئامېرىكىدىنمۇ قىممەت ئىكەن.
تاكسىچى: شىنجاڭدا نېفىت بار، ئەمما مايىنىڭ ھەممىسى ئىچكىرىگە كېتىدىغان تۇرسا ماي قىممەت بولىدۇ-دە. بىز شوپۇرلارغا تەس ھازىر.

جون: سىزچۇ، بىر ئايدا نەچچىلىك پۇل تاپىسىز؟
تاكسىچى: بۇرۇن ياخشى ئىدى. ھازىر قارا تاكسى كۆپىيىپ كەتتى. شۇڭا بىر ئايدا تۆت- بەش مىڭدىن ئاشمايدۇ.
جون: بۇ پۇل بىر ئائىلىگە يېتەمدۇ؟
تاكسىچى: يېتىدۇ، ئەمما ھەممىلا ئائىلە بۇنداق پۇل تاپالمايدۇ. مانا، ئايرودرومغىمۇ كەلدۇق.
جون: ئايرودروم يىراقكەن جۇمۇ.
تاكسىچى: يېڭى يول پۈتسە، يىگىرمە مىنۇتتىلا كەلگىلى بولىدۇ. بۇندىن كېيىن ماشىنا كېرەك بولسا، ماڭا تېلېفون بېرىڭ.
جون: بولىدۇ. مەن يەنە كېلىمەن. شۇ ۋاقىتتا سىزنى ئىزدەيمەن. تاكسى ھەققى نەچچە پۇل بولدى؟
تاكسىچى: 110 كوي.
جون: مانا، ئېلىڭ. سىزگە كۆپ رەھمەت!
تاكسىچى: رەھمەت. ئاق يول بولسۇن!

---

* -كىنا: ئىكەن+particle -ھە
** -غان بىلەن: It expresses 'even though'

Talking with the taxi driver!

In the US and many European countries, it is perfectly normal for passengers not to communicate with the taxi driver beyond telling them their destination and asking about the price. Some passengers even find it annoying or intrusive when the taxi driver speaks to them. In Xinjiang, however, this is not the case; taxi drivers and passengers generally engage in at least some idle conversation during the course of the journey. Passengers who refuse to speak to the taxi driver may be considered rude or snobbish. Likewise, though in most cities in Europe and America a passenger should not sit in the front seat of a taxi unless the back seats are full, it is perfectly normal – even expected – that a male passenger should accompany the driver in the front of the car. This is especially true if the passenger is by himself.

Exercise 13.2:  Write a summary of what you have learned about being a taxi-driver in Xinjiang. Mention the challenging aspects of the job and why they are challenging.

Exercise 13.3:  Listen to some of the questions recorded from the conversation (Exercise 13.1). Give your own answer to each question without pausing the CD. Practice until you feel comfortable answering the questions in the time alloted. You may take some notes on the lines provided below.

4 The Word دەپ to Express Purpose and Objectives

In Chapter 5 you learned different ways to express purpose and objectives. However, there is another way to express purpose with the word دەپ. This word can follow the 1st person optative (wishing) forms to express purpose. Look at the following example.

I came to the bazaar to buy bread. .بازارغا نان ئالاي دەپ كەلدىم

Compare the following sentences:

دۇكانغا ئۇن ئالاي دەپ كەلدىم.
دۇكانغا ئۇن ئالغىلى كەلدىم.
دۇكانغا ئۇن ئېلىش ئۈچۈن كەلدىم.
دۇكانغا ئۇن ئېلىشقا كەلدىم.

All the sentences above might be translated into English as: I came to the store to buy flour.

5 The Word دەپ as Conjunction 'that'

Take a look at the following example from the dialogue:

بىز سىزنى ئۈرۈمچى ۋاقتى سائەت ئالتىدە كېلىدۇ دەپ ئويلاپتىمىز!
We thought that you were coming at six o'clock Urumchi time!

Here the word دەپ serves to denote what the subject of the verb in the following clause thought. Look at more examples:

مەن سىزنى ئۇيغۇر دەپ ئويلاپتىمەن.
I thought that you were a Uyghur.
سىزنى ئالدىراش دەپ بالدۇرراق كەلدىم.
I came earlier because I thought that you were busy.
ئۇنى پولۇغا ئامراق دەپ پولۇ ئېتىۋاتىمەن.
I am cooking Pilaf because I know that he loves pilaf.
ئۇلارنى كەچرەك كېلىدۇ دەپ تاماقنى تېخى باشلىمىدىم.
I thought that they would come later, so I did not start cooking.

Exercise 14:  Look at the following signs at the Urumchi airport and match them with their English equivalents in the table below.

❷

❶

❹

❸

❻

❺

waiting area	
baggage check	
security check	

ticket counter	
passport control	
departure/arrival boards	

Exercise 15: ئۈرۈمچى ئايرودرومىدا

Exercise 15.1: Listen to the dialogue and tell if the following statements are true or false.

خاتا	توغرا

1.جون ئۈچىدىغان ئايروپىلان بۇزۇلۇپ قالدى.

2. سودىگەر جوننى ئامېرىكىلىق ئۇيغۇر دەپ ئويلىدى.

3. سودىگەر جوننىڭ ئۇيغۇرچىسىنى ئاڭلاپ ھەيران قالدى.

4. ئەخمەت ئوتتۇرا ئاسىياغا بېرىشنى خالىمىدى.

5. شىنجاڭدا پاسپورت ئېلىش بەك تەس.

Exercise 15.2: Listen to the conversation again, and fill in the words missing from the transcript.

(ئۇيغۇر) سودىگەر: نى خاۋ! چۇ بېيجىڭما؟*

جون: سىز ئۇيغۇرمۇ؟

سودىگەر: ۋوي، سىزمۇ ئۇيغۇرما؟

جون: ياق، مەن ئامېرىكىلىق.

سودىگەر: ئەمىسە سىز ________________ ئوخشىمامسىز؟

جون: ياق، مەن ئۇيغۇر ئەمەس، ئۈرۈمچىدە بىر يىل ئۇيغۇرچە ئۆگەندىم.

سودىگەر: ________________ ! ئۇيغۇرچىڭىز بەك ياخشىكەنە.

جون: رەھمەت. مەن بىر يىل ئۇيغۇر دوستلىرىم بىلەن ياشىدىم. ھەر كۈنى دېگۈدەك ئۇيغۇرچە سۆزلىدىم.

سودىگەر: چەتئەللىكلەر ھەجەپ________________ دەيمىنا. ماۋۇ خىتايلار شىنجاڭدا ئون يىل تۇرسىمۇ "ياكېشى" دىن باشقا گەپنى ئۆگىنەلمەيدۇ. سىز بىر يىلدىلا ھەممە گەپ نى________________.

جون: كۆپ مەشق قىلسا، ئۆگىنىش تەس ئەمەس. ھە راست، سىزنىڭ ئىسمىڭىز نېمە؟

سودىگەر : ئىسمىم ئەخمەت. سىزنىڭچۇ؟

جون: مېنىڭ ئۇيغۇرچە ئىسمىم يالقۇن.

ئەخمەت: يالقۇن... ياخشى ئىسىم ________________. سىزمۇ سائەت توققۇزنىڭ ئايروپىلانىدا ئۇچامسىز؟

جون: شۇنداق. مېنىڭ ئايروپىلانىم بېيجىڭ ۋاقتى سائەت توققۇزدا ئۇچماقچى ئىدى. مانا ئەمدى بىر نەچچە سائەت ساقلايدىغان ________________.

ئەخمەت: يامغۇر ياغسا، ئايروپىلان دائىم مۇشۇنداق كېچىكىپ قالىدۇ.

جون: مۇنداق دەڭ. مەن تېخى ئايروپىلان ________________ ئوخشايدۇ دەپ ئويلاپتىمەن.

ئەخمەت:___________________ ئۈرۈمچىدە بۇنداق ئىشلار كۆپ... سىز بېيجىڭغا ئوقۇغىلى ماڭدىڭىزمۇ؟

جون: ياق، مەن ئامېرىكىغا قايتىمەن. ئامېرىكىدىكى ئوقۇشۇم تېخى تۈگىمىدى.

ئەخمەت: سىز ئامېرىكىدا نېمە __________________ ئوقۇيسىز؟

جون: مېنىڭ كەسپىم ئوتتۇرا ئاسىيا ____________________.

ئەخمەت: سىز ئوتتۇرا ئاسىياغىمۇ باردىڭىزمۇ؟

جون: ياق، تېخى بارمىدىم. سىزچۇ، سىز ئوتتۇرا ئاسىياغا بارغانمۇ؟

ئەخمەت: باراي دەپ ئويلىغان. ئەمما پاسپورتۇم بولمىغاچقا بارالمىدىم.

جون: ئۇيغۇرلارنىڭ پاسپورت ئېلىشى بەك تەس _________________ئاڭلىدىم.

ئەخمەت: بۇنى بىر دېمەڭ. سۆزلەپ كەلسەك گەپ جىق. شۇڭا مەن دائىم بېيجىڭدىلا تۇرىمەن.

*نى خاۋ! چۈ بېيجىڭما؟ : In Chinese: Hello! Are you going to Beijing?

Exercise 15.3: Now answer the following questions.

1. نېمىشقا ئەخمەت چەتئەللىكلەرنى ئەقىللىق دەيدۇ؟
2. نېمىشقا ئەخمەت پاسپورت مەسىلىسىنى تىلغا ئالدۇ؟ سىز بۇ مەسىلىگە قانداق قارايسىز؟
3. نېمە ئۈچۈن ئەخمەت بېيجىڭدا تۇرىدۇ؟
4. سىزنىڭچە، ئەخمەت بېيجىڭدا نېمە ئىش قىلىدۇ؟
5. سىزنىڭچە، نېمە ئۈچۈن يامغۇر ياغسا، ئايروپىلان ئۇچمايدۇ؟
6. "خىتاي" بىلەن "خەنزۇ" سۆزىنىڭ نېمە پەرقى بار؟

Exercise 16: خوتەن قاشتېشى

Exercise 16.1:  Review the following words, then read the second part of the dialogue on the next page.

stone quarrying, masonry	تاشچىلىق
jade trade	قاشتېشى سودىسى
profit	پايدا
to joke	چاقچاق قىلماق

جون: سىز بېيجىڭدا نېمە ئىش قىلىسىز؟
ئەخمەت: تاشچىلىق قىلىمەن.
جون: تاشچىلىق؟ بۇ قانداق خىزمەت؟
ئەخمەت: تاشچىلىق دېگىنىمىز قاشتېشى سودىسى دېگەن گەپ. بىز ئىچكىرىدە قاشتېشى ساتىمىز.
جون: قاشتېشىنى نەدىن ئالىسىز؟ بېيجىڭدا قاشتېشى كۆپمۇ؟
ئەخمەت: ياق، قاشتېشىنى بىز خوتەندىن ئەكېلىپ ساتىمىز.
جون: مەن خوتەنگە بارغاندا قاشتېشى ھاققىدە ئاڭلىغان. خوتەننى "قاشتېشى ماكانى" دەپمۇ ئاتايدىكەن.
ئەخمەت: ھە بەللى، بىلىدىكەنسىز!
جون: قاشتېشىنى نېمىگە ئىشلىتىدۇ؟
ئەخمەت: ئۇنىڭدىن ئاساسەن زىننەت بۇيۇملىرىنى ياسايدۇ.
جون: قىزىق... نېمىشقا قاشتېشىنى شىنجاڭدا ساتمايسىلەر؟
ئەخمەت: قاشتېشىنى ئىچكىرىدە قىممەترەك ساتقىلى بولىدۇ، پايدىسىمۇ كۆپرەك بولىدۇ.
جون: ئەمىسە سىز باي، شۇنداقمۇ؟
ئەخمەت: باي دەپ كەتكىلى بولمايدۇ، ئىشقىلىپ، تۇرمۇشۇم شىنجاڭدىكىدىن ياخشى.
جون: ھازىر سودىڭىز قانداقراق؟
ئەخمەت: ئانچە ياخشى ئەمەس. ھازىر تاشچىلىق قىلىدىغان ئۇيغۇرلار بەك كۆپ. تاش كۆپ، خېرىدار ئاز. شۇڭا بۇندىن كېيىن باشقا بىر ئىش قىلسام بولامدىكىن.
جون: ھازىر يېنىڭىزدا قاشتېشى بارمۇ؟
ئەخمەت: ھەئە، ماۋۇ سومكامدا بىرنەچچە تال كىچىكرەك تاشلار بار. سىزگە كۆرسىتەي. مانا قاراڭ، ماۋۇ ئاق قاشتاش، ماۋۇ يېشىل قاشتاش. ئۇنىڭ تۈرلىرى كۆپ. مانا بۇ سېرىق قاشتاش، مانا قارىسى...
جون: بۇلاردىن قايسىسى قىممەت؟
ئەخمەت: ئېقى بىلەن سېرىقى ئەڭ ئەتىۋارلىق ھېسابلىنىدۇ.
جون: بۇلار قانچە پۇل؟
ئەخمەت: ماۋۇ بىر پارچە تاشنى 20 مىڭ كويغا ئالىدۇ. سىز ئالامسىز؟ سىزگە ئەرزانىراق بېرەي.
جون: ياق، ياق، رەھمەت. مەن ئوقۇغۇچى، مەندە بۇنچىلىك پۇل يوق.
ئەخمەت: ھا..ھا... چاقچاق قىلىپ قويدۇم. بۇ تاشنى خىتايلارغا ساتىمىز. سىزگە ماۋۇ تاشنى سوۋغا قىلاي.
جون: سىز يەنە چاقچاق قىلىۋاتامسىز؟
ئەخمەت: چاقچاق قىلمىدىم. بۇ سىزگە سوۋغىتىم بولۇپ قالسۇن.
جون: ئەمىسە مەن سىزگە ئازراق پۇل بېرەي.
ئەخمەت: ياق، ياق، بۇ مېنىڭ كۆڭلۈم. بىز ئادەتتە سوۋغات ئۈچۈن پۇل ئالمايمىز.
جون: ئەمىسە سىزگە كۆپ رەھمەت.

Exercise 16.2: Discuss the following questions with your classmates.

1. نېمىشقا ئۇيغۇرلار قاشتېشىنى ئۆز يۇرتىدا ساتماي ئىچكىرىگە ئاپىرىپ ساتىدۇ؟
2. نېمىشقا ئەخمەت جوندىن قاشتېشى ھەققىنى ئالمايدۇ؟

Uyghur Migrant Workers in Beijing

Increasing unemployment among non-Han Chinese in Xinjiang has forced more and more Uyghurs to immigrate temporarily to inner China, and particularly Beijing, seeking a better life and better education for their children. The number of Uyghur immigrating to Beijing has jumped dramatically in recent years. This is due in large part to the capital's relatively free markets, an increased regulation of its political sector, and a growing demand for typically Xinjiang-ese luxury goods such as furs, tanned animal hides, Uyghur cuisine, and jade. These Uyghur migrants' new lives in Beijing have been entirely unproblematic, however, migrants are often the target of prejudice. Uyghurs are stereotyped as pickpockets or drug dealers by many Han Chinese. As a result, Uyghurs in Beijing are sometimes denied entry into shops and hotels, and their children sometimes have trouble registering for schools.

Exercise 17: يولۇچىلار دىققىتىگە!

Exercise 17.1:  Now you will hear a flight announcement. Listen to it twice and answer the questions that follow.

1.Why was the flight delayed?

a. weather-related issues   b. technical difficulties

c. runway congestion   d. cigarette smoking caused a fire

2. Why do people have to go to gate 22?

____

Exercise 17.2: Listen to the announcement one more time. While listening, look at the flight information summary below. Update all the necessary information according to the announcment.

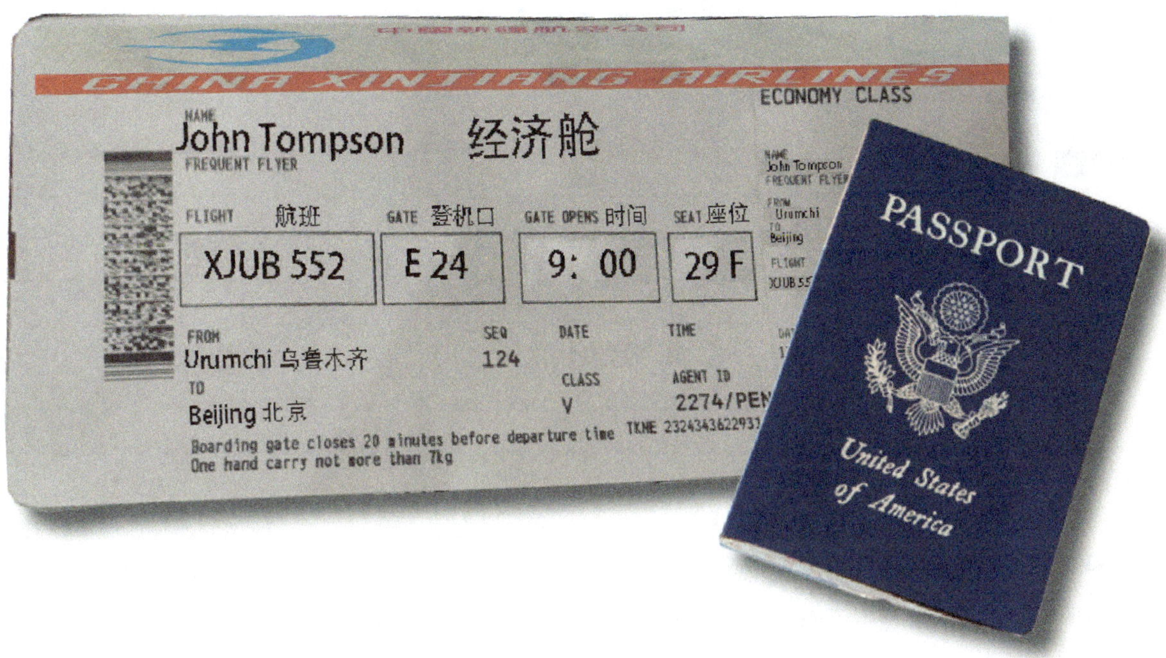

Exercise 18: سەپەر تەسىراتلىرىم

Exercise 18.1: Think of a recent trip you took. Describe a scene from this trip in detail. Mention the people you saw, the things they were doing, and anything unusual or surprising you noticed about them.

Exercise 18.2:  John is on the plane writing his last blog post. Read the last entry and answer the questions on the next page.

Uyghur John's Blog

ئامېرىكىلىق ياڭقونىڭ تورتۇراسى

Search

كۈندە بىر ماقال:
ئۆلمىگەن جاندا ئۈمىد بار.

مانا، سەپىرىم ئاياغلاشتى دېسەمۇ بولىدۇ. بىرتەرەپتىن مەن بەك خوشال، چۈنكى ئامېرىكىنى خېلى سېغىندىم. ئاتا - ئانامنىمۇ كۆرمىگىلى بىر يىل بوپتۇ. ئەمما يەنە بىرتەرەپتىن كۆڭلۈم ئازراق يېرىم، چۈنكى ئۈرۈمچىگىمۇ خېلى كۆنۈپ قاپتىمەن... يەنە كېلىشكە پۇرسەتلەر چىقامدىكىن؟ بۇ يەرنىڭ تاماقلىرىنى، مېۋە- چېۋىلىرىنى تازا سېغىنىمەندە... بايا ئايرودرومدا نۇرغۇن خەنزۇلارنى كۆردۈم. ئۇلارنىڭ ھەممىسى دېگۈدەك قولىغا ئاز دېگەندە بىر يەشىك مېۋە كۆتۈرۈۋاپتۇ. قارىماققا، ئۇلارمۇ شىنجاڭ مېۋىلىرىگە ئامراق ئوخشايدۇ. بەزىلىرى نان، قاق، كىشمىشلەرنى ئېلىۋاپتۇ.... مەن بىلەن بىللە بۇ ئايروپىلانغا بىر نەچچە چەتئەللىكلەرمۇ چىقتى. ئۇلارنىڭ قولىدا گىلەم، دۇتار، بىر نەچچە پارچە رەسىم كۆردۈم...

ئايروپىلاندا بىر نەچچە ئۇيغۇرمۇ بار. ئەخمەتكامىنىڭ ئېيتىشىچە، ئۇيغۇرلار بېيجىڭغا ئىش ئىزدەپ بارىدىكەن. ئۇنىڭ گېپىگە قارىغاندا، ئۇيغۇرلار بېيجىڭدا كۆپ قىيىنىلىدىكەن.
شۇ بىچارىلەرگە ئۆز يۇرتىدا ئىش تېپىلمىسا.... ئۈرۈمچىدە نۇرغۇن خەنزۇلار ياشايدىكەن.
ئۇلارنى ھۆكۈمەت قانداق ئىشقا ئورۇنلاشتۇرىدىكىن تاڭ؟

ئۇيغۇرلار ئاجايىپ خەلق ئىكەن. ئۆزىنىڭ زۆرۈر ئىشى بولسىمۇ، ئۇنى قويۇپ، سىزگە ياردەم بېرىدىكەن. مېھمانلارنى بەكمۇ ھۆرمەتلەيدىكەن. رېستورانغا بىللە بېرىپ قالسىڭىز، ئىقتىسادىي شارائىتى ئانچە ياخشى بولمىسىمۇ، تاماقنىڭ پۇلىنى سىزگە تۆلەتكۈزمەيدىكەن، "سىز مېھمان" دەپلا تۇرىدىكەن. بۇنداق چاغلاردا ئادەم بەك خىجىل بولىدىكەن، چۈنكى ئامېرىكىلىقلاردا بۇنداق ئادەت يوق، ھەركىم ئۆزىنىڭ تامىقىنىڭ پۇلىنى ئۆزى تۆلەيدۇ.

بۇ قېتىملىق سەپىرىم ناھايىتى ئۈنۈملۈك بولدى. ئۇيغۇرچەمنى خېلىلا ياخشىلىۋالدىم، ئەمدى كېرەكلىك ماتېرىياللارنى قىينالماي ئوقۇيالايمەن. نۇرغۇن كىتابلارنى پوچتا ئارقىلىق سېلىۋەتتىم. مەن بارغۇچە كىتابلىرىممۇ يېتىپ كېلەر... ئۆزۈمگە يەنە بىر ئېلېكترونلۇق لۇغەتمۇ ئالدىم. ئۇ بەك قولاي ئىكەن. ئۇنى يانچۇقۇمغا سېلىپ يۈرسەممۇ بولىدىكەن...

تاماقنىڭ پۇرىقى كېلىۋاتىدۇغۇ... ھازىر تاماق بېرىدىغان ئوخشايدۇ. قورسىقىمنىڭ قانچىلىك ئاچقانلىقىنى مانا ھازىر بىلدىم. تاماقنى يەپ ئازراق ئۇخلىۋالاي.... خەير- خوش، ئۈرۈمچى! سېنى بەكمۇ سېغىنىمەن!

1. The following two sentences have been removed from the text. Which paragraph do they belong to? Mark their place in the text with an asterisk *.

هېچ كىم بۇ يەردىن قوزۇق كەتمەيدىكەندە...

ئۆزىنىڭ ۋاقتىنى، ياردىمىنى هېچ قاچان ئايىمايدىكەن.

2. John posed some questions that he left unanswered. What is your opinion about the following issues?

ئۈرۈمچىدە نۇرغۇن خەنزۇلار ياشايدىكەن. ئۇلارنى هۆكۈمەت قانداق ئىشقا ئورۇنلاشتۇرىدىكىن تاڭ؟

3. Explain the following expression:

كۆڭلۈم ئازراق يېرىم

What does John mean when he uses it? Have you ever been in a situation where you could have used this expression? Explain.

4. Why does John think his trip was productive?

5. How productive were you in this course? Evaluate your work, explain your reasoning, and provide evidence to support your self-assessment. Write at least 7 sentences in Uyghur about what you have learned and accomplished.

Pulling it all together خۇرجۇندا

In this section, you will reinforce your knowledge and check the progress you have made during chapters 11 and 12 by completing a limited selection of focused exercises.

Exercise 19: خوتەننىڭ قول سانائىتى

Exercise 19.1: In this video Samat talks about handicraft culture in Khotan. Watch it and tell if the following statements are توغرا or خاتا.

خاتا	توغرا

1. خوتەن - گىلەمچىلىك بازىسى.
2. خوتەندە گىلەمچىلىك ماشىنىلاشمىغان.
3. خوتەن گىلەملىرى قول ھۈنىرىگە تايىنىپ ئىشلىنىدۇ.
4. خوتەندە يىپەك توقۇمىچىلىقى ئۇزۇن تارىخقا ئىگە.
5. خوتەن گىلەملىرى پۈتۈن جۇڭگو بويىچە ئەڭ داڭلىق.
6. خوتەنلىكلەر تۇرمۇشتا كېرەكلىك بولغان نەرسىلەرنى ئۆزلىرى ئىشلەپ چىقىرىدۇ.

Exercise 19.2: Watch the video one more time and answer the following two questions.

1. Why does the narrator mention سەددىچىن سىپىلى in his narration?
2. Why does he talk about Khotan's location and transportation at the end of the video?

Exercise 20: خوتەندە باغۋەنچىلىك

Exercise 20.1:  In this video segment Samat talks about gardening in Khotan. Listen to the video and list all the names of fruits you hear in his narration.

Exercise 20.2: Watch the video one more time and answer the following questions.

1. Why does he mention Turpan grapes in this video?
2. What does he say about چىلان? Why do people grow it in Khotan?
3. How does he explain the development of gardening in Khotan. Why is it more developed than farming?

Exercise 21:  What have you learned about Khotan? Use all the information you have gathered from Chapter 11 and 12 and take your notes below.

Artisanship:

____

____

Symbols:

____

____

Dialect:

____

____

Naming culture:

____

____

Gardening:

____

____

خوتەندىكى ھېيتگاھ مەسچىتى

خوتەندىكى مەلىكاۋات قەدىمىي شەھىرى

Exercise 22:  You want to stay at a hotel in Khotan. Fill out the online form below. What other information do you see on this page?

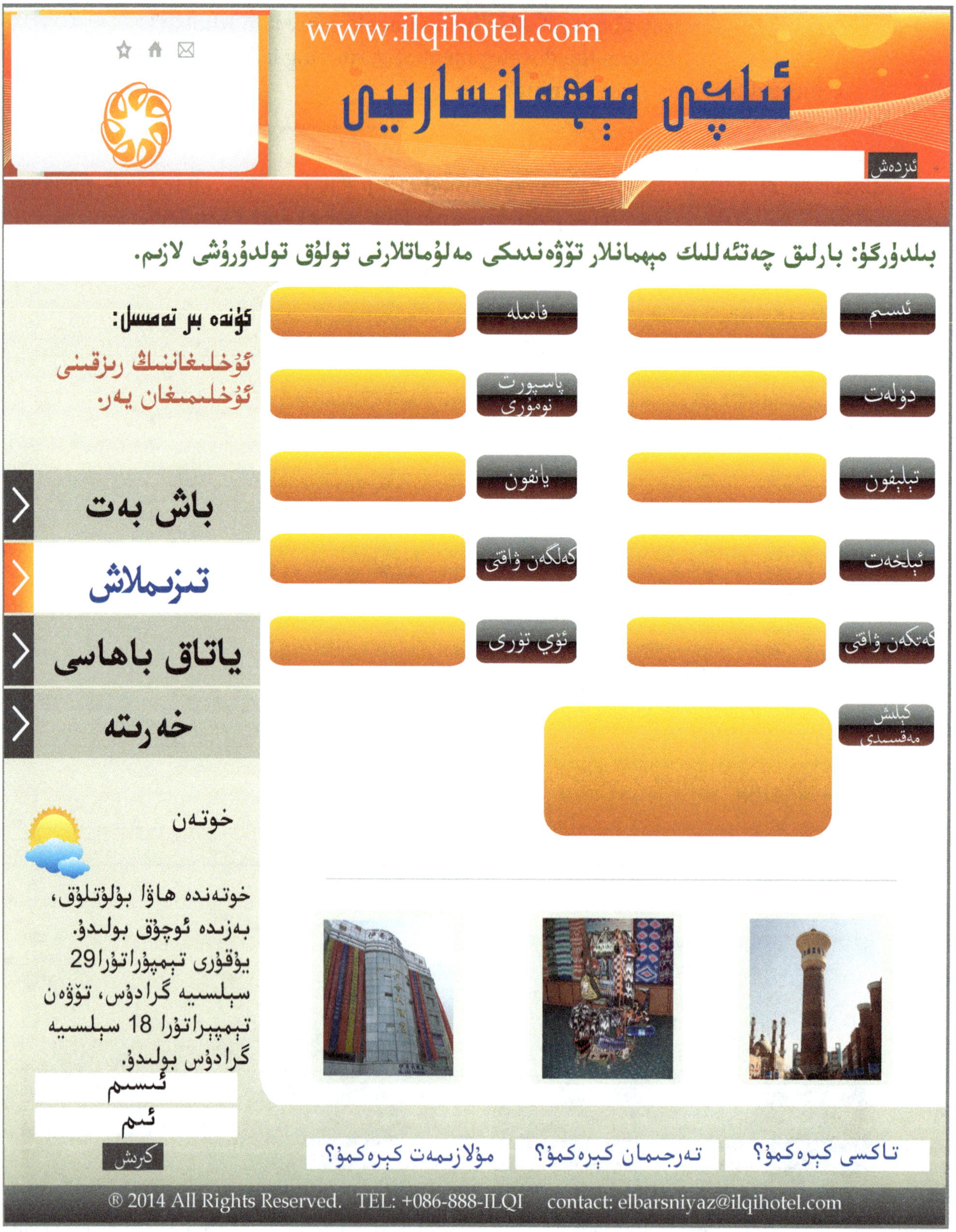

www.ilqihotel.com

ئىلچى مېھمانسارىيى

ئىزدەش

بىلدۈرگۈ: بارلىق چەتئەللىك مېھمانلار تۆۋەندىكى مەلۇماتلارنى تولۇق تولدۇرۇشى لازىم.

كۈندە بىر تەمسىل:

ئۇخلىغاننىڭ رىزقىنى ئۇخلىمىغان يەر.

باش بەت

تىزىملاش

ياتاق باھاسى

خەرىتە

ئىسىم		فامىلە	
دۆلەت		پاسپورت نومۇرى	
تېلېفون		يانفون	
ئېلخەت		كەلگەن ۋاقتى	
كېتكەن ۋاقتى		ئۆي تۈرى	
كېلىش مەقسىدى			

خوتەن

خوتەندە ھاۋا بۇلۇتلۇق، بەزىدە ئوچۇق بولىدۇ. يۇقىرى تېمپېراتۇرا 29 سېلسىيە گرادۇس، تۆۋەن تېمپېراتۇرا 18 سېلسىيە گرادۇس بولىدۇ.

ئىسىم

ئىم

كىرىش

تاكسى كېرەكمۇ؟ | تەرجىمان كېرەكمۇ؟ | مۇلازىمەت كېرەكمۇ؟

 TEL: +086-888-ILQI contact: elbarsniyaz@ilqihotel.com

Exercise 23: ئۈرۈمچىدە تۇرغىنىمدا

Exercise 23.1:  Listen to Colin's narration about his time in Urumchi. Take notes so that you can answer the questions below. Use the expressions in the box as necessary.

1. كولىن ئۈرۈمچىدە تۇرغان كۈنلىرىنى تەسۋىرلەپ نېمە دەيدۇ؟
2. بوش ۋاقىتلىرى چىقىپ قالسا، كولىن بىلەن دوستلىرى نېمە قىلاتتى؟
3. كولىن ئۇيغۇر دوستلىرى بىلەن قانداق ئالاقە قىلىشىپ تۇرۇپتۇ؟

I still remember	ھازىرغىچە ئېسىمدە
through the internet	تور ئارقىلىق
a long-standing friend	قەدىناس دوست

Exercise 23.2: Listen to the passage again, and fill in the blanks with the words and expressions you hear.

ئۈرۈمچىدە تۇرغان ۋاقتىم ناھايىتى __________ ئۆتتى. بولۇپمۇ ئۇيغۇر __________
بىلەن ئۆتكەن كۈنلىرىم. بىكار بولساق توپ __________، ناخشا ئاڭلاپ __________
ئوينايتتۇق، شەنبە - يەكشەنبە كۈنلىرى __________ ئايلىناتتۇق. بەزىدە __________
قىلاتتۇق. ئۈرۈمچىدە ئوقۇغاندىن ھازىرغىچە شىنجاڭغا بارمىغىلى __________ بولاي دېسىمۇ،
شۇ كۈنلەر ھازىرغىچە __________ ئۇيغۇر دوستلىرىم بىلەن تور ئارقىلىق __________
يېزىشىپ، تېلېفون__________ تۇرۇپتۇق. خۇدايىم بۇيرىسا بىر __________ چىقىپ قالسىلا،
ئۈرۈمچىگە بېرىپ كونا قەدىناس دوستلىرىمنى يوقلايمەن!

Exercise 24: خوتەن قاشتېشى

Exercise 24.1:  You have been asked by an American travel magazine to write a short paragraph about Khotan (Hetian) Jade. It should be written for an English-speaking travel audience. Use the information from the dialogue in Exercise 16.1 along with John's blog entry from Chapter 11, Exercise 19 and write a short passage on the next page.

Exercise 24:2: Present your passage in Uyghur translation to your partner.

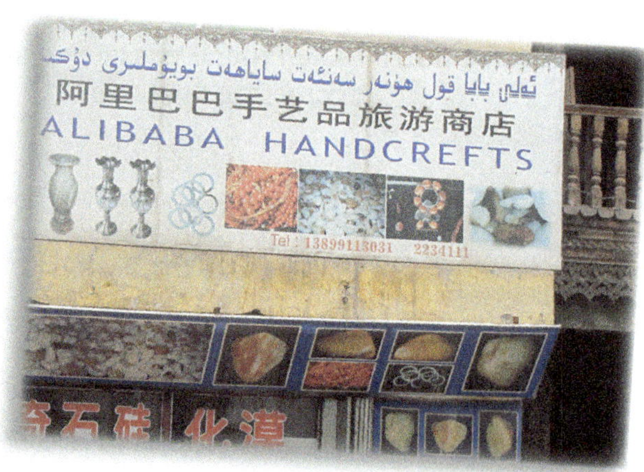

Self-check

Use the following list to check your knowledge of the topics you have covered in chapters 11 and 12. Mark whether you know and can do the following in Uyghur. If you think you may need more work to fully understand something, you can go back to the relevant section in the chapters and review it.

1. I can talk and write about:

The city of Khotan	
The Khotan carpet	
The Khotan ئەتلەس	
The Khotanese dialect	
Gardening in Khotan	
Khotanese naming tradition	
Khotanese jade	
The capital city of Urumchi	
Uyghur migrant workers in Beijing	
My most impressive trip	
The Uyghur comedian Abdukerim Abliz	

2. I can also:

Distinguish the Khotanese dialect	
Talk to the receptionist at a hotel and reserve a room	
Talk to strangers and ask for help	
Describe my desire	

3. I know how to:

Use some proverbs with the word كۆڭۈل	
Write an invitation letter for a farewell party	
Call a taxi agency to order a taxi	
Talk to a taxi driver	
Read signs at the airport in Urumchi	

4. I know the following words and concepts:

	ۋىلايەت		خوتەن قاشتېشى
	تاكسى شىركىتى		كارخانا
	جەلپ قىلماق		بوستانلىق
	قەدىناس دوست		چۆل
	كۆڭۈل		تېرىلغۇ يەر
	مۇلازىمەت		توپا ياغدىغان ئەھۋال
	نېفىت		كۆلەم
	تاشچىلىق		قالايمىقان
	چولپان		قۇرغاق
	ئېسىل		كەمبەغەل بولساڭ گىلەم ئال
	توپا يېغىش ئەھۋالى		شەرق ئۇسلۇبى
	مىننەتدارلىق		شېۋە
	ھەرگىز		لەقەم

5. I can use grammar to ...

Express the idea of 'one moment... and the next' (بىرتۇرۇپ...يەنە بىرتۇرۇپ)	
Express the habitual past with the suffix مىش-	
Make the 1st person of the interrogative present-future form (بارامدىمەن)	
Avoid duplication of the verb forms using the conjunction بولۇپ	
Express desire using the word كەلمەك	
Make suggestive commands using the word جۇمۇ	
Express probability using the suffix ار-/ەر-	
Express purpose with the word دەپ	
Form a clause using the word دەپ	

Vocabulary سۆزلۈك

**Vocabulary is given according to the Uyghur alphabetical order.
The right column precedes the left column on each page.**

unusual; very	ئاجايىپ
habit, custom	ئادەت
kind, sincere	ئاق كۆڭۈل
aviation	ئاۋىئاتسىيە
spiralling road	ئايلانما يول
to apologize	ئەپۇ سورىماق
eccentric, very, really	ئەجەب
superiority	ئەۋزەللىك
petrol, benzene	بېنزىن
poor; unfortunate; unlucky	بىچارە
cleanliness	پاكىزلىق
capital city	پايتەخت
smell	پۇراق
highway	تاشيول
taxi service	تاكسى شىركىتى
railroad	تۆمۈر يول
jail	تۈرمە
to attract	جەلپ قىلماق
animal husbandry	چارۋىچىلىق
exit	چىقىش ئېغىزى
state run	دۆلەت ئىگىلىكىدىكى
national	دۆلەتلىك
agriculture	دېھقانچىلىق
to go through the necessary formalities	رەسمىيەت ئۆتمەك
to flourish	روناق تاپماق
a small glass cup; shot glass	رومكا

to repair	رېمونت قىلماق
to force	زورلىماق
industry	سانائەت
trade	سودا
gift	سوۋغات
to splash water	سۇ چاچماق
to sweep	سۈپۈرمەك
political	سىياسىي
individual	شەخسىي
transport hub	قاتناش تۈگۈنى
unlicensed taxicab	قارا تاكسى
close friend	قەدىناس دوست
construction	قۇرۇلما
an obstacle, hindrance	كاشىلا
to be sad	كۆڭۈل يېرىم بولماق
happily	كۆڭۈللۈك
scale, scope; surface area	كۆلەم
coal	كۆمۈر
to be late	كېچىكمەك
auto manufacturing	ماشىنىسازلىق
administrative region	مەمۇرىي رايون
gratitude	مىننەتدارلىق
county	ناھىيە
oil (crude petroleum)	نېفىت
never	ھەرگىز
wage; right	ھەق
to be astonished	ھەيران قالماق

to look for, to search for	ئىزدىمەك
economic	ئىقتىسادىي
to like; to light	ياقماق
to carry in a pocket	يانچۇققا سېلىپ يۈرمەك
passenger	يولۇچى

government	ھۆكۈمەت
in addition	ئۇنىڭ ئۈستىگە
province	ئۆلكە
productive; efficient	ئۈنۈملۈك
the lap; lower slope	ئېتەك
inside part; China proper	ئىچكىرى

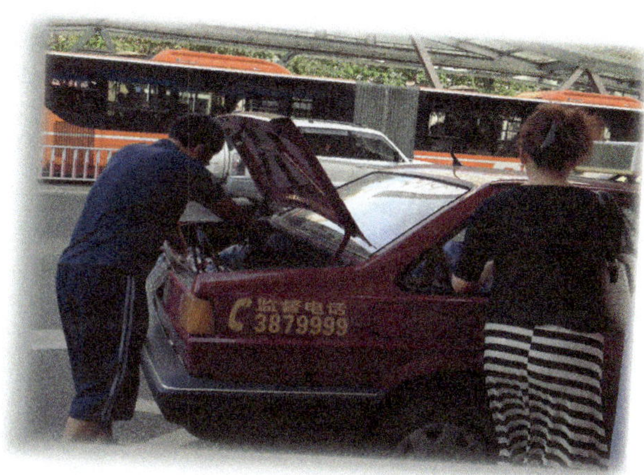

Comprehensive Culture Quiz بىلىق ھوسۇل

You have learned a lot about Uyghur culture from the twelve chapters which comprise this textbook. In this section you will sum up some of the most interesting points from your virtual trip to Xinjiang. Take a brief quiz to check your knowledge of some aspects of Uyghur culture which you touched upon during your studies. Fill in the blanks with the appropriate terms related to Uyghur traditional concepts, customs, and everyday life.

1. Uyghurs bake their traditional bread and samsa in a ________________.
2. The book "دىۋانى لۇغەتىت تۈرك" was written by ________________________.
3. The Forbidden City is called ______________________________ in Uyghur.
4. The Great Wall of China is called ____________________________ in Uyghur.
5. The word سامسپەز means ______________________________.
6. The book "قۇتادغۇ بىلىگ" was written by ______________________________.
7. The most famous Uyghur knives are called ____________________________.
8. The word بەكە means ______________________.
9. كارىز are found primarily in and around _________________________.
10. The famous Heyt Gah mosque is in ___________________________.
11. The word مەدىكار means ______________________________.
12. The land of jade is ____________________________.
13. Tata Tonga is famous for ____________________________________.
14. Xinjiang's most famous baseball team is located in ______________________.
15. مەشرەپ is a type of ____.
16. The word چاقچاق means ______________________________________.
17. Sand Therapy is performed primarily in ___________________________.
18. There are ____________________ steps in a traditional Uyghur wedding .
19. The expression تەزىيە بىلدۈرمەك means ____________________________.
20. Gojahmet Sadvaqasov is best known as ____________________________.
21. Dolqun Yasin is best known as ______________________________.
22. Abdukerim Abliz is best known as ________________________________.

Appendix A

Transcripts of Listening Exercises

PRELIMINARY CHAPTER

Exercise 2.1

مېنىڭ ئىسمىم جون. ئۇيغۇرچە ئىسمىم يالقۇن. مەن ئامېرىكىلىق. 1982 - يىلى 4 - ئاينىڭ 25 - كۈنى نيۇ يوركتا تۇغۇلدۇم. 2005 - يىلى جورجتاۋۇن ئۇنىۋېرسىتېتىنى پۈتتۈردۈم. 2007 - يىلى يازدا ئىندىيانا ئۇنىۋېرسىتېتىغا كېلىپ ئىككى ئاي ئۇيغۇرچە ئۆگەندىم. 2008- يىلى تۇنجى قېتىم شىنجاڭغا باردىم. ئۇ يەردە ئۈچ ئاي تۇردۇم. بۇ ماكانىنى بەك ياخشى كۆردۈم. پۇرسەت بولسا، ئۇيغۇر دىيارىنى يەنە بىر قېتىم زىيارەت قىلىمەن. مەن ئۇيغۇر تىلىغا قىزىقىمەن. ئىندىيانا ئۇنىۋېرسىتېتىغا كېلىشىمنىڭ سەۋەبى ئۇيغۇر تىلىنى ۋە ئوتتۇرا ئاسىيا تارىخىنى تېخىمۇ ياخشى ئۆگىنىش.

Exercise 4.1

دولقۇن: ياخشىمۇسىز!
ماھنۇر: ياخشىمۇسىز!
دولقۇن: مېنىڭ ئىسمىم دولقۇن، سىزنىڭچۇ؟
ماھنۇر: مېنىڭ ئىسمىم ماھنۇر.
دولقۇن: تونۇشقانلىقىمدىن خۇشالمەن.
ماھنۇر: مەنمۇ خۇشال.
دولقۇن: سىز قەيەرلىك؟
ماھنۇر: مەن تۇرپانلىق. سىزچۇ؟
دولقۇن: مەن خوتەنلىك. ئۈرۈمچىدە ئوقۇيمەن.
ماھنۇر: ھە، مۇنداق دەڭ.
دولقۇن: سىزچۇ؟ سىز نېمە ئىش قىلىسىز؟
ماھنۇر: مەن بۇلتۇر ئوقۇش پۈتتۈردۈم، يېقىندا ئىشقا ئورۇنلاشتىم.
دولقۇن: نەدە ئىشلەيسىز؟
ماھنۇر: ساياھەت شىركىتىدە.
دولقۇن: ياخشى يەردە ئىشلەيدىكەنسىزغۇ.
ماھنۇر: سىز نەدە ئوقۇيسىز؟
دولقۇن: مەن شىنجاڭ پېداگوگىكا ئۇنىۋېرسىتېتىدا ئوقۇيمەن.
ماھنۇر: ئوقۇتقۇچى بولىدىكەنسىز-دە...
دولقۇن: شۇنداق. مەن ئۇيغۇر تارىخىغا بەك قىزىقىمەن... ئاپلا، مېنىڭ دەرسىم بار ئىدى، كېچىكىپ قالسام بولمايدۇ.
ماھنۇر: ماقۇل ئەمىسە. خوش!
دولقۇن: ئامان بولۇڭ! يەنە كۆرۈشەرمىز.

Exercise 8.2

مېنىڭ ئىسمىم ئېلىس ئاندېرسون. ئۇيغۇرچە ئىسمىم نازاكەت. بۇ سۆزنىڭ مەنىسى " نازۇك، لاتاپەت ". مەن ئۆزۈم ئامېرىكىلىق. ئوكلاھوما شتاتىدا تۇغۇلۇپ چوڭ بولدۇم. ھازىر ئىندىيانا ئۇنىۋېرسىتېتىنىڭ مۇزىكا فاكۇلتېتىدا ئوقۇيمەن. مەن ئۇيغۇرچە ئۆگەنگىلى تۆت يىل بولدى. ئۈچ قېتىم شىنجاڭنى زىيارەت قىلدىم. بىرىنچى قېتىم 2004-يىلى يازدا ئۈرۈمچىگە باردىم. ئۇ يەردە شىنجاڭ ئۇنىۋېرسىتېتىدا بىر ئاي ئىنگلىزچە دەرس بەردىم. لېكىن شۇ چاغدا ئۇيغۇرچە بىر سۆزمۇ بىلمەيتتىم. ئامېرىكىغا قايتقاندا ئۇيغۇر تىلى ۋە مەدەنىيىتىگە قىزىقىپ قالدىم. ئىككى يىلدىن كېيىن ئۇيغۇرچە ئۆگىنىشنى باشلىدىم. 2007-يىلى ئىككىنچى قېتىم شىنجاڭغا باردىم. بۇ قېتىم ئىككى يېرىم ئاي قەشقەردە تۇرۇپ ئۇيغۇرچە ئۆگەندىم ھەم مۇزىكا توغرۇلۇق تەتقىقات قىلدىم. شۇ چاغدىمۇ ئۇيغۇرچەم ئانچە ياخشى ئەمەس ئىدى، شۇڭا مەن خېلى قىينالدىم. ئەمما ئۇيغۇرچەم كۈندىن كۈنگە ياخشىلاندى. دائىم ئۇيغۇرلار بىلەن سۆزلەشتىم. 2010-يىلى تەتقىقات قىلىش ئۈچۈن يەنە بىر قېتىم شىنجاڭغا باردىم. ئۈچ ئايچە ئۈرۈمچىدە تۇردۇم. بۇ قېتىم بۇرۇنقىدەك قىينالمىدىم، چۈنكى ئۇيغۇرچەم خېلى ياخشى ئىدى. ئۇيغۇر دوستلىرىممۇ كۆپەيدى. بوش ۋاقتىمدا دوستلىرىم بىلەن شەھەر ئايلاندىم. ئۇلاردىن جانلىق تىلنى خېلى ياخشى ئۆگەندىم. ئۇيغۇر تىلىنى ئۆگىنىش ئاسان ئەمەس. ھەر كۈنى مەشق قىلىشىڭلار كېرەك. ئەمما تىرىشىپ ئۆگەنسەڭلار، شىنجاڭغا بارغاندا قىينالمايسىلەر!

CHAPTER 1

Exercise 10.1

جون: ياخشىمۇسىز!

ئەكبەر: ياخشىمۇسىز!

جون: سىز ئۇيغۇرمۇ؟

ئەكبەر: ھەئە. سىز قانداق بىلدىڭىز؟

جون: قولىڭىزدىكى ئۇيغۇرچە كىتابتىن. سىزنىڭ ئىسمىڭىز ئەكبەرمۇ؟

ئەكبەر: ھەئە، ئىسمىمنى نەدىن بىلىسىز؟

جون: ئوقۇتقۇچىمىز ئېيتقان ئىدى.

ئەكبەر: سىزنىڭ ئۇيغۇرچىڭىز بەك ياخشىكەن.

جون: رەھمەت. يەنە كۆپ ئۆگىنىشىم لازىم.

ئەكبەر: سىزنىڭ ئىسمىڭىز نېمە؟

جون: مېنىڭ ئىسمىم جون. ئۇيغۇرچە ئىسمىم يالقۇن.

ئەكبەر: مۇنداق دەڭ. ياخشى ئىسىم تاللاپسىز.

جون: بۇ قەشقەرلىك دوستۇمنىڭ ئاكىسىنىڭ ئىسمى ئىدى.

ئەكبەر: ياخشى، ياخشى... سىز قايسى فاكۇلتېتتا ئوقۇيسىز؟

جون: مەن تىلشۇناسلىق فاكۇلتېتىدا ئوقۇيمەن. سىزچۇ؟

ئەكبەر: مەن ئاخبارات كەسپىدە.

جون: ئاخبارات؟ ئۇ قايسى فاكۇلتېت؟

ئەكبەر: ژۇرنالىزىم فاكۇلتېتى.

جون: ھە، كەچۈرۈڭ. بىز بۇ سۆزنى ئۆگەنگەن. مەن ئۇنتۇپ قاپتىمەن.
ئەكبەر: سىز ئۇيغۇرچىنى مۇشۇ مەكتەپتە ئۆگەنگەنمۇ؟
جون: ھەئە. مەن ھازىر 2- يىللىقتا ئوقۇۋاتىمەن.
ئەكبەر: سىز شىنجاڭغا بېرىپ باقتىڭىزمۇ؟
جون: باردىم. ئۆتكەن يىلى قەشقەردە ئۈچ ئاي تۇردۇم.
ئەكبەر: ماڭا بارمىغىلى ئۈچ يىل بولدى. ئاڭلىسام، قەشقەر بەك ئۆزگىرىپ كېتىپتۇ.

Exercise 10.3

جون: ھازىر قەشقەرنى چېقىۋاتىدۇ. بىر كونا ئۆينى چاققاندا، بىر كوزا ئالتۇن چىقىپتۇ.
ئەكبەر: نېمە چىقىپتۇ دېدىڭىز؟
جون: ئالتۇن.
ئەكبەر: ھە، كەچۈرۈڭ، مەن خاتا ئاڭلاپتىمەن.
جون: بۇ خەۋەرنى مەن توردىن كۆردۈم. كېيىن ئالتۇن تاپقانلار ئالتۇننى تالىشىپ ئۇرۇشۇپ قاپتۇ.
ئەكبەر: نېمىشقا؟
جون: ئالتۇننى تالىشىپتۇ. كېيىن ئۇ ئالتۇننى ھۆكۈمەت مۇسادىرە قىپتۇ.
ئەكبەر: ھەقىقەتەن قىزىق ئىش بوپتۇ...
جون: سىز بىزنىڭ ئۇيغۇرچە سۆھبەت سائىتىمىزگە قاتنىشالامسىز؟
ئەكبەر: سۆھبەت سائىتى؟ ئۇ قاچان بولىدۇ؟
جون: ھەر جۈمە كۈنى سائەت ئۈچتە ۋاقتىڭىز بارمۇ؟
ئەكبەر: ھەئە، بۇنداق ئىشقا ۋاقىت تاپىمىز ئەلۋەتتە. ئۇ قەيەردە بولىدۇ؟
جون: خەلقئارا بۆلۈمدە.
ئەكبەر: ئەمىسە جۈمە كۈنى شۇ يەردە كۆرۈشەيلى. خوش!
جون: خوش! سىزنى كۈتىمىز.

Exercise 16.1

مېنىڭ ئىسمىم زۆھرە. مەن ناخشا-مۇزىكا ئاڭلاشقا بەك ئامراق. مەن كۆپىنچە ھىندىستان، ئۆزبېكىستان ناخشىلىرىنى ئاڭلايمەن. بەزىدە ئۇيغۇرچە خىپ - خوپ ئوينايمەن. دوستلىرىم مەن ئوينىغان خىپ - خوپنى كۆرۈشنى ياخشى كۆرىدۇ. بىز بەزىدە ياتاقداش قىزلار بىلەن دىسكوخانىغا بېرىپ دىسكو ياكى تانسا ئوينايمىز. بەزىدە ھىندىچە ۋە ئەرەبچە ئۇسسۇلمۇ ئوينايمىز. زېرىكىپ قالساق، كارا ئوكەي مۇزىكىسىغا ناخشا ئېيتىمىز.

****

مېنىڭ ئىسمىم داۋۇت. مەن شىنجاڭ ئۇنىۋېرسىتېتىنىڭ تارىخ فاكۇلتېتىدا ئوقۇيمەن .مەن كىچىكىمدىنلا تارىخقا بەك قىزىققان ئىدىم. شۇڭا ئالىي مەكتەپتە مۇشۇ كەسىپنى تاللىدىم. دەرستىن سىرتقى ۋاقىتلاردا تورغا چىقىپ ئۇيغۇر تارىخىغا دائىر ماتېرىياللارنى ئوقۇشنى ۋە توپلاشنى ياخشى كۆرىمەن. بەزىدە تارىخىي رومانلارنى ئوقۇيمەن. ھازىر تارىخ تېمىسىدىكى ئەسەرلەرنى ئوقۇيدىغانلار كۆپىيىۋاتىدۇ. زېرىككەندە ئۇيغۇر مۇقاملىرىنى ئاڭلايمەن، چۈنكى ئۇيغۇر مۇقاملىرىدا ئۇيغۇرلارنىڭ تارىخى ئەكس ئەتكەن.

CHAPTER 2

Exercise 15.1

(تاك ...تاك)

ئەكبەر: جون! كېلىڭ، كېلىڭ.

جون: قانداق ئەھۋالىڭىز؟

ئەكبەر: ياخشى. كەلگىنىڭىز ياخشى بولدى. بىزدە"ياخشى مېھمان ئاش ئۈستىگە" دېگەن ماقال بار. مەن پولۇ ئېتىۋاتىمەن. كېلىڭ، بىللە يەيمىز.

جون: شۇنداقمۇ؟ مەن پولۇغا بەك ئامراق. قولۇمنى قەيەردە يۇيۇمەن؟

ئەكبەر: ئۇيغۇرلاردا ئۆيگە كەلگەن مېھماننىڭ قولىغا سۇ بېرىلىدۇ. بۇ يەر ئامېرىكا بولغاندىكىن سۇخانىدا يۇسىڭىز بولىدۇ.

جون: بۇ ياخشى ئادەت ئىكەن. ھەر بىر مېھماننىڭ قولىغا سۇ بېرەمدۇ؟

ئەكبەر: شۇنداق. ئۇيغۇرلارنىڭ ئادىتىدە مېھمان بەك ھۆرمەتلىنىدۇ.

جون: ئۇيغۇرلاردا يەنە قانداق ئادەتلەر بار ؟

ئەكبەر: چاي ۋە تاماق ئالدى بىلەن چوڭلارغا بېرىلىدۇ. چاي ياكى تاماق ئىككى قوللاپ سۇنۇلىدۇ ۋە ئىككى قول بىلەن ئېلىنىدۇ.

CHAPTER 3

Exercise 8.2

تەكلىماكان قۇملۇقى- تارىم ئويمانلىقىنىڭ ئوتتۇرىسىغا جايلاشقان. بۇ قۇملۇقنىڭ شەرقتىن غەربكىچە ئۇزۇنلىقى مىڭ كىلومېتىردىن ئاشىدۇ، جەنۇبتىن شىمالغا سوزۇلغان كەڭلىكى تەخمىنەن 400 كىلومېتىر. تەكلىماكان قۇملۇقى شىنجاڭ بويىچە ئەڭ چوڭ قۇملۇق. ئۇنىڭ كۆلىمى 324 مىڭ كۋادرات كىلومېتىر. قۇم بارخانلىرىنىڭ ئېگىزلىكى60-80 مېتىر، ئەڭ ئېگىز جايى 250 مېتىرچە كېلىدۇ. تەكلىماكان ئەسلى "تەركىي ماكان" يەنى "تاشلانغان ماكان" دېگەن سۆزدىن كېلىپ چىققان.

كىشلەرنىڭ ئېيتىشىچە، قەدىمكى زاماندا بۇ يەر گۈللەپ ياشنىغان، سۈيى كۆپ، مەنزىرىسى گۈزەل، ئاۋات بىر ماكان بولغان ئىكەن. ئەمما قۇم كۆچۈش سەۋەبىدىن بۇ يەردىكى كىشلەر ئەسلى ماكانىنى تاشلاپ، تەكلىماكاننىڭ ئەتراپىغا جايلاشقان ئىكەن. شۇنىڭدىن كېيىن كىشلەر بۇ يەرنى "تەركىي ماكان" دەپ ئاتىشىپتۇ. يىللارنىڭ ئۆتۈشى بىلەن تىلدىكى ئىستېمالنىڭ ئۆزگىرىشىگە ئەگىشىپ، بۇ سۆز "تەكلىماكان" غا ئۆزگىرىپتۇ.

Exercise 11.2

جون: ياسىن، بۇ سىزمۇ؟

ياسىن: ھە مەن. سىز كىم؟

جون: بۇ مەن، جون، ئامېرىكىدىن تېلېفون قىلىۋاتىمەن.

ياسىن: ھە جون، قانداق ئەھۋالىڭىز؟ تىنچلىقمۇ؟

جون: رەھمەت. ئىشلىرىم ياخشى. 7- ئايدا مەن شىنجاڭغا بارماقچى.

ياسىن: شۇنداقمۇ؟ بۇ ياخشى گەپقۇ.

جون: سىزنىڭ مەسلىھەتىڭىز كېرەك ئىدى.

ياسىن خوش...

جون: يۇ يوركتىن بېلەتنى قايسى شەھەرگە ئالسام قولايراق بولىدۇ؟
ياسىن: نيۇ يوركتىن بېلەتنى بېيجىڭغىچە ئالسىڭىز ياخشىراق بولىدىغۇ دەيمەن.
جون: شۇنداق قىلاي. بېيجىڭنىمۇ كۆرگۈم بار ئىدى. ئەمما بېيجىڭدا مېنىڭ تونۇشلىرىم يوق. ئۇ يەردە نەگە چۈشسەم بولىدۇ؟
ياسىن: چاتاق يوق! ئۇ يەردە مەن تونۇيدىغان بىر نەچچە بالا بار. ئۇلارغا خەۋەر بېرىپ قويىمەن، ئۇلار ئايرودرومغا چىقىپ سىزنى كۈتۈۋالىدۇ.
جون: رەھمەت سىزگە! بېيجىڭنىڭ داڭلىق ساياھەت ئورۇنلىرىنى زىيارەت قىلماقچى ئىدىم. ئۇنىڭغا قانچىلىك ۋاقىت كېتىدۇ؟
ياسىن: بېيجىڭنى ئۈچ - تۆت كۈن ئايلانسىڭىز بولىدۇ. باللار سىزگە ياردەم بېرىدۇ.
جون: ئۈرۈمچىگە قانداق بارسام بولىدۇ؟
ياسىن: ئۈرۈمچىگە پويىز بىلەن كەلسىڭىز ياخشىراق بولىدۇ، چۈنكى پويىز ھەم ئەرزان، ھەم قولاي. ئۈرۈمچىگە كەلگۈچە نۇرغۇنلىغان جايلارنى كۆرەلەيسىز.
جون: رەھمەت سىزگە، ياسىن!
ياسىن: ئەرزىمەيدۇ. كېلىشتىن بۇرۇن يەنە بىر تېلېفون قىلىڭ.
جون: ئەلۋەتتە، بېلەتنى ئېلىشىم بىلەنلا، تېلېفون قىلىمەن.

Exercise 14.1

قاۋۇل: ياخشىمۇسىز!
جون: ياخشىمۇسىز!
قاۋۇل: سىز ئامېرىكىلىق جونمۇ؟
جون: ھەئە، سىز قاۋۇلمۇ؟
قاۋۇل: ھەئە، مەن قاۋۇل. بېيجىڭغا خوش كەپسىز !
جون: رەھمەت!
قاۋۇل: جون، سىزنىڭ ئۇيغۇرچىڭىز بەك ياخشىكەن!
جون: رەھمەت. مەن ئامېرىكىدا ئىككى يىل ئۇيغۇرچە ئۆگەنگەن.
قاۋۇل: سىز بۇرۇن شىنجاڭغا بارغانمۇ؟
جون: ھەئە، مەن شەرقىي تۈركىستاننى بۇرۇن زىيارەت قىلغان، ئەمما ئۇ چاغدا ئۇيغۇرچە بىلمەيتتىم.
قاۋۇل: ھوي، دىققەت قىلىڭ، بۇ يەردە ھەرگىز "شەرقىي تۈركىستان "دېگىلى بولمايدۇ.
جون: كەچۈرۈڭ، ئۇنتۇپ قاپتىمەن.
قاۋۇل: ئەمدى سىزنى مېھمانخانىغا ئاپىرىپ قوياي. ئاندىن تاماق يەيلى.
جون: قاۋۇل، مەن تېخى مېھمانخانا ئالمىغان، قانداق قىلىمەن؟
قاۋۇل: چاتاق يوق، بۇ يەردە مېھمانخانىغا بېرىپلا ياتاق ئالسا بولىدۇ. قېنى، تاكسى توسايلى.
جون: بېيجىڭدا مېھمانخانا قىممەتمۇ ؟
قاۋۇل: قىممەتلىرىمۇ بار، ئەرزانلىرىمۇ بار. ھە راست، سىز بېيجىڭدىن ئۈرۈمچىگە قانداق بارىسىز؟
جون: ياسىن پويىز بىلەن كەلسىڭىز ياخشى بولىدۇ دەپ ئېيتقان ئىدى.
قاۋۇل: پويىز ياخشى، ئەمما بىر نەچچە كۈن ۋاقتىڭىز كېتىدۇ. سىزگە ئايروپىلان ياخشىمىكىن.

جون: قېنى، بېيجىڭدا بەش - ئالتە كۈن تۇراي، ئاندىن بىر گەپ بولار.
قاۋۇل: پاھ، سىز بۇنداق ئىبارىلەرنىمۇ بىلىدىكەنسىزغۇ! "بىر گەپ بولار" دېگەن گەپنى بەك ئورۇنلۇق ئىشلەتتىڭىز.
جون: شۇنداقمۇ؟ رەھمەت...
قاۋۇل: مانا تاكسى، قېنى ماڭايلى!

Exercise 15.3

جون: ئەسسالامۇ ئەلەيكۇم!
پروفېسسور: ۋەئەلەيكۇم ئەسسالام!
پروفېسسور: سىز ئامېرىكىدىن كەلدىڭىزمۇ؟
جون: ھەئە، شۇنداق.
پروفېسسور: قايسى شتاتتىن كەلدىڭىز؟
جون: ئىندىيانا شتاتىدىن.
پروفېسسور: ئۇيغۇرچىنى نەدە ئۆگەندىڭىز؟
جون: ئىندىيانا ئۇنىۋېرسىتېتىدا ئۆگەندىم.
پروفېسسور: ئامېرىكىدا ئۇيغۇرچە ئۆگىنىدىغانلار كۆپمۇ؟
جون: ئانچە كۆپ ئەمەس.
پروفېسسور: ياخشى، ياخشى... بېيجىڭغا كېلىشتىكى مەقسىتىڭىز نېمە؟
جون: بېيجىڭنى زىيارەت قىلىپ، شىنجاڭغا بارىمەن.
پروفېسسور: مۇنداق دەڭ. شىنجاڭغا قاچان ماڭىسىز؟
جون: ئۈچ - تۆت كۈندىن كېيىن.
پروفېسسور: ئۇ يەردە قانچىلىك تۇرىسىز؟
جون: بىر يىلچە تۇرىمەن.
پروفېسسور: خېلى تۇرىدىكەنسىز. قايسى شەھەرلەرنى زىيارەت قىلماقچىسىز؟
جون: خوتەن، قەشقەر، تۇرپان، غۇلجىلارنى كۆرمەكچىمەن.
پروفېسسور: ياخشى! ئاق يول بولسۇن!

Exercise 15.5

1. سىز ئامېرىكىدىن كەلدىڭىزمۇ؟
2. قايسى شتاتتىن كەلدىڭىز؟
3. ئۇيغۇرچىنى نەدە ئۆگەندىڭىز؟
4. ئامېرىكىدا ئۇيغۇرچە ئۆگىنىدىغانلار كۆپمۇ؟
5. بېيجىڭغا كېلىشتىكى مەقسىتىڭىز نېمە؟
6. شىنجاڭغا قاچان ماڭىسىز؟
7. ئۇ يەردە قانچىلىك تۇرىسىز؟
8. قايسى شەھەرلەرنى زىيارەت قىلماقچىسىز؟

Exercise 18.2

- ئەسسالامۇ ئەلەيكۇم، يۇسۇپكا. قانداق ئەھۋالىڭىز؟
- خۇداغا شۈكرى، بالام. مۇشۇنچىلىك تۇرىۋاتىمەن.
- دادا، خوتەنگە قاچان ماڭىمىز؟
- خۇدا خالىسا يەكشەنبە كۈنى.
- خۇدا بۇيرىسا، كېلەر ھەپتە قارامايغا بېرىپ كېلىمەن.
- ئەمىسە بىللە بارايلى.
- خۇدايىم بۇيرىسا، بىر ئايدىن كېيىن يېڭى ئۆيگە كۆچىمىز .
- ئۆي پۈتتىمۇ؟
- خۇدايىمغا ئامانەت، قىزىم. بارغاندىن كېيىن تېلېفون قىلىشنى ئۇنتۇما!
- خاتىرجەم بول، دادا. بېرىپلا تېلىفون قىلىۋېتىمەن.
- خوش دادا، مەن ماڭدىم.
- خۇدايىمغا ئامانەت، قىزىم.
- ئەھمەدكا، تۇرپان قانداقراق ئىكەن؟
-يازدا تۇرپانغا بېرىشتىن خۇدايىم ساقلىسۇن، ئۇكا. ئوت دېگىنە، ئوت.
- ئاڭلىدىڭمۇ، ياپونىيەدە توققۇز بال يەر تەۋرەپتۇ.
خۇدايىم ساقلىسۇن بۇنداق بالا- قازادىن.
- خۇدايىم توۋا، ئەجەب كېچىكتىڭلار!
- ئاپتوبۇس يولدا بۇزۇلۇپ قالدى.
- خۇدايىم توۋا، بۇ راست ئىشمىكەن؟
- راستكەن. مەنمۇ باشتا ئىشەنمىگەن.

Exercise 20.1

جون: سەددىچىن بۇ يەرگە يىراقمۇ؟
قاۋۇل: ھەئە، شەھەردىن يىراق. بۇ يەردىن 70 كىلومېتىر ماڭىمىز.
جون: "سەددىچىن" دېگەن سۆزنىڭ مەنىسى نېمە؟
قاۋۇل: بۇ پارىسچە سۆز، مەنىسى "چىن دۆلىتىنىڭ توسمىسى" .
جون: نېمشقا بۇنى"توسما" دەيدۇ؟
قاۋۇل: بۇرۇنقى ۋاقىتتا چىن دۆلىتى شىمالدىكى كۆچمەن مىللەتلەرنىڭ ھۇجۇمىنى توساش ئۈچۈن بۇ سېپىلنى سالغان. شۇنىڭ بىلەن كىشىلەر بۇنى"سەددىچىن" دەپ ئاتىغان.
جون: مۇنداق دەڭ. سەددىچىن سېپىلى بېيجىڭدىن باشقا يەنە قەيەردە بار؟
قاۋۇل: سەددىچىن بىر پۈتۈن سېپىل. ئۇ شەنخەيگۇەن شەھىرىدىن يۈمېنگۇەن شەھىرىگىچە سېلىنغان. شۇڭا جۇڭگونىڭ شىمالىدىكى ھەممىلا يەردە سەددىچىن بار.
جون: دېمەك، بۇ سېپىل بۇرۇنقى ۋاقىتتا چېگرا بولغان، شۇنداقمۇ؟
قاۋۇل: توپ - توغرا ئېيتتىڭىز، بۇرۇن شۇنداق بولغان. ھازىر ئۇنداق ئەمەس. مانا سەددىچىنگە كەلدۇق.
جون: پاھ، نېمە دېگەن كۆپ ئادەم!
قاۋۇل: قېنى، ئاۋۇ يەردە رەسىمگە چۈشەيلى.

CHAPTER 4

Exercise 3.2

جون: بۇ ئاشخانىدا خەنزۇچە سۆزلەرنى كۆپ ئىشلىتىدىكەن.

قاۋۇل: بەزى ئاشخانىرغا قارىغاندا بۇ يەردە ئانچە كۆپ ئەمەس. بەزى يەردە "لەڭمەن" دېيىشنىڭ ئورنىغا "بەنمىيەن" دەيدۇ.

جون: نېمىشقا بۇنچە كۆپ خەنزۇچە سۆزلەرنى ئىشلىتىسلەر؟ ئۇيغۇرچە سۆز يوقمۇ؟

قاۋۇل: ئۇيغۇرچە سۆز بار، لېكىن ئۇيغۇرلار هازىر خەنزۇچە سۆزلەرنى ئىشلىتىشكە ئادەتلىنىپ قېلىشۋاتىدۇ.

جون: مەن باياتىن ئاڭلىغانلىرىمنى يېزىۋالاي. سىز "تاڭجاڭ" دېدىڭىز. بۇ نېمە دېگەن گەپ؟

قاۋۇل: هە، ئۇ "كۇتكۇچى" دېگەن مەنىدە.

جون: "تاڭجاڭ"، "خۇيمەن"، "سومەن"، "گاڭپەن"، "بەنمىيەن"، "گويرۇ"، ... هە، يەنە "سوگوزا" دېگەنچۇ؟

قاۋۇل: ئۇ سەي قورۇيدىغان ئۇستا.

جون: هە، يەنە "سەي". بۇ "قورۇما" دېگەن گەپ، شۇنداقمۇ؟

قاۋۇل: هەئە.

جون: سىز بۇيرۇغان "گويرۇ لەڭمەن" ئاچچىق لەڭمەنمۇ؟

قاۋۇل: ئاچچىق، چۈنكى ئۇنىڭغا كۆپ لازا سالىدۇ. لېكىن جۇڭگو تاماقلىرىغا قارىغاندا ئۇيغۇر تاماقلىرى ئانچە ئاچچىق ئەمەس.

جون: مەن لۇغەتتىن "لازا" دېگەن سۆزنى تاپقان. لۇغەتتە ئۇ "مۇچ" دەپ ئېلىنغان.

قاۋۇل: راست دەيسىز. هازىر تىلىمىز بەك بۇزۇلۇپ كېتىۋاتىدۇ. يەنە كېلىپ ئۆزىمىز بۇزۇۋاتىمىز.

Exercise 10.2

1. يېنىڭىزدىكى كىتابنى ئېلىۋېتىڭە.
2. جالال يىغىنغا كەلدىغۇ.
3. ئۇ چېپىنى ئىچپىلا چىقىپ كەتتى.
4. سىز كۆپ ئاۋارە بولماڭە.
5. قىزىڭىزغا گەپ قىلىڭە.
6. ئۇ ماڭا قاراپلا قالدى.
7. بۇ بەك داڭلىق يازغۇچىغۇ، سىز ئۇنى تونۇمامسىز؟
8. ماڭا قاراڭە، سىز زادى كىم بولىسىز؟
9. تۇرپان هازىر ئىسسىق، ئۇ يەرگە كۈزدە بارغان ياخشىغۇ!

Exercise 13.1

مال لەڭسەي مازار داڭلىق مەقبەرە جوڭياڭ مىندا گاۋكاۋ
خېرىدار جوڭبا ئەردوچوزا سودىلىق شاڭچاڭ چاقىرىق داۋاملىق
ساياهەت ناۋاي

CHAPTER 5

Exercise 8.2

ئەسسالامۇ ئەلەيكۇم قەدىرلىك يولۇچىلار! شىنجاڭ ھاۋا يوللىرىنىڭ 389 نۆۋەتلىك ئايروپىلانى سىلەرنى قىزغىن قارشى ئالىدۇ. ئايروپىلانىمىز 15 مىنۇتتىن كېيىن بېيجىڭدىن ئۈرۈمچىگە ئۇچىدۇ. پۈتۈن مۇساپە تۆت سائەت15 مىنۇت. سىزنىڭ، بىزنىڭ، شۇنداقلا ھەممىمىزنىڭ بىخەتەرلىكى ئۈچۈن بىلىشكە تېگىشلىك قائىدىلەرنى دىققەت بىلەن ئاڭلاڭ:

- ئايروپىلان ئۇچۇشتىن بۇرۇن بىخەتەرلىك تاسمىسىنى باغلاشنى ئۇنتۇماڭ
- قولدا كۆتۈرىۋالغان سومكىڭىزنى ئورۇندۇقنىڭ ئاستىغا قويۇڭ.
- جىددىي ئەھۋال يۈز بەرسە ،ئوكسىگېن ماسكىسىنى ئىشلىتىڭ.
- ئوكسىگېن ماسكىسىنى ئىشلىتىش ئۇسۇلى ھاۋاقىزلىرى ھازىر سىلەرگە كۆرسىتىۋاتقان ئۈلگە شەكلىدە بولىدۇ. بۇنىڭ تەپسىلاتى ئۈچۈن ئالدىڭىزدىكى يولۇچىلار قوللانمىسىغا قاراڭ.
- پۈتۈن ئۇچۇش جەريانىدا ئايوپىلانىنىڭ ھەرقانداق يېرىدە تاماكا چېكىشكە بولمايدۇ.
- ئايروپىلان ئۇچۇشتىن بۇرۇن بارلىق ئېلېكترونلۇق ئۈسكۈنىلەرنى ۋاقتىنچە ئۆچۈرۈۋېتىڭ.
- ھاجەتخانىدىكى ئىس - تۈتەك كۆزەتكۈچكە چېقىلماڭ، كۆزەتكۈچنى بۇزغان ياكى بۇزماقچى بولغانلارغا قانۇن بويىچە ئەللىك مىڭ يۈەن جەرىمانە قويۇلىدۇ.
- پۈتۈن ئۇچۇش جەريانىدا ئايروپىلان بۆلمىسىدىكى خىزمەتچىلەرنىڭ قوماندانلىقىغا بويسۇنۇڭ.

بىرەر نەرسىگە ئېھتىياجىڭىز بولسا، ھاۋا قىزلىرىغا ئېيتىڭ.
سەپىرىڭىز ئۈچۈن شىنجاڭ ھاۋا يوللىرىنى تاللىغانلىقىڭىزغا يەنە بىر قېتىم رەھمەت ئېيتىمىز.
سەپىرىڭىز كۆڭۈللۈك بولسۇن!

Exercise 10.1

ياسىن: ۋەي!
جون: ئەسسالامۇ ئەلەيكۇم!
ياسىن: ۋەئەلەيكۇم ئەسسالام! سىز كىم؟
جون: مەن جون.
ياسىن: جون؟ سىز ئۈرۈمچىگە كېلىپ بولدىڭىزمۇ؟
جون: شۇنداق.
ياسىن: قاۋۇل سىزنى سائەت سەككىزدە بارىدۇ دېگەن.
جون: مەن سائەت ئالتىدە كەلدىم.
ياسىن: ئاپلا! مەن خاتالىشىپتىمەن. قاۋۇل سىزنى بېيجىڭ ۋاقتى بىلەن سەككىزدە يېتىپ بارىدۇ دېگەن ئىكەندە. مەن سىزنى ئۈرۈمچى ۋاقتى سائەت سەككىزدە كېلىدۇ دەپ ئويلاپتىمەن.
جون: كېرەك يوق. شىنجاڭ ئۇنىۋېرسىتېتىغا قانداق بارىمەن؟
ياسىن: سىز قەيەردە؟
جون: مەن ھازىر ئايرودرومدا.
ياسىن: ھە، ئۇنداقتا تاكسىغا ئولتۇرۇڭ.
جون: تاكسى قىممەتمۇ؟
ياسىن: ئانچە قىممەت ئەمەس. قىرىق كويغا شىنجاڭ ئۇنىۋېرسىتېتىغا ئەكېلىدۇ.

جون: بەك ئەرزان ئىكەن. 40 كوي 6-7 دوللار دېگەن گەپ. ئەمىسە تاكسىغا ئولتۇراي. سىز بىلەن نەدە كۆرۈشىمىز؟

ياسىن: مەن شىنجاڭ ئۇنىۋېرسىتېتىنىڭ ئالدىغا بېرىپ تۇرىمەن.

جون: ماقۇل ئەمىسە... مانا تاكسىمۇ كەلدى...

Exercise 15.1

جون: ئەسسالامۇ ئەلەيكۇم!

ئارسلان ئاكا: ۋەئەلەيكۇم ئەسسالام، ئوغلۇم. سىز كىم بولىسىز؟

جون: مېنىڭ ئىسمىم جون، مەن ئامېرىكىدىن كەلدىم.

ئارسلان ئاكا: ئامېرىكىدىن؟ ئۇنداقتا ئۇيغۇرچىنى نەدىن بىلىسىز؟

جون: مەن ئۇيغۇرچىنى ئامېرىكىدا ئۆگەندىم.

ئارسلان ئاكا: ئامېرىكىدا ئۇيغۇر تىلىنى ئۆگىنىدۇ دەڭ... ياخشى، ياخشى.

جون: كەچۈرۈڭ، تۇرپانغا بىرىنچى كېلىشىم. ماڭا مېھمانخانا كېرەك ئىدى. قايسى مېھمانخانىغا بارسام بولىدۇ؟

ئارسلان ئاكا: بۇ يەردە بىر نەچچە مېھمانخانا بار. ئەڭ يېقىنى "تۇرپان" مېھمانخانىسى.

جون: بۇ مېھمانخانىغا قانداق بارىمەن؟

ئارسلان ئاكا: بۇ يەردىن ئۇدۇل ماڭسىڭىز، ياشلار يولىغا يېتىپ كېلىسىز. سولغا قايرىلىپ 200 مېتىرچە ماڭسىڭىز، مېھمانخانا كۆرۈنىدۇ.

جون: كەچۈرۈڭ، يەنە بىر قېتىم دەپ بېرەمسىز؟ ياخشى چۈشىنەلمىدىم.

Exercise 19.3

قەشقەر ھازىر ئۆزگىرىپ كەتتى، ئەمما كونا تارىخىي بىنالار بۇ شەھەرنىڭ ئۆتمۈشتىكى شانۇ-شەۋكىتىنى تېخىچە ئەسكەرتىپ تۇرىدۇ. مانا مەشھۇر ھېيتگاھ جامەسى. بۇ جامە 1872- يىلى قۇرۇلغان بولۇپ، قەشقەردىكى ئەڭ چوڭ جامە ھېسابلىنىدۇ.

قارىخانىيلار خانلىقى دەۋرىدىكى ئۇلۇغ مۇتەپەككۇر، شائىر يۈسۈپ خاس ھاجىپنىڭ مازىرىغا يېقىنلاشتىم. شائىرنىڭ مەشھۇر ئەسىرى "قۇتادغۇ بىلىك" ئېسىمگە كەلدى...

مانا مەھمۇد قەشقەرى مازىرى. بۈيۈك تىلشۇناس ئالىم 11- ئەسىردە "دىۋانۇ لۇغەت - ئىت تۈرك" ناملىق ئەسىرىنى يېزىپ، پۈتۈن دۇنياغا مەشھۇر بولغان. قانداق ئۇلۇغ زاتلار ئۆتكەن بۇ ماكاندىن...

مانا "ئاپئاق خوجا" مەقبەرەسى. مەزكۇر مەقبەرە 1873- يىلى ياسالغان. بەزى تارىخىي مەنبەلەرگە قارىغاندا ئىپارخان، بوۋىسى ئاپئاق خوجىنىڭ مەقبەرىسى ئىچىگە دەپنە قىلىنغان ئىكەن...

قېنى، قەشقەرنىڭ چوڭ بازىرىغا ئۆتەيلى. نېمىلەر يوق بۇ بازاردا... ئەمگەكچان، مېھنەت سۆيەر خەلقىم... مانا تۈرلۈك قول ھۈنەر بۇيۇملىرى، مىللىي ئۇسلۇبتىكى زىبۇزىننەت بۇيۇملىرىدىن ھالقا، مارجان، ئۈزۈك، بىلەزۈكلەر... مانا قولدا توقۇلغان گىلەملەر، ھەر خىل كىيىملەر، رەختلەر... نېمىدېگەن چىرايلىق ئەتلەسلەر... مانا مىللىي چالغۇ ئەسۋابلار: دۇتار، راۋاب، غېجەك، تەمبۇر، ساپايى، داپ، نەي، سۇناي... سەنئەتكار خەلقىمنىڭ ئون ئىككى مۇقامى خىيالىمدىن ئۆتتى. بۇ مۇقاملاردا ئۇيغۇر خەلقىنىڭ ھاياتى، گۈزەل روھىي دۇنياسى، قايغۇ - ھەسرەتلىرى ناخشا، مۇزىكا، ئۇسسۇل ئارقىلىق ئىپادىلەنگەن.

ئەمدى ئۇيغۇر ئاشخانىسىغا كىرەيلى. ئۇيغۇرلار تاماققا ئۇستا خەلق. مانا داڭلىق ئۇيغۇر نانلىرى، لەڭمىنى، سامسا- مانتىلىرى، ئۆپكە- هېسىپلىرى. شائىرىمىز مۇھەممەتجان راشىدىن ئېيتقاندەك: ئۇيغۇرلارنىڭ تائاملىرى بەرگەن لەززەت، ئاغزىڭىزدىن كەتمەي ئايلاپ، يىللاپ تۇرار! بۇ گۈزەل ماكانىنى زىيارەت قىلساڭلا، چوقۇم قەشقەرگە بېرىڭلار!

CHAPTER 6

Exercise 6.2

بۇ تاراق- تۇرۇق نەدىن كېلىۋاتىدۇ؟
شۇ ئارىدا تېلېفون جىرىڭلىدى.
ئۇلار قاقاقلاپ كۈلۈشتى.
بەرگە بىر نەرسە پوككىدە چۈشتى.
بۇ ۋاراڭ- چۇرۇڭدا نېمە ئىش قىلالايسىز؟

Exercise 9.1

ساتقۇچى: ھەي، ئۇكام، مەكەسلە.
جون: مېنى چاقىرىۋاتامسىز؟
ساتقۇچى: ھەئە، سىلىنى. پىچاق ئالامىلا؟
جون: پىچاق ئالىدىغانلىقىمنى نەدىن بىلدىڭىز؟
ساتقۇچى: قارىسام ، چەتئەللىكلەرگە ئوخشايدىكەنلا، بۇ بازارغا كەلگەن ساياھەتچىلەر چوقۇم پىچاق ئالىدۇ ئەمەسمۇ.
جون: مەنمۇ پىچاق ئالاي دەپ كېلىۋېدىم...
ساتقۇچى: ئۇنداقتا مېنىڭ پىچاقلىرىمنى كۆرۈپ باقسىلا.
جون: بۇ يېڭىسار پىچاقلىرىمۇ؟
ساتقۇچى: نەق ئۆزى! پىچاق تونۇيدىكەنلا...
جون: ھە، بىر ئۇيغۇر دوستۇم يېڭىسار پىچاقلىرى ئەڭ ياخشى دېگەن...

Exercise 9.2

ساتقۇچى: قېنى بىرەرىنى تاللىدىلىما؟
جون: ھەممىسى ياخشىدەك تۇرىدۇ. بۇلار نەچچە پۇل؟
ساتقۇچى: ئۆزلىرى بىر دېسىلە. قانچە پۇلغا ئالىلا؟
جون: سىز دەڭە، مەن بىلمەيدىكەنمەن. يەنە ئەرزان دېۋەتسەم خاپا بولۇپسىز...
ساتقۇچى: بازاردا خاپا بولىدىغان ئىش يوق، ئۇكام، دەۋەسلە...
جون: 50 كە بېرەمسىز؟
ساتقۇچى: 50 دېگىنىڭىز دوللارمۇ يا ...؟
جون: دېگىنىم 50 كوي، دوللار ئەمەس...

Exercise 9.3

ساتقۇچى: ياق - ياق، بۇ پىچاقلارنى 50 كويغا بەرگىلى بولمايدۇ. 50 كويغا ئاۋۇ كىچىك بەكىنى ئالسىلا...

جون: بەكە؟ بۇ نېمە؟

ساتقۇچى: ھە، بەكە دېگەن قىسقا پىچاق، ئۇنىڭ تىغىنى دەستە ئىچىگە قايرىپ قويغىلى بولىدۇ. بۇمۇ ياخشى نەرسە، بولۇپمۇ ساياھەتچىلەر ئۈچۈن. ئالسىلا، بەردىم 50 كويغا...

جون: ھە، بۇمۇ بولىدىكەن. مەن بەكىنىمۇ ئالاي.

ساتقۇچى: ئالسىلا،... 50 دوللار بەرسىلە، بۇ پىچاقنىمۇ سىلىگە بېرەي، مېھمان ئىكەنلا. بىز بۇ پىچاقلارنى يۈز دوللاردىنمۇ ساتقان...

جون: مەن بىر ئوقۇغۇچى، مېنىڭ ئۇنچىلىك پۇلۇم يوق...

ساتقۇچى: 200 كويغا ئالالامىلا؟

جون: بۇ قانچە دوللار بولىدۇ؟

ساتقۇچى: 30 دوللارچە بولىدۇ. قانداق، ئالامىلا يا؟

جون: 100 دوللار قانچە يۈەن بولىدۇ؟

ساتقۇچى: يۈز دوللار 680 يۈەن بولىدۇ، 50 دوللار... 340... دېمەك 200 يۈەن 30 دوللار، شۇنداقما؟

جون: شۇنداق ئوخشايدۇ... ماقۇل، مەن بۇ پىچىقىڭىزنى 30 دوللارغا ئالاي...

Exercise 13.4

يېڭىسار پىچىقى - ئۇيغۇرلارنىڭ يەرلىك مىللىي قول- ھۈنەر سەنئىتى بۇيۇملىرى ئىچىدە داڭلىق مەھسۇلاتلارنىڭ بىرى. ئۇ ئەسلىدە يېڭىسارنىڭ ئەنئەنىۋى ئىجادىيىتى بولغاچقا، شۇ جاينىڭ نامىغا ماس ھالدا " يېڭىسار پىچىقى " دەپ ئاتالغان. تارىم بوستانلىقىنىڭ غەربىي جەنۇبىي قىسمىغا جايلاشقان يېڭىسار ناھىيىسىدە پىچاق ياساش ھۈنەر كەسپى ناھايىتى تەرەققىي قىلغان. بۇ يەردە ئىشلەنگەن پىچاقلارنىڭ تۈرى يىگىرمە خىلدىن ئاشىدۇ. 1987- يىلى مەملىكەت بويىچە ھۈنەر- سەنئەت بۇيۇملىرىنى باھالاشتا، يېڭىسار پىچىقى بىرىنچىلىككە ئېرىشكەن. يېڭىسار پىچىقى ياسىلىش شەكلى جەھەتتىن نەپىس ۋە كۆركەم بولۇپ، ئىشلىتىشكە ناھايىتى قولاي. ئۇنىڭ تىغى ئۈچۈن سۇپەتلىك پولات تاللىنىدۇ. ئىشلىتىش ئورنىغا قاراپ، پىچاقنىڭ بىسى ۋە سېپى ھەرخىل شەكىللىك ياسىلىدۇ. ھەر بىر تۈرىنىڭ ئۆزىگە خاس نامى بولىدۇ. مەسىلەن، قاسساپ پىچىقى، ئائىلە پىچىقى، خەنجەر نۇسخىلىق پىچاق، يان پىچىقى، كۆرگەزمە پىچىقى قاتارلىقلار. يېڭىسار پىچىقىنىڭ سېپى ئۈچۈن ھەرخىل ھايۋانلارنىڭ مۈڭگۈزى ۋە سۆڭەكلىرى، مىس، كۈمۈش، قاشتېشى، مەرۋايىت قاتارلىق ئەتىۋارلىق ماتېرىياللار ئىشلىتىلىدۇ. بۇ خام ئەشيالار ئىنچىكە ھۈنەر ئارقىلىق بىر- بىرىگە كىرىشتۈرۈلۈپ گۈزەل سەنئەت بۇيۇمىغا ئايلاندۇرىلىدۇ. يېڭىسار پىچىقىنىڭ ھەممىسىگە ئۆزىگە ماس كېلىدىغان غىلاپ ياسىلىدۇ. غىلاپسىز يېڭىسار پىچىقى بولمايدۇ. غىلاپنىڭ كۆپچىلىكى ھارخىل رەڭلىك كالا خۇرۇمىدىن ياسىلىدۇ. يەنە بەزى غىلاپلار مىس ياكى ئاليۇمىندىن ئىشلىنىپ، يۈزىگە ھەرخىل نەقىش ئويۇلىدۇ. پىچاق قەدىمدىن تارتىپ ئۇيغۇرلارنىڭ ئەنئەنىۋى ئادىتىدە ئەر- يىگىتلەرنىڭ كىچە - كۈندۈز يېنىدىن ئايرىلمايدىغان قورالى بولۇپ كەلگەن. ھاتتە ئۇيغۇرلارنىڭ بېلىنى بەلباغ بىلەن باغلاش ئادىتىمۇ پىچاقنى يانغا ئېسىش ئېھتىياجىدىن كېلىپ چىققان. پىچاقنى ئەرلىك جاسارىتىنىڭ مۇھىم بەلگىسى دەپ بىلىش ئۇيغۇرلارنىڭ مۇھىم ئەنئەنىسى ھېسابلىنىدۇ.

CHAPTER 7

Exercise 5.1

جون: ئەسسالامۇ ئەلەيكۇم!

مۇئەللىم: ۋەئەلەيكۇم ئەسسالام! كىلىڭ، كىلىڭ، سىز جونمۇ؟

جون: ھەئە، مەن جون تومسون.

مۇئەللىم: مىنىڭ ئىسمىم پەرىدە داۋۇت، مەن سىزنىڭ ئۇيغۇر تىلى ئوقۇتقۇچىڭىز بولىمەن. ئىسىڭىزدە بولسا، سىز بىلەن بىر نەچچە قىتىم تىلىفوندا سۆزلەشكەن.

جون: ھەئە، ئىسىمدە بار ئەلۋەتتە. سىزنىڭ ئىسمىڭىزنى تولۇق ئىيتماي پەرىدە مۇئەللىم دىسەم بولامدۇ؟

مۇئەللىم: بولىدۇ، بولىدۇ... ئۈرۈمچىگە قاچان كەلدىڭىز؟

جون: مەن بۇ يەرگە كەلگىلى ئىككى ھەپتە بولدى. قارىسام ئوقۇشقا بىر نەچچە كۈن بار ئىكەن، شۇڭا تۇرپان بىلەن قەشقەرنى زىيارەت قىلىپ كەلدىم. ئۈرۈمچىگە تۈنۈگۈنلا قايتتىم.

مۇئەللىم: مۇنداق دەڭ... سەپىرىڭىز ياخشى بولدىمۇ؟

جون: ھەئە، بەك ياخشى بولدى. تۇرپان، قەشقەرلەرگە باردىم. ناھايىتى كۆپ ئۇيغۇرلار بىلەن سۆزلەشتىم. خىلى كۆپ نەرسىلەرنى ئۆگىنىۋالدىم. ئەمدى ۋاقتىم بولسا، غۇلجا تەرەپلەرنى كۆرگۈم بار...

مۇئەللىم: بۇنى ياخشى ئويلاپسىز. غۇلجىغا چوقۇم بىرىڭ. ھە راست، ساۋاقداشلىرىڭىز بىلەن تونۇشتىڭىزمۇ؟

جون: ياق، تىخى، مەكتەپكە ھازىر كەلدىم. سىنىپتا قانچە ئوقۇغۇچى بار؟

مۇئەللىم: ھازىرچە ئالتە ئوقۇغۇچى ئۆزىنى تىزىملىتىپتۇ.

جون: ئۇلارنىڭ ھەممىسى چەتئەللىكلەرمۇ؟

مۇئەللىم: ياق، ئىككى خەنزۇمۇ بار.

جون: قىزىق، خەنزۇلارمۇ ئۇيغۇرچە ئۆگىنەمدۇ؟

مۇئەللىم: ئۆگىنىدىغانلارمۇ چىقىپ تۇرىدۇ.

جون: قالغان تۆتى قەيەرلىك ئىكەن؟

مۇئەللىم: بىرسى سىزنىڭ يۇرتدىشىڭىز ئىكەن، يەنە بىرسى گىرمانىيەلىك ئىكەن. مەن ئۇنىڭ بىلەن ئۈلۈشكۈن كۆرۈشتۇم. ئۇمۇ تونۇشاي دەپ كەلگەن ئىكەن. قالغان ئىككىسىنىڭ ئىسىملىرىغا قارىغاندا ياپونىيەلىك ئوخشايدۇ.

جون: مۇنداق دەڭ... مىنىڭ ئۇلار بىلەن تىززەك تونۇشقۇم بار. دەرسلىرىمىزنى قاچان باشلايمىز؟

مۇئەللىم: ئۆگۈنلۈككە باشلايمىز.

جون: ياخشى! ئەمسە ئۆگۈنلۈككە كۆرۈشەيلى!

مۇئەللىم: بولىدۇ. خوش!

Exercise 6.3

بۈگۈن ساۋاقداشلار بىلەن شەھەر ئايلىنىمىز دەپ كېلىشكەن ئىدۇق. دەرستىن چۈشۈپلا دۆڭكۆۋرۈك بازىرىدا ئۇچرىشىدىغان بولدۇق. ياسىن ۋاقتىدا كەلدى، ئەمما غەيرەتنى يېرىم سائەت ساقلىدۇق. قورساقلىرىمىز بەكمۇ ئېچىپ كەتتى، شۇڭا ئالدى بىلەن تاماق يەۋالايلى دەپ بىر ئاشخانىغا كىردۇق. مەن بىر تەخسە پولۇ، بىر چىنە قېتىق ۋە خامسەي بۇيرۇتتۇم. ياسىن 10 دانە پېتىر مانتا ۋە 4 زىق كاۋاپ بۇيرۇتتى. غەيرەت بىر تەخسە لەڭمەن ۋە 2 دانە سامسا بۇيرۇتتى. ئاشپەز ئۇستاملار ناھايىتى چاققان ئىكەن. بۇيرۇتقان تاماقلىرىمىز بەك تېز تەييار بولدى. ئاشخانا پاكىز ئىكەن. چىنە- قاچا، چوكىلارمۇ پاكىز يۇيۇلغان. بىز پاراڭلاشقاچ تاماق يېدۇق. كۈتكۈچى چاي دەملەپ كەلدى. تاماقنى يەپ بولغاندىن كېيىن تاماقنىڭ پۇلىنى تۆلىدۇق. جەمئىي 52 كوي بوپتۇ. پۇلنى تۆلەپ، ئۇستاملارغا رەھمەت ئېيتىپ، ئاشخانىدىن چىقتۇق. بازارغا پاراڭلاشقاچ پىيادە ماڭدۇق.

Exercise 9.1

جون: ياخشىمۇسىز!

ياسىن: ياخشىمۇسىز! قانداق ئەھۋالىڭىز؟ قەشقەردىن قاچان قايتتىڭىز؟

جون: ئۈلۈشكۈن قايتتىم.

ياسىن: مۇنداق دەڭ. مەن سىزنى كېلىپلا تېلېفون قىلىدۇ دەپتىمەن.

جون: كەچۈرۈڭ، بەك كەچ كەلگەچكە تېلېفون قىلمىدىم.

ياسىن: كېرەك يوق. مەكتەپكە تىزىملاتتىڭىزمۇ؟

جون: ياق. تۈنۈگۈن ئۇيغۇر تىلى مۇئەللىمىم بىلەن كۆرۈشتۇم.

ياسىن: مۇئەللىم بىلەن كۆرۈشۈش ۋە تىزىملىتىش باشقا باشقا ئىككى ئىش.

جون: شۇنداقمۇ؟ چەتئەللىك ئوقۇغۇچىلار قانداق تىزىملىتىدۇ؟

ياسىن: مەكتىپىمىزدە "چەتئەللىك ئوقۇغۇچىلار ئىشخانىسى" دەپ بىر ئىشخانا بار. سىز شۇ يەرگە بارىسىز.

جون: دەرسلەرنىمۇ شۇ يەردە تىزىملامدۇ؟

ياسىن: ياق، دەرسلەرنى مەكتەپ سىزگە تاللاپ بېرىدۇ. سىز شۇ دەرسلەرنى ئوقۇيسىز.

جون: ئۆزۈم ياقتۇرغان دەرسلەرنى تاللاپ ئوقۇسام بولامدۇ؟

ياسىن: بولمايدۇ. سىز مەكتەپ سىزگە تاللاپ بەرگەننى ئوقۇشىڭىز شەرت!

جون: ياتاقچۇ؟ ياتاقنىمۇ مەكتەپ تاللاپ بېرەمدۇ؟

ياسىن: شۇنداق، چەتئەللىك ئوقۇغۇچىلار چوقۇم مەكتەپنىڭ چەتئەللىك ئوقۇغۇچىلار ياتاق بىناسىدا تۇرۇشى لازىم.

جون: شۇنداقمۇ؟ مېنىڭ ئۇيغۇرلارنىڭ ئۆيىدە تۇرغۇم بار ئىدى.

ياسىن: چەتئەللىكلەر ئۇيغۇرلارنىڭ ئۆيىدە تۇرۇشقا بولمايدۇ. بۇ قانۇنغا خىلاپ.

جون: مېنىڭ ئۈرۈمچىدە بىرقانچە ئۇيغۇر دوستلىرىم بار. مەن ئۇلار بىلەن ئىنتېرنېت ئارقىلىق تونۇشقان. ئۇلارنىڭ ئۆيىگە بارسام بولامدۇ؟

ياسىن: مېھمانغا بارسىڭىز بولىدۇ. بەلكىم ئۇيغۇرلارنىڭ مېھماندوست خەلق ئىكەنلىكىنى بىلىسىز. ئەمما قونۇپ قالسىڭىز ئۆي ئىگىلىرىنى ساقچىلار سوراققا تارتىدۇ.

جون: نېمە؟ "سوراققا تارتىدۇ" دېگىنىڭىز "سوئال سورايدۇ" دېگەن گەپمۇ؟

ياسىن: بىرئاز ئوخشايدۇ. ساقچىلارنىڭ قوپال سوئال سورىشىنى بىز "سوراققا تارتماق" دەيمىز.

جون: مەن سوراققا تارتىشقا بەك ئۆچ!

ياسىن: مېنىڭمۇ سوراق بىلەن خوشام يوق.

Exercise 14.5

ئامېرىكىلىق ئوقۇغۇچىلارغا ئۇيغۇر ئالىي مەكتەپ ئوقۇغۇچىلىرىنىڭ تۇرمۇشى قىزىقارلىق تۇيۇلۇشى مۇمكىن. بۇ يەردە ئوقۇغۇچىلار بىزگە ئوخشاش مەكتەپكە ئوقۇش پۇلى ۋە ياتاق پۇلى تاپشۇرغان بىلەن ئوقۇيدىغان دەرسلەرنى ئۆزلىرى تاللىيالمايدىكەن، تۇرىدىغان ياتاقلىرىنىمۇ ئۆزلىرى تاللىيالمايدىكەن. ھەممىنى مەكتەپ بىر تۇتاش ئورۇنلاشتۇرۇپ بېرىدىكەن. بۇ يەردىكى ئوقۇغۇچىلار ھەر كۈنى ئەتىگەن سائەت سەككىزدىن چۈشكىچە ۋە بەزى كۈنلىرى چۈشتىن كېيىنمۇ بىر ئىككى سائەتتىن دەرس ئوقۇيدۇ. پۈتۈن مەكتەپتىكى ئوقۇغۇچىلار چۈش سائەت 12 دە تەڭلا دەرستىن چۈشكەچكە، بۇ ۋاقىتتا مەكتەپ قورۇسى بەكمۇ قىستاڭچىلىق بولۇپ كېتىدۇ. بۇ ۋاقىتتا پۈتۈن ئوقۇغۇچىلار مەكتەپ ئاشخانىسىغا تاماققا بارىدۇ. تۈنۈگۈن مەنمۇ ئۇيغۇر دوستلىرىم بارىدىغان ئوغۇللار 2 - ئاشخانىسىغا باردىم. تاماقلارنىڭ تۈرى كۆپ، شۇنداقلا باھاسى كوچىدىكى ئاشخانىلاردىن خېلىلا ئەرزان ئىكەن. ئەمما تاماقلارنىڭ سۈپىتى ئانچە ياخشى ئەمەس.

بارلىق ئوقۇغۇچىلار پۈتۈنلەي مەكتەپنىڭ ياتاق بىناسىدا تۇرۇشى لازىم ئىكەن. ئۇيغۇر دوستۇم ياسىننىڭ ياتىقىغا بېرىپ كۆرۈپ باقتىم. بىر ياتاقتا ئالتە ئوقۇغۇچى بىللە تۇرىدىكەن، شۇڭا ھەر بىر ئۆيدە قوش قەۋەتلىك كارۋاتتىن ئۈچى بولىدىكەن. ئەمما ياتاقلاردا مۇنچا ياكى ھاجەتخانا بولمىغاچقا ئوقۇغۇچىلار كوللىكتىپ ھاجەتخانىغا بارىدىكەن. ھەر بىر قەۋەتتە بۇنداق كوللىكتىپ ھاجەتخانىدىن ئىككىسى بولىدىكەن. ئۇلار بۇنى "سۇخانا" دەپ ئاتايدىكەن. ئادەتتە ئۇيغۇر ئوقۇغۇچىلار بىلەن خەنزۇ ئوقۇغۇچىلار بىر ياتاقتا تۇرۇشنى خالىمايدىكەن. ئۇيغۇرلار خەنزۇلارنى "مەينەت" دېسە، خەنزۇلار ئۇيغۇر ئوقۇغۇچىلارنى "ئوغرى" دەيدىكەن. بەزىدە ئۇيغۇر ئوقۇغۇچىلار بىلەن خەنزۇ ئوقۇغۇچىلار سۇخانىدا ئۇرۇشۇپ قالىدىكەن.

بۇ يەردىكى ئوقۇغۇچىلارنىڭ كۈندىلىك مەشغۇلاتى بەك ئاددىي: ئەتىگەن سائەت سەككىزدە دەرسكە بارىدۇ؛ تۆت سائەت دەرستىن كېيىن ئاشخانىغا بارىدۇ؛ تاماقتىن كېيىن ياتاققا ياكى كۇتۇپخانىغا بارىدۇ؛ ھەر چارشەنبە كۈنى چۈشتىن كېيىن ئوقۇغۇچىلارغا ئۆز سىنىپىدا "سىياسى ئۆگىنىش" دەپ يىغىن ئاچىدۇ؛ بۇ يىغىندا ئوقۇغۇچىلار كوممۇنىستىك پارتىيەنىڭ ھەر خىل سىياسەتلىرىنى ئۆگىنىدىكەن، شۇڭا ھېچكىمنىڭ بۇ يىغىن بىلەن خوشى يوق ئىكەن. شەنبە ۋە يەكشەنبە كۈنلىرى ئوقۇغۇچىلار كىر يۇيۇش، مونچىغا بېرىش، بازار ئايلىنىش دېگەندەك ئىشلار بىلەن ئالدىراش بولىدىكەن. ئوقۇغۇچىلار بۇ يەردە تورغا چىقىشقا بەك ئامراق ئىكەن.

مەكتەپنىڭ ئۇدۇلىدا بىرنەچچە تورخانا بار ئىكەن. ئوقۇغۇچىلارنىڭ ھەممىسى دېگۈدەك بوش ۋاقتى بولسىلا تورخانىغا بېرىشنى ياخشى كۆرىدىكەن. توردا ناخشا ئاڭلاش ۋە دوستلىرى بىلەن پاراڭلىشىش ئاساسلىق ئورۇندا تۇرىدىكەن.

كەلگىنىمگە بىر ئاي بولمايلا ئامېرىكىنى ئەجەب سېغىندىم...

Exercise 15.1

جون: ياخشىمۇسىز!

كاتىپ: ياخشىمۇسىز! ياردەم كېرەكمۇ؟

جون: شۇنداق. مەن ئوقۇغۇچىلىق كېنىشكىسى ئالماقچى ئىدىم. قەيەردىن ئالىمەن؟

كاتىپ: مۇشۇ يەردىن ئالىسىز. سىز يېڭى ئوقۇغۇچىمۇ؟

جون: ھەئە.

كاتىپ: قايسى فاكۇلتېتتا ئوقۇيسىز؟

جون: مەن تارىخ فاكۇلتېتىدا ئوقۇيمەن.
كاتىپ: نەچچە مەۋسۇم ئوقۇيسىز؟
جون: ئىككى مەۋسۇم.
كاتىپ: دەرسلىك كىتاب ئالامسىز؟
جون: شۇنداق. ئۇلارنى قەيەردىن سېتىۋالىمەن؟
كاتىپ: مەكتىپىمىزنىڭ كىتابخانىسىدا ھەممە دەرسلىك كىتابلار سېتىلىدۇ.
جون:مەن تېخى بانكا ھېساباتى ئاچمىغان. نەق پۇل تۆلىسەم بولامدۇ؟
كاتىپ: بولىۋېرىدۇ. سىز ماگىستىرلىق ئۇنۋانى ئۈچۈن ئوقۇماقچىمۇ؟
جون: شۇنداق. ھە راست. چەتئەللىك ئوقۇغۇچىلار سۇغۇرتا ئېلىشى شەرتمۇ؟
كاتىپ: ياق، شەرت ئەمەس. لېكىن مەكتەپتىن ياتاق ۋە ئاشخانا كارتىسى ئېلىشىڭىز شەرت.
جون: مۇنداق دەڭ. ئۇلارنىمۇ مۇشۇ يەردىن ئالامدىم؟
كاتىپ: ياق. ئۇلارنى ياندىكى ئىشخانىدىن ئالىسىز.
جون: كۆپ رەھمەت سىزگە.
كاتىپ: ئەرزىمەيدۇ. خوش!
جون: خوش!

Exercise 15.3

ئا. سىز قايسى كەسىپتە ئوقۇيسىز؟
ب. مەن تىلشۇناسلىقتا ئوقۇيمەن.
ئا. فاكۇلتېتىڭىزنىڭ مۇدىرى كىم؟
ب. ئەنۋەر مۇئەللىم.
ئا. ئۇ قايسى ساھە بويىچە ئىشلەيدۇ؟
ب. ئۇ ئالتاي تىللىرىنى تەتقىق قىلىدۇ.
ئا. ئۇ ياخشى مۇتەخەسسىسمۇ؟
ب. ھەئە، ئۇ خېلى داڭلىق چىققان پروفېسسور.
ئا. باكالاۋر ئۇنۋانىنى قايسى مەكتەپتىن ئالدىڭىز؟ ماگىستىرلىقنىچۇ؟
ب. باكالاۋر ئۇنۋانىنى قەشقەر پېداگوگىكا ئۇنىۋېرسىتېتىدىن ئالدىم. ماگىستىرلىقنى شىنجاڭ ئۇنىۋېرسىتېتىدا ئوقۇۋاتىمەن.
ئا. ھەپتىدە نەچچە خىل دەرس ئاڭلايسىز؟
ب. ئون خىلدەك...
ئا. ئىمتىھان نومۇرى قانداق ھېسابلىنىدۇ، نومۇر بويىچىمۇ ياكى ھەرپ بويىچىمۇ؟
ب. نومۇر بويىچە.

CHAPTER 8

Exercise 5.1

مارك: ياتاقنى ئېلىپ بولدىڭىزمۇ؟
ئىلغار: تېخى ئالمىدىم. ياتاقنى مەكتەپ ئۆزى تاللاپ بېرىدۇ دەپ ئويلاپتىمەن.
مارك: ئامېرىكىدا بۇنداق ئىش يوق. ئوقۇغۇچى ئۆزى خالىغان ياتاقنى تاللايدۇ.
ئىلغار: مۇنداق دەڭ... سىزنىڭچە قانداق ياتاقنى ئالسام بولىدۇ؟
مارك: سىزگە قانداق ياتاق لازىم؟
ئىلغار: ماڭا ئەرزانراق ياتاق بولسا بولاتتى.
مارك: قېنى، يۈرۈڭ، مەن سىزنى ياتاق بۆلۈمىگە ئاپىراي. شۇ يەردە مەسلىھەتلىشەيلى!
ئىلغار: شۇنداق قىلايلى! كۆپ رەھمەت سىزگە!

Exercise 7.2

1. سىزنى ئولتۇرۇشقا ئۆزۈم ئاپىراي.
2. ئاياللىرىڭىزنى ئۆيۈمىزگە ئەكېلىڭ، ئۇنىڭ بىلەن تونۇشايلى.
3. قىزىم، كىتابلارنى پەسكە ئەپچۈشۈڭ.
4. دادىڭىز ئۆكىڭىزنى مومىڭىزنىڭ ئۆيىگە ئاپىرىپ قويسۇن.
5. بۇ ئۈستەلنى تۆپىگە ئەچىقامدۇق؟
6. دادا، ۋېلىسىپىتىمنى ئۆيگە ئەكىرىپ قويسام بولامدۇ؟

Exercise 8.3

ياسىن: قېنى باللار، مەن سىلەرگە تونۇشتۇرۇپ ئۆتەي: بۇ بىزنىڭ ئامېرىكىلىق دوستىمىز جون. ئۇ شىنجاڭ ئۇنىۋېرسىتېتىغا ئۇيغۇرچە ئۆگەنگىلى كەلدى.
ئوقۇغۇچى ئا: قارشى ئالىمىز. ئۈرۈمچىگە خۇش كەپسىز!
جون: رەھمەت! مەن ئۇيغۇرلاردىن كۆپرەك دوستۇم بولسىكەن، دەيمەن.
ئوقۇغۇچى ئا: سىزنىڭ ئۇيغۇرچىڭىز ياخشىكەنغۇ! سىز ئۇيغۇرچىنى قەيەردە ئۆگەنگەن؟
جون: مەن ئامېرىكىدا ئىككى يىل ئۇيغۇرچە ئۆگەندىم. بۇ قېتىم بۇ يەرگە بىر يىللىق پراكتىكىغا ئۈچۈن كەلدىم.
ئوقۇغۇچى ب: ئامېرىكىدىمۇ ئۇيغۇرچە ئۆگىتىدىغانلار بارمۇ؟ بەك قىزىقكەن.
جون: ئامېرىكىدا ھەممە تىلنى ئۆگىتىدىغانلار بار.
ساقىي: ئەمسە ئاغىنىلەر سورۇننى باشلىۋەتتۇق. ياسىن بۇ ئامېرىكىلىق دوستىمىزنى ئەكەپتۇ. ھېلى ئۇ بىزگە مايكىل جېكسوننىڭ ناخشىلىرىنى ئېيتىپ بېرىدۇ. قېنى، سورۇنىمىزنىڭ پەيزى بولۇشى ئۈچۈن، خوشە!
جون: مەن ناخشىچى ئەمەس. مەن ناخشا ئېيتالمايمەن.
ياسىن: ئۇ سىزگە چاقچاق قىلىۋاتىدۇ... قېنى، خوشە!
ساقىي: ئەمدى بۇ رۇمكا سىزنىڭ ھۆرمىتىڭىز ئۈچۈن. كەچۈرۈڭ، ئىسمىڭىز نېمىتى؟
جون: جون. ئۇيغۇرچە ئىسمىم يالقۇن.
ساقىي: ياخشى ئىسمىكەن. قېنى ئەمسە سورۇنىمىزنىڭ يالقۇندەك قىزىپ كېتىشى ئۈچۈن، خوشە!
جون: مەن هاراق ئىچمەيمەن.
ساقىي: ياق، ياق. بۇ هاراق ئەمەس، بۇ دېگەن كۆڭۈل!
جون: كۆڭۈل؟ بۇ نېمە دېگەن گەپ؟
ياسىن: سىزنىڭ ھۆرمىتىڭىز، دېگەن گەپ.

جون: رەھمەت. بۇنى چوقۇم ئىچىشىم لازىممۇ؟
ياسىن: ئىچسىڭىز بىز خوشال بولىمىز.
جون: بوپتۇ، ئەمىسە بىر رۇمكا ئىچىپ باقاي.
ياسىن: ئامېرىكىلىقلار ھاراق ئىچەمدۇ؟
جون: ئىچىدۇ، ئەمما مەن ئانچە ھاراق ئىچىپ كەتمەيمەن. بۇ ھاراقنى نېمە دەيسىلەر؟
ياسىن: بۇنى ئاق ھاراق دەيمىز. ئۈزۈم ھارىقىنى قىزىل ھاراق دەيمىز.
جون: ئەمىسە... خوشە!
ساقىي: مانا قاراڭ، بىردەمدىلا" ئاق ھاراق" ، "قىزىل ھاراق "ۋە"خوشە "دېيىشنى ئۆگىنىۋالدىڭىز. مۇشۇنداق قىلسىڭىز ئۇيغۇرچىنى تېخىمۇ ياخشى ئۆگىنىۋالىسىز. خوشە!
جون: ۋاي خۇدايىم، بۇ ھاراق بەك كۈچلۈك ئىكەن!
ياسىن: سەي يەڭ، سەي يېسىڭىز، ھاراقنى باسىدۇ.
جون: ياق، ھازىر ھاراق مېنى باستى.

Exercise 9.1

ياسىن: تۈنۈگۈن كۆپ ئىچىۋەتكەن ئوخشايمىز. سىزمۇ مەست بولۇپ قاپسىز.
جون: ئۇقمايمەن. ئەتىگەن ئويغانسام، سافادا يېتىپتىمەن. بېشىم بەك ئاغرىۋاتىدۇ.
ياسىن: ھاراق چىشلىۋاپتۇ. بۇنىڭ ئۈچۈن پولۇ يەپ ئاندىن بىر ئۇخلىۋەتسىڭىز ئوڭشىلىپ قالىسىز.
جون: مېنى ھېچكىم چىشلىمىدى.
ياسىن: ياق، ئولتۇرۇشتىن كېيىن باش ئاغرىغاننى "ھاراق چىشلىۋاپتۇ" دەيمىز.
جون: شۇنداقمۇ؟ بۇ قىزىق گەپ ئىكەن. سىلەر ئادەتتە ھەر شەنبە ئاشۇنداق ئولتۇرۇش قىلامسىلەر؟
ياسىن : دائىم ئەمەس. بۇرۇن شەنبە ياكى يەكشەنبە كۈنلىرى باشقا ئالىي مەكتەپلەرگە بېرىپ يۇرتلۇقلار ئولتۇرۇشى قىلاتتۇق. كېيىن مەكتەپلەر بۇنى چەكلىۋەتتى.
جون: ھازىر ئۆز مەكتىپىڭلاردا ئولتۇرۇش قىلامسىلەر؟
ياسىن: ياق، ئوقۇغۇچىلار مەكتەپ ياتىقىدا ھاراق ئىچسە بولمايدۇ. شۇڭا تۈنۈگۈنكىگە ئوخشاش سىرتتا ئۆيى بار بالىلارنىڭ ئۆيىدە ئولتۇرىمىز.
جون: ئۇيغۇر ئوقۇغۇچىلار ئادەتتە ئوقۇشتىن سىرتقى ۋاقىتلاردا ئىشلەمدۇ؟
ياسىن: بۇ يەردە ئىشلەيدىغان ئوقۇغۇچىلار ئاز. ئۇنىڭ ئۈستىگە ئىشمۇ جىق ئەمەس.
جون: ئەمىسە ئۇلار قانداق ياشايدۇ؟ مەكتەپ تۇرمۇش پۇلى بېرەمدۇ؟
ياسىن: بۇرۇن بېرەتتى. ھازىر بىزدىن ئالىدۇ. ئوقۇش پۇلى، كىتاب پۇلى، تاماق پۇلى، ياتاق پۇلى دېگەندەك پۇللارنىڭ ھەممىسىنى بىز تۆلەيمىز. مەكتەپ بىزگە بىر تىيىن بەرمەيدۇ.
جون: ئۇنداقتا ئاتا- ئانىڭلار پۇل ئەۋەتىپ بېرەمدۇ؟
ياسىن: ھەئە، ھەممىمىزنىڭ بانكا كارتىسى بار. ئادەتتە ئاتا- ئانىلار ھەر ئايدا شۇ كارتىغا پۇل سېلىپ قويىدۇ.
جون: بىر ئايدا بىر ئوقۇغۇچىغا قانچىلىك پۇل كېتىدۇ؟
ياسىن: مەن يېڭى كەلگەندە بەش- ئالتە يۈز كوي بولسا يېتەتتى. ھازىر ئايغا مىڭ كوي كېتىدۇ. مال باھاسى بەك ئۆسۈپ كېتىۋاتىدۇ. بىلەمسىز، بىر لەڭمەن بۇرۇن ئالتە كويتى. ھازىر 15 كوي.
جون: ئاخشامقى ئولتۇرۇشتا بەك كۆپ تاماق بار ئىدى. ئۇنىڭ پۇلنى كىم چىقاردى؟
ياسىن: بىز ئادەتتە ئولتۇرۇش قىلساق پۇل يىغىش قىلىمىز. ئاخشاممۇ شۇنداق بولدى.
جون: مەن ئاخشام پۇل تۆلىمەپتىمەن. پۇلنى كىمگە بېرىمەن؟

ياسىن: ياق، ياق. سىز خاتا چۈشىنىپ قاپسىز. بىز ئادەتتە مېھمانلاردىن پۇل ئالمايمىز. بۇ ئۇيغۇرلارنىڭ ئادىتى.

جون: بۇنداق قىلساق مەن بەك خىجىل بولۇپ قالىدىكەنمەن.

ياسىن: ھېچ ۋەقەسى يوق. ئامېرىكىغا ماڭىدىغاندا ئۇيغۇر ئاغىنىلىرىڭىزگە بىر خوشلىشىش ئولتۇرۇشى قىلىپ بەرسىڭىز بولىدۇ.

جون: ماقۇل، بۇ ياخشى مەسلىھەت بولدى.

Exercise 22.3

جون: رەيھانگۈل، سىز قانداق قەھۋە ئىچىسىز؟

رەيھانگۈل: مەن سۈتلۈك قەھۋە ئىچىشكە ئامراق. سىزچۇ؟

جون: مەن ئەزەلدىن قەھۋە ئىچمەيمەن.

رەيھانگۈل: شۇنداقمۇ؟ مەن ئامېرىكىلار قەھۋەسىز ياشىيالمايدۇ دەپ ئاڭلىغان.

جون: كۆپ قىسىم ئامېرىكىلىقلار شۇنداق. ئەمما مەن ھازىر ئۇيغۇر بولدۇم!

رەيھانگۈل: باياتىن سىز بىر نەچچە سوئالىم بار دېگەن ئىدىڭىز.

جون: توغرا. مەن ئۇيغۇر ئوقۇغۇچى قىزلارنىڭ دەرستىن سىرتقى ۋاقىتلاردا نېمە قىلىدىغانلىقىنى سوراي دېگەن.

رەيھانگۈل: بولىدۇ. بىز ئادەتتە دەرستىن كېيىن مەكتەپتە بولىمىز.

جون: سىلەر مەكتەپتىن سىرتقا چىقمامسىلەر؟

رەيھانگۈل: چىقىمىز. كۆپىنچە شەنبە ۋە يەكشەنبە كۈنلىرى باشقا يەرلەرگە بارىمىز.

جون: مۇشۇ توغرۇلۇق سۆزلەپ بېرەمسىز؟

رەيھانگۈل: بولىدۇ. بىزنىڭ شەنبە كۈندىكى بىرىنچى ئىشىمىز مەكتەپ مۇنچىسىغا بېرىش. ئوقۇغۇچىلار ياتىقىدا مۇنچا يوق. شۇڭا ياتاق بىناسىدىكى سۇخانىدا كەچلىرى بېشىمىزنى يۇيۇۋالىمىز.

جون: مۇنچىغا چۈشكەندىن كېيىن نەگە بارىسىلەر؟

رەيھانگۈل: قىزلار كۆپىنچە ياتاقداش ۋە ساۋاقداش قىزلار بىلەن بازارغا بارىدۇ، بەزىلەر دۇكان ئارىلايدۇ. بەزىدە ئۇرۇمچىلىك ساۋاقداش قىزلارنىڭ ئۆيىگە بېرىپ ئولتۇرۇش قىلىمىز.

جون: بۇ ئولتۇرۇشلارغا ئوغۇللارمۇ بارامدۇ؟

رەيھانگۈل: بۇنداق ئولتۇرۇشلارغا ئوغۇللارنى چاقىرمايمىز.

جون: دېمەك، قىزلار بىلەن ئوغۇللار بىللە ئولتۇرۇش قىلمايدۇ. شۇنداقمۇ؟

رەيھانگۈل: ياق. ئۇنداقمۇ ئەمەس. بىز بەزىدە ساۋاقداشلىرىمىزنىڭ تۇغۇلغان كۈن ئولتۇرۇشلىرىغا ئوغۇللارنى چاقىرىمىز.

جون: ئوغۇللار بىلەن بىللە ئولتۇرۇش قىلغاندا سىلەرمۇ ھاراق ئىچەمسىلەر؟

رەيھانگۈل: قىزلار ئاساسەن ھاراق ئىچمەيدۇ. لېكىن بەزى قىزلار قىزىل ھاراق ئىچىدۇ.

جون: مۇنداق دەڭ. بۇنداق ئولتۇرۇشلاردا ناخشا ئېيتامسىلەر؟

رەيھانگۈل: بەزىدە ناخشا ئېيتىمىز. لېكىن كۆپىنچە تانسا ئوينايمىز.

جون: تانسا دېگىنىڭىز دىسكومۇ؟

رەيھانگۈل: ياق. بۇ ئوغۇل قىزلار جۈپ بولۇپ ئوينايدىغان تانسا. ياۋروپالىقلار ئوينايدىغان ۋالىسقا ئوخشايدۇ.

جون: بۇ بەك قىزىقكەن. سىلەردە ئولتۇرۇش بولغاندا مەنمۇ بارسام بولامدۇ؟
رەيھانگۈل: ئەلۋەتتە بولىدۇ. ئىمتىھان تۈگىگەندە بىز ئولتۇرۇش قىلىمىز. شۇ چاغدا سىزنى چاقىرايلى.
جون: كۆپ رەھمەت.

Exercise 25

1. بۇ مەكتەپتە دەرسلەرنى ئۆزۈم تاللامدىم يا مەكتەپ ئورۇنلاشتۇرۇپ بېرەمدۇ؟
2. ياتاقنىچۇ، ئۆزۈم تاللامدىم؟ سىزنىڭچە قايسى ياتاقتا تۇرسام ياخشىراق بولىدۇ؟
3. ئوقۇغۇچىلىق كىنىشكىسىنى ئېلىش ئۈچۈن نېمە قىلىشىم كېرەك؟
4. كۇتۇپخانا كارتىسىنى بېجىرىشىم كېرەكمۇ؟ ئۇنىڭ ئۈچۈن نەگە بېرىشىم كېرەك؟
5. يېتەكچى ئوقۇتقۇچىم بىلەن كۆرۈشمەكچى بولسام، ئۇنىڭ بىلەن قانداق ئالاقىلىشىمەن؟
6. تەنتەربىيە زالىغا بارماقچى بولسام، ئۇنىڭغا ئايرىم پۇل تۆلەمدىم؟

CHAPTER 9

Exercise 5.1

دوختۇر: ياخشىمۇسىز! سىزگە نېمە بولدى؟
كېسەل: نەچچە كۈندىن بېرى مىجەزىم يوق قاراڭ. بېشىم ئاغرىپ، كۆڭلۈم ئېلىشىپ، ھېچ ماغدۇرۇم يوق.
دوختۇر: گېپىڭىزگە قارىغاندا قان بېسىمىڭىز ئۆرلىگەن ئوخشايدۇ. قېنى، قان بېسىمىڭىزنى ئۆلچەپ باقايلى... قان بېسىمىڭىز خېلى يۇقىرى ئىكەن. بېشىڭىز ئاغرىغىنىغا نەچچە كۈن بولدى؟
كېسەل: بەش- ئالتە كۈن بولۇپ قالدىغۇ دەيمەن.
دوختۇر: دەرھال دوختۇرغا كۆرۈنمەي باش ئاغرىقىغا چىداپ ئولتۇردىڭىزمۇ؟
كېسەل: باش ئاغرىقىنى توختىتىدىغان دورىلارنى ئىچتىم.
دوختۇر: پايدا قىلدىمۇ؟
كېسەل: پايدا قىلغاندەك تۇرىدۇ، لېكىن ئاغرىقى توختىمىدى، شۇڭا دوختۇرغا بېرىشنى قارار قىلدىم.
دوختۇر: ياخشى قىپسىز. سىزگە ھازىر باش ئاغرىقىنى توختىتىدىغان دورا ئەمەس، قان بېسىمنى چۈشۈرىدىغان دورىلار كېرەك. مەن سىزگە رېتسېپ يېزىپ بېرەي. دورىلارنى بىرىنچى قەۋەتتىكى دورىخانىدىن ئالسىڭىز بولىدۇ.
كېسەل: رەھمەت، دوختۇر.
دوختۇر: دورىلارنى ۋاقتىدا ئىچىڭ. يەنە پەرھىز تۇتمىسىڭىز بولمايدۇ.
كېسەل: ئۇ نېمە دېگىنىڭىز؟
دوختۇر: مايلىق تاماقلارنى يېمەي تۇرۇڭ، كۆپرەك مېۋە- چېۋىلەردىن يەپ بېرىڭ. قېتىق ئىچىڭ. ئىلاجى بولسا ساپ ھاۋاغا كۆپرەك چىقىڭ.
كېسەل: يۇگۇرسەم بولامدۇ؟
دوختۇر: ھازىرچە يۈگۈرمەي تۇرۇڭ، لېكىن كۆپرەك مېڭىپ بەرسىڭىز بولىدۇ.
كېسەل: ماقۇل دوختۇر. رەھمەت سىزگە. خوش!
دوختۇر: خوش. ئامان بولۇڭ!

Exercise 6.1

بىمار: كەچۈرۈڭ دوختۇر، سىزدىن بىر ئىشنى سورىسام بولامدۇ؟
سېسترا: مەن سېسترا، دوختۇر لازىم بولسا چاقىرىپ بېرەي...

بىمار: ياق، ياق، بۇ ئىشنى سىزدىن سورىسامۇ بولىدۇ...مەن دوختۇرخانىدا ياتقىلى ئىككى كۈن بولدى، قاراڭ.
شۇ كۈنىلا كۆرپەمنى ئالماشتۇرۇپ بېرىڭلار دەپ ئىلتىماس قىلغانتىم، ئەمما ھازىرغىچە ئالماشتۇرۇلمىدى...
سېسترا: كۆرپىگە نېمە بوپتۇ؟
بىمار: سىڭلىم، بۇ كۆرپە بەكمۇ مەينەت ئىكەن... قاراڭ، ھەممە يەردە قاننىڭ داغلىرى قېتىپ كېتىپتۇ. بۇنىڭدا يېتىشقا كۆڭلۈم تارتمايۋاتىدۇ. بىر ئامالىنى قىلىپ بەرسىڭىز.
سېسترا: ماقۇل، مەن مۇلازىمەتچىلەرگە دەپ قويىمەن.

Exercise 8.1

بىز ئادەتتە بوش ۋاقتىمىز بولسا پۇتبول ئوينايمىز. ھە راست، بۇ ئەنگلىيەچە پۇتبول، سىلەر ئويناىدىغان ئامېرىكىچە پۇتبول ئەمەس. ئۇيغۇر ئوقۇغۇچىلار ئامېرىكىچە پۇتبولنى ئاساسەن ئۇقمايدۇ، بىز ئۇنى پەقەت كىنولاردا كۆرگەن. بەزىدە چۈشتىن كېيىنلىرى ئوغۇللار ياتاق بىناسى ئارىلىقىدا فاكۇلتېتلار بويىچە كوماندىغا ئايرىلىپ توپ ئوينايمىز. بۇ مۇسابىقە رەسمىي پۇتبول مەيدانىدا بولمىغاندىكىن بىز پۇتبولنىڭ قائىدىلىرىگە ئانچە رىئايە قىلىپ كەتمەيمىز. چۈنكى بىزنىڭ توپ ئوينىشىمىز پەقەت كۆڭۈل خوشى ئۈچۈن. بىز ئادەتتە خەنزۇ ئوقۇغۇچىلار بىلەن توپ ئوينىمايمىز. پۇتبولنى خەنزۇ ئوقۇغۇچىلار بىزچىلىك ئوينىيالمايدۇ، ئەمما داشۆنىڭ مەكتەپ پۇتبول كۇلۇبىدا ئاران ئىككى ئۇيغۇر ئوقۇغۇچى بار. بەزى ئوغۇللار يەنە ۋاسكېتبول ۋە ۋالىبول ئوينايدۇ، ئەمما بۇ يەردە مەيدان تاپماق تەس. شۇڭا توپ ئويناش ئانچە ئاسان ئەمەس. مەكتىپىمىزنىڭ چوڭ تەنتەربىيە سارىيى بار، ئەمما ئۇنى پەقەت مەكتەپ تەنتەربىيە كوماندىسىنىڭ مەشق قىلىشىغا ئىشلىتىدۇ، ئوقۇغۇچىلار كىرىشكە بولمايدۇ.

Exercise 15.2

ئۆز مۇخبىرىمىز: ھاۋانىڭ ئىللىشىغا ئەگىشىپ، شەھىرىمىزنىڭ ھەر قايسى چوڭ يېزا - ئىگىلىك مەھسۇلاتلىرى بازىرى ۋە تاللا بازارلىرىغا يالپۇز، بېدە قاتارلىق ياۋا كۆكتاتلار سېلىندى. شەھەرلىك كېسەللىكلەرنىڭ ئالدىنى ئېلىش - كونترول قىلىش مەركىزىدىكى ئالاقىدار مۇتەخەسسىسلەرنىڭ تونۇشتۇرۇشىچە، ياۋا كۆكتات تەركىبىدە مىنېرال ماددا مول بولۇپ، ئوزۇقلۇق تەركىبى يۇقىرى ئىكەن. تاغلىق رايون، قاقاسلىقلاردا ئۆسكەن ياۋا كۆكتاتلار سالامەتلىككە پايدىلىق بولسىمۇ، لېكىن خىمىيە سانائىتى زاۋۇتىنىڭ ئەتراپى، يول بويى، ئاھالىلەر كۆپ ئولتۇراقلاشقان رايون ھەمدە ئەخلەت دۆۋىلىرى ياكى بۇلغانغان ئۆستەڭ ئەتراپىدا ئۆسكەن ياۋا كۆكتات ئادەمنى ئاسانلا زەھەرلەپ قويىدىكەن. ئەتىياز - باكتېرىيىنىڭ كۆپىيىش مەزگىلى، شۇڭا ياۋا كۆكتاتنى يېيىشتىن بۇرۇن پاكىز يۇيۇپ، سۇغا بىردەم چىلاپ قويغاندىن كېيىن قورۇپ يېيىش، ھەرگىزمۇ خام يېمەسلىك كېرەككەن.

CHAPTER 10

Exercise 4.1

جون: ياسىن، تۈنۈگۈنكى تويغا تەكلىپ قىلغىنىڭلار ئۈچۈن كۆپ رەھمەت سىلەرگە، بەك كۆڭۈللۈك بولدى...
ياسىن: ھە، سىزگە ياققان بولسا، ياخشى بوپتۇ... تويلار بۇ يەردە قىزىيدۇ...
جون: تويدا مەن بىر نەرسىگە ھەيران قالدىم...
ياسىن: سىزنى تويدا نېمە ھەيران قالدۇردى؟
جون: ئۇيغۇرلارنىڭ ھاراق ئىچىشى....
ياسىن: سىلەردە تويدا ھاراق ئىچمەمدۇ؟

جون: ئىچىدۇ، ئەمما بۇنداق كۆپ ئەمەس... بىزدە ئادەتتە پىۋا بىلەن قىزىل ھاراق كۆپ ئىچىلىدۇ. بىراق تۈنۈگۈنكى تويدا قارىسام ھېلىقى زەھەردەك ئاچچىق ھاراقنى تازا ئىچىدىكەن. مەن تېخى مۇسۇلمانلار بۇنچىلىك ھاراق ئىچمەيدۇ دەپ ئويلاپتىمەن...

ياسىن: توغرا، ئەسلىدە بۇنچىۋالا ھاراق ئىچىلمىسە ياخشى بولاتتى، ئەمما ھازىر بۇ يامان ئادەت بولۇپ قالدى. بىزگە بۇ ئادەت خىتايلاردىن ئۆتتىمىكىن...

جون: ئامېرىكىدا مېنىڭ بىر قازاق دوستۇم بار ئىدى، ئۇمۇ "ھاراق ئىچىش ئادىتى بىزگە رۇسلاردىن كەلدى" دېگەن. شۇ چاغدا مەن "رۇسلار سىلەرنى ھاراق ئىچىشكە مەجبۇر قىلغانمۇ؟" دەپ سورىسام، ئۇ كۈلۈپ كېتىپ: "ياق، بىز ئۇلارنىڭ ئىچكىنىنى (ئىچكەنلىكىنى) كۆرۈپ ئىچىشنى باشلىدۇق" دېگەنتى.

ياسىن: توغرا دەيسىز، ھېچ كىم بىزنى مەجبۇرلىمىدى. ھەممە گەپ ئۆزىمىزدە... بۇ ئادەتتىن قۇتۇلساق ياخشى بولاتتى...

جون: ئۆتكەن ئاي مەن بىر ئولتۇرۇشقا بارغانتىم. ئۇ يەردىمۇ ساۋاقداشلار بىر نەچچە بوتۇلكا ھاراق كۆتۈرۈپ كەپتۇ. مەن "بۈگۈن ھاراق ئىچمىسەك بولامدىكىن" دېسەم، بىر دوستۇم: "ھاراق بولمىسا كۆڭۈل ئاچقىلى بولامدۇ" دەپ كۈلۈپ كەتتى. شۇ كۈنى ئىچمەي دېسەممۇ، ئىچىشكە مەجبۇر بولدۇم...

ياسىن: شۇنداق، ئىچمىگەنلەرنى ئۆزىمىز زورلاپ ئىچۈرىمىز...

Exercise 10.3

جون: ياسىن، تۈنۈگۈن مەن ئۇيغۇرلارنىڭ ئەنئەنىۋى تويلىرى توغرۇلۇق بىر ماقالە ئوقۇدۇم. ئۇنىڭدا ھاراق ھەققىدە ھېچ قانداق گەپ يوق. قارىماققا ئەنئەنىۋى تويلاردا ھاراق ئىچىلمەيدىكەن - ھە؟

ياسىن: ھە، شۇنداق، ئەنئەنىۋى تويلاردا ھاراق ئىچىلمەيدۇ. ھاراق دېگەن كاساپەت مۇشۇ يېقىنقى يىللاردا پەيدا بولدى. ئەمما ئۇيغۇرلار جەمئىيىتىدە بۇ ئەڭ ئېغىر مەسىلە ئەمەس. بۇنىڭدىنمۇ يامان ئىشلار بار.

جون: قانداق ئىشلارنى دەيسىز؟

ياسىن: مەسىلەن قىمار ئويناش، نەشە، خېروئىن چېكىش. ھازىر كۆپ ياشلار، بولۇپمۇ ئىشسىز قالغانلار، خېروئىننىڭ ئارقىسىغا كىرىپ، ئۆمرىنى بەربات قىلدى. بۇ كاساپەتنى ياشلىرىمىزغا يەنە ئۆزىمىز ساتىمىز.

جون: سىزمۇ خېروئىن ساتامسىز؟

ياسىن: ياق، ياق، ئۆزىمىز دېگىنىم، ئۇيغۇرلىرىمىز.

جون: مەسلىلەر كۆپ دېدىڭىز. ئۇيغۇرلار جەمئىيىتىدە يەنە قانداق مەسلىلەر بار؟

ياسىن: ھە، "بالا كەلسە قوشلاپ كېلىدۇ، بىر- بىرىنى باشلاپ كېلىدۇ" دېگەندەك، خېروئىن پەيدا بولغاندىن كېيىن ئەيدىز كېسىلىمۇ كۆپەيدى...

جون: ۋاي، كەچۈرۈڭ ياسىن، مەن ئۇنتۇپ قاپتىمەن. بۈگۈن ئابدۇكېرىم ئابلىزنىڭ كېچىلىكى بار ئىكەن، سادىق ماڭىمۇ بېلەت ئەپ قويدۇم دېۋىدى، بارمىسام بولمايدۇ. بىز بۇ توغرۇلۇق كېيىنرەك پاراڭلاشساق بولامدۇ؟

ياسىن: بولىدۇ، بولىدۇ. مەن ئەتە تېلېفون قىلاي، ئاندىن بىللە تاماق يەيلى.

جون: خوش!

Exercise 13.2

ياسىن: سالام جون! قانداق ئەھۋالىڭىز؟

جون: ياخشى. ياسىن، ئۆزىڭىزچۇ؟

ياسىن: ياخشى. كۆتۈبخانىغا ماڭدىڭىزمۇ؟
جون: ھەئە. سىزمۇ كۆتۈپخانىغا بارامسىز؟
ياسىن: ياق. مەن دوختۇرخانىغا ماڭدىم.
جون: دوختۇرخانىغا؟ ئاغرىپ قالدىڭىزمۇ؟
ياسىن: ياق، تاغامنىڭ ئوغلى بالنىستتا ئىدى. شۇنى يوقلىماقچىمەن.
جون: بالنىست؟ بۇ قەيەر؟
ياسىن: ھە، ئۇ «كېسەلخانا» دېگەن مەنىدە... ئىنگلىزچە گەپمىكىن.
جون: ياق، ئىنگلىزچىدە بۇنداق سۆز يوق. بەلكىم رۇسچە بولۇشى مۇمكىن.

Exercise 14.3

جون: ياخشىمۇسىز، ياسىن!
ياسىن: ھە جون، كېلىڭ، كېلىڭ، ياخشىمۇسىز!
ياسىن: (تاغىسىغا قاراپ): تاغا، جون كەلدى!
جون: ئەسسالامۇ ئەلەيكۇم!
ياسىننىڭ تاغىسى: ۋەئەلەيكۇم ئەسسالام جون، كېلىڭ!
جون: كەچۈرۈڭ، يامان ئىش بوپتۇ... بۇنداق ئەھۋالدا نېمە دېيىشنىمۇ بىلمەيمەن...
ياسىن: ھېچقىسى يوق، توغرا دېدىڭىز...
ياسىننىڭ تاغىسى جونغا: كەلگىنىڭىز ئۈچۈن رەھمەت، جون. مانا ئوغلىمىز بىزنى تاشلاپ كەتتى. تەقدىرنىڭ ئىشىغا تەن بەرمىسەك بولمايدۇ، بالام... ئامال يوق. بىزدە: ئاللاھ بەردى، ئاللاھ ئالدى دېگەن گەپ بار ...
جون: بالىڭىز نەچچە ياش ئىدى؟
ياسىننىڭ تاغىسى: ئەمدى ئون ئىككىگە كىرگەنتى...ھەەەي، ئۆلۈم ياشقا قارىمايدىكەن ئەمەسمۇ... رەھمەتلىك ئوغلۇم ھېچ بىر راھەت كۆرمەيلا كۆز يۇمدى، جېنىم بالام (يىغلايدۇ) .... تۇغۇلغاندىن بېرى بالنىستتىن بالنىستقا كۆتۈرۈپ يۈردۇق سېنى، پايدىسى بولمىدىغۇ (يىغلايدۇ)....
جون: كەچۈرۈڭ...
جون(ياسىنغا قاراپ): ياسىن، سىزدىن سورايدىغان بىر نەرسە بار ئىدى...
ياسىن: ئا يەرگە ئۆتۈپ سۆزلىشەيلى.
جون: ياسىن، تاغىڭىزنىڭ ئالدىدا خىجالەت بولدۇم ...
ياسىن: نېمىشقا؟
جون: قاراڭ، مەن ھېچ قاچان بۇنداق مۇراسىملارغا قاتنىشىپ باقماپتىكەنمەن. نېمە دېيىشنىمۇ بىلمەيمەن... بۇ يەردىكى كىشىلەرنىڭ يىغىسىنى كۆرۈپ ئىچىم سېرىلىپ كەتتى، ئەمما نېمە دەپ تەسەللى بېرىشنى بىلمەيمەن...
ياسىن: بىزدە ئادەتتە تەسەللى بېرىش ئۈچۈن "خۇدا رەھمەت قىلسۇن"، "جايى جەننەتتە بولسۇن" دېگەندەك گەپلەرنى قىلىدۇ.
جون: توختاپ تۇرۇڭ، مەن بۇ گەپلەرنى يېزىۋالاي....
ياسىن: سىز يېزىپ تۇرۇڭ، مەن مېھمانلار بىلەن كۆرۈشۈپ قوياي. يېزىپ بولغىنىڭىزدىن كېيىن، ئاۋۇ ئۆيگە كىرىڭ، ھازىر ئاش تارتىلىدۇ...

Exercise 15.2

ئالەمدىن ئۆتمەك   كۆز يۇمماق   ئۇ دۇنياغا سەپەر قىلماق   ھالاك بولماق

ۋاپات بولماق   ئۆلۈپ كەتمەك   تۈگەپ كەتمەك   قازا قىلماق

Exercise 15.3

- خۇدا/ئاللاھ رەھمەت قىلسۇن (قىلغاي)
- ياتقان يېرى جەننەتتە بولسۇن (بولغاي)
- سەۋر قىلىڭ
- ئۆلۈم دېگەن ياش - قېرى دېمەيدىكەن
- كەتكەننىڭ كەينىدىن كەتكىلى بولمايدۇ
- ئاللاھ ئۆزىنىڭ ياخشى بەندىلىرىنى ئاشۇنداق بالدۇر ئېلىپ كېتىدىكەن

Exercise 17.4

بۈگۈن بىر غەلىتە چۈش كۆرۈپتىمەن. چۈشۈمدە مەن بىر خانىش ئىكەنمىشمەن. ئەتراپىمدا نۇرغۇن خىزمەتكارلار خىزمىتىمنى قىلىپ يۈرەرمىش. بىر كۈنى شاھىم ئوۋغا چىقىپ كېتىپتىمىش. شۇ كۈنى يېنىمغا بىر قېرى موماي كېلىپ بۇنداق دەرمىش:

- ھەي، خانىش، مەن سەندىن ئىككى سوئال سورايمەن، ئەگەر ئىككى كۈن ئىچىدە سوئاللىرىمغا توغرا جاۋاب تاپالمىساڭ، شاھىڭ ئوۋدىن قايتىپ كەلمەيدۇ!

قورقۇپ كەتكىنىمدىن ئاغزىمنى ئاچالماي قېتىپلا قاپتىمەن... ئاتراپىمدىكى خىزمەتكارلىرىم غايىب بوپتىمىش....

موماي ماڭا قاراپ جاۋابىمنى ساقلاپ تۇرارمىش...

- ماقۇل، سوئاللىرىڭنى سورا، مەن ئويلاپ باقاي دەپ جاۋاب بېرىپتەنمىش. موماي ماڭا قاراپ "دۇنيادا نېمە قاتتىق، نېمە تاتلىق؟" دەپ سوراپتۇ. شۇنىڭ بىلەن ئويغىنىپ كېتىپتىمەن... خۇدايىم توۋا، بۇ چۈش زادى قانداق چۈش؟

Exercise 22.4

يەنە بىر تەرەپتىن ئېيتقاندا، مۇشۇنداق قويۇق جەمئىيەت تورى ئىچىدە ياشاشنىڭ ياخشى بولمىغان يەرلىرىمۇ بار ئىكەن ۋە بەزى ئىشلار ئۇيغۇرلارغا بەك ئېغىر تەسىر كۆرستىدىكەن. مەن يېقىندا ئۇيغۇرلارنىڭ جەمئىيەتتىكى مەسئۇلىيەتلىرىنىڭ ئېغىرلىقىنى چوڭقۇر ھېس قىلدىم. تويلارنى مىسالغا ئالساق، ئۇيغۇرلار توي ۋە نىكاھنى دۇنيادىكى ئەڭ بەختلىك ئىش دەپ قارايدىكەن. لېكىن، باشقىلارنىڭ تويغا بارىدىغان ۋاقىتلاردا، مەن تونۇيدىغان ئۇيغۇرلارنىڭ كۆپىنچىسى "توي دېگەن ۋاقىتنى سۇدەك ئىسراپ قىلىدىغان بىر پائالىيەت" دەپ تويغا بېرىشنى يامان كۆرىدىكەن. ئۇلارنىڭ تويغا بارغۇسى بولمىسىمۇ، بارمىسام سەت بولىدۇ دەپ بارىدىكەن.

قويۇق جەمئىيەت تورى ئىچىدە ياشاشنىڭ باشقا بىر يامان يېرىمۇ بار. ئۇيغۇرلار شەكىل دېگەن ئۇقۇمغا بەك ئېتىبار بېرىدىكەن. بۇ ھاياتتىكى ھەر قانداق ئىشنىڭ شەكلى بار، لېكىن ئۇيغۇرلارنىڭ شەكىلگە شۇنچە كۆپ ئېتىبار بېرىدىغانلىقىنىڭ يامان تەرىپىمۇ بار دەپ قارايمەن. مەسىلەن، كۆپ قىسىم ئادەملەر باشقىلارغا گەپ قىلغاندا " راست گەپنى دېسەم ياخشى بولمايدۇ" دەپ، راستىنى ئېيتماي، ياخشىچاق بولۇپ يالغان گەپ قىلىپ يۈرىدىكەن. بىز ئامېرىكانلارنىڭ ياخشى بىر يېرىمىز شۇكى، بىز گەپنى ئۇدۇل قىلىدىكەنمىز. توغرىسىنى ئېيتمايدىغان بۇنداق ئىشنى بىر خىل ئالا كۆڭۈللۈك دېسەك بولارمىكىن دەيمەن.

CHAPTER 11

Exercise 8.1

خىزمەتچى: ياخشىمۇسىز!

جون: ياخشىمۇسىز! بىر ئۇيغۇر دوستۇم مۇشۇ مېھمانخانىنى تەۋسىيە قىلىۋىدى. بىرنەچچە كۈنگە ياتاق ئالسام بولامدۇ؟

خىزمەتچى: ئىسمىڭىز نېمە؟

جون: ئىسمىم جون. كەچۈرۈڭ، مەن تېلېفون قىلىپ تىزىملىتىشقا ئۈلگۈرەلمىدىم.

خىزمەتچى: چاتاق يوق.

Exercise 8.3

خىزمەتچى: ياخشىمۇسىز!

جون: ياخشىمۇسىز! بىر ئۇيغۇر دوستۇم مۇشۇ مېھمانخانىنى تەۋسىيە قىلىۋىدى. بىرنەچچە كۈنگە ياتاق ئالسام بولامدۇ؟

خىزمەتچى: ئىسمىڭىز نېمە؟

جون: ئىسمىم جون. كەچۈرۈڭ، مەن تېلېفون قىلىپ تىزىملىتىشقا ئۈلگۈرەلمىدىم.

خىزمەتچى: چاتاق يوق. سىز چەتئەللىك ئوخشىمامسىز؟!

جون: شۇنداق، مەن ئامېرىكىلىق.

خىزمەتچى: ئۇنداقتا سىز باشقا مېھمانخانىغا بېرىشىڭىز لازىم. بۇ مېھمانخانىدا چەتئەللىكلەر تۇرسا بولمايدۇ.

جون: نېمىشقا؟

خىزمەتچى: خوتەندە چەتئەللىكلەر ئۈچۈن ئالاھىدە مېھمانخانا بار، "ئەلچى" مېھمانخانىسى...

جون: مۇنداق دەڭ... سىز دېگەن مېھمانخانا بۇ يەردىن يىراقمۇ؟

خىزمەتچى: يىراق ئەمەس، چوققۇ بازارنىڭ ئارقىسىدا. ھازىر چىقىپلا تاكسى توسسىڭىز بولىدۇ، تاكسى بەش كويغا سىزنى شۇ مېھمانخانىغا ئاپىرىپ قويىدۇ.

جون: رەھمەت.

Exercise 8.4

جون: ياخشىمۇسىز!

خىزمەتچى: ياخشىمۇسىز!

جون: بۇ مېھمانخانىدا بوش ياتاق بارمۇ؟

خىزمەتچى: سىز چەتئەللىكمۇ؟ ئۇيغۇرچىغا ئۇستىكەنسىز... نەدىن كەلدىڭىز؟

جون: مەن ئامېرىكىلىق. مۇشۇ مېھمانخانىدا چەتئەللىكلەرنى ئورۇنلاشتۇرىدۇ دەپ ئاڭلىدىم.

خىزمەتچى: شۇنداق، چەتئەللىكلەر مۇشۇ مېھمانخانىغا چۈشىدۇ.

جون: بىر نەچچە كۈنگە ياتاق ئالسام بولامدۇ؟

خىزمەتچى: بولىدۇ. سىزگە قانداق ياتاق لازىم؟

جون: قانداق ياتاقلار بار؟

خىزمەتچى: ھەر خىل: بىر كىشىلىك، ئىككى كىشىلىك...

جون: بىر كىشىلىكنى ئالاي. قانچە پۇل؟

خىزمەتچى: كۈنىگە 40 دوللار.

جون: ياخشى، بولىدىكەن.

خىزمەتچى: پاسپورتىڭىزنى كۆرۈپ باقاي.
جون: ھازىر، ... مانا.
خىزمەتچى: رەھمەت. ئەمدى ماۋۇ تىزىملىتىش جەدۋىلىنى تولدۇرۇڭ.
جون: رەھمەت سىزگە. ماۋۇ يەرگە نېمە يازىمەن؟
خىزمەتچى: قېنى، ھە، بۇ يەرگە پاسپورتىڭىزنىڭ نومۇرىنى يازىسىز.
جون: مانا، يازدىم، بىر قاراپ چىقسىڭىز.
خىزمەتچى: ياخشى! سىز خوتەندە قانچىلىك تۇرماقچى؟
جون: تېخى بىلمەيمەن. ھازىرچە ياتاقنى ئۈچ كۈنگە ئالسام بولامدۇ؟
خىزمەتچى: بولىدۇ، لازىم بولسا، بىز يەنە ئۇزارتىپ بېرىمىز.
جون: رەھمەت سىزگە.
خىزمەتچى: ئەرزىمەيدۇ. مانا سىزگە ئاچقۇچ. 52 - ياتاق، 2 - قەۋەتتە. يەنە سوئاللىرىڭىز بولسا، شۇ قەۋەتنىڭ مۇلازىمەتچىسىدىن سورىسىڭىز بولىدۇ. ھە، راست، يۈك - تاقلىرىڭىز كۆپمۇ؟
جون: كۆپ ئەمەس، بىرلا چامادانىم بار.
خىزمەتچى: سىز ياتىقىڭىزغا چىقىۋېرىڭ، بىر مۇلازىمەتچى يۈكىڭىزنى ئەچىقىپ بېرىدۇ.
جون: كۆپ رەھمەت سىزگە. يەنە بىر نەرسىنى سورىسام بولامدۇ؟
خىزمەتچى: ئەلۋەتتە، تارتىنماي سوراۋېرىڭ.
جون: مېھمانخانىدا ئاشخانا بارمۇ؟
خىزمەتچى: ھەئە، ئاشخانا 1 - قەۋەتتە. يەنە نېمە لازىم بولسا،1 - قەۋەتتىكى مۇلازىمەتچىدىن سورىسىڭىز بولىدۇ.
جون: رەھمەت سىزگە.
خىزمەتچى: ئەرزىمەيدۇ!

Exercise 13.2

جون: كەچۈرۈڭ، بۇ ئەتراپتا بازار بارمۇ؟
مەتتۇرسۇن: ۋۇي، سىز چەتئەللىكما؟
جون: ھەئە، مەن ئامېرىكىلىق.
مەتتۇرسۇن: يىراقتىن كەلگەن مېھمان ئىكەنسىز، بازارغا سىزنى ئۆزۈم ئاپىراي.
جون: رەھمەت سىزگە. تۈنۈگۈن گىلەم كارخانىسىغا بارغان ئىدىم، بۈگۈن بازارنى ئايلانغۇم كەلدى.
مەتتۇرسۇن: ياخشى بوپتۇ. بازارلىرىمىزنى كۆرمىسىڭىز ھەرگىز بولمايدۇ. يۈرۈڭ، مەن سىزنى چوققۇ بازارغا ئاپىراي، پىيادىلا بارىمىز. بازاردىن نېمە ئالماقچىسىز؟
جون: تۈنۈگۈن ئەتلەس كۆڭلەك كىيگەن ئاياللارنى كۆرۈپ، مېنىڭمۇ ئانامغا بىر پارچە ئەتلەس ئالغۇم كەلدى.
مەتتۇرسۇن: بۇنى ياخشى ئويلاپسىز. خوتەن ئەتلەس ماكانى ئەمەسمۇ... مەن سىزگە ئەڭ ئېسىل ئەتلەسلەرنى كۆرسىتەي.
جون: رەھمەت سىزگە. خوتەندە ئۇيغۇرلار بەك كۆپ ئىكەن...
مەتتۇرسۇن: شۇنداق، بۇ ئۇيغۇرلار ماكانى ئەمەسمۇ، شۇڭا مەكتەپنى پۈتتۈرۈپ بۇ يەردىن كەتكۈم كەلمىدى. ساۋاقداشلىرىمنىڭ كۆپى ھازىر ئۈرۈمچىدە.
جون: ھە راست، مېنىڭ ئىسمىم جون، ئۇيغۇرچە ئىسمىم يالقۇن. سىزنىڭچۇ؟
مەتتۇرسۇن: مېنىڭ ئىسمىم مەتتۇرسۇن.
جون: مەتتۇرسۇن؟ مەن تۇرسۇن دېگەن ئىسمنى ئاڭلىغان، ئەمما مەتتۇرسۇن دېگەننى بىرىنچى قېتىم ئاڭلىشىم.

مەتتۇرسۇن: ھە، خوتەنلىكلەرنى ئۇلارنىڭ ئىسىملىرىدىن بىلىۋالغىلى بولىدۇ.
جون: ئۇلارنىڭ ئىسىملىرى باشقىچمۇ؟
مەتتۇرسۇن: باشقىچە ئەمەس، لېكىن خوتەنلىكلەرنىڭ ئىسىملىرىنىڭ كۆپىنچىسى 'مەت' بىلەن باشلىنىدۇ.
جون: قىزىق، مەن بۇنى بىلمەيدىكەنمەن...
مەتتۇرسۇن: بۇ يەردە كۆپرەك تۇرسىڭىز، خېلى نەرسىلەرنى ئۆگىنىۋالىسىز... مانا بازارغىمۇ
كېلىپ قالدۇق. قېنى، ئالدى بىلەن ئەتلەس بازىرىغا ئۆتەيلى...
جون: شۇنداق قىلايلى!

Exercise 16.1

مەتتۇرسۇن: مانا، ئەتلەس بازىرىغىمۇ كەلدۇق. قاراڭ، چىرايلىق شارپىلار بار ئىكەن.
جون: بۇلارنىڭ رەڭلىرى نېمە دېگەن چىرايلىق!
مەتتۇرسۇن: ئانىڭىز نەچچە ياشلاردا؟
جون: ئانامنىڭ يېشىنى نېمىشقا سورايسىز؟
مەتتۇرسۇن: ئاياللار ئەتلەسنى يېشىغا قاراپ ئالىدۇ.
جون: شۇنداقمۇ؟
مەتتۇرسۇن: شۇنداق. مەسىلەن، يېشى چوڭراق ئاياللار قىزىل رەڭلىك ئەتلەسنى كىيمەيدۇ. ئۇلار كۆك، يېشىل،
دېگەندەك رەڭلەرنى ئالىدۇ. موماياللار قارا ئەتلەس كىيىدۇ.
جون: ئۇنداقتا مەن كۆك رەڭلىكنى ئالاي. ئانامنىڭ كۆزىگە ماس كېلىدۇ.
مەتتۇرسۇن: ھە، قېنى ئاۋۇ ئۇستامنىڭ مېلىنى كۆرۈپ باقايلى.

Exercise 16.2

مەتتۇرسۇن: ئۇستام، ماۋۇ ئەتلەس شارپىلىرىنى نەچچە پۇلغا بېرىتلا؟
دۇكاندار: سەدە كەگەن خېيدانى قاچۇما دېيتۇ. چاغلاپ بەرسىلە.
مەتتۇرسۇن: ئەتلەس سەركەشتە ئەمەستۇ؟
دۇكاندار: ھەنىنىۋاسى دىلخا ئەتلەسيا.
مەتتۇرسۇن: ئەمسە مانى نەچچىگە بېرتلا؟
دۇكاندار: قالىسام خىڭ ئەدەمكەنلا، سىلىگە ئوتتۇز كويدىن بېرېي.
مەتتۇرسۇن: مۇشۇ ئۇز گەپلىرى ئۇچۇن ئىككىنى ئالاي.
دۇكاندار: ئابدان. ئانىكىلىرىغا ئالاملا يا ئاپىلىرىغا ئالاملا؟
مەتتۇرسۇن: ئادىشىمنىڭ ئانىكىسىغا.

Exercise 16.6

بېرىلا -- بىرىتلا
بىر -- بىي
بېرەي -- بىرىي
قارىسىلا -- قالىسىلا

CHAPTER 12

Exercise 1.2

ئۈرۈمچى- شىنجاڭ ئۇيغۇر ئاپتونوم رايونىدىكى ئەڭ چوڭ شەھەر. ئۇ تەڭرىتاغنىڭ شىمالىي ئېتىكىگە، جۇڭغارىيە ئويمانلىقىنىڭ جەنۇبىي چېتىگە جايلاشقان. ئۈرۈمچى شىنجاڭ ئۇيغۇر ئاپتونوم رايونىنىڭ سىياسىي، ئىقتىسادىي، مەدەنىيەت، پەن- تېخنىكا مەركىزى. ئۈرۈمچىنىڭ كۆلىمى 11 مىڭ 440 كۋادرات كىلومېتىر، بۇنىڭ ئىچىدە شەھەر رايونىنىڭ كۆلىمى 51 كۋادرات كىلومېتىر.

ئۈرۈمچى شەھەر ئەتراپى رايونى بىلەن شەھەر رايونىنى ئۆز ئىچىگە ئالىدۇ. شەھەر ئەتراپى رايونى ئۈرۈمچى ناھىيىسى ۋە دۆلەت ئىگىلىكىدىكى ئالتە دېھقانچىلىق، چارۋىچىلىق مەيدانىنى ئۆز ئىچىگە ئالىدۇ. شەھەر رايونى يەتتە مەمۇرىي رايونغا بۆلۈنگەن.

ئۈرۈمچىنىڭ يىللىق ئوتتۇرىچە تېمپېراتۇرىسى 7.3 سېلسىيە گرادۇس، يازدا ئەڭ ئىسسىق بولغاندا، 37 سېلسىيە گرادۇس، قىشتا ئەڭ سوغۇق بولغاندا، نۆلدىن تۆۋەن 32 سېلسىيە گرادۇس بولىدۇ. بۇ يەرنىڭ ۋاقتى بېيجىڭ ۋاقت رايونىدىن ئىككى سائەت كېيىن بولىدۇ.

ئۈرۈمچىدە ھازىر مېتاللىچىلىق، كۆمۈر، ئېلېكتىر، ئېلېكترون، ماشىنىسازلىق، نېفىت - خىمىيە سانائىتى، كۆندىلىك ئىستېمال بۇيۇملىرى، قۇرۇلۇش ماتېرىياللىرى، توقۇمىچىلىق، تېرە-خۇرۇم، قەغەزچىلىك قاتارلىق سانائەت سىستېمىلىرى بار.

ئۈرۈمچى شىنجاڭنىڭ قاتناش تۈگىنى. ئۈرۈمچىنى ھەرقايسى ۋىلايەت، شەھەر، ناھىيە ۋە دېھقانچىلىق- چارۋىچىلىق مەيدانلىرى بىلەن تۇتاشتۇرىدىغان تاشيوللار بار. شۇنداقلا ئۈرۈمچىنى بېيجىڭ، شاڭخەي، چۇڭچىڭ قاتارلىق چوڭ شەھەرلەر بىلەن تۇتاشتۇرىدىغان لەنجۇ – شىنجاڭ تۆمۈر يولى بار. ئۇنىڭدىن باشقا ئۈرۈمچىنى ئىچكى ئۆلكىلەر ۋە چەت ئەللەر بىلەن تۇتاشتۇرىدىغان ھاۋا قاتناش يوللىرىمۇ بار.

ئۈرۈمچى شەھىرى ئۆز ۋاقتىدا يىپەك يولىنىڭ مۇھىم تۈگۈنى بولغان. ئۇ تارىخىي ۋە جۇغراپىيىلىك ئورنىنىڭ ئەۋزەللىكى، كۆپ مىللەتلىك قۇرۇلمىسى بىلەن مەملىكەت سىرتى ۋە ئىچىدىكى نۇرغۇنلىغان ساياھەتچىلەرنى ئۆزىگە جەلپ قىلىپ كېلىۋاتىدۇ. ھازىر ئۈرۈمچى ئەڭ روناق تاپقان ساياھەت رايونلىرىنىڭ بىرى.

Exercise 2

ئۈچ ، ئۈچ پۈتۈن ئوندىن ئىككى، ئۈچ پۈتۈن يۈزدىن ئەللىك ئالتە
سەككىز، سەككىز پۈتۈن ئوندىن سەككىز، سەككىز پۈتۈن يۈزدىن يەتتە
ئالتە، ئالتە پۈتۈن ئوندىن بەش، يىگىرمە تۆت پۈتۈن ئوندىن ئالتە
يىگىرمە تۆت، يىگىرمە تۆت پۈتۈن ئوندىن ئۈچ ، يىگىرمە تۆت پۈتۈن يۈزدىن ئاتمىش يەتتە
بىر يۈز ئىككى، بىر يۈز ئىككى پۈتۈن ئوندىن تۆت، بىر يۈز ئىككى پۈتۈن يۈزدىن ئوتتۇز توققۇز

Exercise 3.2

ئەزىز دوستلىرىم،

ۋاقىت نېمىدېگەن تېز ئۆتۈپ كەتتى. خۇدايىم بۇيرىسا، بىر نەچچە كۈندىن كېيىن ئامېرىكىغا قايتىمەن. راستىنى ئېيتسام، ئۈرۈمچىگە بەك كۆنۈپ قاپتىمەن. سىلەر بولغىنىڭلار ئۈچۈن بۇ يەردىكى ۋاقتىم بەك كۆڭۈللۈك ئۆتتى. مەن سىلەردىن بەك مىننەتدارمەن. سىلەر مېنى كۆپ مېھمان قىلدىڭلار. شۇڭا كېتىشتىن بۇرۇن ھەممىڭلارنى مەن ئامراق بولغان "قەشقەر رېستورانى"غا چاقىرىپ مېھمان قىلاي دەيمەن. سىلەر مېنى مېھمان دەپ ھېچ قاچان پۇل تۆلەتكۈزمىدىڭلار، ئەمما بۇ قېتىم سىلەر مېنىڭ مېھمىنىم بولۇڭلار. تاماقنىڭ پۇلىنى مەن تۆلەيمەن، بولامدۇ؟ قالغان گەپلەرنى كېيىن

دېيىشەرمىز. مۇشۇ شەنبە سائەت يەتتىلەردە كۆرۈشسەك قانداق؟
جاۋابىڭلارنى كۈتۈپ،

جون

Exercise 4.1

ياسىن: شۇنداق قىلىپ كېلەر ھەپتە ئامېرىكىغا قايتىمەن دەڭ... ۋاقىت نېمىدېگەن تېز ئۆتىدۇ - ھە!

جون: راست. بىردەمدىلا بىر يىل ئۆتۈپ كېتىپتۇ. لېكىن مەن بەك جىق نەرسىلەرنى ئۆگىنىۋالدىم.

ياسىن: بىزمۇ سىزدىن جىق نەرسە ئۆگەندۇق.

مۇختەر: جون، سىزگە بۇ يەردە قايسى ئىش ئەڭ ياقتى؟

جون: ياقتى؟ مەن چۈشەنمىدىم.

مۇختەر: يەنى قايسى ئىشنى سىز ئەڭ ياخشى كۆردىڭىز؟

جون: ھمم... ماڭا ئەڭ ياققان ئىش - ئۇيغۇرلار بەك ئاق كۆڭۈل ئىكەن.

مۇختەر: ئامېرىكىلىقلار ئاق كۆڭۈل ئەمەسمۇ؟

جون: ياق، بىزمۇ ئاق كۆڭۈل، ئەمما يەنىلا پەرق چوڭ ئىكەن.

Exercise 4.2

قاۋۇل: جون، ئۈرۈمچىدە سىز ئەڭ ھەيران قالغان ئىش نېمە بولدى؟

جون: «شىنجاڭ ئۇيغۇر ئاپتونوم رايونى» دېگەن بىلەن بۇ يەردە ھېچقانداق ئاپتونومىيە يوق ئىكەن.

مۇختەر: ھەي باللار، ئاستىراق گەپ قىلىڭلار. يەنە تۈرمىگە چۈشمەيلى، جۇمۇ.

مېجىت: جون، سىز ئۇيغۇرلارنىڭ ئۆيلىرىگە باردىڭىزمۇ؟

جون: باردىم. قەشقەردە نۇرغۇن ئۆيلەردە مېھمان بولدۇم. تويلارغىمۇ باردىم.

مېجىت: مۇشۇ جەرياندا سىز ھەيران بولغان بىرەر ئىش بولدىمۇ؟

جون: بۇنداق ئىشلار جىق. مەن بەك ھەيران قالغان بىر ئىش بار: ئۇيغۇرلارنىڭ ئاياللىرى سەھەردە ئۆينىڭ ئالدىدىكى يولنى سۈپۈرۈپ سۇ چاچىدىكەن. ئەمما ئۇ يول شەخسىي يول ئەمەس، ئۇنىڭدا ھەممە ئادەم ماڭىدۇ.

مېجىت: بۇ راست. ئۇيغۇرلار "يولنىڭ يۈزىنى ئاچسا، خۇدايىم شۇ كىشىنىڭ بەختىنى ئاچىدۇ" دەيدۇ.

جون: مۇنداق دەڭ... مەن بۇنى ئۇيغۇرلاردىكى پاكىزلىق دەپ چۈشىنىپتىمەن... راستىنى دېسەم مەن ئۇيغۇرلارنىڭ ھاراق ئىچىشىنى ياخشى كۆرمىدىم.

مېجىت: ئۇنداقتا بۇ سىزگە ئەڭ ياقمىغان ئىش بوپتۇ- دە.

جون: شۇنداق. ماڭا بۇ زادىلا ياقمىدى. ئۇيغۇرلار ھاراقنى كۆپ ئىچسە بەك زىيانلىق.

Exercise 4.3

جون: بۈگۈنمۇ ھاراق ئىچەمدۇق؟

قاۋۇل: ئەمدى بۇ ئۇزىتىش ئولتۇرۇشى بولغاچقا، ئازراق ئىچەيلى. سىزمۇ ئازراق ئىچىڭ.

جون: ئاق، ھاراق بەك ئاچچىق ئىكەن. مەن پىۋا ئىچسەم بولامدۇ؟

قاۋۇل: چاتاق يوق، ئەمما ئاۋۋال ماۋۇ بىر رۇمكا ئاق ھاراقنى ئېلىڭ، بۇ بىزنىڭ كۆڭلىمىز.

جون: رەھمەت، ئەمىسە مۇشۇ بىر رۇمكا ھاراقنى دوستلۇقىمىز ئۈچۈن ئىچەي...

مېجىت: ھەي قاۋۇل، ھاراقنى زورلىما، جۇمۇ. بۇنداق قىلساڭ، جون ئۈرۈمچىگە ھەرگىز كەلمەيدۇ!

Exercise 4.4

مىجىت: ھەي قاۋۇل، ھاراقنى زورلىما، جۇمۇ. بۇنداق قىلساڭ جون ئۇرۇمچىگە ھەرگىز كەلمەيدۇ!
جون: ياق، مەن يەنە كېلىمەن. مەن ئۇيغۇرلارنى، شىنجاڭنى ياخشى كۆرىمەن. ئەمما ھازىر مەكتەپنى پۈتتۈرۈشۈم لازىم، ئاندىن خىزمەت تېپىشىم كېرەك.
مۇختەر: خىزمەتكە چىقسىڭىز بەلكىم ئۇرۇمچىگە كېلەلمەيسىز.
جون: خۇدايىم بۇيرىسا، خىزمەتكە چىقىپ توي قىلسام، ئائىلەمنى ئېلىپ شىنجاڭغا ساياھەت قىلغىلى كېلىمەن.
مىجىت: ئۇنداق بولسا شۇ چاغدا مېنى ئىزدەڭ، جۇمۇ، مەن سىزنى غۇلجىغا ئاپىراي.
جون: رەھمەت. مېنىڭ غۇلجىغا، يەنە ئالتاي، قارىماي، خوتەنلەرگە بارغۇم بار. ھە راست، ياسىن، ئەتە مەن ئامېرىكىدىكى تۇغقانلىرىمغا بىرئاز سوۋغات ئالماقچىتىم. سىزنىڭ ۋاقتىڭىز بولامدۇ؟
ياسىن: بولىدۇ. ئەتە مەن بىكار. سائەت نەچچىدە بازارغا بارىسىز؟
جون: سائەت ئونلاردا بارساق بولامدۇ؟
ياسىن: چاتاق يوق. ئەمىسە ئەتە سائەت ئوندا مەن ياتىقىڭىزغا باراي.
جون: سىزگە كۆپ رەھمەت! قېنى، دوستلار، تاماقنى سىلەر بۇيرىتىڭلار، ئەمما تاماقنىڭ پۇلىنى بۈگۈن مەن تۆلەيمەن.
ياسىن: ئۇنداق قىلساق بولماس، سىز مېھمان تۇرسىڭىز...
جون: ياق، ياق، مەن سىلەرنى مېھمان قىلاي، بۇ مېنىڭ كۆڭلۈم...

Exercise 5.1

1. قايسى ساياھەت سىز ئۈچۈن ئەڭ قىزىق بولدى؟
2. ساياھەت جەريانىدا سىز ھەيران بولغان بىرەر ئىش بولدىمۇ؟
3. قايسى شەھەرلەرنى زىيارەت قىلدىڭىز؟
4. قايسى شەھەر سىزگە ئەڭ ياقتى؟ نېمىشقا؟
5. شۇ شەھەرنى قىسقىچە تەسۋىرلەپ بېرەمسىز؟

Exercise 11.1

ياسىن :ئالدىغان نەرسىلەرنىڭ ھەممىسىنى ئالدىڭىزمۇ؟
جون :ھەئە، مېنىڭچە بولدى...كۆپ نەرسە ئالمايمەن دېگەنتىم، ئەمما بۇ بازارغا كىرگەندە ئادەم ئۆزىنى تۇتۇۋالالماي قالىدىكەن...
ياسىن :بۇ يەردىن ئامېرىكىغا قۇرۇق قول بىلەن بارغىلى بولماس...
جون :ئۇغۇ شۇ، ئەمما بۇلارنى ئەكەتمەكمۇ چوڭ گەپتە...مەن بۇ يەردىن بېيجىڭغا ئۇچىمەن ئەمەسمۇ، شۇڭا يۈكۈم يىگىرمە كىلودىن ئاشسا بولمايدۇ.
ياسىن :ھە، توغرا، توغرا ...ئەمما بېيجىڭدىن يەنە بەزى نەرسىلەرنى ئېلىۋالسىڭىز بولىدۇ...
جون :ياقەي، بولدى. مۇشۇ نەرسىلەرنى ئەكەتسەممۇ چوڭ گەپ...
ياسىن :چامادانلىرىڭىزنى قاچان تەييارلايسىز؟
جون :بۈگۈن كەچتە تەييارلايمىكىن...
ياسىن :ياردەم لازىم بولسا، دەڭ، مەن قارىشىپ بېرەي.
جون :سىزنى ئاۋارە قىلغۇم يوق...ھېلىمۇ شۇنچە ۋاقتىڭىزنى ئالدىم.
ياسىن :ياق، ياق، ئاۋارە بولىدىغان ئىش يوق...

جون :ماقۇله، ئەمىسە ياتاقىا بىللە بارىلى.
ياسىن :ئەكېتىدىغان پىچاقلىرىڭىز كۆپمۇ؟
جون :ئۈچ پىچىقىم بار.
ياسىن :ئۇلارنى چامادانغا سېلىۋالسىڭىز ياخشىراق بولارمىكىن؟
جون :ھەئە، ئۆتكەن قېتىم بىر پىچىقىمنى يېنىمغا سېلىۋالغانتىم، ئايرودرومدا ئېلىۋالدى...
ياسىن :پىچاقنى كۆرسە ئۆتكۈزمەيدۇ...
جون :شۇنداقكەن...
ياسىن :ھە راست، ئايرودرومغا قانداق چىقىسىز؟
جون :شۇ ئىشنى سىز بىلەن مەسلىھەت قىلماقچىتىم .بۈگۈن كەچتە تاكسى زاكاز قىلىپ قويساق بولامدۇ؟
ياسىن :بولىدۇ، شۇنداق قىلىلى .مەن ئۆزۈم تېلېفون قىلىپ بىر تاكسى بۇيرىتاي...

Exercise 12.1

ئەر: ۋەي!
ياسىن: ئەسسالامۇ ئەلەيكۇم. بۇ دۆڭكۆۋرۈك ساياھەت تاكسى شىركىتىمۇ؟
ئەر: شۇنداق. تاكسى كېرەكمۇ؟
ياسىن: ھەئە. بۈگۈن لازىم ئىدى.
ئەر: ھازىر دەمسىز؟
ياسىن: ياق، بۈگۈن كەچتە لازىم.
ئەر: سائەت نەچچىگە بولسۇن؟
ياسىن: كەچ سائەت يەتتىگە.
ئەر: ئادرېسىڭىزنى دەۋېتەمسىز؟
ياسىن: شىنجاڭ ئۇنىۋېرستېتى 8 - ياتاق بىناسى.

Exercise 13.3

1. سىز چەتئەللىك ئوخشىمامسىز؟
2. پاھ، ئۇيغۇرچىغا ئۇستا بوپ كېتىپسىز!
3. ھازىر ھەممە ئادەم خەنزۇچە ئۆگىنىۋاتسا سىز نېمىشقا ئۇيغۇرچە ئۆگىنىسىز؟
4. بىزنىڭ تىلىمىزنى ئۆگىنىپ نېمە قىلىسىز؟
5. سىز قەيەرلىك؟
6. ئامېرىكىدا تاكسى نەچچە پۇل؟
7. سىز ئادەتتە تاكسىغا كۆپ چىقامسىز؟

Exercise 15.1

(ئۇيغۇر) سودىگەر: نى خاۋ! چۈ بېيجىڭما؟
جون: سىز ئۇيغۇرمۇ؟
سودىگەر: ۋوي، سىزمۇ ئۇيغۇرما؟
جون: ياق، مەن ئامېرىكىلىق.
سودىگەر: ئەمىسە، سىز ئامېرىكىلىق ئۇيغۇر ئوخشىمامسىز؟
جون: ياق، مەن ئۇيغۇر ئەمەس، ئۈرۈمچىدە بىر يىل ئۇيغۇرچە ئۆگەندىم.

سودىگەر: خۇدايىم توۋا! ئۇيغۇرچىڭىز بەك ياخشىكەنە.

جون: رەھمەت. مەن بىر يىل ئۇيغۇر دوستلىرىم بىلەن ياشىدىم. ھەر كۈنى دېگۈدەك ئۇيغۇرچە سۆزلىدىم.

سودىگەر: چەتئەللىكلەر ھەجەپ ئەقىللىقكەن دەيمىنا. ماۋۇ خىتايلار شىنجاڭدا ئون يىل تۇرسىمۇ «ياخشى» دىن باشقا گەپنى ئۆگىنەلمەيدۇ. سىز بىر يىلدىلا ھەممە گەپنى ئۆگىنىپسىز.

جون: كۆپ مەشق قىلسا ئۆگىنىش تەس ئەمەس. ھە راست، سىزنىڭ ئىسمىڭىز نېمە؟

سودىگەر : ئىسمىم ئەخمەت. سىزنىڭچۇ؟

جون: مېنىڭ ئۇيغۇرچە ئىسمىم يالقۇن.

ئەخمەت: يالقۇن... ياخشى ئىسىم تاللاپسىز. سىزمۇ سائەت توققۇزنىڭ ئايروپىلانىدا ئۇچامسىز؟

جون: شۇنداق. مېنىڭ ئايروپىلانىم بېيجىڭ ۋاقتى سائەت توققۇزدا ئۇچماقچى ئىدى. مانا ئەمدى بىر نەچچە سائەت ساقلايدىغان ئوخشايمەن.

ئەخمەت: يامغۇر ياغسا ئايروپىلان دائىم مۇشۇنداق كېچىكىپ قالىدۇ.

جون: مۇنداق دەڭ. مەن تېخى ئايروپىلان بۇزۇلغان ئوخشايدۇ دەپ ئويلاپتىمەن.

ئەخمەت: ئەتىيازدا ئۈرۈمچىدە بۇنداق ئىشلار كۆپ... سىز بېيجىڭغا ئوقۇغىلى ماڭدىڭىزمۇ؟

جون: ياق. مەن ئامېرىكىغا قايتىمەن. ئامېرىكىدىكى ئوقۇشۇم تېخى تۈگىمىدى.

ئەخمەت: سىز ئامېرىكىدا نېمە كەسىپتە ئوقۇيسىز؟

جون: مېنىڭ كەسپىم ئوتتۇرا ئاسىيا تەتقىقاتى.

ئەخمەت: ئوتتۇرا ئاسىياغىمۇ باردىڭىزمۇ؟

جون: ياق، تېخى بارمىدىم. سىزچۇ، سىز ئوتتۇرا ئاسىياغا بارغانمۇ؟

ئەخمەت: باراي دەپ ئويلىغان. ئەمما پاسپورتۇم بولمىغاچقا بارالمىدىم.

جون: ئۇيغۇرلارنىڭ پاسپورت ئېلىشى بەك تەس دەپ ئاڭلىدىم.

ئەخمەت: بۇنى بىر دېمەڭ. سۆزلەپ كەلسەك گەپ جىق. شۇڭا مەن دائىم بېيجىڭدىلا تۇرىمەن.

Exercise 17.1

ئۈرۈمچىدىن بېيجىڭغا ئۇچىدىغان 552 - قېتىملىق ئايروپىلان يولۇچىلىرى دىققەت! ئۈرۈمچىدىن بېيجىڭغا ئۇچىدىغان 552 - قېتىملىق ئايروپىلان ھازىر ئۇچۇش تەييارلىقىنى پۈتتۈردى.

ئۇچۇش يولىدا كۆرۈلگەن كاشىلا تۈپەيلىدىن ئايروپىلانىمىز ئۈچ سائەت كېچىكتى. بۇنىڭ ئۈچۈن جۇڭگو دۆلەتلىك ئاۋىئاتسىيە شىركىتىگە ۋاكالىتەن يولۇچىلاردىن ئەپۇ سورايمىز. ئايروپىلان 30 مىنۇتتىن كېيىن ئۇچىدۇ. يولۇچىلارنىڭ تېزدىن 22 - چىقىش ئېغىزى ئارقىلىق ئايروپىلانغا چىقىش رەسمىيەتلىرىنى ئۆتىشىنى سورايمىز.

Exercise 23.1

ئۈرۈمچىدە تۇرغان ۋاقتىم ناھايىتى كۆڭۈللۈك ئۆتتى. بولۇپمۇ ئۇيغۇر دوستلىرىم بىلەن ئۆتكەن كۈنلىرىم. بىكار بولساق توپ ئويناپتىمىز، ناخشا ئاڭلاپ ئۇسسۇل ئويناپتىمىز، شەنبە – يەكشەنبە كۈنلىرى بازار ئايلىناتتۇق. بەزىدە ساياھەتمۇ قىلاتتۇق. ئۈرۈمچىدە ئوقۇغاندىن ھازىرغىچە شىنجاڭغا بارمىغىلى بەش يىل بولاي دېسىمۇ، شۇ كۈنلەر ھازىرغىچە ئېسىمدە. ئۇيغۇر دوستلىرىم بىلەن تور ئارقىلىق خەت يېزىشىپ، تېلېفون قىلىشىپ تۇرۇپتۇق. خۇدايىم بۇيرىسا بىر پۇرسەت چىقىپ قالسىلا، ئۈرۈمچىگە بېرىپ كونا قەدىناس دوستلىرىمنى يوقلايمەن!

Appendix B

Transcripts of Video Exercises

PRELIMINARY CHAPTER

Exercise 5.1

- مېنىڭ ئېتىم نازۇگۇم، مېنىڭ يېشىم 18 دە. مەن شەرقشۇناسلىق لېتسىيەدە ئوقۇيمەن، ياپون تىلىنى ئۆگىنىمەن.
- نەچچىنچى يىلى تۇغۇلدىڭىز؟ قايسى شەھەردە تۇغۇلدىڭىز؟

1992 - يىلى 26 - نويابىردا تۇغۇلغانمەن. مەن تاشكەنت شەھىرىدىن. بىرىنچى سىنىپنى مۇشۇ يەردە پۈتتۈرۈپ، كېيىن قازاقىستانغا كەتكەنمىز. ئاشۇ يەردە ئالتە يىل ياشاپ، يەنە قايتىپ كەلدۇق. كېيىن 8 - ۋە 9 - سىنىپنى بۇ يەردە پۈتتۈرۈپ لېتسىيەگە ئوقۇشقا كىردىم. ھازىر بىرىنچى كۇرستا ئوقۇۋاتىمەن.

Exercise 10.1

باتۇر : ھەي نازاكەت!
نازاكەت: ۋىي باتۇر، بۇ سىزمىتىڭىز ؟ قانداق ئەھۋالىڭىز ؟
باتۇر: ياخشى، ئۆزىڭىزچۇ؟
نازاكەت: ۋاي ياخشى! ئالدىراش كۆرۈنىسىز، نەگە ماڭدىڭىز؟
باتۇر: خەلقئارا بۆلۈمگە.
نازاكەت: ۋۇي! ئۇ يەردە نىمە قىلىسىز ؟
باتۇر: ئاڭلىشىمچە، خەلقئارا بۆلۈم چەتئەللىك ئوقۇغۇچىلارنى چىكاگوغا ساياھەتكە ئاپارماقچى ئىكەن. شۇڭا ئۆزەمنى تىزىملىتىپ قوياي دېگەن ئىدىم.
نازاكەت: ئەمدى سىزمۇ چەتئەللىك بولۇپ قالدىڭىزمۇ؟
باتۇر: ياق، ياق. ئامرىكىلىق بولغىنىم بىلەن چىكاگوغا تېخى بېرىپ باقماپتىمەن. شۇڭا مۇشۇ پۇرسەتتىن پايدىلىنىپ، چىكاگونى كۆرۈپ كېلەي دېۋىدىم.
نازاكەت: ھە، ئامرىكىلىقلارمۇ بارساق بولامدىكەن؟
باتۇر : ئەلۋەتتە، سىزنىڭمۇ بارغۇڭىز بارمۇ؟
نازاكەت: بار، بىر ئادەمگە نەچچە پۇل ئىكەن؟
باتۇر: 50 دوللار.
نازاكەت: سىلەر قاچان ماڭماقچى؟
باتۇر: شەنبە كۈنى سەھەر سائەت 6 دە.
نازاكەت: ھە، قاچان قايتماقچى؟
باتۇر: كەچ سائەت 9 دا چىكاگودىن بۇ ياققا ماڭىدىكەنمىز.
نازاكەت: ۋاي، ئۇنداق بولسا مەنمۇ باراي.
باتۇر: ئەمىسە يۈرۈڭ ، خەلقئارا بۆلۈمگە بىللە بارايلى.

Exercise 19.1

ئەسسالامۇ ئەلەيكۇم ، مېنىڭ ئىسمىم باھادىر، مەن ئامرىكىلىق. 1985 - يىلى مىسۇرى شىتاتىدا تۇغۇلدۇم . مېنىڭ ئۇكام ۋە ئىككى سىڭلىم ۋە ئەلۋەتتە دادام ۋە ئاپام بار. ئۇلار ھازىرمۇ مىسۇرى شىتاتىدا ئىشلەيدۇ. مەن بولسام سەككىز يېرىم يىلدىن بۇرۇن ئىندىيانا شىتاتىغا كەلدىم، ئوقۇش ئۈچۈن. بۇ يەردە كىچىك ئۇنىۋېرسىتېتتا تارىخ فاكۇلتېتىدا ئوقۇدۇم. مېنىڭ كەسپىم خەلقئارا مۇناسىۋەت ئىدى. 2010 - يىلى ئۇنىۋېرسىتېتنى پۈتتۈردۇم، ئەمما ئىش تاپالمىدىم. شۇڭا ئاخىرى مەن دوستۇم بىلەن ئىشلىدىم. ئۇنىڭ بىر كىچىك ئويۇنلار دۇكىنى بار ئىدى. بىر يىلدىن كېيىن مەن ئۆيلەندىم. ئاندىن مەن ئاسپىرانتۇرىنى باشلىدىم. ھازىر مەن ئىندىيانا ئۇنىۋېرسىتېتىنىڭ يېقىن شەرق بۆلۈمىنىڭ ئوقۇغۇچىسى. مەن تارىخ، مەدەنىيەتلەر ۋە تىللارغا قىزىقىمەن. شۇڭا مەن ئەرەب، فارىس ۋە ئۆزبېك تىللىرىنى ئوقۇغان. ھازىر مەن ئۇيغۇرچىنى ئۆگىنىۋاتىمەن. ئۇنىۋېرسىتېتنى پۈتتۈرگىنىمدىن كېيىن مەن بۇ تىللارنى ئىشلىتىدىغان خىزمەت تاپماقچى.

CHAPTER 2

Exercise 11.1

ئەسسالامۇ ئەلەيكۇم. بۇ بىزنىڭ ئائىلىمىز، بۇ بىر ئۇيغۇر ئائىلىسى. مېنىڭ ئىسمىم زۇلپىقار. بۇ مېنىڭ ئايالىم، ئايالىمنىڭ ئىسمى قەلبىنۇر. بۇ مېنىڭ ئوغلۇم. ئوغلۇمنىڭ ئىسمى ئويغان. ئوغلۇم بۇ يىل بەش ياشقا كىردى. بىز ئۈرۈمچىدىن كەلدۇق. ئۈرۈمچىدە مېنىڭ ئاپام، ئاكىلىرىم، سىڭلىلىرىم بار. مېنىڭ ئايالىم كۇچادىن. ئايالىمنىڭ ئانىسى، تاغىسى كۇچادا. مېنىڭ بىر تاغام قەشقەردە. مېنىڭ مومام قەشقەردە تۇرىدۇ. بوۋام ئۆچ ... ئۈچ يىل بۇرۇن تۈگەپ كەتكەن. ھازىر ئۈرۈمچىدە مېنىڭ ئالتە ئاكام، ئىككى سىڭلىم بار. بىزنىڭ ئائىلە ناھايىتى (ئۈرۈمچىدىكى ئائىلىمىز) ناھايىتى چوڭ بىر ئائىلىدۇر. ھەر بىر ئائىلىدە نەچچىدىن نەۋرە بار. مېنىڭ بىر بالام بار، ئوغۇل، ئىسمى ئويغان.

Exercise 11.2

مېنىڭ قېيىنئاپام، قېيىنئاتام كۇچا ناھىيىسىدە. قېيىنئاتام تىجارەتچى، قېيىنئاپام ئائىلە ئايالى. مېنىڭ ئۆزەمنىڭ بىۋاستە ئۈرۈق - تۇغقانلىرىدىن ئۈرۈمچىدە بەزىلەر خىزمەتچى بولۇپ ئىشلەيدۇ، بەزىلەر ئوقۇغۇچى، بەزىلەر تىجارەتچى. مەسىلەن، مېنىڭ چوڭ ئاكام سودىگەر؛ ئىككىنچى ئاكام ئۇ يەككە تىجارەتچى، كىچىكرەك تىجارەت بىلەن شۇغۇللىنىدۇ؛ بىر ئاكام ئۈرۈمچى شەھرىدە ئوتتۇرا مەكتەپ ئوقۇتقۇچىسى؛ بىر سىڭلىم چەتئەل شىركىتىدە ئىنگلىزچە تەرجىمان؛ بىر ئىنىم ئۈرۈمچىدە تەھرىر بولۇپ ئىشلەيدۇ. ئۇنىڭدىن باشقا ئۇچتۇرپان ناھىيىسىدە بىر سىڭلىم بار. سىڭلىم تىجارەت بىلەن شۇغۇللىنىدۇ.

Exercise 13.1

مومای: ۋاي كەلسىلە
تۇرئەخمەت: ئەسسلامۇ ئەلەيكۇم! چوڭ ئاپا. ياخشىمۇسىز، چوڭ ئاپا!
مومای: رەخمەت. ياخشى كەلدىڭمۇ؟

موماي: ۋاي-ۋۇي ئەك كىچىكى تۆرەخمەت بۇ.
ئەر: ماڭا قاراپ گەپ قىلىپ بېرىڭ، ئاپا. ماڭا قاراپ گەپ قىلىڭلار، قانچىنچى نەۋرىڭىز بۇ؟
موماي: ئەڭ كەنجە نەۋرىدە، بۇ نەۋرىنىڭ كەنجىسى
ئەر: نەۋرىنىڭ كەنجى نەۋرە...
موماي: 18 -، ئۆزى يىگىرمە نەچچىنى كۆردۈم ئۇچى ئۆلۈپ كەتتىغۇ. ھازىر بارنى دەۋاتىمەن دە. 18- نەۋرە بۇ.
ئەر: بۇ ئەمدى بوۋىسىنىڭ ئېتىنى مۇناسىپ نىمە قىلسۇن ئەمدى.
موماي: ھە، ئۇنىڭ فامىلىسىنى ئات قىلغان بۇنىڭغا تۆرەخمەت دەپ دېگەن گەپنى، ئېتى تۆرەخمەت بۇنىڭ فامىلىسى تۆرەخمەتوۋ، 8 - سىنىپتا ئوقۇۋاتىدۇ. ياخشى ئوقۇغىن دەپ تەرەپ تەرەپتىن دەپ تۇرىمىز بۇنىڭغا. بۇ دائىم ئۇيغۇرلارنى سوراپ بېشىمنى ئايلاندۇرىۋېتىدۇ. ئۇيغۇرلارنىڭ تارىخىنى تولا سورايدۇ. ئا نېمە ما نېمە قىلىپ، كىم بىلىدۇ نېمە بولىدىكىن...
ئەر: تارىخچى بولىدۇ بۇ.

Exercise 19.2

قىز: ئالدى بىلەن ئۆزىڭىزنى قىسقىچە تونۇشتۇرسىڭىز.
ئوغۇل: بولىدۇ. مېنىڭ ئىسمىم ئۆندىري. مېنىڭ ئۇيغۇرچە ئىسمىم ئۆتكۈر. مەن 1985 - يىلى چېخىيەدە تۇغۇلغان.
قىز: ئائىلىڭىزدە كىملەر بار؟
ئوغۇل: بىزنىڭ ئائىلىمىز چوڭ ئەمەس. بىز ئۈچ جان. دادام ئالىي مەكتەپتە خىمىيە مۇئەللىمى. ئاپام شەھەرلىك ھۆكۈمەتتە ئىشلەيدۇ. مەن دوكتورلۇق ئۇنۋانى ئۈچۈن ئوقۇۋاتىمەن.
قىز: خاتالاشمىسام چېخ جۇمھۇرىيىتىدە ئۇيغۇر يوق. سىزنىڭ ئۇيغۇرچە ئۆگىنىشىڭىزگە نېمە سەۋەب بولدى؟
ئوغۇل: بەش يىل ئاۋۋال موسكۋادا بىرنەچچە ئۇيغۇر سودىگەر بىلەن ئۇچرىشىپ قالدىم. ئاڭلىسام، ئۇلار جۇڭگودىن كەپتۇ، لېكىن ئۇلارنىڭ چىرايى خەنزۇلارغا ئوخشىمايدىكەن. شۇنىڭ بىلەن ئۇلارغا قىزىقىپ قالدىم. كېيىن بىر دوستۇمنىڭ ياردىمى بىلەن ئازراق ئۇيغۇرچە ئۆگەندىم.
قىز: شىنجاڭغا باردىڭىزمۇ؟
ئوغۇل: باردىم. 2007 - يىلى ئۇرۇمچىگە بېرىپ شىنجاڭ ئۇنىۋېرسىتېتىدا ئىككى مەۋسۇم ئۇيغۇرچە ئوقۇدۇم. شۇ چاغدا تۇرپان ۋە قۇمۇلغا باردىم. 2009 - يىلى يەنە بىر قېتىم شىنجاڭغا باردىم. بۇ جەرياندا قەشقەر، خوتەن، ئالتاي، ۋە غۇلجىغا باردىم.
قىز: ئامېرىكىغا كېلىشىڭىزنىڭ مەقسىدى نېمە؟
ئوغۇل: يېقىندا فۇلبرايت ئوقۇش مۇكاپاتىغا ئېرىشىپ، ئىندىيانا ئۇنىۋېرسىتېتىغا بىر يىللىق زىيارەتچى ئوقۇغۇچى بولۇپ كەلدىم. بۇ يەردە دىسسېرتاتسىيەمنى ئىشلەۋاتىمەن. دىسسېرتاتسىيەمنىڭ ماۋزۇسى "ھازىرقى زامان ئۇيغۇر ئەدەبىياتىنىڭ تەرەققىيات مەسىلىلىرى".
قىز: كەلگۈسى پىلانلىرىڭىز ھەققىدە سۆزلەپ بەرسىڭىز.
ئوغۇل: مەن ئۇيغۇر تىلىغا ۋە ئۇيغۇر مەدەنىيىتىگە بەك ئامراق. كەلگۈسىدە داۋاملىق ئۇيغۇرلار ھەققىدە تەتقىقات قىلىشنى خالايمەن. مۇمكىن بولسا ئۇيغۇرلار ھەققىدە بىرنەچچە كىتاب يازىمەن.
قىز: ئەتە قۇربان ھېيت. قۇربان ھېيت مۇناسىۋىتى بىلەن ئۇيغۇرلارغا ئېيتىدىغان يۈرەك سۆزىڭىز بارمۇ؟
ئوغۇل: يۈرەك سۆزۈم بار. گۈزەل ئۇيغۇر تىلى يوقالمىسۇن. ئۇيغۇرلار مەڭگۈ ياشىسۇن!
قىز: رەھمەت!
ئوغۇل: ئەرزىمەيدۇ.

CHAPTER 4

Exercise 6.3

گۆشنىڭ سۆڭەكلىرىنى ئايرىپ شورپا قاينىتىمىز. شورپىنىڭ كۆپۈكىنى ئالىمىز. شورپىغا پىياز، پەمىدور ۋە تۇز سالىمىز. شورپا تەييار بولغىچە، پىياز، گۆش ۋە ئاشكۆكى توغرايمىز. ئاندىن قارىمۇچ، زىرە ۋە تۇز سېلىپ قىيما تەييارلايمىز. خېمىرغا تۇخۇم سېلىپ تۇزلۇقراق سۇدا يۇغۇرىمىز. خېمىرنى چەيلەيمىز. ئاندىن زۇۋۇلا ئۈزۈمىز. زۇۋۇلىنى ئالدى بىلەن قولدا چوڭايتىمىز، ئاندىن نوغۇچتا نېپىز يايىمىز. خېمىرنى يېيىپ بولغاندىن كېيىن قاتلاپ جىلىت كېسىمىز. ھەر بىر جىلىتنىڭ ئىچىگە ئاز - ئازدىن قىيما سېلىپ چۆچۈرە تۈگۈمىز. چۆچۈرىنى تۈگۈپ بولغاندىن كېيىن قايناۋاتقان شورپىغا سېلىپ، قازاننىڭ ئاغزىنى ياپىمىز. قازان قاينىغاندا ئاغزىنى ئېچىپ، ئوتنى پەسلىتىپ، چۆچۈرە پىشقۇچە يەنە ئۈچ - تۆت مىنۇت قاينىتىمىز. چۆچۈرە پىشقاندا چىنىگە ئۇسۇپ، ئاشكۆكى سېلىپ، يەيمىز.

Exercise 8.2

ئەر: نېمە ئىش قىلىۋاتىسەن؟
ئوغۇل: تونۇرغا ئوت سالماقچى.
ئەر: تونۇرغا ئوت سېلىپ نېمە ئىش قىلماقچى؟
ئوغۇل: سامسا ياقىمەن.
ئەر: سامسا... نەنىڭ سامسىسى بۇ؟
ئوغۇل: شىنجاڭنىڭ.
ئوغۇل: قوي گۆشى، پىياز، ئاندىن قارىمۇچ، تۇز، ئاندىن قىيما قىلىپ...
ئايال: ھازىر بۇ ئۇكىمىز نېمە قىلىۋاتىدۇ؟
ئوغۇل: جىلتە ئېچىۋاتىدۇ، جىلتە.... بىسمىللارەھمانىرىيىم، مانا... سامسا!
ئوغۇل: ھوييييييي! ئە(ر)كەك قوينىڭ سامسىسى، ھە!
ئوغۇل: سامسا يېقىۋاتامسىز، سامسا؟ ئەمتاخۇن، سامسىمۇ بۇ مانتىمۇ ؟
ئوغۇل: سامسا، سامسا!
ئوغۇل: يېقىڭە!
ئايال: سامسا بىلەن مانتىنىڭ نېمە پەرقى بار؟
ئوغۇل: سامسىنى قانداق پىشۇرىدا؟
سامسىپەز: سامسىنى تونۇردا پىشۇرىمىز؛
ئوغۇل: مانتىنى؟
سامسىپەز: مانتىنى قاسقاندا پىشۇرىمىز.
ئوغۇل:ھە، گەپ قىلىڭە، گەپ قىلىڭە!
ئوغۇل: مۇشۇنى يېقىپ بولغاندىن كېيىن ئوتتۇز مىنۇتتىن كېيىن ئاستا پىشىپ چىقىدۇ.
سامسىپەز: ھەسەنجان....
ئوغۇل: كەلسىلە خېرىدار، قومۇراپ بېرەي، سوغۇق سۇغا لىككىدە گومۇراپ بېرەي!
سامسىپەز: ھوييييت! ئۇستام ياقسا ئالمايتكەن، مانا بىزلا ياقساق قالمايدىكەن،.. ھە...
ئوغۇل: مانا، مانا، ھە ئەكەك قوينىڭ، ھوييييييت، ھوييييييت... ياغ دەريا سامسا، ھە، قالايمىقان
تۆتماڭلار...

Exercise 13.2

Excerpt 1:

شىنجاڭدا ساياھەت قىلىدىغان جايلار بەك كۆپ. مەسىلەن، تۇرپاندىكى ئىدىقۇت شەھرى ئەڭ داڭلىق. بۇ يەرگە تۇرپان شەھرىدىن ئىككى سائەتتە بىر جوڭبا ماڭىدۇ. قەشقەرگە بارىدىغانلار ئاپاق غوجا مازىرىغا بارىدۇ. مەھمۇت قەشقىرى مازىرى ھەم يۈسۈپ خاس ھاجىپ مەقبەرىسىگە چىقىدىغانلارمۇ جىق. ئۈرۈمچىدە ئاساسەن سەنشىخاڭزا ۋە ئەردوچوزىلاردا ئۇيغۇرلار كۆپ. يوخاۋ تەرەپلەردە شاڭچاڭلار جىق. چاۋشىلاردا جا... جا مال ناھايىتى ئاز. سودا قىلىشقا بەك ياخشى.

Excerpt 2:

مەن ئاتۇش شەھىرلىك 1 - ئوتتۇرا مەكتەپنى پۈتتۈرگەندىن كېيىن گاۋكاۋغا قاتناشتىم. ئەسلى بىرىنچى ئارزۇيۇم يىكى داشۆدە ئوقۇش ئىدى. كېيىن جوڭياڭ مىندادىن چاقىرىق كەلدى. شۇنىڭ بىلەن 2008 - يىلى بېيجىڭغا كەلدىم. ھازىرقى ئوقۇشۇم يەنە ئىككى يىلدىن كېيىن پۈتىدۇ. مۇمكىن بولسا يەنە داۋاملىق ھالدا يەنجۇشېڭ ۋە بوشى بولغىچە ئوقۇغۇم بار.

Excerpt 3:

ئاشخانىدا 18 ئادەم بار: ئىككى كاۋاپچى، بىر ناۋاي، بىر سامسىپەز، ئالتە فۇۋۇيەن، لەڭسەيخانىدا بىرەيلەن بار، چوڭ سەيخانىدا ئىككى، مەنجاڭخانىدا ئىككى، پېيسەيخانىدا ئۈچ.

CHAPTER 5

Exercise 13.1

باراڭدا، بۇ يەردە ھازىر ئالتە يەتتە خىل ئۈزۈم بار، بىزنىڭ مۇكەممەل بولغان ئۈزۈمدىن. بۇنىڭ ئىچىدە كىشمىش، قاشقىر، قىزىل ئۈزۈم، بىجاقىي، ھە، قاپاق سايىۋى، ئاندىن كېيىن غۇنچە ئۈزۈم قاتارلىقلاردىن، ئۈزۈملەردىن تەشكىللەنگەن. مانا ئەمدى كۆپىنچىسى مۇشۇ ساياھەتچىلىككە دەپ... ئومۇمەن دېھقانلار كىشمىشنى، يۈزدە توقسان پىرسەنت كىشمىشنى تىكىدۇ. نېمە ئۈچۈن دېسە كىشمىشنى ھۆل، قۇرۇق يېگىلى بولىدۇ، ھەم مۇكەممەل، ئۈزۈن ساقلىغىلى بولىدۇ.

Exercise 13.2

ئايال: مۇشۇ تۇرپاننىڭ ئۈزۈملىرىدىن تەييارلىنىدىغان ۋىنو ئىكەن.
ئەر: ھە، ۋىنو ، ھە، ھە....
ئايال: تۇرپاننىڭ ئۈزۈملىرى ناھايىتى مەشھۇر.
ئەر: تۇرى جىق. مەسىلەن، سىلەرنىڭ ئۇ قازاق تەرىپىدى، قازاقىستان تەرىپىدە، ئۆزەكلەرنىڭ كۆپىنچىسى كاۋكازدىن كىرىدۇ، كۆپىنچىسى گرۇزىيە تەرەپتىن كىرىدۇ، ئۆزەكلارنىڭ ئاز. بىز كۆپىنچىسى بىز چىقىرىدىغان، بىر مەزگىلدە، بىز چىقارغان. ھازىر سىلەر كۆپىنچىسى، قازاقىستان تەرەپتىن بىزگە كونۋېرت كىرىدۇ، كورۋېكا كىرىدۇ، بىز ۋىنونىڭ ياخشى ماتېرىياللىرىنى بىز ھازىر

بىر قىسمىنى چىقىرىش تەييارلىقىنى قىلىۋاتىمىز.

ئايال: قايسى ۋىنو ياخشى؟ ئاق ۋىنومۇ، قىزىلمۇ؟

ئەر: بىزنىڭ بۇ يەردە مەسىلەن، ئۈزۈملەردىن رىيسلىڭنىڭ بار، كابىرنو - سوبېرنيو كىينونىڭ بار، ما(ۋۇ) سابۇرىي دەيدىغان ئۈزۈملەردىن... مۇكەممەل ئەمدى، ياۋروپا ئۈزۈملىرى ئاساسىي جەھەتتىن بىزدە بار. بىزنىڭ قولىمىزدىكىسى ھازىرقىسى ماۋۇ رېيسلىڭنىڭ ماۋۇمۇ بولىدۇ، ئاندىن كېيىن ماۋۇ قىزىل گۈلنىڭمۇ بولىدۇ. ئايسۋاينمۇ بار. بۇ ھازىر قازاق تەرەپلەردە ئاز بۇ ھاراقلار. بۇنى "پۇتاۋجيۇ" دەپ قويىدۇ، بىزنىڭ بۇ يەردە. ئەمدى ياۋروپاچە "ئايسۋاين" دەپ، ھازىر كانادا... كانادانىڭ، ئاشۇ تەرەپلەرنىڭ كۆپرەك بوۋاتىدۇ (بولىۋاتىدۇ). مۇنداق، مۇز، سوغاق تېمپېراتۇرىدا ياسىغان.

ئايال: قىزىل ئۈزۈمدىن قىزىل ۋىنو، ئاق ئۈزۈمدىن ئاق ۋىنو، شۇنداقمۇ؟

ئەر: ھە، ئاشۇنداق چىقىدۇ. ئۈزۈمنىڭ تەركىبى ئوخشىمايدۇ. مەسىلەن، رېيسلىڭ دېگەن ئۈزۈم بارغۇ، ئاق كېلىدۇ، دۇنيادا داڭقى بار. ئۇنىڭدىن ئاق ئۈزۈم ھارىقى چىقىدۇ. بىزنىڭمۇ بار، مانا، رېيسلىڭ دەيدىغان. تېتىپ باقساڭلار بولىدۇ ئازراق. قىزىل گۈلنىڭمۇ بار، تېخى ياخشى.

ئايال: بۇ ۋىنولار چەتئەلگە چىقامدا؟

ئەر: ھە، يۆتكىگىلى بولىدۇ، لېكىن بىز ئىمپورت - ئېكسپورت قىلىپ چىقارمىدۇق. ھازىرچە كۆپىنچە كىشىلەر كېلىپ مۇشۇ يەردىن ئېلىپ كەتكەنلەر كۆپ.

ئايال: قايسى ۋىنونى بەكرەك ئالىدۇ؟

ئەر: قايسى تەرەپنىڭ؟ ياۋروپانىڭمۇ ياكى نەنىڭ؟

ئايال: ياۋروپانىڭ.

ئەر: ياۋروپانىڭ... ئادەتتە مۇشۇ "دراي رېد ۋاين" نى بەكرەك ئالىدۇ. مۇشۇنداق بىر قىزىل بىرى بار.

ئايال: ھە، قىزىلنى.

ئەر: قىزىلنى، شېكەرسىزنى.

Exercise 16.2

كارىز- بوستانلىقتىكى مۆجىزە. شۇنداقلا ئۇيغۇرلار ئەقىل پاراستىگە تايىنىپ ئىجاد قىلغان كەشپىيات. تۇرپاندا "ئەر ئۆلسە چىراق ئۆچىدۇ، كارىز ئۆلسە ئەل كۆچىدۇ" دېگەن ماقال بار. بۇ ئۇيغۇرلارنىڭ كارىزغا بولغان مۇھەببىتىنىڭ ناھايىتى چوڭقۇرلۇقىنى كۆرسىتىدۇ. تۇرپان قەدىمىي يىپەك يولىدىكى مۇھىم تۈگۈن. بۇ يەردە ناھايىتى قەدىمكى زاماندىن باشلاپ ئىنسانلار ياشىغان. تۇرپاننىڭ ياز پەسلى ناھايىتى ئىسسىق بولغاچقا، سۇنىڭ پارغا ئايلىنىش مىقدارى ئىنتايىن يۇقىرى. قەدىمكى ئۇيغۇرلار بۇنىڭ ئالدىنى ئېلىش ئۈچۈن سۇنى يەرنىڭ ئاستىدا ماڭدۇرۇش ئۇسۇلىنى ئىجاد قىلغان. جۇڭگو تارىخنامىلىرىدا تۇرپاندىكى كارىزلارنىڭ بۇنىڭدىن ئىككى مىڭ يىل ئىلگىرىلا مەۋجۇت بولغانلىقى ئېيتىلىدۇ. كارىز كۆپلىگەن يەر ئاستى قۇدۇقلىرىنى بىر بىرىگە ئۇلاپ ياسىغان يەر ئاستى ئۆستىڭى. بۇنىڭدا سۇ يەر ئاستىدا ئاقىدۇ ۋە سۇ پارغا ئايلانمايدۇ. تۇرپان كارىزلىرىدا ئاۋۋال يەردىن قۇدۇق كولىنىدۇ، ئاندىن ئاۋۋالقى قۇدۇق بىلەن كېيىنكى قۇدۇق يەر ئاستىدىن كولانغان ئېرىق ئارقىلىق بىرى بىرىگە ئۇلىنىدۇ. قۇدۇقلارنىڭ چوڭقۇرلۇقى ئوخشىمايدۇ. باش تەرەپتىكى قۇدۇقلار چوڭقۇرراق، كېيىنكىسى تېيىزراق بولىدۇ. تۇرپاندىكى ئەڭ ئۇزۇن كارىز 11 كىلومېتىر كېلىدۇ. بۇ كارىزدا ئىككى يۈزدىن ئارتۇق قۇدۇق بار. تۇرپاندىكى كارىزلارنىڭ ئومۇمىي ئۇزۇنلۇقى بەش مىڭ كىلومېتىردىن ئاشىدۇ. شۇڭا بەزىلەر ئۇنى "يەر ئاستى سەددىچىن سېپىلى" دەپ ئاتايدۇ.

CHAPTER 6

Exercise 8.1

كۈلالچىلىق - ئۇيغۇرلاردا ئۇزاق تارىخقا ئىگە ئەنئەنىۋى ھۈنەرلەرنىڭ بىرى. ئۇيغۇر كۈلالچىلىقىدا بارلىق ساپال بۇيۇملار قولدا ياسىلىدۇ. ساپال بۇيۇملارنى ياسايدىغان ئۇستىلار "كۈلالچى" دەپ ئاتىلىدۇ. كۈلالچىلار ئاۋۋال سېغىز توپىدا لاي ئېتىدۇ، ئاندىن ئۇچار چاق ئارقىلىق ساپال بۇيۇملار ياسىلىدۇ. كۈلالچىلار ھېچقانداق ئېلېكتىر ئەسۋابى ئىشلەتمەيدۇ. ئەمما ئۇلار ياسىغان ساپال بۇيۇملارنىڭ شەكلى چىرايلىق ۋە ئۆلچەملىك چىقىدۇ. ئۇيغۇرلاردىكى ساپال بۇيۇملارنىڭ شەكلى ئاددىي، ئەمما گۈزەللىك قىممىتى يۇقۇرى. ئۇيغۇر كۈلالچىلىقىدا قەدىمىي شەكىل ۋە ئۇسلۇپ كۆپ ئىشلىتىلىدۇ. رەڭ بېرىلگەن ساپال بۇيۇملار سەككىز يۈز سېلسىيە گرادۇسلۇق خۇمداندا ئۈچ - تۆت سائەت پىشۇرىلىدۇ. ئۇيغۇر ئۇستىلار ياسىغان ساپال بۇيۇملارغا دائىم گۈل- گىياھلارنىڭ رەسمى ياكى باشقا نەقىشلەر سىزىلىدۇ. ئۇيغۇرلار ئىسلام دىنىغا ئېتىقاد قىلىدىغان بولغاچقا، ساپال بۇيۇملارغا جانلىق ھايۋانلارنىڭ ۋە ئادەملەرنىڭ رەسمى سىزىلمايدۇ. ئۇيغۇر كۈلالچىلىقىدا ساپال بۇيۇملارغا كۆپىنچە بىر خىل رەڭ بېرىلىدۇ. كۆپىنچە جىگەر رەڭ، سېرىق رەڭ، توپا رەڭ، يېشىل رەڭ ئىشلىتىلىدۇ. بۇ رەڭلەر ئاساسەن تەبىئى مېنىرال ماددىلاردىن يەرلىك ئۇسۇلدا ياسىلىدۇ.

CHAPTER 7

Exercise 19

مېنىڭ ئىسمىم زۇلپىقار. مەن ئۇيغۇر. شىنجاڭ ئۇنىۋېرسىتېتىدا ئىشلەيمەن. شىنجاڭ ئۇنىۋېرسىتېتىدا ھاياتلىق ئىلمى ئىنىستىتۇتى، ئاخباراتشۇناسلىق ئىنىستىتۇتى، فىلولوگىيە ئىنىستىتۇتى قاتارلىق بىرقانچە ئىنىستىتۇتلار بار. مەن ئوقۇتىلىق قىلىپ ئۆزۈم بۇرۇن ئوقۇغان ھەم ئىشلىگەن فىلولوگىيە ئىنىستىتۇتى توغرۇلۇق توختىلاي. فىلولوگىيە ئىنىستىتۇتىدا تارىخ فاكۇلتېتى، فولكلور قاتارلىق بىرقانچە كەسپلەر بار. مەن 1992 - يىلدىن 1996 - يىلغىچە شۇ فىلولوگىيە ئىنىستىتۇتىدا ئوقۇغان. مەن ئوقۇغان ۋاقىتتا دەرسلەر ئۇيغۇرچە ئۆتۈلەتتى، ئىمتىھانلار ئۇيغۇرچە ئېلىناتتى. دەرسلەر، ھە، خېلى بىر تۈركۈم دەرسلەر ئۇيغۇرچە سۆزلىنەتتى.

ئەمما ھازىر دەرسلىك پىلانىدا ئۆزگىرىش بولغانلىق تۈپەيلىدىن ئاساسلىق دەرسلەر خەنزۇ تىلىدا ئۆتۈلىدىغان بولدى، ئىمتىھانلارمۇ خەنزۇ تىلىدا ئېلىپ بېرىلىدىغان بولدى. مەسىلەن، ھازىرقى ئەھۋالدا ئۇيغۇر ئەدەبىياتىدىن باشقا كەسپلەر ئاساسەن خەنزۇ تىلىدا ئۆتۈلىدۇ. بىز ئوقۇغان ۋاقىتتا، ھە، پۈتكۈل ئەدەبىيات، فولكلور دەرسلىرىنىڭ ھەممىسى ئۇيغۇرچە ئۆتۈلەتتى. دەرسلەر ئۇيغۇرچە سۆزلىنەتتى، ئىمتىھانلار ئۇيغۇرچە ئېلىناتتى. ھازىر بۇ ئەھۋالدا ئۆزگىرىش بولدى.

ھازىر ئوقۇغۇچىلارنىڭ كۆپىنچىسى خەنزۇچىنى ياخشى بىلىدۇ، دەرسلەرنىڭ كۆپىنچىسى خەنزۇچە ئۆتۈلىدۇ. ئەدەبىيات نەزەرىيەسى قاتارلىق دەرسلەر، فولكلور قاتارلىق دەرسلەر خەنزۇچە ئۆتۈلىدۇ. ئۇيغۇر ئەدەبىياتى قىسمىغا ئائىت بىر تۈركۈم ئاز ساندىكى دەرسلەر ئۇيغۇرچە ئۆتۈلىدۇ. ئەمما، ھە، قارىساق، مۇشۇ يىگىرمە يىلدىن بۇيان شىنجاڭ ئۇنىۋېرسىتېتىنىڭ قۇرۇلمىسىدا، شىنجاڭ ئۇنىۋېرسىتېتىنىڭ قارمىقىدىكى فىلولوگىيە ئىنىستىتۇتىنىڭ تەركىبىدە نۇرغۇن ئۆزگىرىشلەر بولدى: فاكۇلتېتلار ئىسلاھ قىلىندى؛ يېڭى - يېڭى كەسپلەر قېتىلدى؛ ئارىلىقتا فىلولوگىيە ئىنىستىتۇتىغا

جەمئىيەتشۇناسلىق فاكۇلتېتىمۇ قېتىلدى. ھازىر فىلولوگىيە ئىنستىتۇتىدا ئۇيغۇر ئەدەبىياتى بويىچە، ئۇيغۇر ھازىرقى زامان ئەدەبىياتى بويىچە، ئۇيغۇر كىلاسسىك ئەدەبىياتى بويىچە ، فولكلور كەسپى بويىچە ماگىستىرلىق، دوكتۇرلۇق تەربىيىلەش ئورۇنلىرى بار. يەنە شۇنداقلا پوست دوكتۇرلۇق ئورنىمۇ بار. ئۇ يەردە ھازىر دوكتۇر ئاسپىرانتلار، ماگىستىر ئاسپىرانتلار ئوقۇۋېدۇ. بىرقانچە ماگىستىرلىق تۈرى ئاسپىرانت تەربىيىلەش مەركەزلىرى بار، ئوقۇتقۇچىلار، ئوقۇغۇچىلارمۇ كۆپ. شىنجاڭ ئۇنىۋېرسىتېتىدا ھازىر تەخمىنەن يىگىرمە مىڭغا يېقىن ئوقۇغۇچى، ئون مىڭغا يېقىن ئوقۇتقۇچى ۋە باشقا ئىشچى - خىزمەتچىلەر بار.

CHAPTER 8

Exercise 24.1

گۈلچېھرە: مەن گۈلچېھرە. قانداق ئەھۋالىڭىز؟ قايتىدىن كۆرۈشۈپ قويايلى.
ئوقۇغۇچى: ياخشىمۇسىز!
گۈلچېھرە: ياخشى. بۇ مەكتەپتە ئوقۇۋاتامسىز؟
ئوقۇغۇچى: ھەئە، مەن مۇشۇ مەكتەپتە ئوقۇۋاتىمەن. سىز يېڭى ئوقۇغۇچى ئوخشىمامسىز؟
گۈلچېھرە: مەن مۇشۇ مەكتەپنى پۈتتۈرۈپ يېقىندا خىزمەتكە چىققان.
ئوقۇغۇچى: ھە، شۇنداقمۇ؟
گۈلچېھرە: سىزنى دوستۇم گۈلى تونۇشتۇرغانتى، شۇ مۇشۇ مەكتەپكە كېلىپ ئىزدىسىڭىز بولىدۇ دەپ. سىز ئىنگلىزچىنى ئۆگىنىۋېتىپسىز، ئاڭلىسام. بۇ جەھەتتىن ماڭا ياردەم بېرەلەمسىزكىن.
ئوقۇغۇچى: ئەلۋەتتە، قولۇمدىن كەلگىنىچە ياردەم قىلىمەن.
گۈلچېھرە: ئەمدى، سىزنىڭ ئوقۇشتىن باشقا خىزمەت ئىشلىرىڭىز بارمۇ ياكى بىكار ۋاقىتلىرىڭىز خېلى كۆپمۇ؟
ئوقۇغۇچى: ھە، بىكار ۋاقىتلىرىم بار، شۇ ۋاقىتلاردا ئۈچرىشىپ بىللە دەرس قىلساق بولىدۇ، بىر-بىرىمىزگە ياردەملىشەلەيسەك بولىدۇ.
گۈلچېھرە: بەك ياخشى بولدى. شەنبە، يەكشەنبە قانداق بولار؟
ئوقۇغۇچى: ھە بولىدۇ، سائەت قانچىلاردا بىكار بولىسىز، شەنبە يەكشەنبىدە؟
گۈلچېھرە: مېنىڭ ئادەتتە شەنبە كۈندە كىتابخانىغا بېرىپ ئانچە - مۇنچە ماتېرىيال كۆرىدىغان ئادىتىم بار. شەنبە كۈنى چۈشتىن كېيىنلىرى بىكار بولىمەن. شەنبە كۈنى ۋاقتىڭىز بولسا، بىرگە ئۈچراشساق، ئۆزئارا پىكىر ئالماشتۇرساق قانداق دەيسىز؟
ئوقۇغۇچى: ياخشى، بولىدىكەن... شەنبە چۈشتىن كېيىنلىرى ماڭىمۇ ناھايىتى مۇۋاپىق. شۇ ۋاقىتتا كۆرۈشسەك بولغۇدەك.
گۈلچېھرە: يەنە بىر نەرسىنى سوراپ باقسام، ھە، مەكتىپىڭلاردا (سىز ئوقۇۋاتقان ھازىرقى مەكتەپتە) بۈرۈن ئىنگلىزچە كلاس بوقتى. ھازىر بېكىدىن ئىنگلىزچە سىنىپ قېتىۋ. بۇ سىنىپنىڭ باھاسى قانچىلىك: بۇ قىممەتمۇ ياكى...؟
ئوقۇغۇچى: مەن ئۇنى ئېنىق ئۇقمايدىكەنمەن. مەكتەپنىڭ... بېشىدا... باشلانغاندا پۇلنى تۆلىگەنتۇق.
گۈلچېھرە: ئادەتتە سىز شەنبە، يەكشەنبە كۈنلىرىڭىزنى قانداق ئۆتكۈزىسىز؟

ئوقۇغۇچى: مەن شۇ دوستلىرىم بىلەن، ئۆيدىكىلەر بىلەن، ئۇنىڭدىن باشقا ۋاقتىم چىقسا دەرس تەييارلاپ، كىنو كۆرۈپ دېگەندەك شۇنداق ئۆتكۈزىمەن. بۇنىڭدىن كېيىن بىللە ئۆگىنىپ ياردەم قىلساق بىر - بىرىمىزگە، ياخشى بولىدۇ.
گۈلچېھرە: رەھمەت سىزگە، تونۇشقىنىمدىن بەك خوش بولدۇم.
ئوقۇغۇچى: مەنمۇ ناھايىتى خۇرسەن.
گۈلچېھرە: يەنە كۆرۈشەيلى.
ئوقۇغۇچى: ماقۇل.
گۈلچېھرە: تېلېفونلىرىمىزنى ئۆزئارا ئالماشتۇرۇۋالامدۇق؟
ئوقۇغۇچى: ئەلۋەتتە، مېنىڭ نومۇرۇم...

Exercise 24.3

گۈلچېھرە: ئاران ئۇچراشتۇق، بىر ھەپتە بوپتۇ كۆرۈشمىگىلى.
ئوقۇغۇچى: راست، مەنمۇ دەرسلەر بىلەن بەك ئالدىراش بولۇپ كەتتىم.
گۈلچېھرە: بىزنىڭ ئىشىمىزمۇ شۇنداق ئالدىراش. ئاران بىر شەنبە يەكشەنبە كەلدى، بىرەر يەرگە بېرىپ بىللە، پاراڭلىشىپ كەلسەك ياخشى بولامدىكىن دەيمەن.
ئوقۇغۇچى: ئەلۋەتتە ياخشى بولاتتى، سىزنىڭمۇ بىرەر پىكرىڭىز بارمۇ؟
گۈلچېھرە: ھىممم. مېنىڭچە كىنو كۆرۈپ كېلەمدۇق - يا؟
ئوقۇغۇچى: ئۇنداق قىلساقمۇ ياخشى بولىدىكەن. قايسى كىنولارنى قويۇۋاتقاندۇ؟
گۈلچېھرە: ئامېرىكىنىڭ "باتۇر يۈرەك" دېگەن بىر كىنوسىنى چىقىپتۇ دەيدۇ. شۇنى بىر كۆرسەك بولامدىكىن.
ئوقۇغۇچى: مەنمۇ ئاڭلىدىم شۇ كىنونى، شۇنداق ياخشى ئىشلىنىپتۇ دەپ. شۇنى كۆرۈپ كېلەيلى ئەمىسە. سائەت قانچىدىكەن؟
گۈلچېھرە: يەتتىدە بىرسى باركەن، توققۇزدا باركەن. قايسىنىڭغا بارساق بولار؟
ئوقۇغۇچى: خالىسىڭىز ھازىر تاماق ئېتىپ يەپ ئۆيدە، ئاندىن توققۇزدىكىسىگە بارساق قانداق بولار؟
گۈلچېھرە: تېخى ياخشى. مېنىڭمۇ قوسقىم ئاچتى.
ئوقۇغۇچى: پولۇ ئېتەيلى دەپ ئويلىغانتىم. سىز قانداق ئويلايسىز؟
گۈلچېھرە: بولىدۇ. ئۇنداق بولسا. سەۋزىنى مەن توغراپ بېرەي.
ئوقۇغۇچى: چاتاق يوق. مەن دۇملەيمەن. بىردەمدىلا قولمۇ - قول ئېتىۋېتىمىز. تاماقنى يەپ بولۇپ چىقىپ كىنو كۆرۈپ كېلەرمىز.
گۈلچېھرە:" تەڭ يېگەن تاماق تەنگە سىڭىدۇ"... ئەلۋەتتە، تېخىمۇ خوشاللىق بولىدۇ بىللە يېسەك... بىللە كىنو كۆرۈپ... ھە، كەچتە سىزنى ئۆزەم ئاپىرىپ قويىمەن ئۆيىڭىزگە، ئەنسىرىمەڭ. مەن ماشىنا ھەيدەپ ئاپىرىۋەتسەم بولىدۇ.
ئوقۇغۇچى: ئۇنداق قىلساق تېخى ياخشى بولىدىكەن.
گۈلچېھرە: ئەجەپ ياخشى. تاماققا تۇتۇش قىلايلى!
ئوقۇغۇچى: ماقۇل ئەمىسە، خوش!

CHAPTER 9

Exercise 16.2

خوتەندە ئۇيغۇر تىبابىتى باشقا رايونلارغا قارىغاندا نىسبەتەن تەرەققىي قىلغان. ئەمدى ئۇيغۇر تىبابىتىنىڭكى خوتەندە تېززاق تەرەققىي قىلىشىدىكى سەۋەب خوتەنلىكلەر دۇچ كەلگەن شۇ تەبىئى مۇھىتىنىڭكى سالامەتلىككە بولغان زىيىنى تۇپەيلىدىنمۇ ياكى باشقا سەۋەبلەر تۇپەيلىدىنمۇ تىبابەت نىسبەتەن بەكراق تەرەققىي قىلغان. ئۇندىن كېيىن خوتەنلىكلەرنىڭكى يېمەك- ئىچمەك ئادىتى، تۇرمۇش ئۇرپ - ئادىتى باشقا بوستانلىقلاردىن سەل پەرقلىنىدۇ. بۇ يەردىكى مۇھىم پەرقلەردىن بىرسى خوتەنلىكلەر يېمەك ئىچمەكتە ئاساسەن مۇشۇ مېۋە - چېۋە ئىستېمال قىلىشقا ئادەتلەنگەن. مېۋە - چېۋە ئىستېمال قىلغانلىق ۋە ئۇنىڭدىن كېيىن مۇشۇ گۆش ئىستىمالىغا نىسبەتەن بېرىلگەنلىك بىلەن نۇرغۇن ئادەمنىڭكى مۇشۇ تىبابەت بىلىملىرى ئومۇملاشقانلىقى تۇپەيلىدىنمۇ خوتەندە ئۇزۇن ئۆمۈر كۆرگۈچىلەر ئىنتايىن جىق كۆرۈلىدۇ. بىر ۋاقىتلاردا پۈتۈن جۇڭگودىكى ئۇزۇن ئۆمۈر كۆرگۈچىلەرنىڭ تەخمىنەن قىرىق پىرسەنتىگە يېقىنى خوتەن ۋىلايىتىگە يىغىلغان دېگەن مەلۇماتلارنى كۆرگەن. ھازىرغا نىسبەتەن خوتەن پۈتۈن جۇڭگودىكى ئۇزۇن ئۆمۈر كۆرگۈچىلەر ئەڭ جىق رايون دەپ قارىلىدۇ. بۇنداق بولۇشنىڭ سەۋەبى بىرسى تىبابەتنىڭ تەرەققىي قىلغانلىقى، ئىككىنچىسى، ئۇلىنىڭكى (ئۇلارنىڭكى) يېمەك - ئىچمەك ئادىتىدىكى ئۆزگىچىلىك، ئۈچىنچىسى، خوتەننىڭكى تەبىئي شارائىتىدىكى باشقا يەرلەرگە ئوخشىمايدىغان قىينچىلىق تۇپەيلىدىن مۇشۇنداق بىر ئالاھىدىلىك كېلىپ چىققان بولۇشى مۇمكىن دەپ ئويلايمەن.

Exercise 17

Part 1

مەن مۇشۇ ئۆزۈم بولسا ئابدۇغېنى. ئىككى مىڭ، بىر مىڭ توققۇز يۈز توقسەن تۆتىنچى يىلى خوتەن ئۇيغۇر تىبابەت ئالىي تېخنىكومىنى پۈتتۈرۈپ مۇشۇ ئۇيغۇر تىبابەت دوختۇرخانىسىغا خىزمەتكە چۈشتۈم. ئۇيغۇر تىبابەت دوختۇرخانىسىغا خىزمەتكە چۈشتۈم. بۇ جەرياندا مەن مۇشۇ ئۆزەم ھەم خىزمەت قىلىش ئارقىلىق مۇشۇ تۇرپاندا مۇشۇ قۇم ساھەسىگە قىزىقتىم. قۇم ساھەسىگە قىزىقىپ، قۇم بىلەن داۋالاشنىڭ شۇنداق قىممىتىنىڭ يۇقىرىلىقىنى ھېس قىلدىم. بۇ جەرياندا دەسلەپتە ئۇيغۇر تىبابەت بىلەن داۋالايدىغان بىر دورىلىق مۇنچا- شور مۇنچا دەپ بىر مۇنچا ئېچىش قارارىغا كېلىپ مۇشۇ ئىسسىق دورا-دەرمانلار بىلەن ئادەملەر خاھىشى بولغاندا كېلىپ يۇيىنىدىغان ئاشۇنداق ئىشلارنى ھاسىل قىلدىم. بۇنىڭغا بىر قىسىم مۇناسىۋەتلىك ئورۇنلاردىن رەسمىيەتلەرنى ئۆتەپ، پاتېنتلارنى ئېلىپ بىر زاۋۇت قۇردۇم. مۇشۇ جەرياندا مۇشۇ قۇم بىلەن داۋالاشنىڭ مۇھىملىقىنى ھېس قىلىپ، مۇشۇ 2006 - يىلى مەن ئۆز ئالدىمغا بىر مۇستەقىل مۇشۇ 200 مو قۇمنى بىر يەرگە ئېلىپ مۇشۇ بىر كۆرۈشۈپ ھەم مۇشۇ يىگىرمە مودەك قورو-جاينى ئۆزۈم مۇشۇ ئىقتىسادىم بىلەن سەپ (سېلىپ) بىر قورۇ جاي ھاسىل قىلدىم.

Part 2

بۇ جەرياندا مەن مۇشۇ ئون نەچچە يىلدىن بېرى مۇشۇ قۇم بىلەن داۋالاشنىڭ ئىنتايىن مۇھىملىقىنى بولۇپمۇ مۇشۇ رېماتىزىم، سوغۇقتىن بولغان رېماتىزىم، يەنى مۇشۇ سوغى (سوۋۇقى) ئېشىپ كەتكەنلىكتىن بولغان ھەر خىل يەل تېشىش، قىچىشىش، بەدەن سوغاپ (سوغۇلۇپ) كېتىش ھەم مۇشۇ شۇنداقلا مۇشۇ سوغى (سوۋۇقى) ئېشىپ كېتىشتىن بۆرەك ئاجىزلىقى دەيمىز، ساپ ئاياللار كېسەللىكلىرى بولسۇن، مۇشۇ قان بېسىمى يۇقىرىلىق قاتارلىق مۇشۇ بىر قىسىم سوغۇقتىن بولغان كېسەللىكلەرگە نىسبەتەن قۇمنىڭ ناھايىتى ئۇنۇمىنىڭ ياخشىلىقىنى ھېس قىلدىم.

Part 3

ھەم مۇشۇ قۇمغا چۈشۈش جەرياندا بىز قۇمغا چۈشكەن بىمارلاردىن، بولۇپمۇ قۇمغا چۈشكەندە دىققەت قىلىدىغان ئىشلار توغرىلىق ناھايىتى تولا ئاشۇ كەلگەن ئادەملەرنىڭ ھەممىسىگە چۈشەندۈرىمىز ھەم مۇشۇ قۇمغا چۈشكەندە ھاۋا ئىسسىق كۈنلەردە، بولۇپمۇ سائەت چۈشتىن، ئەتىگەن سائەت توققۇزدىن ئون بىرگىچە، چۈشتىن كېيىن بولسا سائەت ئۈچ يېرىمدىن مۇشۇ سەككىزلەرگە.. يەتتە سائەت... شىنجاڭ ۋاقتى سائەت يەتتىلەرگىچە مۇشۇ قۇمغا چۈشۈپ، چۈشىدىغانلىقىنى، ھەم بۇ قۇمغا چۈشكەن چاغدا بىر ئورۇندا ئون بەش مىنۇت يىگىرمە مىنۇت ئولتۇرۇپ يەنە بىر ئورۇنغا يۆتكىلىش كېرەكلىكى، ھەم مۇشۇ .. ئۇنداق قىلمىغان چاغدا سوغۇق ھاۋا بەدەنگە ئۆتۈپ كېتىپ بەلكىم رېماتىزىمنى مۇنداق قوزغاپ قويۇش ئېھتىماللىقى بارلىقىنى چۈشەندۈرىمىز. ھەم شۇنداقلا مۇشۇ يۈرىكى ئاجىز كىشىلەردە سائەت بەشتىن كېيىن چۈشۈشىنى يەنى سالقىن مۇنداق سالقىنراق، تولا سايىلىق يەردە چۈشۈشىنى ئۇلارغا نەسىھەت قىلىمىز ھەم مۇشۇ ئىشلارغا دىققەت قىلىشنى ئېيتىمىز. بولۇپمۇ قان بېسىمى تۆۋەن، قان ئاز، مۇشۇ بولۇپمۇ ئايال كىشىلەردە مۇشۇ قۇمغا چۈشكەندە ھە كۆپرەك مۇشۇ كەچلىكى چۈشۈشنى، بەك ئاجىزلاپ كەتكەن كىشىلەر ئىسسىق ۋاقىتتا چۈشكەندە كۆتۈرەلمەي بۇ ھېلىقى ھۇشىدىن كېتىدىغان ياكى ھۇشسىز بولۇپ كېتىدىغان ئەھۋاللار كېلىپ چىقىدۇ. شۇڭلاشقا بۇ ئىشلارنى ئالاھىدە چۈشەندۈرۈپ، بۇ توغرىلىق ئۇلارغا مەسلىھەتلەرنى بېرىمىز. يەنە مۇشۇ قۇمغا چۈشكەن چاغدا مۇشۇ يۈرىكى سالىدىغان، قان بېسىمى يۇقىرى كىشىلەر ئەمدى چۈشۈشكە ئالاھىدە دىققەت قىلمىسا بولمايدۇ. چۈنكى بۇنداق كېسەللەر چۈشكەن چاغدا يۈرەككە قان يېتىشمەيدىغان ياكى يۈرەك سىلىپ كېتىپ ئايلىنىپ كېتىدىغان ئىشلار كېلىپ چىقىدۇ. باشقا، قۇمغا كۆمۈلگەن چاغدا، بولۇپمۇ مۇشۇ كۆكرەك ساھەسىنىڭ ئاستىنقى قىسمىنى كۆمۈش كېرەك، چۈنكى ئۇنداق قىلمىغاندا مۇشۇ كۆكرەكنىڭ يۇقىرقى قىسمىنى كۆمگەندە يۈرەك، باشقا رەئىس ئەزالار بولغاچقا، ئۇلارنى كۆمگەن چاغدا ئۇ يەرلەر ئىسسىقلىققا چىدالماي يا ئايلىنىپ كېتىدىغان ياكى كۆڭلى ئاينىپ بىئارام بولىدىغان ئىشلار كېلىپ چىقىدۇ. شۇڭلاشقا بۇ ئىشلارغا ئالاھىدە دىققەت قىلىمىز. بولۇپمۇ بەدەننىڭ تۆۋەن قىسمىنى، كۆكرەك قىسمىنىڭ ئاستى قىسمىنى كۆمۈش ھەمدە ئون بەش يىگىرمە مىنۇتتىن ئوشۇق بىر ئورۇندا ئولتۇرماسلىق ھەمدە يۆتكىلىپ كۆمۈلۈش دېگەندەك ئەھۋاللارنى ئالاھىدە چۈشەندۈرىمىز.

Part 4

- بۇ سىڭلىمىز كىم ؟

- بۇ سىڭلىمىز يېڭى كەلگەن، مۇشۇ غۇلجىدىن كەلگەن بىمار. مۇشۇ پۇتى ئاغرىپ، رېماتىزىم تەسرىدىن داۋالىنىشقا كەلگەن. ئەمدى ئىككى- ئۈچ كۈن بولدى، ئەمدى مۇشۇ قۇمغا چۈشۈپ ئاز تولا دارىلارنى يەپ ئۆزى مۇنداق قۇمغا چۈشۈپ داۋالىنىۋاتىدۇ.

Part 5

مۇشۇ قۇمغا چۈشكەن بىمارلارنى، مەسىلەن: بىز قۇمغا چۈشۈشتىن بۇرۇن ئالدىن سالامەتلىكنى تەكشۈرەپ (تەكشۈرۈپ)، چۈشۈشكە كېرەكمۇ - كېرەك ئەمەسمۇ... بۇ ئەھۋالنى تېپ (تېپىپ) بولغاندىن كېيىن، قۇمغا چىققان چاغدا مۇشۇ بىمارلارغا ئىسسىق مايلاردىن بېرىپ مايلاشقا بېرىمىز. ئۇ مايلارنى پۇتلىرىغا قۇمنىڭ ئۈستىگە چىقىپ سۈرۈپ، ئون يىگىرمە مىنۇت بەدەنگە سىڭدۈرغاندىن كېيىن قۇمغا قايتىپ چۈشۈپ مۇشۇ دارىنىڭ (دورىنىڭ)، قىممىتىنىڭ مۇشۇ پايدىلىق ئۈنۈمدارلىقىنى ئاشۇرىدۇ. بۇ ئارقىلىق ئۆزىنىڭ كېسىلىگە شىپالىق تەسىرىنىڭ ناھايىتى تېززەك بولىدىغانلىقىنى ھېس قىلىپ شۇڭلاشقا مايلارنى ئىشلىتىدۇ، ئىسسىق دورىلارنى يەيدۇ، ئۆزىگە مۇناسىۋەتلىك دورىلارنى يەپ داۋالىنىپ كېتىدۇ. ئەمدى مۇشۇ قۇمغا كىرىشنىڭكى داۋالىنىش باسقۇچى بولۇپ، ئەڭ ئاز بولغاندا ئون بىر كۈن، قۇمغا چۈشكەن كىشىلەر ئون بىر كۈن، ئون بەش كۈن... ئون ئۈچ ... ئون بىر كۈن، ئون ئۈچ كۈن، ئون بەش كۈن، ھەتتا 21 كۈن چۈشۈپ بىر داۋالىنىش كۇرسى دەپ قايتقان بىمارلار ئاشۇلارغا ناھايىتى دىققەت قىلىدۇ. ئەمدى قۇمغا چۈشكەن كېسەللەر ئەمدى بىرىنچى يىلى ئون بىر كۈن، ئىككىنچى يىلى ئون ئۈچ كۈن، ئۈچىنچى يىلى ئون بەش كۈن مۇنداق چۈشىدىغان ئەھۋاللارمۇ بار.

CHAPTER 11

Exercise 9.1

خوتەن ۋىلايىتى شىنجاڭ ئۇيغۇر ئاپتونوم رايونىدىكى يەر كۆلىمى ئەڭ چوڭ رايونلارنىڭ بىرسى. شىنجاڭدىكى يەر كۆلىمى ئەڭ چوڭ رايون بايىنغولىن موڭغۇل ئاپتونوم ئوبلاستى، ئىككىنچىسى خوتەن ۋىلايىتى. خوتەن ۋىلايىتىنىڭكى ئومۇمىي نوپۇسى ئىككى مىليونغا يېقىن. بۇ يەردە 96 % دىن 97 % گە قەدەر ئادەم(لەر) پۈتۈنلەي ئۇيغۇرلار ئولتۇراقلاشقان. ئۇ شىنجاڭ ئۇيغۇر ئاپتونوم رايونىنىڭكى جەنۇبى قىسمىغا جايلاشقان. خوتەن ۋىلايىتى مۇشۇ دۆلەتلەردىن ھىندىستان، پاكىستاننىڭ بىر قىسىم جايلىرى بىلەن چېگرىلانسا، ئۆلكىلەردىن مۇشۇ تىبەت بىلەن چېگرىلىنىدۇ. ئەمدى خوتەن ۋىلايىتىنىڭكى پۈتكۈل زېمىن كۆلىمىدىن قارىغان ۋاقتىنىڭ ئۆزىدە بوستانلىق كۆلىمى بىلەن چۆل كۆلىمىنى سېلىشتۇرغاندا بوستانلىقنىڭ نىسبىتى ئىنتايىن تۆۋەن. لېكىن، ئاھالە زىچلىقى مەملىكەت بويىچە ئىنتايىن يۇقىرى. دېھقانلارغا كىشى بېشىغا توغرا كېلىدىغان تېرىلغۇ يەر كۆلىمى شىنجاڭ ئۇيغۇر ئاپتونوم رايونىدا نىسبەتەن ئاز ھېسابلىنىدۇ. گەرچە يەر جىق بولغان بىلەن، خوتەن سۈيى نىسبەتەن قىس رايون. ئۇنىڭدىن كېيىن، خوتەننىڭكى ئاھالىكىدىن ئېلىپ ئېيتقان ۋاقتىنىڭ ئۆزىدە، خوتەننىڭكى جۇغراپىيەلىك ئاھىدىلىكى شىنجاڭنىڭ باشقا رايونلىرىدىن سەل پەرقلىنىدۇ.

خوتەن نىسبەتەن ئىسسىق. ئىسسىق بولۇش بىلەن بىرگە ئۇ يەر ئىنتايىن قۇرغاق. قۇرغاق بولغانلىقى تۈپەيلىدىن بىر يىلدىكى 365 كۈننىڭكى تەخمىنەن 150 كۈنى، 200 كۈنى ئەتراپىدا خوتەندە توپا ياغىدىغان ئەھۋال بار. خوتەننىڭكى تېلېۋىزىيە ئىستانسىسىدا ھاۋارايىدىن مەلۇمات بەرگەن ۋاقىتنىڭ ئۆزىدە "خوتەندە سۇس توپا ياغىدۇ" دېگەندەك مەلۇماتلار بېرىلىدۇ.

CHAPTER 12

Exercise 6.4

مىشەدە بىر كويكەن پايپاق،
ئى يەدە قىممەتكەن پايپاق،
ئا(ل)غانلار ئېپ بولدى پايپاق،
ئا(ل)مىغانلار خاپ (خاپا) بولدى،
پايپاق.
ئانىغا پايپايق بىر كويما،
دادىغا پايپاق بىر كويما،
ئاھ باللا، جېنىم باللا،
پايپاق بىر كويكەن باللا،
پايپاق نوچىكەن باللا،
پايپاق گاڭگۇڭكەن باللا،
مىشەگە كېلىۋېلىڭلا باللا،
مىشەدە بىر كويكەن پايپاق،
ئى يەدە قىممەتكەن پايپاق،
ئا(ل)غانلار ئەپ بولدى پايپاق.
ئا(ل)مىغانلار خاپ (خاپا) بولدى،
پايپاق.
ئاھ باللا، جېنىم باللا،
پايپاق بىر كويكەن باللا،
پايپاق نوچىكەن باللا،
پايپاق گاڭگۇڭكەن باللا،

ئىشەدە ئىككى كويكەن پايپاق،
مىشەدە بىر كويكەن پايپاق،
ئى يەردە ئىككى كويكەن پايپاق،
مىشەدە بىر كويكەن پايپاق.
ئاھ باللا، جېنىم باللا،
پايپاق ئې(لى)ۋې(لى)ڭلا باللا،
پايپاق بىر كويكەن باللا،
پايپاق ھەر خىلكەن باللا،
ئالغانلار ئېپ بولدى پايپاق،
ئا(ل)مىغانلار خاپ (خاپا) بولدى،
پايپاق،
ئانىغا پايپاق بىر كويما،
دادىغا پايپاق بىر كويما،
ھەر خىل پايپاق بىر كويما،
ھەر ياڭزا پايپاق بىر كويما،
ئانىغا پايپاق بىر كويما،
دادىغا پايپاق بىر كويما،
ئاھ باللا، جېنىم باللا،
پايپاق بىر كويكەن باللا،
پايپاق نوچىكەن باللا،
پايپاق گاڭگۇڭكەن باللا...

Exercise 19.1

خوتەن قول سانائىتى ئىنتايىن تەرەققىي قىلغان يۇرت. خوتەن تارىختىن بۇيان ئۆزىنىڭكى گىلەملىرى بىلەن ئىنتايىن مەشھۇر. ھازىر پۈتۈن شىنجاڭدىكى گىلەمچىلىك بازىسى ھېسابلىنىدۇ. بۇ يەردىكى مۇشۇ گىلەمچىلىك ھازىرغا قەدەر ماشىنىلاشمىغان، پۈتۈنلەي قول ھۈنىرىگە تايىنىپ ئىشلىنىدۇ. شۇڭا بەزىلەر مۇشۇ خوتەندە قولدا توقۇلغان گىلەملەرنى جۇڭگودىكى سەددىچىن سېپىلى ياكى باشقا قۇرۇلۇشلار بىلەن سېلىشتۇرۇشقا بولىدىغان بىر خىل ئەمگەك دەپ قارايدۇ. ئەمدى خوتەننى تىلغا ئېلىشقا بولىدىغان ئىككىنچى بىر ئالاھىدە مەھسۇلات خوتەننىڭ ئەتلەسلىرى.

خوتەندە مۇشۇ پىلە يېپەك توقۇمىچىلىقى ئۇزۇن تارىخقا ئىگە، شۇڭا خوتەندە مۇشۇ ئەتلەسچىلىك ئۆزىگە خاس بىر خىل يەرلىك يېنىك سانائەت ياكى قول سانائەتنى كەلتۈرۈپ چىقارغان. بۇلارىن باشقا خوتەندە ھەرخىل تۇرمۇشقا كېرەكلىك بولغان نەرسىلەرنىڭ ھەممىسىنى ئۆزى ئىشلەپ ئۆزى تەمىنلەيدىغان بىر ھالەتنى بارلىققا كەلتۈرگەن. بۇنداق بولۇشىدىكى سەۋەب خوتەن بوستانلىقى مۇشۇ تەكلىماكان ئويمانلىقى بىلەن قاراقۇرۇم تاغلىرىنىڭ ئوتتۇرىسىغا جايلاشقان بىر ئارالغا ئوخشايدىغان جاي. ھازىر قاتناشنىڭ قولايلىق بولۇپ كەتكەنلىكى تۈپەيلىدىن خوتەنگە بارماق نىسبەتەن ئوڭاي. بۇرۇنقى ۋاقىتلاردا، بولۇپمۇ ماشىنا قاتنىشى بارلىققا كەلمىگەن ۋاقىتلاردا خوتەندىن ئايرىلىپ ئىككىنچى بىر بوستانلىققا بېرىش ئۈچۈن يىگىرمە كۈندەك ۋاقىت كېتەتتى. ھازىر مۇشۇ سەۋەبتىن خوتەنلىكلەرنىڭكى مۇشۇ ھەممە نەرسىلەرنى ئۆزى ئىشلەپچىقىرىپ ئۆزى تەمىنلەيدىغان بىر خىل يەرلىك ئالاھىدىلىكنى بارلىققا كەلتۈرگەن دەپ قاراشقا بولىدۇ.

Exercise 20.1

خوتەندە باغۋەنچىلىك ئىنتايىن تەرەققىي قىلغان. پۈتكۈل شىنجاڭ ئۇيغۇر ئاپتونوم رايونىغا داڭلىق بولغان مېۋىلەردىن ياڭاق بار. ئەمدى ياڭاقچىلىق ئادەتتە خوتەننىڭكى تۈۋرۈك كەسپىلىرى ھېسابلىنىدۇ. لېكىن ياڭاقتىن باشقا يەنە ئۆرۈك، ئانار، چىلان قاتارلىق مېۋىلەرمۇ خوتەننىڭكى نىسبەتەن غوللۇق مېۋىلىرى ھېسابلىنىدۇ. لېكىن دەپ قويۇشقا تېگىشلىككە بىر ئالاھىدىلىك، خوتەندە مۇشۇ شىنجاڭ ئۇيغۇر ئاپتونوم رايونىدا تېرىشقا ماس كېلىدىغان ھەرقانداق مېۋە - چېۋىنى تاپقىلى بولىدۇ. مەسلەن، تۇرپاننى "ئۈزۈمچىلىك ماكانى" دەيدۇ. لېكىن پۈتكۈل تۇرپاندىكى ئۈزۈمچىلىكنىڭ كۆلىمىنى يىغسا، خوتەندىكى ئۈزۈمچىلىككە تەڭ كەلمەيدۇ. يېقىندىن بۇيان خوتەندە مۇشۇ چىلان تېرىش، بولۇپمۇ سورتى ياخشى چىلانلارنى تېرىش بارلىققا كەلدى.

بۇ چىلانلارنىڭ قەنت تەركىۋى ئىنتايىن يۇقىرى، دانىسى يوغان، بازاردا ناھايىتى قارشى ئېلىنىدۇ. شۇڭا خوتەننى باغۋەنچىلىك ئىنتايىن تەرەققىي قىلغان يۇرت، دەپ قاراشقا بولىدۇ. ئەمدى خوتەننىڭ باغۋەنچىلىكىنىڭكى تەرەققىي قىلىشتىكى سەۋەب خوتەندە مۇشۇ سۇ قىس بولغانلىقى تۈپەيلىدىن يېزا ئىگىلىك مەھسۇلاتلىرىنىڭ مول ھوسۇلى نىسبەتەن تۆۋەن.

شۇڭا خوتەنلىكلەر باغۋەنچىلىكنى تەرەققىي قىلدۇرۇشقا تايىنىپ كۈچەيگەن. ئاندىن كېيىن يەر ئاز، سۇ قىس بولغانلىقى تۈپەيلىدىن دېھقانچىلىققىلا تايىنىپ قالسا، تۇرمۇشى بارغانسېرى نامراتلىشىپ كېتىدۇ. شۇڭا ئۇلار يېزا ئىگىلىكىگە تايىنىشتىن باشقا يەنە ھوسۇلى نىسبەتەن ياخشى، كىرىمى يۇقىرى بولغان باغۋەنچىلىكنى ئۆزىنىڭكى مۇھىم بىر ئالاھىدىلىكى قىلىپ تاللىغان. شۇڭا خوتەننىڭ ھەرقانداق بىر جايىغا بارسا، بىر باغ تېپىش مۇمكىن. خوتەندە ئومۇمەن يېرى بار ھەرقانداق بىر ئائىلە چوڭ بولسۇن، كىچىك بولسۇن، بىرەر بېغى بولىدۇ.

Uyghur - English Glossary ئۇيغۇرچە - ئىنگلىزچە لۇغەت

Note: The right columns precedes the left column on each page.

	ئا
to take, to carry	ئاپارماق
disaster	ئاپەت
famous	ئاتاقلىق
mounted	ئاتلىق
to name; to be dedicated to	ئاتىماق
unusual; very	ئاجايىپ
weakness	ئاجىزلىق
key	ئاچقۇچ
covetous	ئاچكۆز
to search	ئاختۇرماق
finally	ئاخىرى
buddy	ئاداش
habit	ئادەت
to make a habit	ئادەت قىلماق
to be used to	ئادەتلەنمەك
fair	ئادىل
barley	ئارپا
extra	ئارتۇق
superfluity	ئارتۇقچىلىق
wish, desire	ئارزۇ
to wish	ئارزۇلىماق
to mix	ئارىلاشتۇرماق
to lend	ئارىيەتكە بەرمەك
minority groups	ئاز سانلىق مىللەت
free	ئازاد
to decrease in number	ئازايماق
in accordance with	ئاساسلانماق
to be a priority	ئاساسلىق ئورۇندا تۇرماق
flammable	ئاسان كۆيىدىغان
graduate student	ئاسپىرانت

gradually	ئاستا- ئاستا
to preserve; take good care of	ئاسرىماق
hanging carpet	ئاسما گىلەم
cook, chef	ئاشپەز
coriander, cilantro	ئاشكۆكى
to increase	ئاشماق
to cause pain	ئاغرىتماق
friend	ئاغىنە
to tie on white (to show mourning)	ئاق باغلىماق
kind, sincere	ئاق كۆڭۈل
to turn white	ئاقارماق
to flow, to leak	ئاقماق
consequence; result	ئاقىۋەت
to warn	ئاگاھلاندۇرماق
to contact	ئالاقىلاشماق
special	ئالاھىدە
to glare at	ئالايماق
to pass away	ئالەمدىن ئۆتمەك / تۈگەپ كەتمەك / ۋاپات بولماق / كۆز يۇمماق / قازا قىلماق
gold	ئالتۇن
to replace	ئالماشماق
to change	ئالمىشىش
higher education	ئالىي مائارىپ
your Majesty	ئالىيلىرى
solution	ئامال
security	ئامانلىق قوغدىغۇچى
public gathering	ئاممىۋى يىغىلىش
pomegranate	ئانار
inhabitants	ئاھالە
prosperous	ئاۋات

we will see	بىر گەپ بولار
a lot	بىر مۇنچە
to sit idle	بىكار تۇرماق
bracelet	بىلەيزۈك
architecture	بىناكارلىق
directly	بىۋاستە
direct relative	بىۋاستە تۇغقان
پ	
to fit	پاتماق
talk/chat	پاراڭ
exploding	پارتلايدىغان
piece; a measure word for book	پارچە
to be revealed	پاش بولماق
cleanliness	پاكىزلىك
axe	پالتا
to put out the welcoming carpet	پاyانداز سالماق
a capital city	پايتەخت
benefit	پايدا - مەنپەئەت
to have good effect; get a profit	پايدا قىلماق
useful, beneficial	پايدىلىق
to be proud of	پەخىرلەنمەك
to be on a diet	پەرھىز تۇتماق
moral character	پەزىلەت
gloves	پەلەي
badminton	پەي توپ
splendid, wonderful	پەيز/پەيزى
Prophet	پەيغەمبەر
smell	پۇراق
opportunity	پۇرسەت
for having an opportunity	پۇرسەت چىقماق
to take advantage of an opportunity	پۇرسەتتىن پايدىلانماق
do not loose a chance	پۇرسەتنى قولدىن بەرمەڭ
to pay	پۇل تاپشۇرماق

pocket knife	بەكە
to determine (to do something)	بەل باغلىماق
mark, emblem	بەلگە
oasis	بوستانلىق
to slaughter	بوغۇزلىماق
dyestuff, tincture	بوياق
single	بويتاق
to obey	بويسۇنماق
according to	بويىچە
to dye	بويىماق
during this time	بۇ جەرياندا
as before	بۇرۇنقىدەك
damage	بۇزغۇنچىلىق
to get broken	بۇزۇلۇپ قالماق
wheat	بۇغداي
spring	بۇلاق
robbery	بۇلاڭچىلىق
polluted	بۇلغانغان
so much	بۇنچىۋالا
kidney	بۆرەك
cradle	بۆشۈك
section	بۆلمە
flourishing	بۈك- باراقسان
alfalfa	بېدە
to decorate	(-نى) بېزىمەك
to occupy	بېسىۋالماق
to be dedicated to	(-غا) بېغىشلانماق
petrol, benzene	بېنزىن
to be disturbed, to be concerned	بىئارام بولماق
poor; unfortunate	بىچارە
safety belt	بىخەتەرلىك تاسمىسى
evil ways (in Islam)	بىدئەت
to dispose	بىر تەرەپ قىلماق
in association, as one	بىر تۇتاش
at one moment	بىر تۇرۇپ

messenger, matchmaker	ئەلچى
farewell	ئەلۋىدا
hard working	ئەمگەك
hard working	ئەمگەكچان
reality, practice	ئەمەلىيەت
tradition	ئەنئەنە
fig	ئەنجۈر
to anxious	ئەندىشە قىلماق
to worry	ئەنسىرىمەك
to pay attention	ئەھمىيەت بەرمەك
superiority	ئەۋزەللىك
generation	ئەۋلاد
AIDS	ئەيدىز
ب	
brave	باتۇر
pigeon soup	باچكا تاڭ
almond	بادام
trellis	باراڭ
to come into existence	بارلىققا كەلمەك
to put out for sale, to sell, to peddle	بازارغا سالماق
a stage, step	باسقۇچ
leader, manager	باشقۇرغۇچى
invitation	باغاق
to tie	باغلىماق
gardener	باغۋەن
to raise; to take care of	باقماق
calamity	بالا- قازا
hospital	بالنىست / كېسەلخانا / دوختۇرخانا
bank account	بانكا ھېساباتى
to value	باھالىماق
just now	باياتىن
to exercise	بەدەن چېنىقتۇرماق
physical capability	بەدەن قۇۋۋىتى
to ruin, to destroy	بەربات قىلماق
striped heavy silk	بەقەسەم

to bother	ئاۋارە قىلماق
aviation	ئاۋىئاتسىيە
related to	ئائىت
family member	ئائىلە ئەزاسى
spiralling road	ئايلانما يول
to revolve; to become	ئايلانماق
ئە	
to provide a ride	ئەپچىقىپ قويماق
a pity	ئەپسۇس
unfortunatly	ئەپسۇسكى
regrettable, unfortunate	ئەپسۇسلىنارلىق
to apologize	ئەپۇ سورىماق
around	ئەتراپ
valuable, precious	ئەتىۋارلىق
eccentric	ئەجەب
badly behaved, immoral	ئەخلاقسىز
rubbish	ئەخلەت
trash bin	ئەخلەت ساندۇقى
manners; etiquette	ئەدەب- ئەخلاق
impolite, rude	ئەدەبسىز
a literary work	ئەدەبىي ئەسەر
spirit, ghost	ئەرۋاھ
member	ئەزا
since long ago	ئەزەلدىن
to recall	ئەسكە كەلمەك
work	ئەسەر
to remind somebody of something	ئەسلەتمەك
century	ئەسىر
to capture	ئەسىر ئالماق
intelligence, perceptiveness	ئەقىل - پاراسەت
to reflect	ئەكس ئەتمەك
opposite of	ئەكسىچە
to follow	ئەگەشمەك

iron	تۆمۈر
railway	تۆمۈريول
to contribute	تۆھپە قوشماق
type	تۈر
group	تۈركۈم
jail	تۈرمە
to spit	تۈكۈرمەك
to pass away	تۈگەپ كەتمەك / ئالەمدىن ئۆتمەك/ ۋاپات بولماق / كۆز يۇمماق / قازا قىلماق
knot	تۈگۈن
ten thousand	تۈمەن
even more	تېخىمۇ
more	تېخىمۇ كۆپ
folk doctor	تېۋىپ
folk medicine	تىبابەت
medicine, therapy	تىبابەتچىلىك
to study hard	تىرىشىپ ئۆگەنمەك
to register	تىزىملاتماق
to register	تىزىملىتىپ قويماق
tailor	تىككۈچى
to mention	تىلغا ئالماق
to wish	تىلىمەك
peace	تىنچلىق
ج	
to get prepared	جابدۇنماق
a punishment, penalty	جازا
to be punished	جازالانماق
bravery	جاسارەت
spoken language	جانلىق تىل
stubborn	جاھىل
to be responsible	جاۋابكار بولماق
to be located	جايلاشماق
schedule	جەدۋەل
to fine	جەرىمانە قويماق
process	جەريان
corpse	جەسەت

belonging	تەۋە
an heirloom, cherished	تەۋەررۈك
to recommend	تەۋسىيە قىلماق
preparation	تەييارلىق
to gather	توپلىماق
to be gathered	توپلاشماق
agreement	توختام
net	تور
ceiling	تورۇس
hindrances	توسقۇنلۇق
partition	توسما
rabbit	توشقان
to carry, to transport	توشۇماق
to think it right	توغرا تاپماق
to cut	توغرىماق
a sort of bread	توقاچ
weaving, knitting	توقۇمىچىلىق
to fill	تولدۇرماق
undergraduate	تولۇق كۇرس
high school	تولۇق ئوتتۇرا مەكتەپ
tandoor	تونۇر
to introduce	تونۇشتۇرماق
a letter of introduction, recommendation	تونۇشتۇرۇش خېتى
get to know	تونۇشماق
to get acquainted	تونۇشۇۋالماق
to marry	توي قىلماق
to connect	تۇتاشماق
life necessity	تۇرمۇش ئېھتىياجى
to be born	تۇغۇلماق
fur hat	تۇماق
the first time	تۇنجى قېتىم
sense, feeling	تۇيغۇ
to feel	تۇيماق
to throw out, pour out	تۆكمەك
camel	تۆگە

to see the fun, to watch the entertainment	تاماشا كۆرمەك
the customs	تاموژنا
to invite someone to dance	تانسغا تارتماق
coffin	تاۋۇت
natural science	تەبئى پەن
natural	تەبئىي
to research	تەتقىقات قىلماق
experience	تەجرىبە
approximately	تەخمىنەن
to develop (something)	تەرەققىي قىلماق
sequence	تەرتىپ
discipline	تەرتىپ - ئىنتىزام
translation	تەرجىمە
to translate	تەرجىمە قىلماق
biography	تەرجىمىھال
to expressing condolences	تەزىيە بىلدۈرمەك/ كۆڭۈل ئېيتماق
to comfort, placate	تەسەللى بەرمەك
to imagine	تەسەۋۋۇر قىلماق
to be approved	تەستىقلانماق
influence	تەسىر
to affect	تەسىر قىلماق
to influence	تەسىر كۆرسەتمەك
to constitute	تەشكىل قىلماق
destiny, fate	تەقدىر
to distribute	تەقسىملىمەك
to investigate	تەكشۈرمەك
to emphasize, stress	تەكىتلىمەك
request	تەلەپ
to request	تەلەپ قىلماق
luck	تەلەي
fortunately	تەلەيگە يارىشا
to teach	تەلىم بەرمەك
to provide, supply	تەمىنلىمەك
to consent to	تەن بەرمەك

to graduate	پۈتتۈرمەك
whole	پۈتۈن
completely	پۈتۈنلەي
knife-maker or seller	پىچاقچى
to make threads from silk worm	پىلىدىن يىپ ئېگىرمەك
on foot	پىيادە
pedestrian	پىيادىلەر
ت	
to instruct, to urge	تاپىلىماق
banging, crashing	تاراق - تۇرۇق
since then	(... دىن) تارتىپ
to argue	تارتىشماق
shy	تارتىنچاق
to feel embarrassed	تارتىنماق
to be dispersed	تارقالماق
speed of spreading	تارقىلىش سۈرئىتى
very; clean	تازا
to clean / wash	تازىلىماق
accidental	تاسادىپىي
stone	تاش
abondoned land	تاشلانغان ماكان
to drop, throw away, cast	تاشلىماق
highway	تاشيول
sack	تاغار
single; odd	تاق
to close; to lock	تاقىماق
to take a taxi	تاكسى توسماق
Taxi Service	تاكسى شىركىتى
waiter	تاڭجاڭ
to argue	تالاشماق
to choose	تاللاپ بەرمەك
to choose	تاللىماق
wall carpet	تام گىلىمى
to enjoy (oneself in), to have fun	تاماشا قىلماق

to live in ease	راھەت كۆرمەك
to speak fluently	راۋان سۆزلىمەك
to put into order	رەتلىمەك
cloth	رەخت
small, narrow street with shops	رەستە
officially	رەسمىي شەكىلدە
to go through the formalities	رەسمىيەت ئۆتىمەك
color	رەڭ
to get angry at	رەنجىمەك
late (refers to a deceased person)	رەھمەتلىك
to fast	روزا تۇتماق
the Ramadan festival	روزا ھېيت
a small glass cup	رومكا
to flourish	روناق تاپماق
spirit, soul	روھ
spiritual world	روھىي دۇنيا
mental state	روھىي ھالەت
prescription; recipe	رېتسېپ
to repair	رېمونت قىلماق
to pay attention to, to comply with, to observe	رىئايە قىلماق
competition	رىقابەت
legend	رىۋايەت
ز	
actually, really	زادى
to mock	زاڭلىق قىلماق
to make fun of	زاڭلىق قىلماق/ مازاق قىلماق
poison	زەھەر
to poison	زەھەرلىمەك
olive	زەيتۇن
to force	زورلىماق
necessity	زۆرۈرىيەت
to be bored	زېرىكمەك

brick	خىش
contrary to, against	خىلاپ
various	خىلمۇ - خىل
د	
tightrope walker	دارۋاز
tightrope walking	دارۋازلىق
stain, dirt, filth	داغ
field research	دالا تەكشۈرۈشى
to treat	داۋالىماق
to continue	داۋاملاشتۇرماق
to bury	دەپنە قىلماق
immediately	دەررۇ
immediately	دەرھال
gate	دەرۋازا
bunch	دەستە
to step	دەسسىمەك
to infuse (tea) to brew	دەملىمەك
time, epoch, period	دەۋر
hell	دوزاق
friendly	دوستانە
a corner	دوقمۇش
oven	دۇخوپكا
show owner	دۇكاندار
to be born	دۇنياغا كەلمەك
state	دۆلەت
state run	دۆلەت ئىگىلىكىدىكى
national	دۆلەتلىك
pile	دۆۋە
round, circular	دۈگىلەك
to braise	دۇملىمەك
agriculture	دېھقانچىلىق
to pay attention	دىققەت قىلماق
ر	
willingness; blessing	رازىلىق
true	راست
cancer	راك

to attract	جەلپ قىلماق
to gather	جەم بولماق
heaven	جەننەت
an aspect, view	جەھەت
courage, bravery	جۈرئەت
pair	جۈپ
emergency	جىددىي
emergency room	جىددىي قۇتقۇزۇش بۆلۈمى
to ring, jingle, ding	جىرىڭلىماق
to plant saplings	جىرىم/كۆچەت تىكمەك
hepatitis	جىگەر ياللۇغى
a crime, offense	جىنايەت

چ

to chop; to dig out; to run	چاپماق
to be tired	چارچىماق
animal husbandry	چارۋىچىلىق
time	چاغ
to crack; lightning	چاقماق
to call	چاقىرماق
clean of dust	چاڭ - توزاڭدىن خالىي
musical instruments	چالغۇ ئەسۋابلار
suitcase	چامادان
to clap, to applaud	چاۋاك چالماق
tea-seller	چايپۇرۇش
foreigner	چەتئەللىك
to be limited, to be bounded by	چەكلەنمەك
a limit, boundary	چەكلىمە
definitely	چوقۇم
to grow up	چوڭ بولماق
star	چولپان
strainer	چويلا
tennis	چويلا توپ
a fable, fairy tale	چۆچەك
dumpling soup	چۆچۈرە
side, perimeter	چۆرە
kettle	چۆگۈن
a desert	چۆل
to turn into a wilderness	چۆلدەرەپ قالماق
concept	چۈشەنچە
border	چېگرا
wrestling	چېلىشىش
enduring	چىدامىلىق
to endure, be able to stand	چىدىماق
putrescent things	چىرىيدىغان بۇيۇملار
exit	چىقىش ئېغىزى
to dip into	چىلىماق
grassy area	چىملىق
fly (insect)	چىۋىن

خ

error	خاتالىق
memory; diary	خاتىرە
staff	خادىم
to be insulted	خارلانماق
raw materials	خام ئەشيا
a rough calculation	خام چوت
queen	خانىش
calligraphy	خەتتاتلىق
map	خەرىتە
dagger	خەنجەر
good news	خوش خەۋەر
to be happy	خۇرسەن بولماق
leather	خۇرۇم
to be addicted	خۇمار بولماق
dough	خېمىر
to be embarrassed, to be ashamed	خىجالەت بولماق
to be ashamed, embarrassed	خىجىل بولماق

rule, regulation	قائىدە
to return	قايتماق
sorrow	قايغۇ - ھەسرەت
grave	قەبرە
cemetery	قەبرىستان
firm, an absolute	قەتئىي
step	قەدەم
to take a step	قەدەم ئالماق
to value, esteem	قەدىرلىمەك
ancient	قەدىمكى
close friend	قەدىناس دوست
debt	قەرز
to borrow	قەرز ئالماق
to swear	قەسەم قىلماق (ئىچمەك)
sweets (such as cube sugar, candy)	قەنت- گېزەك
story, floor	قەۋەت
to accept	قوبۇل قىلماق
animal pen	قوتان
weapon	قورال
to be afraid	قورقماق
courtyard	قورۇ
fried fish	قورۇلغان بېلىق
to fry	قورۇماق
lamb's skin	قوزا تېرىسى
bi -, double	قوش
double layered	قوش قەۋەتلىك
to agree	قوشۇلماق
to defend, protect	قوغدىماق
handicraft products	قول - ھۈنەر بۇيۇملىرى
convenient	قولايلىق
hand fabricated	قولدا توقۇلغان
bridesmaid, the best man (at a wedding)	قولداش
to use	قوللانماق
to support	قوللىماق
commanding	قوماندانلىق
to spend the night	قونۇپ قالماق

the Forbidden City	شەھرىستان / خان سارىيى
mutton soup	شورپا
at that time	شۇ چاغدا
since then	شۇنىڭدىن تارتىپ
dialect	شېۋە
curing, healing	شىپالىق
	غ
goose	غاز
to vanish, to disappear	غايىب بولماق
strange	غەلىتە
peculiar	غەيرىي
sheath	غىلاپ
	ق
ability, skill	قابىلىيەت
to cover	قاپلىماق
a transport hub	قاتناش تۈگۈنى
transportation	قاتناش ۋاستىلىرى
to participate in	قاتناشماق
to commute, to travel back and forth	قاتنىماق
to escape	قاچماق
unlicensed taxicab	قارا تاكسى
to help	قاراشماق
to welcome	قارشى ئالماق
pine tree	قارىغاي
to be in mourning	قارىلىق تۇتماق
to look	قارىماق
butcher	قاساپ
jade	قاشتېشى
barren land	قاقاسلىق
to laugh heartily	قاقاقلاپ كۈلمەك
disturbance, chaos	قالايمىقانچىلىق
to leave	قالدۇرماق
blood pressure	قان بېسىمى
to launch, to develop	قانات ياياماق
an illegal matter	قانۇنغا خىلاپ

trade	سودا
to trade	سودا قىلماق
to greet	سوراشماق
to interrogate	سوراققا تارتماق
an occasion, gathering	سورۇن
to stretch out; extend	سوزۇلماق
to lock up	سولىماق
fried noodles	سومەن
gift	سوۋغات
to splash water	سۇ چاچماق
swimming	سۇ ئۈزۈش
to water	سۇغارماق
insurance	سۇغۇرتا
to extract	سۇغۇرماق
dynasty	سۇلالە
noodle soup	سۇيۇقئاش
bone	سۆڭەك
conversation hour	سۆھبەت سائىتى
very clear	سۈپ- سۈزۈك
to sweep	سۈپۈرمەك
picture	سۈرەت
city wall	سېپىل
to chew gum	سېغىز چاينىماق
to miss	سېغىنماق
comparative	سېلىشتۇرما
fully cooked	سىڭىپ پىشماق
to try	سىناپ باقماق
to test, try out	سىناشماق
political	سىياسىي
ش	
condition	شارائىت
scarf	شارپا
a type of thin silk	شايى
individual	شەخسىي
shape	شەكىل
to be formed	شەكىللەنمەك
to tour a city	شەھەر ئايلانماق

territory	زېمىن
intellect, intelligence	زېھىن
jewellery	زىبۇزىننەت بۇيۇملىرى
to throb, to give a sharp and stabbing pain	زىڭىلدىماق
to visit	زىيارەت قىلماق
harmful; deleterous	زىيانلىق
س	
happiness	سائادەت
handle; pure	ساپ
pottery	ساپالچىلىق / كۇلالچىلىق
to become yellow	سارغايماق
to play on musical instruments	ساز چېلماق
to preserve	ساقلىماق
to get preserved	ساقلىنىپ قالماق
weighty words	سالمىقى بار گەپ
samsa maker	سامسىپەز
industry	سانائەت
industrial factory	سانائەت زاۋۇتى
field, area of knowledge	ساھە
tour company	ساياھەت شىركىتى
tourist attractions	ساياھەت ئورۇنلىرى
tool	سايمان
the Great Wall	سەددىچىن
numb	سەزمەس
jumping	سەكرىمەك
honest, sincere	سەمىمىي
art	سەنئەت
art sciences	سەنئەت پەنلىرى
health department	سەھىيە خىزمىتى
reason	سەۋەب
to be patient, to forbear, to endure	سەۋر قىلماق
a fried dish	سەي \ قورۇما

machine manufacturing	ماشىنسازلىق
strength, vigor	ماغدۇر
proverbs	ماقال - تەمسىل
article	ماقالە
to agree	ماقۇل بولماق
a place, area, home	ماكان
oil, cream	ماي
funds	مەبلەغ
to be obliged	مەجبۇر بولماق
to force	مەجبۇرلىماق
obligation, duty	مەجبۇرىيەت
culture	مەدەنىيەت
religious school	مەدرىس
day laborer	مەدىكار
deceased	مەرھۇم(ە)
delicious	مەززىلىك
period of time	مەزگىل
content	مەزمۇن
to get drunk	مەست بولماق
advice	مەسلىھەت
responsible, in charge	مەسئۇل
responsibility	مەسئۇلىيەت
exercise; operation	مەشغۇلات
to practice	مەشق قىلماق
goal	مەقسەت
campus	مەكتەپ قورۇسى
to inform	مەلۇم قىلماق
report	مەلۇمات
based on some information	مەلۇماتلارغا ئاساسلانغاندا
princess	مەلىكە
country	مەملىكەت
an administrative region	مەمۇرىي رايون
meaning	مەنا
source	مەنبە
a view, scenery	مەنزىرە

happily	كۆڭۈللۈك
scale, scope	كۆلەم
coal	كۆمۈر
to welcome guests	كۈتۈۋالماق
to live	كۈن كەچۈرمەك
diary	كۈندىلىك خاتىرە
daily routine	كۈندىلىك مەشغۇلات
from day to day	كۈندىن كۈنگە
to be late	كېچىكمەك
no problem	كېرەك يوق
to become wider	كېڭەيمەك
to agree	كېلىشمەك
to do the laundry	كىر يۇيۇش
bed sheet	كىرلىك
raisin	كىشمىش
cloth for a garment	كىيىملىك
گ	
gas reserves	گاز زاپىسى
witness	گۇۋاھچى
ل	
to find a partner	لايىق تاپماق
design	لايىھە
nickname	لەقەم
full	لىق
very quickly	لىككىدە
م	
salary	مائاش
mattress	ماتراس (كۆرپە)
self-boasting	ماختانچاق
to compliment	ماختىماق
physical, material	ماددىي
necklace	مارجان
tomb	مازار
to match up with	ماس كەلمەك
to suit; to match	ماسلاشماق
to drive a vehicle	ماشىنا ھەيدىمەك

karez (underground irrigation channel)	كارىز
bed carpet	كارىۋات گىلىمى
trouble, bad luck, misfortune	كاساپەت
craftsman	كاسىپ
hindrance	كاشىلا
a stick, bat	كالتەك
baseball	كالتەك توپ
dove	كەپتەر
to cut	كەسمەك
major	كەسىپ
humble	كەمتەر
to be discriminated	كەمستىلىش\ كەمستىلمەك
a village	كەنت
one after another	كەينى - كەينىدىن\ ئارقا - ئارقىدىن
jar	كوزا
to dig	كولىماق
a group, club	كۇرژۇك
to increase	كۆپەيمەك
to lift	كۆتۈرمەك
to move	كۆچمەك
nomad	كۆچمەن
to copy	كۆچۈرمەك
exhibition	كۆرگەزمە
spectator	كۆزەتكۈچ
to notice	كۆزى چۈشمەك
to become green, to go moldy	كۆكەرمەك
to have fun	كۆڭۈل ئاچماق
to care for	كۆڭۈل بۆلمەك
to want	كۆڭۈل تارتماق
entertainment	كۆڭۈل ئېچىش پائالىيىتى
to feel nauseous	كۆڭۈل ئېلىشمەك\ ئاينىماق
to be sad	كۆڭۈل يېرىم بولماق

dense, thick	قويۇق
to rescue	قۇتقۇزۇش
to get away from, to avoid	قۇتۇلماق
well	قۇدۇق
to sacrifice	قۇربان بېرىش
the Korban festival	قۇربان ھېيت
to establish	قۇرماق
mainland	قۇرۇقلۇق
construction	قۇرۇلما
to be established	قۇرۇلماق
sand therapy	قۇم بىلەن داۋالاش
sand shift	قۇم كۆچۈش
desert area	قۇملۇق
tail fat	قۇيرۇق ياغ
to pour	قۇيماق
to be frozen (from fear, surprise or shock)	قېتىپ قالماق
to itch	قىچىشماق
to make blushed	قىزارتماق
enthusiastic, fervent	قىزغىن
to interest someone in something	قىزىقتۇرماق
to be interested in	قىزىقماق
stop light	قىزىل چىراق
to liven up, to reach a height	قىزىماق
crowded	قىستاڭچىلىق
brief	قىسقىچە
to gamble	قىمار ئوينىماق
filling; ground	قىيما
to suffer; to be tortured	قىينالماق
to cut, snip	قىيماق
ك	
chicken coop	كاتەك
small production unit	كارخانا

palace	ئوردا
forest	ئورمان
to arrange, to organize	ئورۇنلاشتۇرۇپ بەرمەك
to perform	ئورۇنلىماق
nutritional components	ئوزۇقلۇق تەركىبى
thief	ئوغرى
to steal	ئوغرىلاپ كەتمەك
buzkashi (a game played on horseback, in which two teams compete for a dead)	ئوغلاق تارتىشىش
to give an injection	ئوكۇل سالماق
to get better, to recover	ئوڭشالماق
to cluster around	ئولاشماق
to be common, to become widespread	ئومۇملاشماق
to hunt	ئوۋغا چىقماق
basin	ئويمانلىق
to be dug out	ئويۇلماق
	ئۇ
to encounter	ئۇچراشماق
to encounter	ئۇچرىماق
to fly	ئۇچماق
to fight	ئۇرۇشۇپ قالماق
to see off	ئۇزاتماق
teacher	ئۇستاز
Uyghur dance	ئۇسسۇل
style	ئۇسلۇب
to understand; to know	ئۇقماق
concept	ئۇقۇم
then	ئۇنداقتا
a title, name; degree	ئۇنۋان
besides that	ئۇنىڭ ئۈستىگە
to unite	ئۇيۇشماق
	ئۆ
sharp	ئۆتكۈر
to pass	ئۆتمەك

condition	ھال
to perish, to die	ھالاك بولماق
earring	ھالقا
to get excited	ھاياجانلانماق
zoo	ھايۋاناتلار باغچىسى
saw design	ھەرە چىشلىق
never	ھەرگىز
times	ھەسسە
wage; right; the truth	ھەق
to carry for free	ھەقسىز توشۇماق
truth	ھەقىقەت
truly	ھەقىقەتەن
to solve	ھەل قىلماق
to cooperate	ھەمكارلاشماق
everyone	ھەممەيلەن
to be surprised	ھەيران بولماق
to be astonished	ھەيران قالماق
magnificent	ھەيۋەتلىك
to lose consciousness, faint	ھوشىدىن كەتمەك
courtyard	ھويلا
attack	ھۇجۇم
document	ھۆججەت
to wail, to sob	ھۆركىرەپ يىغلىماق
government	ھۆكۈمەت
the (government) authorities	ھۆكۈمەت ئەمەلدارلىرى
craft; skill	ھۈنەر
craftsman	ھۈنەرۋەن
to be reckoned	ھېسابلانماق
that	ھېلىقى
	ئو
surgery	ئوپېراتسىيە
fire; grass	ئوت
to burn up	ئوت كەتمەك
to light a fire	ئوت ياقماق
vegetables	ئوتياش \ كۆكتات
stove	ئوچاق

measure	مىقدار
A.D.	مىلادى
traditional, national	مىللىي
national tradition	مىللىي ئەنئەنە
national character	مىللىي تۇس
gratitude	مىننەتدارلىق
ن	
bad	ناچار
to show, demonstrate	نامايان قىلماق
unknown	نامەلۇم
poor	نامرات
county	ناھىيە
bread maker; baker	ناۋاي
to breath	نەپەس ئېلىش\ئالماق
delicate	نەپىس
feast in honor of deceased	نەزىر
advice	نەسىھەت
marijuana, hashish	نەشە
to smoke marijuana	نەشە چەكمەك
pear	نەشپۈت
songs and music	نەغمە- ناۋا
exact	نەق
on the scene	نەق مەيدان
to be decorated	نەقشلەنمەك
decoration	نەقىش
to sign in (in hospital	نومۇر ئالماق
numerous	نۇرغۇنلىغان
style, form	نۇسخا
occasional	نۆۋەتلىك
wedding	نىكاھ توي
oil	نېفت
ھ	
haram (not permitted in Islam)	ھارام
cart driver	ھارۋىكەش
a mourner	ھازىدار
to produce; to obtain	ھاسىل قىلماق

to prohibit	مەنئى قىلماق
neighborhood	مەھەللە
result, outcome	مەھسۇل
products	مەھسۇلات
existing	مەۋجۇت
dirty	مەينەت
a measure word for land area	مو
expert, specialist	مۇتەخەسسىس
ceremony	مۇراسىم
complicated	مۇرەككەپ
to be cold, to become cold	مۇزلاپ كەتمەك
competition	مۇسابىقە
to confiscate	مۇسادىرە قىلماق
punch	مۇشت
fixed, stable	مۇقىم
stipend	مۇكاپات پۇلى
service	مۇلازىمەت
tower	مۇنار
related	مۇناسىۋەتلىك
stage, podium	مۇنبەر
regular, full time	مۇنتىزىم
bath room	مۇنچا
appropriate	مۇۋاپىق
miracle	مۆجىزە
shoulders	مۈرە
property	مۈلۈك
hospitality	مېھماندوستلۇق
disable	مېيىپ
temperament; feeling, mood	مىجەز
heritage	مىراس
copper	مىس
coppersmith	مىسكەر
rumors, gossip	مىش- مىش (گەپ)
to blow one's nose (out)	مىشقىرماق

to keep-in-the-pocket	يانچۇققا سىلىپ يۈرمەك
cell phone	يانفون
to return	يانماق
wild	ياۋا
wild birds	ياۋايى قۇشلار
feast in honor after seven days	يەتتە نەزرى
basement	يەر ئاستى ئۆيى
earthquake	يەر تەۋرەش
earthquake	يەر تەۋرىمەك
to untie, to take off (clothes)	يەشمەك
with one knee underneath	يەكتىز
to win	يەڭمەك
air	يەل
to develop a fungus infection	يەل تاشماق
a cover, cover sheet	يوپۇق
blanket	يوتقان
big	يوغان
to disappear	يوقاپ كەتمەك
to visit	يوقلىماق
passenger	يولۇچى
homeland	يۇرت
infectious, contagious	يۇقۇملۇق
wool	يۇڭ
tamarisk	يۇلغۇن
to wash	يۇماق
cough	يۆتەل
set of books	يۈرۈشلەشكەن دەرسلىك
to happen	يۈز بەرمەك
luggage	يۈك - تاق
load up	يۈك ئارتماق
lofty, noble	يۈكسەك
to lead	يېتەكلىمەك
countryside	يېزا
an agricultural	يېزا- ئىگىلىك

respect, honour	ئىززەت
to express	ئىزهار قىلماق
smoke	ئىس - تۈتەك
to use, consume	ئىستېمال قىلماق
consumption	ئىستىمال
wastefulness	ئىسراپچىلىق
hot food	ئىسسىقلىق
violin	ئىسكرىپكا
to use	ئىشلەتمەك
ability	ئىقتىدار
economic	ئىقتىسادىي
owner	ئىگە
to possess	ئىگىلىمەك
if it is possible	ئىلاجى بولسا
application, request	ئىلتىماس
to request; to apply	ئىلتىماس قىلماق
management	ئىلمىي باشقۇرۇش
valid document	ئىناۋەتلىك كىنىشكىسى
conscientious, thankful	ئىنساپلىق
anthropology	ئىنسانشۇناسلىق
ي	
nuclear test	يادرو سىنىقى
cultural relics	يادىكارلىق
if you remember	يادىڭىزدا بولسا
to be injured	يارىلانماق
written history	يازما تارىخ
pillow	ياستۇق
age	ياش قۇرامى
burning oil - accompanied by prayers for the dead	ياغ پۈراتماق
wood	ياغاچ
carpenter	ياغاچچى
scarf	ياغلىق
to light; like	ياقماق
walnut skin	ياڭاق پوستى
potato	ياڭيۇ
peppermint	يالپۇز

to talk too much (slang)	ۋالاقلىماق
promise	ۋەدە
prefecture	ۋىلايەت
street sign	ۋىۋىسكا
	ئې
the lap; lower slope	ئېتەك
care, consideration	ئېتىبار
to pay attention	ئېتىبار بەرمەك
field	ئېتىز
farmland	ئېتىزلىق
faith	ئېتىقاد
brook	ئېرىق
aesthetic thought	ئېستېتىك تەپەككۇر
valuable	ئېسىل
mouth; a measure word for a room	ئېغىز
to taste, to try	ئېغىز تەگمەك
corral	ئېغىل
to flow	ئېقىپ تۇرماق
plateau	ئېگىزلىك
e-mail	ئېلخەت
careful, cautious	ئېھتىياتچان
need, requirement	ئېھتىياج
	ئى
temple	ئىبادەتخانا
expression	ئىبارە
to express	ئىپادە قىلماق
to express	ئىپادىلىمەك
to unite	ئىتتىپاقلىشىش
to invent	ئىجاد قىلماق
invention	ئىجادىيەت
social science	ئىجتىمائىي پەن
inside; China proper	ئىچكىرى
to be full of regrets, remorse	ئىچى سىرىلىپ كەتمەك
to look for, to search for	ئىزدىمەك

goat	ئۆچكە
to put out, to erase	ئۆچۈرمەك
custom	ئۆرپ - ئادەت
duck	ئۆردەك
billow	ئۆركەش
apricot	ئۆرۈك
mutual	ئۆزئارا
to change	ئۆزگەرمەك
changes	ئۆزگىرىش
of his own accord, voluntarily	ئۆزلىكىدىن
self-opinionated	ئۆزۈمچىل
a stream, small water channel	ئۆستەڭ
to increase	ئۆسۈپ كەتمەك
roof	ئۆگزە
the day after tomorrow	ئۆگۈن
cave	ئۆڭكۈرا غار
measure	ئۆلچەم
to measure	ئۆلچىمەك
province	ئۆلكە
death toll	ئۆلۈش نىسبىتى
a visit to a bereaved family	ئۆلۈم پەتىسى
to build house	ئۆي سالماق
to marry	ئۆيلەنمەك
	ئۈ
triangle	ئۈچ بۇلۇڭ
ring	ئۈزۈك
vineyard	ئۈزۈمزارلىق
superior, greater	ئۈستۈن
tools	ئۈسكۈنە
pearls and jewels	ئۈنچە - مارجان
fertility, productivity	ئۈنۈمدارلىق
productive; efficient	ئۈنۈملۈك
	ۋ
noise	ۋاراڭ - چۇرۇڭ (ۋاڭ-چۇڭ)
to yell	ۋارقىرىماق

to loose	يېتتۇرۇپ قويماق
to tear, to rip	يىرتماق
to hold a meeting	يىغىن ئاچماق
a horse	يىلقا

to lose	يىڭىلمەك
thread, string	يىپ
the Silk Road	يىپەك يولى
silk-growing	يىپەكچىلىك

English - Uyghur Glossary ئىنگلىزچە- ئۇيغۇرچە لۇغەت

A	
abandoned land	تاشلانغان ماكان
ability	قابىلىيەت، ئىقتىدار
accept, to	قوبۇل قىلماق
accidental	تاسادىپىي
according to	بويىچە
actually, really	زادى
A.D.	مىلادى
addicted, to be	خۇمار بولماق
administrative region, an	مەمۇرىي رايون
adopt, to	قوللانماق
advice	نەسىھەت
aesthetic thought	ئېستېتىك تەپەككۇر
affect, to	تەسىر قىلماق
afraid, to be	قورقماق
against	خىلاپ، قارشى
age	ياش، ياش قورامى
agree, to	قوشۇلماق
agreement	توختام
agricultural	يېزا - ئىگىلىك
agriculture	دېھقانچىلىق
AIDS	ئەيدىز
air	ھاۋا؛ يەل
alfalfa	بېدە
almond	بادام
ancient	قەدىمكى
animal husbandry	چارۋىچىلىق
animal pen	قوتان
anthropology	ئىنسانشۇناسلىق
anxious, to be	ئەندىشە قىلماق
apologize, to	ئەپۇ سورىماق
application	ئىلتىماس
appropriate	ماسلىشىش / ماسلاشماق

appropriate for, to be	مۇۋاپىق
approved, to be	تەستىقلانماق
approximately	تەخمىنەن
apricot	ئۆرۈك
architecture	بىناكارلىق
argue, to	تارتىشماق، دەۋالاشماق
around	ئەتراپ
arrange/organize, to	ئورۇنلاشتۇرۇپ بەرمەك
art	سەنئەت
article	ماقالە
art sciences	سەنئەت پەنلىرى
ashamed, embarrassed, to be	خىجىل بولماق
as before	بۇرۇنقىدەك
aspect, view	جەھەت
astonished, to be	ھەيران قالماق
attack	ھۇجۇم
at that time	شۇ چاغدا
attract, to	جەلپ قىلماق
aviation	ئاۋىئاتسىيە
axe	پالتا
B	
bad	ناچار
badly behaved	ئەخلاقسىز
badminton	پەي توپ
baker	ناۋاي
banging	تاراق - تۇرۇق
bank account	بانكا ھېساباتى
barley	ئارپا
barren land	قاقاسلىق
baseball	كالتەك توپ
based on some information	مەلۇماتلارغا ئاساسلانغاندا

basement	بەر ئاستى ئۆيى
basin	ئويمانلىق
bath house	مۇنچا
bath room	مۇنچا؛ ھاجەتخانا
become green, go moldy	كۆكەرمەك
become wide, to	كېڭەيمەك
become yellow, to	سارغايماق
bed carpet	كارىۋات گىلىمى
bed sheet	كىرلىك
belong, to	تەۋە
benefit	پايدا - مەنپەئەت
besides that	ئۇنىڭ ئۈستىگە
better, recover, to get	ئوڭشالماق
bi-, double	قوش
big	يوغان
billow	ئۆركەش
biography	تەرجىمىھال
blanket	يوتقان
blood pressure	قان بېسىمى
blow one's nose (out), to	مىشقىرىش / مىشقىرماق
blush, turn red, to	قىزارماق
bone	سۆڭەك
border	چېگرا
bored, to be	زېرىكمەك
born, to be	دۇنياغا كەلمەك، تۇغۇلماق
borrow, to	قەرز ئالماق
bother, to	ئاۋارە قىلماق
boundary	چەك، چېگرا
bracelet	بىلەيزۈك
braise, to	دۇملىمەك
brave	باتۇر
bravery	جاسارەت
bread maker	ناۋاي
breath, to	نەپەس ئېلىش / ئالماق

brick	خىش
bridesmaid, the best man (at a wedding)	قولداش
brief	قىسقىچە
brook	ئېرىق
broth	سۇيۇقئاش
buddy	ئاداش
build house, to	ئۆي سالماق
bunch	دەستە
burning oil - accompanied by prayers for the dead (usually by ladies)	ياغ پۇرىتىش
burn up, to	ئوت كەتمەك
bury, to	دەپنە قىلماق؛ كۆممەك
butcher	قاسساپ
C	
calamity	بالا - قازا
calligraphy	خەتتاتلىق
call, to	چاقىرماق
camel	تۆگە
campus	مەكتەپ قورۇسى
cancer	راك
capital city	پايتەخت
capture, to	ئەسىر ئېلىش / ئالماق
care	ئېتىبار
care for, to	كۆڭۈل بۆلمەك
careful, cautious	ئېھتىياتچان
carpenter	ياغاچچى
carry for free, to	ھەقسىز توشۇماق
carry, to	ئاپارماق
cart driver	ھارۋىكەش
cause pain, to	ئاغرىتماق
carving	نەقىش
cave	ئۆڭكۈر \ غار
ceiling	تورۇس

cell phone	يانفون
cemetery	قەبرىستان
century	ئەسىر
ceremony	مۇراسىم
changes	ئۆزگىرىش
change, to	ئۆزگەرمەك
chaos	قالايمىقانچىلىق
chew gum, to	سېغىز چايناش / چايناماق
chicken coop	كاتەك
choose, to	تاللىماق
chop, to	چاپماق
cilantro	ئاشكۆكى
city wall	سېپىل
clap, applaud, to	چاۋاك چالماق
cleanliness	پاكىزلىك
clean of dust	چاڭ - توزاڭدىن خالىي
clean/ wash, to	تازىلىماق
close friend	قەدىناس دوست
close, lock, to	تاقىماق
cloth	رەخت
cloth for a garment	كىيىملىك
cluster around, to	ئولاشماق
coal	كۆمۈر
coffin	تاۋۇت
cold, to become cold, to be	مۇزلاپ كەتمەك
color	رەڭ
come in existence, to	بارلىققا كەلمەك
comfort, to	تەسەللى بېرىش / بەرمەك
commanding	قوماندانلىق
common, to become widespread, to be	ئومۇملاشماق
commute, to	قاتنىماق
comparative	سېلىشتۇرما
competition	مۇسابىقە

completely	پۈتۈنلەي
complicated, complex	مۇرەككەپ
compliment, to	ماختىماق
concept	چۈشەنچە
condition	شارائىت
confiscate, to	مۇسادىرە قىلماق
connect, to	تۇتاشماق
consent, to	تەن بەرمەك
consequence	ئاقىۋەت
considered	ھېساپلانماق
consideration	ئېتىبار
constitute, to	تەشكىل قىلماق
construction	قۇرۇلما
consumption	ئىستىمال
contact, to	ئالاقىلاشماق
content	مەزمۇن
continue, to	داۋاملاشتۇرماق
contrary to	خىلاپ
contribute, to	تۆھپە قوشماق
convenience	قولايلىق
convenient	قولاي
conversation hour	سۆھبەت سائىتى
competition	رىقابەت
cook, chef	ئاشپەز
cooperate, to	ھەمكارلاشماق
copper	مىس
coppersmith	مىسكەر
copy, to	كۆچۈرمەك
coriander	ئاشكۆكى
corner	دوقمۇش
corpse	جەسەت
corral	ئېغىل
cough	يۆتەل
counted as, to be	ھېسابلانماق
country	مەملىكەت
countryside	يېزا
courage	جۈرئەت

courtyard	قورۇ
cover, cover sheet	يوپۇق
cover, to	قاپلىماق
covetous	ئاچكۆز
crack, to	چاقماق
cradle	بۆشۈك
craft	ھۈنەر
craftsman	ھۈنەرۋەن
crashing	تاراق - تۇرۇق
crime, offense	جىنايەت
crowded	قىستاڭچىلىق
cultural relics	يادىكارلىق
culture	مەدەنىيەت
curing, healing	شىپالىق
custom	ئۆرپ - ئادەت
cut, snip, to	توغرىماق
D	
dagger	خەنجەر
daily routine	كۈندىلىك مەشغۇلات
damage	بۇزغۇنچىلىق
dance	ئۇسسۇل
day laborer	مەدىكار
death toll	ئۆلۈم نىسبىتى
debt	قەرز
deceased	مەرھۇم (ە)
decorate, to	(-نى) بېزىمەك
decrease in number, to	ئازايماق
defend, protect, to	قوغدىماق
definitely	چوقۇم
delicate	نەپىس
delicious	مەززىلىك
demand	تەلەپ
dense, thick	قويۇق
desert	چۆل
desert area	قۇملۇق
design	لايىھە
destiny, fate	تەقدىر

determine (do something), to	بەل باغلىماق
develop a fungus infection, to	يەل تېشىش
develop, to	تەرەققىي قىلماق
dialect	شېۋە
diary	خاتىرە
dignity	ئىززەت
dig, to	كولىماق
dig out, to	چاپماق
dip in, to	چىلىماق
directly	بىۋاستە
direct relative	بىۋاستە تۇغقان
dirty	مەينەت
disable	مېيىپ
disappear, to	يوقاپ كەتمەك
disaster	ئاپەت
discipline	تەرتىپ - ئىنتىزام
discriminated, to be	كەمستىلىش / كەمستىلمەك
dispersed, to be	تارقالماق
dispose, to	بىر تەرەپ قىلىش
distribute, to	تەقسىملىمەك
disturbance	قالايمىقانچىلىق
disturbed, concerned, to be	بىئارام بولماق
document	ھۆججەت
doorplate	ۋىۋىسكا
double	قوش
double layered	قوش قەۋەتلىك
dough	خېمىر
dove	كەپتەر
drive a vehicle, to	ماشىنا ھەيدىمەك
drop, throw away, cast, to	تاشلىماق
drunk, to get	مەست بولماق
duck	ئۆردەك
dug out, to be	ئويۇلماق

during this time	بۇ جەريانىدا
dye	بوياق
dyestuff, tincture	بوياق
dye, to	بويىماق
dynasty	سۇلالە
E	
earring	ھالقا
earthenware jar	كوزا
earthquake	يەر تەۋرەش
economic	ئىقتىسادىي
e-mail	ئېلخەت
embarrassed, to be	تارتىنماق
emergency	جىددىي
emergency room	جىددىي قۇتقۇزۇش بۆلۈمى
emphasize, stress, to	تەكىتلىمەك
encounter, to	ئۇچراشماق
endure, be able to stand, to	چىدىماق
enduring	چىداملىق
entertainment	كۆڭۈل ئېچىش پائالىيىتى
enthusiastic	قىزغىن
error	خاتالىق
escape (from), to	قۇتۇلماق
escape, to	قاچماق
established, to be	قۇرۇلماق
establish, to	قۇرماق
ethnic minority	ئاز سانلىق مىللەت
even more	تېخىمۇ
everyone	ھەممەيلەن
evil ways (in Islam)	بىدئەت
exact	نەق
excellent	ئېسىل
excited, to get	ھاياجانلانماق
exercise	مەشق
exercise, to	بەدەن چېنىقتۇرماق
exhibition	كۆرگەزمە

existing	مەۋجۇت
exit	چىقىش ئېغىزى
experience	تەجرىبە
expert, specialist	مۇتەخەسسىس
exploding	پارتلايدىغان
expressing condolences, to	تەزىيە بىلدۈرمەك / كۆڭۈل ئېيتماق
expression	ئىبارە
express, to	ئىپادىلىمەك / ئىزھار قىلماق
extra	ئارتۇق
extract, to	سۇغۇرماق
F	
fable, fairy tale	چۆچەك
fair	ئادىل
faith	ئېتىقاد
family member	ئائىلە ئەزاسى
famous	ئاتاقلىق
farewell	ئەلۋىدا
farmland	ئېتىزلىق
fast, to	روزا تۇتماق
feast in honor after seven days	يەتتە نەزىرى
feast in honor of deceased	نەزىر
feel embarrassed, to	تارتىنماق
feeling	تۇيغۇ
feel nauseous, to	كۆڭۈل ئېلىشمەك / ئايىنماق
feel, to	تۇيماق
fertility, productivity	ئۈنۈمدارلىق
fervent	قىزغىن
field	ئېتىز
field (area of knowledge)	ساھە
field research	دالا تەكشۈرۈشى
fig	ئەنجۈر
fight, to	ئۇرۇشۇپ قالماق

filling; ground	قىيما
fill, to	تولدۇرماق
finally	ئاخىرى
find a partner, to	لايىق تاپماق
fine	ئېسىل
fine, to	جەرىمانە قويماق
fire; grass	ئوت
firm, absolute	قەتئىي
fit, to	پاتماق
fixed, stable	مۇقىم
flammable	ئاسان كۆيىدىغان
flourishing	بۈك - باراقسان
flourish, to	روناق تاپماق
flow, leak, to	ئاقماق
fly (insect)	چىۋىن
fly, to	ئۇچماق/ئۇچۇش
folk doctor	تېۋىپ
folk medicine	خەلق تىبابىتى
follow, to	ئەگەشمەك
forbear, to	سەۋر قىلماق
force, to	زورلىماق
foreigner	چەتئەللىك
forest	ئورمان
for having an opportunity	پۇرسەت چىقماق
formed, to be	شەكىللەنمەك
form, organize, to	تەشكىل قىلماق
fortunately	تەلەيگە يارىشا
free	ئازاد؛ ئەركىن
fried dish	سەي\قورۇما
fried fish	قورۇلغان بېلىق
fried noodles	سومەن
friend, a	ئاغىنە
friendly	دوستانە
from day to day	كۈندىن كۈنگە
frozen (from fear, surprise or shock), to be	قېتىپ قالماق
fry, to	قورۇماق
full (bus)	لىق
full of regrets, remorse, to be	ئىچى سىرىلىپ كەتمەك
fully cooked	سىڭىپ پىشماق
funds	مەبلەغ
fur hat	تۇماق
G	
gamble, to	قىمار ئويناش / ئويناماق
gardener	باغۋەن
gas reserves	گاز زاپىسى
gate	دەرۋازا
gathered, to be	توپلاشماق
gather, to	توپلاش
generation	ئەۋلاد
get acquainted, to	تونۇشۇۋالماق
get away from, avoid, to	قۇتۇلماق
get broken	بۇزۇلۇپ قالماق
get prepared	جابدۇنماق
get to know	تونۇشماق
gift	سوۋغات
give an injection, to	ئوكۇل سېلىش / سالماق
glare at, to	ئالايماق
gloves	پەلەي
goal	مەقسەت
goat	ئۆچكە
gold	ئالتۇن
good news	خوش خەۋەر
goose	غاز
go through the formalities, to	رەسمىيەت ئۆتمەك
government	ھۆكۈمەت
gradually	ئاستا - ئاستا
graduate student	ئاسپىرانت
graduate, to	پۈتتۈرمەك

grassed area	چىملىق
gratitude	مىننەتدارلىق
grave	قەبرە
greet, to	سوراشماق
group	تۇركۇم
group, club	كۇرژۇك
grow up, to	چوڭ بولماق
H	
habit	ئادەت
hand fabricated	قولدا توقۇلغان
handicraft products	قول - هۈنەر بۇيۇملىرى
handle; pure	ساپ
hanging carpet	ئاسما گىلەم
happen, to	يۈز بەرمەك
happily	كۆڭۈللۈك
happiness	سائادەت
happy, festive	كۆڭۈللۈك
happy, to be	خۇرسەن بولماق
haram (not permitted in Islam)	هارام
hard working	ئەمگەكچان
harmful	زىيانلىق
have fun, to	كۆڭۈل ئاچماق
have good effect, to	پايدا قىلماق
health department	سەھىيە خىزمىتى
heaven	جەننەت
heirloom, cherished	تەۋەررۈك
hell	دوزاق
help	ياردەم
helpless; poor	بىچارە
help, to	قاراشماق
hepatitis	جىگەر ياللۇغى
heritage, legacy	مىراس
higher education	ئالىي مائارىپ
high quality; excellent	ئېسىل
high school	تولۇق ئوتتۇرا مەكتەپ

highway	تاشيول
hindrance	توسقۇنلۇق، كاشىلا
hold a meeting, to	يىغىن ئاچماق
homeland	يۇرت
honest, sincere	سەممىي
horse, a	يىلقا
hospital	بالنىست / كېسەلخانا / دوختۇرخانا
hospitality	مېهماندوستلۇق
hot food	ئىسسىقلىق
humble	كەمتەر
humiliated, to be	خارلانماق
hunt, to	ئۇۋغا چىقماق
I	
if it is possible	ئىلاجى بولسا
illegal	قانۇنغا خىلاپ
imagine, to	تەسەۋۋۇر قىلماق
immediately	دەررۇ
immoral	ئەخلاقسىز
impolite, rude	ئەدەبسىز
in accordance with	ئاساسلانماق
in association, together	بىر تۇتاش
increase, to	ئۆسۈپ كەتمەك
individual, private	شەخسىي
industrial factory	سانائەت زاۋۇتى
industry	سانائەت
infectious, contagious	يۇقۇملۇق
influence	تەسىر
influence, to	تەسىر كۆرسەتمەك
inform, to	مەلۇم قىلماق
infuse (tea), brew, to	دەملىمەك
inhabitants	ئاھالە
injured, to be	يارىلانماق
in mourning, to be	قارىلىق تۇتماق
in that case	ئۇنداقتا
inside; China proper	ئىچكىرى
instruct, urge, to	تاپىلىماق

insulted, to be	خارلانماق
insurance	سۇغۇرتا
intellect	زېھن
interest someone in something, to	قىزىقتۇرماق
interested in, to be	قىزىقماق
interrogate, to	سوراققا تارتماق
introduce, to	تونۇشتۇرماق
invention	ئىجادىيەت
invent, to	ئىجاد قىلماق
investigate, to	تەكشۈرمەك
invitation	باغاق
invite someone to dance, to	تانسىغا تارتماق
iron	تۆمۈر
itch, an	قىچىشىش
J	
jade	قاشتېشى
jail	تۈرمە
jar	كوزا
jewelry	زىبۇزىننەت بۇيۇملىرى
join together	ئۇيۇشۇش
jumping	سەكرەش / سەكرىمەك
just now	باياتىن
K	
karez (underground irrigation channel)	كارىز
keep in the pocket, to	يانچۇققا سېلىپ يۈرمەك
kettle	چۆگۈن
key	ئاچقۇچ
kidney	بۆرەك
kind, sincere	سەمىمي
knife-maker or seller	پىچاقچى
knot	تۈگۈن
know, to	ئۇقماق
L	
labor	ئەمگەك

lamb's skin	قوزا تېرىسى
landscape	مەنزىرە
late (refers to a deceased person)	رەھمەتلىك
late, to be	كېچىكمەك
laugh heartily, to	قاقاقلاپ كۈلمەك
leader, manager	باشقۇرغۇچى
lead, to	يېتەكلەش
leather	خۇرۇم
leave, to	قالدۇرماق
legend	رىۋايەت
lend, to	ئارىيەتكە بەرمەك
letter of introduction, recommendation	تونۇشتۇرۇش خېتى
life necessity	تۇرمۇش ئېھتىياجى
lift, to	كۆتۈرمەك
light a fire, to	ئوت يېقىش / ئوت ياقماق
lightning, to	چاقماق
limit	چەكلىمە
limit, to	چەكلىمە
limited/bounded by, to be	چەكلەنمەك
literary work	ئەدەبىي ئەسەر
live in ease, to	راھەت كۆرمەك
liven up, reach a height, to	قىزىماق
live, to	كۈن كەچۈرمەك
load up	يۈك ئارتماق
located, to be	جايلاشماق
lock up, to	سولىماق
lofty, noble	يۈكسەك
look for, search for, to	ئىزدىمەك
look, to	ئىزدىمەك
lose, to	يېڭىلمەك
lose consciousness, faint, to	ھوشىدىن كەتمەك
lot	بىر مۇنچە

luck	تەلەي
luggage	يۈك - تاق
M	
machine manufacturing	ماشىنسازلىق
magnificent	ھەيۋەتلىك
mainland	قۇرۇقلۇق
major	كەسىپ
make a habit, to	ئادەت قىلماق
make fun of, to	زاڭلىق قىلماق / مازاق قىلماق
make threads, to	يىلىدىن يىپ ئېگىرىش
management	ئىلمىي باشقۇرۇش
manners; etiquette	ئەدەب - ئەخلاق
map	خەرىتە
marijuana, hashish	نەشە
mark, emblem	بەلگە
marry, to	توي قىلماق
match up with, to	ماس كەلمەك
mattress	ماتراس (كۆرپە)
meaning	مەنا
measure	ئۆلچەم
measure, to	ئۆلچىمەك
measure word for land area	مو
medicine, therapy	تىبابەتچىلىك
meet, to	كۈتۈۋالماق
member	ئەزا
memory	خاتىرە
mental state	روھىي ھالەت
mention, to	تىلغا ئالماق
messenger, matchmaker	ئەلچى
method	ئامال
minority groups	ئاز سانلىق مىللەت
miracle	مۆجىزە
miss, to	سېغىنماق

mix, to	ئارىلاشتۇرماق
mock, to	زاڭلىق قىلماق
moral character	پەزىلەت
more	تېخىمۇ كۆپ
mounted	ئاتلىق
mourner	ھازىدار
mouth	ئېغىز
move, to	كۆچمەك
multiply	كۆپەيمەك
musical instruments	چالغۇ ئەسۋابلار
mutton soup	شورپا
mutual	ئۆزئارا
N	
name, to; dedicated, to be	ئاتىماق
national	دۆلەتلىك
national character	مىللىي تۈس
national tradition	مىللىي ئەنئەنە
natural	تەبىئىي
natural science	تەبىئى پەن
nearby	ئەتراپ
necessity	زۆرۈرىيەت
necklace	مارجان
need, requirement	ئېھتىياج
neighborhood	مەھەللە
net	تور
never	ھەرگىز
nickname	لەقەم
noise	ۋاراڭ - چۇرۇڭ (ۋاڭ - چۇڭ)
nomad	كۆچمەن
no problem	چاتاق يوق
not loose a chance, to	پۇرسەتنى قولدىن بەرمەك
notice, to	كۆزى چۈشمەك
nuclear test	يادرو سىنىقى
numb	سەزمەس
numerous	نۇرغۇنلىغان

O	
oasis	بوستانلىق
obey, to	بويسۇنماق
obligation, duty	مەجبۇرىيەت
obliged, to be	مەجبۇر بولماق
occasional	نۆۋەتلىك
occasion, gathering; place (for meetings),	سورۇن
occupy, to	بېسىۋالماق
occur, happen, to	يۈز بەرمەك
officially	رەسمىي شەكىلدە
of his own accord, voluntarily	ئۆزلىكىدىن
oil	نېفت
oil (cream)	ماي
olive	زەيتۇن
on a diet, to be	پەرھىز تۇتماق
one after another	كەينى - كەينىدىن / ئارقا - ئارقىدىن
on foot	پىيادە
on the scene	نەق مەيدان
operation	مەشغۇلات
opportunity	پۇرسەت
opposite of	ئەكسىچە
outer ring road	ئايلانما يول
oven	دۇخوپكا
overcrowding	قىستاڭچىلىق
owner	ئىگە
P	
pair	جۈپ
palace	ئوردا
participate in, to	قاتناشماق
partition	
pass away, to	تۈگەپ كەتمەك / ئالەمدىن ئۆتمەك / ۋاپات بولماق / كۆز يۇمماق / قازا قىلماق
passenger	يولۇچى

pass, to	ئۆتمەك
patient, to be	سەۋر قىلماق
pay attention, to	ئېتىبار بەرمەك
pay, to	پۇل تاپشۇرماق
peace	تىنچلىق
pear	نەشپۈت
pearls and jewels	ئۈنچە - مارجان
peculiar	غەيرىي
pedestrian	پىيادىلەر
peppermint	يالپۇز
perform, to	ئورۇنلىماق
period of time	مەزگىل
perish, die, to	ھالاك بولماق
petrol, benzene	بېنزىن
physical capability	بەدەن قۇۋۋىتى
physical, material	ماددىي
picture; speed	سۈرەت
piece; a measure word for book	پارچە
pigeon soup	باچكا تاڭ
pile	دۆۋە
pillow	ياستۇق
pine tree	قارىغاي
pity	ئەپسۇس
placate, to	تەسەللى بېرىش / بەرمەك
place; area	ماكان
place (for meetings), an occasion, gathering	سورۇن
plant saplings, to	جىرىم / كۆچەت تىكىش
plateau	ئېگىزلىك
play on musical instruments	ساز چېلىش
pocket knife	بەكە
poison	زەھەر
poison, to	زەھەرلىمەك

political	سىياسىي
polluted	بۇلغانغان
pomegranate	ئانار
poor	نامرات
possess, to	ئىگىلىمەك
potato	ياڭيۇ
pottery	ساپالچىلىق / كۇلالچىلىق
pour, to	قۇيماق
practice, to	مەشق قىلماق
prefecture	ۋىلايەت
preparation	تەييارلىق
prepare for smth, to	جابدۇنماق
prescription; recipe	رېتسىپ
preserved, to get	ساقلىنىپ قالماق
preserve, to	ساقلىماق
princess	مەلىكە
process	جەريان
produce; obtain, to	ھاسىل قىلماق
product	مەھسۇلات
productive; efficient	ئۈنۈملۈك
products	مەھسۇلات
prohibit, to	مەنئى قىلماق
promise	ۋەدە
property	مۈلۈك
Prophet	پەيغەمبەر
prosperous	ئاۋات
proud (of), to be	پەخىرلەنمەك
proverbs	ماقال - تەمسىل
provide, supply, to	تەمىنلىمەك / تەمىنلەش
province	ئۆلكە
public gathering	ئاممىۋى يىغىلىش
punch	مۇشت
punished, to be	جازالانماق
punishment, penalty	جازا
put in order, to	رەتلىمەك
put out for sale, sell, peddle, to	بازارغا سالماق
put out the, to welcoming carpet	پايانداز سالماق
put out, erase, to	ئۆچۈرمەك
Q	
queen	خانىش
R	
rabbit	توشقان
railroad	تۆمۈريول
railway	تۆمۈريول
raise, to	باقماق
raisin	كىشمىش
raw materials	خام ئەشيا
reality, practice	ئەمەلىيەت
reason	سەۋەب
recall, to	ئەسكە كەلمەك
receive; accept, to	قوبۇل قىلماق
receive (guests), meet, to	كۈتۈۋالماق
reckoned, to be	ھېسابلانماق
recommend, to	تەۋسىيە قىلماق
reflect, to	ئەكس ئەتمەك
register, to	تىزىملىتىپ قويماق
regrettable, unfortunate	ئەپسۇسلىنارلىق
regular, full time	مۇنتىزىم
related	مۇناسىۋەتلىك
related to	ئائىت
religious school	مەدرىس
remind somebody of something, to	ئەسلەتمەك
repair, to	رېمونت قىلماق
replace, to	ئالماشماق
report	مەلۇمات
report, to	مەلۇم قىلماق
request; apply	ئىلتىماس قىلماق
request, to	تەلەپ قىلماق

rescue, to	قۇتقۇزۇش
research, to	تەتقىقات قىلماق
responsibility	مەسئۇلىيەت
responsible, in charge	مەسئۇل
responsible, to be	جاۋابكار بولماق
restrict, to	چەكلىمەك
result, outcome	مەھسۇل
return, to	قايتماق
revealed, to be	پاش بولماق
revolve; become, to	ئايلانماق
revolve, rotate, to	ئايلانماق
ring	ئۈزۈك
ring, jingle, ding, to	جىرىڭلىماق
robbery	بۇلاڭچىلىق
roof	ئۆگزە
rough calculation	خام چوت
round, circular	دۈگىلەك
rubbish	ئەخلەت
ruin, destroy, to	بەربات قىلماق
rule, regulation	قائىدە
rumors, street talk, gossip	مىش - مىش (گەپ)
S	
sack	تاغار
sacrifice, to	قۇربان بېرىش
sad, to be	كۆڭۈل يېرىم بولماق
safety belt	بىخەتەرلىك تاسمىسى
salary	مائاش
samsa maker	سامسىپەز
sand shift	قۇم كۆچۈش
sand therapy	قۇم بىلەن داۋالاش
saw design	ھەرە چىشلىق
scale, scope	كۆلەم
scarf	ياغلىق
scarf	شارپا
schedule	جەدۋەل
search, to	ئىزدىمەك

section	بۆلمە
security	ئامانلىق قوغدىغۇچى
see off, to	ئۇزاتماق
see the fun, to	تاماشا كۆرمەك
self-boasting	ماختانچاق
self-opinionated	ئۆزۈمچىل
sense, feeling	تۇيغۇ
sequence	تەرتىپ
service	مۇلازىمەت
set of books	يۈرۈشلەشكەن دەرسلىك
shape	شەكىل
sharp	ئۆتكۈر
sheath	غىلاپ
shoulders	مۈرە
show, demonstrate, to	نامايان قىلماق
show owner	دۇكاندار
shy	تارتىنچاق
shy, to	تارتىنماق
side, perimeter	چۆرە
silk-growing	يىپەكچىلىك
since long ago	ئەزەلدىن
since then	شۇنىڭدىن تارتىپ
since then	...دىن تارتىپ
single	بويتاق
single, odd	تاق
sire	ئالىيلىرى
sit idle, to	بىكار تۇرماق
skill	قابىلىيەت
slaughter, to	بوغۇزلىماق
small glass cup	رومكا
small, narrow street (with shops on either side)	رەستە
small production unit	كارخانا
smell	پۇراق
smoke	ئىس - تۈتەك

smoke marijuana, to	نەشە چېكىش / چەكمەك
social science	ئىجتىمائىي پەن
solution	ئامال
solve, to	ھەل قىلماق
so much	بۇنچىۋالا
songs and music	نەغمە - ناۋا
sorrow	قايغۇ - ھەسرەت
sort of bread	توقاچ
source	مەنبە
speak fluently, to	راۋان سۆزلىمەك
special	ئالاھىدە
specialization; major	كەسىپ
spectator	كۆزەتكۈچ
speed of spreading	تارقىلىش سۈرئىتى
spend the night, to	قونۇپ قالماق
spirit, ghost	ئەرۋاھ
spirit, soul	روھ
spiritual world	روھىي دۇنيا
spit, to	تۈكۈرۈش / تۈكۈرمەك
splash water, to	سۇ چاچماق
splendid, wonderful	پەيز / پەيزى
spoken language	جانلىق تىل
spread, to	تارقالماق
spread, to be	تارقالماق
spring	بۇلاق
staff	خادىم
stage, podium	مۇنبەر
stage, step	باسقۇچ
stain, dirt, filth	داغ
star	چولپان
state	دۆلەت
state run	دۆلەت ئىگىلىكىدىكى
status	ھال
steal, to	ئوغرىلاپ كەتمەك
step	قەدەم
step, to	دەسسىمەك

stick, bat	كالتەك
stipend	مۇكاپات پۇلى
stone	تاش
stop light	قىزىل چىراق
storey, floor	قەۋەت
stove	ئوچاق
strainer	چويلا
strange	غەلىتە
stream	ئۆستەڭ
stream, small water channel	ئۆستەڭ
street sign	ۋىۋىسكا
strength, vigor	ماغدۇر
stretch out, to	سوزۇلماق
striped heavy silk	بەقەسەم
stubborn	جاھىل
study hard, to	تىرىشىپ ئۆگەنمەك
style	ئۇسلۇب
style, form	نۇسخا
suffer, to	قىينالماق
suitcase	چامادان
superfluity	ئارتۇقچىلىق
superior, greater	ئۈستۈن
superiority	ئەۋزەللىك
support, to	قوللىماق
surgery	ئوپېراتسىيە
surprise, to	ھەيران بولماق
swear, to	قەسەم قىلماق (ئىچمەك)
sweep, to	سۈپۈرمەك
sweets (such as cube sugar, candy)	قەنت - گېزەك
swimming	سۇ ئۈزۈش
T	
tail fat	قۇيرۇق ياغ
tailor	تىككۈچى
take advantage of	پۇرسەتتىن پايدىلانماق

take a step, to	قەدەم ئالماق
take out, carry out, to	ئەپچىقىپ قويماق
take, carry, to	ئاپارماق
take a taxi, to	تاكسى توسماق
talk/chat	پاراڭ
talk too much, to (slang)	ۋالاقلىماق
tamarisk	يۇلغۇن
tandoor	تونۇر
taste, to	ئېغىز تەگمەك
taste, try, to	ئېغىز تەگمەك
Taxi Service	تاكسى شىركىتى
teacher	ئۇستاز
teach, to	تەلىم بەرمەك
tear, rip, to	يىرتماق
tea-seller	چايپۇرۇش
temperament	مىجەز
temple	ئىبادەتخانا
tennis	چويلا توپ
ten thousand	تۇمەن
territory	زېمىن
test, try out, to	سىناشماق
that	ھېلىقى
the customs	تاموژنا
the day after tomorrow	ئۆگۈن
the first time	تۇنجى قېتىم
the Forbidden City	شەھەرىستان / خان سارىيى
the (government) authorities	ھۆكۈمەت ئەمەلدارلىرى
the Great Wall	سەددىچىن
the Korban festival	قۇربان ھېيت
the lap; lower slope	ئېتەك
the Ramadan festival	روزا ھېيت
the Silk Road	يىپەك يولى
thief	ئوغرى
think it right, to	توغرا تاپماق

thread, string	يىپ
throb, give a sharp, stabbing pain, to	زىڭىلدىماق
throw out, pour out, to	تۆكمەك
tie on white (show mourning), to	ئاق باغلىماق
tie, to	باغلىماق
tightrope walker	دارۋاز
tightrope walking	دارۋازلىق
time	چاغ
time, epoch, period	دەۋر
times	ھەسسە
tired, to be	چارچىماق
title, name; degree	ئۇنۋان
tomb	مازار
tool	سايمان
tools	ئۇسكۈنە
tools, weapons	قورال
tour a city, to	شەھەر ئايلانماق
tour company	ساياھەت شىركىتى
tourist attractions	ساياھەت ئورۇنلىرى
tower	مۇنار
trade	سودا
trade, to	سودا قىلماق
tradition	ئەنئەنە
traditional, national	مىللىي
translate, to	تەرجىمە قىلماق
translation	تەرجىمە
transport, to	توشۇماق
transportation	قاتناش ۋاستىلىرى
transport hub	قاتناش تۈگۈنى
trash bin	ئەخلەت ساندۇقى
travel back and forth, to	قاتنىماق
treat, to	داۋالاش / داۋالىماق
trestle	باراڭ
triangle	ئۈچ بۇلۇڭ

trouble, bad luck, misfortune	كاساپەت
true	راست
truly	ھەقىقەتەن
truth	ھەقىقەت
try, to	ئىغىز تەگمەك
turn in a wilderness, to	چۆلدەرەپ قالماق
turn white, to	ئاقارماق
type	تۈر
type of thin silk	شايى
U	
understand, to	چۈشەنمەك / ئۇقماق
unite, to	ئىتتىپاقلىشىش
unknown	نامەلۇم
unlicensed taxicab	قارا تاكسى
untie, take off (clothes), to	يەشمەك
unusual; very	ئاجايىپ
unset, to be	رەنجىمەك
use, consumption	ئىستېمال قىلماق
used to, to be	ئادەتلەنمەك
useful, beneficial	پايدىلىق
use, to	ئىشلەتمەك
V	
valuable, precious	ئەتىۋارلىق
value, esteem, to	قەدىرلىمەك
value, to	باھالىماق
vanish, disappear, to	غايىب بولماق
various	خىلمۇ - خىل
vegetables	ئوتياش / كۆكتات
very; clean	تازا
very clear	سۈپ - سۈزۈك
very quickly	لىككىدە
view, scenery	مەنزىرە
village	كەنت
vineyard	ئۈزۈمزارلىق
violin	ئىسكرىپكا

visit, to	يوقلىماق
visit to a bereaved family	ئۆلۈم پەتىسى
W	
wage; right	ھەق
wail, sob, to	ھۆركىرەپ يىغلىماق
waiter	تاڭجاڭ
wall carpet	تام گىلىمى
walnut skin	ياڭاق پوستى
want, to	كۆڭۈل تارتماق
warn, to	ئاگاھلاندۇرماق
wash, to	يۇماق
wastefulness	ئىسراپچىلىق
watch, to	تاماشا قىلماق
water, to	سۇغارماق
way, method	ئامال
weakness	ئاجىزلىق
weapon	قورال
weaving, knitting	توقۇمىچىلىق
wedding	نىكاھ توي
weighty words	سالمىقى بار گەپ
welcome, to	قارشى ئالماق
well	قۇدۇق
we will see	بىر گەپ بولار
wheat	بۇغداي
whole	پۈتۈن
wild	ياۋا
wild birds	ياۋايى قۇشلار
willingness; blessing	رازىلىق
win, to	يەڭمەك
wish, desire	ئارزۇ
wish, to	تىلىمەك
with one knee underneath	يەكتىز
witness	گۇۋاھچى
wood	ياغاچ
wool	يۇڭ
work	ئەسەر

worry, to	ئەنسىرىمەك
wrestling	چېلىشىش
wretched; unfortunate	بىچارە
written history	يازما تارىخ

Y	
yell, to	ۋارقىرىماق
yellow	سېرىق
Z	
zoo	هايۋاناتلار باغچىسى